Frederick William IV and
the Prussian Monarchy

Frederick William IV

Frederick William IV and the Prussian Monarchy 1840–1861

David E. Barclay

CLARENDON PRESS · OXFORD

1995

Oxford University Press, Walton Street, Oxford OX2 6DP
Oxford New York
Athens Auckland Bangkok Bombay
Calcutta Cape Town Dar es Salaam Delhi
Florence Hong Kong Istanbul Karachi
Kuala Lumpur Madras Madrid Melbourne
Mexico City Nairobi Paris Singapore
Taipei Tokyo Toronto
and associated companies in
Berlin Ibadan

Oxford is a trade mark of Oxford University Press

Published in the United States
by Oxford University Press Inc., New York

British Library Cataloguing in Publication Data
Data available

Library of Congress Cataloging in Publication Data
Data applied for
ISBN 0–19–820430–2

1 3 5 7 9 10 8 6 4 2

Typeset by Jayvee, Trivandrum, India
Printed in Great Britain
on acid-free paper by
Biddles Ltd., Guildford & King's Lynn

For Gordon A. Craig

PREFACE

Frederick William IV, King of Prussia from 1840 to 1861, was perhaps the most important German monarch between Frederick the Great and William II. An immensely complicated and contradictory personality, he was a man for whom aesthetic, religious, dynastic, and ideological values took precedence over considerations of *Realpolitik*. Many of his contemporaries thus believed that Frederick William inhabited a Romantic, anachronistic dream world utterly out of touch with its times. The well-known writer David Friedrich Strauß expressed those sentiments with particular flair and piquancy in his 1847 pamphlet, *The Romantic on the Throne of the Caesars*. Ostensibly an analysis of Julian the Apostate, Strauß's essay represented a thinly veiled critique of the King of Prussia and his attempts to transform his society into a 'Christian-German' state. And ever since the middle of the nineteenth century, Strauß's image of the 'Romantic on the throne' has influenced most historians' perceptions of that monarch. So have the writings of older generations of German historians, from Ranke, Treitschke, and Sybel to Meinecke, Hintze, and Schnabel. From their works emerged an image of a king who was gifted and intelligent, but erratic, indecisive, unstable, and, in the end, a hapless and even tragic failure. That image has persisted, with slight variations, down to the present.

Although this study focuses on Frederick William IV, it is not a biography in the traditional sense. Rather, it is an attempt to reconsider Frederick William's reign in the context of new questions and new problems. The last few years have witnessed a revival of interest in conservative political movements, the cultural representations of conservative values, the adaptive strategies of conservative élites, and the 'invention' of traditions by those élites in the nineteenth century. Although historians have in fact long been aware of the tenacity of monarchical values and of effective royal authority in nineteenth-century Prussia, they have paid remarkably little attention to the actual character and significance of monarchical structures there, especially in the 'pre-Bismarck' period before 1862. This book attempts partially to redress that situation. It concerns the nature of the monarchical institutions of Prussia at a time when that state was beginning its transition to parliamentarism and industrialism. Above all, it attempts to consider the interaction between constantly evolving monarchical and courtly institutions on the one hand and larger processes of cultural, social, economic, and political change on the other. It thus intends to contribute to our understanding of the structures of the nineteenth-century European state and the ways in which conservative élites were able to adapt themselves to those structures.

To understand monarchical structures, it is, of course, necessary to understand the monarch himself. In a semi-absolutist setting, the ruler was not simply the creature of bureaucratic, court, military, or agrarian élites; rather, he was at the very centre of the Prussian state, and his personality and his decisions could have a major effect on Prussian society at large. With the exceptions of Frederick II and William II, however, historians have until recently devoted remarkably little scholarly attention to the actual occupants of the Prussian throne. Only in the past few years have some scholars begun to work more intensively on various aspects of Frederick William IV's reign; and this is the first book-length study to appear in English. It is not surprising, therefore, that many historians still base their judgements of that monarch on the views of older historians, who regarded Frederick William's reign as an unhappy prelude to the triumphant unification of the *Reich* in 1871. That way of thinking has itself become anachronistic, and it is time to assess Frederick William IV within the context of his own times, circumstances, assumptions, and possibilities, free of the rancour of late nineteenth-century political and ideological disputes.

Frederick William was in fact very much a child of his times, and very much a modern monarch. He was also an ideologue who was sensitive to the importance of the new 'publics' that were emerging in European society, and therein, I argue, lay much of his modernity. In this book I contend that Frederick William IV was far more consistent than older historians believed; in short, he was engaged in what I have called an anti-revolutionary 'monarchical project', which he viewed as the only real alternative to the revolutionary forces that had been unleashed in Europe since 1789. To sustain his project he sought to create a sacral tradition of monarchy, sustained by 'organic', corporative political institutions, in a Prussia where such traditions had never been deeply rooted. Much of my book consists of an attempt to assess the consequences of Frederick William's monarchical project for the development of Prussian political institutions and cultural values in the middle of the nineteenth century. Among other things, I conclude that, measured according to his own criteria, he was far more successful than most historians have realized.

This study consists of ten chapters, each of which begins with a relatively detailed description of one or two major events that illustrate its main themes. The opening chapter considers the condition and evolution of monarchical institutions in nineteenth-century Europe as a whole; it concludes with an evaluation of the Prussian monarchy to 1840, the year of Frederick William IV's accession to the throne. Chapter 2 then introduces Frederick William himself. In it I emphasize the impact on the young Crown Prince of Berlin Romanticism and the post-1815 religious 'Awakening' (*Erweckungsbewegung*) in Germany. Both of these movements decisively shaped his views of monarchical authority and the form of his monarchical project, which, I suggest, he always regarded from both an ideological and an aesthetic perspective. The next three chapters discuss the first years of Frederick William's reign up to the February Patent of 1847. Chapter 6 then considers Frederick William's response to the revolutionary events of 1847-8, while Chapter 7 analyses the emergence, structure, and significance of the counter-revolutionary court Camarilla from March to December of 1848. Chapter 8 focuses on Frederick William IV and the 'national question'. It treats the King's complex relationship with Joseph Maria von Radowitz, the Camarilla's brilliant arch-rival and Frederick William's closest adviser during the revolutionary years, and concludes with a description of the abortive Prussian Union project and the Olmütz crisis of 1850. The last two chapters then present a detailed analysis of the reaction decade and the ways in which mon-archical institutions and values survived in a post-revolutionary, parliamentary-constitutional Prussian state.

The preparation of this book has taken up much of the past decade, and it gives me a great deal of pleasure to acknowledge the financial, personal, and intellectual assis-tance that I have received during those years. I am especially grateful to the Alexander von Humboldt-Stiftung (Bonn-Bad Godesberg) for a generous research-fellowship which made this project possible in the first place. The completion of the project was facilitated by a Summer Stipend from the National Endowment for the Humanities (Washington, DC) and support from the Kalamazoo College Faculty Development Program, for which I am most appreciative. I should also like to thank the staffs of the various libraries and archives where I conducted my research: in addition to the archives listed in the Bibliography, they include the Senatsbibliothek in Berlin; the Universitätsbibliothek of the Freie Universität Berlin; the library of the Friedrich-Meinecke-Institut and the microfilm collection at the Otto-Suhr-Institut (both at the Freie Universität Berlin); the libraries of the University of Michigan in Ann Arbor; Dwight Waldo Library at Western Michigan University in Kalamazoo; and especially Upjohn Library at Kalamazoo College. Eleanor Pinkham and her staff were always more than willing to assist me with every facet of my work, from ordering obscure volumes on interlibrary loan to taking pho-tographs for me while on vacation in Rome! I also owe a special debt of gratitude to the staff of the former Zentrales Staatsarchiv in Merseburg; Dr Meta Kohnke and her colleagues, especially Frau 'Olé' and Herr Templer, were invariably helpful and generous to me during my long sojourns in that city.

A German version of this study is being published by Siedler Verlag in Berlin. My thanks also go to Wolf Jobst Siedler and his staff for their encouragement and assis-tance.

As on so many previous occasions, the Historische Kommission zu Berlin was my 'home away from home' during my visits to Germany. Dr Jürgen Schmädeke und Frau Monika Koch were gracious and hospitable hosts there; my thanks also go to the late Dr Wolfgang Treue, Professor Klaus Zernack, and Professor Wolfram Fischer, the Historische Kommission's most recent chairs. Dr Manfred Jehle and Professor Monika Neugebauer-Wölk (now of the Martin-Luther-Universität Halle-Wittenberg) provided me with especially important advice and assistance. Dr Felix Escher, also of the Historische Kommission, is an inexhaustible source of informa-tion on the history of Berlin and the Mark Brandenburg; I have profited immensely from my many conversations with him. My thanks go as well to Ursula Kinzel and Sigrid Kleinschmidt for their help throughout the project.

A book of this sort could not have been completed without advice, criticism, and suggestions from colleagues and friends in various places. Professor Hermann Beck, Professor James Brophy, Professor Eric Dorn Brose, Professor Günther Grünthal,

Dr Hans-Christof Kraus, Dr Frank-Lothar Kroll, Professor James Retallack, Professor Hermann-Josef Rupieper, Professor Martin Sperlich, Dr Thomas Stamm-Kuhlmann, and Dr Gerd-H. Zuchold have all read (or heard) big chunks of this study. I am grateful for their help, and I have benefited more than they can possibly imagine from years of stimulating conversation with them. Dr Jürgen von Gerlach—a descendant of several individuals discussed in the pages that follow—has followed this project with enthusiasm and interest for many years. I owe an especially large debt of gratitude to four colleagues and friends from Kalamazoo College. Professor Hardy Fuchs has read and commented on various German versions of my work, while my History Department colleague, Professor David Strauss, has read every draft of this study with care, patience, and sensitivity. David Curl helped me with the illustrations, for which I am very appreciative; and Professor Joe K. Fugate was invariably able to answer complex questions about translations from nineteenth-century German. I am also indebted to many other individuals who have helped me in important ways at various times. They include John Ackerman, the late Professor Walter Bußmann, Karl Eisbein, Alfred Gobert, Professor Gerd Heinrich, Professor Larry Eugene Jones, Marcus Kiefer, Professor Patricia Kollander, Professor Karl Möckl, Dr Wolfgang Neugebauer, Dr Heinz Schönemann, Professor Ernst Schraepler, Dr Johann Karl von Schroeder, Wolf Jobst Siedler, Professor Heinz Sperlich, and Inge Staffa, as well as Janet Riley and Sandra Webber in Kalamazoo. I thank them all. I am also grateful to Oxford University Press and to Tony Morris and Anna Illingworth, the Press's history editor and assistant history editor.

Finally, I should like to thank two individuals to whom I owe incalculable personal and intellectual debts. Professor Otto Büsch of the Freie Universität Berlin and the Historische Kommission zu Berlin was a valued teacher, counsellor, colleague, and friend for more than twenty years. After I received my Humboldt stipend he served as my official host and *wissenschaftlicher Betreuer* in Berlin, and he supported my efforts with good humour, infectious enthusiasm, and unflagging energy. I simply could not have completed this book without his help; sadly, he died before he could see it. He will be sorely missed.

Professor Gordon A. Craig has been a personal, professional, and intellectual inspiration to me for almost a quarter of a century. Indeed, any merit that this book may have is largely due to his influence. My interest in the Prussian *Vormärz* was first sparked by a memorable seminar which he offered at Stanford in 1971. In the intervening years I have continued to benefit from his wise counsel, his incisive criticisms, his insightful suggestions, and his generous support; and it is to him that I affectionately dedicate this book.

D.E.B.

Kalamazoo
May 1994

CONTENTS

NOTE ON SOURCES AND TRANSLATIONS

EAST GERMAN ARCHIVES

Much of the research for this study was undertaken between 1986 and 1993 in archives located in the former German Democratic Republic: specifically, the Nationalgalerie in the former East Berlin, the Staatsarchiv Potsdam, the Zentrales Staatsarchiv Potsdam, and, most notably, the Zentrales Staatsarchiv, Dienststelle Merseburg. The Zentrales Staatsarchiv Potsdam has been integrated with the former West German Bundesarchiv, and is now the Bundesarchiv, Abteilungen Potsdam. After the *Wende* in 1989–90, the Merseburg archive temporarily remained in that city as a branch of the Geheimes Staatsarchiv Preußischer Kulturbesitz. Beginning in 1993, however, its collections were returned to Berlin. (Before the Second World War the Merseburg records had been located in Berlin-Dahlem and Berlin-Charlottenburg.) In this study, I shall continue to distinguish between the old Merseburg holdings (GStA Merseburg) and the collections in Berlin-Dahlem (GStA Berlin). The former Staatsarchiv Potsdam, located in Frederick William IV's Orangerie in the park of Sanssouci, has reverted to its earlier name and is now the Brandenburgisches Landeshauptarchiv. In the autumn of 1994 the drawings of Frederick William IV, formerly located in the Sammlung der Zeichnungen in the East Berlin Nationalgalerie, were transferred to the Plankammer of the Stiftung Schlösser und Gärten Potsdam-Sanssouci. I have used these new names throughout this study. It is not likely that the classification system used by the former East German archives will be changed in the near future; so, even where, as in the case of the Merseburg collection, the archives have been physically removed from one city to another, the interested scholar should still be able to locate individual documents to which I refer in the text.

THE GERLACH PAPERS

Leopold von Gerlach (1790–1861) was for years the powerful Adjutant-General to Frederick William IV and leader of the influential court 'Camarilla' that shaped much of Prussian state policy during and after the 1848 revolution. It has been assumed for several decades that his papers were lost at the end of the Second World War. Thus scholars were obliged to use a highly edited version of his diaries that had been published by his daughter in 1891. Since the late 1970s, however, the Gerlach-

Archiv (a collection of Gerlach family documents housed in the Institute of Political Science at the University of Erlangen) has owned thirty-four volumes of typescript transcripts of Gerlach's papers. I was the first scholar to evaluate these documents systematically; after a year of 'detective' work, I was able to demonstrate not only the transcripts' veracity but also that they had been prepared in the 1920s and the 1930s. The old Potsdam Reichsarchiv had planned to produce an annotated edition that was never published, partly because of unfavourable economic conditions after 1929. The transcripts include both Gerlach's unexpurgated diary and his voluminous correspondence with dozens of prominent personalities, many of whom figure in this study. I was also able to determine that the former Zentrales Staatsarchiv Potsdam (now the Bundesarchiv, Abteilungen Potsdam), the successor to the Reichsarchiv, still owns a second (and, in fact, more complete) set of these transcripts, which only became available a few years ago; as far as I can tell, I was the first Western scholar to peruse that set. Throughout this study I have usually referred to the Erlangen set.

TRANSLATIONS

Frederick William IV had a highly idiosyncratic prose style which does not always make for easy translation. His rather emphatic letters usually included chains of exclamation points, which I have retained in my translations, as well as multiple underlinings, which I have indicated in italics.

LIST OF ILLUSTRATIONS

Frontispiece: Frederick William IV. Lithograph by Valentin Schertle after painting by Franz Krüger, 1844 (Bildarchiv Preußischer Kulturbesitz).

ABBREVIATIONS

'Abschriften'	Abschriften des Nachlasses Leopold von Gerlachs
ADB	*Allgemeine Deutsche Biographie*
AKO	Allgemeine Kabinetts-Ordre (General Cabinet Order)
BA Frankfurt/M.	Bundesarchiv, Außenstelle Frankfurt am Main
BA Potsdam	Bundesarchiv, Abteilungen Potsdam (formerly Zentrales Staatsarchiv Potsdam)
BayHStA	Bayerisches Hauptstaatsarchiv, Munich
BLHA	Brandenburgisches Landeshauptarchiv, Potsdam (formerly Staatsarchiv Potsdam)
BPH	Brandenburg-Preußisches Hausarchiv
CEH	*Central European History*
FBPG	*Forschungen zur Brandenburgischen und Preußischen Geschichte*
FW IV	Frederick William IV
GHA	Geheimes Hausarchiv, Abteilung III, of Bayerisches Hauptstaatsarchiv, Munich
GA	Gerlach-Archiv, Erlangen
GLA	Generallandesarchiv, Karlsruhe
GStA Berlin	Geheimes Staatsarchiv Preußischer Kulturbesitz, Berlin
GStA Merseburg	Geheimes Staatsarchiv Preußischer Kulturbesitz, Abteilung Merseburg (formerly Zentrales Staatsarchiv, Dienststelle Merseburg)
HA	Hausarchiv
HHStA	Österreichisches Staatsarchiv, Vienna: Haus-, Hof- und Staatsarchiv
HZ	*Historische Zeitschrift*
JGMOD	*Jahrbuch für die Geschichte Mittel- und Ostdeutschlands*
NDB	*Neue Deutsche Biographie*
NPZ	*Neue Preußische [Kreuz-] Zeitung*
PRO	Public Record Office, Kew
StaBi	Staatsbibliothek Preußischer Kulturbesitz, Berlin
ZfG	*Zeitschrift für Geschichtswissenschaft*

I
The Nineteenth-Century Prussian Monarchy in its European Context

A Tournament in Potsdam and a Continent of Monarchs

The Crown Prince of Prussia, the future Frederick William IV, had never exactly cut a dashing or martial figure. Fat, balding, extremely near-sighted, and a poor rider to boot, he always felt more at home in the company of artists and architects than in the glittering world of court society. So he must have presented an odd sight indeed when, on 13 July 1829, he appeared with his younger brothers at the courtyard of the Neues Palais, near Potsdam, on horseback and costumed as a medieval knight. The occasion was the Festival of the Enchantment of the White Rose, a grandiose birthday celebration for the Crown Prince's sister, the visiting Russian Empress Alexandra Feodorovna. The festivities included the re-enactment of an 'old German tournament', with high-ranking Prussian princes and aristocrats dressed as 'knights' riding a series of quadrilles and engaging in chivalric competition for the honour of receiving the victor's prize from the Empress's hands. One observer, Countess Elise Bernstorff, wrote unconvincingly that the Crown Prince 'fits into his costume as though he has never worn another; he sits astride his steed as though he has never ridden another; he regards everything serenely and confidently, either as if he were confident of victory or unconcerned with the victor's prize'. The latter assumption was closer to the truth; in fact, the Crown Prince did not receive any of the prizes that were awarded that day, which included golden chains, silver beakers, and Turkish sabres.[1]

As incongruous as the sight of the Crown Prince must have been, just as unusual was the idea of a medieval tournament itself, especially in the courtyard of one of Frederick the Great's late Rococo palaces in the park of Sanssouci. In the making for some time, its details had been worked out by the Crown Prince's uncle, Duke Carl of Mecklenburg-Strelitz, a man who was especially enamoured of grand royal ceremonies. Karl Friedrich Schinkel, the foremost German architect of the nineteenth century, had been involved with the plans, as had Baron Friedrich de la Motte Fouqué, a writer of popular Romantic epics set in the Middle Ages. One of them, *The Magic Ring*, had profoundly affected the Russian Empress—then known by her German name as Princess Charlotte—and her siblings when it had appeared back in 1812. With her enthusiasm for the Middle Ages, Charlotte had taken the white rose as her personal device—hence the selection of that flower as the festival's symbol.

---

[1] Gräfin Elise von Bernstorff geborene Gräfin von Dernath, *Ein Bild aus der Zeit von 1789 bis 1835: Aus ihren Aufzeichnungen*, 2nd edn. (2 vols.; Berlin, 1896), ii: *1823 bis 1835*, 143; Ernst Lewalter, *Friedrich Wilhelm IV.: Das Schicksal eines Geistes* (Berlin, 1938), 305–6.

The festival itself consisted of three parts, of which the first, the 'medieval' tournament, is of special interest. A drum roll and a fanfare announced the arrival of the Empress in the tribunal and the beginning of the festival. A chief herald approached her and received her permission to be paid homage by a group of 'knights'. Thereupon, to the continued accompaniment of fanfares, the first group of four 'knights' appeared: the Crown Prince and his three brothers. The Crown Prince was preceded by the banner of Prussia and was followed by two pages who carried his lance and his shield. The knights were attired in armour of light silver or gold, over which they wore a knee-length tunic, emblazoned with each individual's own heraldic device. Each knight also wore an armband in the colours of his lady. After a series of events with lance, sword, and spear, the four princes retired from the scene and were replaced by the next four knights, and so on, until all forty knights participating in the event had done their part. Then they joined together into a single quadrille, again involving manœuvres with lance and sword; finally, the tournament ended with a grand parade of all the knights. The judges, who had been counting points, then distributed the various victors' prizes. These events were followed later in the day by a series of *tableaux vivants* and a court ball in the Neues Palais.[2]

Presiding benignly over the whole splendid—and expensive—occasion was the King himself. Normally a man of almost legendary lugubriousness, Frederick William III actually appeared to be enjoying himself on this occasion. Always devoted to his family, he was now surrounded by his four sons and his three daughters, along with their spouses, most notably the imposing Tsar Nicholas I himself. Frederick William III was a survivor. Indeed, few monarchs of his or any age had endured calamities and humiliations of the sort which had been his lot between 1806 and 1814: the military collapse of 1806 and the royal family's ignominious flight from Berlin; the crushing Treaty of Tilsit, followed by two years of French military occupation, during which time the royal family remained in the far east of the kingdom; the death of the King's beloved wife, Queen Luise, at the age of only 34, in 1810; the gamble of 1812–13, when Prussia had been drawn into the new anti-Napoleonic coalition, a decision which, despite its fortuitous outcome, had been fraught with risk and danger. Frederick William III had borne heavy burdens, and he was prematurely aged. Now, in 1829, who could gainsay him an opportunity to play the role of beaming patriarch on the occasion of his Imperial daughter's visit?

But the Festival of the White Rose was far more than just a glittering show, and more than simply an ephemeral display of Hohenzollern family togetherness. It was, in fact, a carefully orchestrated exercise in royal self-affirmation and in the *public* representation of monarchical values. It was an occasion on which the entire Prussian court could be seen symbolically to embrace centuries-old chivalric virtues of obedience, loyalty, and sacrifice—virtues which seemed to stand in such stark contrast to the gross excesses of the French Revolution and the fiendish usurpations of Bonaparte. The festival also affirmed the special ties that bound the Hohenzollerns

[2] Bernstorff, *Bild*, ii. 141–4; Lewalter, *Friedrich Wilhelm IV.*, 305–6; Walter Bußmann, *Zwischen Preußen und Deutschland: Friedrich Wilhelm IV. Eine Biographie* (Berlin, 1990), 86–8.

to the Romanovs. Those ties went beyond dynastic marriages. They had helped throw off the Napoleonic yoke, and now, a decade and a half later, they symbolized the apparent triumph of monarchism and legitimism over the forces of revolution. In short, the Festival of the White Rose was one example of the ways in which nineteenth-century monarchies continued, like their predecessors, to make use of rituals and ceremonies in an attempt to 'express an idealized image' of monarchical rule.[3]

Despite his appreciation of the importance of ceremony and ritual, Frederick William III was himself a painfully shy man not usually given to gaudy display. Born in 1770, he was a product of the age of sentiment, with its emphasis on simplicity, domestic virtues, and, above all, the free development of the individual personality. Thus he required for himself a private sphere, a distinction between his private life and his public functions that would have been well-nigh inconceivable to a seventeenth- or eighteenth-century monarch. For Frederick William III, though, grave royal ceremonies were irksome affairs that had to be endured, and he was only really happy when he could escape from the centre of things and retreat into the bosom of his family. When he was in Berlin he preferred to stay in the Crown Prince's palace rather than in the enormous royal palace nearby; but above all he liked to get away to his rustic estate at Paretz, near Potsdam, a collection of unadorned buildings where he could live like an ordinary squire.[4]

Indeed, on a certain level Frederick William III represented the prototype of a new kind of post-revolutionary monarch. At a time when the principles of the 'revolution' seemed to have been defeated and the principles of dynastic legitimism were being everywhere proclaimed, many monarchs had become increasingly austere—some would say 'bourgeois'—in their tastes, self-perceptions, and lifestyles. A voluptuary like Britain's George IV was the exception rather than the rule during the Restoration era. More typical were people like Frederick William III or the Austrian Emperor Francis I, famous for his strolls through Vienna, his friendly conversations with his subjects, and his willingness to let family members follow the tuggings of their hearts rather than the demands of their station.[5] (Thus he permitted his brother, Archduke John, to marry the daughter of a provincial postmaster.) Superficially, at least, Louis-Philippe, 'King of the French'—rather than 'King of France'—after the July Revolution of 1830, was the very incarnation of the 'bourgeois monarch', with his umbrella, his sharp business-acumen, his self-created role as *paterfamilias* of his large brood, and his dislike for the structures of the old Bourbon court. And then, of course, after their marriage in 1840 there were those models of familial rectitude,

---

[3] Richard Wortman, 'Rule by Sentiment: Alexander II's Journeys through the Russian Empire', *American Historical Review*, 95 (1990), 746.

[4] Heinz Dollinger, 'Das Leitbild des Bürgerkönigtums in der europäischen Monarchie des 19. Jahrhunderts', in Karl Ferdinand Werner (ed.), *Hof, Kultur und Politik im 19. Jahrhundert: Akten des 18. Deutsch-französischen Historikerkolloquiums Darmstadt vom 27.–30. September 1982* (Bonn, 1985), 349–52; Thomas Stamm-Kuhlmann, 'War Friedrich Wilhelm III. von Preußen ein Bürgerkönig?', *Zeitschrift für historische Forschung*, 16 (1989), 445–6, 448–50, 452–7.

[5] Hannes Stekl, 'Der Wiener Hof in der ersten Hälfte des 19. Jahrhunderts', in Karl Möckl (ed.), *Hof und Hofgesellschaft in den deutschen Staaten im 19. und beginnenden 20. Jahrhundert* (Boppard am Rhein, 1990), 17–20.

Victoria and Albert. Even a traditional despot like Nicholas I, unrestrained by any kind of bourgeois public opinion, emphasized the simple asperities of his military lifestyle, his devotion to the Empress and her family, and his earnest efforts to prepare his son for the burdens of high office. The contrast to the behaviour of many earlier European rulers was enormous.[6] In the words of one historian, 'Rituals tell us about beliefs, but they tell us even more about ways of life.'[7] And in adhering to the 'rituals of bourgeois life', the monarchs of post-Napoleonic Europe seemed to be serving notice that, in the age of *bourgeois conquérants*, middle-class ways of living were infiltrating even the most resilient bastions of monarchical and aristocratic exclusiveness.

Despite these examples, it would nevertheless be misleading to exaggerate the extent of monarchical *embourgeoisement* during the nineteenth century. For all his self-doubts and simple tastes, for all his love of privacy and trivial 'middle-class' diversions, Frederick William III was never a bourgeois monarch.[8] Nor, indeed, were any of his fellow monarchs, including the ones we have just mentioned. Their ways of life may have seemed impeccably bourgeois and respectable, at least superficially. Nor can there be any doubt that, in an age in which bourgeois publics were becoming increasingly important, most of these monarchs came into frequent contact with their bourgeois subjects. But acceptance of a supposedly middle-class way of life did not necessarily entail the acceptance of a bourgeois consciousness. Even the 'Citizen-King' Louis-Philippe never forgot that he 'sprang from the noblest family in Europe, and had buried in the depths of his soul a full measure of hereditary pride, certainly not considering himself like any other man'.[9] What was true of Louis-Philippe applied at least as much to his fellow monarchs, including the King of Prussia, who also knew that he was not 'like any other man'. Nor indeed was he. He was more than simply a president for life, or the permanent head of a bureaucratic apparatus. Moreover, he and most of the other dynastic rulers on the Continent after 1815 faced a formidable and unique task: to reconstitute—or, in some cases like the Netherlands, Belgium, or Greece, to constitute for the first time—monarchical institutions and monarchical authority in societies where they could no longer simply be taken for granted.

In a revolutionary age, monarchs could not justify themselves simply through the fact of their existence. Nor could they be content to point to their utility as first servants of their states, or as enlightened guarantors of public order and efficient administration. The convulsions that had attended a quarter century of revolution, war, and Napoleon had changed everything. Although post-Napoleonic Europe had apparently embraced the cause of traditional monarchy and dynastic legitimacy, all

---

[6] Stamm-Kuhlmann, 'Bürgerkönig', 352–6.

[7] Anne Martin-Fugier, in Michelle Perrot and Anne Martin-Fugier, 'The Actors', in Michelle Perrot (ed.), *A History of Private Life*, iv: *From the Fires of Revolution to the Great War*, trans. Arthur Goldhammer (Cambridge, Mass., 1990), 134–6.

[8] Stamm-Kuhlmann, 'Bürgerkönig', 458–9.

[9] Alexis de Tocqueville, *Recollections*, trans. George Lawrence, ed. J. P. Mayer and A. P. Kerr (Garden City, NY, 1970), 6.

the rulers of the Continent, including the mighty Tsar himself, were acutely aware that the French Revolution represented a watershed in human history, that their positions could never again be wholly secure, and that they had been permanently placed on the defensive, ideologically and politically.[10]

One of the greatest challenges to traditional forms of monarchical authority was the idea of popular sovereignty, to which the Revolution had given such drastic and dramatic expression after 1789. That idea, which would forever alter the relationship of dynastic monarchs to their state, was not simply going to disappear after the Corsican had been sent to St Helena and the monarchs were back on their thrones.[11] The rulers of Europe responded to the idea of popular sovereignty in several ways. Some—such as the British, Dutch, Belgian, and Bavarian crowns, but also the restored Bourbon monarchy in France and its Orleanist successor—agreed to various kinds of constitutional or parliamentary limitations on their prerogatives. For others, notably the great bureaucratic-military monarchies of Central and Eastern Europe, any concession to demands for popular representation on a constitutional or parliamentary basis was anathema.

The powerful appeal of the idea of popular sovereignty also attested to the increasingly rapid differentiation and politicization of European societies after 1789. Those processes in turn often altered the relationship between the crown, on the one hand, and new structures of civil society and of educated, culturally autonomous, bourgeois publics on the other. There were, of course, sharp regional variations from one part of Europe to another. The caricatures of royalty that appeared in the British press and in the French press after 1830 would have been unthinkable in Russia. On the whole, however, organized public opinion was a factor most European rulers could no longer ignore, and one which had to enter into their political calculations. Similarly, the relationship between monarchs and other institutional expressions of public authority—parliaments and constitutions in some parts of Europe, highly articulate bureaucratic or aristocratic élites in others—also became increasingly complicated. Thus European rulers after 1815 continued to face real challenges and limits to what has been described as 'crown autonomy', that is, 'the extent to which rulers could use state policies to realize their interests'.[12] With the exception of the tsars and the 'Caesarist' Napoleon III, European monarchs faced limitations, restrictions, and challenges unknown to their absolutist forebears.[13]

Despite these challenges, in the decades after 1815 the monarchies of Europe were able quite successfully to reconstitute—or constitute for the first time—the bases of effective monarchical authority in their states. In recent years historians have

[10] Adrianus Petrus Johannes van Osta, *De europese monarchie in de negentiende eeuw: Het britse en duitse model* (Diss.; Utrecht, 1982), 14–15, 19–39; Heinz Gollwitzer, *Ludwig I. von Bayern: Königtum im Vormärz. Eine politische Biographie* (Munich, 1986), 30–43.

[11] See the detailed discussions in Reinhard Bendix, *Kings or People: Power and the Mandate to Rule* (Berkeley, Calif., 1978), and F. H. Hinsley, *Sovereignty*, 2nd edn. (Cambridge, 1986), esp. chs. 3 and 6.

[12] Edgar Kiser, 'The Formation of State Policy in Western European Absolutisms: A Comparison of England and France', *Politics and Society*, 15 (1986–7), 260.

[13] Gollwitzer, *Ludwig I.*, 766–7.

increasingly recognized that the period from 1815 to 1914 witnessed a resurgence of the prestige and popularity of monarchy in many European societies; and with that resurgence came a veritable cult of monarchy that reached exaggerated proportions in the latter decades of the century, from Queen Victoria's jubilees to what has been described as the 'monstrous' 'late flowering of court culture' in Wilhelmine Germany. In fact, however, what might be described as the 'monarchical revival' in nineteenth-century Europe had already begun during the Restoration, when the crowned heads of the Continent seemed far more vulnerable, far more defensive, and far more modest in their habits and pretensions.[14] Even with the ultimate triumph of republicanism in France after 1875, or the disappearances of the Papal States and the Kingdom of Naples in 1860–1, Europe as a whole remained a continent of hereditary rulers throughout the entire century, and with landed aristocrats those rulers remained the linchpin of an Old Regime which, as Arno J. Mayer has argued, persisted in many parts of Europe until the First World War.[15] In fact, Europe had rarely seemed more monarchical than in the nineteenth century. Under Napoleon's aegis, for example, the territories of Bavaria, Württemberg, and Saxony had become kingdoms, and that status was maintained under the Vienna peace. Similarly, the Netherlands had become a hereditary monarchy under the House of Orange at the end of the Napoleonic wars; Belgium and Greece imported rulers from other European princely houses after gaining their independence; Bulgaria and Romania followed suit a few decades later. Even in thoroughly constitutional states, sufficient opportunities usually existed 'to permit talented individuals on the throne to play a significant role'.[16] Ludwig I of Bavaria, who ruled a state with a constitutional charter from 1825 to 1848, is a good example, as are two scions of the House of Saxe-Coburg-Gotha: Leopold I, King of the Belgians after 1831, and his nephew, Prince Albert. If a constitution turned out to be too confining, there were always other opportunities elsewhere, as Leopold II showed later in the century with his free-lance projects in the Congo basin.[17] Indeed, in constitutional monarchies even mediocre rulers could sometimes play critical, if often negative, roles, as the unhappy history of Italy's four Savoyard kings after 1861 demonstrates.[18]

Reviving Monarchy: Principles, Pageantry, and Court Politics

How did they do it? How does one explain the monarchical revival after Napoleon, and what were some of its characteristics? Of course, the nature of that revival varied considerably over time and location; and the essential difference between constitu-

[14] Philip Mansel, *Louis XVIII* (London, 1981), 413; Karl Ferdinand Werner, 'Fürst und Hof im 19. Jahrhundert: Abgesang oder Spätblüte?', in id. (ed.), *Hof, Kultur und Politik*, 48: John C. G. Röhl, 'Hof und Hofgesellschaft unter Kaiser Wilhelm II.', in id., *Kaiser, Hof und Staat: Wilhelm II. und die deutsche Politik* (Munich, 1987), 78.
[15] Arno J. Mayer, *The Persistence of the Old Regime: Europe to the Great War* (New York, 1981), 129–52.
[16] Gollwitzer, *Ludwig I.*, 767.
[17] For an excellent study which locates Leopold II squarely in the context of these problems, see Georges-Henri Dumont, *Léopold II* (Paris, 1990).
[18] Denis Mack Smith, *Italy and its Monarchy* (New Haven, Conn., 1989).

tional and neo-absolutist monarchies remained fundamental. The latter were able to draw upon older sources of monarchical power which had remained fairly intact, despite the traumas of the Napoleonic era. Their rulers remained the supreme warlords of their societies, and, as 1848 was to prove, they could continue to count on the loyalty of their armed forces. They were the ultimate source of bureaucratic decision-making and of preferment in the state service, and they also enjoyed direct control over vast quantities of land and money. Their relations with other powerful élites, most notably the landed aristocracies who usually populated officers' corps and high state office, were not as troubled as in previous centuries; after the French Revolution, nobles were far less inclined to engage in *frondes* against their rulers.[19] Moreover, in many parts of Europe those traditional landed élites adapted themselves quite skilfully to the economic and political requirements of the post-revolutionary age—another factor which contributed to the success of the monarchical revival itself.[20]

The crowned heads of Europe were able to draw not only upon 'traditional' forms of monarchical authority but also upon modern forms of ideological persuasion to sustain their political positions. Above all, as products of an ideological age, many of them learned from their enemies and made surprisingly effective use of modern ideological appeals and of ritualized modes of ideological discourse to ward off what they regarded, especially before 1848, as the omnipresent threat of revolution. The Festival of the White Rose was one small example of the ways in which monarchical values were being recast and, in many cases, newly created in the years after Waterloo. Other examples were much more important, especially the attempt to provide a new kind of doctrinal basis for kingship. Some of these efforts even antedated Napoleon's final disappearance: for example, Novalis's 1798 collection of aphorisms on 'Faith and Love, or the King and the Queen', with its rapturous evocation of the hereditary monarch's central moral role as 'the genuine life-principle of the state', or Tsar Alexander I's equally hazy and exalted notions of the Holy Alliance.[21] More substantive were ideological programmes like the doctrine of 'Official Nationality' in Russia after 1825, which tried to establish a kind of 'counter-nationalism' rooted in loyalty to the Tsar and the historically validated principles of autocracy.[22] Especially important for Central Europe, though, was a set of ideological and juridical doctrines called the 'monarchical principle'

---

[19] Mayer, *Persistence*, 146–62; Panajotis Kondylis, *Konservativismus: Geschichtlicher Gehalt und Untergang* (Stuttgart, 1986), 236–46.

[20] Volker Press, 'Adel im 19. Jahrhundert: Die Führungsschichten Alteuropas im bürgerlich-bürokratischen Zeitalter', in Armgard von Reden-Dohna and Ralph Melville (eds.), *Der Adel an der Schwelle des bürgerlichen Zeitalters 1780–1860* (Stuttgart, 1988), 1–19, esp. 5–6, 8, 11–13. See also Dominic Lieven, *The Aristocracy in Europe, 1815–1914* (New York, 1992).

[21] 'Novalis' [Friedrich von Hardenberg], 'Glauben und Liebe oder Der König und die Königin', in id., *Fragmente und Studien: Die Christenheit oder Europa*, ed. Carl Paschek (Stuttgart, 1984), 42–58; Friedrich Meinecke, *Cosmopolitanism and the National State*, trans. Robert B. Kimber (Princeton, NJ, 1970).

[22] Nicholas V. Riasanovsky, *Nicholas I and Official Nationality in Russia, 1825–1855* (Berkeley, Calif., 1967).

(*monarchisches Prinzip*), which for an entire century, from 1815 to 1918, served as 'the central category' of German public law.[23]

Although it had both German and French antecedents, especially in the French *Charte* of 1814, the concept of the monarchical principle was first articulated in the Bavarian constitutional charter of 1818, which stated that 'The King is the head of state; he unifies in his person all the legitimate power of the state and exercises them under the conditions established by the present constitution.'[24] These were notions that came to be anchored in the constitutional arrangements of many of the member states of the German Confederation after 1819. The fact that what came to be called the monarchical principle was first described in a constitution is quite revealing; for it was essentially a restatement of the continued justification of monarchical sovereignty in a 'revolutionary' age, as well as a tacit recognition of the fact that things like constitutions and parliaments were not going to disappear. Thus it presupposed the existence of a powerful rival or alternative ideological construct, the 'democratic principle' of popular sovereignty and the division of powers.[25]

A set of ideological categories that had been unknown before the Atlantic revolutions of the late eighteenth century, the monarchical principle was the product of an age in which monarchy had been desacralized and demythologized, and in which, moreover, the utility of secular, enlightened despotism could no longer automatically be assumed.[26] Indeed, the very fact of its emergence after 1814–15 as a cluster of abstract and rather slippery ideological principles attests to the vulnerability and defensiveness of monarchy in those years, and to the desire of the ideological defenders of monarchy to emphasize the stability of a hereditary system as opposed to the chaos and instability of revolutionary republican regimes. At the same time, as its application to the Bavarian and other south German constitutions suggests, it could also be used to justify compromises with constitutionalism.[27] In a constitutional monarchy dominated by the monarchical principle, the prerogatives of the crown should take priority over the forces which might seek to limit those powers (for example, through control over budgets). 'The monarchical principle thus states that, as in older forms of continental absolutism, the unitary power of the state rests in the ruler's hands.'[28] The monarchical principle was not synonymous with absolutism. In constitutional monarchies based on the monarchical principle, the crown had to agree to certain limitations on its absolute power, especially in the sphere of judicature, civil liberties, and the rights of 'historically' constituted estates of the realm; but

[23] Hans Boldt, *Deutsche Staatslehre im Vormärz* (Düsseldorf, 1975), 15.   [24] Quoted ibid. 19.

[25] Ibid. 16–17; Heinrich Otto Meisner, *Die Lehre vom monarchischen Prinzip im Zeitalter der Restauration und des Deutschen Bundes* (Aalen, 1969; orig. Breslau, 1913), 3; Dieter Grimm, *Deutsche Verfassungsgeschichte 1776–1866: Vom Beginn des modernen Verfassungsstaats bis zur Auflösung des Deutschen Bundes* (Frankfurt am Main, 1988), 113–16; Matthew Bernard Levinger, 'Imagining a Nation: The Constitutional Question in Prussia, 1806–1825' (Ph.D. thesis; Chicago, 1992), ch. 6, esp. 297–304.

[26] Meisner, *Lehre*, 161; Otto Brunner, 'Vom Gottesgnadentum zum monarchischen Prinzip: Der Weg der europäischen Monarchie seit dem hohen Mittelalter', in id., *Neue Wege der Verfassungs- und Sozialgeschichte*, 2nd edn. (Göttingen, 1968), 179.

[27] Meisner, *Lehre*, 198–215; Boldt, *Staatslehre*, 16, 32–3; Dollinger, 'Leitbild', 328–9.

[28] Brunner, 'Gottesgnadentum', 182.

the crown's executive authority, and its power to initiate legislation, remained immense.[29]

Such arguments were powerfully advanced by one of the most forceful and imaginative conservative thinkers of the nineteenth century, Friedrich Julius Stahl, in an influential 1845 pamphlet entitled simply *The Monarchical Principle*. While contrasting the monarchical principle of the German states with the parliamentary principle in Great Britain, Stahl also contended that it was necessary and legitimate to make concessions to public opinion and to modern ideas of national representation. One of the central problems that Continental monarchies faced, Stahl argued, was how to accommodate royal power to the requirements and structure of the modern state, in which old-fashioned, patrimonial institutions were no longer tenable. Monarchy and political representation were thus, in his view, eminently reconcilable, though in his system the balance would always be tilted toward the former. The monarchical principle stood for something more substantial than monarchical sovereignty, for in Great Britain the queen was sovereign but did not rule. The monarchical principle was thus an ideological and constitutional guarantee that, even under constitutional conditions, the monarch would continue to rule and not simply reign. By making a compromise with constitutionalism, in other words, it might be possible to neutralize democratic demands for genuine popular sovereignty.[30]

For monarchs and their supporters, however, it did not suffice to devise often abstruse ideological defences for monarchical authority. As Stahl had realized, it was also necessary to recognize and appeal to public opinion. Thus nineteenth-century rulers and their advisers, both in genuinely parliamentary monarchies and in neo-absolutist states, were increasingly determined to construct an effective public image of the majesty, power, and stability of monarchy, and of the mutuality of affection (and obligation) between caring ruler and devoted subjects. In some cases this involved the adaptation and modernization of older practices, such as royal patronage for the arts, or lavish spending on architectural and public-works projects. As with so much else, the extent and effect of that support varied considerably over time and place, and could be decisively influenced by a ruler's individual personality. In addition, the presence of a large, independent, art-consuming bourgeois public, the emergence of the modern artistic avant-garde, the growing importance

[29] Boldt, *Staatslehre*, 33–8. One recent historian argues that many of the emerging bourgeois publics in Europe embraced the idea of a monarchy which could serve either as a guarantor of social stability or as the symbol of bourgeois notions of the state: that is, a state based on constitutional principles and individual rights as opposed to bureaucratic decree or ascriptive 'rights'. In Germany, she contends, bourgeois liberals before 1848 came to see their monarchs as projections of their own wishes, the symbols of a state organized according to liberal principles and dominated by a bourgeois 'political nation'. Monika Wienfort, *Monarchie in der bürgerlichen Gesellschaft: Deutschland und England von 1640 bis 1848* (Göttingen, 1993), 169–203.

[30] Friedrich Julius Stahl, *Das monarchische Princip: Eine staatsrechtlich-politische Abhandlung* (Heidelberg, 1845). See also the recent commentaries in Boldt, *Staatslehre*, 196–206; Wilhelm Füßl, *Professor in der Politik: Friedrich Julius Stahl (1802–1861). Das monarchische Prinzip und seine Umsetzung in die parlamentarische Praxis* (Göttingen, 1988), 44–50; Robert M. Berdahl, *The Politics of the Prussian Nobility: The Development of a Conservative Ideology 1770–1848* (Princeton, NJ, 1988), 368–70.

of the notion of *l'art pour l'art*, and increasing competition from other public authorities undercut traditional forms of royal patronage of art and culture after the French Revolution. Still, royal support for artists and architects remained extremely important after 1815, and many monarchs appreciated its utility for their own public images.[31]

If royal patronage of the arts was one example of the way in which 'older' forms of monarchical self-representation and propaganda could be modernized, so too were royal ritual and ceremonial. In recent years historians and other scholars have become increasingly sensitive to the complex reciprocal relationships between structures of power, authority, and dominance, on the one hand, and, on the other, the non-verbal signs, symbols, and modes of ritualized discourse through which those relationships are mediated and interpreted.[32] Thus ritual, ceremonial, and etiquette—to use the sociologist Edward Shils's important distinctions—have come to be seen as critically important ingredients of those processes through which the legitimacy of any political system is forged and sustained.[33] Ritual and ceremonial have been fruitfully described as modes of exercising power 'along the cognitive dimension'—so that royal pageantry, pomp, and spectacle became ways of explaining, justifying, impressing, and mediating. Ritual tries at once to project certain 'right' or 'authoritative' notions of what is important and to deflect people's attention from alternative notions, 'since every way of seeing is also a way of not seeing'.[34]

Viewed in this light, the rituals and ceremonies of nineteenth-century monarchs were not simply exercises in anachronistic showmanship, pale reflections of the grand occasions that had been such conspicuous features of pre-1789 monarchies. Rather, rituals and ceremonies remained critically important opportunities for monarchs and their supporters to project an authoritative image of monarchy to increasingly segmented, differentiated, and secularized nineteenth-century publics. Above all, it was through ritual and ceremonial that modern monarchs continued, like their

[31] A. G. Dickens, 'Epilogue', in id. (ed.), *The Courts of Europe: Politics, Patronage and Royalty 1400–1800* (London, 1977), 326–7; Robin Lenman, 'Painters, Patronage and the Art Market in Germany 1850–1914', *Past and Present*, 123 (May 1989), 109–40, esp. 114–17.

[32] Of special importance are the recent essays collected in Sean Wilentz (ed.), *Rites of Power: Symbolism, Ritual, and Politics since the Middle Ages* (Philadelphia, 1985); David Cannadine and Simon Price (eds.), *Rituals of Royalty: Power and Ceremonial in Traditional Societies* (Cambridge, 1987); and János M. Bak (ed.), *Coronations: Medieval and Early Modern Monarchic Ritual* (Berkeley, Calif., 1990).

[33] Shils describes ritual as 'a stereotyped, symbolically concentrated expression of beliefs and sentiments regarding ultimate things. . . . An elaborate etiquette has much in common with ritual in its rigidly stereotypical structure, in its specification of actions, and in its symbolization of differing appreciation of the charismatic qualities embodied in great authority, power, and eminence. But etiquette is at the periphery of the relation to sacred things while ritual is at the centre.' Shils goes on to argue that ceremonial 'belongs to the same family of rigidly stereotyped actions but is closer to ritual than to etiquette because it has more cognitive content. . . . Its occurrence is more concentrated than that of etiquette.' Edward Shils, 'Ritual and Crisis', in id., *Center and Periphery: Essays in Macrosociology* (Chicago, 1975), 154–5.

[34] Steven Lukes, 'Political Ritual and Social Integration', in id., *Essays in Social Theory* (New York, 1977), 68. Cf. David Cannadine, 'Introduction', in Cannadine and Price (eds.,), *Rituals*, 12; Isabel V. Hull, 'Prussian Dynastic Ritual and the End of Monarchy', in Carole Fink, Isabel V. Hull, and MacGregor Knox (eds.), *German Nationalism and the European Response, 1890–1945* (Norman, Okla., 1985), 14, 16.

forebears, to validate their claims to remain at the 'active' or 'animating centers' of their societies.[35]

Of course, in the nineteenth century it was not always easy to make such claims stick. As we have already noted, monarchy in the Western world had almost completely lost its sacral or numinous character, and occasional attempts to reassert that mystic quality—the coronation of Charles X at Reims in 1825 is the best example—often encountered indifference or derision.[36] Moreover, royal ritual and ceremonial tended, as a whole, to be rather unimpressive and even comical in the decades just after 1815. Pompous occasions were not really appropriate in an age that emphasized the importance of simplicity and naïve domestic pleasures. But the use, effectiveness, and grandeur of royal rituals and ceremonies grew steadily throughout the century. Up to the 1870s, for example, royal ceremonies in Great Britain were almost laughably mismanaged. Grand royal ceremonial only began to emerge in that country with the monarchy's transformation into an institution that was at once politically weak and a symbol of imperial glory.[37] In short, grand royal ritual was only possible in Great Britain when the monarchy itself had clearly lost much of its day-to-day political significance. The political situation in many other parts of Europe was, of course, notably different; but there, too, monarchical ritual and ceremonial became increasingly splendid and awe-inspiring as the century progressed.

The use of ritual or ceremonial in the nineteenth century often entailed the refurbishment or modernization of older practices. Official travels were one example. From time immemorial, of course, rulers had undertaken royal progresses and official entries through their realms in order to take symbolic—and, in many cases, actual—possession of them.[38] In many parts of Europe, however, royal journeys had dwindled in significance by the eighteenth century, and they had increasingly come to serve utilitarian purposes: inspections, reviews, or the fulfilment of traditional obligations towards powerful élite groups.[39] Indeed, some eighteenth-century monarchs barely left their main places of residence. George III, for example, never travelled north of Worcester and never visited his possessions in Hanover.[40] Before 1789 Louis XVI only left the Île-de-France once, to go to Cherbourg.

After 1815, however, both the functions and the frequency of royal travel began to change; and, as was so often the case in the nineteenth century, other European monarchs followed the lead of the Bonapartes. Both Napoleons travelled frequently and extensively throughout France; as plebiscitary dictators attuned to public opinion, they understood the importance of being seen by their subjects. Official

[35] Clifford Geertz, 'Centers, Kings, and Charisma: Reflections on the Symbolics of Power', in Wilentz (ed.), *Rites of Power*, 14, 15.

[36] But see the sympathetic and thorough account by Landric Raillat, *Charles X: Le Sacre de la dernière chance* (Paris, 1991), esp. chs. 2 and 9.

[37] David Cannadine, 'The Context, Performance and Meaning of Ritual: The British Monarchy and the "Invention of Tradition", c. 1820–1977', in Eric Hobsbawm and Terence Ranger (eds.), *The Invention of Tradition* (Cambridge, 1983), 106–7, 109, 117, 121. Cf. Thomas Richards, 'The Image of Victoria in the Year of Jubilee', *Victorian Studies*, 31 (1987), 7–32, on the 'commodification' of the Queen's image.

[38] Geertz, 'Centers', 16–29.   [39] Wortman, 'Rule', 745–6.

[40] Richard Mullen and James Munson, *Victoria: Portrait of a Queen* (London, 1987), 59.

journeys now presented an opportunity to enhance the popular image of royalty, to personalize the bonds between ruler and common folk, to integrate provincial aristocracies more effectively with the monarchical centre, and to extend the charisma of monarchy beyond the narrow confines of court and capital.[41] The political impact of royal tours, with all the impressive ceremonial that usually accompanied them, depended to a large extent on the personality of the monarch and the purpose of the trip. As we shall have ample opportunity to observe in this study, Frederick William IV was a tireless traveller who quickly understood the new opportunities that the railway offered to him; and, like his Russian nephew Alexander II, he was adept at using those occasions to project an image of himself as benevolent and loving father of his people. In fact, he was probably even more successful at this than the Tsar. In contrast to 'Sasha', Frederick William was a brilliant speech-maker and witty raconteur with an almost instinctive sense for the right word on the right occasion.

To be sure, frequent royal travels did not necessarily result in an improved public image of monarchy. During the first years of his reign after 1820, for example, George IV travelled far more often than his father, but his constant presence in the public eye did little to enhance his horrible public reputation or improve his low popularity. Frederick William IV's great-nephew, the German Emperor William II, was notorious for his frenetic travels, and after 1894 he spent less than half his time in Berlin or Potsdam. But his extensive trips were often private affairs, escapes from the responsibility of day-to-day work which rarely brought him into contact with his subjects. In stark contrast to William II, the Austrian Emperor Francis Joseph (another nephew of Frederick William IV) was well known for his iron self-discipline and punctilious adherence to duty. His numerous tours through his diverse domains were thus extremely ritualized, standardized, and rather old-fashioned affairs, marked by removable triumphal arches, processions of girls strewing flowers, concerts, gala receptions, and visits to local museums and hospitals. Through their fixed and ritualized quality, however, Francis Joseph's trips conveyed the message that the dynastic bond was the glue that held the Empire together; while the Emperor himself, with his extremely impressive appearance and almost overwhelmingly majestic bearing, was his own best advertisement. As Charles de Gaulle, that twentieth-century republican monarch, always realized, dignity and distance were essential ingredients of successful monarchical representation.[42]

Modernized ceremonial occasions like official royal tours had various purposes; but one of them, in a century in which nationalism was an increasingly potent political force, was to project an image of the monarch as symbol of the nation.[43] In multi-

---

[41] Philip Mansel, *The Court of France 1789–1830* (Cambridge, 1988), 153–4; Wortman, 'Rule', 745–71.

[42] John Cannon and Ralph Griffiths, *The Oxford Illustrated History of the British Monarchy* (Oxford, 1988), 541; Isabel V. Hull, *The Entourage of Kaiser Wilhelm II 1888–1918* (Cambridge, 1982), 33–40; Jean-Paul Bled, *Franz Joseph*, trans. Teresa Bridgeman (Oxford, 1992), 209–10, 220–1.

[43] For an early example of the use of the royal image to mobilize patriotic sentiment, see Linda Colley, 'The Apotheosis of George III: Loyalty, Royalty and the British Nation 1760–1820', *Past and Present*, 102 (Feb. 1984), 94–129.

national entities like the Habsburg Monarchy, rulers sought to emphasize the unity of the state, and the dynasty's role as guarantor of that unity. Above all, it had now become necessary for monarchs to show that they were heads of state and society, and not merely the most exalted members of a particular caste or estate. One of the most vivid manifestations of the unity of the European state during and after the French Revolution was, of course, the army. By the first quarter of the nineteenth century most monarchs usually appeared in uniform on ceremonial occasions. What a change from the previous century, when uniforms had been associated with military monarchies like those of Sweden or Prussia![44] The increasing use of uniforms by Continental monarchs (and, to a lesser extent, their British counterparts) may well have reflected both a 'nationalization' and 'militarization' of nineteenth-century monarchy; but it also reflected something else. By wearing a uniform, the monarch was symbolically suggesting that he too was subordinate to the abstract entity called the state: another indication of the ways in which the distinctions and the relations between monarch and state were becoming clearer.[45]

Thanks to things like royal tours, the dispersal of popular royalist literature, and increasingly rapid communications, royal ritual and ceremonial were becoming more accessible to ordinary men and women in nineteenth-century Europe. Still, the real focus of that ritual and ceremonial remained, as it had been for centuries, the court. During the early modern period, courts had been the stage on which the great theatre of royal power had been acted out, and it was there that the complex interplay between pageantry and power, and between display and dominance, had been most obvious. Court society was thus one of the most influential élite 'social formations' during the heyday of monarchical absolutism, and it has deservedly been the subject of many analyses by historians and sociologists.[46] But how significant were royal courts in the nineteenth century? As we have already seen, the culture of simplicity and sentiment, as well as the individual personalities of many rulers in the late eighteenth and early nineteenth centuries encouraged a decline of the courts as the loci of symbolic power and as the driving force of society. Lavish court display, after all, hardly seemed compatible with the simple life-styles of supposedly bourgeois monarchs. The monarchical revival after 1815, however, witnessed a gradual but steady reversal of this trend, with a renascence of the size of courts, a return to splendid court ceremonial, and a reaffirmation of the importance of court society. As with so many things, nineteenth-century monarchs looked to their enemy, the Corsican usurper, as model and inspiration in their efforts to re-create imposing courts. Recent studies have emphasized the powerful monarchist streak in Napoleon I, and during the First Empire the court of France attained a size and magnificence

[44] Philip Mansel, 'Monarchy, Uniform and the Rise of the *Frac* 1760–1830', *Past and Present*, 96 (Aug. 1982), 111, 113.

[45] Werner, 'Fürst und Hof', 45; Mansel, 'Uniform', 124–5; Nigel Arch and Joanna Marschner, *Splendour at Court: Dressing for Royal Occasions since 1700* (London, 1987), 74–99.

[46] Among many studies of absolutist courts as instruments of royal policy, see esp. the classic analysis by Norbert Elias, *The Court Society*, trans. Edmund Jephcott (New York, 1983).

unparalleled since the days of the Sun King. And that imperial court in turn set the tone for what has aptly been described as a 'return to grandeur' at other European courts after the Congress of Vienna.[47]

European courts had always been highly complex social formations which performed a number of distinct functions, many of which varied over time and place. Thus the Spanish and Austrian courts had long been known for their elaborate etiquette and their extreme social exclusiveness, while in Prussia the court had dwindled to insignificance after the death of Frederick I in 1713. During the heyday of the absolutist court system, many courts had used ritual and ceremonial to focus attention on the sacral, almost magical quality of kingship, while serving simultaneously as the kingdom's military, political, and diplomatic nerve-centre. Courts had also been the arbiters of good taste and civility, the social setting which connected the crown with other élite groups, foreign and domestic. By the nineteenth century, however, a number of these functions had been attenuated or had even disappeared. With the growing differentiation between monarchical institutions and the state, many administrative activities which had been located at the court— for example, the supervision of royal lands—were now taken over by bureaucratic hierarchies outside the court. Similarly, it was no longer possible to project a semi-divine image of monarchical authority, despite the continued insistence by some nineteenth-century rulers that their power literally had a heavenly sanction. Finally, the growing financial and cultural autonomy of non-aristocratic élite groups meant that nineteenth-century courts had to compete with alternative sources of social authority, prestige, and status. The experiences of the courts of France after 1815, though not necessarily 'typical', illustrate these developments with special clarity.

During the Bourbon Restoration (1814/15–30), the French court enjoyed an unprecedented popularity and a social influence in Paris which it had rarely known under the Old Regime. Now focused on the Tuileries, in the heart of the capital, rather than on Versailles, it became the focal point of an urban-based aristocratic society while simultaneously opening itself to non-noble influences.[48] Thus it was no longer as exclusive as its predecessors—or, to put it more precisely, it now defined exclusivity in a new way. In the words of its historian, 'Official rank, not social class, was now the basis of the court of France.'[49] Moreover, the relative openness of the Restoration court meant that it had become a meeting-place for various élite groups within French society. The court was, of course, intimately bound up with the high politics of the day, while its grandeur and size made it 'a model for the other courts of Europe'. Though the Restoration court could not forestall the events of July 1830, there can be little doubt that it contributed to the relative popularity and stability enjoyed by the Bourbon regime until its last years. Louis-Philippe, however, decid-

---

[47] Philip Mansel, *The Eagle in Splendour: Napoleon I and his Court* (London, 1987), 205; cf. id., *Court of France*, 188.

[48] Anne Martin-Fugier, *La Vie élégante ou la formation du Tout-Paris 1815–1848* (Paris, 1990), 392.

[49] Mansel, *Court of France*, 128.

ed to dispense with a court almost entirely, which only intensified the alienation of several important élite groups from his regime.[50]

The absence of a vigorous court life during the July Monarchy helped to accelerate a process which, ironically, had already begun during the heyday of the Restoration court and which illustrates one of the major problems faced by all nineteenth-century courts: the development of alternative centres of prestige, high fashion, and élite social life which no longer derived their inspiration from the world of the court. The privatization of *le monde*, its separation from the court and from high politics, was largely completed during the 1830s and 1840s in France. Luxury and leisure, rather than a relationship to the court, thus became the defining characteristics of a depoliticized high society in nineteenth-century Paris, and its centres were to be found not in the Tuileries but in places like the aristocratic Faubourg Saint-Germain. Of course, there were still plenty of people in Paris society who hankered after a glamorous court; and, after his election to the presidency of the Second Republic in December 1848, Louis-Napoleon Bonaparte began to reconstruct one. With his establishment of the Second Empire in 1852, Napoleon III's court became for a time the most dazzling and splendid in all of Europe. Still, the nature and character of the court had changed fundamentally since the Restoration: 'In 1820, the *monde* was defined as everyone who was linked to the court. By 1849 the relationship had reversed itself.' Thereafter the court would be one institution of high society, but not the definer of it.[51]

Despite such constraints and qualifications, the size, splendour, and social radiance of many European courts increased throughout the century. Napoleon III's was grand, but so too was the court of Francis Joseph in Austria, which contrasted sharply with the dullness and simplicity of court life during the reign of his two predecessors. The renascence of a magnificent court life almost seems to have represented a conscious strategy on the part of Habsburg élites after the upheavals of 1848–9. To signal the defeat of the revolution and the political centrality of the monarch it seemed necessary to resurrect an elaborate ceremonial structure which could draw attention to the awe-inspiring majesty of Emperor and dynasty. The strategy of using the court system to establish a cult of monarchy around Francis Joseph corresponded to the period of neo-absolutism from 1849 to 1859, when Austria had no constitution, and political decision-making was focused on the Emperor and his advisers. Thus Francis Joseph's court, in the tradition of royal establishments elsewhere in Europe, fulfilled a whole range of political, symbolic, and social functions. It remained the gravitational centre around which orbited the activities of the grand aristocracy, which in turn helped set the tone for the rest of Vienna's social life until at least the 1890s. Known for its formality and rigid etiquette, the Habsburg court's organizational structure was immense, from the exalted aristocratic officials of the Emperor's

[50] Ibid. 129–49, 189–93, 194. For a different view, see Suzanne d'Huart, 'La Cour de Louis-Philippe', in Werner (ed.), *Hof, Kultur und Politik*, 77–85.

[51] Martin-Fugier, *La Vie élégante*, 391; see also Louis Girard, 'La Cour de Napoléon III', in Werner (ed.), *Hof, Kultur und Politik*, 155–65; L. Girard, *Napoléon III* (Paris, 1986), 199–214.

maison civile and *maison militaire* all the way down to dozens of pages, lackeys, cooks, gardeners, tailors, barbers, and coachmen.[52]

The court of the Habsburg Emperor was not necessarily the most spectacular example of the expansion of official monarchical institutions in the nineteenth century. That dubious honour is probably reserved for the Prussian-German court of William II, which experienced a gargantuan 'inflation' of its personnel and its finances after 1888.[53] But even at earlier dates, in smaller states, and on a more modest scale, many nineteenth-century monarchs appreciated the advantages of a vigorous court life.[54] In all nineteenth-century monarchies, constitutional or otherwise, courts continued to serve a number of critically important ends. They functioned as the symbolic focus of monarchy, the principal instrument through which monarchical values could be articulated and transmitted. They were the guarantors of social rank, and, in many cases, the institution which mediated between the monarch, his advisers, and other élite groups. In semi-absolutist or pre-constitutional regimes, courts continued to play a central political role, as we shall have ample opportunity to observe in this book. Where the distinction between the crown and the state had not been fully drawn, where popular representations were non-existent or attenuated, and where ultimate decision-making power continued to reside in the throne, the court constituted the field of play upon which vying interests and individuals fought for the monarch's attention and competed to influence his choices.

The Prussian Monarchy to 1840

During the first half of the nineteenth century, Prussia was, with Austria and Russia, one of the three most important examples of a semi-absolutist, non-constitutional monarchical state. But what kind of absolutism was it? What kind of monarchy was it? And how does the Prussian monarchy fit into the complex picture that we have just been drawing? How was the Prussian monarchy affected by the kinds of developments that we have just been describing? These are questions that will recur in the chapters that follow. But to help us set the scene, let us briefly summarize the evolution and character of Prussia's monarchical system up to the late 1830s, shortly before Frederick William IV's accession to the throne.

Karl Marx wrote in 1843 that 'the king constitutes the system in Prussia'.[55] This comment was not much of an exaggeration. Indeed, throughout the seventeenth and

---

[52] Bled, *Franz Joseph*, 211–23; Brigitte Hamann, 'Der Wiener Hof und die Hofgesellschaft in der zweiten Hälfte des 19. Jahrhunderts', in Möckl (ed.), *Hof und Hofgesellschaft*, 61–78.

[53] Röhl, 'Hof und Hofgesellschaft', esp. 241–6, 248, 250–61.

[54] On the courts of smaller monarchs, esp. in Central Europe, see Gollwitzer, *Ludwig I.*, 328–34; Paul Sauer, *Der schwäbische Zar: Friedrich, Württembergs erster König* (Stuttgart, 1984), 381–94; Gisela Herdt, 'Der württembergische Hof im 19. Jahrhundert: Studien über das Verhältnis zwischen Königtum und Adel in der absoluten und konstitutionellen Monarchie' (Diss.; Göttingen, 1970); Max Brunner, *Die Hofgesellschaft: Die führende Gesellschaftsschicht Bayerns während der Regierungszeit König Maximilian II.* (Munich, 1987); Karl Möckl, 'Hof und Hofgesellschaft in Bayern in der Prinzregentenzeit', in Werner (ed.), *Hof, Kultur und Politik*, 183–235; and Möckl (ed.), *Hof und Hofgesellschaft*.

[55] Karl Marx to Arnold Ruge, May 1843, quoted in Siegfried Bahne, 'Die Verfassungspläne König

[*cont. on p. 17*]

eighteenth centuries Brandenburg-Prussia had been the very quintessence of the dynastic state. A creation of the dynasty and its servitors in the army and the bureaucracy, it was an artificial hotchpotch of diverse territories accumulated over the course of many generations. Thus the only basis for any kind of shared or common identification with the larger entity called 'Prussia' was the king himself.[56]

A relative newcomer among the great powers of Europe, Prussia was the incarnation of the modern, rational, 'machine' state of the eighteenth century. Its ruling dynasty, which only achieved royal status in 1701, had never been endowed with the kinds of sacral significance that had long surrounded the French or Habsburg courts. The first King 'in' and later 'of' Prussia, Frederick I, was obsessed with pageantry, and determined to create a court that in pomp and splendour would be second to none.[57] His two successors, Frederick William I and Frederick II, did not share his enthusiasm for gaudy display, and only rarely availed themselves of opportunities for the lavish representation that elsewhere served to enhance an absolutist ruler's political authority. The two great eighteenth-century Prussian kings did maintain a rudimentary court-structure, however, and on unavoidable occasions even the misanthropic and anti-social Frederick II had to subject himself to a regimen of court balls and official etiquette. On the whole, though, Frederick shared his father's well-known contempt for court ceremonial, while holders of formal court offices never enjoyed much influence during his reign. To be sure, under both Frederick William I and Frederick II considerable influence *could* be amassed by individuals with access to the court and through it to the king's informal entourage, the Soldier King's boisterous *Tabakskollegium* being one of the better-known examples.[58] Above all, though, it was through the structures of the administration and the army that the Hohenzollern kings were able to consolidate and sustain effective royal authority in the years before 1786. In the words of one scholar, 'Whereas Louis XIV had ruled surrounded by court nobles engaged in status display (and in displaying their status as they exalted his), Frederick the Great ruled as the first among a vast number of officials.'[59] According to many historians, the foundations had thus been laid by the time of Frederick's death in 1786—and certainly no later than 1794, with the introduction of the Prussian Law Code—for Prussia's transition from 'royal' to 'bureaucratic' absolutism.[60]

Friedrich Wilhelms IV. von Preußen und die Prinzenopposition im Vormärz' (*Habilitationsschrift*; Bochum, 1970), 129.

[56] Bernd von Münchow-Pohl, *Zwischen Reform und Krieg: Untersuchungen zur Bewußtseinslage in Preußen 1809–1812* (Göttingen, 1987), 410–11.

[57] Ingrid Mittenzwei and Erika Herzfeld, *Brandenburg-Preußen 1648–1789: Das Zeitalter des Absolutismus in Text und Bild*, 3rd edn. (Berlin, 1990), 159; Linda Frey and Marsha Frey, *Frederick I: The Man and his Times* (Boulder, Col., 1984), 66–91.

[58] Theodor Schieder, *Friedrich der Große: Ein Königtum der Widersprüche* (Frankfurt am Main, 1983), 46–7, 50–4, 57–9.

[59] Gianfranco Poggi, *The Development of the Modern State: A Sociological Introduction* (Stanford, Calif., 1978), 76.

[60] There is a large literature on these developments, but see above all Hans Rosenberg, *Bureaucracy, Aristocracy, and Autocracy: The Prussian Experience 1660–1815* (Cambridge, Mass., 1958); Hubert C.

[*cont. on p. 18*]

Twenty years after Frederick's death the Fred50erician state collapsed on the bat-
tlefields of Jena and Auerstädt, and for a long time after 1806 the Prussian monarchy
under Frederick William III faced an 'existential crisis' of unparalleled depth and
intensity; at various times it seemed that the monarchy itself might cease to exist. But
several developments came to the rescue of the state and the dynasty, most notably
the celebrated Prussian reform movement.[61] The reformers, including Baron vom
Stein and his great rival, Prince Karl August von Hardenberg, were certainly not
unanimous in their views about what should be done to resolve the situation; but they
agreed that a radical break with the structures of the Frederician system was essential. Among the most important of those structures was the now-discredited cabinet
system, through which the king had made policy decisions based on consultations
with non-responsible cabinet councillors, rather than with a modern-style cabinet of
ministers responsible for specific portfolios.[62] The result of these pressures for
change was the series of reforms undertaken between 1807 and 1819: the restructuring of the military, Stein's emancipation of the peasants and his reorganization of
municipal government, Hardenberg's economic and financial reforms, and a series
of administrative changes at the very top of the Prussian state. Hardenberg in particular envisaged a streamlined, unitary, bureaucratic system which would be able to
adjust quickly to the exigencies of modern times. In 1810 he became State Chancellor
(*Staatskanzler*), a position without precedent in Prussian history, and as the country's '*Ersatzkönig*' he managed to concentrate a great deal of power in his own hands.
Frederick William III, whose self-confidence had never been especially great, at first
seemed willing to follow Hardenberg's lead, so that the Chancellor's position has
been compared to that of the great political cardinals in seventeenth-century
France.[63]

Thus it seemed that the royal absolutism embodied in the old cabinet-system had
been replaced by an 'absolutism of the State Chancellor'.[64] The reformers' ideas necessarily implied a diminution of the monarch's capacity for personal rule, though

Johnson, *Frederick the Great and his Officials* (New Haven, Conn., 1975); and Reinhart Koselleck, *Preußen zwischen Reform und Revolution: Allgemeines Landrecht, Verwaltung und soziale Bewegung von 1791 bis 1848*, 3rd edn. (Stuttgart, 1981).

[61] The most up-to-date surveys of the Prussian reform movement can be found in Thomas Nipperdey, *Deutsche Geschichte 1800–1866: Bürgerwelt und starker Staat* (Munich, 1983), 33–69; Hans-Ulrich Wehler, *Deutsche Gesellschaftsgeschichte* (Munich, 1987–), i: *Vom Feudalismus des Alten Reiches bis zur defensiven Modernisierung der Reformära*, 397–485; James J. Sheehan, *German History 1770–1866* (Oxford, 1989), 291–310; Levinger, 'Imagining a Nation'; and Bernd Sösemann (ed.), *Gemeingeist und Bürgersinn: Die preußischen Reformen* (Berlin, 1993).

[62] Otto Hintze, 'Das preußische Staatsministerium im 19. Jahrhundert', in id., *Gesammelte Abhandlungen*, iii: *Regierung und Verwaltung: Gesammelte Abhandlungen zur Staats-, Rechts- und Sozialgeschichte Preußens*, ed. Gerhard Oestreich, 2nd edn. (Göttingen, 1967; orig. 1908), 530–7; Münchow-Pohl, *Zwischen Reform und Krieg*, 432–5.

[63] On Hardenberg's reforms, see above all Barbara Vogel, *Allgemeine Gewerbefreiheit: Die Reformpolitik des preußischen Staatskanzlers Hardenberg (1810–1820)* (Göttingen, 1983).

[64] For much of the material in the following paragraph, see Thomas Stamm-Kuhlmann, *König in Preußens großer Zeit: Friedrich Wilhelm III. Der Melancholiker auf dem Thron* (Berlin, 1992), 312–18, 323–9.

they certainly had no intention of utterly eliminating his executive prerogatives or transforming him into a constitutional monarch. Ultimately, as Hardenberg himself appreciated, the Chancellor's own position depended upon his relationship to the king, much as Bismarck's did later in the century. Hardenberg was also no democrat, although he did support the idea of a system of political representation for the king-dom as a whole.[65] The idea of such a representation was broached in his Finance Edict of 1810; and five years later, shortly before the battle of Waterloo, Frederick William III solemnly promised to establish representative institutions for the entire Prussian state, including the new territories that had just been acquired at the Congress of Vienna.[66] More than anything else, though, Hardenberg remained a bureaucratic centralizer. Accordingly, in 1817 his government established a Council of State (*Staatsrat*), to be composed of the royal princes, ministers, and other members named by the king. It was foreseen as a 'supreme advisory authority' for legislative and administrative decisions, a kind of substitute parliament which, at least accord-ing to theory, would be strongly influenced by bureaucrats.[67] In short, when Hardenberg called for 'democratic principles in a monarchical government', what he really meant, in the words of one scholar, was 'freedom for individuals in the eco-nomic and social realm—and virtually unlimited power for the state in the conduct of public affairs'.[68]

Given Hardenberg's views, it is not surprising that the reform era and its after-math witnessed an acceleration of the process of 'differentiation between crown and state'. Under Frederick William I, for example, the substantial royal demesnes (*Domänen*) had been regarded as the inalienable property of the royal house. Now, however, they were in effect nationalized: that is, they were now considered to be state property which could be disposed of as the state saw fit. The income from state-controlled lands would be used to pay for the expenses of crown and court. According to the Law on State Debts (*Staatsschuldengesetz*) of 1820, an annual sub-sidy of 2.5 million Taler, derived from the profits of the *Domänen*, was to be used as a 'royal feoffment in trust' (*Kronfideikommiß*) to meet the public expenses of the court and the royal house.[69] This *Kronfideikommiß* was in some ways analogous to the 'civil lists' which pay for royal expenses in constitutional monarchies, though in Prussia it was not subject to any kind of parliamentary control.

The Prussian royal house could still draw upon substantial private resources. The king's privy purse (*Schatulle*) was steadily augmented from the profits of his private estates (*Schatullgüter*), while Frederick William III's notorious miserliness made it

---

[65] Matthew Levinger, 'Hardenberg, Wittgenstein, and the Constitutional Question in Prussia 1815–22', *German History*, 8 (1990), 257–77.

[66] Ibid. 261–2; Sheehan, *German History*, 420–1; Stamm-Kuhlmann, *König*, 409–15.

[67] Nipperdey, *Deutsche Geschichte*, 37; Herbert Obenaus, *Anfänge des Parlamentarismus in Preußen bis 1848* (Düsseldorf, 1984), 95–100.

[68] Sheehan, *German History*, 305.

[69] Thomas Stamm-Kuhlmann, 'Der Hof König Friedrich Wilhelms III. von Preußen 1797 bis 1840', in Möckl (ed.), *Hof und Hofgesellschaft*, 278–80; Obenaus, *Anfänge*, 122–8. Although the noun *Fideikommiß* is usually rendered into English as 'entail', Rudolf Braun's translation of it as 'feoffment in

[*cont. on p. 20*]

possible to create a 'crown reserve' (*Krontresor*) of three million Taler out of the unspent portions of *Kronfideikommiß* subsidies. Those reserves were to be used as an emergency fund for members of the royal family. There was also a *Hausfideikommiß*, which Frederick William I had set up for his younger sons and their descendants, and a similar *Königlich-Prinzliches Fideikommiß* for the younger sons of Frederick William III.[70]

The distinction between the king's functions as a public figure and a quasi-private individual was not, however, entirely unambiguous. In 1819, for example, a Ministry of the Royal House was established, which until 1848 was responsible both for managing the royal family's private business and for administering various state affairs. And to complicate matters even further, the *Hausminister* from 1819 to 1851, Prince Wilhelm Ludwig Georg von Sayn-Wittgenstein-Hohenstein, was Frederick William III's closest personal confidant and also, as Lord Chamberlain (*Oberkammerherr*), occupant of the highest formal court office. In short, during the reign of Frederick William III the monarch had by no means simply become one organ of the state among many others. At the very least, he remained *primus inter pares*.

Wittgenstein's relationship to the King exemplified the continued importance of royal power and the limits of Hardenberg's own. In fact, after 1810 the state chancellor had encountered stubborn opposition to his policies, not only from the landed representatives of local and corporative or 'estatist' (*ständisch*) interests but also within the high bureaucracy and among the circle of Frederick William's informal advisers at court.[71] That opposition ultimately forced Hardenberg to agree to a number of compromises and also resulted in a dilution of the King's constitutional promise of 1815. Prussia thus remained a pre-constitutional state without a system of popular political representation. The same Law on State Debts which had regulated royal finances also provided that the government would only assume new debts with the approval of a national representative body, or 'estates of the realm' (*Reichsstände*).[72] Not surprisingly, this motivated the parsimonious King and his equally thrifty advisers to pursue policies of extreme financial stringency for many years, while the constitutional pledges of 1815 remained unfulfilled.

Many historians have suggested that as a result of the compromises and shortcomings of the reform era, post-1815 Prussia in effect became a 'state of officials' (*Beamtenstaat*), dominated by a caste of bureaucrats who viewed themselves in Hegel's terms as a 'general estate', that is, as the representatives of universal, nonparticular interests. In the absence of a real constitution, then, bureaucratic absolutism functioned as a kind of 'intra-administrative' constitutionalism which, though authoritarian, nevertheless pursued reformist and modernizing socio-

---

trust' seems especially useful in this case: see his 'Taxation, Sociopolitical Structure, and State-Building: Great Britain and Brandenburg-Prussia', in Charles Tilly (ed.), *The Formation of National States in Western Europe* (Princeton, NJ, 1975), 277.

[70] Hermann Schulze, *Die Hausgesetze der regierenden deutschen Fürstenhäuser* (Jena, 1883), iii, pt. 2, 619–21; Stamm-Kuhlmann, 'Hof'.

[71] B. Vogel, *Gewerbefreiheit*, 195; Berdahl, *Politics*, 123–54.   [72] Levinger, 'Hardenberg', 274.

economic policies.[73] Recent research indicates, however, that the reality of the post-reform Prussian state was more complex and even paradoxical. The bureaucracy itself was by no means homogeneous or monolithic, but rather divided between 'liberal' and 'conservative' factions. Above all, conservatives within the government—especially the Council of State and the cabinet, or 'State Ministry' (*Staatsministerium*)—were able to thwart many of Hardenberg's reforms after 1815, and thereafter formed the core of what amounted to a 'government party' during the last two decades of Frederick William III's reign. Moreover, this party often had substantial disagreements with those extra-governmental conservatives who represented the 'old-corporative' (*altständisch*) views of many, but by no means all, Junker estate-owners in East Elbia. The latter group emphasized its attachment to traditional, local or provincial institutions, simultaneously expressing a deep aversion to administrative centralism and all forms of 'bureaucratic despotism'. Thus they never became fully reconciled with those 'governmental' or 'bureaucratic' conservatives who after the 1820s occupied a number of key positions at the highest levels of the Prussian state.[74]

In addition to these lines of division, there were other splits and fissures among the various élite groups that dominated Prussian society in the early nineteenth century. These divisions were influenced by a whole range of factors, including age, occupation, education, friendship patterns, regional origin, and religious confession. As a result, major differences often cut across individual élite groups; thus, for example, some common-born but influential members of the educated bourgeoisie (*Bildungsbürgertum*) supported state initiatives to encourage industrial and technological innovation, while others were out-and-out technophobes who worried about the socially disruptive effects of technological change.[75] Similarly, not all Junkers in the countryside were unrelenting foes of Hardenberg's reforms; historians have paid rather too much attention to the ideas of Friedrich August Ludwig von der Marwitz, the brilliant defender of patrimonial corporativism and agrarian particularism, and not enough to those of *grands seigneurs* like Friedrich Abraham Wilhelm von Arnim-Boitzenburg, who quickly realized that the innovations of the reform period could be turned to the advantage of traditional ruling groups.[76]

Indeed, so complex were the lines of division within the Prussian state that one historian posits the existence of two distinct blocs—one reformist, one reactionary—composed of several distinctive subgroupings in Restoration and *Vormärz* Prussia.

[73] This argument is summarized in Jonathan Sperber, 'State and Civil Society in Prussia: Thoughts on a New Edition of Reinhart Koselleck's *Preußen zwischen Reform und Revolution*', *Journal of Modern History*, 57 (1985), 278–80.

[74] Barbara Vogel, 'Beamtenkonservativismus: Sozial- und verfassungsgeschichtliche Voraussetzungen der Parteien in Preußen im frühen 19. Jahrhundert', in Dirk Stegmann, Bernd-Jürgen Wendt, and Peter-Christian Witt (eds.), *Deutscher Konservatismus im 19. und 20. Jahrhundert. Festschrift für Fritz Fischer zum 75. Geburtstag und zum 50. Doktorjubiläum* (Bonn, 1983), 19–24.

[75] On all these matters, see esp. Eric Dorn Brose, *The Politics of Technological Change in Prussia: Out of the Shadow of Antiquity, 1809–1848* (Princeton, NJ, 1993).

[76] Klaus Vetter, 'Der brandenburgische Adel und der Beginn der bürgerlichen Umwälzung in Deutschland', in Reden-Dohna and Melville (eds.), *Adel*, 285–303.

'Each cut across class planes, penetrated occupational enclaves, dissected the ministerial cabinet and Council of State, bridged the civilian bureaucracy and army, and extended from state into society.' In this setting, the king was able to position and manœuvre himself among several contending élite groups, and the result was a 'precarious' balance, with the monarch and his closest advisers at the fulcrum.[77] In short, monarchical authority in Prussia had not been fundamentally shaken by the General Law Code of 1794, the military collapse of 1806–7, or the reform movement thereafter. The king still occupied the strategic centre of the state, and was thus in a position at least 'formally to control the three pillars of absolutist ruling practice [*Herrschaftspraxis*]': the military, the making of foreign policy, and the administration.[78]

Although Frederick William III was known neither for his vigour nor for his decisiveness, he had always jealously guarded the ultimate decision-making prerogatives of his office. That became especially clear after Hardenberg's death in 1822. His would-be successor and political enemy, the bureaucratic conservative Otto von Voß-Buch, himself died shortly thereafter; and the office of Chancellor was not renewed. The old system of cabinet government, which the reformers had so vehemently excoriated, had been replaced by a more modern cabinet of ministers called the State Ministry (*Staatsministerium*). Each minister was responsible for a particular department of state (for example, war, justice, or religious affairs and education), and was expected to follow the government's general political line. After 1822–3, however, the State Ministry was not guided by any sort of prime minister; nor did the individual ministers report directly to the king on their activities. Direct communication between the monarch and the State Ministry was the responsibility of only one or two ministers, who in later years came to be called 'cabinet ministers' (*Kabinettsminister*). In the absence of a powerful and dominating personality like Hardenberg, the king himself thus remained at centre stage; and the old system of cabinet government persisted, though in an altered form. By 1823 the king's privy or Civil Cabinet had been divided into two departments (*Abteilungen*); the First Department was responsible for reporting directly to the monarch on the most pressing non-military matters, while the Second Department was essentially a secretarial bureau. The head of the First Department enjoyed almost exclusive rights to present reports directly to the monarch; most other ministers rarely saw the king.[79]

Under the morose and withdrawn Frederick William III, the court itself was only rarely (as in 1829) a dazzling showcase for monarchical splendour; but it continued

[77] Brose, *Politics*, 251–2, 256, 259.
[78] Hans-Ulrich Wehler, *Deutsche Gesellschaftsgeschichte* (Munich, 1987–), ii: *Von der Reformära bis zur industriellen und politischen 'Deutschen Doppelrevolution' 1815–1845/49*, 300.
[79] The discussion here follows the standard accounts of Heinrich Otto Meisner, 'Zur neueren Geschichte des preußischen Kabinetts', *FBPG* 36 (1924), 40–52; id., 'Die monarchische Regierungsform in Brandenburg-Preußen', in Richard Dietrich and Gerhard Oestreich (eds.), *Forschungen zu Staat und Verfassung: Festgabe für Fritz Hartung* (Berlin, 1958), 234–9; Walther Hubatsch (ed.), *Grundriß zur deutschen Verwaltungsgeschichte 1815–1945*, ser. A: *Preußen*, xii, pt. a: *Preußische Zentralbehörden*, ed. Friedrich Wilhelm Wehrstedt (Marburg, 1978), 162–3.

to function as a locus of political power. As we have just seen, it was difficult to reach the king through governmental or bureaucratic channels. Access to the monarch came mostly through the court, and with it access to influence in the Prussian state as a whole. This was vividly demonstrated by the careers of Frederick William's closest confidants and advisers during the 1820s and 1830s. With the partial exception of Adjutant-General Job von Witzleben, this 'kitchen cabinet' of royal confidants was unremittingly hostile to the innovations of liberal reformers, and after Hardenberg's death such reformers had to look outside the court for sources of political support. In particular, the House Minister, Prince Wittgenstein, played a critically important role in helping to shape the politics of monarchical restoration and reaction in Prussia.

In the early 1820s Crown Prince Frederick William had worked closely with several members of his father's circle of friends in a joint effort to undercut Hardenberg's reform efforts.[80] But that had been a marriage of political convenience. The Crown Prince loved his father, and was always a dutiful and obedient son; but the two men were temperamental opposites, and the Crown Prince's own vision of monarchy had an exalted, even mystic streak which was incomprehensible to his sober, unimaginative father. Moreover, the future king leaned more toward the anti-absolutist, corporative-estatist (*ständisch*) views of a Ludwig von der Marwitz than toward the governmental absolutism of a Wittgenstein or a Metternich. The Crown Prince was never a rebel, nor did he chafe after the responsibilities of the high office that awaited him. Still, tensions between rulers and their heirs are a well-nigh inescapable feature of absolute or semi-absolute monarchies, and Prussia in the 1830s was no exception. In the last decade of his life Frederick William III mostly wanted to be left alone, and to many outside observers it seemed that the state was in the grip of a creeping paralysis. People like Wittgenstein were afraid of the impending change at the top, and determined to limit its effects. In what was called the 'Crown Prince's Circle' (*Kronprinzenkreis*), however, there was a general expectation that the future Frederick William IV would re-establish the foundations of the monarchical system by breaking utterly with the spirit of bureaucratic absolutism, whether of Hardenbergian or conservative provenance, and reinstitutionalizing decentralized, estatist political structures.

Who, then, was the Crown Prince, the man upon whom so many hopes and fears rested in the 1830s? What were his views of monarchy and the nature of the monarchical system, especially in the context of the upheavals and transformations that we have described in this chapter? Frederick William IV will, of course, be the protagonist of this book, and it is to his early life and the evolution of his world-view that we shall devote our attention in the next chapter.

---

[80] Paul Bailleu, 'Kronprinz Friedrich Wilhelm im Ständekampf 1820', *HZ* 87 (NS 51; 1901), 67–73.

2
Monarchy as *Gesamtkunstwerk*:
The Education of Frederick William IV,
1795–1840

A Church for a King

On 24 September 1848 the King and Queen of Prussia walked down the hill from the palace of Sanssouci to attend the consecration of the nearby Friedenskirche. The first religious service at that 'Church of Peace' took place in a time of profound and sweeping changes in the structure of the Prussian state—changes to which Frederick William IV had only superficially accommodated himself. In March of that year, in the midst of the revolution that had swept through Berlin, he had made a number of concessions to revolutionary demands; and now, in the early autumn, it seemed that Prussia was about to be transformed into a constitutional, parliamentary monarchy with a responsible ministry. But the King had largely dissociated himself from that process; indeed, during most of the spring and summer he had rarely been in his turbulent capital, preferring instead the relative peace and calm of his usual summer residence at Sanssouci, Frederick the Great's villa near Potsdam. It was from Sanssouci, with all its evocations of Prussia's greatest monarch, that Frederick William IV and Queen Elisabeth proceeded to the new Friedenskirche on that Sunday morning in early autumn.[1]

If Sanssouci is perhaps the best-known physical symbol of the Frederician age in Prussia, then the neighbouring Friedenskirche is the clearest architectural embodiment of the character and values of Frederick William IV. Above all, it reflects both his deep-seated religious beliefs and his lifelong passion for architecture. The Prussian monarch was convinced that a return to the principles of early Christianity was an essential aspect of his struggle against the 'unbelief' (*Unglaube*) and 'indifference' (*Gleichgültigkeit*) of his own age. Moreover, he believed that the early medieval basilica was the most appropriate architectural expression of his determination to build a 'Christian state' in Prussia as a bulwark against the revolutionary spirit of the nineteenth century. As a young man he had assiduously studied the great Gutensohn/Knapp collection of etchings of early Roman basilicas, and his attachment to the basilica style had grown even more intense after his first visit to Rome in 1828.[2] In 1834 Frederick William had obtained a twelfth-century mosaic from the

---

[1] See the description of the consecration ceremony in W. Riehl, 'Die Friedenskirche bei Sanssouci', *Mittheilungen des Vereins für die Geschichte Potsdams*, 2 (1866), 62–3.

[2] Gerd-H. Zuchold, 'Friedrich Wilhelm IV. und die Byzanzrezeption in der preußischen Baukunst', in Otto Büsch (ed.), *Friedrich Wilhelm IV. in seiner Zeit: Beiträge eines Colloquiums* (Berlin, 1987), 221; Eva

[*cont. on p. 25*]

church of San Cipriano in Murano (near Venice), which was about to be demolished, and by the early 1840s he had decided to use the mosaic as the focal point of a new church for his court in Sanssouci.[3] After 1841 the King and his court architect, Ludwig Persius, designed the Friedenskirche, the cornerstone of which was laid in 1845. Set in a magnificent landscape created by the great garden designer Peter Joseph Lenné, the Friedenskirche is reminiscent of the early medieval churches of San Clemente and Santa Maria in Cosmedin in Rome. In the apse of the Friedenskirche is the Murano mosaic, a majestic Byzantine depiction of *Christos Pantocrator*, Christ enthroned as judge of the world. None of this was coincidental, or the result of purely aesthetic preference on the King's part.[4] The Friedenskirche was to be the programmatic expression, in stone and glass, of Frederick William IV's vision of monarchy, of the essence of the Prussian state, and of himself as *Primas* of German Protestantism. The King's church was supposed to symbolize the state's very essence, while the Murano mosaic itself evoked Frederick William's notion of his own ordination through the grace of God.[5] In the year of revolution, then, the King's church stood as physical testimony to his unbroken attachment to a view of his office that was at once intensely ideological and shaped by essentially aesthetic considerations.

Ludwig Dehio reminded us some years ago that in order to understand Frederick William IV, it is necessary to regard him primarily as an artist, not as a politician.[6] Other observers have suggested that Frederick William was first and foremost a man of the church, preoccupied with religious questions, to which everything else was secondary.[7] In fact, as the Friedenskirche demonstrates, there is some truth to both points of view. Dehio was right to suggest that the King was essentially an artist; but what makes his artistic endeavours interesting and important is the fact that he was the ruler of a great European power, in a position to impose, or attempt to impose, his ideas upon millions of his subjects. Accordingly, it is impossible to separate or distinguish clearly among his aesthetic/architectural, religious, and political concerns. They all spring from the same source, and are all bound together. Frederick William IV was an almost classic example of the artist in politics, of a man whose political views and aesthetic judgements reciprocally influenced each other; and therein lies much of his historic significance. He was an ideologue who based his political judgements on interrelated aesthetic, ideological, and religious categories.

Börsch-Supan, commentary to Ludwig Persius, *Das Tagebuch des Architekten Friedrich Wilhelms IV. 1840–1845*, ed. Eva Börsch-Supan (Munich, 1980), 131; FW (IV) to Crown Princess Elisabeth, Rome, 23 Oct. 1828, GStA Merseburg, HA Rep. 50 J Nr. 995 Fasz. 6, Bl. 37ᵛ.

   [3] FW (IV) to King Ludwig I of Bavaria, 21 Jan. 1834, GHA, Nachlaß König Ludwig I., II/A/11.

   [4] For a description of the Friedenskirche, see esp. Sibylle Badstübner-Gröger, *Die Friedenskirche zu Potsdam*, 4th edn. (Berlin [East], 1986).

   [5] Zuchold, 'Byzanzrezeption', 224.

   [6] Quoted in Gerd Heinrich, *Geschichte Preußens: Staat und Dynastie* (Frankfurt am Main, 1981), 347.

   [7] Walter Bußmann, 'Friedrich Julius Stahl', in Martin Greschat (ed.), *Gestalten der Kirchengeschichte*, ix: *Die neueste Zeit* (Stuttgart, 1985), 328.

Moreover, Frederick William IV adhered fiercely and unrelentingly to his ideological tenets and to his various *Lieblingsprojekte*. To be sure, many contemporaries and later historians have emphasized his erratic behaviour, his inconsistency, and his unpredictability.[8] Other, equally insightful contemporaries always called attention to his ideological and political stubbornness, as one diplomat reported in 1852: 'The King of Prussia will never give up any of the views concerning the governance of state and church with which he mounted the throne in the year 1840, and which he pursued until 1848.'[9] In adhering so stubbornly to a particular set of ideological principles, Frederick William demonstrated that he was a child of his times. In an age of ideology, Frederick William IV was himself an ideologue who proceeded, in the name of preserving Prussia's traditions, to invent an ideology for the Prussian monarchy. As we have just seen, those ideological notions were themselves the product of several long-term factors, all of which antedated his accession to the throne in June 1840: the specific circumstances of his own biography, especially his long years as politically ineffectual heir to the throne; the impact upon him of the views of his circle of confidants and advisers, almost all of whom rose to positions of considerable political influence after 1840; and general cultural and intellectual currents in Germany between about 1800 and 1840. As a result of all these factors, Frederick William assumed his throne on 7 June 1840 with a vision of himself, his office, the Prussian state, Prussian society, and the German nation that had been shaped over the course of several decades.

Aesthete and Heir: The Prussian Crown Prince, 1795–1823

Frederick William's ideological and aesthetic politics were rooted, above all, in the particular circumstances of his own life before 1840. Those circumstances can be rather easily traced, as there are few sovereigns in modern history about whose childhood, adolescence, and early adulthood we are better informed.[10] Born in Berlin on 15 October 1795, Frederick William IV was the oldest of seven surviving children of Frederick William III (who himself succeeded to the throne in 1797) and Queen Luise, formerly a princess of Mecklenburg-Strelitz. Frederick William IV was only eighteen months older than his brother William, who succeeded him as king in 1861 and became German emperor in 1871. For a number of years Frederick William and William had the same teachers, of whom the most important was the progressive educator Friedrich Delbrück, the princes' tutor from 1800 to 1809.[11]

---

[8] K. A. Varnhagen von Ense, *Tagebücher*, ed. Ludmilla Assing, 2nd edn., i. 385 (26 Dec. 1841).

[9] Wilhelm Freiherr Rivalier von Meysenbug to Ludwig Freiherr Rüdt von Collenberg-Bödigheim, 7 Sept. 1852, GLA, Abt. 48/2649.

[10] Ernst Lewalter, *Friedrich Wilhelm IV.: Das Schicksal eines Geistes* (Berlin, 1938); and Frank-Lothar Kroll, *Friedrich Wilhelm IV. und das Staatsdenken der deutschen Romantik* (Berlin, 1990), are crucial for an understanding of Frederick William's life before 1840.

[11] Friedrich Delbrück, *Die Jugend des Königs Friedrich Wilhelm IV. von Preußen und des Kaisers und Königs Wilhelm I.: Tagebuchblätter ihres Erziehers Friedrich Delbrück (1800–1809)*, ed. Georg Schuster (3 vols.; Berlin, 1907).

The first eleven years of Frederick William's life were marked by an atmosphere of blissful familial stability and intimacy. Frederick William III utterly rejected the flamboyant lasciviousness and frivolous *Mätressenwirtschaft* that had characterized his own dissolute father's eleven-year reign, and he remained devoted to his queen. German nationalist propagandists later apotheosized Luise as the 'Prussian Madonna', mainly because of her sufferings after 1806 and her early death in 1810; but she was indeed characterized by a remarkable depth of insight, strength of character, and family loyalty. The Prussian Crown Prince and his younger siblings were thus brought up to love and respect their parents, which for European royal children was by no means usual or self-evident. Neither Frederick William IV nor William I, nor indeed any of their younger brothers and sisters, were ever involved in serious or enduring quarrels with their parents. The intense and often bitter family conflicts of the eighteenth-century Hohenzollerns were unknown to the children of Frederick William III and Luise.

For their part, the royal couple, and especially the Queen, were influenced in their views on their childrens' education by late eighteenth-century attitudes towards simplicity and sensibility, by the notion that childrens' abilities should be allowed to develop and express themselves naturally.[12] These were ideas to which Friedrich Delbrück himself adhered, and were among the reasons why he was entrusted with the education of the two oldest royal princes. The young Crown Prince formed an intense bond with Delbrück, who accompanied his charges to Königsberg and Memel when the royal family was forced to flee to the east after Prussia's disastrous defeat at Napoleon's hands in 1806–7. In 1810, despite the Crown Prince's tearful entreaties, Delbrück was replaced by Johann Peter Friedrich Ancillon, a well-known pastor and author of various historical and philosophical treatises. Ancillon, the Queen hoped, would provide a more sharply focused learning-environment for her oldest son. Although he remained attached to Delbrück, the Crown Prince also became devoted to Ancillon, with whom he maintained a close relationship (and extensive correspondence) until the latter's death in 1837. Whilst Delbrück and Ancillon were responsible for the princes' general education, they also received instruction from such notables as Barthold Niebuhr, the great historian; Carl von Clausewitz, the military theorist; and Friedrich Karl von Savigny, renowned for his 'historical school of law'. Savigny, who later served as a minister under Frederick William IV, seems to have had a strong influence on the Crown Prince's early and vehement rejection of natural law as the basis of public authority, and his emphasis on the primacy of the 'historical' and the 'traditional'.[13]

Frederick William's basic personality traits, talents, and intellectual interests developed at a very early age. To the consternation of his father, and in sharp contrast to his brother William, the young heir to the Prussian throne never developed an aptitude for military affairs. The Prince's unsoldierly ways grew even more marked

---

[12] Ludwig Dehio, *Friedrich Wilhelm IV. von Preußen: Ein Baukünstler der Romantik* (Munich, 1961), 10.

[13] Kroll, *Friedrich Wilhelm IV.*, 40–4; Lewalter, *Friedrich Wilhelm IV.*, 138–42.

as he grew older; as an adult he was both corpulent and exceedingly near-sighted, which created difficulties for him at military reviews.[14] Frederick William IV thus grew up to be probably the least martial monarch in Prussian history. Instead, he early on demonstrated both a passion and a talent for drawing and architecture. Equally notable were his deep religious sensibilities and a personality that was charming, voluble, and imaginative, but undisciplined and given to emotional excess. In one of her last letters to her oldest son, Queen Luise voiced concerns that were echoed by his contemporaries for decades: 'The ability to suppress your desires and resist your passions is utterly absent in you, and this point was quite impermissibly neglected during your education. Listen to my maternal voice, my dear Fritz; think carefully about what I tenderly repeat to you so often; tame the youthful *fire* with which you want to *have* everything that *you like*, and with which you immediately demand the *means* to *attain* everything that you think of for yourself.'[15]

The irruption of Napoleon's armies into Prussia radically transformed the lives of the royal children. Forced with the rest of his family to flee to the eastern parts of their kingdom, and to live for some time under personally complicated and politically precarious conditions, the young Frederick William began to develop, towards France and towards 'the Revolution', a violent antagonism that persisted throughout his life and indeed became one of his ideological preoccupations. Typical of his views is a letter of May 1832 to his brother-in-law, Prince (later King) John of Saxony, in which he writes with horror of 'the *revolution*, that monster, which first saw the light of the world forty years ago, and which, were I apocalyptically inclined, I would immediately compare to the Beast *par excellence*, or to the Whore who lay down with kings and made them drunk from her chalice'.[16] Not surprisingly, Frederick William's hatred of Napoleon and of Bonapartism developed early and remained inextinguishable.[17] After Napoleon's defeat in 1814–15 the Crown Prince's antipathy extended even to Paris itself, which he regularly denounced in his letters from that place as a 'sink of corruption'.[18] As late as the mid-1850s, reported one of his aides-de-camp in his memoirs, the King was almost invariably a pleasant and charming conversationalist, 'except that things boiled over in him whenever he got around to the Napoleonic period, and in talking about Napoleon I he used strong expressions that were otherwise alien to him'.[19]

[14] Peter Paret, *Clausewitz and the State* (New York, 1976), 201. Frederick William often joked about being fat. Among his family nicknames were 'Dicky' ('Fatty') and '*der Butt*' ('the halibut'). His letters are full of self-caricatures in which he unsparingly depicts himself as a kind of spheroid; in many drawings he adds a fish-tail, in reference to his nickname.

[15] Luise, Königin von Preußen, *Königin Luise von Preußen: Briefe und Aufzeichnungen 1786–1810*, ed. Malve Gräfin Rothkirch (Munich, 1985), 545–6.

[16] FW (IV) to Prince John of Saxony, 31 May 1832, in Johann Georg, Herzog zu Sachsen (ed.), *Briefwechsel zwischen König Johann von Sachsen und den Königen Friedrich Wilhelm IV. und Wilhelm I. von Preußen* (Leipzig, 1911), 127.

[17] Kroll, *Friedrich Wilhelm IV.*, 160–6; Konrad Kettig, *Friedrich Wilhelms IV. Stellung zu Frankreich bis zur Errichtung des 2. französischen Kaiserreiches (2. Dezember 1852)* (Berlin, 1937), 9–22.

[18] Kroll, *Friedrich Wilhelm IV.*, 160.

[19] Friedrich von Bismarck-Bohlen, 'Aufzeichnungen aus meinem Leben als Flügeladjutant Seiner Majestät König Friedrich Wilhelm IV.' (MS, 1880), GStA Merseburg, HA Rep. 50 F 1 Nr. 6, Bl. 10.

During the years just before the liberation war of 1813–14 the young Crown Prince presented further evidence of two inclinations that helped define his personality: his unquenchable love for drawing and architecture, and his enthusiasm for Romantic literature. Even as a small boy Frederick William's artistic talent had manifested itself in numerous sketches and drawings; and by 1810 the Crown Prince had almost certainly become acquainted with Carl Friedrich Schinkel (1781–1841), Germany's greatest nineteenth-century architect and a man who exerted a profound influence on the later King's vision of architecture and its aesthetic/ideological context.[20] Indeed, Frederick William's educators were rather concerned that his love of drawing, often expressed in fantastic and imaginary landscape compositions, could become a form of escapism that would divert him from the hard task of learning how to rule. In a frequently cited, undated letter from 1811 or 1812, Ancillon warned his young charge,

As I unfortunately still won't be seeing you for a few days, I fear that those pleasant evenings will be lost to Your Highness, because I can already see you spending the whole time with a pencil in your hand. For a future Schinkel this would be a very useful activity; but because the state does not consist of a Gothic temple, and because no people has ever been ruled on the basis of Romantic pictures, this perpetual drawing is becoming a pure waste of your precious time.[21]

Ancillon's reference to 'Gothic' buildings and 'Romantic pictures' points to yet another aspect of Frederick William's development in the years just before 1813: his growing enthusiasm for the German Middle Ages, coupled with a deep interest in the imagery and literature of European Romanticism. Frederick William has always been described as a Romantic. In fact, Romanticism (however that slippery term may be defined) is only one aspect of a highly complex world-view that the Crown Prince had developed by about 1830. Still, it was an essential aspect; indeed, even before the liberation war, Frederick William had succumbed to the enchantments of Romantic literature, from Ludwig Tieck to the *Arabian Nights*.[22] Above all, though, the Crown Prince came to have a passion for the writings of Friedrich de la Motte Fouqué.

Fouqué (1777–1843) is largely forgotten today, and in any case is almost totally unknown outside the German-speaking world.[23] Like Ancillon, he was a descendant of the Huguenot *réfugiés* whom the Great Elector had invited to settle in the Mark Brandenburg after Louis XIV's revocation of the Edict of Nantes in 1685. An indefatigable editor of anthologies and journals, Fouqué was also a tireless producer of plays, short stories, and novels. Specializing in vivid Romantic narratives, often based on legends and tales of the Mark Brandenburg, he derived his stories and

[20] L. Dehio, *Friedrich Wilhelm IV.*, 13–14.
[21] Paul Haake, *Johann Peter Friedrich Ancillon und Kronprinz Friedrich Wilhelm IV. von Preußen* (Munich, 1920), 32–3.
[22] Kroll, *Friedrich Wilhelm IV.*, 35–6.
[23] For biographical details, see Arno Schmidt, *Fouqué und einige seiner Zeitgenossen: Biographischer Versuch* (Zurich, 1987; orig. 1958).

characters almost exclusively from an imagined, dreamy, often fantastic notion of the Middle Ages, redolent with images of knights, damsels, rocky crags, dark forests, castles, and all the rest. Although he always remained a second-rate writer, Fouqué enjoyed a tremendous if brief vogue from about 1810 to 1815, when Romantic-patriotic enthusiasm for the German Middle Ages and for the Gothic style as '*vater-ländische Kunst*' was at its zenith within certain literary and intellectual circles.[24] Especially successful was *The Magic Ring* (*Der Zauberring*), published in 1812, which was eagerly devoured by the Crown Prince in the year of the liberation war.[25] The story concerns a Swabian knight, Hugh von Trautwangen, and his wanderings through the world, during the course of which he sired numerous children, who later become involved in complex struggles with each other.[26] Full of swordplay and courtly romance, *The Magic Ring* at first may seem to be politically innocuous. In fact, however, it contained a subtle, yet powerful, ideological message: the historic duty of a reinvigorated German nation to rescue Europe from the chaos of revolution; and a vision of a political system based on 'the existence of a patriarchal order, God-given differences of social status, and a people closely bound to its ruling house by love, loyalty, and obedience'.[27] Although Frederick William's feelings about Fouqué later became more measured and even distant, there can be little doubt that the author of *The Magic Ring* represented the most important single literary influence on him.[28] Fouqué's evocation of an organic medieval world, of the special bonds between ruler and ruled that had supposedly typified the Middle Ages, encouraged the tendency on Frederick William's part to think of his future responsibilities in terms of feelings, allusions, and images. An evocative, pictorial language or *Bildersprache* typified Fouqué's style; and the architecturally gifted Crown Prince showed himself to be more receptive to pictorial imagery than to the language of abstract reason or logical syllogism. From an early age he was inclined to respond to political issues more on the basis of exalted passion than of measurement or careful calculation.

That tendency received sustenance from Prussia's participation in the great anti-Napoleonic coalition of 1813, which the Crown Prince himself described as a 'crusade'. For Frederick William as for so many others of his generation, the events of 1813–15 represented a personal and political watershed. 'Fritz' accompanied his father into the field, where he experienced military action for the first time, and travelled across Germany and on to Paris in 1814. In many ways the experiences of 1813–15 served as a kind of Grand Tour or *Bildungsreise* for the heir to the Prussian

---

[24] Günter de Bruyn, 'Ein märkischer Don Quijote', in Friedrich de la Motte Fouqué, *Ritter und Geister: Romantische Erzählungen*, ed. Günter de Bruyn (Frankfurt am Main, 1981), 285, 287.

[25] Kroll, *Friedrich Wilhelm IV.*, 46–7; Lewalter, *Friedrich Wilhelm IV.*, 107–9.

[26] Friedrich Baron de la Motte Fouqué, *Fouqués Werke*, iii: *Der Zauberring*, ed. Walther Ziesemer (Berlin, n.d.).

[27] Frank-Lothar Kroll, 'Politische Romantik und romantische Politik bei Friedrich Wilhelm IV.', in Büsch (ed.), *Friedrich Wilhelm IV. in seiner Zeit*, 97.

[28] FW IV to Gustav Adolf von Rochow, 23 Jan. 1843, GStA Merseburg, HA Rep. 50 J Nr. 1169, Bl. 7–8.

throne.[29] It was in those years that he became acutely aware of his own German patriotism, a feeling which, not surprisingly, became associated for him with visual images derived from his travels. His letters, especially to Ancillon and to his siblings William, Carl, and Charlotte, bear vivid testimony to the ecstatic feelings with which he discovered historic German landscapes, especially along the Rhine. In July 1815 Frederick William journeyed through the Rhineland, which Prussia had just acquired at the Congress of Vienna. His reaction to that region bordered on the delirious, as he confessed in his diary: 'I immersed my right hand in the Rhine and crossed myself. What a divine stream! This width! These banks! . . . How elegant this Rhine appears from the hill!! What a stream!!! After the Jordan and the Ganges and the Nile it is the first of the world!!!'[30] Indeed, for his entire adult life Frederick William's German patriotism was intimately bound up with 'Rhineland Romanticism', much of which became focused on the campaign to finish Cologne Cathedral.

That project is exceptionally important for an understanding of how Frederick William IV's aesthetic and ideological approach to politics developed. Construction on Cologne Cathedral had begun in 1248, but it had never been completed; indeed, nothing at all had been done since 1560.[31] In the first years of the nineteenth century, though, the national-patriotic appropriation of the Gothic Revival in Germany gave a new impetus to plans for the cathedral's completion in an appropriately Gothic style.[32] These ideas were taken up with gusto and tenacity by Sulpiz Boisserée, who, with his brother Melchior, was a well-known Cologne art-collector and devotee of the Gothic style.[33] In 1808 Sulpiz Boisserée began a series of detailed drawings of the cathedral which culminated fifteen years later in the publication of a great collection of eighteen copper engravings known as the *Domwerk*.[34] Five years later the Boisserée brothers met the Prussian Crown Prince and immediately gained a lifelong ally.[35] During the summer of 1814 Frederick William was able to visit Cologne for the first time, and as a result of his stay he became an ecstatic proponent of plans to complete the cathedral. In Sulpiz Boisserée's own words, Frederick William 'wanted to complete the cathedral right away. And when we walked around the choir he could not contain himself anymore.'[36] After two more visits in 1815 and 1817 Frederick

---

[29] See Herman Granier (ed.), *Hohenzollernbriefe aus den Freiheitskriegen 1813–1815* (Leipzig, 1913); and id. (ed.), *Prinzenbriefe aus den Freiheitskriegen 1813–1815: Briefwechsel des Kronprinzen Friedrich Wilhelm (IV.) und des Prinzen Wilhelm (I.) von Preußen mit dem Prinzen Friedrich von Oranien* (Stuttgart, 1922).

[30] Haake, *Ancillon*, 75; Kroll, *Friedrich Wilhelm IV.*, 33–4.

[31] W. D. Robson-Scott, *The Literary Background of the Gothic Revival in Germany: A Chapter in the History of Taste* (Oxford, 1965), 159.

[32] Thomas Nipperdey, 'Der Kölner Dom als Nationaldenkmal', *HZ* 233 (1981), 595–613, esp. 595–6, 604–6.

[33] Robson-Scott, *Gothic Revival*, 155–61.   [34] Ibid. 275–82.

[35] Thomas Parent, *Die Hohenzollern in Köln* (Cologne, 1981), 28–9; Ursula Rathke, 'Die Rolle Friedrich Wilhelms IV. von Preußen bei der Vollendung des Kölner Doms (Teil I)', *Kölner Domblatt*, 47 (1982), 130–6.

[36] Quoted in Rathke, 'Vollendung I', 155; and Robson-Scott, *Gothic Revival*, 290.

William's ideas for the cathedral began to take on an increasingly clear and 'irreversible' character, and one which clearly anticipated the cathedral's final appearance at the time of its completion in 1880.[37]

The Cologne Cathedral project shows that, for Frederick William IV, architecture was always bound up with other values and concerns. To be sure, Frederick William's own Gothic enthusiasms began to fade after 1821.[38] More important than his short-lived *Gotikbegeisterung* was his intense, if diffusely emotional, national feeling, and his belief that such national feeling was inevitably bound up with religious obligations and the ethical requirement of loyalty to God-given historical traditions, and above all the traditions of the Holy Roman Empire.[39] Frederick William IV's German nationalism was inseparable from his vision of a medieval empire sustained by shared Christian and monarchical values. That empire had been one of the victims of 'the revolution', but all his life Frederick William hankered for its return; and his vision of an organic, historic, God-fearing Christian empire helps explain much of his political behaviour after 1840.[40]

Finally, Frederick William's involvement with the Cologne Cathedral venture points to yet another crucial aspect of his developing personality and world-view. One recent scholar suggests that the young and deeply impressionable Crown Prince was drawn to Boisserée's plans because the cathedral represented for him a 'total work of art, composed of music, architecture, painting, and religious ceremony', a work of art which evoked 'a "transcendent" feeling' in him.[41] The concept of the *Gesamtkunstwerk*, that typical product of the nineteenth-century German Romantic imagination, can serve as a metaphor for Frederick William IV's developing understanding of his royal office and his life's work. It is neither surprising nor coincidental that the Crown Prince endorsed the work of Carl Maria von Weber, and that he unsuccessfully pleaded for that composer's appointment as General Music Director for the Prussian monarchy in the 1820s. Weber's advocacy of a 'German-national' musical style had been epitomized in *Der Freischütz*, which enjoyed a sensational Berlin première in 1824; and as early as 1816 Weber had called for a fusion of all the arts 'in which every feature and every contribution . . . are moulded together in a certain way and dissolve to form a new world'.[42] Such an idea appealed mightily to Frederick William's vivid imagination. As Friedrich Meinecke put it, Frederick William thought of 'the state as a work of art in the highest sense of that word. As an artist he thought widely and generously; he wanted to admit and incorporate into his cathedral those spiritual forces and persons who in any way recognized his kingdom.'[43] Art, architecture, ritual, religious emotion, kingship, public duties, patriotic

---

[37] Rathke, 'Vollendung I', 160.   [38] L. Dehio, *Friedrich Wilhelm IV.*, 19.

[39] On the connection between Christianity and the national movement in Germany, see Nipperdey, 'Kölner Dom', 606–13.

[40] Kroll, *Friedrich Wilhelm IV.*, 131–6.   [41] Rathke, 'Vollendung I', 157.

[42] Quoted in John Warrack, 'Gesamtkunstwerk', in Denis Arnold (ed.), *The New Oxford Companion to Music* (2 vols.; Oxford, 1983), i. 759.

[43] Friedrich Meinecke, *Das Leben des Generalfeldmarschalls Hermann von Boyen* (2 vols.; Stuttgart, 1896, 1899), ii. 483. See also Frederick William's politically revealing sketches of medieval kings,

[*cont. on p. 33*]

enthusiasm, piety towards an imagined medieval past, all were bound up together in Frederick William's imagination; all were constituent parts of a grand and unified, if fragile and ultimately unstable and unrealizable, structure. For all its apparent contradictions, Frederick William IV's personality was not inconsistent or divided against itself. Rather, like Wagner and other contemporaries, the King of Prussia was sustained by a singular, if ultimately unattainable, vision. And for Frederick William IV, religion was the cement that would bind together his *Gesamtkunstwerk*.

Frederick William's aesthetic and political coming of age coincided with a movement of religious renewal in Germany known as the 'Awakening' (*Erweckungsbewegung*). With its origins in the late eighteenth century, and no doubt influenced by the Romantic currents of the first years of the new century, the Awakening represented a thoroughgoing rejection of the genial scepticism and rationalism of the Enlightenment. Although rooted in older traditions of German Pietism, the Awakening in the first half of the nineteenth century nevertheless represented something new. Thus it is most useful, perhaps, to speak not of 'pietist' but of 'neo-pietist' tendencies in the Awakening, with its emphasis on an intense, private, and rather emotional devotionalism, on preaching and prayer, on a reliance on Scripture as the ultimate religious authority, and on a life-style based on rigorous and constant self-examination and penance (*Buße*).[44] It was a regionally and confessionally diverse phenomenon, which appealed to Catholics and Protestants alike. In Prussia, however, especially in Pomerania and Berlin, it became a historically significant force thanks to its association with young aristocrats, most of whom belonged to Frederick William IV's generation and some of whom became his close advisers and confidants. Indeed, it was very often shared religious feeling that drew them to Frederick William in the first place. For all its variegated and even diffuse character, the Awakening was generally characterized by a deep hostility to theological and political rationalism, and thus it is not surprising that Awakened Christians often embraced monarchical conservatism in the name of an 'organic' traditionalism. Still, despite its apparent traditionalism the Awakening was itself not traditional; as a product of the nineteenth century, responding to nineteenth-century conditions, it represented something new in German life. The Awakening helped to reconcile two traditional opponents in German Protestantism, pietism and orthodoxy, both of

emperors, and knights in Stiftung Schlösser und Gärten Potsdam-Sanssouci, Plankammer (hereafter Plankammer Potsdam-Sanssouci), Sammlung Friedrich Wilhelm IV., II-1-Ce-20, and Mappe X, Umschläge A–C. Cf. Rathke, 'Vollendung I', 141, 144; ead., 'Die Rolle Friedrich Wilhelms IV. von Preußen bei der Vollendung des Kölner Doms (Teil II)', *Kölner Domblatt*, 48 (1983), 62–3.

[44] One of the best introductions to the Awakening remains Franz Schnabel, *Deutsche Geschichte im neunzehnten Jahrhundert*, iv: *Die religiösen Kräfte*, 3rd edn. (Freiburg, 1955), 297–309. See also Friedrich Wilhelm Kantzenbach, *Die Erweckungsbewegung: Studien zur Geschichte ihrer Entstehung und ersten Ausbreitung in Deutschland* (Neuendettelsau, 1957), esp. 9–26, 82–133; John E. Groh, *Nineteenth Century German Protestantism: The Church as Social Model* (Washington, DC, 1982), 100–38; Christopher M. Clark, 'The Politics of Revival: Pietists, Aristocrats, and the State Church in Early Nineteenth-Century Prussia', in Larry Eugene Jones and James Retallack (eds.), *Between Reform, Reaction, and Resistance: Studies in the History of German Conservatism from 1789 to 1945* (Providence, 1993), 31–60.

which were now joined in common opposition to rationalism, Enlightenment, and liberalism. Like Frederick William's own conservatism, the Awakening cannot be regarded as 'simply a relic of antiquity, a compilation of traditional forces, of "conservatives" . . . it is not an old-style but rather, if anything, a new conservatism'.[45] Perhaps because of its very modernity, the Awakening also lent itself to a 'surrogate' nationalism, an alternative to liberal, parliamentary, or republican nationalism.[46]

As with the young Frederick William, participation in the anti-Napoleonic crusade played a key role in the lives of many of the 'Awakened' aristocrats who later worked closely with him.[47] After Waterloo, a number of pious young officers began to meet once a week at the tavern of an innkeeper named Mai, and thus this circle of friends came to be known as the *Maikäferei* (loosely and not very evocatively translatable as 'May-Bug Society').[48] Although the *Maikäferei* was fairly short-lived, quite a few of its earnest members, bound together by ties of friendship and, later, of marriage, continued to meet regularly in each others' homes for discussion and devotions. Many of those individuals later occupied powerful and influential positions in the government of Frederick William IV.[49]

It is almost impossible to exaggerate the importance of the Awakening for an understanding of the personality of Frederick William IV, the views of many of his key advisers, and the character of his government. The neo-pietism of 1815 or 1820 was not changeless, and Frederick William's advisers of 1840 or 1850 were no longer the enthusiastic young officers they once had been. But the connection between neo-pietism and Restoration-era monarchical conservatism persisted and even deepened after 1815, and played a pivotal role in Frederick William's own definition of his future office. Unlike many of the Awakened young officers who became his close friends, Frederick William could never point to a single, overpowering experience of conversion. He did not need to be 'won over' to neo-pietist ways. Virtually from the time that he first became aware of religion, the Crown Prince adhered to his faith piously and with a deep emotional intensity; he had always been hostile to rationalist preaching.[50] Although Frederick William IV is best known to history as a 'Romantic on the throne', Hans-Joachim Schoeps's characterization of him as an 'Awakened Christian on the throne' is perhaps even more appropriate.[51]

[45] Thomas Nipperdey, *Deutsche Geschichte 1800–1866: Bürgerwelt und starker Staat* (Munich, 1983), 424–5.

[46] Groh, *Protestantism*, 118–20.

[47] Walter Wendland, 'Studien zur Erweckungsbewegung in Berlin (1810–1830)', *Jahrbuch für brandenburgische Kirchengeschichte*, 19 (1924), 23; Otto Graf zu Stolberg-Wernigerode, *Anton Graf zu Stolberg-Wernigerode: Ein Freund und Ratgeber König Friedrich Wilhelms IV.* (Munich, 1926), 11–15; Kantzenbach, *Erweckungsbewegung*, 82–93.

[48] See most recently Robert M. Berdahl, *The Politics of the Prussian Nobility: The Development of a Conservative Ideology 1770–1848* (Princeton, NJ, 1988), 246–7; Clark, 'Revival', 35–42.

[49] Wendland, 'Erweckungsbewegung', 25, 26; Anneliese Kriege, 'Geschichte der Evangelischen Kirchen-Zeitung unter der Leitung Ernst-Wilhelm Hengstenbergs (vom 1. Juli 1827 bis zum 1. Juni 1869) (Ein Beitrag zur Kirchengeschichte des 19. Jahrhunderts)' (Diss.; Bonn, 1958), 2–3.

[50] Wendland, 'Erweckungsbewegung', 60.

[51] Hans-Joachim Schoeps, 'Der Erweckungschrist auf dem Thron: Friedrich Wilhelm IV.', in Friedrich Wilhelm Prinz von Preußen (ed.), *Preußens Könige* (Munich, 1971), 159–72.

By the time he had attained his twenty-first birthday, then, the major aesthetic, ideological, moral, and religious elements that defined Frederick William's *Gesamt-kunstwerk* were already in place: a deep emotionalism (*Schwärmerei*), a capacity for Romantic ecstasies, and a receptivity to Romantic fantasies; a related tendency to deal with the world in terms of visual images; a passion and a talent for architecture, which could provide visual expression to his political, religious, and aesthetic views; an abhorrence of 'the revolution' and all its works; an intense if somewhat diffuse German patriotism, based upon his admiration of the corporative institutions of the medieval Empire; a reverence for *all* institutions that could be regarded as 'historic', 'traditional', and 'organic'; a belief in the divinely ordained quality of his future royal office; and, finally, fervent religious feelings, expressed above all in his desire to renew the spirit of early Christianity and transform Prussia into a Christian state. But almost a quarter of a century was to pass before he could attempt to lay the institutional foundations of his *Gesamtkunstwerk* into place. Between 1815 and 1840 the Crown Prince had only limited opportunities to play an effective public role, most notably as chair of the Crown Prince's Commission (*Kronprinzenkommission*) from 1820 to 1823.

As we have already noted, the reformers who after 1806 had tried to transform and modernize Prussia found themselves in an increasingly embattled situation after 1815. The reformers' influence had reached its zenith with the King's promise of a constitution in 1815.[52] Thereafter, Chancellor Hardenberg and his allies faced growing opposition, not only from their old adversaries among the landed nobility but also from Frederick William III's circle of advisers at court; they included Police Minister (and, after 1819, Minister of the Royal House) Prince Wittgenstein, Otto von Voß-Buch, and the former royal tutor, Ancillon. A crucial facet of Hardenberg's post-1815 constitutional planning concerned local and regional (*Kreis*) government ordinances, for which his advisers had provided legislative drafts by 1820.[53] In late 1820 the anti-Hardenberg opposition convinced the King to appoint a commission, chaired by the Crown Prince, to review the new proposals.[54]

The Prince did not need much convincing to take up the cudgels against Hardenberg, whose politics he had come to detest. (Indeed, many years later he could still write disdainfully of the 'barren legacy of the legislation of that liberal-despotic debauchee Hardenberg, under which, unhappily!!!!!!!, Papa's name stands'.)[55] Especially loathsome, according to the Crown Prince, were Hardenberg's efforts to eliminate particularism and create a unitary state out of Prussia's historically disparate provinces. Frederick William certainly believed in the divine basis of his father's royal authority; but at the same time he vigorously defended the 'historic rights' of local and provincial institutions. Above all, he advocated political

---

[52] Nipperdey, *Deutsche Geschichte*, 67; Herbert Obenaus, *Anfänge des Parlamentarismus in Preußen bis 1848* (Düsseldorf, 1984), 81–3.

[53] Obenaus, *Anfänge*, 128–36; Berdahl, *Politics*, 196–8.   [54] Obenaus, *Anfänge*, 141.

[55] FW IV to his sister Charlotte (Empress Alexandra Feodorovna of Russia), 21 Jan. 1845, GStA Merseburg, HA Rep. 50 J Nr. 1210 Vol. III, Bl. 17ᵛ.

representation on the basis of 'historically' defined, corporative bodies and estates (*Stände*), rather than on a modern, parliamentary basis. The claims of parliaments to universal representation were specious, Frederick William believed; what deserved to be represented were the rights and liberties of historical estates. The proper monarchical state was thus a *Ständestaat*, not a centralized state. The Crown Prince's strong views on these matters had been fortified after 1815 by his reading of Carl Ludwig von Haller's *Restauration der Staatswissenschaft* (*Restoration of the Science of the State*, 1816–22), which he had begun to study in 1818.[56] Haller, a Swiss writer, depicted the state as a *patrimonium*, organized on familial lines, with the sovereign as patriarch. At the same time, he argued, all authority is based on property, and all holders of property themselves partake of patrimonial rights, which may not be circumscribed by kings or parliaments or bureaucrats. In Haller's system, all power is thus limited by the central reality of property and by a web of patrimonial authorities.[57] In one historian's words, 'This curious doctrine resonated with special power among the East Elbian nobility. It provided a justification for the system of manorial domination (*Gutsherrschaft*) and its public privileges. It also provided a justification for regionalist and traditional estatist (*altständisch*) opposition to the bureaucracy, to the absolutist and anti-feudal tradition of the Prussian state, and to that state's tendency to accept the values of liberal modernity'.[58] Influenced by ideas of this sort, Frederick William rejected all forms of 'absolutism', of which one of the most insidious, to his mind, was 'bureaucratic' absolutism of the Hardenberg sort.[59] Whatever its provenance, Frederick William believed, 'absolutism' was synonymous with policies of 'mechanistic' centralization, with the elimination of tradition and historically conditioned distinctiveness. Thus absolutism was in its essence revolutionary, the evil twin of 1789.

The Crown Prince's Commission was appointed in December 1820 and made its recommendations concerning local-government ordinances in March 1821. Later that year it was called together again to consider the problem of political representation at the provincial level. The commission released its final report in the spring of 1823; the result was the establishment of a network of diets for the eight provinces (*Provinziallandtage*) in 1823–4. These diets represented a kind of *Ersatz* for Frederick William III's constitutional promises of 1815. Each provincial diet was to be organized on a *ständisch* basis, with political representation based on corporative group interests; property-owning peasants, towns, and landowning nobility were to constitute Curias in each diet.[60] The arrangements for the provincial diets represented a complete victory for the restorationist politics of Frederick William III's confidants, and a major set-back for the centralizing and modernizing tendencies symbolized by Hardenberg, who himself had died in 1822.

[56] Kroll, *Friedrich Wilhelm IV.*, 26–7. Frederick William had also read Edmund Burke, whose *Reflections on the Revolution in France* he described in 1818 as 'one of the most divine books'. Ibid. 79–80.
[57] Berdahl, *Politics*, 232–46.   [58] Nipperdey, *Deutsche Geschichte*, 318.
[59] Lewalter, *Friedrich Wilhelm IV.*, 212, 218–21; Kroll, *Friedrich Wilhelm IV.*, 82–5, 90–3.
[60] Obenaus, *Anfänge*, 141–9, 151–209.

Although the Crown Prince detested Hardenberg's politics, he never became a member of his father's circle of conservative advisers after 1815. Indeed, people like the cautious and miserly Wittgenstein were suspicious of the heir's impressionable personality and extravagant ways;[61] and after the Crown Prince's Commission had finished its work, the Crown Prince himself was increasingly relegated to the political margins. Although he remained a member of the Council of State, he was never really taken into his father's political confidence, nor was he effectively trained after the 1820s for his future role. If anything, his isolation from political decision-making increased as the years went on. Like so many heirs to thrones before and after him, in the 1820s and 1830s the future Frederick William IV got married and increasingly devoted himself to private pursuits. In his case, this meant the cultivation of a circle of friends and confidants—many of whom remained close to him after his accession to the throne—and the further refinement of his intellectual and aesthetic interests, particularly in architecture and religion. Although these may have constituted private pursuits in the 1820s and 1830s, after 1840 they were to have important public consequences.

Years of Waiting, 1823–1840

In 1823, the same year that the Crown Prince's Commission finished its work, the Crown Prince himself got married to Princess Elisabeth Ludovika, daughter of the Bavarian King Max I Joseph, and half-sister of the heir to the Bavarian throne, the future Ludwig I. Although, as we have seen, European monarchs in the early nineteenth century increasingly attempted to define a new zone of privacy in their lives, the choice of a spouse still remained a matter of considerable political importance and delicacy. In the case of the Prussian Crown Prince, though, the choice was even more complicated, for he insisted that, public duty notwithstanding, he would only select a mate on the basis of mutual love and affection. In marriage, as in everything else, for Frederick William IV the public and private spheres overlapped. He had first met Elisabeth, or Elise as she was usually called, in 1819, when he had been dispatched on a 'bridal inspection' (*Brautschau*) to southern Germany. Elise had been born in 1801, and was one of five sisters, the 'Bavarian princesses', whose marriages were a matter of high state policy. The Prussian Crown Prince was rather quickly attracted to Elise, but the courtship lasted several years, and it sometimes seemed that the marriage would never take place. In the new age of familial values and private affection, Fritz and Elise wanted to be sure of their feelings for each other. Then there was another, even more pressing problem: the matter of Elise's Catholicism, unacceptable for a future Queen of Prussia. Ironic scepticism or indifference in religious affairs, which had been so typical of aristocratic and royal

---

[61] Hans Branig, *Fürst Wittgenstein: Ein preußischer Staatsmann der Restaurationszeit* (Cologne, 1981), 188; Leopold von Gerlach, 'Aus der Familiengeschichte Leopold von Gerlachs', in Hans-Joachim Schoeps (ed.), *Aus den Jahren preußischer Not und Erneuerung: Tagebücher und Briefe der Gebrüder Gerlach und ihres Kreises 1805–1820* (Berlin, 1963), 103.

attitudes in the eighteenth century, had largely disappeared by the time of the Restoration era; and for Elise, religious belief was a matter of the deepest moment, one which took precedence over the tuggings of the heart or the demands of politics. By 1823, however, these problems had been temporarily ironed out. Frederick William III agreed that Elise would not have to convert immediately to the Evangelical faith. For her part, she agreed to submit to instruction in Evangelical beliefs, and any conversion would take place on the basis of 'free conviction' rather than political calculation.[62] After the official marriage-ceremony in Munich, in November Elise travelled to Berlin, where the municipal government welcomed her with one of its grandest receptions in decades.[63]

The new Crown Princess turned immediately to her instruction in Evangelical beliefs, a drawn-out and, for her, painfully difficult process that lasted several years. Finally, in 1829, she consented to a formal conversion to her husband's faith.[64] Rumours persisted for decades, though, that this conversion had not been genuine. Those stories were almost certainly groundless, but they unquestionably diminished Elisabeth's popularity among many Protestants in Prussia and elsewhere. The future queen's ability to play an important representational role at the court or in public was hampered not only by her rather morose and withdrawn personality and her religious difficulties but also by her health, which was shaky from the very beginning and got steadily worse.[65] She rarely accompanied her husband on his numerous inspection trips and other journeys, and when she did travel, it was usually to visit relatives in Saxony, Bavaria, or Austria. The marriage between the Crown Prince and Elise remained childless, which later gave rise to widespread and often rather malicious claims that Frederick William was impotent.[66] By about 1830 it had become clear that no child would be forthcoming and that Frederick William's younger brother William would be his heir. If the marriage between Frederick William and Elisabeth lacked the erotic passion that characterized the relationship between Queen Victoria and Prince Albert, it was nevertheless based on a genuine and enduring love un-

---

[62] Wittgenstein and Graf Bernstorff to Frederick William III, 30 Sept. and 1 Nov. 1823, GStA Merseburg, Geheimes Zivilkabinett 2.2.1. Nr. 3037 Bl. 1–2ᵛ, 11; draft of marriage contract, 17 Oct. 1823, BayHStA, Abt. II, Bayer. Gesandtschaft Berlin 505.

[63] *Ordnung der Feierlichkeiten, welche bei Gelegenheit der Vermählung Seiner Königlichen Hoheit des Kronprinzen mit Ihrer Königlichen Hoheit der Prinzessin Elisabeth von Bayern auf Befehl Seiner Majestät des Königs statt finden sollen*, GStA Berlin, BPH Rep. 50 Nr. 249.

[64] See the documents in GStA Merseburg, HA Rep. 50 N Nr. 11, esp. Bl. 114–22; and Caroline von Rochow geborene von der Marwitz and Marie de la Motte-Fouqué, *Vom Leben am preußischen Hofe 1815–1852*, ed. Luise von der Marwitz (Berlin, 1908), 148–50, 157–64; Lewalter, *Friedrich Wilhelm IV.*, 249–51, 255.

[65] In a letter of 18 Jan. 1824 to her brother Ludwig she reports that 'my health has hardly been able to recover from all the exertions; I am unwell and have got quite thin'. GHA, Nachlaß König Ludwig I., I/A/10. The only biographical study devoted to Elisabeth is by Wilhelm Moritz Freiherr von Bissing, *Königin Elisabeth von Preußen (1801–1874): Ein Lebensbild* (Berlin, 1974). It is, however, disappointingly thin. The title incorrectly states that she died in 1874, when in fact she died in 1873.

[66] e.g. see the allusion to FW's childlessness in Heinrich Heine's poem, 'Der Kaiser von China'. In his diary entry for 14 Dec. 1844, Varnhagen mentions a 'fearful satiric poem' on the subject of Frederick William's extravagance: 'To be sure, it adds, he doesn't spend anything on mistresses, and for good reason!' Varnhagen von Ense, *Tagebücher*, ii. 414.

usual by the standards of most royal marriages. Elise herself was an anchor of stability for her excitable husband; moreover, as we shall see, it would be a grave error to underestimate her political significance after 1840. Although she lacked the political ambitions and instincts of William's wife, Augusta, Elisabeth did have certain political interests, and especially after 1848 she was an invaluable ally of the reactionary court Camarilla.

In the years after their marriage, Fritz and Elise increasingly surrounded themselves with a group of friends and intimates who came to be known as the Crown Prince's Circle. As that appellation suggests, most (though by no means all) of these friends shared Frederick William's religious and political views. Many of them had already befriended each other before meeting the Crown Prince, and it was often as a result of that network of friendships that they became acquainted with him in the first place. Moreover, many members of the *Kronprinzenkreis* were soldiers; despite Frederick William's singularly unmartial ways and interests, it was inevitable that an heir to the Prussian throne would be surrounded by men from the military, even if, in the words of one critical court chronicler, 'The soldiers who composed the King's entourage were more inclined to pray than to fight.'[67] Indeed, from an early age Frederick William preferred to be surrounded by military men who shared his religious inclinations. An example of the military 'zealots' (*Frömmler*) who were closest to him was his adjutant after 1816, Karl von Roeder (1787–1856), a man of little intellectual or military distinction but with a highly developed ethical consciousness, an intense religious faith, and a willingness to criticize the Crown Prince to his face.[68]

Where the friendship between Frederick William and Roeder was based on mutual respect and shared religious feeling, the friendship between the heir to the throne and the equally pious Count Carl von der Groeben (1788–1876) was far more intense and emotional. The Crown Prince once described Groeben as 'a model of pure morality' and as 'my *loyal, tested, beloved* friend'; and, apart from Elisabeth herself, there was probably no one else in Frederick William IV's entourage to whom he was more deeply attached, just as there was no one else who returned that affection more uncritically and unconditionally. Contemporary and historical judgements on Groeben vary widely. While some contemporaries praised his martial skills, others regarded him as a 'charming salon-type without notable military abilities'.[69]

As a young man Groeben had been influenced, like so many of his generation, by 'Christian-German' enthusiasms; but unlike many of his conservative peers later in

[67] Eduard Vehse and 'Vehse redivivus', *Illustrierte Geschichte des preußischen Hofes, des Adels und der Diplomatie vom Großen Kurfürsten bis zum Tode Kaiser Wilhelms I.* (2 vols.; Stuttgart, n.d. [1901]), ii: *Von Friedrich Wilhelm II. bis zum Tode Kaiser Wilhelms I.*, 277.

[68] Ernst Ludwig von Gerlach, diary entry for 10 Mar. 1827, in 'Ungedrucktes aus dem Tagebuch Ludwig von Gerlachs 1826–1829', in Hans-Joachim Schoeps (ed.), *Neue Quellen zur Geschichte Preußens im 19. Jahrhundert* (Berlin, 1968), 129; cf. Roeder's voluminous correspondence with FW IV : GStA Merseburg, HA Rep. 50 J Nr. 1174.

[69] FW (IV) to Frederick William III, 2 Apr. 1834, GStA Merseburg, HA Rep. 50 J Nr. 1006 Vol. III, Bl. 114^v; Graf Thun to Graf Buol, 13 June 1853, HHStA, P.A. III, Karton 48, VIII. Interna Preußens, fol. 31^r.

life, he always remained attached to German national sentiments. Groeben never became a political general, however, but remained a soldier first and foremost. After distinguishing himself in the campaigns of 1806–7 and 1813–15, Groeben served under Gneisenau at the new Prussian garrison in Koblenz, where he became a confidant of that distinguished officer as well as a close friend of Carl von Clausewitz. (Groeben later helped to edit Clausewitz's collected works.) In 1824 Groeben became Chief of the General Staff of the Second Army Corps in Stettin, which was nominally commanded by the Crown Prince.[70] That was the beginning of a remarkable friendship between the two men that lasted until Frederick William's death. As late as 1853, the Austrian minister to Berlin described Groeben as a 'man whom the King loves like "a bride", and with the same religious views and enthusiastic tendencies. The King corresponds with him constantly and has such an intimate relationship with him that they have sworn to say the same prayers at the same time every day . . .'.[71]

Also from the military, but much more obviously 'political' in their interests and inclinations, were Leopold von Gerlach (1790–1861) and Joseph Maria von Radowitz (1797–1853). Gerlach first met the Crown Prince while serving as a staff officer in April 1813.[72] The scion of an old family that had been ennobled in 1735, Gerlach was the son of Berlin's first mayor, Leopold von Gerlach the Elder. The younger Leopold was one of four remarkable brothers, all of whom shared intensely conservative views on state, society, and religion. Wilhelm (1789–1834) was a jurist in Frankfurt an der Oder. Otto (1801–49) was the socially engaged pastor of a church in an impoverished section of the Prussian capital; as a result of his activities among the poor he was called the 'Wesley of Berlin'.[73] The third brother, Ernst Ludwig (1795–1877), will figure prominently in this account. A veteran of the liberation war and, like his brother Wilhelm, a jurist, Ludwig was active after 1815 both in the *Maikäferei* and the Awakening. A difficult, overbearing, uncompromising, yet powerful and in many ways brilliant personality, Ludwig von Gerlach became an unbending advocate of Hallerian patrimonialism and Evangelical orthodoxy.[74] In contrast to Frederick William IV, Ludwig was rarely susceptible to Romantic enthusiasms, and unlike Leopold he was never a close personal friend of the monarch; in any case, he spent most of the 1820s and 1830s away from Berlin, pursuing his career in Naumburg, Halle, and Frankfurt an der Oder. During those years he began to develop a flair for using modern forms of publicity and controversy in order to promote his political and religious ideas. In 1827 he was one of the founders of Ernst

[70] Rochow and de la Motte-Fouqué, *Leben*, 186–7; Alexander Scharff, 'General Carl Graf von der Groeben und die deutsche Politik König Friedrich Wilhelms IV.', *FBPG* 48 (1936), 3; Paret, *Clausewitz*, 258; Kurt von Priesdorff (ed.), *Soldatisches Führertum* (10 vols.; Hamburg, 1937–42), v. 222–4.

[71] Graf Thun to Graf Buol, 13 June 1853, HHStA, P.A. III, Karton 48, VIII. Interna Preußens, fol. 31ʳ–31ᵛ.

[72] Leopold von Gerlach to FW IV, 21 Sept. 1856, GStA Merseburg, HA Rep. 50 J Nr. 455, Bl. 148ᵛ; Leopold von Gerlach, 'Familiengeschichte', in Hans-Joachim Schoeps (ed.), *Aus den Jahren*, 103.

[73] Ibid. 21, 28.

[74] For biographical details, see, above all, Hans-Christof Kraus, 'Ernst Ludwig von Gerlach: Politisches Denken und Handeln eines preußischen Altkonservativen' (Diss.; 2 vols.; Göttingen, 1991).

Wilhelm Hengstenberg's *Evangelische Kirchen-Zeitung*, one of Prussia's most influential conservative newspapers (and regularly perused by the Crown Prince).[75] After 1830–1 he also became involved with the efforts of another conservative newspaper, the *Berliner Politisches Wochenblatt*, to propagate the idea of a 'Christian-German' state in Prussia.[76] Much of the direct political influence that Ludwig was to enjoy after 1840, though, stemmed from the close relationship between his brother Leopold and Frederick William IV.

Leopold was five years older than Ludwig, and had pursued a professional military career. Although, as we have already seen, he had met the Crown Prince in 1813, he only entered the circle of Frederick William's intimates after the late 1820s. In 1826 he was named adjutant to Prince William, the Crown Prince's younger brother, and accompanied him on various trips abroad.[77] By 1828 he had resumed his correspondence with the Crown Prince, and by 1830 was appearing almost daily in Frederick William's company. Certainly his access to the Prince was eased as a result of his own close friendship with another member of the *Kronprinzenkreis*, Carl von Voß–Buch (1786–1864). The son of Otto von Voß–Buch, one of Hardenberg's more relentless opponents, the younger Voß shared the Gerlachs' political and religious views. A rather difficult and taciturn person, Voß nevertheless became the Crown Prince's civil adjutant in 1828 and thus a key member of his circle.[78] After 1830, Leopold von Gerlach was also increasingly active in that same circle. His relationship to Frederick William became an intense one, although, as we shall see, it was always exceptionally complex and ambivalent. Moreover, it was only after 1842 and especially after 1848 that his personal influence reached its zenith.

Another military man associated with the Gerlach-Voß group was the remarkable Joseph Maria von Radowitz. Born in 1797 to a Catholic family of Hungarian origin, Radowitz had first fought in 1813 for Jérôme Bonaparte's Kingdom of Westphalia.[79] Thereafter he had served in the armed forces of Electoral Hesse, but in 1823 he applied for a position in the Prussian army. His superiors quickly became aware of his formidable intellectual skills, and so he became tutor in mathematics and military science to Prince Albrecht, Frederick William III's youngest son. This position brought him into unexpectedly rapid contact with high officials of the court and of Berlin society; and in June 1824 he met the Crown Prince in Potsdam. Immediately mesmerized by Frederick William's personality, Radowitz became one of his most

---

[75] Kriege, 'Kirchen-Zeitung', 35–55, 62–3; Berdahl, *Politics*, 252–3.

[76] Berdahl, *Politics*, 258–63; Hermann Beck, 'Conservatives, Bureaucracy, and the Social Question in Prussia (1815–1848)' (Ph.D. thesis; Los Angeles, 1988), ch. 1; id., 'Conservatives and the Social Question in Nineteenth-Century Prussia', in Jones and Retallack (eds.), *Between Reform, Reaction and Resistance*, 67–74.

[77] Leopold von Gerlach, 'Familiengeschichte', in Hans-Joachim Schoeps (ed.), *Aus den Jahren*, 102–3.

[78] Ibid. 38.

[79] After many decades, the best biographical studies of Radowitz remain Paul Hassel, *Joseph Maria von Radowitz*, i: *1797–1848* (Berlin, 1905); and Friedrich Meinecke, *Radowitz und die deutsche Revolution* (Berlin, 1913).

fervent admirers, while for his part Frederick William declared in 1829 that there were 'few people more noble, pure, or sagacious' than Radowitz.[80] Indeed, along with Elisabeth and Groeben, Radowitz was one of the later King's most intimate friends. At first Radowitz was closely associated with the Gerlach circle, as a result of which he was actively involved with the *Berliner Politisches Wochenblatt*.[81] By the middle of the 1830s, though, their relationship had begun to cool, and signs of personal and political estrangement had already appeared.

By no means all of Frederick William's friends and advisers from his years as Crown Prince were military men. For example, yet another of his close confidants for several decades was Count Anton zu Stolberg-Wernigerode (1785–1854), a nobleman notable not only for his aristocratic demeanour—he was described by contemporaries as one of the last *grands seigneurs* of the old school—but also for his unimpeachable integrity and strength of character. Acquaintances and observers were less sure of his intellectual abilities and political skills. Stolberg had known the Crown Prince since Frederick William's childhood, but their relationship began to develop steadily after 1815.[82] With Frederick William's accession to the throne, the two men became virtually inseparable.

Although most of the Crown Prince's associates shared, with varying degrees of nuance and intensity, *ständisch*-conservative political views, this was never uniformly the case. Frederick William was a man possessed of genuine and far-reaching intellectual abilities, and especially during the 'long years of waiting' as Crown Prince he loved to surround himself with interesting conversation-partners.[83] Accordingly, of central importance to Frederick William's life were the tea salons or 'tea evenings' that often took place in Elise's chambers at the royal palaces in Berlin or Potsdam, or in the princely couple's summer retreat near Potsdam. These *Abendgesellschaften* usually consisted of lectures or readings, with the Crown Prince simultaneously listening and drawing on a sketching-pad. Participants in the tea evenings often included notable personalities from the arts, literature, music, the sciences, or academic life, such as the poet Ludwig Tieck, the historian Leopold (von) Ranke, and, of course, the garden designer Lenné and the architect Schinkel. Certainly the most notable of Frederick William's friends from the scientific world was the naturalist Alexander von Humboldt (1769–1859), who could scarcely be described as religiously or politically conservative. Humboldt had met the Crown Prince in 1805 after returning from his expedition to South America, but it was only after 1830 that their relationship became closer. In that year Humboldt accompanied Frederick William on a trip to visit his brother-in-law, Tsar Nicholas I, in St Petersburg, and in the following year the two men again travelled together, this time to Warsaw. They

---

[80]   Hassel, *Radowitz*, 178; FW (IV) to Frederick William III, 4 June 1829, GStA Merseburg, HA Rep. 50 J Nr. 1006 Vol. III, Bl. 8.

[81]   Hassel, *Radowitz*, 213–18.

[82]   Rochow and de la Motte-Fouqué, *Leben*, 223–6; Stolberg-Wernigerode, *Stolberg-Wernigerode*, 16.

[83]   Ernst II., Herzog von Sachsen-Coburg-Gotha, *Aus meinem Leben und aus meiner Zeit* (3 vols.; Berlin, 1887–9), i. 612.

began to see each other even more frequently after 1835, and by the time Frederick William became king, Humboldt was appearing at his table almost daily.[84]

One measure of Frederick William's attachment to Alexander von Humboldt was the fact that the ageing naturalist was permitted to use a bedroom in the Crown Prince's summer residence, the villa of Charlottenhof in the park of Sanssouci. Essentially completed in 1826–7, Charlottenhof testifies to the development of Frederick William's architectural tastes after 1815, especially his predilections for Italianate neoclassicism as well as the careful integration of buildings into landscapes. As noted earlier, his Gothic phase was relatively short-lived, and by 1821 it was essentially over. He had always been interested in classical antiquity, and like so many educated Germans of his time, he was a passionate admirer of Italy; for years he tried in vain to convince his father to let him visit Rome, the architectural history of which he had already thoroughly studied. By the 1820s he had become increasingly involved with projects to reshape the Potsdam landscape with buildings that were inspired by classical Roman villas. In the first part of that decade he drafted plans for a large neoclassical palace to be called 'Belriguardo'; he wanted it to be built on a hill across the Havel directly south of Sanssouci, and as an axial pendant to that older edifice. The designs for Belriguardo, which Frederick William hoped to take up as his official residence, are reminiscent of a Roman imperial palace; like the Friedenskirche some years later, they suggest a clear link between the Crown Prince's architectural notions and his grandiose political conceptions. Many of Frederick William's ideas, however, including this one, never came to fruition, largely because of the extreme frugality of Prussian court authorities under Frederick William III.[85]

The Crown Prince's ardour for architecture was never dampened by such disappointments, and evidence abounds of his close connection in those years to various projects of Schinkel and Lenné. His younger brother, Prince Carl (1801–83), shared his passion for art and architecture, and the Crown Prince was keenly interested in the development of Carl's summer residence at Klein-Glienicke. Historically associated with Potsdam but located in what is now the most south-westerly corner of Berlin, the estate of Klein-Glienicke was acquired for Prince Carl in 1824. Carl immediately engaged Peter Joseph Lenné to design the park along the lines of an English landscape-garden, while by 1827 Schinkel and his pupils had transformed the house itself into an antique Roman country villa of the sort described by the younger Pliny towards the end of the first century.[86] For many years the Crown

---

[84] Conrad Müller, introd. to Alexander von Humboldt, *Alexander von Humboldt und das preußische Königshaus: Briefe aus den Jahren 1835–1857*, ed. Conrad Müller (Leipzig, 1928), 56–66; Hanno Beck, *Alexander von Humboldt*, ii: *Vom Reisewerk zum 'Kosmos' 1804–1859* (Wiesbaden, 1961), 180–1.

[85] Hans Hoffmann and Renate Möller, *Schloß Charlottenhof und die Römischen Bäder*, 2nd edn. (Potsdam-Sanssouci, 1985), 52, 82; Frederick William's drawings and sketches for Belriguardo in Plankammer Potsdam-Sanssouci, Sammlung Friedrich Wilhelm IV., Mappe III, Heft 1, Umschlag B; Klaus von Krosigk and Heinz Wiegand, *Glienicke* (Berlin, 1984), 17; Helmut Engel, 'Friedrich Wilhelm IV. und die Baukunst', in Büsch (ed.), *Friedrich Wilhelm IV. in seiner Zeit*, Baukunst', 162–3; L. Dehio, *Friedrich Wilhelm IV.*, 28.

[86] Michael Seiler, 'Die Entwicklungsgeschichte des Landschaftsgartens Klein-Glienicke 1796–1883' (Diss.; Hamburg, 1986), 111–19.

Prince was closely associated with the whole process of planning for his brother's villa. Moreover, the development of Klein-Glienicke initiated an outburst of building activity that continued for over thirty years and resulted in the transformation of the Potsdam region, with its pine forests, rivers, and lakes, into an Italianate Arcadia, one of the finest and most aesthetically gracious ensembles of architecture and garden design in Europe. Frederick William played a decisive role in its realization. Deprived of the opportunity to implement his political and religious visions, the Prussian Crown Prince turned with gusto to his architectural pursuits. Frederick William's dreams for his beloved Potsdam landscape, site of the 'divine' Sanssouci, are expressed especially clearly in a remark he made to Lenné shortly after becoming king: 'The Duke of Dessau made his land into a garden. I cannot do that, because my land is too large. But it might be possible gradually to make a garden out of the vicinity of Berlin and Potsdam; I could live for another twenty years, and in that period of time it is possible to accomplish something.'[87]

The collaboration among Frederick William, Schinkel, and Lenné is especially apparent in the design and execution of Charlottenhof, the Crown Prince's own antique villa. The park, with its existing house, was acquired by Frederick William III for his oldest son in early 1826, and immediately thereafter Lenné received the assignment to redesign the park, while Schinkel and his assistant Persius—in other words, the same team that designed Glienicke—set out to transform the existing structure into a classical villa, including on its front a long terraced portico. Frederick William was centrally involved in the whole project, preparing dozens of sketches and suggestions for its execution. The result was one of the most successful and pleasing examples in nineteenth-century Europe of the 'marriage' of English-style garden design with neoclassicist architecture. It is also impossible to determine whether Charlottenhof is essentially the achievement of Frederick William IV or of Schinkel. Rather, it attests to a continuous and fruitful collaboration between the two men.[88] Charlottenhof quickly became Frederick William's favourite retreat; to the Crown Prince it was known as 'Siam', and in letters to relatives the heir to the Prussian throne would self-mockingly refer to himself with titles such as 'Lord Dicky Butt of Siam'.[89] It was in this idyllic setting, with its Romantic evocations of the classical world, that the *Abendgesellschaften* of the Crown Prince's Circle continued throughout the summer months of the late 1820s and into the 1830s.

In 1828 the Crown Prince himself was finally able to realize his dream of going to Italy. Because of her poor health, Elise had to remain in Bavaria; Frederick William was accompanied by Ancillon and Groeben. His journey took him to Genoa, to the sights of Tuscany, thence to Rome. He had already studied that city's antiquities so

[87] Quoted in L. Dehio, *Friedrich Wilhelm IV.*, 87. See also August Kopisch, *Die königlichen Schlösser und Gärten zu Potsdam: Von der Zeit ihrer Gründung bis zum Jahre MDCCCLII* (Berlin, 1854), 161–220; Georg Poensgen, *Die Bauten Friedrich Wilhelms IV. in Potsdam* (Berlin, 1930); and Friedrich Mielke, *Potsdamer Baukunst: Das klassische Potsdam*, 2nd edn. (Frankfurt am Main, 1991), 139–81.

[88] Mielke, *Baukunst*, 129–34.

[89] Lewalter, *Friedrich Wilhelm IV.*, 283–9; Engel, 'Baukunst', 165; FW (IV) to Prince Johann of Saxony, 14 Aug. 1828, in Johann Georg, Herzog zu Sachsen and Hubert Ermisch (eds.), *Briefwechsel*, 30.

well that they reminded him of some of his own architectural projects. Still, Rome confirmed him in his architectural and aesthetic notions, and, like so many other Germans, he succumbed utterly to a passionate love of the place (he once called it '*Romsucht*').[90] During his stay in Rome Frederick William forged a close relationship with his guide there, yet another individual who was to play a vital role in his life for many years to come: Christian Carl Josias Bunsen (1791–1860), at the time Prussian minister to the Holy See. Bunsen was an intellectual polymath, as we shall see in a later chapter; he played a pivotal role, for example, in the establishment of the renowned German Archaeological Institute in Rome. Moreover, like his princely guest, he was deeply religious, committed to a rediscovery through careful scholarship of the spirit and energy of early Christianity. Bunsen increasingly became convinced that that spirit was architecturally best evoked by the basilica style. It was thus almost inevitable that Bunsen and the future King of Prussia should strike up an intense friendship; and in subsequent years Bunsen's political advancement was due largely to Frederick William's interventions on his behalf.[91]

Frederick William returned from Italy in December 1828, having visited Naples, Ravenna, and Venice along the way.[92] By that time he was 33 years old, and the views, feelings, attitudes, and friendships to which he adhered for the rest of his life had, for the most part, already been shaped. Nevertheless, as he moved into mature adulthood, there seemed little likelihood that the Crown Prince would soon get a chance to play an active role in Prussia's affairs. For his part, Frederick William insisted that the ecstatic expectations and enthusiasms of his youth had been extinguished: 'The attainment of ideal conditions is something which long ago disappeared from my calculations and expectations', he claimed, perhaps a trifle disingenuously, in 1829.[93] But in fact, until his accession to the throne he loved to spin out his 'reveries about the future';[94] he continued to surround himself with his friends and confidants; and, of course, he pursued his architectural interests. He also amplified his ideas, which reached all the way back to the time of the liberation war, for a Protestant cathedral in Berlin. The cathedral, he hoped, would take the form of a great basilica that would be unmatched anywhere in the world.[95] And though his proposals, like so many others in those years and thereafter, came to nought, he was still able to initiate some realizable projects, of which perhaps the most notable was the restoration of Burg Stolzenfels on the Rhine—an undertaking

[90] FW IV to Alfred von Reumont, 10 Feb. 1851, GStA Merseburg, HA Rep. 50 J Nr. 1130, Bl. 14ᵛ.
[91] FW (IV) to Frederick William III, 4 Mar.1839, GStA Merseburg, HA Rep. 50 J Nr. 1006 Vol. III, Bl. 239ᵛ.
[92] Lewalter, *Friedrich Wilhelm IV.*, 289–302; L. Dehio, *Friedrich Wilhelm IV.*, 59–61.
[93] FW (IV) to Ludwig I, 13 Aug. 1829, GHA, Nachlaß König Ludwig I., 86/6/8.
[94] FW (IV) to Crown Prince Max (II) of Bavaria, 6 Apr. 1840, GHA, Nachlaß König Max II., 83/2/409.
[95] L. Dehio, *Friedrich Wilhelm IV.*, 104–10; Engel, 'Baukunst', 163–4; and esp. Carl-Wolfgang Schümann, *Der Berliner Dom im 19. Jahrhundert* (Berlin, 1980), 21–50; and Karl-Heinz Klingenburg, *Der Berliner Dom: Bauten, Ideen und Projekte vom 15. Jahrhundert bis zur Gegenwart* (Berlin [East], 1987), 56–60, 74–95.

that testified to the persistence of Frederick William's devotion to Rhineland Romanticism, to a patriotic vision of Germany's medieval greatness, and to monarchical self-representation.[96]

Stolzenfels was a ruined castle high over the Rhine which the city of Koblenz presented to Frederick William in 1823. It was decided to restore the ruin as a Gothic edifice which could serve as a residence for Frederick William and Elisabeth during their stays in that region. Both Schinkel and the Koblenz official Johann Claudius von Lassaulx were involved with plans for the restoration. It promised to be expensive, however, and serious work only began in 1835; Frederick William himself, whose understanding of financial matters was always rather doubtful, had to borrow substantial sums from the Prussian state bank, the *Seehandlung*, to pay for the project.[97] Despite its huge costs, it was especially dear to his heart, and by 1845 it was essentially completed. Stolzenfels was the very incarnation of Frederick William's ideas of what a medieval castle on the Rhine should look like, with its high Gothic towers and arcades, its Gothic chapel, its statue of the young Siegfried from the *Nibelungenlied*, and its cycles of paintings with scenes evoking chivalric values. Thus, like most of Frederick William's buildings, it represented at once an aesthetic and an ideological statement, an affirmation of monarchical sentiments and anti-revolutionary, 'chivalric' values.[98]

And so, as some thoughtful contemporary observers noted, Frederick William remained loyal to the views, feelings, and emotions that had inspired his youth. Many of those contemporaries also continued to be concerned about his excitability, his nervous unsteadiness and unpredictability, his rashness, his frequent indecisiveness, and his flights of fancy. In a letter to Metternich of July 1840, Prince Wittgenstein concluded that Frederick William 'certainly has the best intentions and the most benevolent sentiments: but nature has equipped him with an ingenious fantasy, and that is a foe which is difficult to overcome, especially if one is not indifferent to popularity'.[99] Even some of his closest associates, like Leopold von Gerlach or Carl von Voß-Buch, were always strongly critical of the Crown Prince's personal shortcomings. Other notable individuals, however, were transfixed by his scintillating intelligence, unshakeable moral and religious standards, and personal amiability. Among his many enthusiastic admirers were people like the great reformer Baron vom Stein, the historian Barthold Niebuhr, and Theodor von

---

[96] Ursula Rathke, 'Schloß- und Burgenbauten', in Eduard Trier and Willy Weyres (eds.), *Kunst des 19. Jahrhunderts im Rheinland* (Düsseldorf, 1980), ii: *Architektur II. Profane Bauten und Städtebau*, 349.

[97] GStA Berlin, I. Hauptabteilung Rep. 109 Nr. 3982, Bl. 36a, 37.

[98] Ursula Rathke, *Preußische Burgenromantik am Rhein: Studien zum Wiederaufbau von Rheinstein, Stolzenfels und Sooneck (1823–1860)* (Munich, 1979), 46–115; ead., 'Ein Sanssouci am Rhein: Bemerkungen zur Entwicklung der preußischen Burgenromantik am Rhein', in Renate Wagner-Rieger and Walter Krause (eds.), *Historismus und Schloßbau* (Munich, 1975), 90, 91–7; Werner Bornheim gen. Schilling, 'Stolzenfels als Gesamtkunstwerk', in Trier and Weyres (eds.), *Kunst des 19. Jahrhunderts*, ii. 329–41; id., *Schloß Stolzenfels*, 3rd edn. (Mainz, 1980).

[99] Wittgenstein to Metternich, 9 July 1840, HHStA, St. K. Preußen, Karton 177, Noten 1840, fol. 24ʳ. See also Branig, *Wittgenstein*, 193.

Schön, the veteran governor of East Prussia and disciple of Kant. Goethe himself had professed in 1828 that he placed 'great hope' in the Prussian Crown Prince: 'According to everything which I know of him and hear of him, he is a very considerable person!'[100]

Still, for many insightful observers Frederick William remained an enigma. Much of his effusiveness and many of his enthusiasms, whether spoken or epistolary, seem contrived and quite consciously theatrical; and in the supposed openness with which he dealt with courtiers, friends, and strangers alike, there was always an element of calculation and even dissimulation. In her memoirs of life at the Prussian court, Caroline de la Motte-Fouqué wrote of 'a certain veiled something' in the Crown Prince's character, while in 1842 one of his oldest associates, Gustav Adolf von Rochow, sighed with exasperation: 'I have been in his immediate vicinity for twenty-three years, and I never know what he wants; he is perpetually having *arrière-pensées* . . .'[101] Frederick William IV always hid behind a mask of his own devising, and even in his most intimate letters he rarely let the mask down. Virtually all the great German historians of the late nineteenth and early twentieth centuries tried to get behind the mask, and some of their characterizations, most notably those by Ranke, Treitschke, and Valentin, became classics. But for all that, he remains an enigmatic and in some ways shadowy and elusive figure.[102]

For now, it is impossible to reach final conclusions about the personality of this remarkable and paradoxical man. It must be reiterated, however, that his basic set of attitudes and beliefs were expressed in a vision of his life's work as a *Gesamtkunstwerk*, as a consciously formed 'artifice'. And a crucial aspect of that *Gesamtkunstwerk*, as we have seen, was his unyielding faith in the divinely ordained nature of the office that he would one day inherit. If anything, his mystical conviction of *Gottesgnadentum*, of the sacral quality of monarchy, intensified as the years went by. In March 1840, reported Carl von Voß-Buch, the Crown Prince developed 'the idea that kings occupy an office established by God, like that of bishops, but different in all other ways. All other offices had been created and given out by human beings. Naturally I disagreed with that qualitative difference, and said to him that he was getting close to the ideas of James I. But I did not manage to do anything more than point out to him that I did not share his opinion.' Indeed, noted Voß with concern, 'It is remarkable how ideas of this sort permeate him . . . He seeks and finds something sacramental everywhere, and every day I increasingly get into

---

[100] Johann Peter Eckermann, *Gespräche mit Goethe in den letzten Jahren seines Lebens*, 3rd edn. (Berlin [East], 1987), 582.

[101] Caroline de la Motte-Fouqué, in Rochow and de la Motte-Fouqué, *Leben*, 170; E. L. von Gerlach, diary (13 Dec. 1842), GA, Tagebücher Ernst Ludwig von Gerlachs, vol. ii/b.

[102] One historian, Willy Andreas, went so far as to suggest that Frederick William showed signs of a 'reactive, unstable psychopath': Willy Andreas, *Die russische Diplomatie und die Politik Friedrich Wilhelms IV. von Preußen* (Berlin, 1927), 13 n. 2. More recently, the historian Dirk Blasius has also described Frederick William as a 'psychopathological personality'—by which, however, he means not a 'sick' personality, but one which sharply deviates from the norm or the average. His analysis draws on the theories of the psychiatrist Kurt Schneider. Dirk Blasius, *Friedrich Wilhelm IV. 1795–1861: Psychopathologie und Geschichte* (Göttingen, 1992).

disagreements with him about these things, which could perhaps become questions of vital significance.'[103]

Three months later Frederick William III was dead, and the former Crown Prince, in his forty-fifth year, had become King of Prussia. An artist now occupied the centre of the Prussian state. In the words of one of his contemporaries, the poet and critic Robert Prutz, 'And now the royal purple is being spread over the seething chaos of an artist's soul! and the fate of a whole realm is bound up with the unruly flights of his fantasy!'[104]

---

[103] Voß to Leopold von Gerlach, 5 Mar. 1840, in 'Briefe von Carl von Voß an Leopold von Gerlach 1839–1843', in Hans-Joachim Schoeps (ed.), *Neue Quellen*, 269.

[104] Robert Prutz, *Zehn Jahre: Geschichte der neuesten Zeit. 1840–1850*, i (Leipzig, 1850), 170.

3
The Structures of 'Personal Rule', 1840–1846

Building a Cathedral and Building a Monarchy

In the late summer of 1842, two years after his accession to the Prussian throne, Frederick William IV journeyed to the Rhine to celebrate the resumption of work on Cologne Cathedral. The King was received to great public acclaim, and he himself was overjoyed. At last, it seemed, one of his favourite projects, which he had supported for years, was about to become reality. On 4 September, after attending Evangelical services and a pontifical mass in the cathedral, Frederick William participated in the dedication of the edifice's new cornerstone. He then surprised and delighted the public with one of those gripping and unexpected speeches which had become his speciality. His taciturn father had never addressed any large gathering of his civilian subjects; nor, indeed, had any Prussian sovereign before him. But Frederick William IV understood that he lived in a different age, one which required new forms for the representation of monarchical values. He was thus the first Prussian ruler regularly to deliver public speeches, and he was brilliant at it. In one of his best performances ever, the King now hailed the 'spirit of German unity and strength' which had sustained the cathedral project from the beginning, and concluded with an emotional salute to the city of Cologne which elicited an ecstatic, even tearful response from the audience.[1]

One of Cologne's most prominent visitors during the cathedral celebration was the Austrian representative, the ageing but ageless Prince Metternich, himself a native Rhinelander. Not surprisingly, Metternich regarded Frederick William's emotional and sentimental appeal to German national feeling with a jaundiced eye. He was also deeply sceptical about Frederick William's plans to transform the Prussian monarchy from within. Determined to convince Metternich of his worthy intentions, the King of Prussia invited the veteran statesman to visit him at his Rhineland castle, Burg Stolzenfels, after the festivities were over. In explaining his policies, Frederick William presented a view of the Prussian state which the Austrian Chancellor later described as 'quite remarkable'. It would be impossible, Frederick William said, 'to come up with any kind of concept that could describe the political entity called Prussia. This thing has no historical basis; it consists of an agglomeration of territories, which themselves once had such a basis and then lost them.' Now they constituted a single but artificial unit held together by a powerful oligarchy of officials. 'In this situation', he continued, 'it is not possible to speak of

---

[1] Friedrich Wilhelm IV., König von Preußen, *Reden und Trinksprüche Sr. Majestät Friedrich Wilhelm des Vierten, Königes von Preußen* (Leipzig, 1855), 30–2. The best account of the *Dombaufest* of 1842 can be found in Thomas Parent, *Die Hohenzollern in Köln* (Cologne, 1981), 50–61.

anything that might logically be described as "reform", because one can only reform—that is, improve—something which already exists. In Prussia, however, we have to create something new, because what already exists there is an absurdity.' Metternich was less than enchanted by Frederick William's discourse, noting several days later that the King 'is interfering with all the gears of the machine', and that his effort to 'reshape' Prussia was almost certain to fail, mostly because of his personality. Above all, the Chancellor asserted, Frederick William demonstrated a tendency which 'I can only describe as "artistic" ', and which invariably would lead him and his followers 'in new directions invented by themselves'.[2]

These two incidents—the King's speech in Cologne and his conversation with Metternich at Burg Stolzenfels—vividly illustrate Frederick William IV's notions regarding his royal office and his royal mission. He had used the occasion of the Cologne celebrations to help orchestrate a gigantic ideological festival, a popular affirmation of monarchical values. As Franz Schnabel once noted, 'King Frederick William IV possessed a distinct awareness of the needs of his time and of other humans.' Accordingly, he sought to modernize and transform older religious rituals into a new kind of public festival, one designed to advertise his own blend of monarchical, *ständisch*-corporative, and Christian-national values as an alternative to the values proclaimed by the great secular festivals of the French Revolution—occasions which had been echoed in Germany by the Wartburg and Hambach festivals in 1817 and 1832.[3] In other words, Frederick William IV was engaged in a deliberate attempt to lay the foundations of a new, counter-revolutionary 'political religion' in Prussia.[4]

In his conversation with Metternich, Frederick William had identified the most complex aspect of what may be called his monarchical project: how to create and sustain an anti-revolutionary, monarchical tradition in a state without a 'historical basis'. Despite his Romantic effusions, Frederick William knew his Prussian history well, and he was entirely capable of looking at it with some clarity and dispassion. In contrast to his father's ageing advisers, he and several of his friends recognized that the maintenance of the post-1815 *status quo* was no longer possible. In the first years of his reign, Frederick William IV was aware that powerful forces of change were transforming Prussian society, and in a rather vague sort of way he understood that a new kind of public (*Öffentlichkeit*) was emerging within that society, that the quiescence of the 1820s and 1830s was gone, and that the nostrums of bureaucratic absolutism no longer sufficed to hold in check the forces of change.

After mounting the throne he devoted most of his career to one central project: to create and then sustain the monarchical principle of effective, sovereign royal authority in an increasingly secular, public mass age. He was never able, however, to differentiate clearly between the private and public aspects of his role, nor did he ever

    [2] Alfred Stern, 'König Friedrich Wilhelm IV. von Preußen und Fürst Metternich im Jahre 1842', *Mitteilungen des Instituts für österreichische Geschichtsforschung*, 30 (1909), 127–8, 134.
    [3] Franz Schnabel, *Deutsche Geschichte im neunzehnten Jahrhundert*, iv: *Die religiösen Kräfte*, 3rd edn. (Freiburg, 1955), 156–7.
    [4] Thomas Nipperdey, 'Der Kölner Dom als Nationaldenkmal', *HZ* 233 (1981), 611.

manage to understand the difference between old-fashioned paternalism and more modern forms of public authority. Still, he sensed that it would be necessary to provide some sort of public basis for monarchical authority in Prussia, and in the years after 1840 he tried to lay the foundations of a monarchy that would be at once popular and genuinely sovereign, without concessions to 'French' forms of parliamentarism or constitutionalism.[5] For all his Romantic, allegedly backward-looking qualities, Frederick William IV was both a child of his times and Prussia's first *modern* king, a man who tried to recast and modernize monarchical institutions by, among other things, creating or 'inventing' a monarchical tradition in Prussia.

There can be little doubt that Frederick William's monarchical project—his *Gesamtkunstwerk*, as we called it in the last chapter—was immensely complex and that it was fraught, as Metternich warned, with endless paradoxes and contradictions. Frederick William was an ideologue, and could not, he thought, avail himself of the techniques or indeed make concessions to the twin devils of 'bureaucratic despotism' and 'revolutionary' constitutionalism. Accordingly, he tried to modernize the Prussian monarchy and create an anti-revolutionary monarchical tradition by appealing to the antique, semi-mythical values and institutions of a pre-absolutist Germany. That Germany was, to his mind, a medieval world of corporative or *ständisch* freedom, based on a hierarchical and paternalistic social order, infused with Christian humility, and sustained by the harmonious union of prince and people. In that world, he believed, the prince was a sacral being, endowed by God with certain unique gifts and insights. As many critics argued, and as Frederick William himself seemed to admit in his 1842 conversation with Metternich, there was little basis in Prussia's *real* historical experience for such an exalted, almost mystical view of monarchical authority. Indeed, in contrast to many Western European states, there were relatively few elements of a sacral tradition in the Prussian monarchy. By appealing to what he believed were older German practices to legitimize his monarchical project, Frederick William was breaking with the actual traditions of his own state. But it was a project that was deeply rooted in his own personality, and it seemed to be the only route open to him if he were to resist the revolutionary challenge and renew both the monarchy and Prussian society at large.

To evaluate Frederick William's monarchical project and its outcome, it will be necessary to consider, first, the public image of kingship that he tried to project and, second, his actual conduct during his first years in office. The former can be illustrated by examining his behaviour on the occasion of the first great public acts of his reign, the ceremonies of fealty in Königsberg and Berlin. The latter can be illuminated by examining the formal and informal structures of power at the top of the Prussian state and the reciprocal interaction between those structures and the King. Above all, the relationship between the King and his advisers will shed a great deal of

[5] Stern, 'Friedrich Wilhelm IV.', 134; Carl von Voß-Buch to Leopold von Gerlach, 10 June 1843, GStA Merseburg, Rep. 92 Graf Karl von Voß-Buch Nr. 16 Bd. III, Bl. 94; Leopold von Gerlach to Ernst Ludwig von Gerlach, June 1841, in Hans-Joachim Schoeps, 'Unbekanntes aus dem Gerlachschen Familienarchiv', in id., *Ein weites Feld: Gesammelte Aufsätze* (Berlin, 1980), 274.

light on Frederick William's notions of how a king should rule. Then we shall briefly consider some of his earliest attempts to create an institutional basis for his monarchical project: his efforts to transform the court, renew the nobility, and reaffirm the medieval concept of 'service'.

The Rituals of Homage: Königsberg and Berlin, 1840

Frederick William IV succeeded to the throne on 7 June 1840 under peaceful and undramatic circumstances. The old King had been sinking for several months, and his entire family, including the Tsar and Empress of Russia, were gathered at his bedside in Berlin's royal palace when he died—'like a patriarch', as the new Queen put it.[6] During the spring of 1840 the Crown Prince found it difficult to face his impending succession, and his father's death filled him with genuine grief and an overwhelming sense of the task that confronted him; he did not enter upon his office with a sense of destiny or of hubris.[7]

Despite the King's private grief and political concerns, the first weeks and months of his reign represented a public honeymoon of almost ecstatic proportions.[8] Those groups that had long been pressing for fundamental change in Prussia's social, cultural, and political circumstances now believed that their time had come, and many of Frederick William's first measures seemed to sustain that supposition: the naming of Alexander von Humboldt and the veteran reformer Hermann von Boyen to the Council of State; signs of favour for German nationalists like Ernst Moritz Arndt, 'Turnvater' Jahn, or Ferdinand Freiligrath; the designation as Minister of Religious and Educational Affairs (*Kultusminister*) of Karl Friedrich Eichhorn, a driving force behind the economically progressive Prussian customs union (*Zollverein*) and described as *la bête noire de Metternich*; the summoning of Ludwig Tieck and the Brothers Grimm, lately persecuted for their political beliefs, to Berlin. According to Peter von Meyendorff, the Russian minister to Berlin, all these changes 'give a certain liberal colouration to the new reign'.[9] But the high point of those first months, a point that established Frederick William as a modern monarch determined to turn public celebrations to political advantage, came with the official ceremonies of homage (*Huldigungen*) in Königsberg and Berlin in the autumn of 1840.

As a relatively new kingdom, Prussia lacked a tradition of sacral coronation-ceremonies. Indeed, Frederick I, the first 'King in Prussia', had been the only

---

[6] Leopold von Gerlach, diary (24 June 1840; 10 May 1842), GA, 'Abschriften', iv. 2.

[7] FW IV to Friedrich Adolf von Willisen, 9 June 1840, GStA Merseburg, HA Rep. 50 J Nr. 1580, Bl. 59; FW IV to Ludwig I, 18 June 1840, GHA, Nachlaß König Ludwig I., 85/3/2; FW IV to Prince John of Saxony, 20 June 1840, in Johann Georg, Herzog zu Sachsen, and Hubert Ermisch (eds.), *Briefwechsel zwischen König Johann von Sachsen und den Königen Friedrich Wilhelm IV. und Wilhelm I. von Preußen* (Leipzig, 1911), 166.

[8] Heinrich von Treitschke, *Deutsche Geschichte im neunzehnten Jahrhundert*, 2nd edn., v: *Bis zur März-Revolution* (Leipzig, 1894), 3–60, on 'Die frohen Tage der Erwartung'.

[9] Herman von Petersdorff, *König Friedrich Wilhelm der Vierte* (Stuttgart, 1900), 33–4; Meyendorff to Nesselrode, 21 July 1840, in Peter von Meyendorff, *Ein russischer Diplomat an den Höfen von Berlin und Wien: Politischer und privater Briefwechsel 1826–1863*, ed. Otto Hoetzsch (3 vols.; Berlin, 1923), i. 123.

Prussian monarch to stage an official coronation. Other rituals had, however, been retained by subsequent monarchs, most notably the homage in Königsberg of the estates of East and West Prussia (which lay outside the boundaries of the old Empire and of the newer German Confederation), and in Berlin of the other estates of the realm. Accordingly, in late August 1840 Frederick William set out for the eastern parts of his kingdom, accompanied by a vast retinue of adjutants, court officials, and members of the royal family.[10]

The events in Königsberg consisted of two separate functions. First, from 5 to 9 September the provincial diet of the province of Prussia gathered together as a special 'diet of homage' (*Huldigungslandtag*), presented a memorial to the King, and then was confirmed in certain antique privileges.[11] In most respects, the whole affair seemed to go well. There were glittering public dinners, concerts, and regattas, culminating with a public festival on the evening of the ninth which included elaborate *tableaux vivants* depicting scenes from East Prussian history. The actual oath of homage took place the following day in the courtyard of the royal palace. Gathered around the throne were some 30,000 spectators, as well as the representatives of the estates of East Prussia, West Prussia, and Posen. After their solemn oath, the King for his part swore to be 'a righteous judge; a loyal, careful, and merciful Prince; a Christian King'.[12]

Ordinarily, these sorts of events, with their 'historic' and 'medieval' emphasis on the mutual loyalty of crown and subjects, would have inspired Frederick William to effusive and enthusiastic outbursts. But the whole affair had been complicated by the Prussian diet's memorial to the King, which had reminded the new ruler of his father's unfulfilled constitutional pledges of 1815. As one recent historian has noted, the diet received Frederick William with unfeigned enthusiasm and support. But that enthusiasm was based on the expectation that, in his role as *Landesvater* and 'first citizen of the state', the new King would be morally obliged to fulfill Frederick William III's constitutional promises.[13] Frederick William had in fact been inclined to announce in Königsberg the convocation of 'estates of the realm' (*Reichsstände*) along lines that his father had once envisaged, but his conservative advisers had dissuaded him from that course. After his arrival in Königsberg the matter had been raised in difficult meetings involving Theodor von Schön, the distinguished governor of the Prussian province, a veteran reformer and long-time confidant of the

[10] GStA Merseburg, Geheimes Zivilkabinett 2.2.1. Nr. 32564, Bl. 31ᵛ–32ᵛ, 107–10, 198ᵛ–199ᵛ.

[11] Herbert Obenaus, *Anfänge des Parlamentarismus in Preußen bis 1848* (Düsseldorf, 1984), 528; Wolfgang Neugebauer, 'Die Protokolle des ost- und westpreußischen Huldigungslandtages von 1840', *JGMOD* 41 (1993), 235–62.

[12] See the detailed, if fulsome, account in Karl Streckfuß, *Der Preußen Huldigungsfest, nach amtlichen und andern sichern Nachrichten und eigener Anschauung zusammengestellt* (Berlin, 1840), 29–58, and suppls. A–D; also the documents in GStA Berlin, BPH Rep. 50 Nr. 205, and GStA Merseburg, Geheimes Zivilkabinett 2.2.1. Nr. 32564, Bl. 237–40, 243.

[13] Monika Wienfort, *Monarchie in der bürgerlichen Gesellschaft: Deutschland und England von 1640 bis 1848* (Göttingen, 1993), 186–9.

erstwhile Crown Prince, and enemy of Frederick William's conservative friends.[14] The King's own response to the diet seemed benign and accommodating. While praising his father's accomplishments, most notably the 1823 legislation on provincial diets, he also indicated that he was open to the prospect of change in the future; in the concerns of the diet, he said, he had 'recognized with a warm heart and joyful pride your expression of the most noble and unalloyed sentiments of deeply rooted loyalty'.[15] The King's remarks were vague if positive-sounding; as Treitschke put it in a well-known passage, the ground had been laid 'for a fateful, mutual misunderstanding' over questions of constitutional reform.[16]

Frederick William himself seems not to have been overly concerned at that point about the possibilities or the dangers of such misunderstandings. And in any case, the King's reception in Königsberg was exceeded in enthusiasm by the second ceremony in Berlin itself. Indeed, the *Huldigung* in Berlin was one of the great popular triumphs of Frederick William's entire reign. On 21 September the King entered his capital through a special triumphal arch to scenes of tumultuous popular acclaim and excitement.[17] The actual ceremony of homage, however, took place on 15 October, the King's birthday. Despite pouring rain, about 60,000 spectators, the *Bürgerschaft* of Berlin, and representatives of the six western provinces of the kingdom, had gathered in the Lustgarten in front of the royal palace. The ritual began inside the palace with a ceremony of homage from the clergy and from those 'mediatized nobles'— that is to say, aristocrats who had enjoyed special privileges under the Holy Roman Empire and its replacement, the German Confederation—who lived within what was now Prussian territory. Then came the turn of the squires (*Ritterschaft*) of the six provinces, who had gathered in the palace's White Hall, and to whom he presented an extemporaneous speech promising a 'simple, paternal, genuinely German and Christian government'.[18] Finally, the King moved to the special throne that had been erected in front of the palace. About 20,000 of the spectators were there to deliver their oaths of fealty. Once again, before the oath was taken, the King addressed the multitude, calling upon them to help him with his efforts 'to develop ever more gloriously those abilities which have gained Prussia, with its population of only fourteen million, a place among the Great Powers of the earth . . . namely, honour, loyalty, the desire to attain light, justice, and truth, and the ability to stride forward with both the wisdom of age and the heroic strength of youth'.[19]

In an age which loved public declamation, virtually everyone who heard this speech was overwhelmed by it, and through it Frederick William had orchestrated

---

[14] See below, Ch. 5; and above all Hans Rothfels, *Theodor v. Schön, Friedrich Wilhelm IV. und die Revolution von 1848* (Halle, 1937), 107–11.

[15] Friedrich Wilhelm IV., *Reden und Trinksprüche*, 23–4.   [16] *Treitschke, Deutsche Geschichte*, v. 46.

[17] Maximilian Graf von und zu Lerchenfeld to Ludwig I, 22 Sept. 1840, BayHStA, MA III 2618; Lord William Russell to Lord Palmerston, 28 Sept. 1840, PRO, FO 64/229; K. Streckfuß, *Huldigungsfest*, 58–76.

[18] K. Streckfuß, *Huldigungsfest*, 91; cf. Walter Bußmann, 'Eine historische Würdigung Friedrich Wilhelms IV.', in id., *Wandel und Kontinuität in Politik und Geschichte: Ausgewählte Aufsätze zum 60. Geburtstag*, ed. Werner Pöls (Boppard am Rhein, 1973), 294–9.

[19] K. Streckfuß, *Huldigungsfest*, 97.

his reign's greatest public-relations success.[20] Always the artist, he had painted his own '*Historienbild*' of a Christian-German monarchy in harmony with God, in a sacral union with its people, and devoted to the preservation of peace and Christian order.[21] What Satanic revolution, what contemptible constitution, what diabolical parliament could prevail against him?

Through his speeches in Königsberg and Berlin Frederick William was doing something quite unprecedented in Prussian history: applying his formidable rhetorical skills in a public forum to explain and justify his views. Previous Prussian rulers felt neither the necessity nor the inclination to make public appeals to sustain their authority, which had required no justification and in any case had manifested itself in terms of effective service to the state. For Frederick William IV, though, times had changed. In a revolutionary age effective monarchical authority required both ideological programmes and propaganda offensives. The Königsberg and Berlin ceremonies were both of these. Frederick William IV was trying to create a sacral tradition of kingship in a state which, as he knew perfectly well, did not really have one.[22] And therein lay his very modernity; as a child of his age, he felt obliged to use appeals both to ideology and to emotion in order to sustain monarchical sentiment. If monarchy was to have a future, he believed, it would have to move beyond the repressive *status quo* embodied by Metternich and Wittgenstein.

Managing Monarchy: Friends, Advisers, and Relatives

Given his exalted, even mystic views of his office, how did Frederick William IV propose to rule? How, in other words, would monarchical power manifest itself in a state in which that power had always been very real and very substantial, despite the comparative absence of pompous monarchical ritual? In his declining years, Frederick William III had relied heavily on the advice of a small number of intimates, most notably Wittgenstein and Cabinet Minister Count Lottum, who themselves were closely attuned to the old King's own wishes. So was the powerful Interior Minister, Gustav Adolf von Rochow; though an old friend of the Crown Prince and at one time a fervent apostle of '*ständisch* freedom', he had become the very incarnation of the bureaucratic despotism which the new monarch despised.

Yet Wittgenstein and Rochow retained their offices after June 1840. Frederick William IV begged Wittgenstein to stay, despite that old intriguer's dislike of his policies, while Rochow's power and influence were probably never greater than in the first weeks and months of the new reign. Still, everyone knew that the management of royal affairs would change soon enough, if only because the new King was so voluble and so enamoured of diverse company. To many observers it seemed that he was frightfully inefficient and too easily distracted, which in turn undermined his

[20] Leopold von Gerlach, diary (3 June 1842), GA, 'Abschriften', iv. 8; Otto Graf zu Stolberg-Wernigerode, *Anton Graf zu Stolberg-Wernigerode: Ein Freund und Ratgeber König Friedrich Wilhelms IV.* (Munich, 1926), 34.

[21] Bußmann, 'Würdigung', 297.

[22] Ernst Lewalter, *Friedrich Wilhelm IV.: Das Schicksal eines Geistes* (Berlin, 1938), 359.

attempt to develop an effective system of personal rule. During the summer of 1840 he spent most of his time away from Berlin, at Sanssouci, his regular abode at that time of the year. There he tried to manage state affairs while maintaining that atmosphere of intellectual openness and conviviality which had sustained him as Crown Prince. Carl von Voß–Buch, who served as a kind of informal civil adjutant to the monarch, complained in October 'that the King is really very preoccupied with trifling matters. . . . Right now he is improvising his decisions. Things can't go on that way.'[23] Voß argued that the real problem lay with the system of 'cabinet government' as it had developed by 1840, though surely the situation was complicated by Frederick William's quirky work-habits and the perception that he was open to a wide and often contradictory range of influences.[24]

During the first six years of his monarchy the countervailing influences that streamed in upon Frederick William IV came from essentially six groups, and it was from among them that individuals and factions competed for the King's favour and support. Five of these groups were official, while one was unofficial. They included the cabinet; the ministry; court officials; the King's military entourage; the royal family; and the King's personal friends and confidants, mostly from his days as Crown Prince. None of these groups effectively dominated the others or monopolized the monarch's attention in the first years of his reign. Thus the distribution of power at the top of the Prussian state, as well as the emergence of political factions (which tended to cut across these groups), was an enormously complicated affair.

As we saw in the first chapter, after Hardenberg's death in 1822 the Civil Cabinet and the State Ministry had become overlapping but distinct entities, with the power of the former increasing at the expense of the latter. The Treasury Minister, Count Lottum, had accumulated considerable influence thanks to his position as 'Cabinet Minister' and head of the Civil Cabinet's First Department. Lottum died shortly after Frederick William IV's accession to the throne, and was promptly replaced by the new King's old friend, General Ludwig Gustav von Thile.[25]

Thile (1781–1852) was the first 'Cabinet Minister' officially to bear that title, apart from the Foreign Minister, who had always been so designated. The scion of a military family, he was himself a soldier who had achieved distinction during the liberation war both for his organizational skills and his personal bravery.[26] After the war he was so affected by the Awakening that he became a fervent religious zealot; in the Berlin of the 1840s he was popularly called 'Bible Thile'.[27] He had never made any secret of his antipathy to politics and the life of the court, and at one point had even

---

[23] Voß to Leopold von Gerlach, 3 Oct. 1840, GStA Merseburg, Rep. 92 Graf Karl von Voß–Buch Nr. 16 Vol. II, Bl. 80ᵛ.

[24] Treitschke, *Deutsche Geschichte*, v. 13–14.

[25] AKO, FW IV to Thile, 26 Oct. 1840, GStA Merseburg, Geheimes Zivilkabinett 2.2.1. Nr. 3692, Bl. 11g.

[26] *ADB*, xxxviii. 28–32 (Friedrich Meinecke).

[27] Eduard Vehse and 'Vehse redivivus', *Illustrierte Geschichte des preußischen Hofes, des Adels und der Diplomatie vom Großen Kurfürsten bis zum Tode des Kaisers Wilhelm I.* (2 vols.; Stuttgart [n.d.]-[1901]), ii. 277; Treitschke, *Deutsche Geschichte*, v. 19.

considered becoming a missionary in North America.[28] Although he was utterly devoid of personal ambition and was generally regarded as an 'upright and capable man', Thile was also utterly unprepared for the position to which Frederick William called him.[29] Curiously, he managed to arouse more hostility among some conservative observers than among liberals. The acerbic liberal diarist Varnhagen, the Pepys of Prussia, once described Thile as 'the most effective of the ministers, because he has beliefs and convictions', while the influential Russian emissary Meyendorff detested him as an *enragé piétiste*.[30]

His position was made even more difficult by the King himself. Not only did Thile have to familiarize himself with a vast body of information about which he had no knowledge or experience, he also had to serve as the bridge between King and Cabinet on the one hand and the Ministry on the other. In addition, Frederick William's working methods were bound to create difficulties. For all his charm and kindliness, the King had a tendency to regard his advisers as 'instruments' (*Werkzeuge*) of his own will. Leopold von Gerlach often complained that Frederick William acted 'as though royalty were descended from a different Adam', and that as a result he was 'utterly indifferent to the people who work with him'.[31] Although Thile had always got on well with his sovereign, as early as December 1840—even before assuming all of Lottum's functions—he was finding it difficult to get the information he needed for his daily reports to the King.[32] As we have already seen, the monarch was also easily diverted by time-consuming trivialities which irked a conscientious man like Thile. After a year in office he had become 'the very image of overwork and exhaustion', sighing to Ludwig von Gerlach that the King 'really does make things very difficult when he quarrels with his ministers about whether a village is called Grieb*au* or Grieb*ow*'.[33]

Thile strove to make the best of his situation, trying on various occasions to get the King to organize his work more efficiently. In 1842 he proposed in a long memorandum that the report on the Civil Cabinet's activities be divided among several regular members of the State Ministry, all of whom would now have direct access to the King, who in turn would enjoy 'the invaluable advantage of being able to draw upon their multifaceted, practical experience'. Had this arrangement been institutionalized, Frederick William would have in effect become his own Prime Minister, but

[28] Voß to Leopold von Gerlach, 18 May 1841, GStA Merseburg, Rep. 92 Graf Karl von Voß-Buch Nr. 16 Vol. III, Bl. 12.

[29] Trauttmansdorff to Metternich, 28 Jan. 1841, HHStA, St.K. Preußen, Karton 177, Politische Berichte 1841, fol. 25ᵛ.

[30] K. A. Varnhagen von Ense, *Tagebücher*, ed. Ludmilla Assing, 2nd edn. ii. 241 (23 Dec. 1843); Meyendorff to Nesselrode, 10 Sept. 1841, *Briefwechsel*, i. 187.

[31] Leopold von Gerlach to Theodor Heinrich Rochus von Rochow, 25 July 1850 (draft), GStA Merseburg, Rep. 92 Leopold von Gerlach Nr. 10, Bl. 139–139ᵛ; Leopold von Gerlach, diary (2 Nov. 1847), GA, 'Abschriften', v. 28; cf. Varnhagen von Ense, *Tagebücher*, iii. 446 (30 Sept. 1846).

[32] Voß to Leopold von Gerlach, 8 Dec. 1840, GStA Merseburg, Rep. 92 Graf Karl von Voß-Buch, Nr. 16 Vol. II, Bl. 90.

[33] Ernst Ludwig von Gerlach, diary (10 Dec. 1841), GA, Tagebücher Ernst Ludwig von Gerlachs, vol. ii/b.

within six weeks he had grown tired of it.[34] Thereafter Thile arranged for Albrecht von Alvensleben-Erxleben, who had recently resigned as Finance Minister, to serve as a second Cabinet Minister and share his reporting responsibilities. In 1844 Alvensleben left for good, and was replaced by the Westphalian aristocrat Ernst von Bodelschwingh, whose political instincts and inclinations were much more highly developed than Thile's. As we shall see, Bodelschwingh was able to use his access to the King to become one of the most powerful men in Prussia between 1845 and 1848.[35]

The State Ministry itself—that is, the 'cabinet' in the modern sense of that word—was remarkable for its instability and factionalism during the *Vormärz* years: that is, the years just before the outbreak of the revolution of March 1848. At the beginning of Frederick William's reign its dominant personalities were Interior Minister Gustav Adolf von Rochow (1792–1847) and Finance Minister Albrecht von Alvensleben-Erxleben (1794–1858). Both men had held their offices since the mid-1830s. They were proud, prickly individuals, and they fell out quickly with the new monarch. Rochow became involved in a series of disputes with Frederick William over the latter's notions regarding the *ständisch*-corporative representation of group interests, which he regarded as dangerous and impractical.[36] Moreover, as a result of the Königsberg events of September 1840, Rochow also became involved in a bitter personal feud with the East Prussian statesman Theodor von Schön, who, for all his reform-minded, liberal views, was one of the King's favourites. Rochow deeply resented what he regarded as Frederick William's preference for Schön, and he also had become disgruntled with the King's scattershot, disjointed style of working.[37] Finally, in the middle of 1842 both Schön and Rochow resigned from their respective positions, though Rochow stayed on as Deputy President of the Council of State until his early death in 1847.[38]

Where Rochow had once been the King's close friend, Finance Minister Alvensleben had always regarded Frederick William as an 'impractical ideologue' and an 'arrogant fantast'.[39] Immensely wealthy and well-known both for his manage-

---

[34] Voß to Leopold von Gerlach, 23 Mar. 1841, GStA Merseburg, Rep. 92 Graf Karl von Voß-Buch Nr. 16 Vol. III, Bl. 14ᵛ.

[35] FW IV to Alvensleben, 18 Feb. 1842, GStA Merseburg, HA Rep. 50 J Nr. 26, Bl. 22–22ᵛ; Trauttmansdorff to Metternich, 24 Feb. 1842, HHStA, St.K. Preußen, Karton 180, Politische Berichte 1842, fol. 154ʳ. See also Otto Hintze, 'Das preußische Staatsministerium im 19. Jahrhundert', in id., *Gesammelte Abhandlungen*, iii: *Regierung und Verwaltung: Gesammelte Abhandlungen zur Staats-, Rechts- und Sozialgeschichte Preußens*, ed. Gerhard Oestreich, 2nd edn. (Göttingen, 1967; art. orig. pub. 1908), 569–70, and Heinrich Otto Meisner, 'Zur neueren Geschichte des preußischen Kabinetts', *FBPG* 36 (1924), 55–6.

[36] Voß to Leopold von Gerlach, 2 Apr. 1841, GStA Merseburg, Rep. 92 Graf Karl von Voß-Buch Nr. 16 Vol. III, Bl. 16ᵛ.

[37] Ernst Ludwig von Gerlach, 7 Apr. 1842, GA, Tagebücher Ernst Ludwig von Gerlachs, vol. ii/b.

[38] See the correspondence in GStA Merseburg, Rep. 92 Gustav Adolf von Rochow A I Nr. 5, esp. FW IV's letter of 9 Apr. 1842 and his AKO to Rochow of 1 May 1842, Bl. 1-3 and 32-32ᵛ; Caroline von Rochow and Marie de la Motte-Fouqué, *Vom Leben am preußischen Hofe 1815–1852*, ed. Luise von der Marwitz (Berlin, 1908), 411–59.

[39] Ludwig von Gerlach, 17 Oct. 1842 and 10 Apr. 1843, GA, Tagebuch Ernst Ludwig von Gerlachs, vol. ii/b; id., 'Warnung vor Abwegen. Also: Recht aus Gott', Easter Sunday 1842, GA, 'Abschriften', xvii. 40.

rial efficiency and his rude manners, Alvensleben was an aristocrat of the old school who 'never goes to church but instead shows up with great regularity at Prince Wittgenstein's card table'.[40] Such a throw-back to the eighteenth century was pre-destined for conflict with the new King, and, like Rochow, he left the State Ministry in the spring of 1842. As we have already seen, Frederick William at first prevailed upon Alvensleben to stay on as Deputy Cabinet Minister to help Thile with his reports; but he resigned from that post in 1844 and thereafter steadfastly refused to work again on the King's behalf.[41]

Although the resignations of Rochow and Alvensleben were particularly signifi-cant, the entire Ministry remained remarkably unstable before 1848. There were, for example, four foreign ministers during those years, four finance ministers, and three interior ministers, which made it very difficult to sustain any kind of coherent pol-icy. So confused was the situation that in March 1842 Thile reported that 'only now is he [the King] beginning to organize his government'.[42] The most stable ministries were the Ministry for Legal Revision, administered from 1842 to 1848 by the great legal scholar Friedrich Karl von Savigny; the *Kultusministerium*, where Friedrich Eichhorn held sway uninterruptedly from 1840 to 1848; and the War Ministry, presided over from 1841 to 1847 by the veteran reformer Hermann von Boyen.[43] The situation only began to stabilize after 1845, with the emergence of Foreign Minister Baron Karl von Canitz and Interior Minister Ernst von Bodelschwingh as the King's principal ministerial confidants.

Where the Ministry was remarkable for its high turnover-rate, the official struc-tures of the court and the royal entourage were a different matter, particularly at their highest levels. Although he sometimes winked at the trivialities of court etiquette, Frederick William was none the less determined to demonstrate the splendour and raise the visibility of his court. Accordingly, he was greatly interested in such things as the details of court liveries or the organization of his official retinue (*Hofstaat*); and it was not surprising that court officials played an exceedingly important role in his reign.[44]

The King was frequently in contact with high-ranking officials in the Ministry of the Royal House and with members of his retinue. As we noted in Chapter 1, the

[40] *ADB*, i. 376; Herman von Petersdorff, 'Graf Albrecht von Alvensleben-Erxleben', *HZ* 100 (1908), 272–7; Trauttmansdorff to Metternich, 3 Nov. 1841, HHStA, St.K. Preußen, Karton 177, Politische Berichte 1841, fol. 184ʳ; Ludwig von Gerlach, 'Warnung vor Abwegen. Also: Recht aus Gott', Easter Sunday 1842, GA, 'Abschriften', xvii. 40.

[41] FW IV to Alvensleben, 26 August 1841, GStA Merseburg, HA Rep. 50 J Nr. 26 Bl. 3–4; Petersdorff, 'Alvensleben', 280–4.

[42] Ernst Ludwig von Gerlach, diary (16 Mar. 1842), GA, Tagebücher Ernst Ludwig von Gerlachs, vol. ii/b; cf. Reinhart Koselleck, *Preußen zwischen Reform und Revolution: Allgemeines Landrecht, Verwaltung und soziale Bewegung von 1791 bis 1848*, 3rd edn. (Stuttgart, 1981), 637.

[43] Walther Hubatsch (ed.), *Grundriß zur deutschen Verwaltungs geschichte 1815–1945*, ser. A: *Preußen*, xii, pt. a: *Preußische Zentralbehörden*, ed. Friedrich Wilhelm Wehrstedt (Marburg, 1978), 102, 115, 135, 140.

[44] Prinz Kraft zu Hohenlohe-Ingelfingen, *Aus meinem Leben: Aufzeichnungen*, ii: *Flügeladjutant unter Friedrich Wilhelm IV. und König Wilhelm I. 1856–1863*, 8th edn. (Berlin, 1909), 16; Franckenberg to Grand Duke Leopold, 15 Feb. 1841, GLA, 48/2595.

House Ministry especially reflected the semi-public, semi-private nature of the Prussian monarchy. Wittgenstein, House Minister since 1819, had always been notorious for his exceptionally stringent financial management. As a result, the Prussian court was a rather lean operation by the standards of other European monarchies.[45] This was a consequence not only of Wittgenstein's tightfistedness but also, as the reader will recall, of the real spending-limits imposed by Frederick William III and transmitted to his heirs. Chief among these was the royal feoffment in trust, an entailed fund which, as noted earlier, was set at 2.5 million Taler annually.

The court's very complex finances were largely the responsibility of Ludwig von Massow (1794–1859), scion of an old Mark Brandenburg family and an acquaintance of Frederick William for decades. Although regarded in Berlin society as rather stolid and boring, he was a singularly effective financial manager who had first served as Marshal (*Hofmarschall*) to the Crown Prince, and after 1835 to the King himself.[46] After 1840 he became Intendant of the Royal Gardens, and in 1844 was assigned to the House Ministry. He was also responsible for overseeing the King's privy purse, which derived substantial annual revenues from several sources, including the King's private estates near Potsdam and at Erdmannsdorf in Silesia. Although Frederick William spent lavishly from these funds, they were efficiently administered by the King's Privy Chamberlain (*Geheimer Kämmerier*), Eduard Schöning, who was also his private secretary.[47] By the nature of their positions, both Massow and Schöning enjoyed regular access to the King; Massow later became an influential member of the court 'Camarilla', while the King often used Schöning as a go-between in delicate political matters.

As House Minister and Lord Chamberlain (*Oberkammerherr*), Wittgenstein was the highest-ranking member of the court; and, despite the gap in age and sentiments that separated him from Frederick William IV, he remained in his twin posts until his death in 1851.[48] Day-to-day court administration, however, was in the hands of the Marshal of the Court. During his entire reign Frederick William had only two marshals. The first, Ludwig von Meyerinck, served in that capacity until 1845, when he became ill and was replaced by Count Alexander von Keller (1801–79), Stolberg's son-in-law. Like Massow, Keller enjoyed a reputation for unflappability and sound financial management; and, also like Massow, he became an active member of the Camarilla in 1848.[49]

---

[45] Hans Branig, *Fürst Wittgenstein: Ein preußischer Staatsmann der Restaurationszeit* (Cologne, 1981), 205, 207–14.

[46] David E. Barclay, 'Gartenintendant und konservativer Hofpolitiker: Ludwig von Massow (1794–1859)', *Mitteilungen der Pückler Gesellschaft*, NS 9 (1993), 6–30.

[47] See Schöning's memoirs in GStA Merseburg, HA Rep. 50 G 3 Nr. 5.

[48] Branig, *Wittgenstein*, 192–6, 200–3; FW IV to Wittgenstein, 22 July 1840, GStA Berlin, BPH Rep. 192 Wittgenstein III, 14, 1a, Bl. 19.

[49] 'Kurz gefaßte Charakteristik der in Berlin gegenwärtigen, Ihre Königliche Majestät von Preußen umgebenden Personen vom Hof-Staat, von der Verwaltung u. von der Armee', n.d., BayHStA, Bayer. Gesandtschaft Berlin 641 (Politische Korrespondenz 1850).

Another court official who played a prominent role in the royal entourage was Baron Rudolph von Stillfried-Rattonitz (later Count Stillfried-Alcantara, 1804–82), Vice-Master of Ceremonies after 1843 and Supreme Master of Ceremonies after 1853. Frederick William and Stillfried were cut from the same cloth. They had met in Silesia in 1830, and had quickly discovered shared interests in medieval history and genealogy. Thereafter Stillfried undertook a series of studies of the Hohenzollern family which led to the discovery of important caches of medieval documents in southern Germany. Those discoveries in turn formed the basis for the publication, after 1840, of the highly regarded *Monumenta Zollerana* volumes on Hohenzollern history.[50] A vain and pompous social climber, Stillfried was not a popular figure at the Prussian court; he was thus a particularly good example of Frederick William's willingness to advance the careers of certain personal favourites who were otherwise politically 'unconnected'.

The King always liked to be surrounded by old friends and familiar faces. Count Anton zu Stolberg-Wernigerode, in 1840 Governor of the province of Saxony, had been one of his intimates for years, and shortly after his accession to the throne the new monarch summoned Stolberg to Berlin. In December 1840, at Wittgenstein's urging, Stolberg joined the State Ministry and was seconded to the House Ministry. Inevitably, like everyone else in the entourage Stolberg complained about the negative effect on his own work of the King's volatile, unsteady, disorganized work-habits.[51] A conscientious but not especially efficient administrator, Stolberg was constantly overburdened by his work and his master's numerous distractions. Moreover, his relationship with Wittgenstein quickly became strained, and in 1846 he severed his official connection to the House Ministry, though he continued to occupy a seat in the *Staatsministerium*.[52] Far more important than Stolberg's official position, however, was his unofficial function as indispensable friend, go-between, and adviser to the King. Few other individuals enjoyed such ready access to the monarch; and many observers noted during the first years after 1840 that Stolberg was Frederick William's special '*homme de confiance*', 'the confidant of the ruler and the *dépositaire* of his views'.[53] To the extent that the King listened to anyone, he listened to him. But Stolberg's views on concrete issues were often vague, and intellectually he was no match for people like Bunsen, Radowitz, the Gerlachs, or Voß-Buch. Rather, he was one of those high-born aristocrats like Carl von der

[50] *ADB* xxxvi. 246–7; Alfred von Reumont, *Aus König Friedrich Wilhelms IV. gesunden und kranken Tagen*, 2nd edn. (Leipzig, 1885), 203–5; FW (IV) to Ludwig I, 10 April 1837, GHA, Nachlaß König Ludwig I., 85/3/2; Rolf Bothe, *Burg Hohenzollern: Von der mittelalterlichen Burg zum national-dynastischen Denkmal im 19. Jahrhundert* (Berlin, 1979), 68–71.

[51] AKO, FW IV to *Staatsministerium*, 30 Dec. 1840, GStA Berlin, I. Hauptabteilung Rep. 90 Nr. 1935; Stolberg-Wernigerode, *Stolberg-Wernigerode*, 31–2, 34, 36.

[52] AKO, FW IV to *Staatsministerium*, 14 Nov. 1842, GStA Berlin, I. Hauptabteilung Rep. 90 Nr. 1935; FW IV to Stolberg, 17 Aug. 1843, ibid., BPH Rep. 192 Wittgenstein II, 1, 12, Bl. 36–7; AKO, FW IV to *Staatsministerium*, 7 Apr. 1846, ibid., I. Hauptabteilung Rep. 90 Nr. 1935; Stolberg-Wernigerode, *Stolberg-Wernigerode*, 35–6; Branig, *Wittgenstein*, 205–6.

[53] Stolberg-Wernigerode, *Stolberg-Wernigerode*, 34; Trauttmansdorff to Metternich, 3 Nov. 1841, HHStA, St. K. Preußen, Karton 177, Politische Berichte 1841 I–XII, fol. 183ᵛ.

Groeben who impressed the King mightily with the simple intensity of his religious faith, his ethical values, and his monarchical loyalties. Frederick William was himself often moved by feeling, emotion, and intuition; and people like Groeben and Stolberg, though far less complex in their own psychological make-ups, always appealed to that side of his personality. Stolberg was thus perceived as a man who shielded the King from unpleasant realities, and for that reason he aroused the antipathy of conservative circles around Rochow.[54]

A King of Prussia was, of course, expected to maintain a substantial military entourage, and Frederick William IV was no exception. Although he was probably the least martial monarch in Prussian history, there was no way that he could escape, or even conceive of escaping, the embrace of military values, institutions, and advisers; and after 1848 the *maison militaire* acquired a great deal of political significance.[55] Like its civilian counterpart, the military entourage also enjoyed considerable stability in the *Vormärz* years. The King of Prussia was quite literally surrounded by soldiers twenty-four hours a day. These were the aides-de-camp or 'adjutants in service' (*dienstthuende Flügeladjutanten*). At any given time there were four to six of these officers, most of whom were majors or colonels. Each was expected to serve uninterrupted three-day stints as the monarch's 'eyes, pen, and notebook'.[56] The real institutional heart of the military entourage, though, was the *Generaladjutantur*.

There were seven adjutants-general (*Generaladjutanten*) in 1840, and by 1847 their number had grown to ten. As with the *Flügeladjutanten*, there were some differences between those officers who were titular adjutants and those who actually functioned as 'reporting adjutants-general' or 'adjutants-general in service' (*vortragende* or *dienstthuende Generaladjutanten*).[57] Thile, for example, continued to hold the title of adjutant-general after 1840, even though he restricted his activities almost entirely to civilian matters. Like the Cabinet Minister, the 'reporting adjutants-general' enjoyed direct access to the King, which meant that, potentially at least, the power of their office was very great indeed; but they did not use that power very much before 1848. Frederick William had inherited his father's old adjutant, General Lindheim, but Lindheim left in 1841 and was replaced by August Wilhelm von Neumann-Cosel, who served both in that position and as head of the important

---

[54] Voß to Leopold von Gerlach, 18 Mar. and 2 Apr. 1841, 10 June 1843, GStA Merseburg, Rep. 92 Graf Karl von Voß-Buch Nr. 16 Vol. III, Bl. 12–12ᵛ, 16ᵛ, 94–94ᵛ; Leopold von Gerlach to Ludwig von Gerlach, 8 May 1842, GA, Fasz. CS; Treitschke, *Deutsche Geschichte*, v. 18; Rochow and de la Motte-Fouqué, *Leben*, 225.

[55] Gordon A. Craig, *The Politics of the Prussian Army 1640–1945* (New York, 1955), 94; see also Gerhard Ritter, *Staatskunst und Kriegshandwerk: Das Problem des 'Militarismus' in Deutschland*, i: *Die altpreußische Tradition (1740–1890)*, 3rd edn. (Munich, 1965), 230.

[56] Hohenlohe-Ingelfingen, *Aus meinem Leben*, ii. 7. The total number of *Flügeladjutanten* varied between eight and fourteen, but that usually included several individuals who held the title but performed other duties.

[57] Generals *à la suite* were also traditional members of the military entourage, but they declined in significance during the *Vormärz* years. Manfred Kliem, 'Genesis der Führungskräfte der feudal-militaristischen Konterrevolution 1848 in Preußen' (Diss.; Berlin [East], 1966), 109c.

Personnel Division in the War Ministry.[58] Neumann seems to have had virtually no political interests, and little influence upon Frederick William; and so he tended to limit his advice to purely military affairs. Only in 1848 did the real political potential of the *Generaladjutantur* begin to manifest itself.

Finally, two other less officially organized groups which were in a position to influence the King were his own family and his private circle of old friends. Queen Elisabeth's political role was at first rather limited.[59] During the first years of her husband's reign she continued to be plagued by poor health, and only after 1848 did her political activity become significant. The King was devoted to his wife, but his relations with the rest of his family—especially his three younger brothers—were often rather difficult, though that was nothing new among the Hohenzollerns.[60] Shortly after his accession, Frederick William had bestowed the title 'Prince of Prussia' upon his brother William, a designation which the younger brother and heir of the childless Frederick II had also borne.[61] Nevertheless, the two brothers were temperamental opposites, and their relationship was usually strained; accordingly, as we shall see below, the Prince of Prussia constantly schemed to undermine the King's political reform projects in the 1840s and continued to disagree with him vehemently in the 1850s.

Frederick William's second brother, Prince Carl (1801–83), was notorious for his uncompromisingly absolutist views, and like William he regarded the King's various projects with great suspicion. (Frederick William once wrote to his sister that Carl considered him 'a silly instrument in the hands of revolutionaries'!)[62] Carl shared his oldest brother's artistic and aesthetic interests, as well as his love of Italy, where he spent much of his time in the 1840s. Despite significant scholarly attainments as a collector and historian of art, Carl was nevertheless a frequent source of embarrassment to the King. Susceptible to shady confidence-tricksters and speculative intrigues, Carl became embroiled in a series of financial scandals—one of them involving an omnibus company in Berlin, another the logging of mahogany along the Nicaraguan coast—that were covered up only with great difficulty, leaving Carl deeply in debt and without much time for politics. So desperate was Carl's situation, in fact, that the King worried in late 1847 that, were it to become public, it might have the same politically destabilizing effect as the notorious Lola Montez scandal in Bavaria.[63]

[58] Kurt von Priesdorff (ed.), *Soldatisches Führertum* (10 vols.; Hamburg, 1937–42), v. 311–14.

[59] Varnhagen von Ense, *Tagebücher*, iii. 312 (28 Feb. 1846).

[60] Leopold von Gerlach to Ludwig von Gerlach, 12 Jan. 1842, GA, Fasz. CS; Thile to FW IV, 17 Mar. 1845, GStA Merseburg, Rep. 92 Ludwig Gustav von Thile C 7, Bl. 64–64^v.

[61] AKO, FW IV to *Staatsministerium*, 14 June 1840, GStA Berlin, I. Hauptabteilung Rep. 90 Nr. 1889.

[62] FW to Charlotte (Alexandra Feodorovna), 28–9 Dec. 1847, GStA Merseburg, HA Rep. 50 J Nr. 1210 Vol. III, Bl. 60; also Wilhelm Moritz Freiherr von Bissing, 'Sein Ideal war der absolut regierte Staat: Prinz Carl von Preußen und der Berliner Hof', *Der Bär von Berlin: Jahrbuch des Vereins für die Geschichte Berlins*, 25 (1976), 124–44; and Margret Schütte, 'Prinz Friedrich Carl Alexander von Preußen', in Verwaltung der Staatlichen Schlösser und Gärten Berlin (ed.), *Schloß Glienicke: Bewohner, Künstler, Parklandschaft. Schloß Glienicke 1. August bis 1. November 1987* (Berlin, 1987; exhib. cat.), 191–209.

[63] FW IV to Charlotte (Alexandra Feodorovna), 28–9 Dec. 1847, GStA Merseburg, HA Rep. 50 J Nr.
[cont. on p. 64]

William and Carl were wed to two sisters, the Weimar princesses Augusta (1811–90) and Marie (1808–77). Of the two, Augusta, in later years one of Bismarck's premier *bêtes noires*, was by far the more significant. When she was 12 years old, Goethe had described her as 'an utterly charming and creative creature, who already has quite original ideas and whimsies'. Highly nervous, sceptical, and politically engaged, she combined an imperious, rather aloof nature with an admiration of French literature and British political institutions. Her *mariage de convenance* with William had hardly been made in heaven, and they never managed to develop much affection for each other. As a young man William complained about his wife's irreligiosity, and decades later, after becoming King of Prussia and German Emperor, he quite enjoyed their frequent separations. Nevertheless, her political influence over her husband, who was much more impressionable and malleable than many people realized, was especially significant after 1848.[64]

The King's youngest brother, Prince Albrecht (1809–72), had virtually no political influence or interest. As a very young man he had married Princess Marianne of the Netherlands, but the two took an almost instant dislike to each other. After Marianne became involved with a huntsman at one of Albrecht's estates, an incredibly convoluted separation and divorce followed, made even more complicated by Albrecht's deep attachment to a woman of aristocratic but lowlier status. Given Frederick William's commitment to 'Christian values' and to strengthening the sanctity of the marriage bond, his own brother's spectacularly unsuccessful marriage was painfully embarrassing. Thus he responded to Albrecht's problems with outbursts of almost hysterical anger, though in the end he reluctantly agreed to the divorce and to his brother's remarriage.[65]

Of all Frederick William's siblings, the one to whom he felt closest was his sister Charlotte, the wife of Tsar Nicholas I and now officially known as Alexandra Feodorovna. Although he always professed to love his imperial brother-in-law, Frederick William was rather intimidated by the Tsar's imposing appearance, authoritatively held views, and hostility to his own policies; thus he often used his extensive correspondence with Charlotte as a conduit to Nicholas. Charlotte herself had long ceased to be the Romantic enthusiast of her adolescent years, and had become thoroughly 'Russian', a firm supporter of her husband's absolutism. She was also notorious for being haughty and spoiled. Leopold von Gerlach described her

1210 Vol. III, Bl. 55–60^v, and the files of the official investigation in GStA Merseburg, HA Rep. 59 I F 11 Bd. 1. For Prince Carl's activities as a collector and historian of art, see esp. Gerd-H. Zuchold, *Der 'Klosterhof' des Prinzen Karl von Preußen im Park von Schloß Glienicke in Berlin* (2 vols.; Berlin, 1993).

[64] Karl Heinz Börner, *Kaiser Wilhelm I. 1797 bis 1888: Deutscher Kaiser und König von Preußen. Eine Biographie* (Cologne, 1984), 47–50; Cécile Lowenthal-Hensel, Lucius Grisebach, and Horst Ludwig, *Preußische Bildnisse des 19. Jahrhunderts: Zeichnungen von Wilhelm Hensel* (Berlin, 1981; exhib. cat.), 114; Lamar Cecil, *Wilhelm II: Prince and Emperor, 1859–1900* (Chapel Hill, 1989), 5. See also Augusta, Deutsche Kaiserin, *Aus dem literarischen Nachlaß der Kaiserin Augusta*, ed. Paul Bailleu and Georg Schuster, 2nd edn. (Berlin, 1912); and Marie von Bunsen, *Kaiserin Augusta* (Berlin, 1940).

[65] The documentation on Albrecht's separation and divorce is voluminous; see GStA Berlin, BPH Rep. 192 Wittgenstein III, 6, 1–12.

trenchantly as a 'curious woman, vain, frivolous, capricious, and obstinate; but there was an element of faith and depth to her'.[66] Frederick William spent years trying to convince her (and, through her, Nicholas) of the correctness of his various projects, but without much success.

After ascending the throne Frederick William continued to communicate with a wide range of acquaintances on an unofficial basis. Most were cronies and associates from the old days, and he frequently sought their advice on a variety of subjects for which they were not officially competent. Not surprisingly, this quickly gave rise to fears, especially within the court, the State Ministry, and the bureaucracy that the King was susceptible to manipulation by 'non-responsible advisers' (*unverantwortliche Ratgeber*).[67] But before 1848 those concerns were exaggerated. Although some of the King's old friends, like Stolberg and Carl von Voß-Buch, did in fact occupy formal or semi-formal court positions, their actual ability to influence policy depended upon the King's own moods and inclinations, and they were often left in the dark about crucial issues.[68] Moreover, many of the individuals whose opinions the King valued most were absent from court for extended periods in the years just after 1840. In early 1842, for example, he remarked that only Radowitz and Leopold von Gerlach really understood him, but those men had been posted outside Berlin for some years.[69] Radowitz spent many years as a Prussian military envoy and diplomat in Frankfurt am Main and Karlsruhe. Gerlach, unhappy with his own military assignment outside Berlin, threatened in 1842 to resign and return to the family estates. His ultimatum, which was probably a bluff, had the desired effect. He was given command of the First Guard Landwehr Brigade in Berlin, a bit of a sinecure that left him plenty of time to involve himself with affairs of high politics.[70] Though he did see the King regularly after 1842, his influence still remained rather limited.

Much of Frederick William's converse with his old friends and associates centred on non-political matters. Already a middle-aged man when he acceded to the throne, he had become settled in his ways and tried to maintain his old life-style. That style included his tea evenings and regular conversations with notable figures from the arts and sciences, though these activities had lost much of their earlier allure and vitality.[71] As in the old days, Alexander von Humboldt remained one of the King's most regular companions, often serving as lecturer or reader at the tea evenings.[72] Despite all the antagonism that he aroused among neo-pietists and other conservatives, Humboldt remained absolutely indispensable to the King, who revelled in the old naturalist's disquisitions on virtually every subject. Humboldt himself continued

[66] Leopold von Gerlach, diary (18 Nov. 1860), GA, 'Abschriften', xvi. 80.

[67] Rochow and de la Motte-Fouqué, *Leben*, 345.

[68] Voß to Leopold von Gerlach, 18 Mar. and 19 Apr. 1841, GStA Merseburg, Rep. 92 Graf Karl von Voß-Buch Nr. 16 Vol. III, Bl. 12 and 21.

[69] E. L. von Gerlach, diary (16 Jan. 1842), GA, Tagebücher Ernst Ludwig von Gerlachs, vol. ii/b.

[70] Leopold von Gerlach, diary (21 June 1842), GA, 'Abschriften', iv. 19–38.

[71] Leopold von Gerlach, diary (24 Feb. 1845), ibid., iv. 157.

[72] *Gespräche Alexander von Humboldts*, ed. Hanno Beck (Berlin [East], 1959), 238–9.

to use his contacts with the monarch to further the careers and support the aspirations of numerous academic protégés.[73]

Other eminences who regularly joined Frederick William's company were the aged poet Ludwig Tieck, the painter Peter (von) Cornelius, the historian Leopold (von) Ranke, the art historian and diplomat Alfred von Reumont, the composer Felix Mendelssohn, and the Danish sculptor Bertel Thorvaldsen. The King was especially fond, though, of the poet and painter August Kopisch, who had lived in Italy for many years and had discovered the Blue Grotto on the island of Capri. Like Humboldt, he became a fixture during summers at Sanssouci.[74] And, of course, architects were invariably in the King's company. Unhappily, the genius Schinkel was already ill when Frederick William mounted the throne, and he died the following year. Thereafter, the King spent an enormous amount of time with Schinkel's most talented disciples, Ludwig Persius (1803–45) and August Stüler (1800–65).

Although Frederick William once described Stüler as 'Schinkel's best pupil', it was Persius who, before his untimely death of typhus at the age of 42, enjoyed the King's special confidence.[75] Together the two men dominated official architecture in Prussia for many years. In several cases they helped to initiate and execute projects which had been close to the Crown Prince's heart for a long time, especially in the area of church restoration and design. In the early 1840s, Persius completed the beautiful basilica-style Church of the Saviour (Heilandskirche) on the shores of the Havel at Sacrow, near Potsdam; it served as a kind of preliminary study to the Friedenskirche, which in turn was to be Frederick William's court church.[76] After 1840 the King remained passionately involved with his various architectural projects; Persius's diary bears witness to the astonishing amount of attention that Frederick William devoted to these matters.[77] But not everyone approved of the monarch's architectural proclivities. The ever-critical Varnhagen, for instance, once wrote: 'The King's love of new building-projects is enormous, but it is almost

[73] *Alexander von Humboldt und das preußische Königshaus: Briefe aus den Jahren 1835–1857*, ed. Conrad Müller (Leipzig, 1928), 72–3; Alexander von Humboldt, *Vier Jahrzehnte Wissenschaftsförderung: Briefe an das preußische Kultusministerium 1818–1859*, ed. Kurt-R. Biermann (Berlin [East], 1985), 11–13, 18–21.

[74] Franckenberg to Grand Duke Leopold, 7 June 1841, GLA, Abt. 48/2595; L. H. Fischer, 'Ludwig Tieck am Hofe Friedrich Wilhelms IV.', in id., *Aus Berlins Vergangenheit: Gesammelte Aufsätze zur Kultur- und Litteraturgeschichte Berlins* (Berlin, 1891), 107–41; Reumont, *Aus gesunden und kranken Tagen*, 165–8.

[75] FW IV to Theodor von Schön, 1 May 1844, GStA Merseburg, HA Rep. 50 J Nr. 1413 Vol. II, Bl. 15–16; FW IV to Prince Carl, 21 July 1845, GStA Berlin, BPH Rep. 50 Nr. 307. On Persius, see esp. Sabine Heintzenberg and Manfred Hamm, *Ludwig Persius: Architekt des Königs* (Berlin, 1993).

[76] FW IV to Prince Carl, 10–11 Nov. 1840, GStA Merseburg, HA Rep. 50 J Nr. 986, Bl. 10; GStA Merseburg, HA Rep. 50 H Nr. 4; Georg Dehio and Ernst Gall (eds.), *Handbuch der deutschen Kunstdenkmäler: Bezirke Berlin/DDR und Potsdam*, new edn. by Abteilung Forschung des Instituts für Denkmalpflege (Munich, 1983), 388–9; L. Dehio, *Friedrich Wilhelm IV. von Preußen: Ein Baukünstler der Romantik* (Munich, 1961), 100–1; Volker Duvigneau, 'Die Potsdam-Berliner Architektur zwischen 1840 und 1875. An ausgewählten Beispielen' (Diss.; Munich, 1966), 44–8; Friedrich Mielke, *Potsdamer Baukunst: Das Klassische Potsdam*, 2nd edn. (Frankfurt am Main, 1991), 147–8.

[77] Ludwig Persius, *Das Tagebuch des Architekten Friedrich Wilhelms IV. 1840–1845*, ed. Eva Börsch-Supan (Munich, 1980), *passim*.

entirely limited to churches, palaces, and buildings for art, that is, buildings for display. It differs utterly from Napoleon's love of new building-projects, which was directed mainly towards useful technologies—roads, canals, harbours, etc.'[78] Even today, some critics contend that the King's numerous projects, especially in the vicinity of Potsdam, were essentially statements of Frederick William's private aesthetic sense, a sense that was increasingly out of touch with the cultural and political currents of the mid-nineteenth century. The King's architecture, they contend, expressed 'highly personal' yearnings that did not reflect any particular political or ideological programme.[79]

Such an argument misses the point. It is certainly true that Frederick William's aesthetic notions were highly personal; nevertheless, his buildings were at once a private 'refuge' and a larger, public statement of his vision of monarchy. It has been said that, aesthetically, the King lived 'in a world based on an imperial imagination'.[80] Politically, he inhabited a similar world, one which was partially defined by his response to late antique and Byzantine imperial monarchy, with the monarch himself consecrated by God and endowed with a divine, mystic calling.[81] Inevitably, these feelings expressed themselves in a highly personalized notion of monarchy and, ironically for a *ständisch* conservative, in a tendency towards absolutist modes of governing. Certainly there is a deep contradiction between Frederick William's personalized, absolutist style on the one hand and his denunciations of bureaucratic absolutism on the other, or between his personal arbitrariness and his veneration of historical, corporative institutions that limited arbitrary royal power. In short, Frederick William was quite remarkably persistent in his *pursuit* of his monarchical project, but that project itself was fraught with contradictions and tensions.

Frederick William was groping for an alternative to modernity that was itself simultaneously modern and anti-modern. He sought to renew monarchical authority in a situation where a historically conditioned social harmony could displace the divisions of modern society, and in which there would be a perfect congruence between the monarchical will and the wishes of a grateful people. In the words of the insightful Count Trauttmansdorff, Austrian envoy to Berlin, the King's actions were the result 'of the partly medieval, partly modern views which have been brewing in his soul for many years'. On the one hand, Trauttmansdorff noted, the King was carried along by a powerful sense of his royal calling, 'often talks like a real Ultra, and more than anyone else is utterly convinced of the necessity of obedience to monarchical authority'. On the other hand, though, he wanted to please modern public opinion, and the results, the Count feared, would be calamitous: 'What can be said about the future shape of things in a state which derives its impulse from a ruler who oscillates between medieval and liberal views, who wants to combine monarchism with popular favour, and who is confident that he has the miraculous power

---

[78] Varnhagen von Ense, *Tagebücher*, ii. 321 (1 July 1844).   [79] Mielke, *Baukunst*, 143.
[80] Ibid. 142; see also E. Börsch-Supan, intro. to Persius, *Tagebuch*, 11.
[81] Gerd-H. Zuchold, 'Friedrich Wilhelm IV. und die Byzanzrezeption in der preußischen Baukunst', in Otto Büsch (ed.), *Friedrich Wilhelm IV. in seiner Zeit: Beiträge eines Colloquiums* (Berlin, 1987), 224.

and the genius to balance these efforts, to the advantage instead of the disadvantage of the state!'[82]

Managing Monarchy: Rivalries, 'Personal Rule', and the Creation of a Chivalric Tradition

The complexities and contradictions of Frederick William's monarchical project confused friend and foe alike, and contributed significantly to the atmosphere of instability at the top of the Prussian state after 1840. Indeed, the first eight years of his reign, especially the years before 1844–5, were marked by bitter and often obscure jockeying for influence and advantage among the King's disparate advisers and associates. Because of the monarch's predilection for talking to great numbers of people, including his unofficial friends, many observers quickly became convinced that Frederick William was lurching towards a system of rule by informal kitchen cabinet or camarilla.[83] When one looks carefully at the summit of the Prussian state in the last *Vormärz* years, however, one does not encounter rule by camarilla, but rather an amorphous, fluid structure of temporary coalitions and overlapping factions which only partially stabilized after early 1845. Factional rivalries were complicated, of course, by the fact that the majority of the King's advisers were of the same generation, came from similar social backgrounds, had shared many of the same formative experiences (for example, military service in the liberation war), had known each other for a long time, and were often related through intermarriage. After 1840, however, the confusing new directions in which the King was moving disrupted older patterns of friendship and political sentiments among the King's advisers, and indeed within Prussia's ruling élite as a whole.[84]

Despite these complexities, it is still possible to identify several more or less distinct groupings or circles—'faction' would be too strong a word—among the King's advisers. The group to which the King felt personally and politically closest in the first years of his reign could be called the 'ministerial pietists', of whom Thile and Stolberg were initially the main representatives. Allied with them was the controversial, uncompromisingly reactionary Hessian statesman Ludwig Friedrich Hassenpflug (1794–1862), who entered Prussian state service as a judicial official in 1841; within three years he had become a member of the Council of State.[85] To their number should also be added the deeply pious Justice Minister Karl Albrecht

---

[82] Trauttmansdorff to Metternich, 9 Mar. 1841, HHStA, St. K. Preußen, Karton 177, Politische Berichte 1841 I–XII, fol. 148ᵛ; and 10 May 1842, ibid., Karton 180, Politische Berichte 1842, fol. 186ᵛ–187ʳ.

[83] e.g. see Meyendorff to Nesselrode, 22 Apr. 1842, in Meyendorff, *Briefwechsel*, i. 232; Lerchenfeld to Ludwig I, 2 Nov. 1845, BayHStA, MA III 2623. Cf. Ernst Rudolf Huber, *Deutsche Verfassungsgeschichte seit 1789*, 3rd edn. (Stuttgart, 1988), ii: *Der Kampf um Einheit und Freiheit 1830 bis 1850*, 483.

[84] Leopold von Gerlach to Ludwig von Gerlach, 8 May 1842, in Hans-Joachim Schoeps, 'Unbekanntes aus dem Gerlachschen Familienarchiv', in id., *Ein weites Feld: Gesammelte Aufsätze* (Berlin, 1980), 276–7.

[85] *ADB*, xi. 1–9; Leopold von Gerlach to Ernst Wilhelm Hengstenberg, 21 Dec. 1840, StaBi, Nachlaß Ernst Wilhelm Hengstenberg.

Alexander Uhden (1798–1878), who began in the early 1840s as a Cabinet Councillor and rose to ministerial rank by 1844.[86] We have already seen that Thile was mainly interested in religious matters, and otherwise overburdened with administrative details, while Stolberg was less than vigorous or creative in his advice to the King. This group thus generally accommodated itself to the King's will, and was usually willing to sustain his *ständisch* political projects. Above all, they also shared the King's intense religious feelings. Rather unfairly if not surprisingly, the 'pietists' called down upon themselves the invective of people on both the left and the right, particularly those 'Metternichean' bureaucrats and conservatives who had support- ed the policies of Wittgenstein and the late King. Thus Trauttmansdorff wrote dis- dainfully in 1841 of 'these bigots who are going around with a clientele of hypocrites', while his Russian colleague, Peter von Meyendorff, complained four years later that 'We are living here in an atmosphere full of religious elements, in a theological morass.'[87]

Closely connected to the 'ministerial pietists' was Baron Ernst Senfft von Pilsach (1795–1882). Without a formal state position until 1845, Senfft was one of the prime examples of an informal adviser to Frederick William IV, and of the web of friend- ships and familial alliances that connected the King's advisers to each other.[88] A native of the county of Mark in Westphalia, he had entered Prussian military service in 1813, and there forged friendships that were crucial for his later career. After the war he was swept along by the currents of the Awakening and became especially close to people like Carl von der Groeben, the Gerlachs, and Adolf von Thadden, the dis- tinguished neo-pietist aristocrat. He followed Thadden to Pomerania, where he became prominent as an estate owner and lay preacher. In 1825 he married Ida von Oertzen, whose sisters were themselves married to Thadden and Ludwig von Gerlach.[89] Four years later, he met the Crown Prince, who was immediately impressed by Senfft's religious zeal and after 1840 often solicited Senfft's advice. One of those rather bluff, direct men whom Frederick William always particularly respected, Senfft was no moss-backed reactionary. He was an almost frenetically active agricultural modernizer, and, after the early 1840s, a fervent devotee of railway building. He also urged the new King to fulfil his father's constitutional promises of 1815 as quickly as possible.[90] His influence on the King could sometimes be critical. In 1841, for example, it was he who urged the King to proceed with a confrontation that led to Alvensleben's resignation as Finance Minister, for which Leopold von Gerlach never forgave him.[91]

[86] *ADB*, xxxix. 765–7; Lerchenfeld to Ludwig I, 2 Nov. 1845, BayHStA, MA III 2623.
[87] Trauttmansdorff to Metternich, 28 Jan. 1841, HHStA, St. K. Preußen, Karton 177, Politische Berichte 1841 I–XII, fol. 25ᵛ; Meyendorff to Nesselrode, 27 Feb. 1845, in Meyendorff, *Briefwechsel*, i. 303.
[88] *ADB*, liv. 316–29 (Herman von Petersdorff); Herman von Petersdorff, 'Oberpräsident v. Senfft-Pilsach', in id., *Deutsche Männer und Frauen: Biographische Skizzen vornehmlich zur Geschichte Preußens im 18. und 19. Jahrhundert* (Berlin, 1913), 151–66; Paul Haake, 'Ernst Freiherr Senfft von Pilsach als Politiker', *FBPG* 53 (1941), 43–90, 296–323.
[89] For his extensive correspondence with Ludwig von Gerlach, see GA, Fasz. 2/a.
[90] Haake, 'Senfft', 54–5.
[91] Petersdorff, 'Alvensleben-Erxleben', 280–1; id., 'Oberpräsident', 154.

Leopold von Gerlach himself was the moving spirit of the rather loosely defined 'Gerlach group', which also included his brother Ludwig, Carl von Voß–Buch, the journalist Ernst Wilhelm Hengstenberg, the Halle historian Heinrich Leo, and the Evangelical church official Carl Friedrich Göschel. They were critical of the 'absolutist' practices of the pre-1840 government, and shared many of the new King's fundamental religious and political beliefs. They were also deeply pessimistic about the King's rash and contradictory policies, and were concerned about his inability to translate his ideas into effective action or choose appropriate advisers. Indeed, they became increasingly convinced that the rampant confusion in Frederick William's government was leading Prussia not to *ständisch* freedom but to constitutionalism. Ludwig's criticism of the King was especially barbed during those years.[92] At no time, though, did the Gerlach group really join those who directly opposed the King, to whom Leopold felt closely bound by ties of personal obligation, affection, and intellectual respect. Rather, Leopold hoped that the King would finally turn to a fixed and clearly defined '*conseil*' as an alternative to both absolutism and constitutionalism.[93] Gerlach also clearly thought of his group—or, as he called it on at least one occasion, 'our party'—as the core of an effective 'coalition' around which an effective government could be built: 'In no way can we simply be in opposition right now', he admonished his more intransigent brother in 1842, 'but for the time being we have to agree with that otherwise silly saying, "*measures not men*" . . .'[94]

Far more bitter in their opposition to the King were, as we have seen, Alvensleben and Rochow, who can be included in the camp of 'ministerial conservatives', which overlapped closely with the group around the Prince of Prussia and his supporters, including Wittgenstein and Prince Carl. Finally, all of these groups, with the possible exception of the 'ministerial pietists', sometimes suspected that the King was favourably disposed towards liberalism in general and towards the camp of the 'ministerial liberals' in particular: Schön, Boyen, and, later, Eduard Flottwell, Finance Minister from 1844 to 1846. In fact, of all the groups at the summit of the Prussian state after 1840, the 'ministerial liberals' were almost certainly the weakest and the most vaguely defined, especially after Schön's resignation in 1842. On the whole, though, the King favoured no particular group to the exclusion of any other, though ultimately the 'ministerial pietists' probably exercised the most immediate and obvious influence. In fact, Frederick William could not bear to part with *any* of his advisers, even when they were actively working against him (Wittgenstein), had been involved in rows with him (Alvensleben), or figured in bitter intra-governmental disputes (Rochow and Schön). He always liked to hear contradictory advice; moreover, he could sometimes be quite effective at playing off his advisers to his own

[92] Hans-Christof Kraus, 'Das preußische Königtum und Friedrich Wilhelm IV. aus der Sicht Ernst Ludwig von Gerlachs', in Büsch (ed.), *Friedrich Wilhelm IV. in seiner Zeit*, 57–66; Kraus, 'Gerlach', i. 188–99, ii. 141–8.

[93] Leopold von Gerlach to Ludwig von Gerlach, 12 Jan. 1842 and 26 July 1844, GA, Fasz. CS; Leopold von Gerlach to Canitz, 13 Jan. 1842 (draft), GA, 'Abschriften', xvii. 32–5; Leopold von Gerlach to Alvensleben (draft), 6 Jan. 1842, ibid. 36–8.

[94] Leopold von Gerlach to Ludwig von Gerlach, 31 July 1842, GA, Fasz. CS.

advantage. More often, though, as Joseph Maria von Radowitz once pointed out in a brilliant characterization, the King's personnel decisions frequently reflected his poor judgement of other human beings:

The King really is decisive, nor does he shrink back from dangers that might crop up when he takes a road that he knows to be correct. But at the same time he suffers from an inexplicable weakness or lack of clarity regarding people. Thus his judgement depends more on personal likes or dislikes than on objective considerations. Accordingly, one finds the most oddly diverse kinds of people among those whom he likes.[95]

The Prussian political system from 1840 to about 1845 could thus be described as an unstable and amorphous absolutism, in which different individuals, groups, and factions vied, without much apparent success, for influence over a monarch who confounded and annoyed all of them. Indeed, probably at no other time after 1806 was Prussia closer to a system of outright personal rule by a monarch than in the years between 1840 and 1845.[96] But monarchical absolutism was even less appropriate for the circumstances of the mid-nineteenth century than bureaucratic absolutism; even if Frederick William had been less mercurial and erratic, his system of personal rule would still have been inherently unstable. After 1845, with the rise of Bodelschwingh and Canitz, a slightly more stable system of governance began to emerge, but it had to contend immediately with overwhelming pressures for social, economic, and ulti-mately political change.

Despite the confusion and uncertainty that surrounded him, Frederick William IV was nevertheless determined to press ahead with his efforts to reconstitute effective monarchical authority in Prussia. To that end, in the early 1840s he initiated several efforts to revitalize the institutional infrastructure of the monarchical system and cre-ate an élite cadre of loyal supporters. The easiest reform was the reorganization and expansion of the official court entourage, which took place in 1843–4. The King hoped that his measures would add new prestige and draw more attention to a court which had been notable mainly for its dullness and lack of grandeur. Until 1843 the officials of the court (*Hofchargen*) had been divided into two categories, the *Große Hofchargen* and ordinary *Ober-Chargen*. Now they were to be divided into three cat-egories; new, grand-sounding titles were created for some of them; and their numbers increased, from eleven in 1841 to seventeen in 1847.[97] The reorganization of the offi-cial retinue did not really have the desired effect; undaunted, the King tried again in 1853. The restructuring of the court may have had little impact or influence, but it did point to the importance that Frederick William attached to the symbols of mon-archical authority. It also pointed to his preoccupation with questions of rank and hierarchy. Thus his attempt to revitalize the nobility as an adjunct of a reinvigorated

---

[95] Paul Hassel, *Joseph Maria von Radowitz*, i: *1797–1848* (Berlin, 1905), 75.

[96] Meyendorff to Nesselrode, 19 Dec. 1841, in Meyendorff, *Briefwechsel*, i. 199; Lewalter, *Friedrich Wilhelm IV.*, 377.

[97] FW IV to Wittgenstein, 5 Dec. 1843, GStA Berlin, BPH Rep. 192 Wittgenstein III, 14, 1a, Bl. 29; Thile to Wittgenstein and Stolberg, 9 Dec. 1843, GStA Merseburg, HA Rep. 192 Georg Wilhelm von Raumer IV A, Bl. 142–3.

monarchy was much more significant than the restructuring of the court, while the failure of these efforts suggests that there were real limits to royal absolutism and personal rule even in the years before 1848.[98]

Frederick William was convinced that ownership of noble estates (*Rittergüter*), especially entailed, hereditary estates, was crucial to the maintenance of a healthy nobility, above all to that 'honour' characteristic of true aristocrats. He also was inclined to make it difficult for commoners to acquire noble status, and felt that at the same time the titles of those individuals who *were* newly ennobled should only be transmitted to those direct descendants who possessed landed estates. The old Prussian practice of awarding noble titles to all the children of a nobleman would no longer necessarily pertain to new nobles, such as those who had been elevated at the homage ceremonies in Königsberg and Berlin. Rather, it would be restricted to that designated male heir who had maintained the noble estate or its equivalent.[99]

Critics immediately charged that Frederick William was trying to create an English-style nobility which had never existed in Prussia and which was completely contrary to German traditions. Indeed, his proposals encountered especially stiff opposition from the entire State Ministry, most notably from Rochow. Among other things, several ministers argued, the King's notions would seriously restrict opportunities for advancement among those worthy officials who might not be in a position to acquire noble estates: a fact which the King was probably well aware of, given his distaste for officialdom. In March 1841 the Ministry urged the King to give up his ideas and 'in the future not to follow the principle of limited and conditional inheritability of noble status'.[100] But Frederick William IV was not one to give in so easily, especially in matters that were dear to his heart. A Commission for Noble Affairs was created in 1841 to consider his ideas, and over the next six years a succession of discussions took place, some of them including the King himself. The draft of a new law emerged in 1847, but further discussion stalled at that point.[101] The King doggedly persisted in his ideas, even after the revolution of 1848 and Prussia's transition to constitutionalism; by 1851, however, he had reluctantly given up the idea of limited inheritability of noble titles. As a result of these endless and inconclusive debates, none of the individuals who had been awarded noble titles in 1840 were actually able to receive them until 1854![102]

[98] Johann Karl von Schroeder, 'Standeserhöhungen in Brandenburg-Preußen 1663–1918', *Der Herold: Vierteljahrsschrift für Heraldik, Genealogie und verwandte Wissenschaften*, 9 (1978), 1–18, esp. 7, 10–11; Robert M. Berdahl, *The Politics of the Prussian Nobility: The Development of a Conservative Ideology 1770–1848* (Princeton, NJ, 1988), 326–33.

[99] For Frederick William's views, see FW IV to Gustav Adolf von Rochow, 10 Sept. and 15 Oct. 1840, GStA Berlin, I. Haubtabteilung Rep. 90 Nr. 2007, Bl. 24, 25–25ᵛ; FW IV to Wittgenstein and Stolberg, 23 Feb. 1843, ibid., Bl. 117–119ᵛ. On the ennoblements of 1840, see the documents in GStA Merseburg, Geheimes Zivilkabinett 2.2.1. Nr. 928 and 929, and GStA Berlin, I. Hauptabteilung Rep. 90 Nr. 1968.

[100] See the discussion in the Ministry, 16 Mar. 1841, GStA Berlin, I. Hauptabteilung Rep. 90 Nr. 2007, Bl. 85; *Votum* of Rochow, 10 Dec. 1840, ibid., Bl. 32–47ᵛ. See also Stephan Kekulé von Stradonitz, 'Gedanken über eine Um- und Ausgestaltung des Adelswesens in Deutschland', *Deutsche Revue*, 35/1 (Jan.–Mar. 1910), 294–305, esp. 299–301.

[101] Berdahl, *Politics*, 328–33.

[102] AKO, FW IV to Staatsministerium, 8 Feb. 1851, GStA Berlin, I. Hauptabteilung Rep. 90 Nr. 2007

[*cont. on p. 73*]

Not only was it essential, Frederick William thought, to maintain the noble sense of 'honour', but it was also important to reinvoke that spirit of selfless service which, he believed, had typified the Middle Ages. Accordingly, he also invested a considerable amount of attention in the first years of his reign to the creation or modification of quasi-medieval 'orders'. The first and most successful example was the establishment in 1842 of a *Pour le mérite* order for arts and sciences, which was to be a civilian adjunct to the decoration that Frederick II had created. Frederick William always regarded Frederick the Great with a mixture of ancestral veneration and moral disapproval. Having succeeded to the throne exactly a century after that great monarch's own accession, Frederick William was the first ruler since Frederick's death to live in Sanssouci on a regular basis; during Frederick William's reign Frederick's collected works were published, and in 1851 a monument to him was completed on Unter den Linden in Berlin. Yet Frederick William also deplored his forebear's notorious irreligiosity and believed that, where Frederick had been renowned for his military accomplishments, he himself should strive to be a guarantor of European peace.[103] Thus the Friedenskirche, or Church of Peace, begun exactly a century after Sanssouci, was consciously designed as an ideological counterpoint to the Enlightened scepticism embodied in Frederick's villa. By the same token, Frederick William conceived the idea of expanding Frederick's old military order, the *Pour le mérite*, to include a Peace Class, that is, an order of civilians who had distinguished themselves in arts, letters, and sciences. The order's 'chapter' would contain thirty German and twenty non-German members. Alexander von Humboldt was the new order's first Chancellor; its first members included many notables, among them Metternich, the mathematician Gauß, the astronomer Sir John Herschel, the painter Dominique Ingres, the scientists Michael Faraday and Louis Daguerre, and the musicians Liszt, Meyerbeer, Mendelssohn, and Rossini. Although the order was occasionally criticized at the time, it still thrives today—which is more than can be said for the Prussian military decoration, or for that matter Prussia itself.[104]

In the years before 1848 the King also sought to breathe new life into older orders, one of which, the Order of the Swan, was re-established in 1843–4 as a semi-religious order devoted to works of Christian charity. In addition, he wanted to reorganize the Order of the Black Eagle, the highest order in the Prussian state, which was reserved for Prussian and foreign potentates and for the very highest Prussian officers and bureaucrats. Established by Frederick I upon the creation of the Prussian monarchy in 1701, it had fallen under the administrative rubric of the General Commission on Orders, which was also responsible for all the other decorations awarded by the

Bl. 161–161ᵛ; 'Beschluß . . . betreffend die Ausfertigung der Adels-Briefe', 11 Mar. 1854, ibid., Bl. 239–40.

[103] Leopold von Gerlach to Hengstenberg, 21 Dec. 1840, StaBi, Nachlaß Ernst Wilhelm Hengstenberg, Briefe Leopold von Gerlachs.

[104] FW IV to Metternich, 29 May 1842, GStA Merseburg, HA Rep. 50 J Nr. 839, Bl. 78–9; AKO, FW IV, 31 May 1842, GStA Berlin, I. Hauptabteilung Rep. 90 Nr. 2247, Bl. 7; list of first members, in GStA Merseburg, Geheimes Zivilkabinett 2.2.1. Nr. 2092, Bl. 13–15; Walter Bußmann, *Zwischen Preußen und Deutschland: Friedrich Wilhelm IV. Eine Biographie* (Berlin, 1990), 343–4.

Prussian government. In 1844, though, Frederick William decided that this must change, as he wished 'to restore to the highest order of the monarchy that dignity which its statutes articulated but which has declined over the course of time'.[105] In 1846–7 the statutes were revised and old ceremonies were reintroduced, along with the Chapter of the Order (*Ordenskapitel*) and its old offices. Finally, in early 1848 the affairs of the order were removed from the purview of the General Commission on Orders and transferred to the Chancellor of the order, Prince Wittgenstein. In undertaking these actions, Frederick William hoped to rekindle what he feared had become a diminished sense of knightly brotherhood and devotion to service among the state's most distinguished servants.[106] Less than a month after the order's final reorganization, Prussia was swept by revolution.

Even before his accession to the throne in 1840, Frederick William IV had become convinced that urgent action was necessary if Prussia were to evade the snares and seductions of 'the revolution'. To do that, though, it would be necessary to *create* a strong *counter*-revolutionary tradition, based both on popular support and on an affirmation of the divinely ordained nature of kingship as the only alternative to despotism. This was a tall order in a state which, as Frederick William recognized, consisted of a collection of territories without uniformly binding traditions, customs, or outlooks. His attempts, in the first years of his reign, to evoke a common tradition based on monarchical values elicited criticism and confusion among Prussia's dominant élites, including many of his own advisers. That situation was partly a consequence of his own erratic, contradictory, 'fantastic' personality. But too many contemporary observers and too many subsequent historians have focused far too much on the contradictions of that personality. In the things that mattered most to him, as we have seen, Frederick William was quite consistent. Erich Marcks once insightfully remarked that Frederick William was 'consistent in the innermost of his being, but inconsistent in every individual act' that he undertook.[107] Above all, he was consistent in his devotion to his monarchical project, with which he had pressed ahead in the first years of his reign, despite the confusion, alarm, and distrust that it often aroused among his advisers. He had tried to use the public stage to galvanize public support for the monarchical cause; he had continued to use his architecture both as a private affirmation and as a public statement of his beliefs; he had sought to transform court and nobility, and he had tried to reawaken a sense of chivalric commitment to higher causes and the greater good. Above all, though, the centrepiece of Frederick William's monarchical project between 1840 and 1848 was his attempt to transform Prussia into a 'Christian state'. That attempt will be the subject of the next two chapters.

[105] AKO, FW IV to Wittgenstein, 15 May 1844, GStA Merseburg, Rep. 92 Familienarchiv von Massow Nr. 14, Bl. 82–82ᵛ.

[106] AKO, FW IV to General-Ordens-Kommission, 23 Oct. 1846, GStA Merseburg, Geheimes Zivilkabinett 2.2.1. Nr. 1959, Bl. 11; AKO, FW IV to General-Ordens-Kommission, 20 Feb. 1848, GStA Berlin, I. Hauptabteilung Rep. 90 Nr. 2012.

[107] Erich Marcks, *Der Aufstieg des Reiches: Deutsche Geschichte von 1807–1871/78* (2 vols.; Stuttgart, 1936), i: *Die Vorstufen*, 225.

4
Monarchy and Religious Renewal in Prussia, 1840–1850

The King's Special Friend

Frederick William IV always needed special confidants who were 'outsiders', people who were not products of traditional Prussian aristocratic, bureaucratic, or military backgrounds, people who were never quite at home in the circumscribed world of the Berlin–Potsdam élite. Radowitz was a good example. Although he married into the Prussian aristocracy and served with distinction as a Prussian officer, his Catholic and Hungarian backgrounds always lent him a bit of an 'exotic' air. In the 1850s, as we shall see, Frederick William relied heavily on the counsel of two more outsiders: the Berlin police chief, Carl Ludwig von Hinckeldey, and the Director of Berlin's Institute for the Deaf and Mute, Carl Wilhelm Saegert. Frederick William's 'outsider' friends invariably aroused controversy, then and thereafter; but few were more controversial than Christian Carl Josias Bunsen (1791–1860).

Virtually everything that has been written about Bunsen emphasizes the wildly divergent feelings and opinions that he aroused among his contemporaries.[1] One of the most successful dilettantes in nineteenth-century Germany, Bunsen was a diplomat, an extraordinarily active scholar, and, above all, a patron of the scholarly activity of others. Married to an Englishwoman, he spent much of his life in England, serving there as Prussian envoy from 1842 to 1854. He had many admirers in Great Britain, including Sir Robert Peel and W. E. Gladstone. Like Alexander von Humboldt, with whom he enjoyed a friendly relationship, Bunsen selflessly encouraged the careers of young academics. One of the most talented, the Sanskrit scholar Max Müller, insisted that there are not 'many Saints whose real life, if sifted as the life of Bunsen has been, would bear comparison with that noble character of the nineteenth century'.[2]

But Bunsen also had many virulent detractors. His one-time mentor, the historian Barthold Georg Niebuhr, came to regard him as an ambitious intriguer. The

[1] Klaus D. Groß, 'Die deutsch-englischen Beziehungen im Wirken Christian Carl Josias von Bunsens (1791–1860)' (Diss.; Würzburg, 1965), 1–11; id., 'Der preußische Gesandte in London: Bunsens politisches und diplomatisches Wirken', in Erich Geldbach (ed.), *Der gelehrte Diplomat: Zum Wirken Christian Carl Josias Bunsens* (Leiden, 1980), 13–14; Walter Bußmann, *Zwischen Preußen und Deutschland: Friedrich Wilhelm IV. Eine Biographie* (Berlin, 1990), 161, 169; Hans Becker, 'Christian Carl Josias von Bunsen: Sein politisches und diplomatisches Wirken im Dienste Preußens und des Deutschen Bundes', in Hans-Rudolf Ruppel, Frank Foerster, and Hans Becker (eds.), *Universeller Geist und guter Europäer: Christian Carl Josias von Bunsen 1791–1860. Beiträge zu Leben und Werk des 'gelehrten Diplomaten'* (Korbach, 1991), 103–6.
[2] Groß, 'Gesandte', 15; Kurt Schmidt-Clausen, *Vorweggenommene Einheit: Die Gründung des Bistums Jerusalem im Jahre 1841* (Berlin, 1965), 187; F. Max Müller, 'Bunsen', in id., *Chips from a German Workshop* (London, 1870), 362.

astute if acerbic Varnhagen detested him, describing him in 1844 as 'a contemptible rascal, a loathsome character, insipid and without any inner spirit; in his semi-transparent slime he has crawled out onto state and church, and has polluted both of them'.[3] This is a harsh and really quite unfair judgement, but it suggests the intensity of feeling that Bunsen could arouse in friend and foe alike. Those feelings were themselves a result of Bunsen's unique position. As an ordinary Prussian diplomat he would have drawn relatively little attention to himself. But he was an exceptional man who found himself in an extraordinary situation, thanks to his close friendship with the King of Prussia. Through that relationship he was able to influence the King's ideas on church, state, and the relationship between the two. In the last *Vormärz* years, religious controversy often served as a substitute or camouflage for political debate. Religious ideas were fraught with political implications and had a significance that transcended the obscure disputes of theologians, or what Germans call *Theologengezänk*. His contemporaries thus believed that Bunsen was in a key position to affect the King's thinking on some of the most critical issues of the day.

The friendship between Frederick William and Bunsen was rooted in a number of shared interests and personality traits. Both were 'generalists', with an inexhaustible interest in a wide range of subjects. They belonged to the same generation, and had been shaped by similar intellectual, cultural, and political forces. Above all, they were both interested in the history and structure of the early church, questions of liturgy and church organization, religious art and architecture, and the renewal of modern Christianity—and they shared a deep love of Italy. As an Awakened Christian, Frederick William was fiercely committed to the establishment of a Christian state in Prussia as a bulwark against the corruptions of the modern age. The reform of the Evangelical Church and of relations between church and state was thus a central component of his monarchical project, and in it Bunsen played a critical role, especially in the 1830s and early 1840s. But despite this remarkable relationship between King and diplomat, there were real limits to Bunsen's influence. After 1842 the ideas and attitudes of the two men began to drift apart. As an Anglicized German and originally a strong advocate of strict Tory views, Bunsen gradually began to adopt a moderately Whiggish perspective. Frederick William, though, remained attached to his own highly distinctive notions, as we shall see in his attitudes towards liberal forces in German Protestantism, in the evolution of his ideas on church organization, and above all in his response to the General Synod of the Evangelical Church in 1846.

Bunsen's Early Life and Career, 1791–1842

Bunsen was not originally a Prussian subject; he was born into respectably bourgeois, though financially straitened, circumstances in the Waldeck region of western

---

[3] Schmidt-Clausen, *Einheit*, 19–20; K. A. Varnhagen von Ense, *Tagebücher*, ed. Ludmilla Assing, 2nd edn., ii. 401 (25 Nov. 1844).

Germany. In 1808 he went to Marburg to study theology, but after only a short stay there he moved on to Göttingen, where he continued his studies of theology, philology, and history. While attending university he supported himself by teaching at the local *Gymnasium* and by serving as a private tutor to an American student, William Backhouse Astor, son of the fabulously wealthy John Jacob Astor. He also gained a reputation for academic brilliance during those years; in 1812 a prize essay on Athenian inheritance-law also won him a doctorate from Jena. Unlike most of Frederick William IV's other close advisers, he did not fight in the liberation war; rather, in 1814 he visited the Netherlands and Denmark to study Old Icelandic. By that time he had already developed a keen interest in philology, and especially in the 'affinity of language' as a key to understanding the early history of humanity. In 1815 he made his way to Berlin, where he met Schleiermacher and Niebuhr, 'and became more and more determined in his own plan of life, which was to study oriental languages in Paris, London, or Calcutta, and then to settle at Berlin as Professor of Universal History'.[4] Bunsen was never short of either optimism or ambition.

In 1816 he was called to Paris to serve again as companion to young Astor, who had returned from a visit to the United States. Bunsen devoted several months in Paris to the study of Persian and Arabic with the great orientalist, Silvestre de Sacy, and then journeyed to Florence to rejoin Astor, who had preceded him there. At that time his plan was to continue on to India to study Sanskrit, but Astor's father unexpectedly summoned him back to America, leaving Bunsen stranded in northern Italy, without prospects and without funds. He always had a remarkable capacity, however, for rebounding from disappointment and deriving advantage from defeat. Aware that Barthold Niebuhr was now in Rome as Prussian minister to the Holy See, Bunsen made his way to that city in late 1816. Niebuhr made arrangements for him to continue his studies of oriental languages and to make extra money as a tutor. It was in those circumstances that he met and married an Englishwoman, Frances Waddington, whose family was staying in Rome at the time. In 1818 he became Niebuhr's secretary. Bunsen was to remain in the Prussian diplomatic service for the next thirty-six years of his life; in 1822 he became Legation Counsellor, and in 1824 Niebuhr's successor as minister to the Holy See, a post he occupied until 1838.[5]

The first decade and a half of Bunsen's life in Rome were immensely happy, and his residence at the Palazzo Caffarelli on the Campidoglio—now part of the Capitoline Museum complex—gained renown both as a centre of sociability and as a seat of learning. His interest in ancient languages and civilizations persisted; and Rome was

[4] F. M. Müller, 'Bunsen', 368–9.

[5] On Bunsen's early life, see, *inter alia*, Frances Baroness Bunsen, *Memoirs of Baron Bunsen, Late Minister Plenipotentiary and Envoy Extraordinary of His Majesty Frederic William IV at the Court of St. James. Drawn Chiefly from Family Papers by his Widow*, 2nd edn. (2 vols.; London, 1869), i. 1–163; ead., *Christian Carl Josias Freiherr von Bunsen: Aus seinen Briefen und nach eigener Erinnerung geschildert von seiner Frau*, ed. Friedrich Nippold, i: *Jugendzeit und römische Wirksamkeit* (Leipzig, 1868), chs. 1–4; Augustus J. C. Hare, *The Life and Letters of Frances Baroness Bunsen* (2 vols.; New York, 1879), i. 91–164; F. M. Müller, 'Bunsen', 362–75; *ADB*, iii. 541–3; Hans-Rudolf Ruppel, 'Christianus Carolus Josias Bunsen Corbacho-Waldeccensis', in Ruppel *et al.* (eds.), *Universeller Geist*, 17–48; H. Becker, 'Bunsen', 107–11.

the natural setting for him to undertake studies of classical archaeology and the history of early Christianity. The history of early Christian basilicas in Rome aroused his particular interest. Most notably, perhaps, he played a key role in the foundation of the German Archaeological Institute in Rome and the Protestant Hospital near the Tarpeian Rock.[6] Finally, his involvement with problems of Christian liturgy and ecclesiastical organization gained him the favour of Frederick William III, who met Bunsen when he visited Rome with Princes William and Carl in 1822.

Frederick William III shared Bunsen's fascination with liturgical matters, and indeed was virtually obsessed with their details. Under his aegis Prussian Protestantism had been reorganized, and during the Reform Era it had essentially become a state church. At the King's behest, Lutheran and Reformed (Calvinist) denominations joined together in 1817 into a single union; and in 1822, the same year that he visited Italy, he introduced a controversial liturgy (*Agende*) for use in the new Evangelical Church.[7] He was thus genuinely interested in Bunsen's sympathetic if not entirely uncritical reaction to his innovations. Bunsen himself always had a remarkable capacity for ingratiating himself with his superiors without appearing to be a fawning courtier; both Frederick William III and his son appreciated Bunsen's ability to speak frankly to them. As a result, Bunsen's career flourished, soaring to new heights when he was summoned to Berlin for extended consultations in late 1827. There he continued his liturgical conversations with the King; and it was on that occasion that he finally met the Crown Prince.[8]

The future Frederick William IV and the bourgeois diplomat were immediately drawn to each other. Their friendship deepened during the Crown Prince's first trip to Italy the following year. Frederick William's high regard for his new friend was immediately apparent, and after their tour of Rome the Crown Prince asked Bunsen to accompany him almost as far as the Swiss border. Thereafter the two men communicated only sporadically, but after 1834 their relationship became closer and they wrote more frequently, with Frederick William remarking to his friend on one occasion that 'Reading your communiqués has been a *real* tonic for me.'[9] By the late 1830s, however, the Prussian government had become embroiled in a major conflict with the Roman Catholic Church which ended with Bunsen's dismissal from his post. The issue concerned mixed marriages, that is, the Catholic Church's recognition of marriages between Catholics and non-Catholics, and the religious upbringing of the children of such marriages. Out of this dispute emerged the so-called 'Cologne Troubles' (*Kölner Wirren*), a major church–state conflict which threatened to poison relations between the Prussian state and the Catholic inhabitants of the recently acquired Rhineland and Westphalia.[10]

---

[6] F. Bunsen, *Bunsen: Aus seinen Briefen*, i. 347–52.

[7] Robert M. Bigler, *The Politics of German Protestantism: The Rise of the Protestant Church Elite in Prussia, 1815–1848* (Berkeley, Calif., 1972), 37–9.

[8] F. Bunsen, *Bunsen: Aus seinen Briefen*, i. 275–334; Groß, 'Beziehungen', 20–1.

[9] FW (IV) to Bunsen, 7 June 1838, GStA Merseburg, HA Rep. 50 J Nr. 244a, Bl. 27.

[10] For the most accessible analysis of the conflict, see Ernst Rudolf Huber, *Deutsche Verfassungsgeschichte seit 1789*, 3rd edn. (Stuttgart, 1988), ii: *Der Kampf um Einheit und Freiheit 1830 bis 1850*,

[*cont. on p. 79*]

After 1815 it had seemed that any problems between the Catholic Church and the Protestant-dominated Prussian state would be fairly easily resolved. Popes Pius VII, Leo XII, and Pius VIII had all been disposed to compromise, while Niebuhr had represented Prussia's interests at the Holy See adroitly and effectively. After 1830, though, the new pope, Gregory XVI, was less inclined to make concessions to other governments; the church as a whole was becoming more militant, more self-confident, and more insistent on protecting itself against state intrusions on its authority and autonomy. Attempts by the Prussian government to find, or if necessary impose, an acceptable solution to the problem of mixed marriages thus encountered scepticism and, ultimately, resistance from the church hierarchy. Bunsen found himself at the centre of a series of complex negotiations, which began in 1830 while Pius VIII was still alive. When Gregory XVI showed an unwillingness to bend to Prussian wishes, Bunsen turned to direct negotiations in 1834 with the Archbishop of Cologne; the two men worked out a temporary (and secret) agreement which Bunsen hoped would resolve the issue amicably. Unfortunately, it had the opposite effect. It seemed to many Catholics that the Prussian government was trying to hatch a secret deal behind the backs of the papacy. Catholic opinion in the Rhineland and Westphalia became increasingly agitated, especially after the old Archbishop's death in 1835 and his replacement by the unyielding Clemens August von Droste-Vischering. In 1837, after further attempts to resolve the mixed-marriage question had failed, the Prussian government—at Bunsen's recommendation—ordered Droste's detention in the fortress of Minden. To many Catholics the Archbishop had become a martyr for his beliefs, and soon the conflict spread from the Rhineland and Westphalia to the Catholic regions of the Prussian East, where the Archbishop of Posen-Gnesen (Poznań-Gniezno) was also arrested. Bunsen himself came under increasingly heavy criticism for his own handling of the affair. With his assertive personality, he had always been a rather poor diplomat, and the Curia had never really trusted him. In the mixed-marriage affair he committed one blunder after another; above all, he had failed to appreciate the Catholic Church's increasingly militant and self-assertive position under Gregory XVI's papacy, and he had been an ineffective negotiator. When he returned to Rome in 1838, the Pope and other high Curia officials refused to see him. The Prussian government had no alternative but to remove him from his post.[11]

The Cologne Troubles themselves persisted until the death of the old King in 1840. As Crown Prince, Frederick William IV had long been respected and even popular in the Rhineland, and as a religious man himself he admired the intensity of

185–255; and the documents in Ernst Rudolf Huber and Wolfgang Huber, *Staat und Kirche im 19. und 20. Jahrhundert: Dokumente zur Geschichte des deutschen Staatskirchenrechts*, i: *Staat und Kirche vom Ausgang des alten Reichs bis zum Vorabend der bürgerlichen Revolution* (Berlin, 1973), chs. 11–13.

[11] For thorough analyses of Bunsen's role in the mixed-marriage controversy, see Rudolf Lill, *Die Beilegung der Kölner Wirren 1840–1842. Vorwiegend nach Akten des Vatikanischen Geheimarchivs* (Düsseldorf, 1962), 16–22, 28–58, and Schmidt-Clausen, *Einheit*, 72–84; for Bunsen's own views, F. Bunsen, *Bunsen: Aus seinen Briefen*, i. 454–506, 556–91.

Droste-Vischering's faith.[12] After mounting the throne Frederick William quickly proceeded to resolve the crisis, essentially acceding to Catholic desires for as much institutional autonomy as possible. Unlike his father's ministers, he realized that both the spiritual and political authority of the papacy had been strengthened during the Restoration era; accordingly, a settlement of outstanding issues could not be reached by negotiations with Rhenish bishops or by ignoring the Pope. The King thus entrusted a Catholic aristocrat, Count Friedrich Wilhelm von Brühl, with a series of delicate missions to the Holy See, which ended with a mutually acceptable settlement in late 1841, in which the Prussian government granted most of the Catholic Church's wishes for self-regulation of its affairs.[13] Though Frederick William IV regarded the ultramontane tendencies of his age with suspicion, he disliked state control of religion even more. Such control was, he believed, a relic of the era of absolutism. The resolution of the Cologne Troubles was thus an essential precondition of his larger project to renew religious life, and with it the moral foundations of state and society in Prussia.[14]

Bunsen himself was sent on an extended holiday to Great Britain, where he spent more than a year; and in late 1839 he was named Prussian minister to Switzerland, with a clear indication that this would only be a temporary way-station until a more significant assignment could come along.[15] Indeed, it became evident to many observers during this period that Bunsen's influence with the Crown Prince was steadily increasing, and that Frederick William was consulting him on a number of important issues.[16] After Frederick William's accession to the throne, Bunsen played an important role in the new King's decision to rehabilitate the writer Ernst Moritz Arndt and to invite the philosopher Schelling, the public-law theorist Friedrich Julius Stahl, and the artist Peter Cornelius to Berlin.[17] Bunsen also supplied Frederick William with interesting news from England and elsewhere. In December 1838, for instance, he called the Crown Prince's attention to Gladstone's new book on *The State in its Relations with the Church*, which Frederick William in turn enthusiastically described as 'grist to my mill'.[18]

Sustained by the ideas of Burke and Coleridge, Gladstone argued in his pathbreaking essay that the state had to be regarded not as a mechanism or as a social convenience but as an organically developing entity. The state was rooted in the nation, and both were inexorably bound to the church. To function properly and morally, therefore, the state had to be closely connected to the church, a connection based in

---

[12] Friedrich Keinemann, *Das Kölner Ereignis: Sein Widerhall in der Rheinprovinz und in Westfalen* (2 vols.; Münster, 1974), i. 29–33, 253–65.

[13] Lill, *Beilegung*, pt 2; E. R. Huber, *Verfassungsgeschichte*, ii. 257–62; Keinemann, *Widerhall*, i. 310–15.

[14] Keinemann, *Widerhall*, i. 232, 233.

[15] FW (IV) to Bunsen, 25 June 1839, in Leopold von Ranke, *Aus dem Briefwechsel Friedrich Wilhelms IV. mit Bunsen* (Leipzig, 1873), 38–9.

[16] Ernst Ludwig von Gerlach, *Aufzeichnungen aus seinem Leben und Wirken 1795–1877*, ed. Jakob von Gerlach (2 vols.; Schwerin, 1903), i. 260.

[17] F. Bunsen, *Bunsen: Aus seinen Briefen*, ii: *Schweiz und England*, 133–47.

[18] Bunsen to FW (IV), 13 Dec. 1838, in Ranke, *Briefwechsel*, 44; Schmidt-Clausen, *Einheit*, 170–1.

turn upon the particular national character or identity embodied in each state. In the case of England, this took the form of a tolerant but still Established church.[19] Gladstone's appeal for a morally renewed state inevitably struck a resonant chord in Frederick William IV, resembling as it did his own vision of a Christian state in Prussia. The new King yearned to do all in his power to invest that vision with reality, and he responded enthusiastically to Bunsen's efforts to encourage institutional co-operation between Anglicans and German Protestants. Those efforts culminated in the establishment of the celebrated Bishopric of Jerusalem in 1841.

The idea of establishing a joint Anglo-Prussian, Protestant bishopric in Jerusalem had long been germinating in Bunsen's mind; now, however, it derived sustenance from his desire to strike out at the Roman Catholic Church, which he regarded as the architect of his humiliation in 1838. Bunsen always remained an activist, and he would not accept his defeat silently. Accordingly, in a letter to Frederick William in December 1838, Bunsen wrote fiercely of his 'campaign against the Pope and his liars—with Britannia as my ally!' (Attached to that letter was an article by Bunsen on 'The Present Papal Conspiracy for the Overthrow of Protestant Thrones'.) During his stay in England he began to develop his ideas on Anglo-German co-operation in consultation with people like Lord Ashley, a prominent member of the Evangelical wing of the Church of England. By 1840, when he returned to England for another long visit, the idea of a joint project in Jerusalem had emerged.[20] The time and the circumstances were propitious for such a project. The Ottoman Sultan had only been able to resist the onslaughts of the great Egyptian leader, Mehemet Ali, with help from the European powers; and, as a consequence, it was generally assumed that the influence of those powers in Ottoman-controlled Palestine would increase.[21] Though Prussia had few concrete interests in that part of the world, it would not be too difficult to interest Frederick William IV in a project to support Christian missions in the Holy Land.

By the autumn of 1840, Bunsen was working out his plans in greater detail. A London missionary society for the conversion of Jews had recently acquired property for a mission station in Jerusalem. Bunsen and his English friends argued that it was desirable 'to transform this private foundation into a national and generally Christian-Evangelical one. This could only happen if the Anglican Church established a bishopric there.'[22] At first Frederick William had sounded out the possibility that the European powers might jointly acquire the Holy Places in Palestine.[23] After discovering that this was not feasible, he decided in early 1841 to invite Bunsen

[19] H. C. G. Matthew, *Gladstone 1809–1874* (Oxford, 1986), 61–5; Schmidt-Clausen, *Einheit*, 170–85.

[20] Schmidt-Clausen, *Einheit*, 88–100; Alfred von Reumont, *Aus König Friedrich Wilhelms IV. gesunden und kranken Tagen*, 2nd edn. (Leipzig, 1885), 97, 98.

[21] Winfried Baumgart, 'Zur Außenpolitik Friedrich Wilhelms IV. 1840–1858', in Otto Büsch (ed.), *Friedrich Wilhelm IV. in seiner Zeit: Beiträge eines Colloquiums* (Berlin, 1987), 133.

[22] Bunsen to F. A. Perthes, 12 Oct. 1841, in F. Bunsen, *Bunsen: Aus seinen Briefen*, ii. 164.

[23] Christiane Schütz, *Preußen in Jerusalem (1800–1861): Karl Friedrich Schinkels Entwurf der Grabeskirche und die Jerusalempläne Friedrich Wilhelms IV.* (Berlin, 1988), 120–1; Groß, 'Beziehungen', 74–5.

to Berlin and then dispatch him to London on a special diplomatic mission. A special 'Instruction' from Frederick William IV was to serve as the basis for Bunsen's negotiations with Sir Robert Peel's government, which began in June 1841. The Prussian envoy was to determine whether the Church of England would be willing to cooperate in the Holy Land with the Evangelical Church of Prussia, because only action could guarantee the position of the Protestant powers there.[24] In his communiqués to the British government, Bunsen constantly emphasized the political advantages that would emerge from a common front of the Protestant powers, which should be entitled to the same rights in the Holy Land as the Catholic and Eastern Orthodox powers. As things currently stood, Protestants in the Ottoman Empire found themselves in a 'disadvantageous and humiliating position'.[25]

The negotiations proceeded very rapidly, and by early August agreement had been reached with the Archbishop of Canterbury and the Bishop of London 'that the Archbishop of Canterbury be authorized by the Crown, to consecrate as Bishop a person, or one of two persons, British subjects, recommended by him, to reside at Jerusalem, and there to exercize [sic] the functions of the members of the two national churches'.[26] After the death or resignation of the first Bishop of Jerusalem, the second would be a Prussian subject, but he would still be consecrated by the Archbishop of Canterbury. The Prussian government would contribute financially to the bishopric. Evangelical congregations in the Holy Land would retain their separate liturgy and language, while recognizing the authority of the Bishop of Jerusalem and thus, through him, of the Archbishop of Canterbury. The British Parliament approved these measures in October 1841, and in November the Archbishop of Canterbury consecrated the first Bishop of Jerusalem, Michael Alexander, and sent him to the Near East to take up his duties.[27]

The Bishopric of Jerusalem was never successful, and was finally dissolved when the Prussian government suspended the agreement in 1886. But it was a tremendous personal and political boost for Bunsen himself, who believed that he had finally been vindicated after his disgrace in 1838. His relationship with Frederick William was firm, and he enjoyed considerable support within highly influential circles in British society. His triumph seemed complete when he learned in November that he was to become Prussian Minister to the Court of St James's.[28] In the weeks that followed, Bunsen enjoyed even more personal triumphs. Following upon the successful conclusion of the Jerusalem negotiations, Frederick William IV travelled to Britain in January 1842 to observe the christening of his godchild, the Prince of Wales (the future Edward VII). Frederick William's well-known charm and graciousness guar-

[24] Ernst Benz, *Bischofsamt und apostolische Sukzession im deutschen Protestantismus* (Stuttgart, 1953), 152–60; Schmidt-Clausen, *Einheit*, 101–9.

[25] Bunsen to Palmerston, 15 July 1841, PRO, FO 64/235, fol. 123–6; FW IV to Bunsen, 12 Aug., 26 Aug., 7 Sept., and 29 Nov. 1841, GStA Merseburg, HA Rep. 50 J Nr. 244a, Bl. 50–56ᵛ.

[26] Bunsen to Palmerston, 5 Aug.1841, PRO, FO 64/235, fol. 151ᵛ.

[27] F. Bunsen, *Bunsen: Aus seinen Briefen*, ii. 158–76, 189–90, 195–207. See also H. Becker, 'Bunsen', 116–19; and Martin Lückhoff, 'Bunsen und Jerusalem', in Ruppel *et al.* (eds.), *Universeller Geist*, 155–66.

[28] Bunsen to Frances Bunsen, 18 Nov.1841, in F. Bunsen, *Bunsen: Aus seinen Briefen*, ii. 190–2.

anteed the trip's success; and certainly it was a clear demonstration to the British of the unusual relationship of trust and confidence that bound the Prussian monarch to his diplomat.[29] Despite that relationship, however, Bunsen still had to reckon with powerful opponents in both Prussia and Great Britain.

In Prussia, much of this opposition came from the ultra-conservatives around Carl von Voß-Buch and his friends like Ernst Wilhelm Hengstenberg and the Gerlachs.[30] One of the major journalistic organs of this group, the *Berliner Politisches Wochenblatt*, had gone through a major crisis at the time of the Cologne Troubles, when it had lost several prominent Catholic contributors. The conservatives associated with the paper tended to blame Bunsen for this set-back.[31] The Gerlachs and their friends were also disturbed by Frederick William's continued determination, sustained by his contacts with Bunsen, to encourage a general institutional renewal of German Protestantism. The young men of the Awakening had, in their middle age, become supporters of Evangelical orthodoxy, and they regarded Frederick William's flirtation with church reform as dangerous and potentially explosive. Ludwig von Gerlach had become especially devoted to the idea that the state, as a creation of God, had a critical role to play in the regulation of religious affairs, and Frederick William's apparent 'softness' in this area worried him. He was especially worried about the dangerous consequences of Frederick William's 'impractical fantasies of being a reformer, for which, as his later government showed, he hadn't any of the most basic qualities'.[32] That same scepticism extended to the King's Jerusalem activities. In the spring of 1842, Otto von Gerlach directed a memorandum to the King in which he tried to explain the concern of many Berlin pastors that the Church of England might ultimately try to absorb their own church; and in July Otto's brother Leopold wrote ominously 'that we are moving towards a time of quick action, that we are going to have to act firmly against the ecclesiastical ideas of the King and Bunsen'.[33]

As usual, the Gerlachs' concerns were exaggerated. Frederick William's own expectations for the Jerusalem project were more modest than Bunsen's, and after the bishopric's creation he was only sporadically interested in it.[34] Bunsen hoped that the project could lay the groundwork for a great affirmation of Protestant unity based on his complex ideas of linking the universal, 'catholic' qualities of Christian belief with the specific traditions of national churches.[35] Frederick William, however, had

---

[29] Victoria to Frederick Wiliam IV, 12 Dec. 1841, GStA Merseburg, HA Rep. 50 J Nr. 359, Bl. 28; FW IV to Victoria, 18 Dec. 1841, ibid., Bl. 28ᵛ–29ᵛ; FW's letters to Elisabeth from his trip, ibid., Nr. 995 Fasz. 16, Bl. 57–58, 116–124.

[30] Voß to Leopold von Gerlach, 2 Apr. and 28 Dec. 1841, GStA Merseburg, Rep. 92 Graf Karl von Voß-Buch Nr. 16 Vol. III, Bl. 16ᵛ, 55.

[31] Schmidt-Clausen, *Einheit*, 215.   [32] E. L. von Gerlach, *Aufzeichnungen*, i. 262.

[33] Hans-Joachim Schoeps, 'Der Widerstand der Berliner Geistlichkeit gegen die Gründung des Bistums zu Jerusalem', in id. (ed.), *Neue Quellen zur Geschichte Preußens im 19. Jahrhundert* (Berlin, 1968), 279–94; Leopold von Gerlach to Ludwig von Gerlach, 1 July 1842, GA, Fasz. CS.

[34] See FW's correspondence with the Bishop of Jerusalem, all of it from 1851–2, in BA Potsdam, 90 Wa 3 Nachlaß Hermann Wagener Nr. 9, Bl. 62–74.

[35] Schmidt-Clausen, *Einheit*, 62–71.

other priorities. In pursuing the Jerusalem project the King was only interested, he insisted, in encouraging missionary activities and in securing the position of the Evangelical Church in the Holy Land. Despite the fears of Otto von Gerlach and other pastors, Frederick William did not envisage the introduction of an English-style hierarchy or 'high-church' practices in Prussia.[36]

Ecclesiastical Reform and the Monarchical State

Despite all the attention it has received over the years, the Jerusalem project was really tangential to Frederick William IV's main interests in the area of Prussian church reform. When it came to renewing the church Frederick William was amenable, as in everything else, to advice, suggestions, and inspiration from a number of quarters. Bunsen's influence was certainly indispensable, and with his wide experience and vast reading he opened the King's eyes both to important historical sources and to non-German ideas about ecclesiastical organization and church–state relations. As we have already seen, Frederick William responded enthusiastically to Gladstone's views, and he was attracted to some of Thomas Arnold's notions as well; and it was Bunsen who had brought both of those men to his attention. There is also indirect evidence that Bunsen acquainted Frederick William with the 'Apostolic Consti-tutions' and the related 'Apostolic Canons', a series of documents on church admin-istration and structure dating from the early Christian era. Though these documents were apparently edited during the era of Constantine the Great, it was widely believed in Bunsen's day that they dated from the first century and that they there-fore described the earliest form of church organization—a form which Frederick William IV was eager to revalidate and revitalize. Indeed, the proximity of Frederick William's views to the models described in these early documents has led one scholar to regard 'these Apostolic Constitutions together with the Apostolic Canons as the most important source, next to the Acts of the Apostles and the Epistles', of the King's ideas.[37]

In issues of ecclesiastical politics Frederick William consulted not only with Bunsen but also with a variety of other confidants and advisers, including the Gerlachs, Voß, Thile, Karl von Roeder, the pietist court-preacher G. F. A. Strauß, and Guido von Usedom, like Bunsen a veteran diplomat and Prussian representative to the Holy See. As the King once wrote to Bunsen, 'My ideal vision of the composi-tion of the church has flowed together like a stream from many sources.'[38] Although

---

[36] Hans-Joachim Schoeps, 'Widerstand', 282; Johannes Heckel, 'Ein Kirchenverfassungsentwurf Friedrich Wilhelms IV. von 1847', in id., *Das blinde, undeutliche Wort 'Kirche': Gesammelte Aufsätze*, ed. Siegfried Grundmann (Cologne, 1964), 435; Benz, *Bischofsamt*, 137; Schmidt-Clausen, *Einheit*, 364–7. Franz Schnabel, *Deutsche Geschichte im neunzehnten Jahrhundert*, iv: *Die religiösen Kräfte*, 3rd edn. (Freiburg, 1955), 535–9, and Gwendolyn Evans Jensen, 'Official Reform in *Vormärz* Prussia: The Ecclesiastical Dimension', *CEH* 7 (1974), 150, exaggerate Frederick William's high-church tendencies.

[37] Hanns Christof Brennecke, 'Eine heilige apostolische Kirche: Das Programm Friedrich Wilhelms IV. von Preußen zur Reform der Kirche', *Berliner Theologische Zeitschrift*, 4 (1987), 247.

[38] E. L. von Gerlach, *Aufzeichnungen*, i. 261; Thile to FW IV, 26 May 1840, GStA Merseburg, HA Rep. 50 E 3 Nr. 14, Bl. 167–172ᵛ; FW (IV) to Bunsen, 24 Mar. 1840, in Ranke, *Briefwechsel*, 47, 49. See

[cont. on p. 85]

he was a lay theologian, Frederick William was an extremely well-informed one; and he did not hesitate to differ with his advisers and develop his own theological and ecclesiastical points of view. This is hardly surprising, for the study of Christian doctrine represented much more to him than a mere intellectual exercise. For Frederick William IV the application of Christian beliefs and values to the world of human affairs was the cornerstone upon which he built his entire ideological edifice. His concepts of monarchy, culture, the state, social organization, Germany and German nationalism, and international relations were all derived from his particular interpretation of Christian doctrine.

Historians have always recognized the centrality of religious considerations to Frederick William IV, and have emphasized his attachment to the idea of a Christian state. What they have not always sufficiently stressed, though, is that for Frederick William Christianity *always* took precedence over the state; the message of Christian salvation was primary, and everything else, especially the state, was secondary.[39] Like Friedrich Julius Stahl, Frederick William IV based his entire understanding of the world on a central religious premiss, without which that understanding would collapse: faith in the saving grace of a *personal* God, a God made flesh, an intercessor for humanity. Stahl and Frederick William believed that humanity would have to make a choice between rationalism and what Stahl called 'the personal, transcendent, revelatory God'. All else, especially his notion of the divine basis of his royal office, flowed from that central insight.[40]

Driven by his determination to confront the rationalist tendencies of the modern world with 'spiritual weapons', Frederick William IV developed his plans to revitalize Evangelical Christianity in Prussia. These ideas can be fairly easily reconstructed, for he left evidence of them everywhere, from the prayers he used in his private devotions to his best-known public speeches. They are also remarkably consistent, evolving gradually but steadily after the early 1820s. Even before he mounted the throne, his ideas had become fixed; indeed, in 1855 he pointed out to Bunsen 'that my views have remained the same since '39'.[41] Frederick William's proposals were a

also Hans-Christoph Kraus, 'Das preußische Königtum und Friedrich Wilhelm IV. aus der Sicht Ernst Ludwig von Gerlachs', in Büsch (ed.), *Friedrich Wilhelm IV. in seiner Zeit*, 59–60.

[39] Ewald Schaper, *Die geistespolitischen Voraussetzungen der Kirchenpolitik Friedrich Wilhelms IV. von Preußen* (Stuttgart, 1938), 58.

[40] Friedrich Julius Stahl, *Zum Gedächtniß Seiner Majestät des hochseligen Königs Friedrich Wilhelm IV. und seiner Regierung: Vortrag gehalten im evangelischen Verein zu Berlin am 18. März 1861* (Berlin, 1861), 4–6; Wilhelm Füßl, *Professor in der Politik: Friedrich Julius Stahl (1802–1861). Das monarchische Prinzip und seine Umsetzung in die parlamentarische Praxis* (Göttingen, 1988), 16; Otto Dibelius, 'Friedrich Wilhelm IV. und die Idee des christlichen Staates', *Die Furche*, 22 (1936), 40–8; Schaper, *Kirchenpolitik*, 55.

[41] Joachim Mehlhausen, 'Friedrich Wilhelm IV: Ein Laientheologe auf dem preußischen Königsthron', in Henning Schröer and Gerhard Müller (eds.), *Vom Amt des Laien in Kirche und Theologie: Festschrift für Gerhard Krause zum 70. Geburtstag* (Berlin, 1982), 193–4; FW IV to Bunsen, 10 June 1855, GStA Merseburg, HA Rep. 50 J Nr. 244a, Bl. 210–211ᵛ. For the evolution of Frederick William's ideas, see his memorandum of 18 Mar. 1822, GStA Merseburg, HA Rep. 50 E 3 Nr. 14, Bl. 53–60ᵛ; FW (IV) to Frederick William III, 26 Nov. 1830, ibid., Bl. 154–164ᵛ; FW (IV) to Bunsen, 21 Mar. to 28 Apr. 1840, ibid., HA Rep. 50 J Nr. 244a, Bl. 34–47ᵛ; his two essays (*Aufsätze*) of 1845 and 1845–6, in E. L. von Gerlach, *Aufzeichnungen*, ii. 444–510; and Heckel, 'Kirchenverfassungsentwurf', 434–53.

product both of his personal desire to restore the ancient practices of the apostolic church and of his wish to transform the relationship between church and state in Prussia. Even in the fifteenth century the Electors of Brandenburg had exercised a great deal of power in church affairs; and after the Reformation the ecclesiastical authority of the secular rulers of Brandenburg-Prussia (*landesherrliches Kirchenregiment*) had become firmly established. Without having quite the status of the King or Queen of England, the Elector and his successors, the Kings of Prussia, functioned in effect as supreme bishop (*summus episcopus*) of the Protestant churches in their domains. In the eighteenth century the autonomy of those churches declined considerably, with Prussia's rulers and bureaucrats increasingly treating them as branches of the state. That tendency reached a climax during the Reform era, when the old church-structure was transformed into an out-and-out extension of the bureaucratic apparatus. The old governing boards of the Lutheran and Reformed Churches were replaced, and ultimate administrative responsibility for their affairs was vested in the Department of Religious Affairs (*Kultusabteilung*) of the Interior Ministry; in 1817 that department became an autonomous ministry, the *Kultusministerium*, responsible for religious and educational matters.[42]

After 1815, the government modified and partially loosened that centralized structure. The Lutheran and Reformed confessions were joined in a single Evangelical state church (*Landeskirche*) in 1817, and, as we have seen, after 1822 Frederick William III introduced a new liturgy for the Evangelical union. The government also appointed new Consistories to help manage church affairs on a regional basis, and after 1829 General Superintendents were named to direct those affairs in each province. The king himself continued to play a crucial role within this still rather centralized structure, as evidenced by Frederick William III's frequent interventions in ecclesiastical matters.[43] Given his antipathy towards bureaucratic despotism, Frederick William IV was convinced that this system, in which the church 'resides in the body of the state', needed to be radically overhauled if German Protestantism were to be truly revitalized.[44] The church should regenerate itself and recast itself from within. If it succeeded in that task, then the unfortunate *landesherrliche Kirchenregiment* could be cast aside, the church would no longer be a pliable instrument of the state, and the king himself could cease to be *summus episcopus*. In his writings on the church Frederick William always stressed his desire to relieve himself of that irksome burden.[45] This office was, he believed, a provisional arrangement that had been made at the time of the Reformation, and it should be ended as the church reformed itself. Until that happened, however, he would have to continue to bear the burden of his ecclesiastical responsibilities.

[42] Otto Hintze, 'Die Epochen des evangelischen Kirchenregiments in Preußen', in id., *Gesammelte Abhandlungen*, iii: *Regierung und Verwaltung. Gesammelte Abhandlungen zur Staats-, Rechts- und Sozialgeschichte Preußens*, ed. Gerhard Oestreich, 2nd edn. (Göttingen, 1967; art. orig. pub. 1906), 84.

[43] Among many sources, see Hintze's classic analysis ibid. 56–96, esp. 56–8, 70–88; and Bigler, *Politics*, pp. ix, 5–11, 20–1, 37–40.

[44] FW IV, second *Aufsatz* of 1845–6, in E. L. von Gerlach, *Aufzeichnungen*, ii. 479.

[45] FW IV, first *Aufsatz* of 1845, ibid. ii. 451.

How, then, could the church be encouraged to change itself, especially considering its demoralized and decrepit state? The King believed that he could encourage the church's internal regeneration by facilitating its reorganization. In a revealing letter to Bunsen in the spring of 1840, Frederick William stated that the monarch should solemnly proclaim that his 'role as Supreme Bishop, though at present undoubtedly *legal*, is a burden to his conscience, because it is even more undoubtedly irreligious and un-Christian'. But at the same time he could only agree to give up his authority to a church which 'is regenerating itself by looking to church history: that is, by applying *the genuine structure of the primitive church to the conditions of the Christian state* in the nineteenth century. It must build itself, *stone for stone*, just like the early church.' But what *was* the 'genuine structure of the primitive church'? If one studied its history, one would see that 'the only possible, the only truly necessary way, had been there for 1800 years, as the legacy of the Apostles'.[46]

To return to apostolic practices would mean to cleanse the church of certain conventions which in his estimation had become untenable. Since the time of Constantine, he argued, three forms of church organization had gradually emerged: the episcopal, the presbyterial, and the consistorial. The first was based on the supreme authority of bishops, the second on representative church bodies, and the third on consistories of pastors. The problem with these forms of ecclesiastical organization was that they all led to the 'separation of clergy and congregation', to the emergence of the clergy 'as a distinct estate of society', which was 'something monstrous'.[47] If one looked back to the time of the early church, though, one would see that the apostles founded individual churches, creating two kinds of 'office' for each church (that is, for all the Christians in a particular community). The holders of both offices—and this was important for Frederick William IV—were ordained by the laying-on of hands. The first office was the ministry itself, originally composed, in apostolic times, of an elder who acted as 'overseer' or *pastor primarius*, a representative of the church to worldly authorities, the bishop in the original sense of the word. Frederick William attached special importance, however, to the second office, that of 'servitors'. This was the office of those deacons and deaconesses who devoted their lives to humble service, who assisted 'the poor, the suffering, and the sick', and who often laid down their lives as martyrs. Like the members of the ministry, deacons and deaconesses were ordained. Finally, according to Frederick William IV, the third element of the early church consisted of lay members of the congregation (*Gemeinde*), who were represented in the management of church affairs by male heads of families.[48] This was the system which Frederick William IV wanted to modify and apply to Prussian conditions.

    [46] FW IV to Bunsen, 24 Mar. 1840, in Ranke, *Briefwechsel*, 50, 65.
    [47] FW (IV), memorandum of 18 Mar. 1822, GStA Merseburg, HA Rep. 50 E 3 Nr. 14, Bl. 54ᵛ–59ᵛ; id., first *Aufsatz* of 1845, in E. L. von Gerlach, *Aufzeichnungen*, ii. 445–8, 452.
    [48] FW IV, first *Aufsatz* of 1845, in E. L. von Gerlach, *Aufzeichnungen*, ii. 456–68; see also Schaper, *Kirchenpolitik*, 79.

His concrete ideas about the ways in which such an 'apostolic' church-organization could be introduced in Prussia passed through several phases. In his 1840 letter to Bunsen he painted, in one of his typical flights of fantasy, a Romantic picture of a Prussia divided into some 350 bishoprics, each about the size of an existing church-superintendent's district, and each corresponding to a church in the apostolic sense. Thirteen or fourteen of these bishops, whose seats coincided with older bishoprics, would be called 'Metropolitans' (for example, the Bishop of Königsberg would become Metropolitan of Samland), and their consistories would become 'Metropolitan Chapters'. The administrative functions of the *Kultusminister* would be assumed by the Prince-Archbishop of Magdeburg, who would be the *Primas Germaniae*. Frederick William himself admitted to Bunsen that these ideas had to be regarded as impracticable 'reveries'.[49] Nevertheless, many historians have tended to regard them as a *programmatic* statement of Frederick William's intentions regarding the church, and thus as yet another example of his detachment from reality.[50] Although he did in fact have an almost limitless capacity for losing himself in day-dreams, his church plans of 1845–6 and 1847 were much more sober and far less fanciful than his effusions of 1840. He was also under no illusion about what it would take to attain his goals, and probably did not expect to see them realized during his lifetime. Thus he compared his essays of 1845–6 to a 'testament', describing them as a 'legacy for coming generations'.[51]

In his revised proposals of the mid-1840s Frederick William made no reference to his Metropolitans or Prince-Archbishops. Instead, he simply reiterated his theories about the organization of the apostolic church and called for the installation of that structure in Prussia. There would still be some 350 'churches' in Prussia, each corresponding, as in his earlier proposal, to existing superintendencies of the Evangelical Church. Each church would be broken into three 'orders' (*Ordnungen*): presbyters, consecrated by ordination; ordained deacons and deaconesses; and the congregation, which would be represented, as in the early church, by morally worthy and upright family fathers. Representatives of all three orders would come together in church synods. One member from each order would then be chosen for the provincial synod, which would also include the provincial consistory. Each provincial synod would in turn elect a representative from each order to sit in the general synod for the whole kingdom. Between 1845 and 1847 Frederick William changed his mind about the composition of this body; in his 1847 proposal it would also include the members of the royal Supreme Consistory (*Oberkonsistorium*), the provincial consistories, and professors of theology from each of the kingdom's universities. The *Kultusminister* would ordinarily sit in the chair, though the king could preside at any time.[52] With

[49] FW (IV) to Bunsen, 24 Mar. 1840, in Ranke, *Briefwechsel*, 61–3.

[50] Schaper, *Kirchenpolitik*, 74–5 n. 4; Schmidt-Clausen, *Einheit*, 309–10; Brennecke, 'Kirche', 240.

[51] FW IV, first *Aufsatz* of 1845, in E. L. von Gerlach, *Aufzeichnungen*, ii. 444, 450–1; see also Brennecke, 'Kirche', 241.

[52] FW IV, second *Aufsatz* of 1845–6, in E. L. von Gerlach, *Aufzeichnungen*, ii. 480–98, 504–6; Heckel, 'Kirchenverfassungsentwurf', 448–53. See also Schaper, *Kirchenpolitik*, 86–100; Schmidt-Clausen, *Einheit*, 323–42, 347–9; Mehlhausen, 'Friedrich Wilhelm IV.', 210–11; Brennecke, 'Kirche', 237–42.

this institutional arrangement, Frederick William argued, it would at last be possible to cast off 'that authority over the church which now (abominably) resides in the secular ruler' and place it in the hands of properly organized apostolic churches.[53] Frederick William concluded that when this step had been taken the Reformation would truly have been completed.[54]

A crucial aspect of Frederick William's church proposals concerns the position of the king as representative of the state *vis-à-vis* the church. He had always felt supremely unqualified for his position as *summus episcopus*. In a conversation with Ludwig von Gerlach, for example, he pointed out, 'I wear boots and spurs, I ride at reviews, and when something isn't right I swear and curse; I can't be a bishop.'[55] At the same time, however, he never deviated from his exalted, mystic-sacral perception of the divine basis of his own office.[56] In some ways that perception might seem to contradict his desire to divest himself of some of his powers. In fact, despite his protestations to the contrary, the King still intended to retain a great deal of say in ecclesiastical affairs while simultaneously stressing his opposition to despotism and absolutism.[57] His dream of an organic renewal of the church was entirely consistent with his more general views regarding politics and the proper organization of state and society. He always emphasized that the church would have to reform itself from within; he would not impose his views upon it, though he would certainly use his own moral example to encourage its renewal. In other words, Frederick William's church-reform proposals paralleled his vision of a Prussian society rejuvenated and immunized against revolutionary doctrines through a corporative, organic-*ständisch* representation of historically defined group interests in which harmony and shared values would replace discord and selfishness. Therein, of course, lay the major problem with the vision. What would Frederick William do, as King, if ordinary human beings declined to renew church, state, and society along the lines that he envisioned? Faced with such difficulties, Frederick William often invoked divine authority to justify what in effect were arbitrary and even autocratic decisions.[58] On other occasions, depending on his mood, he would simply announce that no one had understood him and then withdraw into sullen passivity. Thus one of the major themes of Frederick William's reign was the collision between his loud support of '*ständisch* freedom' and his inclination, when confronted with complexity or disagreement, to revert to a system of 'personal rule', or alternatively to wash his hands of all responsibility and blame his subordinates for his difficulties. But when push came to shove, the preservation of his own authority as monarch always took priority over other considerations.

Frederick William's attitudes towards Prussia's Jewish population clearly illustrate the ambiguities and ironies that attended his vision of *ständisch* reform in church

---

[53] FW IV, second *Aufsatz* of 1845–6, in E. L. von Gerlach, *Aufzeichnungen*, ii. 491.
[54] Ibid. ii. 476.   [55] E. L. von Gerlach, diary (10 Nov. 1845), ibid. i. 435.
[56] Schaper, *Kirchenpolitik*, 55–9.
[57] Heckel, 'Kirchenverfassungsentwurf', 438–9; Schmidt-Clausen, *Einheit*, 352.
[58] Hintze, 'Epochen', 90.

and state. For several generations, Jews in Prussia had been moving slowly—but, it seemed, steadily—towards the achievement of full civil and political emancipation, especially in the wake of an 1812 edict which granted citizenship to Jews. Despite the limitations of that edict and Restoration-era efforts to dilute it further, the most politically active members of Prussia's various Jewish communities eagerly embraced the prospect of full integration and assimilation into an officially secular, civil community, and thus reacted with outrage and dismay to Frederick William's proposals concerning the place of the Jews in a reinvigorated 'Christian-German' state. In a cabinet order of December 1841, the King argued that Jews should always be tolerated in Prussia; nevertheless, Jews constituted a unique national community, and the historical particularities of that community should be respected. Consistent with the *ständisch*-corporative vision that informed all his thinking, he contended that Prussian Jews should be organized into 'corporations', which in turn would name delegates to represent Jewish interests before local authorities. Frederick William further suggested that Jews should no longer be required to perform military service, a clear indication that, in his eyes, Jews and Christians could never enjoy equivalent rights and responsibilities in a *ständisch*, Christian-German state. The whole proposal elicited massive protests from Jewish groups, which branded the prospect of 'segregation' (*Absonderung*) from the rest of the civil community as retrograde, a retreat to the condition of Prussia's Jews before 1790. Interior Minister Rochow and *Kultusminister* Eichhorn also resisted the King's ideas, implying that he had not understood the main trends of Prussian history or the evolving place of the Jewish community within Prussian society. In short, they intimated, he was 'inventing' group rights that were inappropriate to present conditions. Typically, however, Frederick William continued to adhere stubbornly to his ideas; and only in 1848 were Prussia's Jews finally accorded full political, civil, and economic rights.[59]

Frederick William IV adhered stubbornly to other ideas as well. Thus he continued to pursue his church-reform proposals, though their chances of realization were slim. In a conversation with Bunsen in September 1857, just days before the onset of his final illness, the King continued to argue vigorously for the notions that he had developed under radically different political circumstances ten years earlier.[60] It might be suggested that he thought of his church reform in architectonic terms, like the building of a cathedral, which is only natural considering his architectural passions.[61] But this analogy is not entirely exact. In contrast to Bunsen, Frederick

---

[59] AKO, FW IV to *Staatsministerium*, 13. Dec. 1841, GStA Berlin, Rep. 84a Nr. 11951; 'Petition der Berliner Jüdischen Gemeinde der Ältesten und Vorsteher der Judenschaft an das Staats-Ministerium', 7 Mar. 1842, ibid.; and the *Votum* of Rochow and Eichhorn, 12 Apr. and 29 Oct. 1842, ibid. My thanks to Dr Manfred Jehle (Berlin) for making these documents available to me. See also, among many studies, David Sorkin, *The Transformation of German Jewry, 1780–1840* (Oxford, 1987); Reinhard Rürup, *Emanzipation und Antisemitismus: Studien zur 'Judenfrage' der bürgerlichen Gesellschaft* (Göttingen, 1975), esp. 20, 26–8; Thomas Nipperdey, *Deutsche Geschichte 1800–1866: Bürgerwelt und starker Staat* (Munich, 1983), 248–50.

[60] F. Bunsen, *Bunsen: Aus seinen Briefen*, iii. 500–1; FW IV to Bunsen, 30 Sept. 1857, GStA Merseburg, HA Rep. 50 J Nr. 244a, Bl. 218.

[61] Among various sources, see Ernst Lewalter, *Friedrich Wilhelm IV.: Das Schicksal eines Geistes*

[cont. on p. 91]

William said, he did not want to build a new structure; rather, he believed that he had been called to restore structures that already existed.[62] Still, it is not entirely coincidental that he began to work on detailed plans for a great Protestant cathedral in Berlin at the same time that he was developing his church-renewal schemes. A cabinet order of January 1842 started the process, and during the next few years several elaborate plans were worked out, most of which called for a basilica to be built on the Museum Island between Schinkel's museum and the royal palace. But the plans were never realized, and the project was officially suspended after the revolution of 1848. His church-renewal plans suffered a similar fate.[63]

Frederick William never intended to impose his church proposals upon the Evangelical Church, despite Ludwig von Gerlach's fears that he would do just that.[64] At the very beginning of his reign the King had been quite eager to summon a General Synod of the Evangelical Church to discuss his reform ideas; but his advisers had dissuaded him from that step, and so he decided to wait until the initiative for renewal had come from the church itself.[65] There were, however, limits to his passivity, and after 1841 he constantly tried to act as a subtle catalyst of church reform by establishing provisional structures or institutions and by encouraging other activities that might lead to the desired result. He himself described this as a gradual process of '*Granulation*' which he thought would lay the groundwork for more thoroughgoing change. One of the best examples of this 'granulation' process was his attempted resurrection of the Order of the Swan (*Schwanenorden*) in 1843–4.[66]

In the previous chapter we alluded to Frederick William's desire to restore or even create new orders which could reacquaint nineteenth-century Germans with the chivalric, service-oriented ethos of the Middle Ages. Among other things, he believed that such orders, and other organizations devoted to good works and Christian charity, could help alleviate the growing social problems of the 1840s. Accordingly, he hit upon the idea of restoring 'the oldest order of Our house, the Society of the Order of the Swan', which had been established in 1443 but had declined into desuetude. Frederick William wanted to invest the order with new life as an organization of fervent Christians devoted to good works.[67] A typical

(Berlin, 1938), 281–3; L. Dehio, *Friedrich Wilhelm IV. von Preußen: Ein Baukünstler der Romantik* (Munich, 1961), 34–42.

[62] FW IV to Bunsen, 10 June 1855, in Ranke, *Briefwechsel*, 357; cf. Schmidt-Clausen, *Einheit*, 293.

[63] Carl-Wolfgang Schümann, *Der Berliner Dom im 19. Jahrhundert* (Berlin, 1980), 51–84; Karl–Heinz Klingenburg, *Der Berliner Dom: Bauten, Ideen und Projekte vom 15. Jahrhundert bis zur Gegenwart* (Berlin [East], 1987), 96–117; Brennecke, 'Kirche', 242–4.

[64] Hans-Christof Kraus, 'Ernst Ludwig von Gerlach: Politisches Denken und Handeln eines preußischen Altkonservativen' (Phil. Diss.; 2 vols.; Göttingen, 1991), i. 195–7, ii. 145–6.

[65] Heckel, 'Kirchenverfassungsentwurf', 440; FW IV, second *Aufsatz* of 1845–6, in E. L. von Gerlach, *Aufzeichnungen*, ii. 479.

[66] Mehlhausen, 'Friedrich Wilhelm IV.', 201–2.

[67] See Frederick William's proclamation of Christmas Eve 1843, in *Reden und Trinksprüche Sr. Majestät Friedrich Wilhelm des Vierten, Königes von Preußen* (Leipzig, 1855), 254–7; for background on the King's decision, see F. Bunsen, *Bunsen: Aus seinen Briefen*, ii. 296; and esp. Jürgen Reulecke, *Sozialer Frieden durch soziale Reform: Der Centralverein für das Wohl der arbeitenden Klassen in der*

[*cont. on p. 92*]

product of his fertile imagination and of his desire to re-create a spirit of Christian communitarianism in a de-Christianized, individualist age, the Order of the Swan was to be open to all confessions and all orders of society.[68] Frederick William himself admitted in a private communication to *Kultusminister* Eichhorn that the order would in fact be doing things that should be coming directly from the church itself. Specifically, the Order of the Swan should be regarded 'as something provisional' until the church itself had created 'something more spiritual and more complete'. In other words, the Order of the Swan would fulfill the functions of an active diaconate—that is, of a group of ordained men and women devoted to Christian service—until such time as a truly apostolic church had been re-established.[69]

Despite Frederick William's hopes, the Order of the Swan was opposed from the outset not only by liberals and rationalists but also by people like the Prince of Prussia, who regarded it as an ill-conceived expression of his brother's overheated fantasy.[70] Bunsen himself, whom Frederick William consulted extensively in the spring of 1844, hoped that the order could be made to serve practical, attainable ends, and thus appear palatable to the public.[71] In fact, it never managed to get off the ground, and gradually the King was diverted by other, more pressing concerns.[72] The charitable activities that he envisaged for the Order of the Swan were largely carried on, though, by the hospital and nursing school that he established on the Köpenicker Feld in the south of Berlin in 1845. To be administered by Evangelical deaconesses 'in the fashion of deaconesses in apostolic congregations', Bethany House (*Haus Bethanien*), as it came to be called, was one of the most enduring of Frederick William's achievements.[73]

Ecclesiastical Politics in *Vormärz* Prussia: Friends of Light and a General Synod

Although Frederick William had not attained his original object of summoning a General Synod of the church during the first years of his reign, he continued to believe that it would be important to convene smaller synods as consultative bodies. *Kultusminister* Eichhorn was opposed to such synods, and did his best to delay their

---

Frühindustrialisierung (Wuppertal, 1983), 63–4. See also Adolph Stillert, *Der Schwanenorden: Seine Geschichte, Statuten und Bedeutung* (Berlin, 1844), copy in BayHStA, MA III 2622.

[68] *Rundschreiben* of Thile, 1 July 1844, GStA Merseburg, Geheimes Zivilkabinett 2.2.1. Nr. 1945, Bl. 2–4; draft statutes, 24 Dec. 1843, ibid., Bl. 5–12.

[69] AKO, FW IV to Eichhorn, 24 Dec. 1843, GStA Merseburg, HA Rep. 50 E 3 Nr. 14, Bl. 175–6.

[70] Varnhagen von Ense, *Tagebücher*, vi. 254 (6 June 1849); Schnabel, *Deutsche Geschichte*, iv. 536–7; Walter Bußmann, 'Probleme einer Biographie Friedrich Wilhelms IV.', in Büsch (ed.), *Friedrich Wilhelm IV. in seiner Zeit*, 34–5; Reulecke, *Sozialer Frieden*, 64.

[71] Bunsen to Frances Bunsen, 21 Apr. 1844, in F. Bunsen, *Bunsen: Aus seinen Briefen*, ii. 259; also his various memos and reports, ibid. ii. 295–304.

[72] Reulecke, *Sozialer Frieden*, 66–7.

[73] On the foundation of *Haus Bethanien*, see FW's AKO, 15 July 1845, and his decree of 20 Dec. 1851, in Friedrich Wilhelm IV., *Reden und Trinksprüche*, 261–3, 266–7. The young Theodor Fontane worked as a pharmacist at Bethany House; see his interesting description in *Von Zwanzig bis Dreißig*, ed. Walter Keitel (Frankfurt am Main, 1980), 348–61.

convocation, probably because he feared that they would quickly give voice to dangerous constitutional ideas. This was precisely what happened at the district and provincial synods that convened after 1843.[74] And the questions of church organization and representation that emerged at these and other forums were of more than merely ecclesiastical interest. By the mid-1840s, religious discussions had become inseparable from politics in Prussia. Pastors and theologians had become increasingly politicized, and religious disputes had political implications that reached far beyond the church.[75] The tendency to dress what should have been normal politics in theological garb was not lost on Germany's various governments, which in fact were keenly aware of the real political dimension of religious controversy. In August 1845, for example, Cabinet Minister Thile prepared a report for the King in which he warned against liberal tendencies in contemporary religious life and urged the King to move vigorously against them, as they were using religion as a 'convenient banner' to advertise their political doctrines.[76] Despite Thile's warning, Frederick William responded rather unclearly and ambivalently to the new religious discussions and especially the new religious movements of the 1840s. On the whole, as we saw in his response to the Cologne Troubles, he tended to oppose attempts by bureaucrats to persecute religious minorities and impose religious beliefs and practices upon unwilling populations, such as those 'Old Lutherans' who had refused to accept the union of 1817.[77] However, the policies of official Protestantism faced a far more serious challenge in the 1840s from a new association called the 'Friends of Light' (*Lichtfreunde*), one of the most remarkable and interesting religious movements of the *Vormärz* years.

Along with Johannes Ronge's 'German Catholics', who broke with official Catholicism in 1844, the Friends of Light have been described as 'the last blossoms of popular rationalism' in pre-1848 German religious life.[78] The Friends began in 1841 as an attempt by several pastors in the Prussian province of Saxony to defend themselves and like-minded colleagues against the onslaught of neo-pietist orthodoxy. Frederick William IV may have been personally a tolerant man, and entirely capable of tolerant religious measures; after his accession to the throne, however, his advisers and officials, especially Eichhorn in the *Kultusministerium*, proceeded relentlessly to impose the orthodoxy of the official church, extend their own influence over new church appointments, and harass supporters of old-fashioned theological rationalism. At the forefront of this campaign were Ernst Wilhelm Hengstenberg and his associates in the circle of the *Evangelische Kirchen-Zeitung*, including Ludwig von Gerlach.[79] The official censure of a rationalist Magdeburg pastor, Wilhelm Franz Sintenis, in 1840 seemed to be a sign of the times, and spurred

[74] Heckel, 'Kirchenverfassungsentwurf', 440–1; Jensen, 'Reform', 150.

[75] Bigler, *Politics*, 193 *et passim*; Trauttmansdorff to Metternich, 10 May 1846, HHStA, St. K. Preußen, Karton 190, Politische Berichte 1846 V–VIII, fol. 20ʳ–25ʳ.

[76] Memorandum of 16 Aug. 1845, GStA Merseburg, Rep. 92 Ludwig Gustav von Thile C 7, Bl. 88.

[77] John E. Groh, *Nineteenth Century Protestantism: The Church as Social Model* (Washington, DC, 1982), 174–9.

[78] Ibid. 196.   [79] Bigler, *Politics*, 53–75, 155, 190–4.

like-minded colleagues in the region to action, among them the charismatic Leberecht Uhlich and the free-thinking Halle pastor G. A. Wislicenus. In 1841 they and their friends established the 'Protestant Friends', popularly known as the 'Friends of Light'. Membership in the organization was open to laypersons, and well-attended meetings devoted to the discussion of political as well as religious matters quickly began to spring up. By 1845 Uhlich was describing the neo-pietists as a 'hateful party', while he and his colleagues were speaking openly to increasingly large rallies about transforming Protestantism into a genuine 'people's church'.[80]

Frederick William IV at first responded uncertainly to the Friends of Light. His initial inclination had been to do nothing against Uhlich and Wislicenus, but as the debate between the Friends of Light and their enemies, especially in the Hengstenberg camp, escalated, the King's advisers urged him to take quick and decisive action.[81] Finally, in August 1845 further public assemblies of the Friends of Light were forbidden. In that same year, though, Uhlich got permission to become pastor of a large church in Magdeburg, where he continued to be both popular and successful. The conservatives around Hengstenberg and Ludwig von Gerlach thereupon arranged for an investigation of Uhlich and his suspension from church office in September 1847.[82]

Ironically, Uhlich's suspension came almost half a year after the government had issued its Toleration Edict, which had extended the freedom of conscience guaranteed in the Law Code of 1794 to include freedom of confession by declaring that those who refused to accept the precepts of official Protestantism could freely leave the state church and without penalty create new 'religious associations'. With this measure Frederick William may have been interested in making a concession to liberal views of toleration, but he also had other motives: the regenerated apostolic church of the future, he believed, should only include people who in his view were genuine and committed believers. In fact, then, there were real limits to his toleration of divisions within official Protestantism, as his own response to the Uhlich case demonstrated.[83] As long as people obeyed church authorities, he wrote in April

    [80] Ibid. 194–218. See also Hans Rosenberg, 'Theologischer Rationalismus und vormärzlicher Vulgärliberalismus', in id., *Politische Denkströmungen im deutschen Vormärz* (Göttingen, 1972), 41–7; Herbert Obenaus, *Anfänge des Parlamentarismus in Preußen bis 1848* (Düsseldorf, 1984), 595–7; Jörn Brederlow, *'Lichtfreunde' und 'Freie Gemeinden': Religiöser Protest und Freiheitsbewegung im Vormärz und in der Revolution von 1848/49* (Munich, 1976), 26–48.

    [81] Thile to FW IV, 20 Oct. 1844, GStA Merseburg, Rep. 92 Ludwig Gustav von Thile C 7, Bl. 59–60; Adolf Heinrich Graf von Arnim-Boitzenburg to FW IV, Oct. 1844 (draft), BLHA, Pr. Br. Rep. 37 Herrschaft Boitzenburg, Nachlaß Adolf Heinrich Graf von Arnim-Boitzenburg Nr. 3940.

    [82] Heinrich von Treitschke, *Deutsche Geschichte im neunzehnten Jahrhundert*, 2nd edn., v: *Bis zur März-Revolution* (Leipzig, 1894), 360; Bigler, *Politics*, 222–7; Hermann Wagener, *Erlebtes: Meine Memoiren aus der Zeit von 1848 bis 1866 und von 1873 bis jetzt* (2 vols.; Berlin, 1884), i. 3–4; E. L. von Gerlach, *Aufzeichnungen*, i. 494.

    [83] Text of the Toleration Edict in the Patent of 30 Mar. 1847, in E. R. Huber and W. Huber, *Staat und Kirche*, i. 454–5; Ludwig von Gerlach's views in E. L. von Gerlach, *Aufzeichnungen*, i. 478–9. See also the analyses in Treitschke, *Deutsche Geschichte*, v. 358–60; E. R. Huber, *Verfassungsgeschichte*, ii. 279–80; Bigler, *Politics*, 252–3; Groh, *Protestantism*, 199; Nipperdey, *Deutsche Geschichte*, 435; Schmidt-Clausen, *Einheit*, 279–80; Mehlhausen, 'Friedrich Wilhelm IV.', 204–5.

1847, they would not be bothered for their particular views. But Uhlich had gone beyond acceptable limits. He could think whatever he liked, but he could not preach his ideas and remain within the Evangelical Church. Besides, he could always take advantage of the Toleration Edict and leave the church.[84] When Frederick William visited Magdeburg in the autumn of 1847, a deputation of municipal officials presented him a petition signed by 20,000 inhabitants of the city in support of Uhlich and calling, among other things, for liturgical freedom within the church. The King again called attention to his Toleration Edict, and then he pointed out that he was not impressed by 20,000 signatures: 'the history of the church shows that truth never resides in the masses; rather, truth itself must force its way into the masses'.[85]

In his response to the Magdeburg officials Frederick William noted that a 'very free church constitution is being prepared'. He also pointed to his revival of district and provincial synods, and above all to the convening of a General Synod the year before.[86] In fact, however, the meeting of the General Synod had turned out to be a grievous disappointment to him. The Synod was, of course, not a popularly elected body, but was composed of seventy-five lay and clerical delegates designated by the King at the suggestion of provincial authorities. Insightfully described by one scholar as an 'Assembly of Notables', the General Synod included representatives of most of the major conflicting elements within the Evangelical Church.[87] The King had pinned many of his hopes for apostolic reform on this body, which met in the chapel of the royal palace in Berlin in June 1846. Almost immediately, however, things began to go wrong for him. Municipal authorities from several Prussian cities directed addresses to the Synod, calling upon it to implement various liberal reforms in the church. Frederick William denounced these addresses in bitter terms, arguing that, though the church should indeed reform itself from within, 'It should do so not by following the path of false freedom but rather by following the path of lawful freedom. It cannot be reformed on the basis of new or arbitrary teachings, but only on the basis of our ancient faith, upon which the whole Church of Christ has been built, and which has been established for all time.'[88] Even worse, though, was the way in which the Synod itself proceeded in directions that the King found appalling. One Synod committee, for example, prepared a report supporting a general reform of the church's structure, but not at all along the 'apostolic' lines that the King had envisaged. Rather, it called for the Evangelical Church in Prussia's eastern provinces to supplement the existing system of consistories with popularly elected presbyteries at

[84] FW IV to Thile, 19 Apr. 1847, GStA Merseburg, Rep. 92 Ludwig Gustav von Thile C 7, Bl. 172; AKO, FW IV to Eichhorn, 30 Apr. 1847, in *Reden und Trinksprüche*, 223–4.

[85] Friedrich Wilhelm IV., *Reden und Trinksprüche*, 228.   [86] Ibid. 227.

[87] Mehlhausen, 'Friedrich Wilhelm IV.', 205. See also Johannes Heintze, 'Die erste preußische Generalsynode 1846', *Jahrbuch für Berlin-Brandenburgische Kirchengeschichte*, 41 (1966), 122–41; Heckel, 'Kirchenverfassungsentwurf', 440–3; Schaper, *Kirchenpolitik*, 102–4; Groh, *Protestantism*, 207–8; Bigler, *Politics*, 183–5; Jensen, 'Reform', 151.

[88] Statement of 22 June 1846, in Friedrich Wilhelm IV., *Reden und Trinksprüche*, 222; also E. L. von Gerlach, *Aufzeichnungen*, i. 448.

the local level and a hierarchy of synods that would genuinely reflect and represent the opinions of church members.[89] Since 1835 the two westernmost provinces of the kingdom, the Rhineland and Westphalia, had maintained a system of synods based on the free choice of church members, and many elements of that system should now, according to the General Synod, be extended to the rest of the monarchy. Frederick William was horrified by this suggestion. He loathed the Rhenish-Westphalian *Kirchenordnung*, which in his view was based on parliamentary theories of representation.[90] Disappointed with the Synod's failure to come up with ideas that were to his liking, Frederick William dismissed the body on 29 August 1846 without accepting any of its recommendations. The Gerlachs and their allies, including Hengstenberg and the *Evangelische Kirchen-Zeitung*, had bitterly opposed the Synod, and with its dissolution Evangelical orthodoxy had won a clear victory.[91]

Not all of the General Synod's decisions, however, were entirely in vain. In late January 1848 the King did respond positively to its proposal that a Supreme Consistory be set up as the Evangelical Church's top administrative body. It turned out to be exceedingly short-lived. The revolution of March 1848, with its demands for the removal of the heavy hand of the state from church affairs, made the King's decision of January nugatory. Accordingly, in April the Supreme Consistory was dissolved. Equally dead, it seemed, were the King's dreams of an apostolic regeneration of the church. But, as we have observed on several occasions, Frederick William IV was a stubborn man, and not inclined to make permanent concessions to what Friedrich Julius Stahl called 'the negative spirit of the age'.[92] After the revolutions of 1848 and the introduction of a revised constitution in early 1850, the King reverted to his Supreme Consistory idea, and in a decree of 29 June 1850 established a more or less autonomous 'Supreme Evangelical Church Council' (*Evangelischer Oberkirchenrat*) to administer the affairs of the church. At the same time, consistent with his determination to encourage vigorous, autonomous church life at the local level, Frederick William instructed the new Church Council to initiate a reorganization of local church structures in the kingdom's six eastern provinces. It was, however, only completed in 1873, twelve years after the King's death; and he was never able to achieve his dream, so critical to his entire monarchical project, of an anti-revolutionary, Christian-German state based on the apostolic regeneration of religious life.[93]

From his comfortable official residence in London's prestigious Carlton Terrace, Bunsen observed developments in *Vormärz* Prussia with growing disquiet. He was glad to be in London and not in Berlin or Potsdam. He was aware that he had many

[89] E. L. von Gerlach, *Aufzeichnungen*, i. 621–5.   [90] Heckel, 'Kirchenverfassungsentwurf', 442.

[91] E. L. von Gerlach, *Aufzeichnungen*, i. 452; Leopold von Gerlach to Ludwig von Gerlach, 12 May 1847, GA, Fasz. CT; Kraus, 'Gerlach', i. 235–7, ii. 151–3.

[92] E. R. Huber and W. Huber, *Staat und Kirche*, i. 625–7; Heckel, 'Kirchenverfassungsentwurf', 443; Schaper, *Kirchenpolitik*, 103–4.

[93] E. R. Huber and W. Huber, *Staat und Kirche*, ii: *Staat und Kirche im Zeitalter des Hochkonstitutionalismus und des Kulturkampfs 1848–1890* (Berlin, 1976), 299, 314–18.

enemies there, and he was aware too of the exceptional, indeed exhausting, demands that Frederick William IV put upon his advisers; on the occasion of one visit to Potsdam, he wrote to his wife 'that if I stayed here I would go under in a few years'.[94] Moreover, as the years advanced he identified himself increasingly with the culture, values, and political institutions of the country to which he had been sent as guardian of Prussia's interests. But even from the distance of London he remained in close contact with events in Germany, and above all he was still an indispensable adviser to his sovereign.

Bunsen and his royal master never doubted their mutual respect and loyalty, but increasingly they began to realize that their respective views on church and state were moving apart. Indeed, in 1847 Bunsen admitted that since 1843 'the King has moved much more decisively to the right than I have to the left'.[95] As Bunsen moved in the direction of a moderate, constitutional-monarchical liberalism, he became increasingly worried about Frederick William's tendency to ignore what he later called the 'signs of the times'.[96] Thus, as we saw earlier, he worried rightly that the 'medieval' elements in the proposed statutes of the Order of the Swan would condemn it to unpopularity: 'The whole tendency of our age will cause it to be rejected, and it will disappear without trace into history.'[97] But it was above all in the area of constitutional politics and, later, the politics of German unity that the differences between the two friends manifested themselves most obviously.

As early as 1842 Bunsen was becoming convinced that Frederick William's government was out of touch with growing and, in his view, legitimate demands for constitutional reform and representative institutions. He was alarmed by the King's apparent indifference to these matters; so, when he visited the Prussian capital in the spring of 1844, he brought with him various constitutional proposals which Alexander von Humboldt described as 'more enlightened [*freisinniger*] than one would ever have imagined'.[98] Although Bunsen's efforts to convince the King of the urgency of the situation fell on deaf ears, during the next three and half years the indefatigable diplomat produced seven long documents on constitutional reform in Prussia.[99] All were without effect. But, as we already know, set-backs never deterred the Prussian minister to the Court of St James's. Prince Albert once reported that after the explosion of 1848 Bunsen produced at least five detailed versions of a constitution for a united Germany.[100]

In the midst of that revolutionary year, Frederick William again summoned Bunsen back to Prussia to help him get through his various troubles. When he got

---

[94] Bunsen to Frances Bunsen, 20 May 1844, in F. Bunsen, *Bunsen: Aus seinen Briefen*, ii. 265.

[95] Quoted in Groß, 'Beziehungen', 147.

[96] Christian Carl Josias Bunsen, *Die Zeichen der Zeit: Briefe an Freunde über die Gewissensfreiheit und das Recht der christlichen Gemeinde* (2 vols.; Leipzig, 1855–6).

[97] F. Bunsen, *Bunsen: Aus seinen Briefen*, ii. 303.

[98] Varnhagen von Ense, *Tagebücher*, ii. 354 (31 Aug. 1844).

[99] F. Bunsen, *Bunsen: Aus seinen Briefen*, ii. 281–95; Ranke, *Briefwechsel*, 116–20; Groß, 'Beziehungen', 146–7.

[100] Groß, 'Gesandte', 22–3; H. Becker, 'Bunsen', 125–9.

there, Bunsen wrote to his wife, he found that the King's personal feelings for him remained unchanged.[101] But the men's views continued to diverge, and to these differences were added disagreements over Prussia's future role in Germany. In February 1849 Frederick William summed up his relationship in a letter to Prince Albert: 'Bunsen is still my friend and enjoys my complete, old, undivided loyalty. All the same, we are in utter disagreement about *Politica Germanica*.'[102]

So Bunsen remained a special friend, but his real influence was limited. During the decisive years of Frederick William's reign he was not as important as other royal confidants. He was a sounding-board for Frederick William's ideas, rather than a decisive shaper of policy. Despite his disappointments, though, Bunsen remained an optimist, convinced that somehow things would work out for the best. While visiting Berlin in 1844, he wrote that it sometimes seemed that the King and his court were impervious to the gathering crisis, that they were 'gliding down a stream', blissfully unaware of the waterfalls that awaited them. 'Often am I haunted by the spectre of the court and ministry at Paris in 1788–9; but then, I say again, Prussia is not France, and, above all, Frederick William IV is not Louis XVI.'[103] In the next three chapters we shall have an opportunity to assess the adequacy of Bunsen's analysis.

---

[101] Bunsen to Frances Bunsen, 7 Aug. 1848, in F. Bunsen, *Memoirs*, ii. 120.
[102] FW IV to Prince Albert, 13 Feb. 1849, GStA Merseburg, HA Rep. 50 J Nr. 355, Bl. 114.
[103] Bunsen to Frances Bunsen, 20 May 1844, in F. Bunsen, *Memoirs*, ii. 40.

5
Monarchy and Society, 1840–1847

'This Book Belongs to the King'

In Berlin, the great literary event of the summer of 1843 was the appearance of two elegantly bound volumes with the curious title *This Book Belongs to the King* (*Dies Buch gehört dem König*). After all, any book by Bettine von Arnim was bound to attract attention. One of the major literary figures of her age, Bettine or Bettina—she preferred to be called by her Christian name, and that was the way she signed her letters—was one of those writers who remain well-known less for the enduring quality of their prose than for the wit and brilliance of the personality that emerges from that prose and from the testimony of contemporaries. In 1843 she was 58 years old, a widow and matriarch of comfortable means. A native of Frankfurt am Main, Bettine had largely been brought up by her grandmother, Sophie La Roche, a friend of Goethe. She herself had met that Olympian figure for the first time in 1807, and thereafter venerated him with a passion that bordered on the cultic. Her sister Gunda had married the distinguished legal scholar Friedrich Karl von Savigny, while her brother was the celebrated Romantic poet Clemens Brentano. In 1811 she married Achim von Arnim, her brother's collaborator. After Achim's death twenty years later, Bettine launched her own literary career. Her first book, an epistolary novel entitled *Goethe's Correspondence with a Child* (*Goethes Briefwechsel mit einem Kind*), caused a sensation when it appeared in 1835, and thereafter she was one of Germany's most fêted writers.[1] She had long devoted herself to progressive social and political causes, and in early 1840 she decided that it was her duty to write frankly and directly to Frederick William to remind him of his duty to become a 'people's king', to break loose from the strait-jacket that narrow-minded advisers would lay upon him, and create a happy union of crown and people based on genuinely popular and constitutional values.[2] Earlier she had intervened on behalf of the politically persecuted Brothers Grimm, who in fact ended up being called to the Academy in Berlin. Now, Bettine believed, 'We have to rescue the King!' In early 1841 she asked for and received permission to dedicate a book to him. The result was the 'King's Book' of 1843.[3]

---

[1] For Bettine's biography, see *NDB*, i. 369–71; and esp. Ingeborg Drewitz, *Bettine von Arnim: Romantik—Revolution—Utopie* (Munich, 1982; orig. 1969).

[2] Correspondence in Hartwig Schultz (ed.), *Der Briefwechsel Bettine von Arnims mit den Brüdern Grimm 1838–1841* (Frankfurt am Main, 1985), 202–11. Cf. Ludwig Geiger (ed.), *Bettine von Arnim und Friedrich Wilhelm IV.: Ungedruckte Briefe und Aktenstücke* (Frankfurt am Main, 1902), 1–2.

[3] Johann Friedrich Geist and Klaus Kürvers, *Das Berliner Mietshaus 1740–1862: Eine dokumentarische Geschichte der 'von Wülcknitzschen Familienhäuser' vor dem Hamburger Tor, der Proletarisierung des Berliner Nordens und der Stadt im Übergang von der Residenz zur Metropole* (Munich, 1980), 214; Ilse Staff, introd. to Bettine von Arnim, *Dies Buch gehört dem König*, ed. Ilse Staff (Frankfurt am Main, 1982), 15; Geiger (ed.), *Bettine von Arnim*, 14.

The book puzzled a number of critics, for it seemed to be devoid of any kind of coherent structure. Rather, it contained a series of fictitious narratives and dialogues, in which an invented version of Goethe's mother, 'Frau Rat', served as the mouthpiece for Bettine's assorted views, including her vision of the ruler liberated from the shackles of his office and free to be the people's friend. And the people certainly needed a friend. After all, the 1840s were a time of hunger, desperation, and deprivation. Accordingly, at the very end of the book readers encountered a remarkable appendix that was utterly free of the high-blown prose of 'Frau Rat' and her several interlocutors. It contained a simple description of the horrible plight of the inhabitants of the so-called 'Family Houses', dreary tenements crowded together in the 'Vogtland' of north Berlin. The appendix's author was not Bettine herself, but a twenty-three-year-old Swiss student named Heinrich Grunholzer whom Bettine had paid to explore the urban horrors of the rapidly growing metropolis. Grunholzer's description of his experiences was harrowing in its simplicity, directness, and intensity.[4]

Bettine sent a copy of her book to the King, who responded with one of his usual enthusiastic missives, addressing the author as 'Oh child of sweet vines, drenched by summer', but Alexander von Humboldt reported that in fact Frederick William had not understood the book and had only idly leafed through it. Other readers also had a hard time understanding it. Indeed, its obscure style, described by the Interior Minister as 'striking a tone of prophetic ecstasy suitable for a small circle of readers', probably helped to save it from the censors.[5] So Bettine's book elicited a mixed reaction from the public, and a puzzled one from the King. But she was not to be deterred. With her unflagging optimism and untiring zeal, she was determined that both the King and the poor should be rescued. By 1844 she was collecting great quantities of data for a new book on the condition of impoverished Silesian weavers. This *Book of the Poor* (*Armenbuch*) was never published. When the Silesian weavers rose in despair, she became fearful that the King's officials might regard her as implicated in the revolt, and so she decided not to proceed with her plans.[6] In dealing with the Silesian problem, Frederick William IV had not taken the social and political initiatives that she thought were essential. Nevertheless, Bettine remained convinced that the King was a noble figure, a man who still could be rescued, who could, indeed, save his country from disorder.[7]

The story of Bettine von Arnim and the King of Prussia points to the paradoxical and complex situation of monarchical authority in a time of intensifying social conflict, economic uncertainty, and demands for radical political change. Like so many

---

[4] B. von Arnim, *Dies Buch*, 403–43; also in Geist and Kürvers, *Mietshaus*, 9–25, and compared to Grunholzer's diary, ibid. 218–31.

[5] Quoted in Christa Wolf, 'Nun ja! Das nächste Leben geht aber heute an: Ein Brief über die Bettine', in Bettina von Arnim, *Die Günderode* (Frankfurt am Main, 1983), 559; Geiger (ed.), *Bettine von Arnim*, 44–6.

[6] Bettina von Arnim, *Bettina von Arnims Armenbuch*, ed. Werner Vordtriede (Frankfurt am Main, 1981), 42–5.

[7] Ibid. 72–7; Bettine von Arnim to FW IV, 14 Dec. 1844, in Geiger (ed.), *Bettine von Arnim*, 78.

liberals, Bettine von Arnim hoped for radical initiatives from Frederick William IV; and like so many of her contemporaries, she was aware of the vast gulf that divided an increasingly petrified governing system from the great mass of ordinary—and on the whole politically loyal—Prussian subjects. Despite her hopes for Frederick William, however, Bettine barely knew the man, having gone out of her way to avoid meeting him in person. She never understood the King's own monarchical project, which was based on a vision radically different from her own. The actual (and repressive) responses of Prussian authorities in 1843–4 to the growing threat of social upheaval were powerful reminders that timely responses to the problems of the 1840s were not in sight. The government of Frederick William IV was required to react to real social needs and also to intensifying public demands for genuine political participation. What future would the monarchical principle have in a society that was changing so rapidly? It was in response to this question that Frederick William IV would shape his monarchical project.

In his own way, ironically enough, Frederick William did want to be a 'people's king'. Like Bettine, he too yearned for a happy union of prince and people, but he wanted to achieve that union on his own terms. Unhappily for him, few contemporary observers really understood what he was trying to do. One of the few who did was his friend Radowitz, and he was not at all optimistic about the King's chances of success. In a letter of January 1844, Radowitz noted that Frederick William was opposed by all three of the major political forces at work in Prussian society: 'the monarchical absolutists, the liberal constitutionalists, and the radical revolutionary party'. A king who wanted to impose his own vision and his own will in the face of such massive opposition 'will offend everyone, will be misunderstood everywhere, and will be traduced everywhere'. How could Frederick William prevail against such odds? To do so would require 'a political hero, and like military heroes these have always been exceedingly rare'.[8] Could the King be such a heroic individual? Could he succeed in becoming a 'people's king' by the grace of God and not of constitutions or parliaments? How, in other words, would monarchical institutions and monarchical authority adapt themselves to the new age that was dawning? To consider Frederick William's response, we shall first have to assess the crisis of state and society in Prussia in the last years before 1848. Then we shall turn to an evaluation of the *public* techniques by which monarchical values were sustained in the 1840s, before evaluating popular feelings about the King himself. Finally, we shall review Frederick William's own responses to the social and political pressures of the 1840s, and his efforts to shape them according to the precepts of his monarchical project.

Modernizing Monarchy in a Time of Crisis: Ceremony, Ritual, Public Opinion

In 1816, the first year after the peace of Vienna, the expanded Prussian state

---

[8] Radowitz to Karl von Canitz, 8 Jan. 1844, in Gernot Dallinger, *Karl von Canitz und Dallwitz: Ein preußischer Minister des Vormärz. Darstellung und Quellen* (Cologne, 1969), 126.

contained 10.34 million inhabitants. By 1840 that number had grown to 15.1 million, and by 1846 it exceeded 16 million. This astounding growth in population was, of course, unevenly distributed geographically and socially. Although all eight Prussian provinces showed considerable rates of population increase, those rates were higher in the agrarian eastern regions of the monarchy than in the Rhineland and Westphalia. The reform legislation after 1807 had created a more mobile population, and even the post-1819 Restoration regime had not attempted to eliminate, or even seriously control, the free movement of population. Although one should not exaggerate the growth of urban areas relative to society at large, some cities did experience massive population-increases as a result of internal migrations. (Movement away from cities often compensated for movement into them; the total percentage of the urban population in Prussia remained fairly stable at 26 to 28 per cent from 1816 to 1846.) Berlin, whose population grew from less than 200,000 in 1816 to 330,000 in 1840 and 408,000 in 1846, was undoubtedly the most spectacular example of rapid urbanization in those years.[9]

Despite the surge in Prussia's population, the structure of society seemed, at least superficially, to have remained fairly 'traditional'. *Vormärz* Prussia was still dominated by agricultural and, to a lesser extent, artisanal production. According to a recent analysis, 2.8 per cent of the population belonged to the upper stratum of big landowners, officials, prominent businessmen (*Wirtschaftsbürger*), officers, and rentiers, with the middle stratum composing 23.5 per cent of the population. The lower stratum embraced 73.8 per cent of the population, and included agricultural labourers of various kinds, unskilled urban workers, journeymen, economically marginalized artisans like weavers, and, at the very bottom, beggars and the desperately poor, who made up 11 per cent of the total population. The largest single groups were unskilled workers of various kinds, including agricultural day-labourers. Only some 272,000 individuals (3.9 per cent) could be described as industrial workers, to whom 54,000 miners (0.8 per cent) might be added; members of both groups often continued to farm on a part-time basis.[10]

Although Prussia in the 1840s was not yet an urban-industrial society, and although social change there was characterized more by continuity than by disruption, it was also a society which was facing increasingly serious problems and challenges. The entire period from 1815 to 1848 was one of 'radical change, full of tensions', and not, as some older accounts suggest, a 'colourless period of trans-

[9] Wolfgang Köllmann (ed.), *Quellen zur Bevölkerungs-, Sozial- und Wirtschaftsstatistik Deutschlands 1815–1875*, i: *Quellen zur Bevölkerungsstatistik Deutschlands 1815–1875*, ed. Antje Kraus (Boppard am Rhein, 1980), 153–230, esp. 189–94, 225–30; Wolfram Fischer, Jochen Krengel, and Jutta Wietog, *Sozialgeschichtliches Arbeitsbuch*, i: *Materialien zur Statistik des Deutschen Bundes 1815–1870* (Munich, 1982), 22–3, 30, 32, 36–42; Hermann Beck, 'Conservatives, Bureaucracy, and the Social Question in Prussia (1815–1848)' (Ph.D. thesis; Los Angeles, 1988), 151.

[10] Jürgen Kocka, 'Zur Schichtung der preußischen Bevölkerung während der industriellen Revolution', in Wilhelm Treue (ed.), *Geschichte als Aufgabe: Festschrift für Otto Büsch zu seinem 60. Geburtstag* (Berlin, 1988), 367–75.

ition'.[11] And at no time was that radical change more obvious or traumatic than in the 1840s. Moreover, the crisis of that decade was complicated by the coexistence of patterns of social continuity with dramatic social change, of tradition with innovation, of stagnation with breakthrough.[12] Prussia has often been described as a state with a 'Janus face', looking backward and forward at the same time, and for no period is that description more apt than for the 1840s. As a result, it is exceptionally hard to find 'conclusive explanations' for what happened in those years.[13]

Bearing these caveats in mind, for reasons of analytic convenience we shall identify six major characteristics of the 1840s, all of which contributed to the atmosphere of change, instability, and, finally, crisis and revolution that typified those years and confronted the Prussian monarchy with immense challenges:

(1) After 1807 Prussian agriculture had been dramatically transformed. Though it might be an exaggeration to describe that process as an 'agricultural revolution', there can be little doubt that the Prussian countryside, especially in East Elbia, witnessed the emergence of a capitalist agriculture to which many members of the region's old agrarian élite adapted themselves quite successfully, even as they tried to maintain older forms of patrimonial authority over their labourers and other peasants. But losers as well as winners had emerged from that process, which created new forms of insecurity on the countryside.[14] Although the agricultural economy as a whole did well in the half-century from 1825 to 1875, short-term fluctuations could

[11] Hans-Ulrich Wehler, *Deutsche Gesellschaftsgeschichte* (Munich, 1987–), ii: *Von der Reformära bis zur industriellen und politischen 'Deutschen Doppelrevolution' 1815–1845/49*, 547.

[12] See the classic older studies by Werner Conze and Reinhart Koselleck, as well as the still-useful analysis by John R. Gillis, *The Prussian Bureaucracy in Crisis 1840–1860: Origins of an Administrative Ethos* (Stanford, Calif., 1971). Recent general accounts include Herbert Obenaus, *Anfänge des Parlamentarismus in Preußen bis 1848* (Düsseldorf, 1984); Wolfgang Hardtwig, *Vormärz: Der monarchische Staat und das Bürgertum* (Munich, 1985); Wolfram Siemann, *Die deutsche Revolution von 1848/49* (Frankfurt am Main, 1985), pt. 2; Rudolf Vierhaus, ' "Vormärz": Ökonomische und soziale Krisen, ideologische und politische Gegensätze', *Francia*, 13 (1985), 355–68; Hermann Beck, 'Conservatives, Bureaucrats, and the Social Question'; Eric Dorn Brose, *The Politics of Technological Change in Prussia: Out of the Shadow of Antiquity, 1809–1848* (Princeton, NJ, 1993). See also the surveys by Thomas Nipperdey, *Deutsche Geschichte 1800–1866: Bürgerwelt und starker Staat* (Munich, 1983), chs. 3 and 4; Wehler, *Gesellschaftsgeschichte*, ii; and James J. Sheehan, *German History 1770–1866* (Oxford, 1989), ch. 8. For surveys of the literature, see, in addition to Wehler, Dieter Langewiesche, 'Die deutsche Revolution von 1848/49 und die vorrevolutionäre Gesellschaft: Forschungsstand und Forschungsperspektiven', *Archiv für Sozialgeschichte*, 21 (1981), 458–98; id., 'Die deutsche Revolution von 1848/49 und die vorrevolutionäre Gesellschaft: Forschungsstand und Forschungsperspektiven, Teil II', *Archiv für Sozialgeschichte*, 31 (1991), 331–443.

[13] Dieter Langewiesche, *Europa zwischen Restauration und Revolution 1815–1849* (Munich, 1985), 127.

[14] Among the more important publications, see, most recently, Robert M. Berdahl, *The Politics of the Prussian Nobility: The Development of a Conservative Ideology 1770–1848* (Princeton, NJ, 1988), ch. 8; also Erich Jordan, *Die Entstehung der konservativen Partei und die preußischen Agrarverhältnisse von 1848* (Munich, 1914); Klaus Klatte, 'Die Anfänge des Agrarkapitalismus und der preußische Konservativismus' (Diss.; Hamburg, 1974); Hanna Schissler, *Preußische Agrargesellschaft im Wandel: Wirtschaftliche, gesellschaftliche und politische Transformazionsprozesse von 1763 bis 1847* (Göttingen, 1978); Hartmut Harnisch, *Kapitalistische Agrarreform und industrielle Revolution: Agrarhistorische Untersuchungen über das ostelbische Preußen zwischen Spätfeudalismus und bürgerlich-demokratischer Revolution von 1848/49 unter besonderer Berücksichtigung der Provinz Brandenburg* (Weimar, 1984); id., 'Zum Stand der Diskussion um die Probleme des "preußischen Weges" kapitalistischer Agrarentwicklung in der deutschen Geschichte', in Gustav Seeber and Karl-Heinz Noack (eds.), *Preußen in der deutschen Geschichte nach 1789* (Berlin

[cont. on p. 104]

be calamitous. The 1842 harvest was bad, but in 1845–6 the situation became disastrous. The result was an agricultural crisis in the 'Hungry Forties' which has rightly been called the 'last agrarian crisis of the old'—that is, pre-industrial or traditional—order.[15]

(2) That crisis overlapped with, and intensified, a crisis in traditional proto-industry and among the artisanate. Many masters and journeymen were suffering horribly. There can also be little doubt that both the breakdown of old guild regulations and population pressures contributed to a dramatic increase in the numbers of both masters and journeymen by the 1840s, which contributed in turn to widespread fears of 'pauperization' and its consequences. Adaptation was not easy, and the social costs were high.[16] Although many artisans were able, in the long run, to adapt themselves to changing conditions, proto-industry—that is, home production, largely in rural regions, on the basis of the 'putting-out' system—was not. Proto-industry was in its death throes in the 1840s; and the most obvious manifestations of those agonies, such as the Silesian weavers' revolt in 1844, attracted a great deal of concern and attention throughout the entire society.[17]

(3) The crises of traditional sectors of the economy at once overlapped with, and were conditioned by, early industrialization, including technological innovation and the enlargement of market areas. The Prussia that lurched into revolution in 1848 was not yet an industrial society, but the groundwork for an industrial revolution had been laid in a quite literal sense: in 1840 there were 185 kilometres of railways in Prussia, which grew to 815 kilometres by 1843, 1,106 by 1845, and 1,424 by 1847.[18] Moreover, industrial development was already beginning to affect the physiognomy of some Prussian cities. The north of Berlin, home of the desperately poor Vogtland, was also the home of the city's burgeoning machine-building industry, associated largely with the name of August Borsig. As early as 1840, one Berlin newspaper wrote that the 'sight of obelisk-shaped smoke-stacks with their columns of smoke swirling into the heavens' had become one of that city's trademarks.[19]

(4) Historians have long been aware of the reawakening of political discussion in Germany after 1830, and of the linkage of that phenomenon to an increasingly assertive, independent, and self-confident *Bürgertum* that was ready to throw off the shackles of bureaucratic tutelage. The world of the *Bürgertum* and of the 'middle-class' society that it sustained was remarkably diffuse and heterogeneous, embracing small-scale shop-owners, state officials, literati, members of 'free' professions, polit-

[East], 1983), 116–44; id., 'Die Gutsherrschaft: Forschungsgeschichte, Entwicklungszusammenhänge und Strukturelemente', *Jahrbuch für Geschichte des Feudalismus*, 9 (1985), 189–240.

[15] Wehler, *Gesellschaftsgeschichte*, ii. 642–8; Berdahl, *Politics*, 306–8.

[16] Ilja Mieck, 'Von der Reformzeit zur Revolution (1806–1847)', in Wolfgang Ribbe (ed.), *Geschichte Berlins* (Munich, 1987), i: *Von der Frühgeschichte bis zur Industrialisierung*, 542–51; Jürgen Bergmann, *Das Berliner Handwerk in den Frühphasen der Industrialisierung* (Berlin, 1973).

[17] Wehler, *Gesellschaftsgeschichte*, ii. 648–51.

[18] Ibid. ii. 615. For the most up-to-date analysis of the politics of railway-building in *Vormärz* Prussia, see Brose, *Politics*, ch. 7.

[19] Quoted in Mieck, 'Reformzeit', 602.

ically engaged Rhenish capitalists, and more politically passive Berlin *Bierbürger*, to name just a few. Despite that diversity, however, it is possible to speak of a bourgeoisie with at least vaguely shared outlooks and values in the *Vormärz* era. As its social, economic, and cultural significance increased, the bourgeoisie insisted on its right to at least a share in governance, and thereby posed a major challenge to the established order of the Prussian state.[20]

(5) All the elements so far mentioned encouraged what can only be described as a 'revolution of political debate' and discussion in the 1840s, a revolution that was sustained by the loosening of censorship regulations after 1841. Although Prussian newspapers, especially in Berlin, remained both boring and heavily censored, a flood of pamphlet and brochure literature bespoke a reawakened and passionate interest in public affairs. As we saw in the previous chapter, those discussions sometimes took the lightly camouflaged form of religious controversy; but increasingly they took place in overtly secular settings, from clubs and associations to casinos and cafés.[21]

(6) The governing system of Prussia, which has been described as a 'monarchic-aristocratic-bureaucratic condominium', was increasingly unable to control or direct events after 1840. The system still had tremendous reserves of influence and coercive authority, especially on the land and in the military, but its actions were increasingly defensive and confused. As its grip seemed to be loosening, as it failed to respond to social problems or to growing demands for political participation, the entire governing system faced a massive 'legitimation crisis'.[22]

As we have already seen, the linchpin of the entire political system was the monarchy and effective monarchical authority. How could that authority be sustained in a time of intensifying, confusing, and overlapping crises? What future was there for the 'monarchical principle' when the legitimacy of the political system as a whole seemed to be declining? These were critical questions that Frederick William IV had to confront if his monarchical project was to be successful. Reconciling his own vision of monarchy with the problems and demands of a society in transition was an amazingly difficult task, and it was compounded by the powerful opposition to which Radowitz had referred in his letter of 1844. Would Frederick William be capable of that 'heroic' action which Radowitz thought would be necessary?

In the first years of his reign, the King had demonstrated repeatedly that he could be very effective at marshalling 'modern' techniques of opinion formation and manipulation on behalf of his monarchical project. As we saw in Chapter 3, he was

[20] Nipperdey, *Deutsche Geschichte*, 400–1. Cf. Jürgen Kocka (with Ute Frevert) (ed.), *Bürgertum im 19. Jahrhundert: Deutschland im internationalen Vergleich* (3 vols.; Munich, 1988), esp. Kocka's introductory essay, 'Bürgertum und bürgerliche Gesellschaft im 19. Jahrhundert: Europäische Entwicklungen und deutsche Eigenarten', i. 11–76.

[21] On bourgeois associational life see, *inter alia*, David Blackbourn, 'The Discreet Charm of the Bourgeoisie: Reappraising German History in the Nineteenth Century', in id. and Geoff Eley, *The Peculiarities of German History: Bourgeois Society and Politics in Nineteenth-Century Germany* (Oxford, 1984), 195–8.

[22] Wehler, *Gesellschaftsgeschichte*, ii. 660–702.

especially skilful as a 'modernizer of tradition'. The most obvious examples were the two ceremonies of homage in 1840, which combined elements of a coronation, ancient oaths of fealty, and a symbolic royal progress through the realm. But as we also saw, Frederick William invested those rituals with new elements, most notably public rhetoric and ritual conversations that were at once highly structured and intensely emotional. It was almost as though he were combining elements of a royal coronation with a contemporary presidential inauguration.

In an influential essay, Clifford Geertz has described the ways by which rulers, through ceremonies like royal progresses, 'take symbolic possession of their realm' and establish themselves symbolically at the 'active centers' of their societies.[23] Through ceremonies like those in Königsberg, Berlin, and Cologne, Frederick William was consciously trying to establish himself symbolically at the centre of Prussian society; but at the same time he was trying to redefine both the centre itself and its relationship to the rest of society. He did not want to 'take possession' of his realm in the fashion of those absolutist monarchs whose practices he deplored, nor did he fully reject his father's 'bourgeois' claim to a private life separate from his public functions. He was, after all, a nineteenth-century monarch. But he was also interested in the reconstitution of monarchy in Prussia, that is, in redefining Geertz's 'animating centers of society' where 'there is both a governing elite and a set of symbolic forms expressing the fact that it is in truth governing'.[24] That redefinition entailed a new vision of the relationship of the monarchic centre to the rest of society; the reconstitution of monarchy, in short, entailed a redefinition of the whole society.

In a hierarchical, patrimonial, but segmented social order based on the maintenance of corporative, *ständisch*, local liberties, a sacral and benign monarchy would at once evoke and guarantee the unity of the whole. To Frederick William, it would symbolize the 'harmony' and the 'reconciliation of extremes' that his teacher Ancillon had always advocated. With his theatrical personality, Frederick William knew that effective public display could affect public opinion, and so he consciously attempted to occupy centre stage in order to call attention to his monarchical project. Ritual public appearances and the public representation of monarchical authority were among the instruments that he used in his effort to reconstitute monarchical authority in a revolutionary age. Some of those instruments—especially his use of the court and court-based ceremonial—remained 'traditional', while others were made possible by recent technological innovations and thus were more obviously 'modern'. His success at orchestrating them was, however, unclear at best.

As we already know, in European societies the royal court had long been one of the traditional vehicles for representing monarchical authority, reinforcing monarchical values within the aristocratic world of court society, and disseminating those values

---

[23] Clifford Geertz, 'Centers, Kings, and Charisma: Reflections on the Symbolics of Power', in Sean Wilentz (ed.), *Rites of Power: Symbolism, Ritual, and Politics since the Middle Ages* (Philadelphia, 1985), 14, 16.
[24] Ibid. 15.

to the broader society outside the court. Obviously, the impact of the court would be greatest in the official *Residenz* itself. Directly or indirectly, large numbers of Berliners—household servants, musicians, cooks, coach-drivers, gardeners, furriers, clothiers, tailors, jewellers, artists, decorators, shop-owners 'by appointment' to the court, to mention just a few—depended for their sustenance upon the presence of the court and the high society that was attached to it. As at most European courts, the main opportunity to dazzle and impress came with the social season, which began with a great royal *cour* on a Thursday in mid-January. A *cour* was an occasion upon which members of court society paid homage to the King and Queen, either by filing past the royal couple or by gathering in designated rooms of the royal palace to be greeted by the King and Queen as they made their *cercle*. The January *cour*, generally called the 'Queen's *cour*', was one of the latter; it was one of the central events on the calendar of Berlin court society. Any individual who wanted to be invited to subsequent court festivities was obliged to attend the Queen's *cour*. It was an occasion of particular importance for those civilians who had been promoted to sufficiently high rank within the bureaucracy to become *hoffähig*, that is, eligible for presentation to the King and Queen at court.[25]

The Queen's *cour* in January inaugurated an annual social season which continued unabated until Lent with a dizzying round of balls, dinners, and concerts. Some events were sponsored by individual members of the royal family, and others by foreign diplomats or high-ranking members of the court society; on average, between 700 and 1,200 guests attended those festivities that took place at the royal palace, though on special occasions the number could be higher.[26] And, of course, all had to be *hoffähig*. Within the court society (*Hofgesellschaft*), moreover, a hierarchical order of preference was strictly observed. Although everyone at the Prussian court was keenly aware of the importance of precedence and etiquette, the actual rules regarding such matters were remarkably vague and very often based on a kind of oral tradition. In fact, no formal, official statement of the rules of court precedence (*Hofrangordnung*) was published between Frederick I's death in 1713 and the establishment of the *Kaiserreich* in the 1870s.[27] But the general rules were well known: 'For civil officials, eligibility for presentation at court extends down to the second class of councillors (the rank of a lieutenant-colonel to colonel); for the military, however, it extends down to second lieutenants. Noted artists and scholars, especially the members of the Peace Class of the order *Pour le mérite*, also have access to court and can be invited to larger festivities as well as to smaller dinners in town and in the country.'[28] Though civilians

---

[25] [Rudolph Graf von Stillfried-Alcantara], *Ceremonial-Buch für den Königlich Preußischen Hof*, vi: *Ceremonial bei Couren* (Berlin, 1877), 31, 37–8.

[26] Graf Lerchenfeld to Ludwig I, 28 Jan. 1841, BayHStA, MA III 2619; Franckenberg to Grand Duke Leopold, 29 Jan. 1841, GLA, Abt. 48/2595.

[27] Konrad Adolf Freiherr von Malsen, report of 2 Aug. 1853, BayHStA, Gesandtschaft Berlin 522; 'Entwurf zum Rang- u. Ceremoniellreglement' (1809), GStA Merseburg, HA Rep. 192 Georg Wilhelm von Raumer IV A, Bl. 548–561ᵛ; [Stillfried-Alcantara], *Ceremonial-Buch*, x: *Hof-Rang-Reglement* (Berlin, 1878), 31–3, 35–42.

[28] Stillfried to Freiherr von Malsen, n. d. (1853), BayHStA, Gesandtschaft Berlin 522.

of bourgeois origin could thus aspire to be admitted to court, the structure of precedence and prestige was strongly tilted towards the military, with military rank being the basis upon which civilian rank was calculated. Indeed, considerations of military sensitivities were among the reasons why an official-precedence list was not published during Frederick William IV's reign; for no Prussian officer, as Stolberg once pointed out, would wish his rank to be compared to a civilian's.[29]

The primacy of military values at the Prussian court was hardly surprising, but it was not unique. Indeed, by the nineteenth century a 'militarization' of monarchical institutions had taken place all over Europe, and kings now almost always appeared in uniform. In Prussia, the same was expected of any male who was presented at court or who attended court balls.[30] Exceptions could be made, however, for certain powerful and influential personalities, or when urgent situations required the relaxation of normal rules of protocol. Thus Ludwig von Gerlach was permitted to appear at the King's table in Sanssouci in early September 1848 wearing a frock-coat; and when Lord Palmerston visited Berlin on one occasion in the 1850s, he refused to wear a uniform and was received anyway. Like most of his fellow monarchs, Frederick William was fascinated by uniforms, whether worn by soldiers, civilian officials, or servants. He had an extremely exacting eye for their details, and he liked to come up with new designs for them.[31]

On the whole, the social life of the Prussian court in the 1840s and 1850s was not especially sumptuous or grandiose. Although most observers noted in the early 1840s that court society had suddenly become much more lively, that was only in comparison with the rather somnolent final years of Frederick William III. From time to time Frederick William IV's court could put on really grand spectacles at the royal palace, of which the most notable were two masked balls in February 1843 and February 1846; the first was supposed to represent a 'Court Festival at Ferrara' during the Renaissance, while the second was based on German fairy-tales. Both were attended by several thousand guests, and included spectacularly costumed participants and *tableaux vivants*.[32]

Grand occasions of this sort, though, were fairly rare at the court of Berlin and Potsdam. Indeed, apart from these two masked balls and the homage ceremonies of 1840, Frederick William IV's reign offered little to compare even with the more spectacular celebrations of his father's time, such as the magnificent 'Lalla Rukh' festival of 1821 and the Festival of the White Rose in 1829. Although he invariably played the cordial host, and always had a sense of occasion when he thought it was

[29] Stolberg to FW IV, 26 Jan. 1854, GStA Merseburg, Geheimes Zivilkabinett 2.2.1. Nr. 3291, Bl. 23ᵛ.

[30] Philip Mansel, 'Monarchy, Uniform and the Rise of the *Frac* 1760–1830', *Past and Present*, 96 (Aug. 1982), 103–32.

[31] Alexander Graf von Keller to Leopold von Gerlach, 30 Aug. 1848, GA, Fasz. X/K/e. For examples of Frederick William's passion for uniforms, see his drawings and sketches of court uniforms in Plankammer Potsdam-Sanssouci, Sammlung Friedrich Wilhelm IV., Mappe X, Umschlag B.

[32] Franckenberg to Grand Duke Leopold, 2 Mar. 1843, GLA, Abt. 48/2597; Alfred von Reumont, *Aus König Friedrich Wilhelms IV. gesunden und kranken Tagen*, 2nd edn. (Leipzig, 1885), 226–8; GStA Merseburg, HA Rep. 192 Georg Wilhelm von Raumer IV A, Bl. 574-585.

important, Frederick William usually disliked these kinds of gatherings. The Queen herself was not at all inclined to be the focus of social life. Moreover, her poor health and morose personality prevented her from assuming such a role, even if she had wanted to do so. In 1844, for example, she was so ill that the King could not hold any court festivals that season. Both King and Queen were absent from Berlin for several months each year, which led many contemporary observers to believe that the royal couple regarded their participation in the rituals of Berlin court life as a burdensome if seasonal concession to the *amour-propre* of the capital city.[33]

During Frederick William's entire reign, in fact, official court society was not an especially effective vehicle for the representation and transmission of monarchical values or loyalties. Although leading elements of the Berlin *Bürgertum*, especially the growing ranks of the 'aristocracy of wealth' of financiers and manufacturers, were increasingly inclined to mimic the tastes, fashions, and even outlooks of the aristocracy, that tendency was not as widespread before 1848 as it was thereafter. Their numbers remained fairly small, and without the proper title and connection they could not gain direct access to the court itself, which was rightly regarded as a bastion of military-aristocratic exclusiveness. That exclusivity seemed to be on the rise in the 1840s, as aristocrats increasingly tried to set themselves apart from commoners; between 1840 and 1857 only four well-off businessmen (*Wirtschaftsbürger*) were ennobled in Prussia.[34] Many of the most active members of the capital's academic, literary, and artistic communities were thus cut off from the court, and were either indifferent or hostile to it. In the words of one especially insightful contemporary, 'Although the most petty lieutenant can claim to be presented at court, out of the entire faculty of the University of Berlin only the current rector is eligible for the same thing.'[35] In addition, during the *Vormärz* years Berlin court society had little impact on manners or outlooks outside the immediate area of the capital itself, mostly because transport and communications remained slow before 1848.[36] Things would only begin to change as sustained industrial growth, the expansion of railways, and the introduction of a parliamentary system began to attract men of affairs from other parts of the country. Until then, Berlin and its court society remained a closed and rather introverted group, and its influence on public opinion remained very limited. Most Berliners were not terribly interested in it.[37]

The King himself disliked not only the winter social whirl in Berlin but also other traditional court-related activities, though he was always punctilious in their observation. Kings were always expected to participate in hunts, which usually overlapped

[33] Franckenberg to Grand Duke Leopold, 15 Feb. 1841, GLA, Abt. 48/2595, and to Alexander von Dusch, 19 Apr. 1844, GLA, Abt. 48/2641.
[34] Friedrich Saß, *Berlin in seiner neuesten Zeit und Entwicklung 1846*, ed. Detlef Heikamp (Berlin, 1983; orig. 1846), 197; Ilsedore Rarisch, *Das Unternehmerbild in der deutschen Erzählliteratur der ersten Hälfte des 19. Jahrhunderts: Ein Beitrag zur Rezeption der frühen Industrialisierung in der belletristischen Literatur* (Berlin, 1977), 6, 103–6.
[35] Saß, *Berlin*, 196.   [36] Reumont, *Aus gesunden und kranken Tagen*, 215.
[37] Ernst Dronke, *Berlin*, ed. Rainer Nitsche (Darmstadt, 1974; orig. 1846), 29–32; Dora Meyer, *Das öffentliche Leben in Berlin im Jahr vor der Märzrevolution* (Berlin, 1912), 65.

with the main social season at court. They were often significant social events; for example, more than 150 people regularly took part in the annual St Hubert's Day hunt in the Grunewald near Berlin. Frederick William himself was an atrocious huntsman who often made jokes about his ineptitude as a marksman, and sometimes contrived to spend hunting-days indoors, detained by 'pressing' state business. On the whole, he preferred more intimate and intellectually stimulating social gatherings, especially in Potsdam.[38]

Of all the traditional forms of public or semi-public monarchical representation, royal patronage of the arts was by far the closest to Frederick William's heart; and in this area he could be rather lavish.[39] Among other things, he tried to create a livelier cultural atmosphere at court by inviting a number of notable personalities to Berlin and Potsdam, though not always with the positive results that he would have liked. One of those individuals, the aged poet and translator Ludwig Tieck, was responsible for some of the more spectacular successes of the court theatre in the early 1840s, including his productions of *Antigone* in October 1841 and *A Midsummer Night's Dream* two years later in the theatre of the Neues Palais near Sanssouci. Felix Mendelssohn, whom Frederick William was constantly trying to induce to return to his native Berlin, composed the music for both occasions.[40]

Even more enduring, perhaps, was Frederick William's support for Berlin's public museums. Since 1839 the general director of Berlin's state museums had been Ignaz von Olfers (1793–1872), a trained physician who turned out to be a brilliant administrator of the arts. He quickly became one of Frederick William's closest confidants, and, along with Alexander von Humboldt, one of the monarch's most reliable links to the world of the arts and sciences. In 1841 the King charged him with the task of turning the Spree island in the heart of Berlin—now known as the Museum Island—'into a sanctuary of the arts and sciences'. Although, as usual, Frederick William's ideas were too grandiose to be realized, Olfers and the architect Stüler worked together to establish the New Museum behind Schinkel's older edifice.[41]

Of all the 'traditional' forms of monarchical representation in Berlin, one in particular stood out for its effectiveness as a shaper of public opinion: the 'Festival of the Coronation and Orders' (*Krönungs- und Ordensfest*), the 'supreme day of celebration

[38] Stolberg to FW IV, 26 Feb. 1846, GStA Merseburg, HA Rep. 50 J Nr. 1413 Vol. II, Bl. 117; FW IV to Elisabeth, 10 Nov. 1846, GStA Merseburg, HA Rep. 50 J Nr. 995 Fasz. 19, Bl. 118–118ᵛ.

[39] During his reign Frederick William acquired 851 paintings and pieces of sculpture. Not surprisingly, Italian motifs were prominent in many of the paintings. 'Verzeichniß der vom 1. Juli 1840 bis ulto. Dezember 1860 von Sr. Majestät dem hochseeligen Könige erworbenen, dem Königlichen Hofmarschall überwiesenen Kunstwerke', GStA Merseburg, Geheimes Zivilkabinett 2.2.1. Nr. 3036, Bl. 1–39.

[40] L. H. Fischer, 'Ludwig Tieck am Hofe Friedrich Wilhelms IV.', in id., *Aus Berlins Vergangenheit: Gesammelte Aufsätze zur Kultur- und Litteraturgeschichte Berlins* (Berlin, 1891), 113, 121; Hellmut Flashar, 'F. Mendelssohn-Bartholdys Vertonung antiker Dramen', in Willmuth Arenhövel and Christa Schreiber (eds.), *Berlin und die Antike. Aufsätze: Architektur—Kunstgewerbe—Malerei—Skulptur—Theater und Wissenschaft vom 16. Jahrhundert bis heute* (Berlin, 1979), 353–6; Staatliche Archivverwaltung der DDR und Staatliche Schlösser und Gärten Potsdam-Sanssouci (eds.), *Potsdamer Schlösser in Geschichte und Kunst*, 2nd edn. (Leipzig, 1984), 112–14.

[41] Helmut Engel, 'Friedrich Wilhelm IV. und die Baukunst', in Otto Büsch (ed.), *Friedrich Wilhelm IV. in seiner Zeit: Beiträge eines Colloquiums* (Berlin, 1987), 181.

for the Prussian monarchy'.[42] The festival took place every year on that Sunday which came closest to 18 January, the anniversary of Frederick I's coronation in 1701. Its purpose was to distribute honours, decorations, and awards to deserving subjects, from princes and ministers to schoolteachers and village pastors, all gathered together in one spot. With its pomp and majesty, it seemed to be a venerable and history-drenched occasion. In fact, the festival was perhaps the best example of an 'invented' tradition in nineteenth-century Prussia. It could trace its lineage to Frederick I's annual celebrations between 1703 and 1712 in honour of the Order of the Black Eagle; but Frederick William I had greatly disliked his father's Baroque splendour, and had stopped celebrating the festival. His two successors did not revive it. After returning to Berlin in 1809, Frederick William III decided to create a special commission to oversee and co-ordinate the complex affairs of the various 'orders' and decorations that existed in the state, among them the Order of the Red Eagle, which had become the second-highest order of the monarchy. Shortly thereafter, the King decided to hold an annual festival in Berlin to recognize the new members of all orders. He also decreed that the festival should be organized like the meeting of a chapter of a knightly order, but 'extended to all orders and decorations, so that all the knights of the Orders of the Black Eagle and the Red Eagle, as well as holders of the Medal of Military Merit solemnly gather together and, as it were, admit their newly decorated members'.[43]

The first festival at Berlin's royal palace had taken place in 1810, and, with the exception of the years 1813–15, it had taken place every year since.[44] Organized by the General Commission on Orders, it had become a resplendent showpiece for the Prussian monarchy. Nothing quite like it existed anywhere else in Europe. Unlike the practice at other courts, it was a celebration of all those individuals who had received honours or decorations in the previous year, regardless of rank or status. The ceremony always took place in the presence of the King and Queen, all the royal princes, the State Ministry, high-ranking officers, and members of the various orders of the Prussian crown: the Black Eagle, the Red Eagle, and the Knights of St John. The festival began with a religious service, after which the recipients of new honours were presented to the royal couple in the Knights' Hall. The ceremony ended with a great banquet to which, in the 1840s, some 800 guests were usually invited. These ceremonies remained essentially unchanged until January 1848, when Frederick William renewed the chapter of the Order of the Black Eagle and removed its initiation rites from the purview of the Coronation Festival.[45] Though all

[42] [Stillfried-Alcantara], *Ceremonial-Buch*, viii: *Ceremonial bei außerordentlichen Festlichkeiten, 8. Ordensfeste* (Berlin, 1877), 215.

[43] Louis Schneider, *Das Preußische Krönungs- und Ordensfest* (Berlin, 1870), 12, 14 (bound in GStA Berlin, I. Hauptabteilung Rep. 90 Nr. 2087).

[44] 'Notizen über die Feier des Krönungs- und Ordens-Festes bis zum Jahre 1840' (1841), GStA Merseburg, Geheimes Zivilkabinett 2.2.1. Nr. 1947, Bl. 78.

[45] L. Schneider, *Ordensfest*, 42. For a typical description of the pre-1848 ceremonial, see *Vossische Zeitung* (25 Jan. 1847); for post-1848 changes, see e.g. 'Anordnung zur Feier des Krönungs- und Ordens-Festes am 20ten Januar 1856', GStA Merseburg, 2.2.1. Nr. 1947, Bl. 170–1.

recipients of the three highest classes of the Order of the Red Eagle were, almost without exception, high-ranking officers and state officials, the Fourth Class and especially the recipients of the General Badge of Honour included a large number of more humble public servants and private citizens. The opportunity for a village mayor, a letter-carrier, a notary, a pastor, a teacher, a master mason, or a physician to go to Berlin and be decorated by the King was, of course, highly coveted, and surely contributed to the prestige of those individuals in their local communities. They could just as surely be relied on as bastions of monarchist sentiment in those communities. Moreover, during the festival strict rules of social precedence and access to court were suspended, which underscored the honour and distinctiveness of the occasion. The recipients of awards, no matter how humble their station, were treated as the King's guests and thereafter 'as the first within their rank and estate'. Thus, its chronicler writes, the festival brought King and court 'into immediate contact with even the most modest stations in life'.[46]

In addition to the provision of court honours, there were, of course, other 'traditional' instruments of what might be called 'monarchical socialization' in Prussian society. Schools, military service, churches (especially in Protestant regions), *Landräte* and other local notables, all were parts of a web of socialization, surveillance, and social control that was especially effective in small towns and in the countryside; in addition, periodic public events always offered opportunities to reinforce popular attachment to the royal house and the person of the monarch. One of the most important of those public occasions was the celebration of the King's birthday on 15 October.

Following his father's practice, Frederick William IV himself usually spent the first part of his birthday with his family in Potsdam, after which they travelled by steamboat to Frederick William III's beloved retreat at Paretz.[47] But where the King treated his birthday as a private affair, everywhere else it was an occasion for lavish displays of patriotism. In many communities the celebrations often began days before, with a series of musical performances and public speeches at the local school, including declamations by the pupils themselves. At the Trier celebration in 1841, for example, a *Gymnasium* pupil spoke on the theme 'What feelings must inspire a German youth on the birthday of his sovereign?' (According to the laudatory report of the district governor, his speech 'bore witness just as much to the speaker's intellectual development as to the excellence of his convictions'.)[48] Celebrations usually concluded on the great day itself with cannon fire, the ringing of church bells, church services, and, in the evening, the illumination of the town and grand public balls. Public officials, who observed these occasions with great care, generally believed that the birthday celebrations represented useful opportunities to sustain and encourage monarchical values, even among people with otherwise dubious political attitudes.

---

[46] L. Schneider, *Ordensfest*, 3, 4.

[47] [Stillfried–Alcantara], *Ceremonial-Buch*, viii: *Geburtsfeste* (Berlin, 1877), 35–6.

[48] Regierungs-Präsident Trier to Gustav Adolf von Rochow, 18 Oct. 1841, GStA Merseburg, Rep. 77 Tit. 499 Nr. 15, Bl. 3–3ᵛ.

After the 1846 celebration, for example, the Police President of Königsberg reported: 'It appears that on such solemn occasions the portion of the local populace which can be described as "liberal" awakens from its evil dream; and thus the proven loyalty which characterized it until a few years ago regains the upper hand.'[49]

From time to time, though, patriotic celebrations like the King's birthday could be transformed into vehicles of political and social protest. In 1841, for instance, a disturbance disrupted the celebrations in Deutz, just across the Rhine from Cologne. At the climax of the main public ceremony, as the crowd was asked to sing 'Hail to Thee in Victor's Laurels' ('Heil Dir im Siegerkranz'), a group of allegedly drunken young men 'from the estate of tradesmen and artisans' began to whistle and shout, after which they interrupted the singing 'by striking up a filthy parody'; whereupon a fight broke out.[50] On such occasions, of course, the *Vormärz* state could make use of a variety of coercive mechanisms, ranging from censorship to the political 'fortress methods' (*Festungspraxis*) of the police, which tended to treat breakers of 'public order' as violators of military security.[51] One should not exaggerate the extent or ferocity of those police-state measures. Between 1837 and 1847 there were only nine investigations of alleged cases of treason in Prussia, and, of special interest to us, 575 investigations of *lèse-majesté* (*Majestätsbeleidigung*).[52] The sentences handed down to those convicted of the latter offence could, however, be rather harsh. In 1846, for example, a tailor named Joseph Jurowski, from Warmbrunn in Silesia, got drunk and said 'our Prussian Freddy is a scoundrel; the King is a scoundrel and a swindler', and for those remarks got eighteen months in gaol. In that same year a certain August Schneider, a barber's assistant in Posen, got two years for saying to a group of soldiers, 'You can forget about our King; he's one rotten apple.' Several people who were convicted of *lèse-majesté* before 1848 had repeated the widespread rumour that the King had a drink problem. In 1847 a Königsberg clerk named Friedrich Wilhelm Stankewicz was handed a twenty-seven-month sentence for exclaiming, in the course of a discussion of recent unrest in Posen, 'The King is a swindler, a scoundrel, and a drunk; down with that dirty rat!' Balthasar Martin, a judicial official (!) from the Halberstadt area, got the comparatively light sentence of only six months for claiming, while sitting in a tavern, that the King drank 'five or six bottles of champagne a day', and then going on to remark: 'How can the King take care of us? He's a lush, the lush of lushes, he only drinks really potent stuff'.[53] Most cases of *lèse-majesté* were like these: that is, they took the form of careless if essentially harmless utterances in public places. Most individuals who were convicted of that offence were

[49] Polizei-Präsident Königsberg to Bodelschwingh, 16 Oct. 1846, ibid., Bl. 81–81ᵛ.

[50] Ibid., Bl. 8–30.

[51] Alf Lüdtke, *Police and State in Prussia, 1815–1850*, trans. Pete Burgess (Cambridge, 1989); Wolfram Siemann, *'Deutschlands Ruhe, Sicherheit und Ordnung': Die Anfänge der politischen Polizei 1806–1866* (Tübingen, 1985), 8–15, 174–96; Frank J. Thomason, 'The Prussian Police State in Berlin, 1848–1871' (Ph.D. thesis; Johns Hopkins, 1978), 18–23, 93–101; Dirk Blasius, *Geschichte der politischen Kriminalität in Deutschland (1800–1980): Eine Studie zu Justiz und Staatsverbrechen* (Frankfurt am Main, 1983), 33–9.

[52] Blasius, *Geschichte der politischen Kriminalität*, 33.

[53] GStA Merseburg, Rep. 77 Tit. 327 Nr. 9 Bd. 1, Bl. 46–7, 50–50ᵛ, 71–83, 89–97ᵛ.

handicraft workers or manual labourers; and to the extent that any meaningful pattern can be established, they tended to be concentrated in the provinces of Silesia, Posen, Saxony, East and West Prussia, and the Rhineland. Moreover, given the widespread unrest of the 1840s, the number of reported cases of *lèse-majesté* was astonishingly small, although the sources also suggest that many more serious slanders against the King never came to trial.[54]

Court festivals, honours lists, public celebrations, and the threat of coercive sanctions could all be regarded as 'traditional' ways of encouraging monarchical sentiments, or at least outward conformity to monarchical values and institutions. But Frederick William IV was a modern monarch, and during his reign traditional methods of monarchical representation and propaganda could be supplemented with more up-to-date techniques. It was now far easier, for example, to transmit the King's portrait to ordinary subjects. New lithographic methods had made it possible to produce and distribute cheap coloured prints by the tens of thousands, including inexpensive portraits of royal personages. After the 1820s the city of Neuruppin, located in the Mark Brandenburg north of Berlin, became a major centre for the production of lithographs and woodcuts. These so-called *Neuruppiner Bilderbogen* were an immensely successful popular art-form for many decades. The pictures, which were usually accompanied by explanatory texts, often appeared in series, and functioned as a kind of illustrated popular newspaper. Topics ranged from illustrations of popular songs and stories, 'genre' pictures, games and entertainment, devotional pictures, lurid or dramatic depictions of crimes and other public events, and portraits of prominent personalities.[55]

Before 1848 the political views expressed in these mass-produced sheets were predictably orthodox, and depictions of monarchs and royal families, especially the Hohenzollerns, figured prominently among them. Ordinary people who could never dream of travelling to Berlin could now regularly afford pictorial depictions of major events in the life of the Prussian royal house, such as the funeral of Frederick William III, the homage ceremonies of 1840, or scenes of the royal couple attending church after the Queen's recovery from a dangerous illness in 1847.[56] Portraits of the royal family were also, of course, widely distributed, and contributed to both the personalization and popularization of an institution which had previously seemed rather abstract, or at least distant, to large numbers of people. These portraits sometimes bore only a faint physical resemblance to the actual ruler, which led Prussian officials in 1842 to consider controlling their production. They decided against such a step, though, for interesting reasons: 'Ordinary people in the countryside attach a lot of importance to getting a portrait of the King and members of the family for a cheap

---

[54] See the files in ibid., esp. Bl. 1.

[55] Elke Hilscher, *Die Bilderbogen im 19. Jahrhundert* (Munich, 1977); Theodor Kohlmann (with Peter-Lutz Kindermann), *Neuruppiner Bilderbogen* (Berlin, 1981; exhib. cat.), 18–19. The first real illustrated newspaper in Germany, the *Leipziger Illustrirte Zeitung*, appeared in 1843.

[56] Kohlmann, *Bilderbogen*, 28–33. For a general analysis of the way in which *Bilderbogen* could contribute to a 'personalization of the system of dominance' in the nineteenth century, see Hilscher, *Bilderbogen*, 138–41; on the *Bilderbogen* in 1848, see Siemann, *Revolution*, 123.

price. Simply looking at the picture, without regard to any actual resemblance or artistic value, is sufficient for their reverence, love, and loyalty.'[57]

If ordinary people could readily identify with a pictorial representation of a formerly remote and awe-inspiring individual, the actual sight of that individual could be even more exciting. Prussian monarchs had always travelled a lot, but Frederick William IV far outdid all his predecessors. He loved to be in motion, and his court gained the reputation of being one of the most 'mobile' in the Europe of his day.[58] Many of his travels became part of an annual routine: in the spring he moved from Berlin to the palace in Potsdam; from there in the early summer to Sanssouci; thence in August and September to the Baltic island of Rügen and the estate of Erdmannsdorf in the Silesian mountains. Army manœuvres followed in the autumn, after which the King returned to Potsdam, before moving to Charlottenburg palace for the Christmas season.[59] But he also loved less structured travel, especially before 1848. Many of his journeys took him abroad, to England and Russia in 1842, to Denmark, Italy, and Russia in 1845, and again to Italy in 1847. At the same time, though, no other Prussian ruler had ever travelled so extensively through his own domains. The Rhineland, including his beloved Stolzenfels, was a frequent destination, and he often stayed for extended periods in Pomerania and East Prussia as well. He was also the first Prussian ruler since Frederick II to visit the cities of the Altmark west of Berlin.[60] Royal visits were grand and carefully orchestrated affairs, and they were made much easier by the rapid expansion of Prussia's railway network.[61] The increasing frequency of royal visits also necessitated a standardization of the protocol followed on such occasions. Accordingly, a royal decree of 1846 set up uniform guide-lines for provincial officials' behaviour during royal tours.[62]

Frederick William was also an enthusiast for the railways that facilitated his travels, and indeed for a great deal of modern technology in general, contrary though that may seem to his 'medievalist' image.[63] Thus he energetically supported the great Industrial Exposition that took place in Berlin from August to October 1844. Organized under government auspices, the exhibition showcased the achievements of the Prussian-dominated Customs Union (*Zollverein*) and testified to the growing importance of Germany's industrial entrepreneurs. A total of 3,040 firms participated, and more than 250,000 people visited the exposition.[64] It was thus a tremendous

[57] Quoted in Hilscher, *Bilderbogen*, 230; cf. Kohlmann, *Bilderbogen*, 62.

[58] Bismarck-Bohlen, 'Aufzeichnungen', GStA Merseburg, HA Rep. 50 F 1 Nr. 6, Bl. 12.

[59] On his annual travel routine, see, among other things, Franckenberg to Grand Duke Leopold, 23 Nov. 1845, GLA, Abt. 48/2598.

[60] Trauttmansdorff to Metternich, 24 May 1841, HHStA, St. K. Preußen, Karton 177, Politische Berichte I–XII, fol. 320^r–320^v.

[61] Karl Hammer, 'Die preußischen Könige und Königinnen im 19. Jahrhundert und ihr Hof', in Karl Ferdinand Werner (ed.), *Hof, Kultur und Politik im 19. Jahrhundert: Akten des 18. Deutsch-französischen Historikerkolloquiums Darmstadt vom 27.–30. September 1982* (Bonn, 1985), 93.

[62] Decree of FW IV, 13 Nov. 1846, GStA Merseburg, Rep. 77 Tit. 95 Nr. 31 Bd. 1 Bl. 122–3.

[63] Brose, *Politics*, 223–4, 235–9.

[64] Hermann Beck, 'Conservatives, Bureaucracy, and the Social Question', 252–4; Jürgen Reulecke, *Sozialer Frieden durch soziale Reform: Der Centralverein für das Wohl der arbeitenden Klasse in der*

[cont. on p. 116]

success, and on 6 October the King arranged for over 500 exhibitors to be transport-
ed by a special train to Potsdam, where ninety-four royal coaches waited to take them
to the gardens of Sanssouci. After a tour of the grounds they received tea and
refreshment at the Neues Palais and were treated to a special performance of opera
and ballet. The festivities concluded with '*ein splendides Souper*' in the palace.[65]

Three days later, a new organization called the Central Association for the Welfare
of the Labouring Classes was founded in Berlin. Its organizers included businessmen, officials, and critical *Literaten*, though the latter were heavily outnumbered by
the first two groups.[66] The Industrial Exposition coincided with an intensifying
debate on the causes and cure of 'pauperism', a debate that had assumed greater
urgency as a result of the brutal suppression of the weavers' revolt in Silesia.[67]
Though several organizations had already been established to address the growing
problems of poverty and misery in Prussia, the Central Association was by far the
most significant, with a number of prominent and wealthy members. It was also by
no means a radical organization; in fact, in its fundamental outlook the Central
Association represented a Prussian variant of the '*juste-milieu*' philosophy of
France's July Monarchy.[68]

Frederick William IV was not completely impervious to the sufferings of his subjects during the Hungry Forties. His letters from his travels, for example, show that
he was aware of the nature and geographical distribution of hunger in the countryside.[69] There is also some evidence that he appreciated Radowitz's calls in the mid-
1840s for a paternalistic 'social kingdom' that would ease the plight of the poor.
(Leopold von Gerlach once noted that the King had defended Radowitz's views on
an 'alliance with the proletariat, which he said was entirely correct, since one couldn't
simply step all over those people, etc.')[70] To be sure, his attempt to resurrect the
Order of the Swan had shown that he did not exactly understand the real character of
his country's social problems; he always remained convinced that monarchical paternalism and a renewed spirit of Christian charity could respond effectively to the
problem of poverty, and as early as November 1843 he called for private initiatives to
combat pauperism.[71] His first reaction was thus to welcome the establishment of the

---

Frühindustrialisierung (Wuppertal, 1983), 45–54; Hans-Heinrich Müller, 'Industriefest in Berlin:
Heerschau der Industriellen Revolution', in Helmut Bock and Wolfgang Heise (eds.), *Unzeit des
Biedermeiers: Historische Miniaturen zum Deutschen Vormärz 1830 bis 1848* (Cologne, 1986), 237–43;
Mieck, 'Reformzeit', 582–6.

[65] Franckenberg to Dusch, 9 Oct. 1844, GLA, Abt. 48/2642.

[66] Reulecke, *Sozialer Frieden*, 76–83.

[67] The most up-to-date account of those events can be found in Hermann Beck, 'Conservatives,
Bureaucracy, and the Social Question', 229–46; and id., 'State and Society in Pre-March Prussia: The
Weavers' Uprising, the Bureaucracy, and the Association for the Welfare of Workers', *CEH* 25 (1992),
303–31. See also Helmut Bleiber, *Zwischen Reform und Revolution: Lage und Kämpfe der schlesischen
Bauern und Landarbeiter im Vormärz 1840–1847* (Berlin [East], 1966).

[68] Hermann Beck, 'Conservatives, Bureaucracy, and the Social Question', 255.

[69] e.g. see FW IV to Elisabeth, 1 June 1845, GStA Merseburg, HA Rep. 50 J Nr. 995 Fasz. 18, Bl. 33–4;
and 7 June 1845, ibid., Bl. 27.

[70] Leopold von Gerlach, diary (29 May 1851), GA, 'Abschriften', viii. 163.

[71] Reulecke, *Sozialer Frieden*, 59–61.

Central Association in 1844. In an order to Finance Minister Flottwell on 25 October he expressed his 'great and lively interest' in the Association's work and promised it the modest sum of 15,000 Taler.[72] The Finance Minister was known, however, for his mildly liberal sympathies, and he had apparently encouraged the King's positive response to the Central Association. Soon, however, his conservative rivals—most notably Interior Minister Count Adolf Heinrich von Arnim-Boitzenburg and Privy Councillor Ludwig Emil Mathis—launched a full-scale offensive to convince Frederick William that the organization was dangerously subversive. In one of those tactical reversals for which he was notorious and which cost him dearly in the court of public opinion, Frederick William accepted Arnim's views and agreed that the Interior Ministry could monitor the Association's activities by reviewing and ruling on the statutes of its local branches.[73] The victory of Arnim and Mathis was a victory for traditional techniques of bureaucratic absolutism, to which the King himself, despite his declamations to the contrary, often made recourse.

Frederick William's erratic response to the social question and to the emergence of new forms of bourgeois associational and political life demonstrated just how difficult it would be for him to combine 'monarchism with popular favour'. With his almost mystical notions of the divine basis of his office, he wanted to invest Prussian kingship with a numinous quality which it had never had. Moreover, to be a 'people's king' he had to be a *visible* monarch, in contact with, and aware of, the emerging publics of civil society. In some ways, he was able to maintain that visibility through his travels, his speeches, and his genuine capacity to make strangers comfortable in his presence. Being a public and visible monarch was, in short, a complex business in the middle decades of the century. A king who still enjoyed substantive (as opposed to symbolic) power, and who was exposed to the vagaries of public opinion, could hardly be numinous. A fat, near-sighted king who made speeches and travelled by train could not aspire to remote and awe-inspiring stature, especially if he made no pretence to be Olympian or above politics.[74]

Frederick William IV's role as a public, visible monarch was at once politically advantageous and politically risky, depending upon which 'public' one was talking about; for it would certainly be misleading to speak of *one* public opinion in *Vormärz* Prussia. Rather, there were different publics, defined by such categories as region, religion, occupation, or education. Ordinary people in the countryside, especially in the Protestant core-provinces like the Mark Brandenburg and Pomerania, generally remained unquestioningly monarchist; but in towns and cities like Berlin, Königsberg, Cologne, or Breslau, a livelier cultural, political, literary, publicistic, and associational setting, compounded by the uncertainties of the 1840s, helped to create a vigorous and often intensely critical public arena which was not especially

[72] Ibid. 84; Hermann Beck, 'Conservatives, Bureaucracy, and the Social Question', 256.

[73] Reulecke, *Sozialer Frieden*, 87–98; Hermann Beck, 'Conservatives, Bureaucracy, and the Social Question', 272–3.

[74] Heinz Dollinger, 'Das Leitbild des Bürgerkönigtums in der europäischen Monarchie des 19. Jahrhunderts', in Werner (ed.), *Hof, Kultur und Politik*, 337.

susceptible to monarchist sentiments of the sort that Frederick William envisaged. New forms of critical social reportage, political pamphleteering, and penetrating satire were emerging, abetted by the loosening of censorship at the beginning of Frederick William's reign and sustained by high levels of literacy and the increasing politicization of the urban population.[75] Bettine von Arnim's book was only one example of these trends; others included the vigorous political and intellectual life of the Rhineland, the critical descriptions of life in Berlin by Friedrich Saß and Ernst Dronke, or the brilliantly successful satires of Adolph Glassbrenner and other Berlin humorists.[76]

Frederick William IV could scarcely count on much sympathy for his monarchical project among these emerging, critical publics. Although he could still draw on significant reserves of popular loyalty in cities like Berlin, to growing segments of the urban public he seemed at best an irrelevance and at worst a figure of ridicule. To many observers the King of Prussia cut a poor figure indeed. Bettine von Arnim's collaborator, the student Grunholzer, probably expressed the feelings of many of his fellows when he saw Frederick William IV for the first time in 1843: 'The King has a vulgar butcher's face. If I imagine him in an ordinary burgher's clothes, sitting with a long pipe behind a tall glass of pale ale in Günther's Tavern, well—so long, "By the Grace of God".'[77]

One sure sign of the development of a critical public in Prussia, especially in the urban centres, was the emergence of new forms of political caricature after 1842. Physically, Frederick William was made to order for caricaturists; he was the first German monarch to be lampooned in critical pictorial depictions, much like George III in Britain or Louis-Philippe in France before him. In early 1843 a widely circulated caricature depicted the King as a drunken Puss in Boots, waving a champagne-bottle and glass in front of Sanssouci, and trying unsuccessfully to follow in the footsteps of Frederick the Great. That particular cartoon was probably one of the factors that induced the monarch to reimpose censorship of pictures, which was only lifted again in March 1848. Despite such efforts, satirical literature and savage printed caricatures continued to be produced in significant quantities.[78]

The circumstances of the 1840s all worked against Frederick William's monarchical project, as did the general perception that he was erratic and indecisive. And even events that might have worked to his political advantage turned out to be public-relations fiascos. Among the best examples was the way in which he and his govern-

[75] Some figures suggest that by 1840 between 85% and 90% of Berlin's adult population was literate. Mary Lee Townsend, 'The Politics of Humor: Adolph Glassbrenner and the Rediscovery of the Prussian *Vormärz* (1815–48)', *CEH* 20 (1987), 41–2.

[76] See esp. Mary Lee Townsend, *Forbidden Laughter: Popular Humor and the Limits of Repression in Nineteenth-Century Prussia* (Ann Arbor, Mich., 1992).

[77] Quoted in Geist and Kürvers, *Mietshaus*, 230.

[78] Remigius Brückmann, ' "Es ginge wohl, aber es geht nicht": König Friedrich Wilhelm IV. von Preußen und die politische Karikatur der Jahre 1840–1849', in *Berlin zwischen 1789 und 1848: Facetten einer Epoche. Ausstellung der Akademie der Künste vom 30. August bis 1. November 1981* (Berlin, 1981), 147–53; Heinz Dollinger, *Friedrich II. von Preußen: Sein Bild im Wandel von zwei Jahrhunderten* (Munich, 1986), 124–8; Townsend, *Forbidden Laughter*, 162–70, 174–91.

ment handled a bungled assassination-attempt in 1844. On the morning of 26 July 1844, as the King and Queen were preparing to depart for their usual summer holiday in Silesia, a man named Heinrich Ludwig Tschech approached their carriage in the crowded courtyard of Berlin's royal palace and fired two pistol shots at close range. Both shots narrowly missed their targets, and Tschech was immediately arrested. The abortive assassination-attempt of course caused an immediate sensation. It was the first time in generations that anyone had tried to murder a German ruler, although such attempts had not been unusual elsewhere in Europe in the first half of the nineteenth century. There were no political motives for the act of the would-be assassin, an unbalanced former village mayor and failed office-seeker who blamed the King for his personal troubles.[79]

Tschech's crime unleashed a wave of popular sympathy for the royal pair, and when they returned to Berlin two months later, thousands of jubilant onlookers were on hand to greet them as they rode through the city in an open carriage.[80] Although Tschech had shown absolutely no signs of remorse and no inclination to request a reprieve, Frederick William was nevertheless inclined to commute his execution. Certainly many, if not most, Berliners expected such a magnanimous gesture. But the King's ministers insisted that Tschech had to be executed as an example, and Frederick William reluctantly agreed. Finally, in December, Tschech was executed in secret and without any sort of prior announcement. With that act, so reminiscent of bureaucratic absolutism at its worst, a great deal of the popular support that the King had enjoyed earlier in the year immediately vanished.[81]

The failed assassination-attempt apparently had one other long-term consequence. In the same month in which Tschech was executed, Frederick William IV decided to proceed more vigorously to complete the structure of corporative institutions that had been initiated with the provincial diets of 1823. The time had come, he believed, to create a system of *ständisch* representation for the Prussian state as a whole, a system which would stand as a 'truly German' alternative to hated 'French' constitutionalism. There is some evidence to suggest that his escape from the assassin's bullet had convinced him that he was truly destined for great things, and thus he was more determined than ever before to proceed boldly with his plans for *ständisch* reform.[82]

---

[79] FW IV to Prince of Prussia, 26 July 1844, GStA Merseburg, HA Rep. 50 L 2 Nr. 1, Bl. 17–18; Arnim-Boitzenburg to FW IV, 27 July 1844 (draft), BLHA, Pr. Br. Rep. 37 Herrschaft Boitzenburg, Nachlaß Adolf Heinrich Graf von Arnim-Boitzenburg Nr. 3942; Adolf Streckfuß, *500 Jahre Berliner Geschichte: Vom Fischerdorf zur Weltstadt. Geschichte und Sage*, ii, 4th edn. (Berlin, 1886), 908–14; Heinrich von Treitschke, *Deutsche Geschichte im Neunzehnten Jahrhundert*, 2nd edn., v: *Bis zur März-Revolution* (Leipzig, 1894), 268–9.

[80] Franckenberg to Dusch, 27 Sept. 1844, GLA, Abt. 48/2642; Streckfuß, *500 Jahre*, ii. 910.

[81] Trauttmansdorff to Metternich, 18 Dec. 1844, HHStA, St. K. Preußen, Karton 186, Politische Berichte 1844 VII–XII, fol. 318ʳ; A. Streckfuß, *500 Jahre*, ii. 920–1; K. A. Varnhagen von Ense, *Tagebücher*, ed. Ludmilla Assing, 2nd edn., ii. 410–13 (14 Dec. 1844).

[82] Meyendorff to Nesselrode, 22 Jan. 1845, in Peter von Meyendorff, *Ein russischer Diplomat an den Höfen von Berlin und Wien: Politischer und privater Briefwechsel 1826–1863*, ed. Otto Hoetzsch (3 vols.; Berlin, 1923), i. 289; Friedrich Wilhelm IV., *Reden und Trinksprüche Sr. Majestät Friedrich Wilhelm des*

[cont. on p. 120]

Too Little, Too Late? *Ständisch* Reform Thwarted, 1844–1847

Even before Tschech had fired his pistol, Frederick William had decided to move much more rapidly with his plans to transform the political basis of the Prussian monarchy.[83] Interior Minister Count Adolf Heinrich von Arnim-Boitzenburg had been one of the voices which had been urging the King to move more vigorously and decisively to deal with the growing crisis in the country. The provincial diets were becoming much more politicized than in the past, reflecting the tendency of the country as a whole. Something needed to be done, Arnim and others believed; indeed, there were some fears that a chasm was developing between the Prussian state and the unfulfilled expectations of civil society, and that as a result the country might soon become 'ungovernable'.[84]

A financial crisis in the 1840s made the situation even worse. The first stage of industrialization was already beginning to stretch available credit. The new Securities Law of 1844, which was intended to bring order to these affairs, at first made things worse, as small investors lost substantial sums. Above all, despite a favourable balance-sheet, the Prussian government did not have sufficient financial flexibility or creditworthiness to respond quickly to changed circumstances, especially the requirements of railway building. Industrial growth had led to a shortage of capital and credit, a 'tightening of liquidity', which got steadily worse after 1844. The Prussian government was thus confronted with an immense problem. If Prussia were to remain a great power, it would require a network of railways. But who and what would pay for them? Among other things, government loans would be necessary; and according to the State Debt Law of 1820, that would necessitate the summoning of estates of the realm (*Reichsstände*), a national diet.[85] For all his 'fantasies', Frederick William understood this problem more clearly than many of his contemporaries, including his brother and heir, the Prince of Prussia.[86] Throughout 1844 Frederick William had been receiving advice on constitutional matters from three of his closest advisers, Radowitz, Bunsen, and Baron Karl von Canitz, the Prussian envoy to Vienna.[87] By late in the year he had decided to proceed; and at a meeting on 27 December 1844 Frederick William told his advisers that the monarchy was in an 'unhealthy' condition, and

Vierten, Königes von Preußen (Leipzig, 1855), 38; Varnhagen von Ense, *Tagebücher*, iii. 28 (10 Feb. 1845); Treitschke, *Deutsche Geschichte*, v. 270–1.

[83] Friedrich Keinemann, *Preußen auf dem Wege zur Revolution: Die Provinziallandtags- und Verfassungspolitik Friedrich Wilhelms IV. von der Thronbesteigung bis zum Erlaß des Patents vom 3. Februar 1847. Ein Beitrag zur Vorgeschichte der Revolution von 1848* (Hamm, 1975), 56.

[84] Arnim-Boitzenburg to FW IV, 17 May 1844 (draft), BLHA, Pr. Br. Rep. 37 Herrschaft Boitzenburg, Nachlaß Adolf Heinrich Graf von Arnim-Boitzenburg Nr. 3968; Berdahl, *Politics*, 333–4; Obenaus, *Anfänge*, 563–94, 649.

[85] Obenaus, *Anfänge*, 523–4

[86] Siegfried Bahne, 'Die Verfassungspläne König Friedrich Wilhelms IV. von Preußen und die Prinzenopposition im Vormärz' (*Habilitationsschrift*; Bochum, 1971), 68.

[87] Obenaus, *Anfänge*, 650; Dallinger, *Canitz*, 54–8; Bahne, 'Verfassungspläne', 37–8; Paul Hassel, *Joseph Maria von Radowitz*, i: *1797–1848* (Berlin, 1905), 123.

that the steps which had been taken since 1840 to redress that condition had so far been unsuccessful.[88]

What were those steps? Although the King had seemed to respond positively to the constitutional wishes of the provincial diet of East and West Prussia in September 1840, his controversial cabinet order of 4 October 1840 had indicated that he had succumbed to the fierce resistance of the ultra-conservative opposition and that no form of representation for the whole Prussian state was in the offing.[89] Thereafter Frederick William had lurched from one partial concession to another without a clear, consistent, or obvious plan, and his innovations had only encouraged suspicion among conservatives and disappointment among the advocates of constitutional reform. In early 1841 he agreed to a liberalization of the structure of the provincial diets, as a result of which they were to be summoned every two years (instead of every three) and their proceedings were to be published.[90] Though the provincial diets of 1841 proceeded uneventfully, by 1843 several of them had begun to articulate pro-constitutional political demands.[91] In 1842, to avoid calling a national diet, the government had summoned twelve representatives from each provincial diet to convene in Berlin as United Committees (*Vereinigte Ausschüsse*), which were supposed to provide advice on railway financing and related matters. Their powers were strictly limited, and nothing much came of them.[92] So matters stood, with pressures mounting for some form of national political representation, until 1844, when Frederick William decided to plunge ahead more vigorously with his plans.[93] By the end of 1844 the King had decided that all the provincial diets should be summoned to Berlin within three years. The united diets would be permitted broad powers to approve new government debts and taxes.[94] The die, it seemed, had been cast.

The King's ideas about all of these matters had remained essentially unchanged for many years. He wished to move away from the Scylla of bureaucratic despotism while avoiding the Charybdis of constitutionalism. In words that fully echoed the King's own views, Radowitz once declared that 'In the *ständisch* system genuine rights are represented, but a representative system merely represents political opinions'.[95] The provinces and estates of the realm should be confirmed in their historic rights, but the sovereign had the authority to guarantee and develop those rights, based on his own patrimonial authority as divinely ordained monarch.[96] Political

---

[88] Obenaus, *Anfänge*, 651.

[89] See Ch. 3 and the summaries in Berdahl, *Politics*, 317–18; Bahne, 'Verfassungspläne', 7–24.

[90] Bahne, 'Verfassungspläne', 31–2.   [91] Berdahl, *Politics*, 322–4.

[92] Bahne, 'Verfassungspläne', 43b–53b; Trauttmansdorff to Metternich, 14 Nov. 1842, HHStA, St. K. Preußen, Karton 180, Politische Berichte 1842 I–XII, fol. 223^r–234^v; Obenaus, *Anfänge*, 551–63; Keinemann, *Preußen*, 45–51; Berdahl, *Politics*, 325–6; Ernst Rudolf Huber, *Deutsche Verfassungsgeschichte seit 1789*, 3rd edn. (Stuttgart, 1988), ii: *Der Kampf um Einheit und Freiheit*, 488–90.

[93] Leopold von Gerlach to Canitz, 4 December 1844, in Dallinger, *Canitz*, 128–31, and in Stephan Nobbe, 'Der Einfluß religiöser Überzeugung auf die politische Ideenwelt Leopold von Gerlachs' (Diss.; Erlangen, 1970) app. of sources, 112–16; Leopold von Gerlach, diary (15 Dec. 1844), GA, 'Abschriften', iv. 128–9.

[94] Obenaus, *Anfänge*, 651.   [95] Quoted in Bahne, 'Verfassungspläne', 35.

[96] FW IV to Theodor von Schön, 26 Dec. 1840, in Hans Rothfels, *Theodor v. Schön, Friedrich Wilhelm IV. und die Revolution von 1848* (Halle, 1937).

participation was a gift from the king, whose own authority remained effectively untouched. Such ideas had always been basic to Frederick William's view of the world; they constituted the very cornerstone of his monarchical project. But how could they be sustained, given the 'unhealthy' condition of the monarchy by 1844 and his own realization that something definitive and far-reaching had to be done? Frederick William consistently denied that he intended to introduce *Reichsstände*, much less a constitutional charter. His goals, he insisted, remained different. He described them to Leopold von Gerlach on 29 January 1845: 'I wish to knock down the bridge to liberalism for myself and my successors and escape from the sickness which we have caught *à coup des lois* as a result of the laws of 1815, 1820, and 1823. . . . I do not want *Reichsstände*, but instead all eight diets with deputations of noble estate owners, towns, and peasants.' He would then promise 'to do for the *Stände* what every German sovereign is obliged to do for his *Stände*', that is, not to impose new taxes or take out new loans without their approval. The united diets would thereafter be permitted to discuss the question of financing for railways, canals, and roads. He would also agree to summon the United Committees every four years.[97] Such an arrangement would allow him, he thought, to 'circumvent a system of national representation', while 'the *rights of the crown and of the Royal House* will remain untouched'. As a result, he insisted to his worried sister Charlotte, he would make it '*impossible* to proceed along the constitutional road'.[98] His policies would, he maintained, strengthen and not weaken monarchy in all of Germany: 'I will not drop the sceptre from my hands, I will not issue a Charter, I will *never* share my sovereign powers with the estates'.[99]

The weeks and months after December 1844 witnessed an intense debate at the highest levels of court and state on the nature, character, and form of the united diet. That debate in turn was the catalyst for some changes among the King's closest advisers and within the various 'groups' or 'factions' that surrounded the throne. In the early summer of 1845 Interior Minister Arnim-Boitzenburg resigned because of long-simmering disagreements with the King about the practicality and political feasibility of the monarch's plans.[100] The King now turned to Ernst von Bodelschwingh to take over the Interior Ministry, at first on an interim and then on a permanent basis.

The scion of an old aristocratic family from Westphalia, Bodelschwingh (1794–1854) had fought with distinction on the Prussian side during the liberation war, suffering a grave lung-wound which afflicted him for the rest of his life. After the war he

[97] Leopold von Gerlach, diary (29 Jan. 1845), GA, 'Abschriften', iv. 139–40.

[98] FW IV to Charlotte (Alexandra Feodorovna), 21 Jan. 1845, GStA Merseburg, HA Rep. 50 J Nr. 1210 Vol. III, Bl. 17ᵛ; FW IV to Nicholas I, 11 Jan. 1845, in Theodor Schiemann, 'Kaiser Nikolaus I. und Friedrich Wilhelm IV. über den Plan, einen vereinigten Landtag zu berufen', in Verein für Geschichte der Mark Brandenburg (ed.), *Festschrift zu Gustav Schmollers 70. Geburtstag. Beiträge zur brandenburgischen und preußischen Geschichte* (Leipzig, 1908), 278–81.

[99] FW IV to Arnim-Boitzenburg, 18 Dec. 1844, BLHA, Pr. Br. Rep. 37 Herrschaft Boitzenburg, Nachlaß Adolf Heinrich Graf von Arnim-Boitzenburg Nr. 3968.

[100] Arnim-Boitzenburg to FW IV, 23 and 27 May 1845, and AKO, FW IV to Arnim-Boitzenburg, 7 July 1845, ibid., Nr. 3926; Treitschke, *Deutsche Geschichte*, v. 273–5; Bahne, 'Verfassungspläne', 40; Obenaus, *Anfänge*, 652–3.

had climbed rapidly in the service of the Prussian state. Following a distinguished bureaucratic career in the Rhineland, he had gone to Berlin to assume the Finance Ministry after Alvensleben's resignation in 1842. In 1844 he took over Alvensleben's functions as Cabinet Minister, which he retained after becoming Interior Minister. Bodelschwingh had thus rather quickly become the highest-ranking civilian official in Prussia.[101] Although he was known for the extreme simplicity of his personality and the austerity of his tastes, Bodelschwingh was even better known for his prodigious energy and limitless capacity for work. As a result, he soon emerged as unofficial Prime Minister of the King's government.[102]

After the summer of 1845 the State Ministry finally became relatively stable. Even Leopold von Gerlach, usually a stern critic of disorganization and 'lack of principles' in Frederick William's government, had to admit in the autumn that the King at last had a 'compact ministry', though he doubted that the ministers would be able to work with each other for long.[103] Gerlach's comment was elicited by the elevation to Foreign Minister of his old friend Baron Karl von Canitz und Dallwitz, who immediately joined Thile and Bodelschwingh as one of the most influential members of the government.

Canitz (1787–1850) had long been one of the King's special advisers in *ständisch*-constitutional affairs. A professional officer with an engaging personality and a scintillating intellect, Canitz had distinguished himself, like Bodelschwingh, in the Liberation War. He had a quite remarkable capacity for forging friendships with people of varied backgrounds and diverse political persuasions, among them Varnhagen, Wilhelm Grimm, Clausewitz, Gneisenau, Savigny, and Tieck. After the war he had been close to the Crown Prince's Circle, including Carl von Voß-Buch, Carl von der Groeben, and the Gerlachs, especially Leopold. Indeed, it was he who had introduced the young Radowitz to the Gerlach brothers. Although he remained an officer, he had been given several difficult diplomatic assignments in Kassel, Hanover, and, from 1841 to 1845, Vienna. There he had constantly tried, without much success, to represent Frederick William's policies to a worried and increasingly suspicious Metternich. In the summer of 1845 he was called back to Berlin, where in early July he became a member of a special constitutional commission and in September Foreign Minister.[104]

It would be incorrect to describe Bodelschwingh, Canitz, and Thile as a *troika*. Frederick William's governing style remained essentially unchanged after 1845, as many observers despairingly noted. He continued to regard his ministers as

[101] Hans-Joachim Schoeps, 'Aus dem Briefwechsel Friedrich Wilhelms IV. mit dem Staatsminister Ernst von Bodelschwingh', in id. (ed.), *Neue Quellen zur Geschichte Preußens im 19. Jahrhundert* (Berlin, 1968), 370–2; *ADB*, iii. 3–5; and *NDB*, ii. 350–1 (Walter Bußmann).

[102] Ludwig von Gerlach, diary (22 Apr. 1846), in Hans-Joachim Schoeps, 'Ungedrucktes aus den Tagebüchern Ludwig v. Gerlachs 1846 und 1847 mit Briefen seines Bruders Leopold', in id. (ed.), *Neue Quellen*, 333; Leopold von Gerlach, diary (21 May 1846), GA, 'Abschriften', iv. 175; Hans-Joachim Schoeps, 'Staatsminister Bodelschwingh', 371; Leopold von Gerlach to Ludwig von Gerlach, 25 Sept. 1846 and 17 Nov. 1847, GA, Fasz. CT.

[103] Leopold von Gerlach, diary (22 Oct. 1845), GA, 'Abschriften', iv. 170.

[104] Dallinger, *Canitz*, 8–64.

'instruments', he continued to solicit advice from a variety of unofficial as well as official quarters, and he continued to interfere with, or undermine, his ministers' work, all of which made it difficult for the ministers to create that *conseil* which so many of them thought was essential. Thus, for all the real power that he concentrated in his own hands, Bodelschwingh always described himself as 'His Majesty's First Scribe'.[105] Moreover, although the three men essentially supported the King's *ständisch* initiatives, they did so for different reasons and in different ways.[106]

According to Leopold von Gerlach, Thile was less than enthusiastic about constitutional reform, but believed that when the King really decided to do something, it was his duty to help.[107] Bodelschwingh embraced the King's initiatives much more vigorously. Although a loyal servant of the crown, Bodelschwingh was a 'moderate conservative' in his views and was open to genuine, far-reaching political change. Indeed, he almost certainly would have liked to push the monarch much more determinedly down the road of constitutional reform.[108] Among the three men, Canitz's views were closest to the King's own. Leopold von Gerlach was probably correct when he wrote to Canitz in 1846 'that you are the only one of the ministers who has truly grasped the King's idea and agrees with it'.[109] Canitz was also worried that a great deal of time had been wasted, that the King should have proceeded with his plans in 1840, and that 'royal authority has lost ground ever since'.[110] Despite a shared sense of urgency, however, differences arose between Bodelschwingh and Canitz over the nature and extent of the desired reforms, and the two men were never able to work as closely as they might have liked. But their relationship was always cordial. Far more difficult, however, was Canitz's relationship to the King's brothers, who by the autumn of 1845 had become Canitz's 'determined enemies'.[111]

All three of the King's brothers opposed his *ständisch* project, but it was William, the Prince of Prussia and future Emperor, who opposed it most loudly and resolutely. He had long had misgivings about his older brother's plans, and to thwart them he had even formed a tacit political alliance in 1840 with Wittgenstein, Alvensleben, Meyendorff, and, from a distance, Metternich and Nicholas I.[112] By early 1845 the estrangement between the royal brothers had grown quite bitter. Among other things, William tried to claim, on the basis of an unfinished and unsigned 'testament' of Frederick William III, that it was illegal to change the constitution of the state

---

[105] Bahne, 'Verfassungspläne', 73.

[106] Dallinger, *Canitz*, 58, 63–4; Leopold von Gerlach to Canitz, n. d. (1846), in Nobbe, 'Einfluß', app. of sources, 134.

[107] Leopold von Gerlach, diary (3 and 5 Feb. 1845), GA, 'Abschriften', iv. 148, 151.

[108] Dallinger, *Canitz*, 66; Hans-Joachim Schoeps 'Staatsminister Bodelschwingh', 376; Bahne, 'Verfassungspläne', 73–4; Bodelschwingh to FW IV (18 June 1846), in Gustav von Diest, *Meine Erlebnisse im Jahre 1848 und die Stellung des Staatsministers von Bodelschwingh vor und an dem 18. März 1848* (Berlin, 1898), 36–41.

[109] Gerlach to Canitz, n. d. (1846), in Nobbe, 'Einfluß', app. of sources, 135; Dallinger, *Canitz*, 64–7.

[110] Canitz, 'Skelett zum Vortrag im Staatsministerium', 30 June 1846, in Dallinger, *Canitz*, 138–9.

[111] Leopold von Gerlach, diary (6 Nov. 1845), GA, 'Abschriften', iv. 172.

[112] Karl Heinz Börner, *Kaiser Wilhelm I. 1797 bis 1888: Deutscher Kaiser und König von Preußen. Eine Biographie* (Cologne, 1984), 57–64.

without the approval of all the royal princes. Frederick William insisted that he was not changing the constitution, urged the Prince to put aside any thought of an 'unhappy and punishable family opposition', and warned his brother that for a king to be so dependent on the princes would be 'ten times worse' than dependence on the *Stände*. He would respond to such a challenge to his authority, he hinted darkly, the same way their father would have. For his part, William accused 'Fritz' of being insincere and 'ashamed to present his ideas in front of right-minded men'.[113]

So spirited was William's opposition that one historian has described it as part of a 'Princes' Fronde' against the King.[114] William himself always insisted that he was not opposed to political progress as such, but, he warned, too many concessions might jeopardize the crown's prerogatives. He thus opposed granting the *Stände* the right to approve taxes, and he thought that a united diet composed of all 800 members of the provincial diets, as the King had proposed, would be a '*chambre monstre*'. Finally, he also believed that Frederick William's notion of a British-style upper house or 'Curia of Lords' (*Herrenkurie*) was too abstract and impractical for Prussian conditions.[115] Despite his strong feelings, however, the Prince of Prussia's opposition remained largely ineffective. Although he enjoyed considerable backing in the army and among certain old-Prussian conservatives, by 1845 he no longer had powerful allies at the upper levels of court and state. Alvensleben was gone, and Gustav Adolf von Rochow shunted aside. Wittgenstein was old and sick, his once formidable influence reduced almost to nothing. Prince Carl was diverted by his complicated personal difficulties, and Meyendorff's position as the representative of a foreign power required him to be exceptionally discreet. The Prince of Prussia also, obviously, could not count on popular support for his opposition to the King, and in fact, as Thile perceptively foresaw, William's own personal unpopularity redounded to Frederick William's political advantage. Indeed, in Berlin the Prince of Prussia came to be regarded as the very incarnation of opposition to constitutional change, and in the spring of 1845 his coach was stoned while passing through the streets of the capital.[116]

William's more or less open opposition to the King's proposals underscores the importance of the shifts that had taken place at the top of the Prussian court and structures in 1845. The faction or group around the Prince of Prussia had weakened to the point of non-existence. Frederick William himself now had a ministry which, though divided within, was nevertheless a model of stability compared to its predecessors. For all the differences among people like Bodelschwingh, Thile, Canitz, or

[113] FW IV to William, 16 Feb. 1845 (draft), in Bahne, 'Verfassungspläne', 55b; Leopold von Gerlach, diary (2 Mar. 1845), GA, 'Abschriften', iv. 159; William to Friedrich Karl von Savigny, 19 Mar. 1845, in Wilhelm I., Deutscher Kaiser, *Kaiser Wilhelms I. Briefe an Politiker und Staatsmänner*, ed. Johannes Schultze, i: *1830–1853* (Berlin, 1930), 30–1.

[114] Bahne, 'Verfassungspläne', 131.

[115] William to Karl Freiherr von Vincke-Olbendorf, 18 Nov. 1845, in Wilhelm I., *Briefe an Politiker*, i. 34; William to Grand Duchess Maria Pavlovna, 5 Apr. 1845, in Wilhelm I., Deutscher Kaiser, *Kaiser Wilhelms I. Weimarer Briefe*, ed. Johannes Schultze (2 vols.; Berlin, 1924), i. 161; William to Presumptive Grand Duke Karl Alexander, 19 Dec. 1845, ibid., i. 163; Leopold von Gerlach, diary (31 Jan. 1845), GA, 'Abschriften', iv. 142–3.

[116] Börner, *Wilhelm I.*, 65.

Stolberg, and for all Leopold von Gerlach's endless jeremiads about the government's weakness, they got along with the King reasonably well. Gerlach was also worried about the Princes' Fronde, and from the outset he tried to mediate the dispute between the royal brothers. On the whole, he applauded the King's 'truly statesmanlike idea' to call the provincial diets together 'without any reform or any change in the constitution of the state'. He also believed by 1845 that liberal and radical opinion had become so dangerous that it was incumbent upon like-minded friends to overcome their reservations and rally around the monarch. Anything which offered a possible opening to the liberals should be avoided; thus the continuing conflict between King and Prince was a 'calamity for the country' which could have especially dangerous consequences.[117]

Gerlach's efforts as a mediator were not especially successful, but after a few months the Prince of Prussia's opposition to his royal brother's reform efforts began to soften. In March 1846 the regular Commission for Estatist [*ständisch*] Affairs began to hold joint meetings with the State Ministry, with the Prince himself serving as chair. The discussions were vexed and complicated, but by early 1847 a compromise was worked out. William more or less gave up his opposition, and the matter was settled.[118] Canitz, whose views were closest to the King's, prepared the first draft of a royal patent 'concerning *ständisch* institutions'; after some revisions, the patent was released on 3 February 1847.[119]

In the patent the King proclaimed that, in fulfilment of the legislation of 1820 and 1823, the provincial diets of the country would be called together as a United Diet whenever the state required new loans, new taxes, or increased taxes.[120] The United Committees would continue to exist, and would gather in Berlin on a regular basis. Three official decrees, released simultaneously with the patent, described the organization and powers of the United Diet and the United Committees. Five days after the patent's release, the King announced that the first United Diet would meet in Berlin on 11 April.[121] The King who loved 'history' and 'tradition' was about to launch an experiment without precedent or historic parallel in Prussian history. Frederick William was himself aware that he was initiating a new chapter in that history, because, as he wrote to his brother Carl, 'it is the first active response by a conservative power to the principles of popular representation, which have laid hold of so many states and ruined them since the French Revolution'.[122] Would his experiment succeed in putting the relationship between King and people, between monarchy and society, on a new but non-constitutional footing?

[117] Leopold von Gerlach to Ludwig von Gerlach, 7 Feb. 1845, in Nobbe, 'Einfluß', app. of sources, 121; Leopold von Gerlach to Canitz, n. d. (1846), ibid. 134; Leopold von Gerlach to Stolberg, 14 Apr. 1845, GA, 'Abschriften', iv. 168.

[118] Bahne, 'Verfassungspläne', 86–92.   [119] Dallinger, *Canitz*, 67–8.

[120] 'Patent, die ständischen Einrichtungen betreffend', 3 Feb. 1847, in Eduard Bleich (ed.), *Der Erste Vereinigte Landtag in Berlin 1847* (4 vols.; Berlin, 1847; repr. Vaduz, 1977), i. 3–4.

[121] 'Patent wegen Einberufung des Vereinigten Landtages', 8 Feb. 1847, ibid. 10.

[122] FW IV to Carl, 19 Mar. 1847, GStA Merseburg, HA Rep. 50 J Nr. 986, Bl. 25.

6
Monarchy at the Crossroads:
King and Revolution, 1847–1848

A Dreary Day in April

The public mood in Berlin seemed to reflect the weather on Sunday, 11 April 1847, as the United Diet gathered for its official opening. The winter had been long and hard. Food shortages and unemployment were becoming increasingly serious problems; and spring had still not arrived. The day was cold and blustery, with a mixture of snow and freezing rain. Under normal circumstances Berliners would have liked a big public spectacle like the opening of the Diet. They were used to seeing figures like the King and the royal princes; but this particular affair was going to be made more interesting thanks to the hundreds of unfamiliar provincial delegates who had been flocking to Berlin in recent weeks. Most Berliners stayed indoors that morning, however, and only about a thousand spectators braved the chill to observe the delegates as they proceeded in their carriages from the cathedral to the palace to hear the King's speech.

More than 600 of the Diet, divided into a Curia of the Three Estates and an upper house or Curia of Lords, crammed into the palace's White Hall to await the King's entrance.[1] When Frederick William IV entered the hall, the multitude rose and shouted '*Lebehoch*!' three times. Affable as usual, the King greeted delegates all around him and finally mounted the steps to the throne, simple but imposing under its large canopy. He sat down and began to speak. At first he seemed a bit hesitant, even somewhat overcome by the emotion of this unprecedented occasion. After about a minute, however, he pulled himself together and proceeded to speak, clearly, forcefully, and without notes, for more than half an hour.[2]

His listeners quickly realized that the King was not amused. The first months of 1847 had not been kind to him. In February the Queen, who had a long history of respiratory problems, had become dangerously ill, and for several weeks Frederick William had been frantic with worry.[3] Then he found that public

---

[1] On the composition of the United Diet, see Herbert Obenaus, *Anfänge des Parlamentarismus in Preußen bis 1848* (Düsseldorf, 1984), 660–8; Robert M. Berdahl, *The Politics of the Prussian Nobility: The Development of a Conservative Ideology 1770–1848* (Princeton, NJ, 1988), 335; and, above all, Peter Eickenboom, 'Der Preußische Erste Vereinigte Landtag von 1847' (Diss.; Bonn, 1976).

[2] Dora Meyer, *Das öffentliche Leben in Berlin im Jahr vor der Märzrevolution* (Berlin, 1912), 76; Franckenberg to Dusch, 11 Apr. 1847, GLA, Abt. 48/2645; Trauttmansdorff to Metternich, 16 Apr. 1847, HHStA, St. K. Preußen, Karton 192, Politische Berichte 1847 I-V, fol. 28^r-28^v; *Allgemeine Zeitung* (Augsburg), 16 Apr. 1847.

[3] FW IV to Bunsen, 12 Feb. 1847, GStA Merseburg, HA Rep. 50 J Nr. 244a, Bl. 83^v; Elisabeth to Ludwig I, 26 Mar. 1847, GHA, Nachlaß König Ludwig I., 89/2 XIII.

reaction to his February patent had been less than enthusiastic. The Silesian liberal Heinrich Simon had denounced the King's plan in a brilliant pamphlet called *To Accept or to Reject?* (*Annehmen oder ablehnen?*), while other liberals had considered boycotting the Diet, or argued that they should take part in the Diet but should try to change it once they were there. Conservatives were also unhappy, regarding the patent as a dangerous opening to constitutionalism.[4] Among ordinary Berliners, the forthcoming Diet had elicited mixed feelings of perplexity, hostility, and apathy.[5] In the days and weeks before 11 April, Frederick William had become aware that many people actually thought that with his patent of 3 February he had agreed to a kind of constitutional charter, and they thus regarded the Diet itself as a kind of parliamentary assembly.[6] Accordingly, he decided that in his opening speech he needed to clarify a number of misunderstandings and false perceptions.

He began by referring to his father's unfinished business, which he was now going to bring to a close through his own efforts as 'heir of an intact crown . . . with all the freedom provided by the fullness of royal authority'. He thus emphasized that the United Diet would only meet when he, as king, decided that it was necessary. Although some people were calling for a 'revolution in church and state', he was not prepared to tolerate such demands. Prussia's geography and history precluded any kind of written constitution; to survive, a state like Prussia had to be guided and directed 'by One Will'. Then, in one of the most frequently quoted passages of his speech, Frederick William proclaimed 'that no power of the earth will succeed in moving Me to transform that natural relationship between ruler and people . . . into a legalistic or constitutional one; and that I will never ever allow a written piece of paper to come between Our Lord God in Heaven and this country . . . to rule us with its paragraphs as a substitute for our old, sacred loyalty'. The 'Christian people, that simple, true, loyal people' of Prussia, he insisted, 'does not want representatives to share in government; it does not want sovereignty to be divided, or to see the genuine power of its kings broken'.[7]

The liberal Varnhagen and the ultra-conservative Leopold von Gerlach were, as usual, far apart in their own responses to the speech, but they did agree about the delegates' reactions. Varnhagen wrote of a general feeling of 'perplexity, resentment, and bitterness' among its listeners, while Gerlach estimated that three-fifths of the Diet's members rejected the King's arguments. The Austrian envoy, Count Trauttmansdorff, declared that the speech had 'hit the assembly like a thunderbolt. . . . With one blow the *Stände* have seen their hopes and desires

---

[4] Veit Valentin, *Geschichte der deutschen Revolution von 1848–1849* (2 vols.; Cologne, 1977; orig. 1931–2), i. 63–6; Obenaus, *Anfänge*, 668–86; Berdahl, *Politics*, 336–7.

[5] Meyer, *Leben*, 68–9, 71–5.

[6] Stolberg to Radowitz, 9 Mar. 1847, GStA Merseburg, Rep. 92 Joseph Maria von Radowitz d. Ä. 1. Reihe Nr. 56, Bl. 94–94ᵛ.

[7] Eduard Bleich (ed.), *Der erste Vereinigte Landtag in Berlin 1847* (4 vols.; Berlin, 1847; repr. Vaduz, 1977), i. 20–6; Friedrich Wilhelm IV., *Reden und Trinksprüche Sr. Majestät Friedrich Wilhelm des Vierten, Königes von Preußen* (Leipzig, 1855), 41–56.

obliterated; not one happy face left the assembly.'[8] The King's experiment with a *ständisch* united diet, which he had hoped would exorcise the spirit of constitutionalism and parliamentarism, ended unsatisfactorily for everyone, but especially for Frederick William himself. It turned out that Trauttmansdorff had largely been right when he argued in February 1847 that the United Diet would be a battleground 'on which the liberal party will begin its conquests on the constitutional field'.[9] And in March 1848, less than a year after his haughty speech in the White Hall, Frederick William's throne shook beneath him. The revolution which he had feared for so long, which he regarded as the 'satanic' incarnation of evil in the world, had finally arrived. In its wake he had to agree to become a constitutional king and to accept certain constitutional limitations on his power. He also had to agree to the election of a national assembly, which convened in Berlin in May 1848 to draft a written constitution for the kingdom. In the spring and summer of 1848 nothing seemed deader or less timely than the monarchical project of Frederick William IV. He had long resisted what Friedrich Julius Stahl had called the 'negative spirit of the age', and to all appearances he had failed. As he plaintively and self-pityingly put it in a letter to his friend Carl von der Groeben at the end of August 1848, '*I do not rule.* For God's sake don't ever forget that for a moment.'[10]

The dramatic events from February 1847 to the summer of 1848 have often been described, and it is not our purpose here to recapitulate them in great detail. Rather, this chapter will focus primarily on the King, his advisers, and the structures of monarchical authority as they confronted growing pressures for radical, even revolutionary change. As we shall see in Chapter 7, the months after March 1848 also witnessed the first stages of a major organizational and attitudinal reorientation among Prussian conservatives, which in turn necessitated new thinking about the place of the king and of monarchical institutions in Prussian society.

The Last *Vormärz* Months: Aimlessness at the Top

Despite the dismay and consternation that attended his speech at the opening session of the United Diet, Frederick William IV was pleased with what he had said. He had been genuinely surprised at the negative reaction to his February patent, and he was distressed by the tendency of the delegates, after their arrival, to act like real parliamentarians by associating with like-minded colleagues and creating embryonic factions. He was especially offended by growing calls for 'periodicity' (*Periodicität*), that is, a statutory requirement for meetings of the United Diet at regular intervals.[11] The

---

[8] K. A. Varnhagen von Ense, *Tagebücher*, ed. Ludmilla Assing, 2nd. edn. iv. 60 (11 Apr. 1847); Leopold von Gerlach, diary (12 Apr. 1847), GA, 'Abschriften', v. 7; Trauttmansdorff to Metternich, 16 Apr. 1847, HHStA, St. K. Preußen, Karton 192, Politische Berichte 1847 I–V, fol. 56ᵛ, 57ʳ.

[9] Trauttmansdorff to Metternich, 5 Feb. 1847, HHStA, St. K. Preußen, Karton 192, Politische Berichte 1847 I–V, fol. 147ʳ.

[10] FW IV to Groeben, 30 Aug. 1848, GStA Merseburg, Rep. 92 Graf Carl von der Groeben B Nr. 4ᵉ 1848, Bl. 13ᵛ.

[11] Trauttmansdorff to Metternich, 16 Apr. 1847, HHStA, St. K. Preußen, Karton 192, Politische

[*cont. on p. 130*]

Diet itself responded to Frederick William's speech by directing an 'address' to him on 20 April, indicating in carefully couched language that the delegates were simply not satisfied with the limited role that the King foresaw for them, and pointing out that both the King's rights and the rights of the *Stände* were equally sacred. Implicit in the address, and in the debates that preceded it, was the demand for periodicity. The King's answer, though not as confrontational as his opening speech, still seemed less than conciliatory; above all, though, it was confusing and contradictory. The United Diet would have no other rights, he asserted, except those provided for in the legislation of 3 February. That legislation was 'unchangeable in its basics; but We do not regard it for that reason as fully completed, but rather as capable of further development'. Since all God's creation was 'capable of further development', he explained in a letter to his sister, he did not feel 'able to attribute the quality of Final Perfection to my own'.[12] It was not at all clear what Frederick William actually meant by these remarks. What many delegates wanted, however, were concessions in the direction of genuine parliamentary institutions and constitutional reform, which for his part the King was not willing to grant to them. Frederick William had assumed that the Diet's principal function was to discuss loans and other financial affairs, and nothing more. In fact, however, it devoted most of its attention to constitutional matters, including the periodicity question.

Although the Diet's actual political achievements were rather sparse, and its results ambiguous, it did provide an important public forum in which, for the first time, questions of concern for the entire Prussian state could be openly debated. What Frederick William had regarded as the culmination of his attempt to build 'truly German' corporative institutions turned out to be something quite different, a kind of national assembly in the making.[13] And in that setting, many individuals who later played a crucial role in Prussian public life—Ludolf Camphausen, David Hansemann, Alfred von Auerswald, Gustav Mevissen, Hermann von Beckerath, Otto von Bismarck, Otto von Manteuffel, Georg von Vincke, to name just a few—learned a number of important lessons about the art of parliamentary politics.[14] Moreover, as Leopold von Gerlach had feared, Frederick William's government often seemed divided, indecisive, and unsure of itself in its dealings with the United Diet. For example, many liberal delegates, influenced by strong German national feelings, had a keen interest in foreign-policy issues and in the relationship between Prussia and the other German states.[15] On 19 May, during a heated debate on those matters, Foreign Minister Canitz stated that he was not opposed to

---

Berichte 1847 I–V, fol. 56ʳ. Cf. FW IV to Bunsen, 13 Apr. 1847, GStA Merseburg, HA Rep. 50 J Nr. 244a, Bl. 85; FW IV to Charlotte (Alexandra Feodorovna), 18 Apr. 1847, GStA Merseburg, HA Rep. 50 J Nr. 1210 Vol. III, Bl. 45.

[12] FW IV to Charlotte, 12 May 1847, ibid., Bl. 47–47ᵛ.   [13] Berdahl, *Politics*, 346.

[14] Theodore S. Hamerow, *Restoration, Revolution, Reaction: Economics and Politics in Germany, 1815–1871* (Princeton, NJ, 1958), 92.

[15] See Harald Müller, 'Der Blick über die deutschen Grenzen: Zu den Forderungen der bürgerlichen Opposition in Preußen nach außenpolitischer Einflußnahme am Vorabend und während des ersten Preußischen Vereinigten Landtags von 1847', *Jahrbuch für Geschichte*, 32 (1985), 203–38.

accepting petitions from the Diet on foreign-policy questions. The Prince of Prussia, who played a vigorous and assertive role in the Diet's proceedings, was aghast, as were many other conservatives, and Canitz had to retract his statement two days later.[16]

Not all the ministers suffered such embarrassments. Bodelschwingh, who was 'Commissar of the Diet', proved to be a powerful and persuasive speaker; but by 1847 he had become convinced that further constitutional concessions were urgently necessary, and his public defence of the King's ideas thus clashed with his own private convictions.[17] On the whole, though, the King's ministers and their supporters in the Diet were not especially effective in organizing themselves politically or in defending, justifying, and articulating their opinions. In June, shortly before the Diet's adjournment, Leopold von Gerlach wrote that he considered it to be 'an unhappy phase for our country. The King began a necessary and just war with bad troops and with commanders who were inexperienced and clumsy.' Many conservatives would probably have agreed with that assessment.[18] Frederick William quickly lost interest in the Diet's proceedings, perhaps because it had so mightily disappointed his expectations. Towards the end, he was no longer following the debates in detail, relying instead on summary reports from Stolberg.[19] Though he was clearly annoyed by the Diet's activities, he saw no need to change the legislation of 3 February or make concessions to what he continued to regard as the destructive tendencies of his age. After the Diet's adjournment on 26 June Frederick William continued to live and govern as before, even as the social, economic, and political crisis in Prussia was reaching dangerous proportions.

On the very day that the United Diet opened in Berlin, reported the *Augsburger Allgemeine Zeitung*, grain prices in that city had 'experienced a disturbing increase'. A *Wispel* (about two dozen bushels) of wheat now cost 100 Taler, 'which is something unheard of in the annals of Berlin'.[20] The steady rise in food prices was accelerated both by bad harvests and by the spread of potato blight, and by 1847 the situation threatened to become catastrophic. This last great crisis of the old agrarian order was intensified by a new kind of crisis, a downswing in industrial production. The result was a wave of social protest, especially food riots, at the very time that the United Diet was deliberating. The capital itself became the scene of one of the most spectacular outbursts of violence, the 'potato revolution' of 21–3 April 1847, which began with women attacking potato-sellers in the markets of Berlin and only subsided after a show of military

---

[16] Gernot Dallinger, *Karl von Canitz und Dallnitz: Ein preußischer Minister des Vormärz. Darstellung und Quellen* (Cologne, 1969), 70–2. Leopold von Gerlach, diary (23 May 1847), GA, 'Abschriften', v. 17.

[17] Hans-Joachim Schoeps (ed.), *Neue Quellen zur Geschichte Preußens im 19. Jahrhundert* (Berlin, 1968), 374–6.

[18] Leopold von Gerlach to Ludwig von Gerlach, 10 June 1847, ibid. 368.

[19] Varnhagen von Ense, *Tagebücher*, iv. 80 (2 May 1847); Stolberg's reports to FW IV, GStA Merseburg, HA Rep. 50 J Nr. 1413 Vol. II, Bl. 221–30; Valentin, *Revolution*, i. 80–1; Herman von Petersdorff, *König Friedrich Wilhelm der Vierte* (Stuttgart, 1900), 65–6.

[20] *Allgemeine Zeitung* (Augsburg), 16 Apr. 1847.

force.[21] By the summer of 1847, Prussia thus found itself in a precarious, even pre-revolutionary situation.[22]

As in so many other situations of that sort, a variety of overlapping, sometimes contradictory, but on the whole mutually reinforcing factors was pushing Prussia and much of the rest of Central Europe in the direction of revolution. In 1847 very few Prussians, whether bourgeois businessmen, peasants, or urban craftsmen, ever thought seriously of any alternative to monarchy; but the social and political currents of that year suggested that Frederick William IV's particular monarchical project was rapidly becoming an irrelevancy. Moreover, after 1847 the King's advisers seemed aimless and indecisive, unable to respond to the increasingly serious situation in the country. Canitz's position, for example, had been seriously weakened by his gaffe in the United Diet. After the Diet's adjournment he withdrew from the limelight and eschewed substantive foreign-policy initiatives. Bodelschwingh's position continued to be relatively strong, and he used it, though without success, to urge the King to think seriously about genuine constitutional concessions.[23] During those months Leopold von Gerlach became more worried than ever before that the King was becoming too dependent on Bodelschwingh, a 'liberal bureaucrat' who, Gerlach believed, had no respect for the country's established institutions and political structures, an unprincipled man who was the King's 'complete opposite' and yet 'increasingly indispensable' to him.[24] Radowitz, who saw a great deal of the King in late 1847, shared Gerlach's concerns. Neither Bodelschwingh, nor Thile, nor Stolberg could really understand the King's ideas, he thought, or help translate them into meaningful reality. Indeed, the three men together constituted 'the most dangerous company which the King has kept since his accession to the throne'. With their intellectual limitations they failed to 'enter into his ideas, which are often confused and impractical but always stem from proper feelings'. Accordingly, they thought that their major function was to keep the King under control and thus render him 'harmless'. The result, Radowitz believed, was creeping paralysis at a time when creative initiatives were desperately needed.[25]

---

[21] On the *Subsistenzunruhen* of 1847, see esp. Manfred Gailus, 'Soziale Protestbewegungen in Deutschland 1847–1849', in Heinrich Volkmann and Jürgen Bergmann (eds.), *Sozialer Protest: Studien zu traditioneller Resistenz und kollektiver Gewalt in Deutschland vom Vormärz bis zur Reichsgründung* (Opladen, 1984), 77–85; id., *Straße und Brot: Sozialer Protest in den deutschen Staaten unter besonderer Berücksichtigung Preußens, 1847–1849* (Göttingen, 1990), ch. 4.

[22] Wolfram Siemann, *Die deutsche Revolution von 1848/49* (Frankfurt am Main, 1985), 44–8; Gailus, 'Protestbewegungen', 86. On the 'potato revolution' in Berlin, see also Meyer, *Leben*, 81–98; Adolf Streckfuß, *500 Jahre Berliner Geschichte: Vom Fischerdorf zur Weltstadt. Geschichte und Sage*, ii, 4th edn. (Berlin, 1886), 948–51; Hamerow, *Restoration*, 84–7, 93; Ilja Mieck, 'Von der Reformzeit zur Revolution (1806–1847)', in Wolfgang Ribbe (ed.), *Geschichte Berlins* (Munich, 1987), i: *Von der Frühgeschichte bis zur Industrialisierung*, 599–601.

[23] Siemann, *Revolution*, 48; Hans-Ulrich Wehler, *Deutsche Gesellschaftsgeschichte* (Munich, 1987–), ii: *Von der Reformära bis zur industriellen und politischen 'Deutschen Doppelrevolution' 1815–1845/49*, 660–702; Thomas Nipperdey, *Deutsche Geschichte 1800–1866: Bürgerwelt und starker Staat* (Munich, 1983), 401–2; Leopold von Gerlach, diary (2 Nov. 1847), GA, 'Abschriften', v. 30; Hans-Joachim Schoeps (ed.), *Neue Quellen*, 576–7.

[24] Leopold von Gerlach, diary (2 and 16 Nov. 1847), GA, 'Abschriften', v. 28, 31; Leopold von Gerlach to Ludwig von Gerlach, 17 Nov. 1847, GA, Fasz. CT.

[25] Paul Hassel, *Joseph Maria von Radowitz*, i: *1797–1848* (Berlin, 1905), 132–3 (autobiographical essay by Radowitz).

After the late summer of 1847 Frederick William IV appeared to be unconcerned about his failure to transform state, society, and religion in Prussia. Indeed, a kind of deceptive normality and even lethargy characterized his activities in the last nine months before the March revolution. In late June he had not bothered to stay in Berlin for the adjournment of the United Diet, choosing instead to travel to Breslau and dedicate a monument.[26] In August, as usual, he spent a few days on the island of Rügen in the Baltic. Thereafter he travelled to southern Germany and, accompanied by Stolberg, continued to Trieste and Venice. In late September he returned to Bavaria before making his way to the Rhineland and Westphalia for a series of public appearances and troop inspections. Finally, in the autumn he took part in the annual series of royal hunts at Letzlingen Castle, Blankenburg Castle, and Quedlinburg.

In the best of times it was difficult to get the King to concentrate on complex or difficult problems, and during his various travels it was almost impossible to do so. From his diplomatic post in Karlsruhe, for example, Radowitz was aware that pressures for significant political change were rapidly growing in Germany, and he believed that Frederick William could help defuse the situation by proposing far-reaching reforms in the structure of the German Confederation. The King could thus appear to be responsive to nationalist feelings and aspirations, but without succumbing to liberal ideas. In September Frederick William asked Radowitz to accompany him on his tour of the Rhineland and Westphalia, and during a conversation on a steamer between Trier and Koblenz Radowitz tried to convince the King that time was of the essence. But Frederick William was too easily distracted, and only when the royal party had reached Münster in Westphalia did Radowitz have an opportunity to present his ideas systematically. Frederick William asked his friend to prepare detailed reports, but nothing came of them. Thile, cautious as ever, believed that they would unnecessarily alienate Austria; and by the autumn of 1847 Frederick William himself had become more interested in the complex political situation in Switzerland than in issues of Confederate reform.[27]

Since 1707 the French-speaking canton of Neuchâtel had belonged to the Hohenzollerns. It was the only member of the Swiss Confederation ruled by a monarch, and a foreign one at that. Frederick William had visited Neuchâtel in 1842, and with his usual personal susceptibilities had waxed enthusiastic about the Romantic beauties of the landscape and the supposed monarchist sentiments of its people. Thereafter he felt almost fanatically attached to Neuchâtel, and determined to hold on to his possessions there. He was thus wildly agitated when, in the autumn of 1847, Neuchâtel became caught up in the emotions of the *Sonderbund* affair, a conflict between liberal and Catholic cantons that reflected the growing tensions of a Europe on the eve of revolution.

[26] FW IV to Elisabeth, 26 June 1847, GStA Merseburg, HA Rep. 50 J Nr. 995 Fasz. 20, Bl. 5.

[27] Hassel, *Radowitz*, 135–8 (autobiographical essay), 445–6, 452–6; Radowitz to FW IV, 12 Oct. 1847, and Thile to FW IV (n. d.), in Joseph Maria von Radowitz, *Nachgelassene Briefe und Aufzeichnungen zur Geschichte der Jahre 1848–1853*, ed. Walter Möring (Stuttgart, 1922), 1–5; id., *Ausgewählte Schriften und Reden*, ed. Friedrich Meinecke (Munich, 1921), 96–110; Erich Brandenburg, *Untersuchungen und Aktenstücke zur Geschichte der Reichsgründung* (Leipzig, 1916), 7–19.

As a Protestant canton, Neuchâtel was under considerable pressure to contribute to Confederate efforts to suppress the Catholic *Sonderbund*, and when it was refused the Swiss Confederation imposed a fine of 300,000 francs upon the canton. Frederick William was greatly upset by the whole affair, and by what he considered to be the dangerous excesses of liberalism and republicanism in Switzerland, a country that he believed posed a threat to monarchical institutions all over Europe. For weeks he barraged Foreign Minister Canitz with enquiries, demands, and entreaties for concerted diplomatic action against Switzerland. But, again, nothing happened. Finally, at the beginning of March 1848 a republican insurrection in Neuchâtel swept away royal and Prussian institutions in that canton. By that time, however, Frederick William had much more serious problems to face closer to home.[28]

'Satan is on the loose again.' This was Frederick William's first reaction to news of the Paris insurrection that toppled Louis-Philippe from his throne and replaced the July Monarchy with a provisional republic. The King of Prussia wasted no tears on Louis-Philippe, whom he regarded, because of the Paris events of July 1830, as an impertinent usurper. But Frederick William and virtually all of his advisers were certain that a French republic would inevitably pose a threat to the thrones of Europe, and especially to the security of the member states of the German Confederation.[29] The threat was a dual one, they believed: France's revolutionary example could encourage similar insurrections in German territories, while France itself, still lusting for the Rhine frontier, also posed a military danger. Frederick William's first response to the news from Paris was to call upon Queen Victoria, Tsar Nicholas, and Metternich to join with him in a renewed spirit of anti-revolutionary and monarchical solidarity: 'If the principles of the French Revolution are carried out, all crowns will inevitably be shattered and all peoples will be plunged into an age of misery and distress, of lawlessness and godlessness. *We* style ourselves "by the Grace of God", and now we have to prove to the whole world that this is true. The maintenance of peace should be our first, but not our exclusive, goal.'[30] In February and early March he also undertook a series of diplomatic initiatives which he hoped would encourage both monarchical unity against the revolution and the stability of the European political system. The most important were the special missions of Leopold von Gerlach to Copenhagen and Radowitz to Vienna, which Frederick William hoped would 'erect a dike against the devastating floods which are pouring over the continent'.[31] Only with Austria's co-operation, Frederick William believed,

---

[28] Maurice Haesler, *De la situation de Neuchâtel vis-à-vis de la Prusse et de la Confédération suisse (1848–1857)* (Saint-Aubin [Neuchâtel], 1958), 34–57; Jacques Petitpierre, *Neuchâtel et la Confédération suisse devant l'Europe: L'Insurrection royaliste et le Traité de Paris. A propos du centenaire d'une capitulation royale 1856–1857* (Neuchâtel, 1957), ch. 1; FW IV to Canitz, 4 Oct. to 13 Dec. 1847, GStA Berlin, BPH Rep. 50 Nr. 117, 133–45; Edgar Bonjour, *Vorgeschichte des Neuenburger Konflikts 1848–1856* (Berne, 1932), 11–20.

[29] FW IV to Carl von der Groeben, 1 Mar. 1848, GStA Merseburg, Rep. 92 Graf Carl von der Groeben B Nr. 4ᵉ 1848, Bl. 6; FW IV to Stolberg, 27 Feb. 1848, GStA Merseburg, HA Rep. 50 J Nr. 1414, Bl. 28.

[30] FW IV to Groeben, 1 Mar. 1848, GStA Merseburg, Rep. 92 Graf Carl von der Groeben B Nr. 4ᵉ 1848, Bl. 5–5ᵛ.

[31] Radowitz to Marie von Radowitz, 3 Mar. 1848, in Radowitz, *Briefe und Aufzeichnungen*, 9.

would it be possible for that dam to hold.[32] Metternich went along with most of Radowitz's proposals for a special congress of the German Confederation's member states to placate nationalist sentiment by addressing issues of Confederate reform; it was scheduled for late March. The force of events, however, rendered all these arrangements nugatory, and the congress never took place. The solidarity of the legitimist powers, discussions of military options, or plans for Confederate reform could not dispel the gathering storm in the early spring of 1848.[33]

Frederick William's nightmare of a revolutionary contagion emanating from France seemed to show signs of becoming reality in late February and early March, as a wave of demonstrations, petitions, addresses, and popular assemblies spread throughout western and south-western Germany. Indeed, the impetus for a number of these activities had been provided even before the overthrow of the monarchy in Paris. On 12 February, the Baden parliamentarian Friedrich Bassermann had delivered an important speech in the lower house of that grand duchy's assembly in which he had called for concrete steps to achieve German unity on a federal basis.[34] Bassermann's speech showed that liberal demands for constitutional and parliamentary reform, the lifting of restrictions on freedom of the press and assembly, and the unity of the German nation were indissolubly linked. What would be the consequences of such demands for the Restoration-era structures of monarchic and aristocratic authority in the German states? That kind of question acquired a literally burning urgency at the beginning of March, as an elemental popular revolution began to sweep through parts of southern and north-western Germany; among other things, the protesters demanded the total elimination of vestigial feudal privileges.[35]

The first significant signs of radical political protest in Prussia's urban areas came on 3 March, when a mass demonstration in Cologne was dispersed by military intervention.[36] But such repressive measures could not check the spread of popular agitation. Within days petitions, addresses, and demonstrations were being reported from

[32] FW IV to Radowitz, 10 Mar. 1848, in Hassel, *Radowitz*, 492–4.

[33] See Radowitz's reports and letters from his Vienna mission in Radowitz, *Briefe und Aufzeichnungen*, 6–37. For older controversies concerning Frederick William's 'German policies' in Feb.–Mar. and Radowitz's Vienna mission, see Reinhold Koser, 'Friedrich Wilhelm IV. am Vorabend der Märzrevolution', in id., *Zur preußischen und deutschen Geschichte: Aufsätze und Vorträge*, ed. Elisabeth Koser (Stuttgart, 1921; orig. 1899), 288–92, 294–301; Hermann Oncken, 'Zur Genesis der preußischen Revolution von 1848', *FBPG* 13 (1900), 132–41; Felix Rachfahl, 'Österreich und Preußen im März 1848: Aktenmäßige Darstellung des Dresden-Potsdamer Kongreßprojektes', *Historische Vierteljahrschrift*, 6 (1903), 357–86, 503–30, and 7 (1904), 192–260; id., *Deutschland, König Friedrich Wilhelm IV. und die Berliner Märzrevolution* (Halle, 1901), 63–98; Friedrich Meinecke, 'Friedrich Wilhelm IV. und Deutschland', in id., *Preußen und Deutschland im 19. und 20. Jahrhundert: Historische und politische Aufsätze* (Munich, 1918; orig. 1902), 219–20, 224–31; Brandenburg, *Untersuchungen*, 17–56.

[34] Valentin, *Revolution*, i. 337, 340.

[35] See Rainer Koch, 'Die Agrarrevolution in Deutschland 1848: Ursachen—Verlauf—Ergebnisse', in Dieter Langewiesche (ed.), *Die deutsche Revolution von 1848/49* (Darmstadt, 1983), 362–94; Manfred Gailus, 'Zur Politisierung der Landbevölkerung in der Märzbewegung von 1848', in Peter Steinbach (ed.), *Probleme politischer Partizipation im Modernisierungsprozeß* (Stuttgart, 1982), 88–113; id., 'Protestbewegungen', 89–93.

[36] Among several descriptions, see Valentin, *Revolution*, i. 416–17; Nipperdey, *Deutsche Geschichte*, 598; Siemann, *Revolution*, 67.

two other major cities in the Prussian monarchy, Breslau and Königsberg; and the possibility of major disturbances in the Prussian countryside, especially Silesia, had become increasingly real.[37] The prospect of agrarian disturbances, so much more difficult to control than urban outbreaks, was especially horrifying to Prussia's landed élite, which helps explain why, in Adolf von Thadden-Trieglaff's expression, so many of them were 'paralysed by icy fear' in the spring of 1848.[38] That same fear and loss of nerve quickly spread to the governing élite in Berlin and Potsdam, and helps to explain a generalized 'crisis of the political élite at the centre' in March 1848.[39]

Division and discord within the upper reaches of the monarchical establishment only made that crisis worse. The Prince of Prussia and the group around Leopold von Gerlach were for standing firm and resisting pressures for constitutional or other concessions. Because of the supposed military threat from France, on 9 March the King designated William as military governor of the Rhineland and Westphalia, Prussia's two westernmost provinces. It seems fairly certain that at that point both William and Gerlach were thinking almost exclusively in terms of military responses to the growing revolutionary challenge.[40] The Gerlachs also urged the King to name his old nemesis Alvensleben to the Ministry, presumably because of his reputation for toughness and because Bodelschwingh had made it clear that his own resignation was a matter of time.[41] Nothing came of the proposal, and around the tenth of the month Bodelschwingh himself rather fatalistically insisted to Carl von Voß-Buch that 'we are closer to a Hansemann government than you imagine': a reference to the liberal Rhenish businessman David Hansemann, who on 1 March had called for a German parliament, the convocation of the United Diet in Prussia, and new guarantees for freedom of the press and 'popular representation'.[42]

Despite his growing pessimism, Bodelschwingh believed in late February and early March that timely concessions were still possible, and during those weeks he devoted all his energies to convincing Frederick William that he was right.[43] He seemed to enjoy some success. At the minister's urging, for example, the King at last

[37] Wehler, *Gesellschaftsgeschichte*, ii. 713; William J. Orr, jun., 'Königsberg und die Revolution von 1848', *Zeitschrift für Ostforschung*, 26 (1977), 282–4.

[38] Wehler, *Gesellschaftsgeschichte*, ii. 707.

[39] Gerd Heinrich, 'Einleitung', in Karl Ludwig von Prittwitz, *Berlin 1848: Das Erinnerungswerk des Generalleutnants Karl Ludwig von Prittwitz und andere Quellen zur Berliner Märzrevolution und zur Geschichte Preußens um die Mitte des 19. Jahrhunderts*, ed. Gerd Heinrich (Berlin, 1985). p. L.

[40] *Promemoria* of Leopold von Gerlach for Prince of Prussia, 11 or 12 March 1848, GA, 'Abschriften', xviii. 120. See also ibid., vi. 9; and Karl Heinz Börner, *Kaiser Wilhelm I. 1797 bis 1888: Deutscher Kaiser und König von Preußen. Eine Biographie* (Cologne, 1984), 73.

[41] FW IV to Thile, 11 Mar. 1848, GStA Merseburg, Rep. 92 Ludwig Gustav von Thile C Nr. 9, Bl. 63. See also Ernst Ludwig von Gerlach, *Aufzeichnungen aus seinem Leben und Wirken 1795–1877*, ed. Jakob von Gerlach (2 vols.; Schwerin, 1903), i. 507; Leopold von Gerlach, diary (addendum of 15 Feb. 1849), GA, 'Abschriften', vi. 10–11; Leopold von Gerlach to Ludwig von Gerlach, 15 Mar. 1848, in E. L. von Gerlach, *Von der Revolution zum Norddeutschen Bund: Politik und Ideengut der preußischen Hochkonservativen 1848–1866. Aus dem Nachlaß von Ernst Ludwig von Gerlach*, ed. Hellmut Diwald (2 vols.; Göttingen, 1970), ii. 487.

[42] Obenaus, *Anfänge*, 715.

[43] Bodelschwingh to Fallenstein, 30 Mar. 1848, in Gustav von Diest, *Meine Erlebnisse im Jahre 1848 und die Stellung des Staatsministers von Bodelschwingh vor und an dem 18. März 1848* (Berlin, 1898), 15.

acceded to long-standing liberal demands for periodic meetings of the United Diet.[44] Conservative critics of Bodelschwingh, including Leopold von Gerlach and Stolberg, were worried that the King had thus committed himself to a constitutional path, but Bodelschwingh believed that it was important to press on. On 8 March he seems to have converted Frederick William to the idea 'that a constitution cannot be avoided', and simultaneously the government issued a decree loosening censorship regulations. During the next few days the feverishly busy minister began to sketch out a constitutional package that might gain the King's approval; thereafter, Bodelschwingh indicated, he would resign. On the fourteenth Frederick William agreed that the United Diet should meet on 27 April to discuss the increasingly grave situation in the country.[45] It thus seemed that Bodelschwingh's efforts to persuade a reluctant monarch to follow a constitutional path might be rewarded with success. Moreover, he was not entirely alone. Despite his own suspicions of Bodelschwingh, Stolberg had vigorously urged his royal master to agree to the periodicity of the United Diet; and on 11 March the liberal Prussian minister to France, Baron Heinrich Alexander von Arnim-Suckow, arrived in Berlin with a first-hand account of the events in Paris and a warning that Prussia would have to commit itself immediately to a constitutional course.[46]

Growing popular pressure for constitutional reform, articulated in the cafés and other public gathering-places of the capital, underscored the increasing seriousness of the situation. A series of large public meetings had taken place in the Tiergarten, just west of the Brandenburg Gate, on 6–7 March, and had concluded with the preparation of a nine-point address to the King calling for drastic changes in the Prussian state and guarantees of fundamental political rights. The Tiergarten demonstrations continued thereafter, growing larger from day to day, while various representatives of the Berlin city government tried without success to mediate between the demonstrators and royal authorities.[47]

The situation deteriorated dramatically after the thirteenth, when regular troops stationed inside the city fought with demonstrators returning from the Tiergarten. Several people were killed, and during the next few days the demonstrations spread to the streets and squares of the inner city itself. Just as the political élite around Frederick William was divided in its responses to the growing popular movement, so too was the military leadership confused and divided about its own role. The Prince of Prussia, who regarded himself as the voice of the army, had not yet left for the

[44] Speech to the *ständisch* United Committees, 5 Mar. 1848, in *Reden und Trinksprüche*, 66–70; cf. Hans-Joachim Schoeps, (ed.), *Neue Quellen*, 377.

[45] Günter Richter, 'Friedrich Wilhelm IV. und die Revolution von 1848', in Otto Büsch (ed.), *Friedrich Wilhelm IV. in seiner Zeit: Beiträge eines Colloquiums* (Berlin, 1987), 109–11; Friedrich Wilhelm IV., *Reden und Trinksprüche*, 70–1, 280–1; Ernst Kaeber, 'Bodelschwingh und die Berliner Märzrevolution', in id., *Beiträge zur Berliner Geschichte: Ausgewählte Aufsätze*, ed. Werner Vogel (Berlin, 1964), 167–73.

[46] Albrecht von dem Bussche, *Heinrich Alexander von Arnim: Liberalismus, Polenfrage und deutsche Einheit. Das 19. Jahrhundert im Spiegel einer Biographie des preußischen Staatsmannes* (Osnabrück, 1986), 105–10.

[47] Günter Richter, 'Zwischen Revolution und Reichsgründung (1848–1870)', in Ribbe (ed.), *Geschichte Berlins*, ii: *Von der Märzrevolution bis zur Gegenwart*, 607, 611.

Rhineland; he continued to follow an uncompromising line, which led to a nasty public row on the fifteenth with the commander of troops in and around Berlin, the liberal-minded General Ernst von Pfuel, who had irritated the Prince by preventing a clash between soldiers and demonstrators directly in front of the royal palace. Finally, on the sixteenth news of the revolution in Vienna and the fall of Metternich reached Berlin; on that same day the Prussian government agreed to the establishment of 'Protective Commissions' (*Schutzkommissionen*) of unarmed citizens to help resolve potential conflicts between civilians and the authorities. Would measures like these dam the tide of revolution?[48]

Revolution and Aftermath, March–August 1848

It is difficult to gauge Frederick William's own reactions to developments in late February and early March 1848. In the first days after receiving the news from Paris he had responded with some clarity and firmness to the worsening situation in his own kingdom, especially in Upper Silesia, where he wanted to set up a special commission for the duration of the emergency and 'for the purpose of reforms'.[49] On 6 March he wrote with some confidence to Groeben of his decision to grant periodicity; though worried about events in the western parts of the kingdom, he was confident that order could be maintained. Six days later he was no longer so sure of himself: 'The granting of periodicity, etc., has made virtually no impression *at all*. . . . Pray with me as one: that the Lord through his mercy will turn things around in Germany and France!'[50] On the eleventh the King had decided that the situation had become so serious 'that a proclamation "To My People" is unavoidable'.[51] By the fourteenth he admitted to Stolberg that he had become 'completely demoralized'. Never one for sophisticated analyses of complex situations, Stolberg suggested that the King had been consuming too much tobacco and vehemently scolded the monarch for not behaving like a true king and Christian. The following day Frederick William journeyed to Potsdam, where he 'utterly lost his courage' and vowed not to return to Berlin, though he finally pulled himself together and went back to the capital later in the day. He was still thinking of returning to Potsdam, but his advisers urged him not to, and the Queen's fragile health made it difficult in any case.[52]

On that same day Bodelschwingh drafted his formal resignation, stating that he lacked the popularity necessary to carry out essential reforms. Two days later, at a

---

[48] G. Richter, 'Zwischen Revolution und Reichsgründung (1848–1870)' 605–14; id., 'Friedrich Wilhelm IV.', 112–16; Adolf Wolff, *Berliner Revolutions-Chronik: Darstellung der Berliner Bewegungen im Jahre 1848 nach politischen, socialen und literarischen Beziehungen* (3 vols.; Berlin, 1851, 1852, 1854; repr. Vaduz, 1979), i. 14–93; A. Streckfuß, *500 Jahre*, ii. 952–69; Prittwitz, *Berlin 1848*, 48–94.

[49] FW IV to Bodelschwingh, 26 Feb. 1848, GA, Neg J/I/e, Bl. 61–2 (copies from Bodelschwingh'sches Hauptarchiv Bethel).

[50] FW IV to Groeben, 6 and 12 Mar. 1848, GStA Merseburg, Rep. 92 Graf Carl von der Groeben B Nr. 4ᵉ 1848, Bl. 8–11.

[51] FW IV to Thile, 11 Mar. 1848, in Koser, 'Vorabend', 310.

[52] AKO, FW IV to *Staatsministerium*, 14 Mar. 1848, GStA Merseburg, Geheimes Zivilkabinett 2.2.1. Nr. 3692, Bl. 92; Leopold von Gerlach, diary (addendum of 11 Apr. 1849 and entry for 27 Mar. 1848), GA,
[*cont. on p. 139*]

meeting of the Ministry in the presence of the King and the Prince of Prussia, Bodelschwingh persuaded Frederick William and his ministers to agree to royal patents guaranteeing the abolition of censorship, the establishment of a constitutional system in Prussia, and the convocation of the United Diet on 2 April (rather than the twenty-seventh, as originally planned). The King also agreed to ask his former minister, Count Arnim-Boitzenburg, to be Bodelschwingh's successor; in fact, Arnim would head Prussia's first constitutional government.[53]

Arnim himself was summoned to the palace early on the morning of 18 March. He asked for twenty-four hours to think about his new appointment before formally committing himself to it.[54] After ten o'clock that morning the two patents were published, and shortly after noon the King confirmed these measures in audiences with deputations from Cologne and from the Berlin city government. In addition, Minister Thile appeared at the city hall in the early afternoon to reassure other local politicians about the forthcoming transition to a responsible constitutional ministry; like Bodelschwingh and all the other ministers, he too was about to resign.[55]

A group of citizens had earlier planned to hold a mass rally in front of the palace to demand political concessions from the King. Now, it seemed, Frederick William had shown his capacity to make such concessions voluntarily, and despite some confusion the demonstration began to turn into a celebration of thanks. The potential for serious conflict still existed, however; between one and two in the afternoon, General Karl Ludwig von Prittwitz, new leader of the élite Guard Corps, replaced the conciliatory Pfuel as commander of all troops in and around Berlin. With a deserved reputation for toughness, Prittwitz would be less likely to bend to popular pressure.[56] By noon the demonstration had got underway, as several thousand people gathered in front of the palace. The assemblage was entirely peaceful. Frederick William, though, was worried about its political implications. He was also concerned that it might get out of control, and again raised the possibility of leaving the city.[57] But that was no longer an option. Around 1.30 p.m. the King, who had barely been visible in public for weeks, appeared on the palace balcony to wave to the crowd. He could not be heard very well when he began to speak; but copies of the two royal patents were circulating through the multitude, and there could be little doubt that most people were aware of his intentions. At this point, more and more demonstrators began to

'Abschriften', vi. 12, 14; Otto Graf zu Stolberg-Wernigerode, *Anton Graf zu Stolberg-Wernigerode: Ein Freund und Ratgeber König Friedrich Wilhelms IV.* (Munich, 1926), 55–7; G. Richter, 'Friedrich Wilhelm IV.', 110.

[53] Bodelschwingh to FW IV, 15 Mar. 1848, in Diest, *Erlebnisse*, 49–51; Adolf Wolff, *Revolutions-Chronik*, i. 108–17; Kaeber, 'Bodelschwingh', 171–6. See also Heinrich Leo's description of a conversation with Bodelschwingh about these developments in GA, 'Abschriften', xviii. 164; and Ludwig von Gerlach to Leopold von Gerlach, 20 Apr. 1848, ibid. xviii. 14–15.

[54] 'Schreiben des Ministers Graf v. Arnim', in Prittwitz, *Berlin 1848*, 453–4.

[55] Ibid. 113–15; Adolf Wolff, *Revolutions-Chronik*, i. 118–26.

[56] Prittwitz, *Berlin 1848*, 127–9.

[57] FW IV to Bodelschwingh, 18 Mar. 1848, in Karl Haenchen (ed.), *Revolutionsbriefe 1848: Ungedrucktes aus dem Nachlaß König Friedrich Wilhelms IV. von Preußen* (Leipzig, 1930), 48–9; Hans-Joachim Schoeps (ed.), *Neue Quellen*, 415.

call for troops in the vicinity to withdraw, including the soldiers stationed around the palace. Thereupon Frederick William himself ordered the just-appointed Prittwitz to 'take the cavalry and use them to mop up the palace square and finally put an end to the scandalous situation there. The cavalry should, however, proceed at a slow pace and not take up arms.'[58] An enormously confusing and dangerous situation ensued as a squadron of dragoons began to move through the crowd but could not disperse it. At that point grenadiers from the Kaiser Franz Regiment came to their assistance, and in the confusion two shots were discharged, though no one was injured.

That was the catalyst. The crowd broke up amid angry charges that the King had betrayed the people of Berlin, that the constitutional concessions had merely been a sinister cloak to entice the people to the palace and shoot them down. Almost immediately barricades began to go up throughout the city. While the first shots of the March revolution were being fired, Frederick William IV, his generals, his advisers, and their guests were sitting down to dinner in the palace. Within hours the Prussian monarchy seemed to be teetering on the brink of disintegration.[59]

Although the tumultuous and astonishing events of 18–25 March 1848 have often been described, Frederick William IV's own motives and behaviour remain controversial. Why did a king 'by the Grace of God', a man who had abusively rejected the idea of a written constitution, now apparently capitulate so utterly to revolutionary demands for constitutional change? Many historians, among them the celebrated Heinrich von Sybel, attributed the King's actions to weakness and nervous collapse on the afternoon of 18 March and thereafter, a notion partially sustained by Frederick William's later confession to Leopold von Ranke that in the March days he and everyone else had lain 'on our bellies'.

The image of a shattered, weak, incoherent, occasionally sobbing monarch has persisted in the historical literature ever since; but in fact, as recent research has clearly shown, that image is wildly overdrawn. Of course, the pace of events after 18 March was confusing and the news contradictory, while the creaky and inefficient command-structure of the Prussian monarchy was overloaded. The King himself was bombarded on all sides by petitioners, would-be advisers, officers, court officials, delegations of professors and local politicians, and his own relatives. The scenes of confusion in the palace testified graphically to a generalized paralysis of the ruling élites and to the breakdown of the normal structures of the court. The literary critic and local journalist Ludwig Rellstab, who simply entered the palace and proceeded to the King's chambers at 6.30 on the morning of the nineteenth, later described the scene that he encountered: 'Up in the King's antechambers officers of every rank, many General Staff officers, ministers, high state officials, and at the

[58] Prittwitz, *Berlin 1848*, 129.

[59] Among various first-hand accounts see the report of *Flügeladjutant* August von Schöler, 18 Mar. 1848, in Haenchen (ed.), *Revolutionsbriefe*, 49–52; Adolf Wolff, *Revolutions-Chronik*, i. 125–40; Prittwitz, *Berlin 1848*, 130–48. Among innumerable secondary accounts, see esp. A. Streckfuß, *500 Jahre*, ii. 972–6; Rachfahl, *Märzrevolution*, 139–44; Valentin, *Revolution*, i. 426–30; G. Richter, 'Revolution', 614–15.

same time an array of servants and royal lackeys were all milling around in confusion. I also became aware of the princes in that unusual throng. People came, people went, people were asking questions, finding things out, and advising each other.'[60]

In those circumstances it was rather difficult to keep one's head. One of the few who did was Thile, who spent the night of the eighteenth and all day on the nineteenth arranging for the entire state treasury, the crown treasury, and important state papers to be crated up and sent to Potsdam and the fortress of Spandau.[61] According to various eyewitness accounts, the King himself appeared calm and determined; after his meeting on the morning of the nineteenth, Rellstab spoke of 'the high seriousness, the deep emotion, and yet so powerful self-control' that Frederick William displayed in those critical hours.[62] The decisions that he took then were essentially his own; and he demonstrated more self-control than either Bodelschwingh or the Prince of Prussia, who sometimes appeared to be on the verge of panic. Only after noon on the nineteenth did he begin to succumb to self-doubt, remorse, and guilt about his actions.

The bloody fighting in the streets of Berlin continued into the evening of the eighteenth, with the army partially succeeding in establishing its control over the heart of the capital. Gaining and maintaining control over the entire city, however, was a different matter. Although Prittwitz's troops vastly outnumbered the barricade fighters, they were not trained in street-fighting or in dealing with popular insurrections.[63] Therefore, shortly before midnight the General had a confidential discussion with Frederick William in which he stated that it would be possible to maintain control of the centre of Berlin for a few days. If the public mood had not calmed down by that time, it would be necessary to evacuate the city, surround it, and bombard it into submission—a favoured technique of nineteenth-century urban warfare, and one applied with brutal effectiveness in other European cities later in the year. The noncommittal monarch listened, thanked Prittwitz, and returned to his desk. Prittwitz noted the 'comfortable way in which His Majesty sat down at his desk, pulling a furry foot-muff over his feet after taking off his boots and stockings, in order, it seemed, to begin writing another lengthy document'. The document he was drafting was perhaps the most famous of his whole reign: his celebrated appeal 'To My Dear Berliners' (*An Meine lieben Berliner*). Shortly after midnight he sent it to Bodelschwingh, now in his last hours as minister, who in turn took it to the court printer at 3 a.m. Within a few hours, hundreds of copies of the royal proclamation were being posted throughout the city.[64]

---

[60] 'Aus dem Adjutanten-Journal (v. Brauchitsch)', 20 Mar. 1848, in Haenchen (ed.), *Revolutionsbriefe*, 52–3; L. Rellstab, *Zwei Gespräche mit Seiner Majestät Friedrich Wilhelm dem Vierten (am 23sten November 1847, und am 19ten März 1848) in geschichtlichen Rahmen gefaßt* (Berlin, 1849), 63–4. See also Prittwitz, *Berlin 1848*, 226–7 (statement of Friedrich Wilhelm von Rauch); and G. Richter, 'Friedrich Wilhelm IV.', 120.

[61] Bismarck-Bohlen, 'Aufzeichnungen', GStA Merseburg, HA Rep. 50 F 1 Nr. 6, Bl. 6ᵛ; Diest, *Erlebnisse*, 12; Manfred Kliem, 'Genesis der Führungskräfte der feudal-militaristischen Konterrevolution 1848 in Preußen', (Diss:, Berlin [East], 1966), 250–7.

[62] Rellstab, *Gespräche*, 75.   [63] Prittwitz, *Berlin 1848*, 264.   [64] Ibid. 230–2, 259–60.

Why Frederick William decided to extend an olive-branch to an embittered and suspicious citizenry is still not entirely clear. Most contemporaries believed, however, that the sound of fighting near the palace, as well as the entreaties of the liberal Westphalian aristocrat, Baron Georg von Vincke, were decisive. A scion of a distinguished family, the cousin of Bodelschwingh, and a prominent member of the previous year's United Diet, Vincke had just arrived from western Germany, and had observed the street-fighting on his way to the palace. The soldiers were exhausted, he said, and there was little chance of victory; the situation had thus become critically dangerous. The officers in the King's immediate entourage 'laughed at this impertinent and singular speech. Outraged at this, Vincke turned to us and said we wouldn't be laughing the next day.'[65] Vincke later denied that he had urged the King to give in to the revolution. There seems little doubt, however, that his remarks, in conjunction with Frederick William's conversation with Prittwitz, strengthened the monarch in his resolve to avoid further bloodshed.[66]

In his appeal, Frederick William asserted that the events of 18 March had resulted from a misunderstanding, that the joy of the people gathered in the palace square had been disrupted by 'a bunch of rioters'. (In his conversation with Rellstab early on the nineteenth he described the events on the square as a '*coup monté*', organized and directed by outsiders, 'who have hidden themselves in Berlin for a week'.)[67] He called upon the 'residents of my beloved native city' to clear the barricades, in exchange for which 'I give you my word as King that all the streets and squares will be immediately evacuated by the troops, and that military occupation will be limited to essential buildings like the palace, the arsenal, and a few others, and even there for only a short period of time'.[68]

While Berliners were waking up to read the proclamation, a series of confused and complex meetings at the royal palace took place between the King and his advisers (including Bodelschwingh from his old Ministry and Arnim-Boitzenburg from the new one), Police President Julius von Minutoli, and, at various times, shifting groups of city officials, about ways to end the violence.[69] Bodelschwingh seems to have supported an immediate withdrawal of troops, while the Prince of Prussia rejected any concession of that sort. Finally, when word reached the palace that several barricades were being torn down in the Königsstadt district, plans were immediately drawn up for an official order announcing the withdrawal of troops from the scenes of fighting.

[65] Leopold von Gerlach, diary (entry written later in the year), GA, 'Abschriften', vi. 21. See also Adolf Wolff, *Revolutions-Chronik*, i. 198–200; Bodelschwingh to Fallenstein, 30 Mar. 1848, in Diest, *Erlebnisse*, 24.

[66] Bismarck-Bohlen, 'Aufzeichnungen', GStA Merseburg, HA Rep. 50 F 1 Nr. 6, Bl. 6ᵛ; Valentin, *Revolution*, i. 438.

[67] Rellstab, *Gespräche*, 71, 72. Frederick William always remained convinced that outside agitators had been responsible for the revolution: FW IV to Bunsen, 13 May 1848, in Leopold von Ranke, *Aus dem Briefwechsel Friedrich Wilhelms IV. mit Bunsen* (Leipzig, 1873), 185.

[68] Text of the proclamation in Adolf Wolff, *Revolutions-Chronik*, i. 201–2; A. Streckfuß, *500 Jahre*, ii. 995–6; and Prittwitz, *Berlin 1848*, 258–9.

[69] On public reaction to the proclamation, see Varnhagen von Ense, *Tagebücher*, iv. 317 (19 Mar. 1848).

Sometime around 11 a.m. Bodelschwingh brought the order, which he described as his last official act, to the deputation of Berlin city officials.[70]

Although taken in a time of great confusion, there can be little doubt that the King's decision *was* his decision, and that Bodelschwingh was executing his master's order to withdraw troops from the streets and squares of the capital. It represented a clear defeat for Prittwitz and other advocates of a military solution to the revolution, especially the Prince of Prussia. The order itself made little military sense, for it would be extremely difficult, and perhaps impossible, for troops to occupy isolated buildings, such as the palace and the arsenal, while essentially giving up the rest of the city. Early on the morning of the nineteenth, Prittwitz had been 'extremely unpleasantly' surprised when he first received word of the King's proclamation to his 'dear Berliners', especially since, as he put it, 'instantaneously, and without the slightest indication being given to him, it was decided completely to alter the course that had so far been followed'. He had no other choice, he felt, but to obey the King's orders to the letter. There had obviously been a massive failure of communication between the King, the King's ministers, and the King's commanding officer.[71] The King believed, as he had indicated in his appeal to his 'dear Berliners', that the palace and the arsenal would continue to be adequately defended. Prittwitz believed that if the troops began to withdraw from their positions, then they would have to withdraw all the way to their barracks inside Berlin or their encampments outside the city. It would be extremely difficult, if not impossible, for them effectively to guard the palace and the arsenal. At 12.30 p.m. Prittwitz ordered his soldiers to withdraw to their quarters, and soon the palace was guarded by only seven companies of troops (who were themselves withdrawn in the next few days).[72] As one recent historian has put it, to save the army Prittwitz had sacrificed the King to the revolution.[73] The withdrawal of the troops was tantamount to giving up the entire capital. But the only real alternative to withdrawing would have been to destroy the city itself—which Frederick William was not prepared to do.[74]

Like Prittwitz, the Prince of Prussia recognized what was happening, and after a vehement argument with Bodelschwingh late in the morning he became embroiled in an even nastier altercation with his older brother. Varnhagen tells us that William, in an outburst of rage, shouted at the King, 'I've always known that you're a babbler [*Schwätzer*], but not that you're a coward!', whereupon he threw his sword at the King's feet.[75] Later that afternoon Philipp von Wussow, commandant of Stolzenfels

[70] Diest, *Erlebnisse*, 25; G. Richter, 'Friedrich Wilhelm IV.', 122. See also the descriptions of the events of 19 Mar. in Leopold von Gerlach, diary, GA, 'Abschriften', iv. 23–8; Adolf Wolff, *Revolutions-Chronik*, i. 207–25; A. Streckfuß, *500 Jahre*, ii. 1002–11; G. Richter, 'Revolution', 615–18; Prittwitz, *Berlin 1848*, 262–93; Diest, *Erlebnisse*, 31–2; Kaeber, 'Bodelschwingh', 178–80; Philipp von Wussow, 'Denkschrift', GStA Merseburg, HA Rep. 50 E 3 Nr. 53, esp. Bl. 93–117.

[71] Prittwitz, *Berlin 1848*, 262–3; G. Richter, 'Friedrich Wilhelm IV.', 123.

[72] Prittwitz, *Berlin 1848*, 290–326.   [73] G. Richter, 'Friedrich Wilhelm IV.', 124.

[74] Lerchenfeld to King Max II, 27 Mar. 1848, BayHStA, MA III 2626.

[75] Varnhagen von Ense, *Tagebücher*, iv. 325–6. But see the somewhat different account of Friedrich Wilhelm von Rauch in Prittwitz, *Berlin 1848*, 317.

castle in the Rhineland, encountered the Prince in the palace. His anger had turned into apathetic despair. He 'sat quietly, sunk deeply in thought; his usual expression of energetic determination could not be seen in his countenance'.[76] William's hard-line policies had not been pursued, and he himself had become a target of popular fury; indeed, some days later his palace on Unter den Linden would have been pillaged had it not been declared 'property of the nation'.[77] There was even the possibility that he might be forced to renounce his right of succession to the throne. Though at first he was inclined to stay at his brother's side, he finally agreed that he should leave Berlin as quickly as possible, and made his way in disguise to London. His disgrace was complete, and his humiliation boundless; and to rub salt into the wounds, Augusta reported that his brother Carl was interested in the possibility of becoming heir to the throne himself, and had decided to 'fish in troubled waters for himself and his son'. In his London exile the chastened William became a changed man. Presumably under Bunsen's influence, he came around rather quickly to the idea that a constitution for Prussia was unavoidable; and when he reappeared in Berlin in June, it was as the deputy for Wirsitz in the Prussian National Assembly, debating the country's future constitutional shape.[78]

When Frederick William and his advisers realized shortly after noon on the nineteenth that they were essentially at the mercy of the citizens of Berlin, they insisted that they had not meant the troop-withdrawal order to include the effective abandonment of the palace; both the palace and the arsenal should continue to be protected. But by that time it was too late. It was also too late for the royal couple to leave the city.[79] By the afternoon of 19 March it thus seemed that Frederick William IV's monarchical authority had disintegrated. Though there was relatively little republican sentiment in those heady days, the King was constantly made to feel that a new relationship was emerging between monarch and subjects; and, for whatever reasons, he accommodated himself rather quickly to those changes. In the early afternoon he, the Queen, and various generals appeared on the palace balcony before a huge and angry crowd. Frederick William acceded to popular demands that he remove his cap and pay homage as the corpses of the Berliners who had been killed in the street-fighting were brought past him.[80] As one eyewitness wrote graphically if

---

[76] Wussow, 'Denkschrift', GStA Merseburg, HA Rep. 50 E 3 Nr. 53, Bl. 111. See also Prittwitz, *Berlin 1848*, 345–9.

[77] *Allgemeine Zeitung* (Augsburg), 25 Mar. 1848.

[78] On William's exile and return, see Karl Haenchen, 'Flucht und Rückkehr des Prinzen von Preußen im Jahre 1848', *HZ* 154 (1936), 32–95; Karl Heinz Börner, 'Prinz Wilhelm von Preußen: Kartätschenprinz und Exekutor der Konterrevolution', in Helmut Bleiber, Walter Schmidt, and Rolf Weber (eds.), *Männer der Revolution von 1848*, ii (Berlin [East], 1987), 493–8; id., *Wilhelm I.*, 76–85. On Prince Carl's alleged machinations to secure the succession for himself, see, *inter alia*, Leopold von Gerlach, diary (5 May 1848), GA, 'Abschriften', vi. 53. See also Prince of Prussia to Leopold von Gerlach, 16 May 1848, BA Potsdam, 90 Ge 6 Nachlaß Leopold von Gerlach Nr. 40, Bl. 9; Karl-Heinz Börner, 'Prinz Wilhelm von Preußen über die Berliner Märzrevolution 1848', *ZfG*, 41 (1993), 425–36.

[79] Prittwitz, *Berlin 1848*, 313–14 (report of Edwin von Manteuffel).

[80] About 300 civilians had died in the fighting; see the analysis of their social composition in Siemann, *Revolution*, 69.

2. Queen Elisabeth

1. Frederick William IV

4. Joseph Maria von Radowitz

3. Leopold von Gerlach

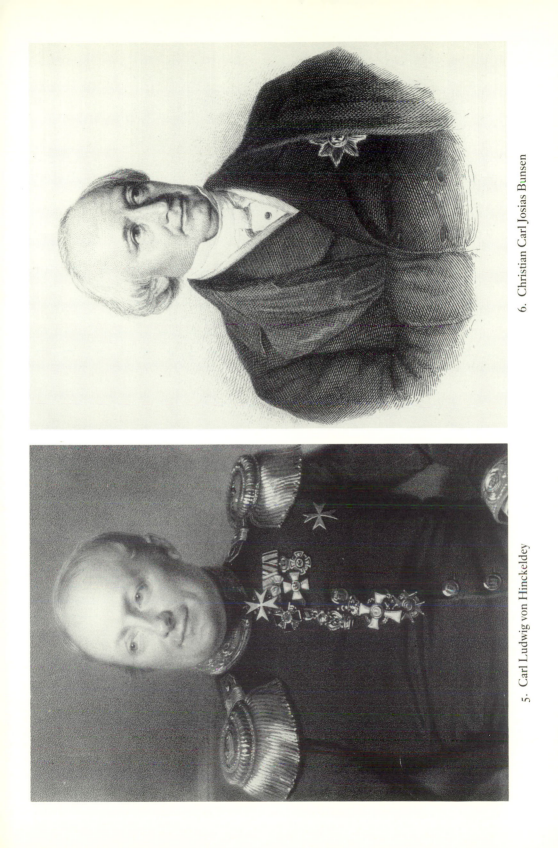

6. Christian Carl Josias Bunsen

5. Carl Ludwig von Hinckeldey

7. Otto von Manteuffel

8.· Ceremony of homage (*Huldigung*), Berlin, 15 October 1840

9. Frederick William IV as drunken Puss-in-Boots vainly attempting to
    follow in the footsteps of Frederick the Great at Sanssouci

10. Ironic self-caricature: Frederick William IV, the unsuccessful
     huntsman, shoots a boar

11. Frederick William IV and the imperial crown in 1849: 'Should I? Shouldn't I? Should I?!' Note champagne-bottle on table

12. Frederick William receives the deputation of the Frankfurt National Assembly, April 1849. He is listening to Eduard Simson; standing next to him is Count Brandenburg

13. Arch of Trimph (*Triumphtor*), 1851, Potsdam-Sanssouci

14. Orangerie, Potsdam-Sanssouci, 1851–1860

15. Friedenskirche, Potsdam-Sanssouci, 1844–1854

melodramatically of the royal couple, 'In the bloodsoaked raiment of the fallen they saw the royal purple lying in dust at their feet.' The Queen, described as 'white with fear and horror', exclaimed at one point, 'The only thing missing now is the guillotine.' Virtually all outside observers agreed that Frederick William IV had been utterly humiliated.[81] Later that afternoon he agreed to the establishment of an armed Citizens' Guard to protect the palace, and he also announced the composition of Prussia's first constitutional government, to be headed by Count Arnim-Boitzenburg.[82] At first Arnim-Boitzenburg also headed the Foreign Ministry on an interim basis, but on the twenty-first the liberal diplomat, Baron Heinrich Alexander von Arnim-Suckow, took over that post.[83]

Two days later, the King made his most spectacular act of public reconciliation with the forces of the new age. At nine in the morning, placards appeared throughout the city, proclaiming that in order 'to save Germany' Frederick William IV had 'placed himself at the head of the entire Fatherland'. At 10 a.m. the new *Kultusminister*, Maximilian Graf von Schwerin-Putzar, the moderately liberal son-in-law of the great theologian Schleiermacher, announced to the students of the university that the King had agreed to support the speedy convocation of an all-German parliament. Schwerin then informed the students that the King of Prussia was about to ride through the streets of Berlin 'bedecked in the German colours', the black-red-gold tricolour of the German national movement.[84] At that same hour the King appeared on the palace balcony and declared to the huge crowd gathered below that he was about to descend and ride through their midst. One of the most unusual, puzzling, and theatrical public displays in the life of that theatrical monarch was unfolding.

Philipp von Wussow has described the scene he saw: 'To the loud applause of the citizens gathered in the palace courtyard, the King mounted his horse at the foot of the winding staircase and began a solemn procession through the city after a German flag was produced by Director Stieber at the King's order; the civic guardsman Krause took it, in order to carry it ahead of the King.'[85] Thereupon Frederick William began to ride through the masses of assembled spectators, 'accompanied by thousands and thousands of cries of *Vivat!*', and into the streets of the capital.[86] Along the way he stopped and delivered short speeches to groups of listeners, and longer addresses to students and professors at the university. In his remarks he expressed his enthusiastic support for the German national cause, but urged caution, and insisted that Prussia was not interested in challenging the legitimacy of other German rulers: 'What you are seeing here, what you are seeing is not an act of usurpation. I don't want to cast any ruler from his throne. We are only aiming to

---

[81] Adolf Wolff, *Revolutions-Chronik*, i. 247–50; Prittwitz, *Berlin 1848*, 329–31; Valentin, *Revolution*, i. 445–7.

[82] Prittwitz, *Berlin 1848*, 336–41.   [83] Friedrich Wilhelm IV., *Reden und Trinksprüche*, 79–80.

[84] Adolf Wolff, *Revolutions-Chronik*, i. 293–4.

[85] GStA Merseburg, HA Rep. 50 E 3 Nr. 53, Bl. 139.

[86] Report of *Flügeladjutant* August von Schöler, 21 Mar. 1848, in Haenchen (ed.), *Revolutionsbriefe*, 53–4.

restore the unity of Germany. . . . I want union and order!' And when someone shouted 'Long live the Emperor of Germany!', the surprised and irritated monarch replied, 'Not that, I won't, I can't.'

After his ride (*Umritt*) was completed, the government released a royal proclamation 'To My People and the German Nation' (*An Mein Volk und an die deutsche Nation*) in which the King stated that he would assume a position of leadership in Germany's hour of need: 'Today I have assumed the old German colours and have placed Myself and My People under the honourable banner of the German Empire. Henceforth Prussia will merge into Germany [*Preußen geht fortan in Deutschland auf*].' Prussia would take the lead in encouraging an 'assembly of German *Stände*' to deliberate on the future shape of the nation, including as one of its first goals the establishment of a popular army. The proclamation concluded with a statement of support for the introduction of 'genuine constitutional governments, with responsible ministries in the individual states; public and oral legal proceedings with juries in criminal cases; equal political and civil rights for all religious confessions; and a genuinely popular, progressive administrative system'.[87] Swept along by the tide of revolution, the King of Prussia was going beyond the promises he had made on 17–18 March.

During the days and weeks after the revolution, the King continued to make sweeping concessions to the popular, constitutional, and national causes. On 22 March he promised the Prussian people genuine electoral reform, and he reiterated his support for the principle of ministerial responsibility.[88] On the twenty-third he received a delegation of his Polish subjects, who warned him that the largely Polish province of Posen faced serious unrest, and urged him to make concessions to Polish national feelings there, to which Frederick William seemed to agree in a cabinet order on the twenty-fourth.[89] Several days earlier a number of Polish political prisoners, including the noted nationalist Ludwik Mieroslawski, had been amnestied. The King's ostensible readiness to accommodate Polish national sentiments was in fact rather non-committal, and Posen found itself in the grip of a large popular uprising which Prussian forces suppressed in May.[90]

On 25 March Frederick William made a quick trip to the palace in Potsdam, where he assembled his Guard officers to assure them that he was not a prisoner of the revolution. He thanked them effusively for their loyalty, and concluded by insisting, to their shock and consternation, that he had never felt more secure than in his palace in Berlin, guarded by loyal civilians. In a frequently quoted passage in his memoirs, Otto von Bismarck describes how this rather careless utterance bewildered and angered the officers, who were deeply upset by the events of 18–19 March and by the King's agreement on 22 March that the army would have to take an oath to the future

---

[87] Adolf Wolff, *Revolutions-Chronik*, i. 294–9; Valentin, *Revolution*, i. 450–1.

[88] Adolf Wolff, *Revolutions-Chronik*, i. 360–3; Hans Mähl, *Die Überleitung Preußens in das konstitutionelle System durch den zweiten Vereinigten Landtag* (Munich, 1909), 30–44.

[89] Adolf Wolff, *Revolutions-Chronik*, i. 368–76.

[90] Karl Heink Streiter, *Die nationalen Beziehungen im Großherzogtum Posen (1815–1848)* (Berne, 1986), 125–35.

Prussian and German constitutions.[91] Finally, on 29 March, following several days of negotiation and vigorous debate about how to include more popular ministers in the new constitutional government, Arnim-Boitzenburg resigned after only ten days in office. He had not been popular since his tenure as Interior Minister from 1842 to 1845; and now he was replaced by the much more politically credible Ludolf Camphausen, a distinguished Rhenish businessman and member of the liberal opposition at the United Diet. David Hansemann, author of the declaration of 1 March on the need for a German parliament, now became Finance Minister and one of the driving forces in the new cabinet.[92]

It was thus under the aegis of a constitutional ministry dominated by moderate liberals that the Second United Diet convened at the beginning of April. It voted overwhelmingly to thank the King for his constitutional concessions, and three days later it passed an electoral law which paved the way for elections to a constituent Prussian National Assembly. Although the elections were indirect (voters would choose electors who would then select deputies), all votes were weighted equally, and the franchise was extended to all adult males who had lived in the same place for six months and were not recipients of poor relief. Voting for the Prussian National Assembly took place in May, at the same time as elections for the Frankfurt National Assembly. The result was an overwhelming electoral defeat for conservative forces; less than 7 per cent of the deputies selected for the new Assembly were landowners.[93] On 22 May the Assembly met for the first time.[94] In his opening speech, Frederick William reminded the deputies that their function was 'to *agree upon* the constitution with me': that is, his assent to a constitutional draft was still essential. But he also assured them that the 'unity of Germany is my fixed goal'.[95]

[91] Bismarck writes of 'a murmuring and a bumping of sabre scabbards' among the officers after the King's speech: Otto von Bismarck, *Die gesammelten Werke*, xv: *Erinnerung und Gedanke: Kritische Neuausgabe auf Grund des gesamten schriftlichen Nachlasses*, ed. Gerhard Ritter and Rudolf Stadelmann (Berlin, 1932), 22. There are at least five different versions of the King's Potsdam address. See also Petersdorff, *Friedrich Wilhelm*, 98–100; Joseph Hansen, *König Friedrich Wilhelm IV. und das liberale Märzministerium Camphausen-Hansemann i. J. 1848* (Trier, 1913), 61; Gordon A. Craig, *The Politics of the Prussian Army 1640–1945* (New York, 1964; orig. 1955), 106; Manfred Messerschmidt, 'Die politische Geschichte der preußisch-deutschen Armee', in *Militärgeschichtliches Forschungsamt* (ed.), *Handbuch zur deutschen Militärgeschichte 1648–1939*, ii: Sect. IV, *Militärgeschichte im 19. Jahrhundert 1814–1890*, pt. 1 (Munich, 1979), 139–40, 144–5; G. Richter, 'Friedrich Wilhelm IV.', 127–8.

[92] FW IV to Elisabeth, 29 Mar. 1848, GStA Merseburg, HA Rep. 50 J Nr. 995 Fasz. 21, Bl. 46; Arnim-Boitzenburg to FW IV, 29 Mar. 1848, in Haenchen (ed.), *Revolutionsbriefe*, 59–60; Mähl, *Überleitung*, 85–108; Jürgen Hofmann, *Das Ministerium Camphausen-Hansemann: Zur Politik der preußischen Bourgeoisie in der Revolution 1848/49* (Berlin [East], 1981), 48–56, esp. 55. On Camphausen himself, see Anna Caspary, *Ludolf Camphausens Leben. Nach seinem schriftlichen Nachlaß* (Stuttgart, 1902), esp. 180–4.

[93] Manfred Botzenhart, *Deutscher Parlamentarismus in der Revolutionszeit 1848–1850* (Düsseldorf, 1977), 132–41, 515–20; Wolfgang Schwentker, *Konservative Vereine und Revolution in Preußen 1848/49: Die Konstituierung des Konservatismus als Partei* (Düsseldorf, 1988). 65.

[94] Ernst Rudolf Huber, *Deutsche Verfassungsgeschichte seit 1789*, 3rd edn. (Stuttgart, 1988), ii: *Der Kamp fum Einheit und Freiheit 1830 bis 1850*, 582–6; Siemann, *Revolution*, 87; Botzenhart, *Parlamentarismus*, 132–41; Mähl, *Überleitung*, 123–227; William James Orr, jun., 'The Foundation of the *Kreuzzeitung* Party in Prussia, 1848–1850' (Ph.D. thesis; Wisconsin—Madison, 1971), 62–7; J. Hofmann, *Ministerium*, 56–86.

[95] Friedrich Wilhelm IV., *Reden und Trinksprüche*, 86.

Prussia really had become a constitutional monarchy, it seemed; and Frederick William IV had given his public assent to this process. Had he abandoned his monarchical project? How can his behaviour in the spring of 1848 be explained? Why had he accepted constitutionalism?

These questions are not new, and have been the subject of scholarly debate for generations. In fact, several psychological, tactical, and ideological factors contributed to Frederick William's behaviour in the spring of 1848, and above all to his supposed conversion to constitutionalism: (1) As we have already noted, the King had been under tremendous pressure from his ministers, especially Bodelschwingh, to offer timely constitutional concessions. When they failed to have the desired effect by around 11 or 12 March, Frederick William became increasingly disillusioned, depressed, and disoriented.[96] But at that point the only alternative—the sustained and massive use of military force—hardly appeared to him to be a desirable or morally defensible option. (2) As a result, Frederick William was confused and overwhelmed by events on 18–19 March, especially when the normal structures of authority and decision-making at the court and in the army became overloaded and collapsed. As Prittwitz observed, Prussians were not accustomed to revolutions. Although the King was not a broken man, or even indecisive (at least on the eighteenth and on the morning of the nineteenth), there is no doubt that he was confused and increasingly uncertain. (3) Though it can never be definitively established, it seems likely that he could rationalize his concessions after 20 March as necessary for two reasons: to play for time, and to hold together what was left of his office's authority, even if this meant agreeing to things that violated his conscience or were obnoxious to him. (4) His homage to those killed in the street-fighting was entirely consistent with his religious views, and his belief in the necessity for all Christians to do penance for their sins.[97] (5) The King quickly came to regret the decisions he had taken in March, and tried to blame them on his advisers and on unavoidable circumstances. In a conversation with Leopold von Gerlach on 13 April, 'the King excused himself for . . . being weak and giving in; constitutionalism had to be recognized *because of Germany*, and in according it such recognition he acted on the express counsel of his ministers, among whom he particularly named Bodelschwingh and Canitz'. Gerlach himself was wary of this remark: 'Does the gentleman want to lie to himself', he wrote in his diary, 'or would he have it believed that he didn't sink as deeply as he really did?'[98]

Despite Gerlach's negative reaction to this explanation, Frederick William's German national feelings should never be underestimated, though they should also not be confused with those of liberal nationalists. Again, final proof is impossible; but it is quite likely that both tactical and ideological reasons induced Frederick William to make concessions to the national cause in 1848. Unity among Germans was desirable and necessary, he believed, especially if it could fend off the revolutionary con-

---

[96] Leopold von Gerlach to Ludwig von Gerlach, 17 and 18 April 1848, in E. L. von Gerlach, *Von der Revolution*, ii. 508–9, 510–11.

[97] Valentin, *Revolution*, i. 446–7.

[98] Leopold von Gerlach, diary (13 April 1848), GA, 'Abschriften', vi. 40–1; emphasis in original.

tagion from France and help salvage what was left of monarchical authority in Central Europe. German unity had to be based on a free agreement among peoples and sovereign princes, and without effective monarchical authority real unity was unattainable. But the prospect of that unity fascinated him in 1848, and in the spring of that year he devoted a great deal of time to spinning out various institutional arrangements for a unified empire. Of course, in the confusion and delirium of March he did get swept along in directions that he would almost certainly not have taken under 'normal' circumstances. For example, Foreign Minister Arnim-Suckow has clearly been identified as the author of the King's proclamation to the German nation on 21 March. Arnim was a firm advocate of Prussian hegemony in Germany, an idea which Frederick William IV could never genuinely accept; and later in the spring of 1848 growing disagreements between monarch and minister demonstrated the real gap that existed between them.[99]

In short, as we shall see in the next two chapters, Frederick William had made concessions which appeared to run contrary to his monarchical project; but in fact he never really repudiated that project. This is not to suggest, however, that Frederick William IV was a monumental tower of strength or that he was a paragon of farsighted determination in the spring of 1848; or, for that matter, that his monarchical project had much chance of success at that point. Far from it: though not broken by the revolution, he certainly did not emerge unscathed from it. In fact, it left deep wounds, and for months after March he was by turns depressed, listless, lachrymose, self-pitying, preoccupied with trivia, sullen, or lethargic. On 29 March Leopold von Gerlach visited the King in Potsdam, and was shocked by what he found: 'His discourses about the March events—a mixture of resignation, weakness, apathy, and desperation—made a frightful impression on me. Everything was confused, listless, and fantastic.'[100] Ludwig von Gerlach reported in mid-June that, according to one mutual acquaintance, 'The King stares into space for hours at a time—then outbursts of rage follow.'[101] Although the King's physical appearance had improved by the late summer, he and the Queen both admitted that their spirits were not much better.[102] Indeed, on 28 August Leopold von Gerlach complained of the King's 'incomprehensible indifference and aversion to all complicated affairs'; and a day later he expressed his deep frustration with what he called Frederick William's 'cowardice and intentional confusion'.[103] During those months the King became increasingly concerned with his own personal safety, as well as that of his brother William. One aspect of the revolutionary shock that intensified in later years was his obsession with security issues and with the regular surveillance of alleged radicals. Berlin Police President Minutoli fed the King's fears in the spring and summer of 1848, and they never went away thereafter. The King who, according to Count

---

[99] Brandenburg, *Untersuchungen*, 59–65.
[100] Leopold von Gerlach, diary (29 Mar. 1848), GA, 'Abschriften', vi. 37.
[101] Ludwig von Gerlach, diary (14 June 1848), in E. L. von Gerlach, *Von der Revolution*, i. 101.
[102] Lerchenfeld to King Max II, 2 Aug. 1848, BayHStA, MA III 2627.
[103] Leopold von Gerlach, diary (28 and 29 Aug. 1848), GA, 'Abschriften', vi. 124, 125.

Trauttmansdorff, had once yearned for popular favour had now become deeply suspicious of his subjects.[104]

He was also disoriented, for as Radowitz once pointed out, no ruler was ever less suited by nature to be a constitutional monarch.[105] He continued to solicit political advice from old friends and former ministers, which led both Thile and Canitz to remind him that they were no longer in service and that, under the new political system, such contacts were inadvisable and could get the King into serious trouble. At the same time his friend Radowitz pointed out to him that, under the changed conditions, he himself should stay away from Berlin and avoid being seen with the King.[106] But Frederick William simply could not bring himself to accept these arguments, and for the rest of his active life his relationships with his constitutional ministers were even more vexed and strained than with their *Vormärz* predecessors. During the spring, summer, and autumn of 1848 he constantly deluged his ministers in Berlin with notes, letters, criticisms, and entreaties on every possible subject; if anything, this inclination got worse as the year went on.[107] Frederick William quarrelled with the cabinet incessantly during the three months of the Camphausen-Hansemann government, and, as he himself admitted, he regularly got 'sick with irritation and annoyance' when he perceived that he was unable to impose his will upon them. Indeed, he tended to regard such differences of opinion as infuriating evidence of the government's wilful 'disobedience'.[108]

As his clashes with the constitutional ministers continued, Frederick William increasingly demonstrated a tendency to withdraw, Achilles-like, into sullen (if temporary) silence, repudiating responsibility for the government's actions, and loudly placing all blame on the ministers if anything went wrong. In April, for example, he querulously declared to Arnim-Suckow, 'If you want to rule without me, that's just

---

[104] See Minutoli's reports to FW of 2 May, 22 May, and 17 June 1848, GStA Merseburg, HA Rep. 50 J Nr. 857, Bl. 2–3, 4–5ᵛ, 6–6ᵛ; and FW IV to Arnim-Suckow, 21 Apr. 1848, GStA Merseburg, Rep. 92 Heinrich Alexander von Arnim B II Nr. 6, Bl. 92ᵛ; cf. Petersdorff, *Friedrich Wilhelm*, 105. In his recent psychological biography of Frederick William IV, Dirk Blasius suggests that the King responded to the March revolution primarily on the level of feelings and emotions, rather than rational calculation; the fear of revolution and the determination to struggle against it decisively shaped his inner life after 1848. In subsequent years his private and deeply emotional recollection of 1848—what Blasius calls the 'delirium of memory' (*Erinnerungsdelir*)—also conditioned his public behaviour. Dirk Blasius, *Friedrich Wilhelm IV. 1795–1861: Psychopathologie und Geschichte* (Göttingen, 1992), 116–17, 169–70, 182–4.

[105] Radowitz, *Briefe und Aufzeichnungen*, 94 (diary, 8 May 1849); cf. Günther Grünthal, 'Zwischen König, Kabinett und Kamarilla: Der Verfassungsoktroi in Preußen vom 5.12.1848', *JGMOD* 32 (1983), 132–3.

[106] Canitz to FW IV and Thile to FW IV, 22 and 28 Mar. 1848, in Haenchen (ed.), *Revolutionsbriefe*, 54–5, 57; Radowitz to FW IV, 28 Mar. 1848, in Hassel, *Radowitz*, 574–5. Cf. Günther Grünthal, 'Bemerkungen zur Kamarilla Friedrich Wilhelms IV. im nachmärzlichen Preußen', in Büsch (ed.), *Friedrich Wilhelm IV. in seiner Zeit*, 40.

[107] e.g. see Erich Brandenburg (ed.), *König Friedrich Wilhelms IV. Briefwechsel mit Ludolf Camphausen* (Berlin, 1906), esp. 101–10; the King's correspondence with Arnim-Suckow in GStA Merseburg, Rep. 92 Heinrich Alexander von Arnim B II Nr. 6; and with Rudolf von Auerswald in GStA Berlin, I. Hauptabteilung Rep. 92 von Auerswald II. Papiere Rudolfs von Auerswald Nr. 5 and Nr. 41.

[108] FW IV to Stolberg, 3 May 1848, GStA Merseburg, HA Rep. 50 J Nr. 1414, Bl. 31; William J. Orr, jun., 'König Friedrich Wilhelm IV. und der Sturz des Ministeriums Auerswald-Hansemann', *JGMOD* 25 (1976), 124.

fine for many reasons—just as long as you do not send any minister to me here to get my agreement.'[109] And in August, in a letter to his friend Groeben, he complained bitterly about everything which had happened 'since the cursed March days' and went on to say, 'If you find inconsistency in the course of government, just remember that we have been blessed with the *monstrum horrendum ingens* of a responsible ministry which takes pride in ruling without and against the king.'[110] Frederick William's angry rejection of responsibility for his government's actions came to be called his policy of 'self-effacement' (*Effacieren*), and after the summer of 1848 it more and more came to be an integral part of his manner of governing, and a way of rationalizing his own accommodation to radical change. Although Leopold von Gerlach, among others, always lamented his sovereign's *Effacieren*, for Frederick William it was psychologically 'an essential precondition for resisting the shock of the revolution. In the final analysis, it was the bridge which enabled Frederick William, with existential reservations, as it were, for his own person, to follow Prussia into the age of constitutionalism.'[111]

And so, in the spring and summer of 1848, Frederick William IV desultorily divided his time between Sanssouci and his city palace in Potsdam. To many observers he appeared to be a broken and beaten man. His monarchical project was, to all appearances, consigned to the dustbin of history. To put it mildly, he was finding it difficult to adjust to constitutional norms, although he had no other alternative. Many of those confidants upon whose advice he had relied for years—Thile, Bodelschwingh, Canitz, Stolberg, Groeben, Radowitz—were gone, though he continued to correspond with the latter three and with his old friend Senfft-Pilsach; and in the late summer of 1848 he was delighted when Bunsen joined him in Sanssouci. The tide of events had rolled over him; he even thought of abdication from time to time. In April and May the Queen herself thought that her husband would step down soon. In fact, she had advised against moving to Sanssouci in the late spring, 'so that it would not be so hard for the King to give it up after his abdication'.[112] And even if he remained King of Prussia, did the monarchical principle have a future? After all, as one poet wrote in 1848, 'Monarchy is dead, though monarchs still live.'[113]

If the King was depressed, angry, and full of self-delusions, the condition of Prussia's traditional governing élites was even worse. The earthquakes of 1848 had caught them quite unprepared, despite the warning shocks of the last *Vormärz* years, and their reactions ranged from confusion and disorientation to depression and, for

---

[109] FW IV to Arnim-Suckow, 10 Apr. 1848, GStA Merseburg, Rep. 92 Heinrich Alexander von Arnim B II Nr. 6, Bl. 84.

[110] FW IV to Groeben, 30 Aug. 1848, GStA Merseburg, Rep. 92 Graf Carl von der Groeben B Nr. 4ᵉ 1848, Bl. 13ᵛ.

[111] Grünthal, 'König', 132; cf. Radowitz to FW IV, 2 Apr. 1848, in Hassel, *Radowitz*, 581.

[112] Leopold von Gerlach, diary (notice of 22 Sept. 1848), GA, 'Abschriften', vi. 55; cf. Orr, 'Foundation', 136.

[113] Quoted in Timothy Garton Ash, 'Eastern Europe: The Year of Truth', *New York Review of Books* 37/2 (15 Feb. 1990), 18.

many, despair and resigned withdrawal. Many aristocrats, officials, and officers, embittered by what they considered to be Frederick William's vacillation and weakness in March, became convinced that he should indeed renounce the throne.[114] According to the well-informed Varnhagen, these feelings were still widespread as late as the spring of 1850: 'Lately there has been a frightful increase in expressions of hatred and contempt for the King among our Guard officers and aristocrats. All his earlier words from the March days are being trotted out and commented upon with resentment. One constantly hears that he is driving the state to ruin, he is unable to govern, he could do nothing better than to abdicate. They add that he could then live entirely for his eccentric artistic hobbies [*Kunstdusel*]; he could also become a Catholic, etc.'[115]

More common, though, than demands for the King's departure was an attitude that combined resignation with stoic defiance. In the words of one aristocrat at the beginning of May, 'Right now I have the feeling that we are sailing on an unknown sea in a ship without a mast or a sail, and that unpredictable popular voices are driving us hither and thither.'[116] Ludwig von Gerlach was similarly pessimistic; but, uncompromising to the end, he was not simply going to accept the revolution as a *fait accompli*. On 27 March he admonished his old colleague Hengstenberg, 'Hold out and do not get soft. I still *have* no hope—but what has happened is a beginning and not an end. We are facing years full of revolution. . . . I am holding out in my own position against attacks both from below and from above, while everyone is cringing before the rabble.'[117]

So Ludwig von Gerlach was not prepared to accept the revolution. Neither was his brother. Neither was Friedrich Wilhelm von Rauch, Prussia's military plenipotentiary to the Russian court, who happened to find himself in Berlin in March. Together with the court officials Ludwig von Massow and Alexander Graf von Keller they formed the core of the 'Camarilla', a body of informal advisers of the King who would try to stem the tide of revolution and restore the structures of monarchical authority in Prussia.

---

[114] Among various sources, see Ludwig von Gerlach, diary (1 Apr. 1848), in E. L. von Gerlach, *Von der Revolution*, i. 88.

[115] Varnhagen von Ense, *Tagebücher*, vii. 114 (28 Mar. 1850). Cf. Herman von Petersdorff, 'Graf Albrecht Alvensleben von Erxleben', *HZ* 100 (1908), 290–1; id., *Friedrich Wilhelm*, 103–5; Grünthal, 'König', 130.

[116] Ludwig Yorck von Wartenburg to Adolf von Willisen, 1 May 1848, quoted in Konrad Canis, 'Der preußische Militarismus in der Revolution 1848', (Diss.; Rostock, 1965), 46–7. Cf. Schwentker, *Vereine*, 57–60.

[117] Ludwig von Gerlach to Hengstenberg, 27 Mar. 1848, StaBi, Nachlaß Ernst Wilhelm Hengstenberg, Briefe Ernst Ludwig von Gerlachs 1829–1867, Bl. 159.

7
Camarilla, Counter-revolution, and Constitution, March–December 1848

Friedrich Wilhelm von Rauch

Friedrich Wilhelm von Rauch's career as a Prussian officer had been rather unusual. Born in Potsdam in 1790, he was the son of a prominent general, and at the age of 13 had become a pupil at the Engineering Academy in his native city. During the liberation war he had served with distinction in a number of battles. Things were slower in the post-war era, however, and his big opportunity only came in 1829, when he became *Flügeladjutant* to Frederick William III. After four years in that position, he was sent to St Petersburg as Prussian Military Plenipotentiary (*Militärbevollmächtigter*), where he quickly gained the confidence, respect, and friendship of Nicholas I. Thereafter Rauch was almost constantly in the Tsar's company, and enjoyed rapid promotion to lieutenant-colonel, colonel, major-general *à la suite*, and, in 1843, adjutant-general to Frederick William IV. His two titles—Military Plenipotentiary to the Tsar and Adjutant-General of the King of Prussia—essentially described his position, which was unique both in the Prussian army and in the world of Prussian diplomacy. Completely independent of the regular Prussian minister to the Russian court, Rauch was directly responsible only to his imperial and royal masters. Conscientious, earnest, unimaginative, and hard-working, he was eminently suited to this difficult task, especially while Frederick William III was still alive. Like that laconic monarch, Rauch was a practical man of few words, and his devotion to the conservative, monarchical, and military values embodied by Nicholas I was boundless. His task of mediating and maintaining contacts between the two courts became more difficult, however, after Frederick William IV ascended to the throne in 1840.[1]

With his poor education and bluff, simple ways, Rauch never had much patience with Frederick William's high-flown political and religious ideas, and certainly he shared the Tsar's concern that the King of Prussia had been playing a dangerous political game in the last *Vormärz* years. Despite that scepticism, and the temperamental and personal gulf that divided the two men, Rauch always remained deeply loyal to Frederick William IV, a feeling which that monarch reciprocated. In a comment to another confidant in early 1849 the King described Rauch incisively: 'Don't expect to find any extraordinary political wisdom, cleverness, artfulness, etc., in him;

---

[1] On the Prussian Military Plenipotentiary and his role at the Russian court, see Gordon A. Craig, 'Military Diplomats in the Prussian and German Service: The Attachés, 1816–1914', *Political Science Quarterly*, 64 (1949), 70–6; Heinrich Otto Meisner, *Militärattachés und Militärbevollmächtigte in Preußen und im Deutschen Reich: Ein Beitrag zur Geschichte der Militärdiplomatie* (Berlin [East], 1957), 67–71; Alfred Vagts, *The Military Attaché* (Princeton, NJ, 1967), 281–300.

don't look for the Russophile or the born aristocrat. Rather, look alone for the Potsdam officer, that is, the *genuinely* unselfish nobleman motivated by *feelings of honour*, the *Prussian* from head to toe.'[2]

In the spring of 1848 Rauch found himself in Berlin, and he did not like what he saw there. He was a man who prized self-control, order, and discipline, and the tumultuous scenes on 18 March were deeply upsetting to him. Like Edwin von Manteuffel, Prince Albrecht's adjutant who quickly became his own protégé, Rauch urged the King and Queen to leave Berlin, but to no avail. Thus, on the following day Rauch had to watch as the King paid homage to the dead of the revolution. He could hardly describe his feelings 'to see his King and Master in the deepest degradation. It was almost more than a true old soldier's heart could bear.' And there was even more to come. On the twenty-first, Frederick William asked Rauch to stay close to him as he rode through the streets of the capital. The Adjutant-General demurred at first, pointing out that he was in civilian attire and did not have access to a uniform. The King insisted, however, and the horrified Rauch later described his reaction to the whole episode: 'I cannot describe the impression that this ride made on me. It seemed to me as if everything had gone mad. . . . Truly, one needed an hour to pull oneself together and get over it all. It was as if I had come from the madhouse.'[3]

That same evening, the King's old friend Stolberg took his leave of the royal couple and prepared to depart for his family estate in Wernigerode. The Queen, who was 'deeply moved' on this occasion, thereupon turned to Rauch and exclaimed, 'You too will probably not be with us much longer, for they will separate us from everyone who is true and faithful to us.'[4] In fact, Rauch did not leave the King's side. Instead of returning to St Petersburg, he remained with Frederick William during the next weeks and months. As one of the King's adjutants-general, he used his right of immediate access to the monarch to good effect, and with Leopold von Gerlach he became one of the leaders of the court Camarilla.

The Camarilla, which has often been described as a 'kitchen cabinet' or *ministère occulte*, has for decades attracted the attention of historians, who have long been fascinated by images of back-room manipulators and *éminences grises* surrounding the monarch, subverting constitutional authority, and directing the state for their own ends. Although there is some truth to this image, we shall see in this chapter that the Prussian Camarilla was not as sinister, powerful, or large as has sometimes been thought. It was, rather, a loosely knit, informal association of like-minded individu-

[2] Marginal comment on letter from Carl Wilhelm Saegert, 7 Jan. 1849, GStA Berlin, BPH Rep. 192 Carl Wilhelm Saegert Nr. 17, Bl. 4. The best capsule description of Rauch can be found in William J. Orr, jun., 'The Foundation of the *Kreuzzeitung* Party in Prussia, 1840–1850' (Ph.D. thesis; Wisconsin-Madison, 1971), 134–6; also Kurt von Priesdorff (ed.), *Soldatisches Führertum* (10 vols.; Hamburg, 1937–42), vi. 30–3; Hans-Joachim Schoeps, 'Berichte aus St. Petersburg', in id. (ed.), *Neue Quellen zur Geschichte Preußens im 19. Jahrhundert* (Berlin, 1968), 441–2; and the characterization in Hermann Wagener, *Die Politik Friedrich Wilhelm IV.* (Berlin, 1883), 59–60.

[3] Excerpts from Rauch's report in Karl Ludwig von Prittwitz, *Berlin 1848: Das Erinnerungswerk des Generalleutnants Karl Ludwig von Prittwitz und andere Quellen zur Berliner Märzrevolution und zur Geschichte Preußens um die Mitte des 19. Jahrhunderts*, ed. Gerd Heinrich (Berlin, 1985), 226, 331, 391–2.

[4] Ibid. 393.

als who wanted to use their access to Frederick William IV in order to achieve certain political ends.[5] Leopold von Gerlach defined it simply as 'an extension of the constitutional ministers'.[6] Its composition shifted over the years after 1848, and it was far from omnipotent. Frederick William IV was too independent—some would say too erratic and unpredictable—to let himself be controlled or directed by one small group of individuals. In fact, Queen Elisabeth was a much firmer and more consistent ally of the Camarilla after 1848, and sometimes her friendship could be crucial. The King himself could only be counted on to support it when he already agreed with its views or when he had to be extricated from an otherwise impossible political situation. Still, during the year of revolution itself the Camarilla's influence was very considerable; that influence reached its zenith in the autumn of 1848, when the Camarilla arranged for Count Friedrich Wilhelm von Brandenburg to become Minister President and challenge the authority of the constituent National Assembly in Berlin.[7] But Brandenburg and his government were not pliant tools of the Camarilla. After effectively annulling the power of the Assembly, the government was able to induce Frederick William to promulgate a new constitution in December 1848, despite the Camarilla's objections. Brandenburg did not believe that it was possible or desirable to turn the clock back to the *ständisch*-bureaucratic monarchy of the Old Regime. Thanks largely to his efforts, Prussia had become committed to a constitutional course; and Frederick William IV would have to adapt his monarchical project to that reality.

In short, the political system that emerged in Prussia after December 1848 was the result of a *compromise* among the country's most powerful élites: the King, the

---

[5] Among recent studies of the Camarilla, see Konrad Canis, 'Der preußische Militarismus in der Revolution 1848' (Diss.; Rostock, 1965), 53–60; Manfred Kliem, 'Genesis der Führungskräfte der feudalmilitaristischen Konterrevolution 1848 in Preußen' (Diss.; Humboldt-Universität zu Berlin, 1966), 390–400; Diwald, intro. to E. L. von Gerlach, *Von der Revolution zum Norddeutschen Bund: Politik und Ideengut der preußischen Hochkonservativen 1848–1866. Aus dem Nachlaß von Ernst Ludwig von Gerlach*, ed. Hellmut Diwald (2 vols.; Göttingen, 1970), i. 55–7; Orr, 'Foundation', 131–6; Richard Schult, 'Partei wider Willen: Kalküle und Potentiale konservativer Parteigründer in Preußen zwischen Erstem Vereinigten Landtag und Nationalversammlung (1847/48)', in Dirk Stegmann, Bernd-Jürgen Wendt, and Peter-Christian Witt (eds.), *Deutscher Konservatismus im 19. und 20. Jahrhundert: Festschrift für Fritz Fischer zum 75. Geburtstag und zum 50. Doktorjubiläum* (Bonn, 1983), 53–4; Günther Grünthal, 'Bemerkungen zur Camarilla Friedrich Wilhelms IV. im nachmärzlichen Preußen', in Otto Büsch (ed.), *Friedrich Wilhelm IV. in seiner Zeit: Beiträge eines Colloquiums* (Berlin, 1987), 39–47; David E. Barclay, 'The Court Camarilla and the Politics of Monarchical Restoration in Prussia, 1848–58', in Larry Eugene Jones and James Retallack (eds.), *Between Reform, Reaction, and Resistance: Studies in the History of German Conservatism from 1789 to 1945* (Providence, 1993), 123–56. Two older works are still very helpful: Erich Jordan, *Die Entstehung der Konservativen Partei und die preußischen Agrarverhältnisse von 1848* (Munich, 1914), 297–368; and Fritz Hartung, 'Verantwortliche Regierung, Kabinett und Nebenregierungen im konstitutionellen Preußen 1848–1918', *FBPG* 44 (1932), 3–17. In the nineteenth century the Spanish term 'camarilla' was first applied to the clique around the dissolute King Ferdinand VII after the Peninsular War: Heinrich Otto Meisner, *Archivalienkunde vom 16. Jahrhundert bis 1918* (Göttingen, 1969), 307. Kliem, 'Genesis', 393–4, differentiates between the *ministère occulte* as a *Gegenregierung* and the Camarilla as a *Nebenregierung*, but that is not analytically very helpful.

[6] Leopold von Gerlach, diary (18 Apr. 1856), GA, 'Abschriften', xiii. 77.

[7] Diwald, introd. to E. L. von Gerlach *Von der Revolution*, i. 57.

Brandenburg government, *and* the Camarilla.[8] The developments that led up to that compromise will be one of the major themes of this chapter. We shall review the processes by which the Prussian monarchy was able to recast and reconstitute itself after the shock of March 1848, and we shall also consider the beginnings of the new relationships between the monarchy and the other constitutive structures of power and authority in Prussian society.

Counsels of Caution, March–September 1848

The beginnings of the Camarilla were hardly spectacular. On 29 March 1848 Leopold von Gerlach visited the King in Potsdam and, as we saw in the previous chapter, he came away deeply depressed. 'I went home heavy with despair', he wrote later; and on the following day, after a night full of bad dreams, he awoke 'with a broken heart' but determined to do something. After some effort, Gerlach was able to locate the veteran court-official Ludwig von Massow, and the two men were then able to arrange an audience with the King through the good offices of Count Keller, the Marshal of the Court. Massow and Gerlach made three suggestions to Frederick William: not to go to Berlin, but to have the ministers confer with him in Potsdam; under no circumstances to permit the moderately liberal General Wilhelm von Willisen to become War Minister; and to break with Foreign Minister Arnim-Suckow. Gerlach later noted that he was already thinking that control over the army and foreign policy were indispensable to the restoration of monarchical authority. 'The King agreed to everything, but how unreliable he is!' Despite Gerlach's well-founded scepticism, Frederick William did write to Ludolf Camphausen that very day to inform the new Minister President that he would not be returning to Berlin. Thereafter at least some 'members' of the Camarilla would be in his vicinity at all times.[9]

There was nothing especially sinister or unusual about this arrangement, for, with the important exception of the Gerlachs, the Camarilla was composed entirely of members of the King's official court-retinue or *maison militaire*. Ludwig von Gerlach remained in his position with the Appellate Court in Magdeburg, while Leopold von Gerlach, though personally close to the monarch, was not officially appointed general *à la suite* until September 1849, and only after Rauch's death in 1850 did he become an adjutant-general.[10] Rauch, however, was an adjutant-general with the right to see the King and present daily reports to him, a function that he shared with the politically insignificant Neumann.[11] Ludwig von Massow, as we know, had occupied a number of important court positions, and in 1848 was serving

[8] Günther Grünthal, 'Zwischen König, Kabinett und Kamarilla: Der Verfassungsoktroi in Preußen vom 5.12.1848', *JGMOD* 32 (1983), 169–71.

[9] Leopold von Gerlach, diary, GA, 'Abschriften', vi. 37–8; Orr, 'Foundation', 139–40; Canis, 'Militarismus', 54; Kliem, 'Genesis', 395.

[10] Leopold von Gerlach, diary (27 Sept. 1849), GA, 'Abschriften', vi. 465; K. A. Varnhagen von Ense, *Tagebücher*, ed. Ludmilla Assing, 2nd edn. vi. 376 (29 Sept. 1849).

[11] Kliem, 'Genesis', 396–7.

as Intendant of the Royal Gardens; because of Wittgenstein's age and infirmities he also functioned as *de facto* Minister of the Royal House. Keller, the son-in-law of Count Stolberg, had been Marshal of the Court for two years. The Camarilla thus remained a compact and informal body throughout 1848. As Leopold von Gerlach wrote several years later, 'Rauch, Massow, Ludwig, and I were the only ones from April 1848 to November 1848. In March and April Neumann had shown himself to be utterly weak and useless. Groeben and Stolberg were gone, while in the Paulskirche'—the meeting-place after May 1848 of the Frankfurt National Assembly—'Radowitz was our opponent.'[12] Keller and, later in the year, Marcus Niebuhr should almost certainly be added to that list, while Baron Ernst Senfft von Pilsach, the ultra-conservative Halle history professor Heinrich Leo, and Edwin von Manteuffel might be regarded as 'associates'.[13]

Of these associates, Edwin von Manteuffel (1809–85) played the most important role in the Camarilla's activities.[14] In 1848 he was just at the beginning of what would become a remarkable career. At the time he was a thirty-nine-year old *Rittmeister*, the son-in-law of the former War Minister Job von Witzleben, and, since 1840, adjutant to Prince Albrecht. Gifted with an exceptional intellectual curiosity, Manteuffel had attended Leopold von Ranke's lectures in the 1840s, and thereafter was a friend of that renowned historian. He combined his keen intellect with fierce energy and a rather quixotic view of himself as a kind of medieval warrior, the chivalric vassal of a personal king to whom his personal obligations took precedence over everything else. Thus he had stayed with the King in the palace on 18–19 March, although Prince Albrecht had already left Berlin and Manteuffel's own pregnant wife was in labour with a son! Frederick William rewarded Manteuffel's loyalty by designating him as a *Flügeladjutant* in early April and promoting him to major in October. His adjutant's position ensured that he would be in ready contact with both the King and Rauch, who admired his scintillating intelligence. After 1848 Manteuffel demonstrated a real flair for hard-nosed political analysis and diplomacy, but in that year itself he essentially served as a courier and go-between. During the summer and autumn months he resided mostly in Berlin, often travelling to Potsdam late in the evening to report to the King.[15]

There can be no doubt that Rauch and Leopold von Gerlach were the two guiding

---

[12] Leopold von Gerlach, diary (12 July 1851), GA, 'Abschriften', viii. 217. Radowitz was elected to the Frankfurt National Assembly in the spring of 1848, hence the reference to the Paulskirche, its meeting-place.

[13] On Leo, see Orr, 'Foundation', 131; *ADB*, xviii. 288–94; Carolyn Rebecca Henderson, 'Heinrich Leo: A Study in German Conservatism' (Ph.D. thesis; Wisconsin-Madison, 1977); and Christoph Freiherr von Maltzahn, *Heinrich Leo (1799–1878): Ein politisches Gelehrtenleben zwischen romantischem Konservatismus und Realpolitik* (Göttingen, 1979), esp. 113–21.

[14] Gordon A. Craig, 'Portrait of a Political General: Edwin von Manteuffel and the Constitutional Conflict in Prussia', *Political Science Quarterly*, 66 (1951), 2.

[15] See, in addition to Craig, Karl Heinrich Keck, *Das Leben des General-Feldmarschalls Edwin von Manteuffel* (Bielefeld, 1890), esp. 82–93; Elisabeth Schmitz, *Edwin von Manteuffel als Quelle zur Geschichte Friedrich Wilhelms IV.* (Munich, 1921), esp. 69–75; Ludwig Dehio, 'Edwin von Manteuffels politische Ideen', *HZ* 131 (1925), 41–71, esp. 48–9; Priesdorff (ed.), *Soldatisches Führertum*, vii. 150–68.

forces of the Camarilla, especially in its first, rather tentative weeks and months. Despite the enormous differences in personality, style, and education between the two men, they were in almost perfect political accord, and there is no evidence that they had any significant disagreements between 1848 and 1850.[16] Rauch enjoyed much better connections in the military than Gerlach, whose fellow officers sometimes regarded him suspiciously as a politician first and a soldier second.[17] Bismarck thought that the 'pragmatic' Rauch's influence was perhaps greater than Gerlach's, while the Russian minister, Peter von Meyendorff, was of the opinion that 'Without Rauch it is difficult to act on the King. Gerlach does not have Rauch's energy, nor, as a consequence, his influence.' Meyendorff also felt that, though Gerlach's 'political principles are as excellent as those of Rauch', he did not have 'the same nerve, the same dexterity of judgement'.[18] Gerlach in fact tended to be rather slow, deliberate, and cautious, with a tinge of fatalism and melancholy. He never had anything like the nervous energy and robust combativeness of his brother or Edwin von Manteuffel, which perhaps explains why he always got on better with the King than either of those men.

To the extent that there were any disagreements within the Camarilla during the spring and summer of 1848, they arose between the Gerlach brothers themselves. Until the autumn of 1848, Ludwig von Gerlach might best be described, like Heinrich Leo or Edwin von Manteuffel, as a kind of 'associate' or 'corresponding' member of the Camarilla. He admitted that he had never felt personally close to the King, and his notion of monarchy and the 'monarchical principle' was always more distanced and abstract than Leopold's.[19] Since at least 1842 or 1843 Ludwig had been convinced that there was not much hope for Frederick William IV, that the King was incapable of the penance, insight, and self-awareness that were essential to a powerful and authoritative monarch.[20] If the monarchical principle were to have any future in Prussia, he believed, the King had to have straight-talking confidants who would not flatter him and who would not be afraid to mention unpalatable truths. Part of the problem, he said, was that the King's own advisers, including himself and his brother, had failed adequately to stand up *to* the King and *for* the King's interests. On 17 March, even before the outbreak of the revolution in Berlin, Ludwig had written to

---

[16] Leopold von Gerlach to Ludwig von Gerlach, 10 June 1850, in E. L. von Gerlach, *Von der Revolution*, ii. 678.

[17] Varnhagen von Ense, *Tagebücher*, vi. 376 (29 Sept. 1849).

[18] Otto von Bismarck, *Die gesammelten Werke*, XV: *Erinnerung und Gedanke: Kritische Neuausgabe auf Grund des gesamten schriftlichen Nachlasses*, ed. Gerhard Ritter and Rudolf Stadelmann (Berlin, 1932), 37, 38; Meyendorff to Nesselrode and to Empress Alexandra Feodorovna (Charlotte), 4 May 1850 and 20 Sept. 1849, in Peter von Meyendorff, *Ein russischer Diplomat an den Höfen von Berlin und Wien: Politischer und privater Briefwechsel 1826–1863*, ed. Otto Hoetzsch (3 vols.; Berlin, 1923), ii. 293 and iii. 382. Cf. Kliem, 'Genesis', 397; id., 'Die Rolle der feudaljunkerlichen Reaktion in der Revolution von 1848/49', *ZfG* 17 (1969), 320; Orr, 'Foundation', 136.

[19] Leopold von Gerlach to Ludwig von Gerlach, 19 May 1848, in E. L. von Gerlach, *Von der Revolution*, ii. 519.

[20] Hans-Christof Kraus, 'Das preußische Königtum und Friedrich Wilhelm IV. aus der Sicht Ernst Ludwig von Gerlachs', in Büsch (ed.), *Friedrich Wilhelm IV. in seiner Zeit*, 87, 90.

Hengstenberg, '*Self-reliant* men, who nevertheless stand with the King, are what he needs. . . . The delicacy which Leopold recommends reminds me of a man who sees his neighbour falling into a fire and thinking that it is too indelicate to grasp him firmly.'[21] The King and all his advisers had to recognize that they were grievous sinners who had to do penance if they and the monarchy were to be rescued.

After the events of 18–19 March, Ludwig stayed at his post in Magdeburg, at some risk to his own safety and despite considerable pressure to step down. Until the early autumn of 1848 he generally stayed away from the Camarilla's deliberations and activities, about which he was at first quite sceptical. During those months his judgements of the King were unremittingly harsh, to his brother Leopold's great dismay and indignation. Ludwig was convinced that the King's behaviour in the March days and thereafter had reduced him to a 'nullity'. From time to time he even compared Frederick William to 'feeble-minded' rulers like the Emperor Ferdinand of Austria.[22] To be identified too strongly with the unhappy monarch, he warned, would be a disservice to the larger monarchical cause. Ludwig hinted after mid-April that the King might well abdicate, and he insisted to his older brother that in such an eventuality real conservatives should hold themselves in reserve by not going down with a discredited monarch: 'Watch out for infection whenever you enter Butt's house. This worries me a lot. Just remember that you and I are also kings.' (The reader will remember that one of the King's nicknames was 'Butt' or 'Butte'.) The latter point was one that Ludwig loved to make in his continuing debates with Leopold; it was derived from Haller's patrimonial ideas about the divine quality of all authority, symbolized originally and most basically in the structures of authority within the family itself. For Ludwig, then, conservative efforts after 1848 should be focused not on rescuing the man Frederick William IV but on restoring divinely ordained authority at *all* levels of society, of which, to be sure, monarchical authority was the most obvious and the most important. For the time being, at least, organized action in the form of a conservative newspaper—one which could help their party prepare for the inevitable conservative reaction—was more important than the King himself.[23] By the late summer of 1848 he was no longer considering the possibility of the King's abdication, not because it had been morally wrong to do so, but simply because no credible successor was available. Even in the autumn, though, he could still write that Frederick William IV reminded him of Richard II or Henry VI of England.[24]

Leopold von Gerlach vigorously disapproved of Ludwig's astringent, rather

---

[21] Ludwig von Gerlach to Hengstenberg, 17 Mar. 1848, StaBi, Nachlaß Ernst Wilhelm Hengstenberg, Briefe Ernst Ludwig von Gerlachs 1829–1867, Bl. 158.

[22] Ludwig von Gerlach to Leopold von Gerlach, 22 June and 29 June 1848, GA, 'Abschriften', xviii, 45, 49; Kraus, 'Königtum', 68; id., 'Ernst Ludwig von Gerlach: Potisches Denken und Handeln eines preußischen Altkonservativen' (Diss.; 2 vols.; Göttingen, 1991), i. 255–65, ii. 193–200.

[23] Ludwig von Gerlach to Leopold von Gerlach, 23 Mar., 12, 16, and 17 Apr., 10 and 25 May 1848, GA, 'Abschriften', xviii. 2, 4, 7, 10, 12, 13a, 20, 31; see also Kraus, 'Königtum', 66–8.

[24] Ludwig von Gerlach, 'Familiengeschichte', in E. L. von Gerlach, *Von der Revolution*, ii. 519; Ludwig von Gerlach to Leopold von Gerlach, 29 June and 26 Oct. 1848, GA, 'Abschriften', xviii. 47–50, 95.

detached approach to monarchy and monarchical values. To Leopold, those values were most obviously embodied in 'a human being of flesh and blood', an actual person who was King by the Grace of God. Ludwig, he once complained, had never been able to understand his attachment to Frederick William as *'mon naturel maître'*. He could never imagine separating himself from that master; his servants had a direct and personal responsibility to him, and to Leopold the very idea of abdication was repellent.[25] People like Alvensleben, who were spreading the idea that the King should step down, were flirting with treason, because the only real alternative to the present king was a republic. One had to make do with the *real* king with whom God has provided us, Leopold argued, and avoid striving after false ideals: 'If authority comes from above, so too does Frederick William IV, and he can only be dismissed from above.'[26] In any case, Leopold insisted, the King's problem was not his objective 'powerlessness' (*Ohnmacht*), but rather his subjective perception of his weakness and his inability, after the shocks of March, to appreciate just how extensive his God-given power really was. He should be shown how to appreciate that power and its use.[27] But no matter what happened, Leopold declared, he would stick with the 'personal king' that God had granted to Prussia.

Rauch and Edwin von Manteuffel shared Leopold's views unreservedly. If anything, Manteuffel's own commitment to the idea of *personal* service to a *personal* sovereign exceeded Leopold's in emotional vigour and intensity.[28] Rauch, too, was fiercely opposed to suggestions that the King should step down; and it is probably not an exaggeration to suggest that his own authority and prestige within conservative and military circles helped to dampen their enthusiasm for abdication. In its first few months, though, the nascent Camarilla had few opportunities to develop its political influence; from April until June its 'members'—Rauch, Leopold von Gerlach, Massow, and Keller—and their associates had to proceed with extreme caution.[29] Opinion in Berlin was sensitive to any rumour that Frederick William might still be turning to his old friends and former ministers for advice—and such rumours began to spread very quickly.[30] These reports became so widespread, in fact, that in early April the Russian envoy Meyendorff fully expected that the constitutional ministers would demand Rauch's removal from the royal entourage; two months later he was surprised to find not only that Rauch was still there but that the ministers supported his continued presence![31] Still, discretion was in order. Keller

[25] Leopold von Gerlach to Ludwig von Gerlach, 29 July 1848, in E. L. von Gerlach, *Von der Revolution*, ii. 554. Cf. Ludwig von Gerlach to Leopold von Gerlach, 1 Aug. 1848, in Herman von Petersdorff, 'Briefe Ludwigs von Gerlach an seinen Bruder Leopold', *Konservative Monatsschrift für Politik, Literatur und Kunst*, 63/1 (Oct. 1905), 73–4.

[26] Leopold von Gerlach to Ludwig von Gerlach, 20 June 1848, in E. L. von Gerlach, *Von der Revolution*, ii. 529; also quoted in Orr, 'Foundation', 138.

[27] Leopold von Gerlach to Ludwig von Gerlach, 23 May 1848, ibid. ii. 524–5.

[28] Keck, *Manteuffel*, 90; Schmitz, *Manteuffel*, 17; L. Dehio, 'Ideen', 50.

[29] Canis, 'Militarismus', 54; Orr, 'Foundation', 140–1.

[30] Varnhagen von Ense, *Tagebücher*, iv. 386 (18 Apr. 1848), 394 (23 Apr. 1848).

[31] Meyendorff to Alexandra Feodorovna (Charlotte), 8 Apr. and 9 June 1848, in Meyendorff, *Briefwechsel*, iii. 336, 347.

had to deny publicly in early June that the King had dined with his ex-ministers Eichhorn, Thile, and Stolberg, and even at the end of August Keller still thought it more advisable for Ludwig von Gerlach to speak with the King at his mid-day luncheon table than in a formal audience, which might give the impression that Frederick William was engaged 'in a confidential discussion with a reactionary'.[32]

Leopold von Gerlach and his friends were all clearly aware of the need for caution in their approaches to the King, and tended to confine their efforts to hints and admonitions to him not to forget just how extensive his royal power and obligations really were.[33] In his conversation with the King on 30 March, Leopold had already suggested that the army and foreign policy were the foundations upon which royal power could be restored. Frederick William should be reminded that under no circumstances could a King of Prussia afford to make concessions that might jeopardize his own control over military and diplomatic affairs. These were the areas that the Camarilla should concentrate on, Gerlach believed; for the time being, however, it should avoid any 'random contact' with the monarch.[34] The time was not yet ripe for a concerted royal response to the challenge posed by the constitutional government.[35] Through these counsels of caution the Camarilla was urging the King to pursue, at least temporarily, essentially the same strategy of self-effacement that Radowitz had supported, despite their supposed opposition to his ideas.[36]

As we saw in the last chapter, Frederick William had found it exceedingly difficult to get along with the constitutional ministers in the Camphausen-Hansemann cabinet. The King was upset with just about everything that the government did, and he wrangled with the ministers over matters ranging from his brother William's treatment to the question of whether or not the opening session of the newly elected Prussian National Assembly should take place in the royal palace. Foreign and German policies were an area of special and vehement disagreement with Foreign Minister Arnim-Suckow, whom the Camarilla suspected of 'Polonomania' and of wanting to drive Prussia into a war with Russia. Arnim in fact did want to make concessions to Polish national sentiments in the province of Posen, adjacent to Russian Poland—an idea which was, of course, anathema to the Tsar's government.[37] Nicholas I also looked askance at Prussia's involvement in the so-called Reich War (*Reichskrieg*) against Denmark, which had begun with the Danish occupation of Schleswig in late March.[38] Prussian troops constituted part of a larger German force which in the late spring, after the dissolution of the old Confederate Diet, became

---

[32] Ludwig von Gerlach, diary (9 June and 30 Aug. 1848), in E. L. von Gerlach, *Von der Revolution*, i. 100, 109; Keller to Leopold von Gerlach, 30 Aug. 1848, ibid. ii. 566–7.

[33] See e.g. Massow to FW IV, 13 May 1848, in Karl Haenchen (ed.), *Revolutionsbriefe 1848: Ungedrucktes aus dem Nachlaß König Friedrich Wilhelms IV. von Preußen* (Leipzig, 1930), 97.

[34] Leopold von Gerlach to Ludwig von Gerlach, 18 Apr. 1848, in E. L. von Gerlach, *Von der Revolution*, ii. 511; cf. Leopold to Ludwig, 16 Apr. 1848, ibid. ii. 506.

[35] Leopold von Gerlach, diary (16 Apr. 1848), GA, 'Abschriften', vi. 43.

[36] Leopold von Gerlach, diary (10 Apr. 1848), ibid. vi. 39.

[37] Karl Heink Streiter, *Die nationalen Beziehungen im Grossherzogtum Posen (1815–1848)* (Berne, 1986), 125–6.

[38] Charlotte to FW IV, n.d. (late Mar. 1848), in Haenchen (ed.), *Revolutionsbriefe*, 92–5.

responsible to the newly emerging 'German central authority' in Frankfurt am Main; there the *Vorparlament* of early spring had paved the way for elections to the Frankfurt National Assembly, which convened in the Paulskirche on 18 May.[39]

The Camarilla shared Nicholas's distaste for concessions to Polish interests in Posen, was worried by the developments in Schleswig-Holstein, and was horrified that the 'crazy' Arnim might drag Prussia into a war with Russia. Frederick William, who was also involved in acrimonious disputes with Arnim about the reorganization of Germany and his own role in a unified state, did not need much convincing from the Camarilla to express his unhappiness with the course of events. At first, the King had not been at all averse to using Prussian troops to resist what he considered to be an unwarranted act of aggression by Denmark.[40] But he quickly realized that the Schleswig-Holstein question could escalate into a European conflict, involving both Britain and Russia, in which Prussia might be dangerously isolated. Above all, though, he wanted to avoid war with Russia over what he thought was, in the final analysis, a rather trivial issue. A quick armistice with Denmark might also free up troops for use against the Poles in Posen, where, in April, military authorities had begun operations against Polish nationalists.[41] The handling of that conflict, which ended in May with a victory for Prussian forces, led to considerable controversy and to new conflicts between ministry and King over the question of the responsibility for, and ultimate control over, the army—undoubtedly the central issue upon which hinged the future of monarchical authority in Prussia. For Frederick William that issue was never negotiable, and here he needed no prodding at all from the Camarilla. 'My army is the basis for the existence of my throne and the preservation of the Fatherland . . . the solid pillar upon which the monarchy rests', he wrote in the spring of 1849; and even in his desperate and depressed mood a year earlier, he never deviated, or could afford to deviate, from that point of view.[42] In early June Frederick William informed the government that there could be absolutely no question of diluting his direct command authority (*Kommandogewalt*) over the army. He insisted that to do so would, in effect, destroy the monarchy itself. In a letter to the cabinet on 4 June, Frederick William asserted that ministerial co-responsibility for the conduct of military affairs would lead to a condition '*which is incompatible with my honour as a human being, a Prussian, and a King, and would lead me directly to abdication*'. The cabinet backed down on this issue, and Frederick William had won a first major victory in his struggle to reconstitute the monarchy on his own terms.[43] It was also a clear

---

[39] Albrecht von dem Bussche, *Heinrich Alexander von Arnim: Liberalismus, Polenfrage und deutsche Einheit. Das 19. Jahrhundert im Spiegel einer Biographie des preußischen Staatsmannes* (Osnabrück, 1986), 168–97, 208–33.

[40] FW IV to Charlotte, 21 Apr. 1848, in Haenchen (ed.), *Revolutionsbriefe*, 82.

[41] FW IV to Arnim, 2 Apr., 7 Apr., 7 May 1848, GStA Merseburg, Rep. 92 Heinrich Alexander von Arnim B II Nr. 6 Bl. 74, 80–80^v, 122–3; von dem Bussche, *Arnim*, 173–5, 210–12.

[42] FW IV to Staatsministerium, May or June 1849, quoted in Canis, 'Militarismus', 220. Cf. Heinrich Otto Meisner, *Der Kriegsminister 1814–1914: Ein Beitrag zur militärischen Verfassungsgeschichte* (Berlin, 1940), 17–18.

[43] FW IV to Staatsministerium, 4 June 1848, in Erich Brandenburg (ed.), *König Friedrich Wilhelms IV. Briefwechsel mit Ludolf Camphausen* (Berlin, 1906), 144–7.

victory for the King's friends at court, and demonstrates both the extent and limits of their influence.

The Camarilla was gradually becoming more assertive in its counsels to the King, as the ministers themselves realized; it was around this time, in late May or early June, that they began to complain of 'outside influences' on the King.[44] What might be regarded as the Camarilla's first significant programmatic statements also date from this same period. In an analysis of the political situation in mid-May, Edwin von Manteuffel contended that conservative forces had been 'forced back but certainly not defeated'. The adherents of a constitutional system were by no means assured of final victory.[45] His associates in Frederick William's immediate entourage shared this assessment; but what should they do to help the King understand that conservative forces were still formidable and that the prospects for a successful monarchical restoration were still favourable? These were the questions which Leopold von Gerlach addressed in an important report that he composed at the end of May, discussed with Massow, and presented to Frederick William on 4 June.[46] Gerlach had concluded that since mounting the throne Frederick William had consistently committed two fundamental errors. First, he had never really deigned to govern; that is, he had never genuinely been interested in the day-to-day problems of governance, but had depended instead on dramatic surprises and sudden announcements to make policy. Second, his system of personal rule had always been full of grievous shortcomings, and he still imagined that he could govern the country without the continued support of trusted aides. This was, Gerlach believed, both false and dangerous. Above all, Frederick William would have to get reliable *Flügeladjutanten* and adjutants-general 'instead of the miserable Neumann', as well as trustworthy War and Foreign Ministers.[47] Accordingly, Gerlach composed his report of 1 June 1848 both to confront Frederick William with the consequences of his errors and to make suggestions for possible solutions.

In it he described in stark and uncompromising terms how confidence in the King and his government had been shattered. As a result of his concessions in March the King had, through his own fault, shackled himself to a constitutional system that had rendered him powerless. His task was thus to liberate himself from this condition by appreciating the power—or the potential power—that he still enjoyed, thereby regaining the country's confidence. This could not be done by relying upon the ministry or its constitutional projects. It was possible that radicals in Berlin might try to proclaim a republic or force Frederick William from office. It was also possible that the French or the National Assembly in Frankfurt's Paulskirche might take decisions which could place Prussia in a dangerous position. In either case, the situation would be tantamount to a state of war, which would not be a bad thing at all: for then

---

[44] Leopold von Gerlach, diary (5 June 1848), GA, 'Abschriften', vi. 73.

[45] Edwin von Manteuffel, manuscript 'Mitte Mai 1848 (Ueber die politische Lage)', GStA Merseburg, HA Rep. 192 M Edwin von Manteuffel D Nr. 5¹, Bl. 4ᵛ.

[46] Leopold von Gerlach, diary (28 May, 31 May, 4 June, 5 June 1848), GA, 'Abschriften', vi. 63, 69–70, 72, 73.

[47] Leopold von Gerlach, diary (28 May 1848), ibid. vi. 63.

the King would be entirely justified in imposing martial law and provisional political institutions upon the country. Until such a situation emerged, however, Frederick William would have to put up with the ministry and with his constitutional promises of March. He should not be afraid of conflicts with his ministers, since he might be able to derive advantages from them. Above all, it would be necessary to follow the Camarilla's advice. The King should, as far as possible, only deal with trustworthy individuals like Rauch, Massow, and Keller. 'He should do everything through them and nothing without them. He should communicate to them everything that he discusses with others . . .'[48] With his natural pessimism, based on years of experience with his sovereign, Gerlach was not at all convinced that Frederick William IV would really follow the Camarilla's advice, and his confidential writings from the spring of 1848 are full of the usual complaints about the King's 'fantasies', 'weakness', 'his customary separation of words from deeds', or his tendency to stick 'with his enemies and not with his friends'.[49] In the case of royal control over the army, however, King and Camarilla were as one, and the Camphausen government did not press the matter. We shall see, however, that in other situations Gerlach's pessimism about the limits of his influence was clearly justified.

In mid-May, at about the time that the army issue was heating up, the Camphausen government prepared its own draft of a possible constitution for Prussia, and in this matter too King and Camarilla were in complete accord. Frederick William immediately denounced that draft, which the cabinet planned to present to the National Assembly after its opening on 22 May, as a 'wretched Belgian piece of work inappropriate to Prussian conditions. . . . Our discussions of it constituted one of the most ghastly hours of my life!'[50] Frederick William took particular umbrage with the document's statements concerning his own office, despite the draft's guarantee of an absolute royal veto over legislation. He insisted on adding a number of new provisions, beginning with a preamble stating that he was King by the Grace of God and that the constitution represented an 'agreement' (*Vereinbarung*) between himself and his subjects. He inserted a paragraph which noted that the army remained under the King's exclusive control. Finally, he also deplored the government's proposals for the composition of the upper house, was especially incensed by the constitutional draft's reference to churches as 'religious societies', and swore that he could never possibly accept such a document. After stormy scenes with his ministers, he reluctantly agreed to sign a revised version on 20 May.[51]

In this case, as in the discussions about the army, King and Camarilla were in complete agreement. Every line of the draft 'breathes cowardice and mindlessness',

---

[48] 'Promemoria von Leopold von Gerlach vom 1. Juni 1848', ibid. xviii. 172–5.

[49] Leopold von Gerlach, diary (6 May, 31 May, 17 May, 31 May 1848, ibid., vi. 53, 69, 58, 70.

[50] Jürgen Hofmann, *Das Ministerium Camphausen-Hansemann: Zur Politik der preußischen Bourgeoisie in der Revolution 1848/49* (Berlin [East], 1981), 126; FW IV to Radowitz, 21 May 1848, in Joseph Maria von Radowitz, *Nachgelassene Briefe und Aufzeichnungen zur Geschichte der Jahre 1848–1853*, ed. Walter Möring (Stuttgart, 1922), 46–7.

[51] J. Hofmann, *Ministerium*, 126–9; constitutional draft with marginal comments of FW IV, ibid. 208–17; Leopold von Gerlach, diary (16 and 17 May 1848), GA, 'Abschriften', vi. 57, 58.

Leopold von Gerlach noted rather curtly when he first saw the document. In a memorandum for the King on 17 May he warned that the 'particularly insidious' designation of churches as voluntary religious societies represented the constitution's most dangerous feature, for once democratic norms were introduced into ecclesiastical affairs the Protestant churches would inevitably splinter into warring sects. Still, Gerlach grudgingly admitted in his report of 1 June, it probably made sense for the King to sign the document, because it was certainly better than anything that the National Assembly might come up with. The King would have to insist that his ministers make no compromise with more radical or democratic forces in the Assembly, and under no circumstances should he agree to any constitutional draft that went beyond the ministerial proposals he had already signed.[52]

Gerlach's suspicions that the National Assembly would be more difficult to deal with, and less willing than the Camphausen government to accommodate itself to Frederick William's concerns, were entirely justified. Indeed, the cabinet itself got involved in a series of misunderstandings with the Assembly, which in turn were aggravated by an intensification of popular radicalism and street violence in Berlin. The radical atmosphere in the city had been steadily on the increase, and got a big boost with the return to the city of the 'Grapeshot Prince' (*Kartätschenprinz*), the unpopular Prince of Prussia, in early June, and by a tepid compromise on a parliamentary resolution 'recognizing' the achievements of the revolution. The disturbances got ugly on 9 June, when a mob surged around the *Singakademie*, the Assembly's meeting-place, and assaulted the physically handicapped Foreign Minister Arnim-Suckow. Finally, on 14 June the pot boiled over as crowds stormed the government arsenal in search of weapons. Arnim himself resigned on the fifteenth.[53] That same day the Assembly declared that it could not accept the cabinet's constitutional draft without amendments and alterations. When it became evident that Camphausen would not be able to gain a majority for his views, he and the rest of the ministry resigned on 20 June.[54]

The King entrusted David Hansemann with the task of putting together a new government, which he quickly did. Although he remained Finance Minister, it was evident that he was also the driving force in the new cabinet. The Minister President was Rudolf von Auerswald (1795–1866), who, like so many East Prussian aristocrats, was mildly liberal in his views; but he had been one of the King's playmates as a child, and had later served as a Hussar officer. The King quickly developed a great deal of confidence in his new Minister President, and hoped that Auerswald would be on his side in any major collision with the Assembly. He had the same hopes for the War

[52] Leopold von Gerlach, diary (8 May 1848), GA, 'Abschriften', vi. 55; id., 'Bemerkungen zum Verfassungsentwurf', 17 May 1848, and 'Promemoria', 1 June 1848, ibid., xviii. 171, 174.

[53] Report of *Staatsministerium*, 10 June 1848, GStA Merseburg, Rep. 92 Heinrich Alexander von Arnim, B II Nr. 6, Bl. 163–4; FW IV to Arnim, 14 June 1848, ibid., Bl. 152–152ᵛ; Arnim to FW IV, 15 June 1848, in Haenchen (ed.), *Revolutionsbriefe*, 110–11.

[54] Manfred Botzenhart, *Deutscher Parlamentarismus in der Revolutionszeit 1848–1850* (Düsseldorf, 1977), 519–22; J. Hofmann, *Ministerium*, 161–7, 221–4, 227–30; Orr, 'Foundation', 142–5; Brandenburg (ed.), *Briefwechsel*, 179–80.

Minister, Baron Ludwig Roth von Schreckenstein, the fourth man to occupy that post since the beginning of the year![55] In fact, by mid-July Frederick William admitted that he had been 'quite taken in' by his two ministers.[56]

Despite his friendly feelings for Auerswald and Roth von Schreckenstein, Frederick William continued to be suspicious of the rest of the cabinet, and certainly neither he nor the Camarilla had any confidence in a man like Hansemann, who was committed to ending the financial and judicial privileges of the Prussian aristocracy. And then there was still the Assembly, which had created a special constitutional commission to modify the Camphausen government's draft constitution. The highly respected democrat Benedict Waldeck chaired the committee, and the constitutional proposal which it presented on 26 July—the 'Charte Waldeck', as its conservative enemies called it—was a much more genuinely progressive and even democratic document than its predecessor in June. It would have provided the King with a suspensive rather than an absolute veto over legislation, and it also called for the introduction of civil marriages, the creation of a truly popular militia or national guard, and the elimination of patrimonial privilege in the countryside.[57]

The composition and the behaviour of the National Assembly had led the King and his advisers to think for some weeks that a major clash might be unavoidable. For years Leopold von Gerlach had been preaching the necessity of a 'firm' and 'reliable' ministry, including a chief minister who would be capable of tough decisions and who would enjoy his complete confidence. The problem now was that there were few obvious or available candidates for such a ministry. Part of the problem, the Gerlachs agreed, was that after the events of March it was difficult to find 'reliable' people who had any confidence in the monarch.[58] Thus people as diverse as the arch-conservative Albrecht von Alvensleben-Erxleben or the mildly liberal Georg von Vincke were sounded out in late June and early July about their willingness to enter the government, but both men had spurned these overtures.[59] The Gerlachs agreed, however, that a strong ministry—that is, a government which would break with Frederick William's old and discredited system of personal rule—was essential if a major confrontation developed between the King and the National Assembly. Since May the King had been thinking about the circumstances that might lead him to move vigor-

---

[55] Hansemann to FW IV, 20 June 1848, in Haenchen (ed.), *Revolutionsbriefe*, 112; William J. Orr, jun., 'König Friedrich Wilhelm IV. und der Sturz des Ministeriums Auerswald-Hansemann', *JGMOD* 25 (1976), 125–7. On Hansemann, see esp. Alan Kahan, 'Liberalism and *Realpolitik* in Prussia, 1830–52: The Case of David Hansemann', *German History*, 9 (1991), 280–307.

[56] Leopold von Gerlach, diary (16 and 18 July 1848), GA, 'Abschriften', vi. 92, 95.

[57] Ernst Rudolf Huber, *Deutsche Verfassungsgeschichte seit 1789*, 3rd edn. (Stuttgart, 1988), ii: *Der Kampf um Einheit und Freiheit 1830 bis 1850*, 730–2; Botzenhart, *Parlamentarismus*, 538–41. On Waldeck, see esp. Ludwig Dehio, 'Benedict Waldeck', *HZ* 136 (1927), 25–57.

[58] Ludwig von Gerlach to Leopold von Gerlach, 17 July 1848, GA, 'Abschriften', xviii. 54.

[59] FW IV to Senfft von Pilsach, 27 June 1848, in Haenchen (ed.), *Revolutionsbriefe*, 115; Orr, 'Foundation', 145–6, 148–9; Leopold von Gerlach, diary (29 June 1848; 6, 11, and 21 July 1848), GA, 'Abschriften', vi. 87–91, 98–101; Vincke to FW IV, 6 and 19 July 1848, in Haenchen (ed.), *Revolutionsbriefe*, 120–5, 129–31; Konrad Canis, 'Ideologie und politische Taktik der junkerlich-militaristischen Reaktion bei der Vorbereitung und Durchführung des Staatsstreiches in Preußen im Herbst 1848', *Jahrbuch für Geschichte*, 7 (1972), 470–1.

ously and decisively against 'the revolution'. As early as the middle of May, he had indicated that he would move quickly if the Assembly were to try to incorporate the principle of popular sovereignty into law, if it were to try to alter the succession to the throne, or if it attempted to proclaim a republic. When the Camphausen government fell apart, Frederick William raised the possibility that the Assembly might deny his own right to dissolve it and then declare itself to be permanent. Haunted all his life by the spectre of 1789, the King said that in such a circumstance he would resume his full powers as monarch and establish a non-responsible government on a dictatorial basis.[60]

Radowitz, to whom the King had communicated these sentiments, continued to urge caution upon his sovereign, pointing out that the idea of popular sovereignty was essentially a 'fashionable expression' which most people thought was perfectly reconcilable with 'respect and love for the crown'.[61] Although Leopold von Gerlach deplored Radowitz's advice and seemed to favour a more confrontational, coercive approach, his concrete suggestions were not substantially different. In an important memorandum written at the end of June he chided Frederick William for his irresoluteness in the immediate past, especially on 9 June, when, after the mob's attack on Arnim, he had missed a good opportunity to proceed vigorously. He also disputed Radowitz's tendency to downplay 'doctrinal' matters such as declarations of popular sovereignty. If the Assembly were to proclaim that it embodied popular sovereignty, then the King should immediately dismiss the cabinet and dissolve the Assembly. He agreed with Radowitz that a huge popular uprising in Berlin would represent the best opportunity for the King to strike. If he persisted in the path of concessions, however, that moment might never come. Then the King himself, Gerlach warned ominously, would be responsible if things did not turn out for the best.[62] Although this missive, which was intended as a riposte to Radowitz's effacement strategy, sounded uncompromising, Gerlach in fact continued to urge caution upon the King throughout July and August. At the end of July, when Frederick William surprised Gerlach by mentioning a plan to send two regiments to Berlin to dissolve the Assembly, the General warned the King that such an 'adventurous' step would be tantamount to a *coup d'état*. He would also need to have in readiness a new cabinet that would enjoy his complete confidence and with which he could work effectively. In other words, he should avoid drastic measures but should work step by step to achieve his goal.[63]

Ludwig von Gerlach's ideas were, as usual, much more blunt, direct, and drastic than his older brother's. By mid-July he had begun to reflect on the possibility of dissolving the Assembly, which would inevitably lead to violence. In that case, a military government would be necessary. In a letter of 17 June he mentioned that such a government might include Prittwitz, Schreckenstein, and perhaps Radowitz, as well

---

[60] FW IV to Radowitz, 21 May and 19 June 1848, in Radowitz, *Briefe und Aufzeichnungen*, 47, 56; see also Leopold von Gerlach, diary (28 May 1848), GA, 'Abschriften', vi. 63.

[61] Radowitz to FW IV, 24 May and 22 June 1848, in Radowitz, *Briefe und Aufzeichnungen*, 48–9, 58–9.

[62] Leopold von Gerlach to FW IV, 28 June 1848, GStA Merseburg, HA Rep. 50 J Nr. 455, Bl. 24–25ᵛ.

[63] Leopold von Gerlach, diary (29 July 1848), GA, 'Abschriften', vi. 104; Leopold von Gerlach to FW IV, 'Promemoria', 29 July 1848, ibid., vi. 106–9 and xviii. 182–3. See also Orr, 'Sturz', 182–3.

as Count Brandenburg, commander of the Sixth Army Corps in Breslau—his first political reference to the man who in the autumn became the Camarilla's choice to head the government and restore the authority of the crown.[64] By late August he was darkly hinting that, given the weakness both of the King and of his political allies, 'at first we'll need a powerful monarchy with a Russian flavour—we're not capable of any other kind of government'. At the same time, though, even he agreed that, for the interim, caution was in order: '*Wait* until ripe fruits fall into the King's lap, and, in the meantime, let us prepare a ministry (Brandenburg, Prittwitz, Bismarck).'[65]

One reason for the Camarilla's caution in July and August may well have been the relative absence, as Leopold suggested in his report of 29 July, of obvious points of conflict with the Assembly. Another was, as always, Frederick William himself, whose mood during those weeks continued to waver between lethargic depression and vehement outbursts of rage at the radical goings-on in Berlin, about which he constantly complained in his communiqués with Auerswald. The Camarilla, especially Ludwig von Gerlach, was keenly aware of its disadvantageous position in those weeks. Despite Ludwig's suggestions, it had no clear alternative to the present government. It also continued to reject the notion of the King's abdication, which even in July was still regarded as a possibility. Thus it had to rely on the steadiness of the King himself, always a risky proposition.

In some respects, however, the situation was gradually improving for the adherents of what Edwin von Manteuffel called 'a carefully considered, carefully prepared Restoration'.[66] A new outburst of popular violence in Berlin on 21 August opened up new possibilities for the Camarilla. As Leopold von Gerlach put it to the Prince of Prussia, 'the excesses in Berlin had, thank God, led us once again to a crisis from which our salvation can emerge or at least begin'. The only problem, he went on, was the King's continuing 'apathy and indifference'.[67] In late August, Prussia unilaterally concluded the armistice of Malmö with the Danes, without having consulted the Frankfurt National Assembly or the provisional central authority in that city. The King's advisers at court had always been suspicious of the nationalist euphoria with which the 'Reich War' had been conducted; and with the conclusion of an armistice, the possibility of a collision with Russia had been reduced. Developments like this were, of course, good news to the Camarilla and other conservatives. Then, in early September, a series of events began to unfold which brought the Camarilla's influence to its zenith.

A Limited Triumph: The Camarilla and the Restoration of Royal Authority, August–December 1848

On 31 July the citizens' militia in the Silesian city of Schweidnitz sought permission

---

[64] Ludwig von Gerlach to Leopold von Gerlach, 17 July 1848, GA, 'Abschriften', xviii. 54; cf. Ludwig von Gerlach to Leopold von Gerlach, 9 July 1848, in Petersdorff, 'Briefe', 71; and Orr, 'Foundation', 152.
[65] Ludwig von Gerlach to Leopold von Gerlach, 28 and 27 Aug. 1848, GA, 'Abschriften', xviii. 73, 71.
[66] Edwin von Manteuffel, 'Anfang Juli 1848 (Ueber Revolutionen)', GStA Merseburg, HA Rep. 192 M Edwin von Manteuffel D Nr. 5², Bl. 7.
[67] Leopold von Gerlach, diary (23 Aug. 1848), GA, 'Abschriften', vi. 123, 124.

to use drum rolls to summon its members to drills. The local regular-army comman-der first granted that permission, then withdrew it, whereupon an angry crowd gath-ered before his house. In the confusion, troops fired upon the crowd without warning, killing fourteen civilians.[68] The bloody incident unleashed a torrent of crit-icism, and on 9 August the Berlin National Assembly considered a proposal by a democratic deputy from Breslau, Julius Stein, calling upon the War Minister to declare 'that officers will distance themselves from all reactionary tendencies', that they should not only avoid conflicts with civilians but also fraternize with them as proof of their devotion to constitutional values. Stein's proposal passed by a large majority, though an amendment suggesting that politically recalcitrant officers should resign was approved by only one vote. The government tried for several weeks to duck this critical issue of civil–military relations, but by 7 September it could no longer be avoided. By a vote of 219–143 the Assembly called upon the gov-ernment to carry out the stipulations of the Stein proposal, whereupon the Auerswald-Hansemann cabinet immediately resigned.[69] To Frederick William IV it seemed that the hour of decision might be fast approaching. The question of parlia-mentary control of the army, an issue that lay at the heart of more than one constitu-tional conflict in Prussia, had finally emerged; and of the attitude of King and Camarilla there could be no doubt. Upon hearing of the vote in the National Assembly, Frederick William wrote to Auerswald, 'The die is cast. For all intents and purposes the republic has been proclaimed, and soon it will be formally as well.' If the National Assembly now tried to behave like the Estates General at the Tennis Court, he would 'disperse it with bayonets'.[70]

Was the time truly propitious for Manteuffel's 'well-considered' restoration? Above all, what would be the response outside Berlin to harsh measures against the National Assembly? Frederick William always insisted, of course, that he could count on the loyalty and love of his subjects. 'I know my people better than you', he had written to Camphausen in May, 'and I know how opinions can shift, especially in turbulent times among a good people, as a result of bold, splendid, decisive, truly Prussian actions by the government and above all by *the King*.'[71] In a confidential memorandum of 4 September 1848, just as the crisis over the Stein proposal was building to a climax, Frederick William expressed confidence that the use of force against his 'disloyal and good-for-nothing' capital would have a 'beneficial' effect throughout the entire country.[72]

It is impossible to say whether or not the King really believed this assertion, nor is it really possible to gauge the extent or limits of his popularity in 1848. The

[68] Manfred Messerschmidt, 'Die politische Geschichte der preußisch-deutschen Armee', in Militärgeschichtliches Forschungsamt (ed.), *Handbuch zur deutschen Militärgeschichte 1648–1939*, ii, sect. IV: *Militärgeschichte im 19. Jahrhundert 1814–1890*, pt. 1 (Munich, 1979), 146; E. R. Huber, *Verfassungsgeschichte*, ii. 735.

[69] Botzenhart, *Parlamentarismus*, 527–32.   [70] Quoted in Orr, 'Sturz', 140.

[71] FW IV to Camphausen, 20 May 1848, in Brandenburg (ed.), *Briefwechsel*, 109.

[72] FW IV, 'Die Lage der Dinge heute 4. September 1848 ist folgende', GStA Merseburg, Rep. 92 Familienarchiv von Massow Nr. 13, Bl. 62.

elimination of censorship on 17 March had precipitated a flood of critical newspapers, satirical journals, placards, pamphlets, caricatures, and cheaply printed broadsides of all kinds.[73] Critical representations of the King figured prominently in much of this literature. We have already seen that Frederick William had been a natural target for caricaturists in the early 1840s; and new images were now added to older depictions of '*der Champagner-Fritze*', the impotent drunkard. Thus the monarch was still portrayed with a champagne-bottle, or even in the shape of one. Now, however, he was often shown in a spiked helmet and either carrying cannons or bombarding his subjects with them after the alleged 'misunderstanding' of 18 March. One especially fearsome cartoon, entitled simply 'Der 18te März 1848', and described sardonically as one of several 'Sketches for Frescoes to Glorify the Most Magnificent Days in the History of the Hohenzollerns', depicts Frederick William sitting on his throne, surrounded by fawning soldiers, empty champagne-bottles, and the emblems 'Intelligenz' and 'Humanität'; in the foreground men, women, and children lie dead or are being massacred by troops.[74] Similar themes were echoed in much of the satirical 'street-corner literature' in Berlin, which took the form both of individual pamphlets and of more or less regularly published journals. Of thirty-five different satirical papers published in 1848, thirty-three represented 'democratic' views, and thus could hardly be regarded as sympathetic to Frederick William IV.[75]

From these samples, largely derived from Berlin, it is difficult to draw any conclusions about the attitudes of ordinary Berliners toward the King after 1848, much less the feelings of other Prussians. In an explosive, rapidly changing time, those feelings were almost certainly volatile, but it is hard to say for sure. There were also significant regional variations. Silesia, for example, was the only part of the country which experienced widespread agrarian disturbances in the spring of 1848, in contrast to other, non-Prussian parts of Germany; and as late as August it was being reported that Silesian villagers and townspeople combined hatred of their local magnates with hostility towards the King himself.[76] In some other regions, such as the Rhineland, much of the population had also become hostile to the monarchy and

---

[73] About a hundred politically oriented newspapers and journals emerged in 1848. Many remained prominent for decades thereafter. Among them were the ultra-conservative *Neue Preußische Zeitung* (popularly known as the *Kreuz-Zeitung*), the liberal *National-Zeitung*, and the democratic *Urwähler-Zeitung* (later known as the *Volks-Zeitung*). Ursula E. Koch, 'Prolegomena zu einer Geschichte des Berliner politischen Witzblattes', in Wilhelm Treue (ed.), *Geschichte als Aufgabe: Festschrift für Otto Büsch zu seinem 60. Geburtstag* (Berlin, 1988), 528–9.

[74] Remigius Brückmann, '"Es ginge wohl aber es geht nicht": König Friedrich Wilhelm IV. von Preußen und die politische Karikatur der Jahre 1840–1849', in Berlin zwischen 1789 und 1848: Facetten einer Epoche. Ausstellung der Akademie der Künste vom 30. August bis 1. November 1981 (Berlin, 1981), 155–9; 'Das Mißverständniß', BA Frankfurt/M., ZSg. 6/515; 'Der 18te März 1848', ibid., ZSg. 6/582.

[75] U. E. Koch, 'Prolegomena', 528–35; Horst Denkler and Claus Kittsteiner (eds.), *Berliner Straßenecken-Literatur 1848/49: Humoristisch-satirische Flugschriften aus der Revolutionszeit* (Stuttgart, 1977).

[76] Ludwig von Massow to FW IV, 19 Aug. 1848, GStA Merseburg, HA Rep. 50 J Nr. 806 Bl. 32ᵛ; Manfred Gailus, 'Zur Politisierung der Landbevölkerung in der Märzbewegung von 1848', in Peter Steinbach (ed.), *Probleme politischer Partizipation im Modernisierungsprozeß* (Stuttgart, 1982), 96–8, who emphasizes the complex motives that lay behind the agrarian disturbances in Silesia.

turned to revolutionary action in the spring of 1848; but in many areas, especially in the Protestant core-provinces, popular monarchism remained deeply rooted and virtually unshaken.[77] In fact, if we can believe contemporary observers like Varnhagen, many members of Prussia's traditional élites were more antagonistic to their monarch than millions of ordinary peasants and urban craftsmen.[78] We have already seen how Frederick William's behaviour in March had elicited feelings of anger, disillusionment, and disorientation precisely among those elements—estate owners, government officials, and officers—which in the *Vormärz* period had been most closely linked to the monarchy. Many members of those élites were so embittered that they never forgave the King for his actions. Prittwitz's memoirs, for example, note that many officers came to regard the Prince of Prussia, for years the commander of the aristocratic Guard units, as their natural and real leader. For many of these individuals, a fiercely loyal adherence to the values of the Prussian monarchy came to symbolize a more general attachment to the symbols and structures of the Old Regime, and could be combined with a distaste for the person of the ruling monarch himself. Alvensleben was just one of many examples, and Ludwig von Gerlach was another.

In the weeks and months that followed the March revolution, Ludwig von Gerlach and his associates found ample confirmation of their *Vormärz* thesis that fellow conservatives had not yet understood the importance of effective party organization or of appeals to public opinion. The conservative, monarchical cause could no longer be served simply by assuming that traditional rulers had a right to rule, by maintaining traditional networks of power and authority, or by equating politics with continued access to the court and the army. The failure of conservatives to organize themselves as a party had already had dire consequences at the United Diet in 1847, Gerlach believed; there the conservatives had essentially abandoned the field to the constitutional liberals. Similarly minded conservatives like Victor Aimé Huber deplored the inability of *Vormärz* conservatives to appreciate the political power of 'doctrines' in the modern world. Although some thinkers like Friedrich Julius Stahl were already laying the foundations of a conservative constitutionalism to replace outmoded *ständisch* concepts, all practical attempts to create an effective conservative 'party' organization had so far met with failure.[79] If monarchical, 'Christian-German' values were to have a future in an age of revolutions, conservatives would have to organize, learn how to exert political pressure, articulate political views, and mobilize public opinion; above all, as Hermann Wagener, one of Ludwig von Gerlach's most important protégés, noted in September 1848, 'we must learn from our enemies' how to organize politically and how to pursue practical, workable goals.[80]

[77] Jonathan Sperber, *Rhineland Radicals: The Democratic Movement and the Revolution of 1848–1849* (Princeton, NJ, 1991), 151–69.

[78] Varnhagen von Ense, *Tagebücher*, v. 238 (15 Oct. 1848).

[79] Wolfgang Schwentker, *Konservative Vereine und Revolution in Preußen 1848/49: Die Konstituierung des Konservativismus als Partei* (Düsseldorf, 1988), 15–16, 18–22, 48–56; also Jordan, *Entstehung*, 153–4.

[80] Hermann Wagener to Otto von Manteuffel, 20 Sept. 1848, GStA Merseburg, Rep. 92 Otto von Manteuffel Tit. II Nr. 151, Bl. 1, 2ᵛ.

After the events of 18–19 March Ludwig von Gerlach was quick to realize that conservatives too could take advantage of the new freedom of the press by creating a popular, overtly political newspaper. It was to that project, and the related project of organizing new conservative political associations, that he devoted most of his prodigious energy during the spring and summer of 1848. The work of the court Camarilla was, in his estimation, of secondary importance. Although the newspaper idea encountered a great deal of scepticism at first, Gerlach was not to be deterred. By 13 April he was thinking of naming it *Das eiserne Kreuz*, and in the next few days he worked feverishly to develop its financial base.[81] On 22 April the decision was taken to found the paper under the name *Neue Preußische Zeitung*; its mast-head, however, bore the iron cross, and thus it was popularly called the *Kreuzzeitung*. Hermann Wagener, formerly a judicial official in Magdeburg, became its first editor.[82] Although people like the Gerlachs, Carl von Voß-Buch, Ernst von Senfft-Pilsach, and others invested heavily in the paper, Wagener and his fellow journalists were able to enjoy substantial editorial freedom. The first sample-issues were published in June, and after 30 June it appeared daily.[83] Within a year the paper was able to triple its circulation from an initial 1,000, a rather impressive figure by the standards of the mid-nineteenth century. Although people like Ernst Wilhelm Hengstenberg were critical of Wagener's 'intellectual and cultural shortcomings', he turned out to be an energetic, caustic, and even ruthless journalist; and under his direction the *Kreuzzeitung* gained a deserved reputation for a style that was at once inflammatory, scabrous, and aggressive. Ludwig von Gerlach remained closely associated with it, especially in the form of his influential monthly reviews of current events. The *Kreuzzeitung* was not a creation of the Camarilla, but thanks to the Gerlachs the two became closely intertwined. The paper itself became the eponymous rallying-point for conservative adherents of what came to be called the *Kreuzzeitung* party after 1848.

Most of the early subscribers to the *Kreuzzeitung* belonged to traditional Prussian élite groups—aristocrats, court and government officials, officers, landowners, and Protestant pastors.[84] But Ludwig von Gerlach and his friends were also interested in shaping and influencing more obviously grass-roots organizations, the numerous conservative societies and associations (*Vereine*) that had begun to pop up in the spring and summer of 1848. At first some conservatives had joined moderately liberal 'Constitutional Leagues' which embraced the idea of a powerful monarchy in a

[81] E. L. von Gerlach, *Aufzeichnungen aus seinem Leben und Wirken (1795–1877)*, ed. Jakob von Gerlach (2 vols.; Schwerin, 1903), i. 525; Ludwig von Gerlach to Leopold von Gerlach, 13, 15, 16, 17, and 18 Apr. 1848, GA, 'Abschriften', xviii. 6, 7, 8–10, 11–12, 13–13b.

[82] Ludwig von Gerlach to Leopold von Gerlach, 24 Apr. 1848, ibid. xviii. 16.

[83] Orr, 'Foundation', 55–87, remains the best account of the paper's establishment. It should now be supplemented by the important letters of Ludwig von Gerlach in GA, 'Abschriften', xviii, and by the papers of Hermann Wagener in BA Potsdam, 90 Wa 3. See also Hermann Wagener, *Erlebtes: Meine Memoiren aus der Zeit von 1848 bis 1866 und von 1873 bis jetzt* (2 vols.; Berlin, 1884), i. 4–19; Schwentker, *Vereine*, 60–2, 175–6; and, above all, Kraus, 'Gerlach', i. 265–9, ii. 200–3.

[84] Schwentker, *Vereine*, 176.

constitutional framework. But by June 1848 more frankly conservative associations—'Patriotic Leagues', 'Prussian Leagues', veterans' societies, and peasants' associations—were emerging on a local basis, especially in Brandenburg and Pomerania, two of the Protestant 'core provinces' of the kingdom. In early July a new group, the Society for King and Fatherland (*Verein für König und Vaterland*), was established in Nauen in an effort to organize like-minded conservatives throughout the entire monarchy. Its members included conservative notables like the Gerlachs, Heinrich Leo, Senfft-Pilsach, and Adolf von Thadden-Trieglaff. Although it enjoyed some success, holding general assemblies and encouraging the establishment of branch organizations in various localities, its attempts to serve as a conservative clearing-house fell short. Many of the grass-roots conservative organizations that emerged in 1848 represented local interests that were loyal to the King, attached to traditional Prussian institutions and outlooks, and thus deeply suspicious of 'democrats' and German nationalism; but they were also reluctant to identify themselves with court ultras in Berlin and Potsdam. 'Conservative yes, reactionary no, was the watchword of most of the societies . . .'[85]

Although they were not as large as the democratic or constitutional societies, by late 1848 the conservative societies in Prussia had enrolled 20,000 members, and by the early summer of 1849 their numbers had swelled to 60,000. They included in their ranks a significant number of peasants, artisans, and shopkeepers who, for one reason or another, felt threatened by the political and economic changes that were transforming Prussian society. In Potsdam, for example, twenty-two of the forty-five members of the local branch of the Society for King and Fatherland were master artisans. In all these associations, diffuse and decentralized though they were, lay the seeds of a modern conservative political movement. They also demonstrated that Frederick William IV's assessment of his kingdom's mood was basically correct: in the small towns and villages of the countryside enormous reservoirs of monarchist sentiment persisted throughout 1848 and thereafter. The mobilization of that sentiment, through such things as addresses and petitions, lent confidence to the conservative cause in the crucial autumn months of 1848.[86] Though it is difficult to say what the individual members of those associations may have thought about Frederick William IV, the kinds of subtle distinctions that Ludwig von Gerlach drew between monarchy and the person of the monarch would almost certainly have been irrelevant to them. The King was simply the King, and one had to be loyal to him.

Attachment to monarchical values could take even more drastic forms. Like England in earlier times, Prussia in 1848 experienced a series of 'Church and King' riots, that is, violent mob activities directed against supposed representatives of liberal, constitutional, or democratic values.[87] One of the most important took place on

[85] Ibid., 97.
[86] Ibid., 142, 156–74, 336–8; Manfred Gailus, *Straße und Brot: Sozialer Protest in den deutschen Staaten unter besonderer Berücksichtigung Preußens, 1847–1849* (Göttingen, 1990), 441–4.
[87] Of eighty-one such disturbances which took place in Germany between 1847 and 1849, seventy took place in Prussia, with the great majority concentrated in Brandenburg, Pomerania, and the province of Prussia. They tended to take place in small cities located in predominantly agrarian regions, especially in

[cont. on p. 174]

20 August in Charlottenburg, then a small town to the west of Berlin that derived much of its livelihood from the adjacent palace of the same name. That evening an angry royalist mob broke up a peaceful meeting of democrats, and in the process assaulted and injured some of its members. This incident in turn contributed to an outbreak of radical violence in Berlin the next day—evidence, perhaps, of an intensifying polarization of public opinion which ultimately worked to the advantage of counter-revolutionary forces.[88]

The first major test of Frederick William's own popularity came in early August, when he undertook his first trip outside the Berlin–Potsdam region since the March revolution, journeying to the Rhineland to attend yet another cathedral celebration in Cologne. On his way he travelled through Magdeburg, where he encountered a friendly crowd and met Ludwig von Gerlach for the first time since March. Similarly cordial receptions along the way to Cologne put him in an exceedingly good mood, especially in the Rhenish metropolis itself, where he enjoyed a triumphal reception.[89] The King shared the limelight there with Archduke John of Austria, whom the Frankfurt National Assembly in the Paulskirche had chosen as *Reichsverweser*—that is, representative of the executive power of a united Germany—in late June. The crowds in Cologne cheered more enthusiastically for Frederick William than for the Archduke. Moreover, at the festival dinner two Prussian princes managed to prevent Heinrich von Gagern, President of the Frankfurt National Assembly, from obtaining a seat of honour next to the King. Frederick William himself, ever the stage-manager of public events, made a point of being genial and accessible to ordinary *Kölsch* citizens. The mood of celebration was so universal that the workers at Karl Marx's *Neue Rheinische Zeitung* left work one day to join in, causing the cancellation of the next issue. The most significant evidence of hostility during Frederick William's stay in the Rhineland came in Düsseldorf, where someone threw manure at his carriage, but otherwise the trip convinced him that the country had calmed down and that support for him was widespread.[90] During the next three months, however, his advisers in the Camarilla often doubted whether that new-found confidence would last very long or could be translated into political success.

The crisis over the Stein resolution and the subsequent resignation of the Auerswald–Hansemann cabinet in early September had caught the Camarilla unprepared. Frederick William himself had reckoned for some days with the possibility of a ministerial crisis, and had even toyed with the idea of engineering a crisis himself in

areas where 'in portions of the lower strata a traditional myth of the "just King", of the "loyal and caring father of the country" was still a vital force'. Ibid. 129–32, 440.

[88] Orr, 'Sturz', 135; Gailus, *Straße und Brot*, 447–8; id., 'Protestbewegungen', 101–2.

[89] FW IV to Charlotte, 1 Sept. 1848, in Haenchen (ed.), *Revolutionsbriefe*, 165; see also Ludwig von Gerlach, diary (12 and 17 Aug. 1848), in E. L. von Gerlach, *Von der Revolution*, i. 106, 107; Leopold von Gerlach to Ludwig von Gerlach, 25 Aug. 1848, ibid. ii. 564; Varnhagen von Ense, *Tagebücher*, v. 165, 169 (17 and 21 Aug. 1848).

[90] Thomas Parent, *Die Hohenzollern in Köln* (Cologne, 1981), 63–8; Sperber, *Radicals*, 310–13; 'Tagebuch des Erzherzogs Johann', 14–15 Aug. 1848, BA Frankfurt/M., FSg. 1/210, fol. 13–15.

order to get rid of Hansemann. He also hoped that a new cabinet of the right would replace the current constitutional draft with a more conservative document. As long, however, as the 'idolatrous theory' of majority rule persisted, such a cabinet could not hope to survive. Thus he would have to dissolve the Berlin Assembly. But what would replace it? A new one on the basis of the electoral law of May 1848, which was what 'almost all of my friends advise'? A return to the United Diet, which is what Frederick William supported? Accordingly, he wrote on 4 September, he would try to stay with the present cabinet as long as possible. If a new cabinet should be necessary, 'Herr Georg von Vincke is the right man', or else, as a second choice, War Minister Roth von Schreckenstein. The King even dispatched Massow to Frankfurt to try to win over Vincke, but to no avail. Roth von Schreckenstein also seems to have removed himself from contention, as did Arnim-Boitzenburg, who had been mentioned as a ministerial possibility despite the King's intense dislike of him.[91]

Despite his failure to find a suitable candidate to head a new government, Frederick William proceeded to draft a series of statements in which he outlined the strategy that he would pursue in the event of a confrontation with the National Assembly. On 11 and 19 September he wrote that he would send a statement to the assembly annulling the vote on the Stein resolution, after which he would force the Assembly to move to the city of Brandenburg and repeal both the constitutional draft and Hansemann's 'confiscatory' laws. Should the Assembly object, it would be dissolved and a new constitution would be imposed by the King himself.[92] Older historians often regarded Frederick William's *Kampfprogramm* of 11 September 1848 as a direct anticipation of the actual course of events after November, and as clear evidence of a determined royal strategy to carry out a *coup d'état* and impose a constitution from above. More recent research has shown, however, that Frederick William found it impossible to pursue a clear or obvious course of action in the autumn of 1848, and he could not adhere to the details outlined in his September programme. Events proceeded along a much more complex path, and to speak of the counter-revolution as a *coup* hatched in advance by King and Camarilla is simplistic.[93]

The Camarilla itself was sceptical about the chances for such a coup. Ludwig von Gerlach had spoken with the King in late August, and after returning to Magdeburg he drafted a 'plan of government' for Frederick William in which he emphasized that only the monarch and no one else was in a position to rescue or destroy the throne. Thus the King needed firm ministers who would stand unshakeably with him in defence of royal authority, even in the face of massive popular unrest.[94] After the

---

[91] Arnim to FW IV, 9 Sept. 1848, and Vincke to FW IV, 14 Sept.1848, in Haenchen (ed.), *Revolutionsbriefe*, 170–5; Canis, 'Militarismus', 166–73; report of Massow, 9 Sept. 1848, GStA Merseburg, Rep. 92 Familienarchiv von Massow Nr. 13, Bl. 67–68ᵛ; Leopold von Gerlach, diary (13 and 15 Sept. 1848), GA, 'Abschriften', vi. 145–6, 147.

[92] 'Kampfprogramm' of 11 Sept. 1848 in Ernst Rudolf Huber (ed.), *Dokumente zur deutschen Verfassungsgeschichte*, i: *Deutsche Verfassungsdokumente 1803–1850* (Stuttgart, 1961), 374; 'Denkschrift König Friedrich Wilhelms IV.', 15 Sept. 1848, in Haenchen (ed.), *Revolutionsbriefe*, 175–8.

[93] Grünthal, 'Zwischen König, Kabinett und Kamarilla', 135–7.

[94] E. L. von Gerlach, 'Regierungsplan für den König, Herbst 1848', in id., *Aufzeichnungen*, ii. 511–18.

Assembly vote on the Stein resolution, Ludwig von Gerlach again travelled to Potsdam and worked out yet another set of proposals to present to the King. It was a remarkably mild document, again stressing the need for a powerful premier upon whom the monarch could rely. Otherwise, the Gerlach brothers agreed, the King should avoid a premature confrontation; he should remain 'moderate, clear-headed, careful, almost passive', but also 'conscientious, fully consistent, and true to his principles'.[95]

In their actual conversation with their royal master on 9 September, Leopold von Gerlach mentioned the possibility of 'a military ministry', to be headed either by Count Brandenburg or Carl von der Groeben. But nothing came of that suggestion, and the Camarilla certainly did nothing to push matters—aware, perhaps, of its own lack of preparation and of the likelihood that Frederick William would probably not stand firm.[96] As Ludwig noted to his brother the day after his return to Magdeburg, 'No one is yet able to discern the King's banner, depend on it, and rally around it. . . . You will have to do all in your power to *organize* the King and the Camarilla—or else all is lost.' In his diary he was even blunter: 'Everything is still as it was. We need heroic deeds, everything is ready, only the hero is missing.'[97]

On 21 September 1848 the King officially appointed General Ernst von Pfuel to head a new ministry. The Camarilla had little to do with this decision, to which, in any case, it had no real alternative.[98] A man of considerable learning and experience, Pfuel (1779–1866) was known both for his personal integrity and his conciliatory, liberal political views. As a young man he had been closely associated with Heinrich von Kleist, and in later years he admitted to Varnhagen, another old friend, that a republic was the best form of government and that he himself was a republican '*in abstracto*'. Such ideas had not prevented him from serving the Prussian crown as a successful officer and as governor of Neuchâtel for many years. Just before the March revolution he had served as commander of troops in Berlin, and in the late spring of 1848 he had played a critical role in bringing hostilities in Posen to a close.[99] He was aware from the very outset that he was assuming the reins of government in a time of crisis, and that his tenure would essentially be an interim one. He had to mediate between a King and an Assembly that were on a collision course, and he even told Leopold von Gerlach that he would probably only stay in office for about two weeks.[100]

[95] 'Vereinbarung der beiden Gerlachs vom 9.9.1848', GA, 'Abschriften', xviii. 194–6.

[96] Leopold von Gerlach, diary (9 Sept. 1848), ibid., vi. 141; Ludwig von Gerlach, diary (9 Sept. 1848), in E. L. von Gerlach, *Von der Revolution*, i. 111–12.

[97] Ludwig von Gerlach to Leopold von Gerlach, 12 Sept. 1848, GA, 'Abschriften', xviii. 77; Ludwig von Gerlach, diary (10 Sept. 1848), in E. L. von Gerlach, *Von der Revolution*, i. 112. Cf. Grünthal, 'Zwischen König, Kabinett und Kamarilla', 137; id., 'Bemerkungen', 42–3.

[98] Leopold von Gerlach, diary (15 and 22 Sept. 1848), GA, 'Abschriften', vi. 148, 153; Leopold von Gerlach to Ludwig von Gerlach, 16 Sept. 1848, in E. L. von Gerlach, *Von der Revolution*, ii. 570–1.

[99] Bernhard von Gersdorff, *Ernst von Pfuel: Freund Heinrich von Kleists, General, Preußischer Ministerpräsident 1848* (Berlin, 1981), esp. 85–129.

[100] Leopold von Gerlach, diary (22 Sept. 1848), GA, 'Abschriften', vi. 153. Cf. Varnhagen von Ense, *Tagebücher*, v. 221 (5 Oct. 1848).

Pfuel immediately offered the hand of conciliation to the National Assembly. One of his first acts was to issue an order, in his function as War Minister, calling upon the army to desist from 'reactionary tendencies' and to encourage good relations between civilians and soldiers. Pfuel had thus effectively demonstrated his support for the main features of the Stein resolution, and both King and Camarilla were aghast.[101] Despite such gestures, the Assembly remained mistrustful of the ministry, the King, and the King's advisers, and so it continued to press for a series of measures guaranteeing civil liberties and equality before the law, including the abolition of the death penalty, the introduction of habeas corpus, and an end to big landowners' hunting-privileges. In the middle of October the Assembly approved a decree eliminating Frederick William's title as King 'by the Grace of God'. No other conceivable measure could have struck more directly at Frederick William's own notion of himself, the nature of his office, and the source of his authority.[102]

Pfuel had not been able to act as a successful mediator. As early as 4 October Frederick William was speaking bitterly of the cabinet's supposed 'treason', and on the seventh Pfuel wrote to the monarch that he could not remain in office if the King was unwilling to accept the constitutional draft of the summer.[103] About a week later the King was unable to persuade the cabinet to support a public statement challenging the Assembly's right to eliminate the reference to the 'Grace of God' in his title. Accordingly, at an official birthday reception on 15 October Frederick William sharply rebuked a delegation from the National Assembly and insisted that a true constitutional system could only be based on 'hereditary authority by the Grace of God'. No compromise on this subject could be possible. Pfuel's situation, made worse by the steady polarization and radicalization of public opinion in Berlin, had become untenable, and the following day the entire cabinet offered to resign. Frederick William agreed to that step, but asked Pfuel to stay on until a new government could be named.[104]

A new Minister President was in fact already waiting in the wings: the King's uncle, Count Brandenburg. 'He was brave and first-rate here', Frederick William enthused, after conferring with Brandenburg on 25 October. 'He will take the position, though unwillingly. But he will just have to.'[105] On 1 November Pfuel reported to the National Assembly that Brandenburg would form a new cabinet. The Camarilla's greatest triumph was about to unfold. As we have already seen, Ludwig von Gerlach had been toying with the prospect of a Brandenburg government since

---

[101] Leopold von Gerlach to Ludwig von Gerlach, 27 Sept. 1848, in E. L. von Gerlach, *Von der Revolution*, ii. 579.

[102] Veit Valentin, *Geschichte der deutschen Revolution von 1848–1849* (2 vols.; Cologne, 1977; orig. 1931–2), ii. 246–51; E. R. Huber, *Verfassungsgeschichte*, ii. 741–5; Canis, 'Ideologie und Taktik', 479–87; Botzenhart, *Parlamentarismus*, 543–4.

[103] Pfuel to FW IV, 7 Oct. 1848, in Haenchen (ed.), *Revolutionsbriefe*, 191–2.

[104] Friedrich Wilhelm IV., *Reden und Trinksprüche Sr. Majestät Friedrich Wilhelm des Vierten, Königes von Preußen* (Leipzig, 1855), 89; Staatsministerium to FW IV, 16 Oct. 1848, and FW IV to Staatsministerium, 20 Oct. 1848, in Haenchen (ed.), *Revolutionsbriefe*, 199–200, 206–7.

[105] FW IV to Charlotte, 25 Oct. 1848, in Haenchen (ed.), *Revolutionsbriefe*, 210.

at least mid-July; and on 29 September, after hearing of Pfuel's 'Anti-Reaction Decree', he insisted to Leopold that the time had come for a ministry composed of Brandenburg, Otto von Bismarck, Hans Hugo von Kleist-Retzow, and Marcus Niebuhr, with the Prince of Prussia as 'generalissimo'. Only a resolute government of that sort, he asserted, would be able to maintain the constitutional autonomy of the crown *vis-à-vis* the Assembly.[106] On 3 October Ludwig arrived in Potsdam and this time stayed for seventeen days. During the next few days and weeks the Camarilla actually did manage, however briefly, to 'envelop' Frederick William and shield him from most 'outside' influences.[107] In the autumn of 1848 the Camarilla was also 'larger' than at any other time. The Halle professor Heinrich Leo and Ernst Senfft von Pilsach often participated in its deliberations, while a new 'member' was added who would thereafter serve for many years as one of Leopold von Gerlach's closest confidants. Marcus Niebuhr (1817–60) was the son of the great historian Barthold Niebuhr; a former official in the *Kultusministerium*, he was also a conservative journalist in Magdeburg who enjoyed Ludwig von Gerlach's enthusiastic patronage.[108]

After falling out with the Pfuel cabinet, Frederick William really had no other alternative but to follow the Camarilla's prescriptions.[109] At a Sanssouci meeting with Rauch and the Gerlachs on 6 October, the King agreed that he was not opposed to Brandenburg, and asked Leopold to travel to Breslau, where his uncle commanded the Sixth Army Corps, in order to sound him out about leading a new government. Gerlach was impressed with what he found there.[110] Would Brandenburg be that 'premier' upon whom the King could rely and for whom the Camarilla had been yearning for so long? The Count had always moved in the highest court circles, and his relationship to the King ensured that he could speak bluntly and with some authority to that impressionable monarch. Only three years older than Frederick William, he was one of the products of Frederick William II's numerous liaisons, and thus was sometimes referred to in private as '*der Bastard Preußens*'. Although he had enjoyed a distinguished military career, he was essentially an unimaginative man who, in Veit Valentin's memorable phrase, had always been 'bored by himself'. He had long professed an ignorance of and distaste for politics, but in October 1848 he succumbed to the Camarilla's entreaties and agreed to assume the reins of government, but only on the condition that he have a completely free hand to direct the cabinet himself. Anything less, he indicated, would compromise his own royal dignity.[111]

---

[106] Ludwig von Gerlach to Leopold von Gerlach, 29 Sept. 1848, GA, 'Abschriften', xviii. 85; Kraus, 'Gerlach', i. 283, ii. 214.

[107] Above all, see the descriptions in Ludwig von Gerlach's diary, in E. L. von Gerlach, *Von der Revolution*, i. 116–29; also Kraus, 'Gerlach', i. 278–9, 287–8, ii. 210–11, 216–17.

[108] Ludwig von Gerlach to Leopold von Gerlach, 22 and 28 Oct. 1848, GA, 'Abschriften', xviii. 94–5, 98; Leopold von Gerlach, diary (1 Nov. 1848), ibid., vi. 210. For biographical details, see *ADB*, xxiii. 662–4; and Orr, 'Foundation', 163–4.

[109] Grünthal, 'Zwischen König, Kabinett und Kamarilla', 144–5.

[110] Leopold von Gerlach to Ludwig von Gerlach, 10 Oct. 1848, in E. L. von Gerlach, *Von der Revolution*, ii. 586–7.

[111] Jordan, *Entstehung*, 351–2; Ludwig von Gerlach, 'Erklärung der Minister' for FW IV, in E. L. von Gerlach, *Von der Revolution*, ii. 581–2. For biographical details on Brandenburg, see Priesdorff (ed.),

[cont. on p. 179]

Brandenburg arrived in Berlin on 17 October, and complications immediately arose. Even before becoming Minister President he had begun to make it clear that he would never be the Camarilla's puppet. Thus he considered the possibility of asking all of Pfuel's ministers to stay in the cabinet, while the Camarilla itself urged a clean break; and after a series of conversations in Berlin and Potsdam the Count began to have serious doubts about taking the job. After several days of intense and exhausting negotiations, the situation was finally resolved by the end of October, when four of the ministers in the Pfuel cabinet expressed their desire to step down for good. Finally, on 1 November the Assembly was informed of Pfuel's departure and Brandenburg's designation as Minister President. That same day Ludwig von Gerlach and Ludwig von Massow arrived in Potsdam. The entire Camarilla, plus Brandenburg, was now assembled in the King's immediate vicinity. Frederick William was himself still playing with the idea of reaching some sort of compromise with the Assembly, but for the Camarilla the time had come to strike a blow against 'parliamentary sovereignty'. As Leopold von Gerlach put it to the new Minister President, 'The main thing now is for you to adopt exactly the opposite kind of system and show in every possible way that the King still rules in this country, and not the Assembly.'[112]

The National Assembly was, of course, horrified at the news of the new government, because its purpose seemed rather obvious. The Assembly even sent a delegation to Potsdam to protest the decision, but to no avail.[113] On the evening of 4 November the Gerlachs, Rauch, Massow, Keller, and Leo gathered in Count Brandenburg's rooms in the Neue Kammern, adjacent to the palace of Sanssouci, where the new Minister President described his plans to name the members of his government and move the Assembly to the city of Brandenburg. While this action was being undertaken, the Count added, Frederick William should hold his tongue and avoid using provocative language; it was crucial, he said, not to give the impression that the government was embarking on a *coup d'état*. In future it would also be necessary to protect the King from 'destructive influences' by more carefully monitoring his audiences: 'A stricter etiquette has to be introduced here.' The participants left the meeting in pouring rain but 'in an elevated mood'.[114] The Camarilla had won at last. Or had it?

Events in Berlin and Potsdam now followed a predictable course. On 8 November

---

Soldatisches Führertum, v. 176–9; Caroline von Rochow and Marie de la Motte-Fouqué, *Vom Leben am preußischen Hofe 1815–1852*, ed. Luise von der Marnitz (Berlin, 1908), 79–80, and Valentin, *Revolution*, ii. 264.

[112] Leopold von Gerlach to Brandenburg, 2 Nov. 1848, GA, 'Abschriften', vi. 211. See also Leopold's diary for the period from 17 Oct. to 3 Nov. 1848, in ibid., vi. 190–214; also Ludwig von Gerlach's 'Journal der Camarilla, Fortsetzung', in E. L. von Gerlach, *Von der Revolution*, i. 131–40, for the days after 1 Nov. Cf. Jordan, *Entstehung*, 354–67; Grünthal, 'Zwischen König, Kabinett und Camarilla', 146.

[113] 'Aufzeichnung des Majors und Flügeladjutanten Frhr. Edwin von Manteuffel über den Empfang der National-Versammlungs-Deputation in Sanssouci am 2. November 1848', GStA Merseburg, HA Rep. 192 M Edwin von Manteuffel B Nr. 2, Bl. 2–3ᵛ; Valentin, *Revolution*, ii. 265–6.

[114] Ludwig von Gerlach, diary (4 Nov. 1848), in E. L. von Gerlach, *Von der Revolution*, i. 133–4; Leopold von Gerlach, diary (5 Nov. 1848), GA, 'Abschriften', vi. 215–17.

the composition of the new government was announced. At first it contained only four members: Count Brandenburg was both Minister President and Foreign Minister; General Adolf von Strotha headed the War Ministry; Adalbert von Ladenberg was *Kultusminister*; and, most importantly, the new Interior Minister was Otto von Manteuffel (1805–82), Edwin's cousin and a man who will play a crucial role in the rest of this study.[115] Ludwig von Gerlach described the next day as a 'grey day with thick fog, but afterwards splendidly bright'. It was also, according to the French revolutionary calendar, the eighteenth of Brumaire—the anniversary of Napoleon I's coup in 1799. Brandenburg appeared before the National Assembly, which was now convening in Schinkel's renowned theatre (*Schauspielhaus*) on the Gendarmenmarkt, and declared that it was adjourned until 27 November, after which it would meet again in the city of Brandenburg.[116] At two o'clock that afternoon, 13,000 troops under the command of General Friedrich von Wrangel entered the city. Wrangel himself rode to the *Schauspielhaus* and informed the assembly that it would have to disperse, which it finally did at 5 p.m. Two days later a state of siege was proclaimed in Berlin.[117] At first some of the delegates tried to resist by proclaiming that the government could not levy taxes as long as the Assembly was not meeting in Berlin, but such acts of defiance were in vain. On 27 November, many delegates assembled in Brandenburg and attempted, among scenes of great commotion, to resume their activity. By then, however, it was too late.[118] On 5 December 1848 Count Brandenburg dissolved the National Assembly and announced the promulgation (*Oktroyierung*) of a new constitution. According to the new document, Frederick William IV remained monarch 'by the Grace of God'; the army was no longer required to take an oath to the constitution; and noble titles were no longer in jeopardy. But in most other respects the new constitution was a remarkably liberal document, one which corresponded less to the King's own political ideals than to the proposals that had been developed by Waldeck's parliamentary commission earlier that year. Most importantly, it provided for a ministry responsible to a parliament elected on the basis of a broadly defined franchise. While the upper house, or First Chamber, was to be selected on the basis of property qualifications, elections to the lower house, or Second Chamber, were to be open to all adult males who were not receiving public poor-relief.[119] Not surprisingly, many observers were taken aback by the government's decision to impose a moderately liberal constitution, but there can be little doubt that it was a clever move which helped to win over wavering moderates to the government's side.

The Camarilla was at best rather passively involved in these developments.

---

[115] Lerchenfeld to King Max II, 9 Nov. 1848, BayHStA, MA III/2628. See also Canis, 'Militarismus', 188–92; E. R. Huber, *Verfassungsgeschichte*, ii. 748–9.

[116] Rauch to Leopold von Gerlach, 9 Nov. 1848, GA, 'Abschriften', xviii. 217.

[117] Lerchenfeld to Max II, 10 Nov. 1848, BayHStA, MA III/2628; Valentin, *Revolution*, ii. 269–71.

[118] Botzenhart, *Parlamentarismus*, 545–50.

[119] See the documents in E. R. Huber (ed.), *Dokumente*, i. 382–94; cf. Friedrich Frahm, 'Entstehungs- und Entwicklungsgeschichte der preußischen Verfassung (vom März 1848 bis zum Januar 1850)', *FBPG* 41 (1928), 288–91.

Ludwig von Gerlach had returned to Magdeburg on 13 November, while Count Brandenburg had been quick to demonstrate his own independence and authority. Leopold von Gerlach noted on 19 November that the ministers already wanted to dissolve the Assembly and impose a constitution, which he and Rauch both opposed. As he then went on to observe: 'Brandenburg avoided talking to me. I find that odd, in view of the curious way in which he entered the government. I can't find fault with him, though, for wanting to show . . . that he is not a creature or tool of the Potsdam Camarilla.'[120] By 26 November Leopold was even reporting that 'the power of the Camarilla has largely been absorbed by the cabinet'.[121] The Camarilla was also ill-informed about the cabinet's exact plans. In 3 December, two days before the Assembly's dissolution, Leopold von Gerlach admitted that he had not spoken with the King about any important issue for a week or more.[122] Brandenburg himself was wary of both the King and the Camarilla. An exponent of an old-fashioned, bureaucratic-military brand of conservatism, he was never able to generate any enthusiasm for his nephew's *ständisch* projects or for the Camarilla's 'Christian-German' ideals. Above all, he believed, the King had to keep the promises he had made in March. Thus he quickly came around to the view that a moderately liberal constitution would be necessary to assuage public opinion after the Assembly's dispersal.[123]

Frederick William at first leaned toward the Camarilla's views, opposing both a dissolution of the Assembly and the imposition of a new constitution. In his euphoria after his victory over 'the revolution', he reverted to his older, *ständisch* ideas, calling for the establishment of an upper house of lords and a lower house arranged according to estates and classes.[124] Brandenburg was exceedingly irritated by royal effusions of this sort. The situation remained delicate, he believed, and as usual Frederick William was making things more difficult. The King had only himself to blame for everything that had gone wrong since March, he said. His own major task was to rescue a country which had been revolutionized thanks to the King's irresponsible behaviour. This task required enormous care and moderation. But Frederick William was up to his old tricks, 'in transports of victory, demanding the impossible, the creation of peers and lords and Old England and who knows what else. I hold everyone in the King's immediate vicinity responsible for this.'[125] The Camarilla, he seemed to imply, should either not interfere with things or else encourage the King to develop more sober ideas.

As the King and the Camarilla both tacitly admitted, however, there was little else to do but go along with the cabinet's decision. After all, the Camarilla agreed, from

---

[120] Leopold von Gerlach to Ludwig von Gerlach, 19 Nov. 1848, in E. L. von Gerlach, *Von der Revolution*, ii. 599. Cf. Leopold's *promemoria* for Brandenburg of 17 Nov. 1848, GA, 'Abschriften', xviii. 226–7, and Ludwig's 'Regierungsplan' of 23 Nov., in *Von der Revolution*, ii. 603–7.

[121] Leopold von Gerlach to Ludwig von Gerlach, 26 Nov. 1848, ibid. ii. 607.

[122] Leopold von Gerlach to Ludwig von Gerlach, 3 Dec. 1848, ibid. ii. 611.

[123] Botzenhart, *Parlamentarismus*, 546; Grünthal, 'Zwischen König, Kabinett und Kamarilla', 163–4.

[124] FW IV, marginal comments on letter from Ernst von Senfft-Pilsach, 29 Nov. 1848, in Haenchen (ed.), *Revolutionsbriefe*, 246.

[125] Brandenburg to Leopold von Gerlach, 24 Nov. 1848, GA, 'Abschriften', xviii. 234; cf. Frahm, 'Verfassung', 283–4.

their standpoint things *had* improved mightily since 10 November, and there were no alternatives to the current ministers. To be sure, Ludwig von Gerlach remained vigorously opposed to both dissolution and promulgation, which he only found out about while riding the train on 6 December.[126] He even conferred with Leopold on the possibility of 'reconstructing the Camarilla and coming up with ministers in reserve', and dashed off a highly critical article for the *Kreuzzeitung*. But it was all to no avail.[127]

Leopold was also disappointed, but he was both more realistic and more fatalistic than his younger brother.[128] He too had opposed dissolution and promulgation, though he understood the reasons behind the government's strategy. He praised the cabinet's 'energy' in restoring public order. Unfortunately, however, the Camarilla could not agree with many of the cabinet's actions and thus should avoid identifying itself too closely with the government. The decision to promulgate a moderate constitution might well pave the way for a new cycle of revolutions and *coups*.[129] Leopold hinted that the Camarilla would hold itself in reserve, but in the meantime it would be necessary to follow the constitutional road. In any case, he consoled himself, the 'dose' of constitutionalism which Prussia had received was 'not too strong'.[130]

Leopold von Gerlach could accept the constitutional path because, as recent research has shown, it was the product of a complex compromise between King and cabinet, between cabinet and Camarilla, within the cabinet itself, and between the government and moderate liberal opinion. Crucial to those compromises was the general perception that the constitution was a 'purely provisional arrangement' which according to its own Article 106 could be amended fairly easily through a simple majority vote of the upper and lower chambers. The King enjoyed an absolute veto over legislation, and his finances would not be subject to popular control through a parliamentary civil list. Above all, Article 105 of the new constitutional draft stipulated that the government could issue legally binding emergency decrees. Interior Minister Otto von Manteuffel, who at first had strongly opposed the promulgation of a constitution, played a critical role in shaping the last measure.[131]

What had happened, in fact, was that both Prussia and Frederick William IV had been brought once and for all into the constitutional age: a reality that the King rejected with every fibre of his being, and one which he hoped to undo as much as

[126] Ludwig von Gerlach, diary (6 Dec. 1848), in E. L. von Gerlach, *Von der Revolution*, i. 143–4; Kraus, 'Gerlach', i. 298–300, ii. 225–6.

[127] Ludwig von Gerlach, diary (8 and 12 Dec. 1848), in E. L. von Gerlach, *Von der Revolution*, i. 145, 146.

[128] Grünthal, 'Zwischen König, Kabinett und Kamarilla', 156–7.

[129] 'Bruchstück eines politischen Résumés von Leopold von Gerlach, Potsdam', 7 Dec. 1848, GA, 'Abschriften', xviii. 252–3; Leopold von Gerlach, diary (3 and 4 Dec. 1848), ibid., vi. 264, 266; and Leopold von Gerlach to Brandenburg, 23 Dec. 1848, ibid., vi. 275–8.

[130] Leopold von Gerlach to Ludwig von Gerlach, 14 Dec. 1848, in E. L. von Gerlach, *Von der Revolution*, ii. 615.

[131] See above all Grünthal, 'Zwischen König, Kabinett und Kamarilla', 123–4, 169–71; id., *Parlamentarismus in Preußen 1848/49–1857/58: Preußischer Konstitutionalismus—Parlament und Regierung in der Reaktionsära* (Düsseldorf, 1982), 29–31; Frahm, 'Verfassung', 286–8.

possible. He had vehemently resisted the Brandenburg government's decision to impose a constitution, and when that step became inevitable he was overwhelmed by despair. Indeed, on 23 November he was so distraught that he declared, 'If I were not a Christian I would take my own life.'[132] A few days later he became embroiled in a frightful scene with Rauch, Massow, and Leopold von Gerlach in which he insisted that the very idea of a constitution was unbearable to him. 'The King was in complete despair', Leopold reported. 'They could declare him mad, he said, they could call him a dog, but he could never agree to sign this thing.'[133] But he really had no choice. Although he would never give up his monarchical project, he would now have to adapt his struggle to the conditions of a constitutional system, and redefine the institutions of monarchy within its parameters.

Despite Frederick William's outbursts of rage, scorn, and despair, he in fact found himself in an exceptionally strong position in the last two months of 1848. The authority of the crown had been restored, and at a fraction of the cost in human lives that accompanied the victorious counter-revolution in the Habsburg lands. Unlike Louis-Philippe, Metternich, Emperor Ferdinand, or his brother-in-law Ludwig I, he was still in office, an outcome which many observers would not have predicted in the late spring or early summer.

It was also obvious that there were still enormous reserves of monarchist sentiment throughout the country, much of which was being mobilized at the local level by the numerous conservative societies which had sprung up since the spring. A convenient opportunity for that sentiment to be organized and publicly displayed came with the official celebration of the royal couple's silver wedding anniversary on 29 November 1848, an occasion for effusive displays of monarchism and Borussian patriotism throughout the country. Even more impressive, though, than the anniversary celebrations was a massive 'address campaign' which followed the King's actions in November and December. Both King and cabinet were flooded with hundreds of addresses and petitions supporting the monarch's actions, many of them from moderately liberal as well as conservative organizations. Although these documents cannot be regarded as a completely accurate gauge of popular sentiment in the kingdom as a whole, they suggest that the Brandenburg government had correctly reckoned that many politically aware Prussians would welcome the idea of a constitution, even one granted unilaterally by the King. Opponents of promulgation like Ludwig von Gerlach were very much in the minority, even among conservatives. Frederick William IV could thus rely not only on an intact army and bureaucracy but also on a huge and powerful segment of public opinion to sustain his actions.[134]

For all his complaining, the King himself began to recognize that the situation was turning to his advantage, despite the fact that the constitution itself still caused him

---

[132] Leopold von Gerlach, diary (23 Nov. 1848), GA, 'Abschriften', vi. 247.

[133] Leopold von Gerlach, diary (5 Dec. 1848, marginal comment), ibid. vi. 267.

[134] See the addresses published after 17 Nov. 1848 in *Preußischer Staats-Anzeiger*; Hans Wegge, *Die Stellung der Öffentlichkeit zur oktroyierten Verfassung und die preußische Parteibildung 1848/49* (Berlin, 1932), ch. 4, esp. 44, 54–9. For reactions in the Rhine Province, see Sperber, *Radicals*, 325–36.

'a little stomach pain'.[135] As he put it in a letter to Stolberg two days after Christmas, 'The struggle of divine right and the divine order has begun, and what the antithesis of them both—the revolution—has driven asunder will again be united by honour regained!'[136]

During the weeks and months after December 1848 Frederick William IV became involved in other kinds of struggles. As we have already noted, his feelings regarding German patriotism and the German national movement were both deep-seated and complex. The revolution of 1848, with all its nationalist pathos and its implications for the future political organization of Germany, was forcing him to move beyond abstract emotions and make some concrete decisions. What should be the relationship between the Prussian monarchy and the rest of Germany? What role should Prussia play in the national reorganization of Germany? What should its relationship be towards Austria? Could a King of Prussia accept an imperial crown, and if so under what conditions? And what role would monarchical institutions play in a unified Germany?

These were some of the critical questions that Frederick William IV confronted in the two years after December 1848. They were crucially significant for his attempt to adapt his monarchical project to changed circumstances. His principal adviser and confidant in these matters was Joseph Maria von Radowitz, once a friend of the Gerlachs and now their bitter rival. The Camarilla knew that Radowitz was a formidable foe, for he occupied a special place in the King's heart. Leopold von Gerlach believed that he and Rauch had been unswervingly loyal to the King in 1848; despite their loyalty, Gerlach sighed in November, 'Bunsen und Radowitz are still his ideals, and in comparison to those two he regards us as cattle.'[137] The relationship between Frederick William and Radowitz, and its implications for the larger relationship between Prussia and the rest of Germany, will be the themes of the next chapter.

[135] FW IV to Bunsen, 13 Dec. 1848, in Leopold von Ranke, *Aus dem Briefwechsel Friedrich Wilhelms IV. mit Bunsen* (Leipzig, 1873), 235.

[136] Otto Graf zu Stolberg-Wernigerode, *Anton Graf zu Stolberg-Wernigerode: Ein Freund und Ratgeber König Friedrich Wilhelms IV.* (Munich, 1926), 123.

[137] Leopold von Gerlach, diary (19 Nov. 1848), GA, 'Abschriften', vi. 238.

8
Nationality, Society, Monarchy: Joseph Maria von Radowitz and Frederick William IV, 1848–1850

Another Special Friend

With no other human being—including Ancillon, Groeben, Stolberg, Bunsen, his sister Charlotte, or even, to an astonishing extent, the Queen herself—did Frederick William IV enter into such an intense and powerful relationship as with Joseph Maria von Radowitz. Frederick William's admiration for his friend's intellect and character was almost literally boundless. 'I am his most intimate and loyal friend, and he is mine,' he asserted on one occasion. Radowitz was the 'intimate friend of my heart and soul,' he insisted. 'Our friendship has been subjected to every imaginable test, but it has emerged victorious and stronger from them.'[1] Even more telling than these effusions, perhaps, was a comparison that Frederick William once drew between Radowitz and Ludwig von Gerlach: 'Both of them build on the same foundations, according to the same principles and for the same cause. But Gerlach is content to breathe no higher than at the altitude of the Righi [a mountain range near Lucerne which rises 1,800 metres above sea-level] while Radowitz is in his element at the height of a Mont Blanc. *That* is why Gerlach bites him in the foot, for no one is *permitted* to see further than he. Everyone is supposed to get *dizzy* where he does. Alas!'[2]

What was the secret of Radowitz's hold over the King of Prussia? Some critical contemporaries believed that the answer to this question was really rather simple. Radowitz, they argued, flattered the King's vanity by providing him with an illusory intellectual structure for his otherwise disconnected and amorphous ideas. Bismarck, for example, loathed Radowitz and dismissed him in his memoirs as the 'clever wardrobe-master' for Frederick William's 'medieval fantasies'.[3] Leopold von Gerlach essentially concurred with Bismarck's assessment, though his own insights were much more penetrating. Radowitz himself was 'intellectually impoverished', Gerlach claimed, in contrast to Frederick William, who had more ideas 'than he can digest and sustain'. Radowitz thus availed himself of the King's own ideas,

---

[1] FW IV, marginal comment on letter from Ernst Freiherr Senfft von Pilsach, 14 Aug. 1850, in Paul Haake, 'Ernst Freiherr Senfft von Pilsach als Politiker', *FBPG* 53 (1941), 82; FW IV to Nicholas I, 23 Sept. 1850, GStA Merseburg, HA Rep. 50 J Nr. 1205, Bl. 127.

[2] FW IV, marginal comment on report from Carl Wilhelm Saegert, 10 Apr. 1851, GStA Berlin, BPH Rep. 192 Carl Wilhelm Saegert Nr. 37.

[3] Lothar Gall, *Bismarck: The White Revolutionary*, trans. J. A. Underwood (2 vols.; London, 1986), i. 63.

embellishing them 'with mathematics and logic, two sciences of which the King has no idea at all'. Frederick William was thus invariably impressed with Radowitz's convincing defence of what were essentially the King's own views, while at the same time dismissing as 'cattle' all those advisers who urged the monarch to focus on mundane, practical issues.[4]

Although Gerlach's observations come close to the mark, neither he nor Bismarck really understood the intensity or the depth of feeling that bound their enemy to their sovereign. Nor, indeed, has anyone else. Although a great deal has been written about Radowitz and his activities as the driving force behind Prussian foreign policy in 1849 and 1850, he remains a rather elusive and mysterious character, and misunderstandings both of his personality and his place in German history still abound.[5] The ultimate explanation of the personal relationship between Frederick William and Radowitz will probably have to be left to a psycho-historian. For now, the most perceptive analysis can still be found in the work of Friedrich Meinecke, who pointed out that Radowitz offered the King something that other confidants, including Gerlach, Stolberg, Thile, or Groeben could not: a universal quality, an opportunity to escape 'from the narrow Prussian milieu' in which, with the notable exceptions of Bunsen and Alexander von Humboldt, all the others were trapped.[6]

As a result both of his own personality and his understanding of the King's, Radowitz managed to avoid being assigned to one of those compartments which Frederick William reserved for most of his other friends and advisers. He understood and sympathized with 'the aesthetic and religious-political' sides of Frederick William's nature.[7] Virtually alone among the King's retinue, he appreciated the nature and the full dimensions of Frederick William's monarchical project. As a result, Radowitz was able to peer more deeply than any other contemporary, including the Queen herself, into the deepest recesses of the King's being. Radowitz's affection for the monarch was unfeigned, but he was not naïve. Though his criticisms of the King were less strident than the Gerlachs', he was under no illusions about Frederick William's limits and weaknesses.[8] Nevertheless, he always remained convinced that Frederick William IV could play a major historical role if he would only grasp the opportunities that awaited him. Like Frederick William, Radowitz was dismayed by the 'negative' spirit of the modern age, and worried about its consequences both for religion and for the future of monarchical authority. Unlike his erstwhile

---

[4] Leopold von Gerlach, diary (3 Aug. and 11 Dec. 1850), GA, 'Abschriften', vii. 151, 244.

[5] As noted earlier in this study, the best biographical accounts remain the studies published by Paul Hassel and Friedrich Meinecke in 1905 and 1913 respectively. Also indispensable is Meinecke's introduction to Joseph Maria von Radowitz, *Ausgewählte Schriften und Reden*, ed. Friedrich Meinecke (Munich, 1921), pp. vii–xxi. Emil Ritter, *Radowitz: Ein katholischer Staatsmann in Preußen. Verfassungs- und konfessionsgeschichtliche Studie* (Cologne, 1948); and Warren B. Morris, jun., *The Road to Olmütz: The Career of Joseph Maria von Radowitz* (New York, 1976), do not go beyond earlier studies.

[6] Friedrich Meinecke, *Radowitz und die deutsche Revolution* (Berlin, 1913), 39.   [7] Ibid.

[8] e.g. see his brief note, 'Meine Politik und der König', 27 Nov. 1851, in Joseph Maria von Radowitz, *Nachgelassene Briefe und Aufzeichnungen zur Geschichte der Jahre 1848–1853*, ed. Walter Möring (Stuttgart, 1922), 390–1.

colleagues at the *Berliner Politisches Wochenblatt*, however, Radowitz believed that Frederick William's destiny and the future of his monarchical project depended on his capacity to respond creatively to the two great 'revolutionary' forces of his age: the social question and the 'principle of nationality'. If Prussia could devise an effective, non-liberal strategy to deal with the problems of modern poverty, if it could succeed in becoming a 'social kingdom', then monarchy itself would emerge stronger, and Frederick William would attain that popularity for which he always yearned.[9] And an imaginative response to the aspirations of the German national movement would, Radowitz believed, lead not only to an expansion of Prussian state power but also to the consolidation of monarchical institutions throughout Central Europe.

Radowitz was thus one of the more imaginative conservative statesmen of his day. He was never the profound thinker that Frederick William believed him to be, nor did he ever approach the originality of such formidable conservative writers as Lorenz von Stein or Friedrich Julius Stahl. Like Stahl, though, Radowitz had an opportunity to put his views into practice. Stahl believed in maximizing monarchical authority by linking conservative values to new parliamentary and constitutional realities. As a sometimes uncomfortable ally of the Gerlachs and a member of the *Kreuzzeitung* party after 1848–9, Stahl became a brilliantly successful parliamentarian; and in the process he helped to redirect and modernize Prussian conservatism. Radowitz's major project in 1849–50—to link conservatism with the national cause—was, in contrast, a failure. His efforts ultimately foundered because his position, like Bunsen's and unlike Stahl's, depended solely upon his relationship to the King. In absolutist times, that might have sufficed. But in nineteenth-century Prussia, especially after December 1848, one needed allies and a more powerful, more *formal* position at court, in the new parliamentary chambers, or in the bureaucratic structure, than Radowitz enjoyed. Frederick William was immensely powerful, but the pre-constitutional days of his 'personal rule' were over.

As in the last *Vormärz* years, the Prussian court and the uppermost levels of the Prussian state remained the scene of complex struggles for power, influence, patronage, and royal favour. The conditions, the ground rules, and the institutional setting for those struggles had, however, changed since 1848. Apart from the King, there was the cabinet, or, to be more precise, individual cabinet members, of whom Count Brandenburg and Otto von Manteuffel were the most important. There were vestiges of the Camarilla, which, however, never again enjoyed the influence it had exercised in the autumn of 1848; allied to the Camarilla was the *Kreuzzeitung* party in the

---

[9] Until recently, Radowitz's social policies, which are crucial to an understanding of his relationship to the King, have been almost completely neglected. On his ideas of a 'social kingdom', see, above all, Hermann Beck, 'Conservatives, Bureaucracy, and the Social Question in Prussia (1815–1848)' (Ph.D. thesis; Los Angeles, 1988), 61–87; id., 'Conservatives and the Social Question in Nineteenth-Century Prussia', in Larry Eugene Jones and James Retallack (eds.), *Between Reform, Reaction, and Resistance: Studies in the History of German Conservatism from 1789 to 1945* (Providence, 1993), 74–81. The older monograph by Walter Früh, *Radowitz als Sozialpolitiker: Seine Gesellschafts- und Wirtschaftsauffassung unter besonderer Berücksichtigung der sozialen Frage* (Berlin, 1937), contains some useful information but has to be used with extreme care because of its ideological coloration.

two chambers of parliament. In addition, as we shall see in Chapter 9, after 1848–9 the King often availed himself of the *Kreuzzeitung* party's rivals in the state security apparatus around the ambitious and ruthless Berlin Police President, Carl Ludwig von Hinckeldey. As always, the army, symbolized by the King's *maison militaire*, remained a formidable power factor at court. In such a setting, a man like Radowitz, who had accumulated many enemies and few friends, did not have much of a chance, and in the midst of the autumn crisis of 1850 the King was forced to let him go. The man who emerged victorious from the two years of fierce struggle at the summit of the Prussian state after December 1848 turned out to be not the King's 'divine friend', but Otto von Manteuffel, the unprepossessing man of the bureaucracy.

Frederick William IV and the National Question

In 1842 Frederick William IV wrote to Metternich that ensuring 'the greatness, power, and honour of Germany' had become his life's main mission.[10] We have already become acquainted with the origins of those feelings. Frederick William's experiences in the liberation war, his immersion in a Romantic world of feeling, aesthetics, intuition, and ecstatic spirituality, and his passion for what he called 'the historic' all conditioned his perceptions of German nationhood. Thus he became an exponent of a monarchical-conservative nationalism which differed markedly both from liberal variants of nationalism and from the anti-national dynastic legitimism of many Restoration-era conservatives. Like many conservatives, and in contrast to those liberals who wanted to create an institutional framework in which inevitable social conflicts could be channelled and regulated, Frederick William dreamed of institutionalizing a harmonious political order in which social conflict would have no place at all. The happy union within each German state of local ruler and *Stände*, each in its own place and performing its own functions, would be paralleled at the level of Germany as a whole by a happy union of princes and peoples, each part of the single German nation, but each retaining its own historically conditioned character and identity.[11] Above all, Frederick William hoped that it would be possible to re-create as much as possible of the old Empire, which had been in 'abeyance' since 1806. By recovering Germany's historic liberties and modernizing its unique traditions, it would be possible, Frederick William hoped, to counteract the sinful, soulless, 'mechanistic' temptations emanating from revolutionary France. Such a revitalized Germany, organized on a monarchic-*ständisch* basis, would be a bulwark of corporative freedom, monarchical loyalty, and Christian piety; and, in contrast to the ravening expansionism of revolutionary France, it would be devoted to the preservation of peace.

As Crown Prince, and even in his first years as King, Frederick William rarely thought about the concrete political arrangements that a united Germany might

---

[10] FW IV to Metternich, 7 Mar. 1842, GStA Merseburg, HA Rep. 50 J Nr. 839, Bl. 75–7.
[11] For a brilliant analysis of the 'conservative idea of the nation', see Panajotis Kondylis, *Konservativismus: Geschichtlicher Gehalt und Untergang* (Stuttgart, 1986), 286–96.

require. Like his Bavarian brother-in-law, Ludwig I, he generally thought of Germany's mission and identity more in cultural than in political or institutional terms.[12] Therefore, it is in his architectural pursuits and in the *pictorial* representations with which he liked to surround himself, rather than in any detailed plan for German political unity, that Frederick William's national feelings expressed themselves most clearly.[13] His beloved Stolzenfels on the Rhine is an excellent example. With its evocations of people like Barbarossa and Rudolf von Habsburg, Stolzenfels demonstrated that, for Frederick William IV as for Ludwig I, it was through history that the national genius of Germany was best and most obviously revealed.[14]

Like so many other Germans, Frederick William was caught up in the wave of patriotic enthusiasm that accompanied the Rhine crisis—that is, French sabre-rattling about the Rhine frontier—at the very outset of his reign. The new King of Prussia believed that the German Confederation had to be more effectively organized in order to counter the continuing threat of French aggression in the west. In early 1841 he was pleased to note, for example, that patriotic feeling in Germany was stronger than at any other time since 1813. At no point in his reign, though, did the legitimist Frederick William think of using what he called the 'sacred fire' of German patriotism to the one-sided advantage of Prussia. As he assured Metternich, Austria would have to be the 'midwife' of the new Germany.[15] Indeed, the renascence of Germany and the imperial majesty of the Habsburgs were, to Frederick William IV, inseparable. As he put it in a letter to Ludwig I in December 1840, 'on the head of the mightiest German prince, the hereditary President of the Confederation . . . I would again like to see what is incontrovertibly the world's most important crown, the crown of Charlemagne. I would like to hear it proclaimed that the Austrian monarch only as Roman Emperor . . . would be President of the Confederation, the first Prince of Germany, the greatest leader of Christendom.'[16] Nothing came of Frederick William's attempts to fan the 'holy fire', and so the reorganization of the German Confederation remained on the back burner until 1847. The efforts that were then undertaken were abortive, as we saw in Chapter 6; Radowitz's memorandum of November 1847 and his Vienna mission of March 1848 had been too little too late, and in the wake of the March revolution it seemed that the German Confederation itself had been swept away for ever.

With his celebrated *Umritt* through the streets of Berlin and his proclamation to the German people on 21 March 1848, Frederick William had pledged Prussia's active support for the cause of German unity. In April and early May, stimulated by several ideas that Britain's Prince Albert had advanced, he devoted a great deal of

---

[12] See Walter Schmitz, '"Der Deutscheste der Deutschen... "': Ludwig I. und die nationale Bewegung', in Johannes Erichsen and Uwe Puschner (eds.), *'Vorwärts, vorwärts sollst du schauen . . . ': Geschichte, Politik und Kunst unter Ludwig I. Aufsätze* (Munich, 1986), ii. 125–52.

[13] Frank-Lothar Kroll, *Friedrich Wilhelm IV. und das Staatsdenken der deutschen Romantik* (Berlin, 1990), ch. 4.

[14] W. Schmitz, 'Ludwig I.', 144–5.

[15] FW IV to Metternich, 10 Jan. 1841, GStA Merseburg, HA Rep. 50 J Nr. 939, Bl. 32–6.

[16] FW IV to Ludwig I, 19 Dec. 1840, GHA, Nachlaß König Ludwig I., 85/3/2. Cf. Kroll, *Friedrich Wilhelm IV.*, 118–20.

time to this cause.[17] Frederick William insisted during those months that Germany's legitimate rulers had to take the initiative to reconstitute Germany, even before the first meeting of the Frankfurt National Assembly in May. Otherwise that '*Sau-Parlament*', as he called it, might lose control of things, thus plunging the country into anarchy and even a republic. Prussia would serve as Supreme Warlord (*Erzfeldherr*) for the entire *Reich*.[18] In sketching these plans, Frederick William succumbed utterly to those 'medieval fantasies' which he so loved and which his advisers so often excoriated. Thus he worked out an elaborate scheme whereby a 'King of the Germans' would be elected to serve as a kind of prime minister to the Habsburg 'Roman Emperor', and he described in loving detail how the King of the Germans would be anointed and crowned at St Bartholomew's Cathedral in Frankfurt am Main. What a spectacle Frederick William's imagination must have conjured up as he prepared these plans, and what an escape they represented from the shocks and humiliations of March![19]

His cabinet, and especially Foreign Minister Arnim-Suckow, quickly brought him down to earth at the beginning of May. Arnim, as we know, had for some time been of the opinion that Prussia should aspire to a German unity under its own hegemony, and he had no sympathy at all for the King's notions. When Frederick William presented his proposals to the Foreign Minister, complained the shocked monarch, 'Arnim declared that he didn't want to have anything to do with them, and why? Because against my own declared and well-motivated will he wants to present *me*!!!!!! with the imperial title. . . . I will *not* accept the crown.'[20] The King claimed to be horrified by the very idea that he might usurp a crown which belonged legitimately to the Habsburgs. A Germany without Austria would be a rump without a head and a third of its historic territory. He would only accept a crown, he said, if it were offered to him by his fellow rulers and if Austria, following Metternich's old policy of 'separation' from Germany, specifically renounced its involvement in German affairs.[21] Frederick William's outrage over the prospect of becoming emperor led to another round of bitter recriminations between the King and the Camphausen cabinet. Angered by the rebuff he had received from his cabinet, the King of Prussia decided to efface himself and, for the time being, withdraw from further involvement in the reorganization of Germany.[22]

Not surprisingly, Frederick William was both scornful and afraid of the Frankfurt

[17] Anton Springer, *Friedrich Christoph Dahlmann* (2 vols.; Leipzig, 1870, 1872), ii. 224–5; Hans-Joachim Netzer, *Albert von Sachsen-Coburg und Gotha: Ein deutscher Prinz in England* (Munich, 1988), 246.

[18] FW IV to Arnim-Suckow, 12 Apr. 1848, GStA Merseburg, Rep. 92 Heinrich Alexander von Arnim B II Nr. 6, Bl. 86–87ᵛ.

[19] FW IV to Friedrich Christoph Dahlmann, 24 Apr. 1848, in Springer, *Dahlmann*, ii. 227; cf. Leopold von Ranke, *Aus dem Briefwechsel Friedrich Wilhelms IV. mit Bunsen* (Leipzig, 1873), 204.

[20] FW IV to Stolberg, 3 May 1848, in Otto Graf zu Stolberg-Wernigerode, *Anton Graf zu Stolberg-Wernigerode: Ein Freund und Ratgeber König Friedrich Wilhelms IV.* (Munich, 1926), 117.

[21] FW IV to Frederick August II, 5 May 1848, in Hellmut Kretzschmar, 'König Friedrich Wilhelms IV. Briefe an König Friedrich August II. von Sachsen', *Preußische Jahrbücher*, 227 (1932), 46; FW IV to Friedrich Christoph Dahlmann, 4 and 15 May 1848, GStA Berlin, BPH Rep. 50 Nr. 512–13.

[22] See his violent letter to Arnim of 7 May 1848, GStA Merseburg, Rep. 92 Heinrich Alexander von Arnim B II Nr. 6, Bl. 122–3.

National Assembly. 'Satan and Adrammelech have their headquarters there!', he wrote to Radowitz after hearing of his friend's election to that body.[23] When the Assembly named Archduke John of Austria as *Reichsverweser*—that is, appointed him to head a temporary executive authority for Germany—at the end of June, Frederick William described the action as 'completely invalid, null and void', but decided to accept it as a *fait accompli*.[24] Throughout the summer, Frederick William and the Prussian authorities continued to treat the Assembly with contempt, refusing to permit the Prussian army to pay homage to the *Reichsverweser* and the national colours in early August and, later that month, unilaterally concluding the armistice of Malmö with Denmark. After November, however, the King became much more directly involved with developments in Frankfurt. His own successes at home, combined with the progress of the Habsburg counter-revolution in the Danube Monarchy, emboldened him to respond more assertively to the 'rebellious' assembly.

The recovery of Austria—signalled by the abdication of the Emperor Ferdinand, his replacement by the eighteen-year-old Francis Joseph, and the determined policies of the Archduchess Sophie and Prince Felix zu Schwarzenberg—forced the Frankfurt National Assembly to deal head-on with the sticky question of the multi-national Habsburg Monarchy's relationship to the rest of Germany. In late October, as Habsburg forces were preparing for the final assault on Vienna, the Assembly voted for a *großdeutsch* solution to the problem of German unity, which would have been tantamount to the fracturing of the Habsburg Monarchy into historically 'German' (including Czech) and non-German parts joined only by personal union to each other. With victory over revolutionary Vienna assured, and confrontation with Hungary looming, Schwarzenberg affirmed a month later in his 'Kremsier Programme' that Austria would continue to remain a unitary political entity. Any real possibility for a *großdeutsch* solution to the German boundary question had thus received the *coup de grâce*. The new Minister President of the provisional *Reich* government in Frankfurt, the respected statesman Heinrich von Gagern, advocated what came to be known as a *kleindeutsch* solution to the German problem, with a 'narrow confederation' of German states clustered around Prussia and surrounded by a looser 'broad confederation' that could include Austria. Schwarzenberg spurned this notion, and in early March 1849 proposed that the entire Habsburg Monarchy be included in any new German political structure. All these developments had enormous consequences for Frederick William IV's perception of the relationship between the Prussian crown and the German nation.[25]

In late November Heinrich von Gagern himself travelled to Berlin to speak with the King about these matters. In view of the complex developments in Austria, there

---

[23] FW IV to Radowitz, 21 May 1848, in Radowitz, *Briefe und Aufzeichnungen*, 46.

[24] FW IV to Archduke John, 3 July 1848, in Georg Küntzel (ed.), *Briefwechsel zwischen König Friedrich Wilhelm IV. und dem Reichsverweser Erzherzog Johann von Österreich (1848–1850)* (Frankfurt am Main, 1924), 1–2.

[25] See the recent accounts of these matters in Heinrich Lutz, *Zwischen Habsburg und Preußen: Deutschland 1815–1866* (Berlin, 1985), 295–307; Thomas Nipperdey, *Deutsche Geschichte 1800–1866: Bürgerwelt und starker Staat* (Munich, 1983), 656–7; Wolfram Siemann, *Die deutsche Revolution von*

[cont. on p. 192]

was a special urgency to Gagern's task: to opt for a *kleindeutsch* solution to the problem of German unity, with the King of Prussia as hereditary German emperor. Gagern tried to convince Frederick William of the potential for revolutionary violence that still existed in the land, of the need for some sort of vigorous action, and of the interesting political possibilities that an imperial crown could offer to the Prussian monarchy and dynasty.[26] Frederick William at first seemed impervious to these ideas, which were associated with what came to be called the *Erbkaiserpartei* in Frankfurt. In those days his thoughts were still focused on the idea of a *trias*, a division of monarchical-executive authority for Germany among Austria, Bavaria, and Prussia. He also remained attached to his old notions of Austria bearing the imperial title and Prussia receiving special responsibility for military affairs. Moreover, he insisted, a crown proffered by the Paulskirche was not a crown at all. A real *Reichsfürst*, he declared, was ten thousand times too good to accept 'an invented crown contrived of dirt and clay' which would reduce him to the status of a Louis-Philippe.[27]

Frederick William's position thus seemed crystal-clear. But was it really? He had, after all, long dreamed of German unity under monarchical auspices. In a conversation with Ludwig von Gerlach in early December 1848 he admitted that the Frankfurt parliament had begun to fulfil a 'youthful dream', and for that reason he did not want it to fall apart.[28] Despite the vehemence with which Frederick William had rejected the crown of the *Erbkaiserlichen*, he was almost certainly protesting too much; in fact, he found it harder to resist Gagern's temptation than he admitted. He still insisted that only his equals could dispose of the crown by offering it to the Austrian Emperor. Should that prince decline the offer, however, then another ruler might in fact be able to accept it.[29] Thus it was with some ambivalence that Frederick William IV regarded the interrelated questions of German unity, the Frankfurt National Assembly, the *Reich* constitution, Austro-Prussian relations, the imperial crown, and the restoration of monarchical authority at the beginning of 1849. That ambivalence—some would call it confusion and contradiction—was complicated

---

1848/49 (Frankfurt am Main), 193–5. For important revisionist arguments, see Roy A. Austensen, 'The Making of Austria's Prussian Policy, 1848–1852', *Historical Journal*, 27 (1984), 861–76; and id., 'Metternich, Austria, and the German Question, 1848–1851', *International History Review*, 13 (1991), 21–37. See further Lawrence Sondhaus, 'Schwarzenberg, Austria, and the German Question, 1848–1851', ibid. 1–20; Alan Sked, *The Decline and Fall of the Habsburg Empire 1815–1918* (London, 1989), 154–7.

[26] Lord Westmorland to Lord Palmerston, 29 Nov. 1848, PRO, FO 64/290; Friedrich Meinecke, *Cosmopolitanism and the National State*, trans. Robert B. Kimber (Princeton, NJ, 1970), 280–8; Erich Brandenburg, *Untersuchungen und Aktenstücke zur Geschichte der Reichsgründung* (Leipzig, 1916), 133–7, 140–4; Veit Valentin, *Geschichte der deutschen Revolution von 1848–1849* (2 vols.; Cologne, 1977; orig. 1931–2), ii. 277–87; Manfred Botzenhart, *Deutscher Parlamentarismus in der Revolutionszeit 1848–1850* (Düsseldorf, 1977), 556–65.

[27] FW IV to Groeben, 4 Dec. 1848, GStA Merseburg, Rep. 92 Graf Carl von der Groeben B Nr. 4ᵉ 1848, Bl. 20ᵛ, 21.

[28] Ludwig von Gerlach, diary (7 Dec. 1848), in id., *Aufzeichnungen aus seinem Leben und Wirken 1795–1877*, ed. Jakob von Gerlach (2 vols.; Schwerin, 1903), ii. 32.

[29] FW IV to Groeben, 4 Dec. 1848, GStA Merseburg, Rep. 92 Graf Carl von der Groeben B Nr. 4ᵉ 1848, Bl. 21; cf. FW IV to Radowitz, 23 Dec. 1848, in Radowitz, *Briefe und Aufzeichnungen*, 68–9.

even further by the divergent tactics and interests of the various groups close to the throne during those months.

First, of course, there was the Camarilla, which by the first months of 1849 no longer functioned as effectively as in 1848. Leopold von Gerlach favoured a simple return to the old German Confederation, with Austria remaining the presiding member; but he was absent from court during much of the first half of 1849, and his influence was correspondingly reduced.[30] Rauch was ill with gout at the same time, and in the spring he was finally able to return to his beloved Russia.[31] Finally, Ludwig von Gerlach was heavily involved in his work for the *Kreuzzeitung* and in domestic politics, especially the two parliamentary chambers which were elected in early 1849. He himself was chosen for the upper or First Chamber, the beginnings of a stormy parliamentary career that was to last for decades. Ludwig believed that it was a mistake for the King to concentrate on German issues so much, when his domestic position still remained unstable. This fascination with Germany, Ludwig believed, was a sure sign that Frederick William had succumbed to Radowitz's advice 'to build himself a nest in the tricoloured Gardens of the Hesperides of his imagination'.[32]

While the Camarilla was diverted, the cabinet itself was pursuing a less than clear or consistent policy during those months. Count Brandenburg was a man who played his cards rather close to his chest, and rarely revealed his hand. It seems fairly clear, though, that throughout much of 1849 and 1850 he behaved as a fairly cold-blooded *Realpolitiker*, trying to use the German national issue to derive maximum political advantage for Prussia. The King himself continued to chafe at the idea of constitutional monarchy and ministerial responsibility, and thus he spent those months perpetually railing against his ministers' 'disobedience'. Brandenburg's own exasperation with the monarch reached new heights: 'I have tried everything with him. I have been rude, I have flattered him, I have been gentle, but always in vain.'[33] Frederick William himself had no confidence in his uncle, Leopold von Gerlach believed, and only kept him on for want of an alternative. Small wonder, then, that with all this confusion Prussian policies towards Austria and the German question were, in the first months of 1849, anything but clear. While the King continued to pursue his objective of a union of Germany's monarchical rulers, including Austria, in January 1849 the cabinet issued a 'Circular Note' that left open an option for Heinrich von Gagern's idea of a Prussian-dominated 'narrow union' excluding Austria.[34]

Despite the disarray at the Prussian court and the mixed signals which were coming out of the Prussian capital, the Frankfurt National Assembly was moving in

[30] Leopold von Gerlach, diary, 10 and 22 Jan. 1849, GA, 'Abschriften', vi. 254, 278.

[31] William J. Orr, jun., 'The Foundation of the *Kreuzzeitung* Party in Prussia, 1848–1850' (Ph.D. thesis; Wisconsin-Madison, 1971), 223.

[32] Ludwig von Gerlach to Leopold von Gerlach, 27 Feb. 1849, GA, 'Abschriften', xix. 7.

[33] Leopold von Gerlach, diary (9 Feb. 1849), ibid. vi. 296.

[34] Leopold von Gerlach, diary (marginal comment from 1857 to entry of 9 Feb. 1849), ibid. vi. 292; Orr, 'Foundation', 219–26; Felix Rachfahl, *Die deutsche Politik König Friedrich Wilhelms IV. im Winter 1848/49* (Munich, 1919), 146–53.

March 1849 to offer Frederick William IV the imperial crown of a unified but non-Austrian Germany. Schwarzenberg's policies in early March—the dissolution of the Austrian parliament, the promulgation of a constitution for the entire Habsburg Monarchy, and the demand that the whole monarchy be included in a unified Germany—really left it with no other choice. On 27 March the Assembly voted by the narrow margin of 267–263 to approve a monarchical constitution; the following day, 290 deputies voted for Frederick William as German Emperor, while 248 delegates abstained. The Assembly then named a delegation of thirty-two parliamentarians, headed by the Prussian deputy Eduard Simson, to travel to Berlin and officially make the offer to the King of Prussia.

Frederick William's discussions with the Frankfurt delegation are among the best-known and most frequently described events of his reign. After months of waffling, the King finally had to make a choice: and he did, though in his usual ambiguous fashion. For months he had been heaping contumely upon the notion that the Assembly had the right to award a crown to anyone. Moreover, despite his own government's Circular Note of 23 January, he insisted that co-operation with Austria remained of paramount importance to him.[35] In a letter to the old patriot Ernst Moritz Arndt, Frederick William thus asserted that the crown of the Paulskirche would represent an 'iron collar of servitude which would turn the son of more than twenty-four rulers, electors, and kings into the serf of the revolution'.[36]

Despite such declamations, it was still not clear just how the King would respond to the parliamentarians. On 3 April he officially received the deputation at his palace in Berlin. Neither he nor his cabinet wanted to reject out of hand a positive Prussian contribution to the creation of a federal state in Germany, and the words of Frederick William's answer were rather conciliatory. His tone, however, was a different matter, and it was clear to everyone that he had finally rejected the crown of the Paulskirche.[37] To his uncle, the cantankerous and tyrannical King of Hanover, he could speak less guardedly. In a letter two days thereafter, Frederick William described the Paulskirche crown, in words that have been quoted in textbooks ever since, as 'a dog collar with which they wanted to chain *me* to the revolution of '48'.[38]

And so the matter seemed to be settled. The King's rejection of the imperial crown had sealed the fate of the National Assembly and its constitutional endeavours.[39] For

---

[35] FW IV to Grand Duke Leopold of Baden, 7 Mar. 1849, in Karl Haenchen (ed.), *Revolutionsbriefe 1848: Ungedrucktes aus dem Nachlaß König Friedrich Wilhelms IV. von Preußen* (Leipzig, 1930), 373, 375.

[36] FW IV to Arndt, 15 Mar. 1849, ibid. 392. See also Friedrich Meusel, 'Ernst Moritz Arndt und Friedrich Wilhelm IV. über die Kaiserfrage', *Hohenzollern-Jahrbuch*, 12 (1908), 231–9.

[37] See the dramatic description of these events in Valentin, *Revolution*, ii. 380–2. For the text of the King's remarks, see Otto von Manteuffel, *Unter Friedrich Wilhelm IV.: Denkwürdigkeiten des Ministers Otto Freiherrn von Manteuffel*, ed. Heinrich von Poschinger (3 vols.; Berlin, 1901), i. 89–91; see also Haenchen (ed.), *Revolutionsbriefe*, 432–3; and Ernst Rudolf Huber (ed.), *Dokumente zur deutschen Verfassungsgeschichte*, i: *Deutsche Verfassungsdokumente 1803–1850* (Stuttgart 1961), 328–9.

[38] FW IV to Ernest August, 5 Apr. 1849, in Haenchen (ed.), *Revolutionsbriefe*, 436; cf. FW IV to Nicholas I, 3 May 1849, GStA Merseburg, HA Rep. 50 J Nr. 1205, Bl. 104.

[39] Bernhard Mann, 'Das Ende der deutschen Nationalversammlung im Jahre 1849', *HZ* 214 (1972), 265–309.

his part, Frederick William IV moved with grim zeal to root out 'the revolution' once and for all. When the Second Chamber, the lower house of the Prussian parliament, voted in late April to proclaim the *Reich* constitution as legally binding in Prussia, the government quickly dissolved it; then, on 30 May, the government promulgated a new electoral law for the lower house, establishing the notorious three-class suffrage-system that remained in effect in Prussia until 1918. The first elections held under the new system took place in July.[40]

Frederick William responded with an especially massive show of force to the wave of popular unrest in support of the *Reich* constitution (*Reichsverfassungskampagne*) in the late spring and summer of 1849.[41] In Prussia popular uprisings took place in Silesia, Westphalia, and the Rhineland, especially in Iserlohn and Elberfeld, where the local militia (*Landwehr*) declared itself absolved of loyalty to the 'absolute crown'. In each of these cases regular Prussian troops were able to restore the government's authority fairly quickly.[42] Things were much more serious, and much more bloody, in the non-Prussian parts of Germany, where both Frederick William and the government of Count Brandenburg were quite happy to use Prussian forces to stamp out 'radicalism' and restore the authority of beleaguered local potentates. Thus Prussian troops played a critical role in suppressing the great Dresden insurrection of early May (in which both Richard Wagner and Mikhail Bakunin participated). Several weeks later, under the command of the Prince of Prussia, the Prussians marched into the Bavarian Palatinate and Baden to suppress republican forces in those regions. After the final surrender of rebel troops in the fortress of Rastatt on 23 July 1849, Prussian military authorities made ruthless use of courts martial and summary executions to snuff out the last embers of revolution.

Frederick William IV derived a grim satisfaction from these proceedings against 'rebellious murderers and bloodhounds', 'those devils incarnate, the filth of all nations'.[43] Though not consistently merciless in his treatment of his enemies, he was certainly harsh. When the renowned Bonn professor and democratic republican Gottfried Kinkel was sentenced to death for high treason, his redoubtable wife Johanna begged the King for mercy. Bettine von Arnim joined with Johanna Kinkel in orchestrating a campaign to save Gottfried's life. The monarch agreed to commute the sentence, but only on condition that Kinkel publicly affirm that he deserved to die and that he was personally entreating the King to spare his life. (The

---

[40] E. R. Huber (ed.), *Dokumente*, i. 397–401; Günther Grünthal, 'Das preußische Dreiklassen-wahlrecht: Ein Beitrag zur Genesis und Funktion des Wahlrechtsoktrois vom Mai 1849', *HZ* 226 (1978), 17–66; id., *Parlamentarismus in Preußen 1848/49–1857/58: Preußischer Konstitutionalismus—Parlament und Regierung in der Reaktionsära* (Düsseldorf, 1982), 66–95.

[41] On the *Reichsverfassungskampagne*, see, most recently and incisively, Siemann, *Revolution*, 207–18; and, for the Rhineland, Jonathan Sperber, *Rhineland Radicals: The Democratic Movement and the Revolution of 1848–1849* (Princeton, NJ, 1991), pt. 3.

[42] Carl von der Groeben to FW IV, 31 May 1849, GStA Merseburg, Rep. 92 Leopold von Gerlach Nr. 6, Bl. 1–6; Brandenburg to FW IV, 12 June 1849, ibid., Bl. 33–8; Leopold von Gerlach to FW IV, 22 June 1849, ibid., Bl. 53–4; Sperber, *Radicals*, 365–86.

[43] FW IV to Adolf von Willisen, 7 May 1849, GStA Merseburg, HA Rep. 50 J Nr. 1580, Bl. 363; FW IV to Alfred von Reumont, 11 May 1849, GStA Merseburg, HA Rep. 50 J Nr. 1130, Bl. 12.

issue turned out to be moot, as Kinkel was spectacularly rescued by his even more famous former student, the future American politician Carl Schurz.)[44] Not surprisingly, the King also arranged an architectural commemoration of his victory over the revolution. In late 1849 he approved the installation of a 'Memorial Monument to the Baden Campaign' adjacent to his brother William's palace at Babelsberg. Still standing, it depicts the Archangel Michael slaying a dragon. And in 1850–1, an Arch of Triumph was constructed as a memorial to the Baden campaign at the foot of a hill to the east of Sanssouci and just a few dozen feet from the Friedenskirche. Designed by August Stüler and Ludwig Ferdinand Hesse according to the King's own plans, it contains a number of terracotta friezes depicting the triumphal homecoming of victorious warriors.[45]

So it seemed that the revolution was truly over, that the counter-revolution had triumphed, and that Frederick William IV and his allies had gained a complete victory over all their foes. But Frederick William was not satisfied. The revolution had brought Germany tantalizingly close to that newer and 'higher' level of unity to which he had so long aspired. Besides, as Friedrich Julius Stahl once noted, Frederick William always believed that his policies—his monarchical project, as we have called it throughout this study—were supposed to represent a positive alternative to the negative forces of the age. Perhaps, the King thought, something useful *could* be salvaged from the wreckage of revolution. Perhaps concrete steps *could* be taken to achieve a kind of German unity along monarchical-conservative lines. In April 1849, just as he was rejecting the crown of the Frankfurt Assembly, he was already giving serious thought to new approaches to the German question.[46] On 3 and 28 April 1849 the Prussian government stated publicly that Frederick William IV was willing to lead a German federal state (*Bundesstaat*), and urged the other German governments to meet with Prussia to consider the preparation of a constitution. The so-called Prussian Union project was unfolding, and with it Radowitz's hour had finally come. On 22 April he was summoned to Berlin from Frankfurt am Main, where he was still serving as a Paulskirche deputy. And one week later Count Brandenburg asked him to meet with the cabinet to discuss Prussia's future role in German affairs.[47]

Radowitz and the Union Project, 1849–1850

Leopold von Gerlach once remarked bitterly that his erstwhile friend Radowitz did

[44] FW IV to Prince of Prussia, 6 Aug. 1849, GStA Merseburg, HA Rep. 50 J Nr. 974, Bl. 29; Valentin, *Revolution*, ii. 538–40.

[45] David E. Barclay, 'Denkmal und Revolutionsfurcht: Friedrich Wilhelm IV. und die Verherrlichung des preußischen Feldzugs in Südwestdeutschland 1849. Monumentale Beispiele im Potsdamer Raum', *Jahrbuch für brandenburgische Landesgeschichte*, 44 (1993), 130–60; Gerd-H. Zuchold, *Die Triumphstraße König Friedrich Wilhelms IV. von Preußen in Potsdam: Das Triumphtor* (Berlin, 1994).

[46] FW IV to Carl Wilhelm Saegert, 3 Apr. 1849, GStA Berlin, BPH. Rep. 192 Carl Wilhelm Saegert Nr. 17; FW IV to Charlotte, 11 Apr. 1849, GStA Merseburg, HA Rep. 50 J Nr. 1210 Vol. III, Bl. 80; FW IV to Ernest August, 5 Apr. 1849, in Haenchen (ed.), *Revolutionsbriefe*, 437; FW IV to Schwarzenberg, 6 Apr. 1849, in Radowitz, *Briefe und Aufzeichnungen*, 78–80.

[47] Konrad Canis, 'Joseph Maria von Radowitz: Konterrevolution und preußische Unionspolitik', in
[cont. on p. 197]

not have a 'Prussian heart'.[48] Despite its petulance, Gerlach's remark contained more than a grain of truth. Like his royal master, Radowitz sensed that Prussia had always been an artificial entity, constantly in need of reshaping and redefinition, while its position as one of the five European great powers remained fragile. The only basis for restructuring Prussia and assuring its future greatness lay, he argued, in a kind of Prussian merger with the rest of Germany. Thus Prussia had a specific German mission, he argued as early as 1840, and nothing should happen in any other German capital 'without our voice being heard and listened to'. Further, because of its 'global' interests Austria could never aspire to the national leadership of Germany. Prussia's politics, therefore, should try to reconcile both the princes and the peoples of Germany to Prussian leadership and Prussian 'moral autonomy' in the country's affairs.[49] Not only should Prussia take the lead in responding to the 'moral' challenges of national leadership, it should also, according to Radowitz, address the growing plight of the poor and the gradual emergence of a new kind of industrial working class; as an advocate of a 'social kingdom' for Prussia, he always thought that the social and national regeneration of Germany were indissolubly linked.[50] In the years immediately after 1847, however, he devoted most of his attention to the national question, and therein, despite his contributions to conservative social thought, lies his real historical significance. The problem of how to reorganize the German Confederation had become an increasingly urgent one for him after the autumn of 1847, as we have already seen; but the events of March 1848 forced him to think even more boldly about how to reconstruct, recast, and redefine the German-speaking world.

After his election to the Frankfurt National Assembly, Radowitz had joined a faction of the extreme right, where he quickly gained a reputation as a thoughtful and persuasive speaker. He also learned important lessons in political compromise, especially with moderate liberal supporters of constitutional monarchy. By early 1849 he had drawn steadily closer to Gagern's *kleindeutsch* notions concerning the establishment of a Prussian-dominated narrow union, with Austria to be included in a looser, broader union, and in the months that followed he made this idea his own. Finally, in late March he had voted with the majority in the Paulskirche to offer the imperial crown to Frederick William IV.[51] At the end of April 1849, the pro-Austrian Foreign Minister Count Heinrich Friedrich Arnim-Heinrichsdorff—the seventh person to hold that post in thirteen months—was sacked after a disagreement with several of

Helmut Bleiber, Walter Schmidt, and Rolf Weber (eds.), *Männer der Revolution von 1848*, ii (Berlin [East], 1987), 468; Radowitz to Gräfin Voß, 22 Apr. 1849, BA Frankfurt/M., FSg. 1/154, Joseph Maria von Radowitz, Bl. 29–31; Radowitz to Marie von Radowitz, 24 Apr. and 25–6 Apr. 1849, in Radowitz, *Briefe und Aufzeichnungen*, 81–2.

[48] Leopold von Gerlach to Brandenburg, 10 and 12 May 1849, in diary (12 May 1849), GA, 'Abschriften', vi. 362.

[49] Radowitz, 'Das Verhältnis Preußens zum Deutschen Bund' (1840), in id., *Ausgewählte Schriften*, 1–2.

[50] Joseph Maria von Radowitz, 'Friedrich Wilhelm IV. und seine Aufgabe', Mar. 1843, GStA Merseburg, Rep. 92 Joseph Maria von Radowitz d. Ä. 1. Reihe Nr. 45d, Bl. 1–16; Hermann Beck, 'Conservatives, Bureaucracy, and the Social Question', 64–5.

[51] Meinecke, *Radowitz*, chs. 2 and 6; Canis, 'Radowitz', 459–65.

his colleagues.[52] Even before Arnim's dismissal, Radowitz had been approached about the possibility of becoming Foreign Minister himself, a prospect which he rejected out of hand. His personal unpopularity and, he feared, his Catholic faith would make such a position politically impossible for him. He also spurned the prospect of succeeding Ludolf Camphausen as Prussian plenipotentiary to the Frankfurt National Assembly. Accordingly, for the next year and a half he held no official position at court or in the Prussian government which in any way corresponded to his real influence over Frederick William IV and over the direction of Prussian state policy. During that period he was in charge of various official negotiations, and in early 1850 he chaired the Administrative Council (*Verwaltungsrat*) of the newly elected Erfurt parliament. Still, he essentially served in an unofficial and 'non-responsible' capacity, and thus his position was an anomalous one: the man who believed that the King should respond creatively and positively to the forces of the modern age, including constitutionalism and responsible government, occupied a non-constitutional position reminiscent of the worst features of the pre-1848 'system of favourites' (*Günstlingswirtschaft*).[53] Although the Gerlachs and other members of the Camarilla are often regarded as the most notorious examples of Frederick William's tendency to surround himself with 'non-responsible' advisers, virtually all of them, with the important exception of Leopold von Gerlach before September 1849, occupied a formal court or state position. It was in fact Radowitz and, as we shall see in a subsequent chapter, a man named Carl Wilhelm Saegert who best exemplify the King's reliance on informal advisers.

Radowitz himself recognized the complexities and ironies of his unique situation. 'My task', he wrote at the end of April 1849, 'is to co-ordinate ideas for the King and the cabinet about the means and ends necessary to deal with our current enormous crisis.'[54] Radowitz was always rather pessimistic about his chances of success, and he was at once a diffident and overly confident politician, better at developing bold insights than at translating such insights into bold policies. His diffidence and his impatience with 'normal' politics were probably products both of his personal situation and of his assessment of the King's personality. Radowitz's health had been poor for many years, and it deteriorated badly in 1850. Moreover, his youngest daughter's death, just at the time that he was critically involved with parliamentary affairs in Erfurt, was an especially cruel blow.[55] Above all, Radowitz was aware that, thanks to his outsider status, he could almost certainly not prevail in Berlin without Frederick William's unqualified support, and even then it would be difficult, for the King was no absolute despot. Radowitz also realized that, despite Frederick William's effusive statements of support, real differences of emphasis and outlook persisted between

[52] Leopold von Gerlach, diary (1 May 1849), GA, 'Abschriften', vi. 352–3.

[53] E. R. Huber, *Deutsche Verfassungsgeschichte seit 1789*, 3rd edn. (Stuttgart, 1988), ii: *Der Kampf um Einheit und Freiheit 1830 bis 1850*, 887.

[54] Radowitz to Marie von Radowitz, 25–6 Apr. 1849, in Radowitz, *Briefe und Aufzeichnungen*, 82.

[55] FW IV to Radowitz, 10 Jan. 1845, GStA Berlin, BPH Rep. 50 Nr. 55; FW IV to Canitz, 7 July 1846, ibid., Nr. 117; Radowitz to Gerhard von Reutern, 16 June 1849, in Radowitz, *Briefe und Aufzeichnungen*, 120–2; Radowitz to FW IV, 28 Jan. 1851, ibid. 381.

them. He was under no illusion about the uphill struggle that he faced, one which he was likely to lose. One of the main things that kept him going, he asserted, was his deep personal attachment to the King.[56]

Radowitz's political base was thus exceedingly fragile; and, as he later admitted, his rejection of the Foreign Ministry deprived him of an institutional affiliation that he might have turned to his advantage. Still, for a comparatively long time he was able to draw upon several reservoirs of support or sympathy for his views. Count Brandenburg was at first wary of him, but was quickly won over to his policy proposals, at least as long as they held out the prospect of maximizing Prussian state power. Indeed, asserted the Minister President in August 1850, Radowitz was 'an insightful and useful adviser'.[57] When, however, it became evident by the autumn of that year that Radowitz's policies might lead to a dangerous confrontation with both Austria and Russia, Brandenburg withdrew his support. Radowitz also had influential allies in the Prince and Princess of Prussia, who had learned from bitter experience that rulers had to adjust themselves to the spirit of the age. William was at first cool to Radowitz's 'liberalism', but his enthusiasm for the Union policy increased steadily, while Augusta quickly became one of Radowitz's most ardent admirers. William's influence, however, was no more decisive in 1850 than in 1846 or 1847.

Much of Radowitz's strategy was based on forging a kind of informal alliance between monarchical, constitutional, and national liberals, on the one hand, and moderate conservatives on the other. He could, of course, count on the special sympathies of those moderate liberals who called for German unity on a *kleindeutsch*, monarchical basis under Prussian auspices. In late June 1849, many of these individuals gathered in the city of Gotha to express their support for a revised *Reich* constitution with an absolute legislative veto for the 'Head of the *Reich*' and a less centralized, more federal structure for Germany as a whole. Their members included a number of prominent liberal notables; because of their meeting-place, they became known as the 'Gotha party', and on the whole they leaned rather strongly toward Radowitz's policies.[58]

Radowitz also succeeded in attracting the sympathies of many grass-roots monarchical conservatives, who, rather like Brandenburg, probably saw in his project a chance to enhance Prussian power and prestige while throttling the last vestiges of revolution. Many of the local conservative associations and societies which had sprung up in 1848 supported Radowitz's Union policy, despite the sustained opposition of prominent ultra-conservatives in Berlin and Potsdam. Radowitz was not at all effective, however, in mobilizing this grass-roots support against the Gerlachs and his other enemies. Nor did he really succeed in building a centrist coalition of

[56] Radowitz to Marie von Radowitz, 1 Nov. 1849, ibid. 137.

[57] Herman von Petersdorff, 'Joseph v. Radowitz und Leopold v. Gerlach', *Deutsche Rundschau*, 130 (1907), 48.

[58] Georg Witzmann, *Die Gothaer Nachversammlung zum Frankfurter Parlament im Jahre 1849 (Das 'Gothaer Parlament'): Eine Studie aus der Vorgeschichte der Reichsgründung und der Jugendzeit des deutschen Parlamentarismus* (Gotha, 1917).

moderate liberals and conservatives. In contrast to people like Ludwig von Gerlach or Otto von Manteuffel, he essentially remained a *Vormärz* court politician.[59]

The constitutional revisions which the Gotha party affirmed had emerged from negotiations which Radowitz pursued in mid-May with representatives of the kingdoms of Bavaria, Hanover, Saxony, and Württemberg. Those discussions were supposed to lay the foundation for Prussia's new Union policy, which called for Austria to be associated loosely, as part of a broader union, with a narrower, Prussian-dominated German union or *Bundesstaat*. The timing seemed propitious. The Austrians were not nearly as hostile to the plan as they later became, and the new Habsburg emissary in Berlin, Count Anton Prokesch von Osten, was actually receptive to some of its features. Although Prokesch realized that Radowitz's aim was to place Prussia 'at the forefront of Germany', he remained confident that a *modus vivendi* remained possible between the two leading German powers.[60] Certainly this represented the hope of Frederick William IV, who constantly and loudly stressed his loyalty to Austria: 'I want to make Austria mightier and greater than ever before', he insisted in August 1849, 'with one wing *over* Germany, with the other *over* Italy, united and strong within.' Radowitz's projects, which he described as '*le salut de l'Europe*', were not at all inimical to Austrian interests.[61]

Despite these developments, the two south German kingdoms were suspicious of Prussia's intentions and remained wary of Austria's exclusion from the planned *Bundesstaat*, and thus they declined to join the Alliance of the Three Kings (*Dreikönigsbündnis*) with Prussia, Hanover, and Saxony on 26 May. Two days later the Alliance's signatories presented a proposed constitution which Radowitz had been instrumental in drafting. The new constitutional document provided explicitly for a 'dual union' in Germany. Decisions for the broader union would be taken by a directory in which Austria and the rest of Germany would each have two votes. The narrow union would include a parliament (*Reichstag*) with a lower house chosen by three-class suffrage and an upper house to represent the interests of the various state governments. Executive authority would reside in a powerful *Reich* Executive who would be assisted by a six-member College of Princes. The new Union constitution thus amounted to a monarchical-conservative variation on the Frankfurt constitution, and it was one with which many moderate liberals could live.[62]

Although twenty-six states had agreed to join the Prussian-dominated Union by

---

[59] Wolfgang Schwentker, *Konservative Vereine und Revolution in Preußen 1848/49: Die Konstituierung des Konservativismus als Partei* (Düsseldorf, 1988), 326–8.

[60] Anton Graf Prokesch von Osten, 'Berlin I', in *Aus den Briefen des Grafen Prokesch von Osten, k. u. k. österr. Botschafters und Feldzeugmeisters (1849–1855)*, ed. Anton Graf Prokesch von Osten (Vienna, 1896), 462, and Prokesch to his wife, 5 May 1849, ibid. 43; Radowitz, 'Diarium', 7 May 1849, in Radowitz, *Briefe und Aufzeichnungen*, 93; Joachim Hoffmann, 'Die Berliner Mission des Grafen Prokesch-Osten 1849–1852' (Diss.; Freie Universität Berlin, 1959), 26–7.

[61] FW IV to Charlotte, 17 Aug. 1849, GStA Merseburg, HA Rep. 50 J Nr. 1210 Vol. III, Bl. 85ᵛ; FW IV to Nicholas I, 3 May 1849, ibid., HA Rep. 50 J Nr. 1205, Bl. 104ᵛ.

[62] E. R. Huber, *Verfassungsgeschichte*, ii. 888; Botzenhart, *Parlamentarismus*, 717–25; Joseph Maria von Radowitz, 'Denkschrift in betreff der Politik Preußens in der deutschen Frage', 12 June 1849, in id., *Briefe und Aufzeichnungen*, 113–18.

the end of the year, it remained an extraordinarily fragile enterprise, and one which encountered difficulties at every turn. Apart from the constant opposition of Austria and Russia, it was also bedevilled by a number of internal problems, among them Radowitz's own inflexible and self-righteous personality, his poor diplomatic skills, the hostility of powerful court and government officials, and the scepticism of the medium-sized German states. By late 1849 Saxony and Hanover had essentially pulled out of the Union, so that it dwindled into a league of north and central German dwarf states aligned with Prussia. In August, much to Frederick William's distress, Schwarzenberg insisted that the German Confederation had only been suspended in the spring of 1848, and he began to press for a resuscitation of the old Federal Diet. Finally, at the end of September he agreed to a compromise formula with Prussia—the 'Interim', as it was called—in which the two states agreed jointly to assume the Archduke John's executive functions until 1 May 1850.[63]

In January 1850, elections proceeded in the Union states for a new Union parliament, which in turn assembled at Erfurt on 20 March. Democratic organizations boycotted the elections, so that the Erfurt parliament consisted almost entirely of moderate, 'Gotha' liberals and extreme conservatives, including prominent members of the *Kreuzzeitung* party such as Friedrich Julius Stahl and Ludwig von Gerlach. Radowitz was chosen to direct the parliament's Administrative Council (*Verwaltungsrat*), but what should have been his hour of triumph resulted instead in confusion and disappointment. A dispute emerged over whether the Union constitution should be approved *en bloc* at the very outset, as the Gotha liberals and the Prussian cabinet desired, or whether it should be open to revision article by article, as the ultra-conservatives wished. The latter induced the King to waver in his support for *en bloc* acceptance; and Radowitz, who also supported the *en bloc* formula, was nevertheless forced publicly to argue on behalf of his sovereign's views. Once again, a compromise was worked out, and at the end of April the Erfurt parliament adjourned; although the Union constitution had been approved, it would not go into effect until it had received the endorsement of the rulers of the individual Union states.[64] To that end, in early May a Congress of Princes (*Fürstenkongreß*) met in Berlin, but to constitutional liberals its results were paltry. Meanwhile, since the early spring of 1850 the King had become steadily more non-committal in his approach to the German question, and, complained Radowitz, he failed to provide decisive leadership at the Berlin conference. Only twelve of the twenty-six Union

---

[63] See, *inter alia*, E. R. Huber, *Verfassungsgeschichte*, ii. 889–92; Canis, 'Radowitz', 476–84; Heinrich Lutz, *Zwischen Habsburg und Preußen: Deutschland 1815–1866* (Berlin, 1985), 315–17; and Siemann, *Revolution*, 218–20.

[64] Meinecke, *Radowitz*, 385–410; Orr, 'Foundation', 438–9, 440–54; Botzenhart, *Parlamentarismus*, 767–76; Wilhelm Füßl, *Professor in der Politik: Friedrich Julius Stahl (1802–1861). Das monarchische Prinzip und seine Umsetzung in die parlamentarische Praxis* (Göttingen, 1988), 224–55; Hans-Cristof Kraus, 'Ernst Ludwig von Gerlach: Politisches Denken und Handeln eines preußischen Altkonservativen' (Diss.; 2 vols.; Göttingen, 1991), i. 335–40, ii. 252–6; critical documents in Radowitz, *Briefe und Aufzeichnungen*, 177–217, 225–35; O. von Manteuffel, *Unter Friedrich Wilhelm IV.*, i. 191–9; and the Erfurt letters of Ludwig von Gerlach, Count Brandenburg, and Otto von Manteuffel to Leopold von Gerlach in GA, 'Abschriften', vol. xx.

states were willing to accept the new constitution. Accordingly, another odd compromise was worked out, this one stipulating that the constitution could not yet be
put into force and that the Union would be 'provisionally' maintained for at least
another two months.[65] During the conference an increasingly pessimistic Radowitz
admitted that his major task was now at the very least 'to keep the German cause . . .
from dying'.[66] In fact, even that modest goal was no longer realizable. The Union
project was already mortally ill, and its death pangs would ruin Radowitz's career and
bring Central Europe to the brink of war.

Radowitz had long had powerful enemies, and by the spring and summer of 1850
their numbers were growing. The Gerlachs and their Camarilla allies—Rauch,
Massow, and Edwin von Manteuffel—were, of course, especially virulent in their
opposition to the King's 'divine' friend. Radowitz also had to contend with the hostility of the Queen, who, he complained, 'views absolutely everything *à la
Kreuzzeitung*, and is especially hostile to the idea of [German] unity'. And, he opined
further, 'The King is open to very dubious influences, to which his character is so
especially susceptible.'[67] For their part, the Camarilla and the Queen thought that
politically Radowitz 'must be cast to the dead'.[68] Not unexpectedly, Ludwig von
Gerlach's critique of Radowitz was much more vitriolic than his older brother's;
while, for his part, Radowitz asserted that Ludwig's newspaper articles against him
'border on high treason'.[69] Still, if Leopold's views were somewhat more circum-
spect, they were just as intensely held. As early as 29 April 1849 he had warned
Brandenburg and Rauch that Radowitz's presence would cause trouble, that
Radowitz had aligned himself with the revolution, and that he was putting his
German interests ahead of his obligations to the Prussian state. And for months
thereafter he incessantly denounced what he called Radowitz's 'cowardice' and 'bad
advice'.[70] Nor did he attempt to hide his views from Radowitz; after the spring of
1849 their correspondence and conversations with each other became steadily more
acerbic.[71]

Gerlach and his friends were, of course, especially displeased with Radowitz's
'*Deutschheit*' and his flirtation with moderate liberals. As firm adherents of the Holy
Alliance and Restoration-era legitimism, they were never emotionally susceptible to
national pathos; nor did they believe that 'fear of the revolution' could justify suc-

[65] See *Protokolle des Fürstenkongresses in Berlin vom 10. bis 15. Mai 1850*, copy in GLA, Abt. 49/2162;
Radowitz's report on the congress, 8–16 May 1850, in Radowitz, *Briefe und Aufzeichnungen*, 239–47; E. R.
Huber, *Verfassungsgeschichte*, ii. 898–900; Meinecke, *Radowitz*, 424–8.
[66] Radowitz to Marie von Radowitz, 11 May 1850, in id., *Briefe und Aufzeichnungen*, 247; Meinecke,
Radowitz, 428.
[67] Radowitz, 'Diarium', 31 May–1 June 1850, in id., *Briefe und Aufzeichnungen*, 108.
[68] Ludwig von Gerlach to Leopold von Gerlach, 10 June 1849, GA, 'Abschriften', xix. 60.
[69] Leopold von Gerlach, diary (15 Aug. 1849), ibid., vi. 437; Kraus, 'Gerlach', i. 309–15, 341–2, ii.
234–8, 257.
[70] Leopold von Gerlach to Rauch and to Brandenburg, 29 Apr. 1849, in Petersdorff, 'Radowitz', 54–5.
[71] Leopold's relations with Radowitz are a major theme of his diary between Apr. 1849 and Nov. 1850;
e.g., his entries for 27 Apr. 1849 and 1 Oct. 1850, in GA, 'Abschriften', vi. 350 and vii. 189–90. See also
Petersdorff, 'Radowitz', 43–61.

cumbing to nationalist 'illusions'. Nationalism was inherently revolutionary, they argued, and nothing could be gained by being in league with it.[72] Leopold von Gerlach himself stated in August 1849 that his 'constant motive is to encourage amity with Austria and Russia in everything and to keep the King on the right track with his ministers'.[73] This did not mean, however, that the Gerlachs shared Frederick William's 'fantasies' about resuscitating the Empire or restoring the imperial crown to the Habsburgs. As a lifelong critic of 'absolutism', Leopold von Gerlach deplored Schwarzenberg's centralizing policies in Austria, which were, he said, Josephinist, absolutist, and 'mechanistic'—exactly the kinds of policies which had made revolution possible in the first place. Nor was Leopold absolutely opposed to the growth of Prussian influence in Germany, or even to certain aspects of the Union. Because of its absolutist nature, he contended, Schwarzenberg's Austria could not lead the struggle against the German revolution as effectively as Prussia, to which smaller, more vulnerable states looked for leadership and assistance. The problem lay with the way in which Radowitz had conducted the negotiations of May 1849, which had offended the sovereign sensibilities of many German rulers and had irretrievably linked the Union to the efforts of the Paulskirche.[74] Accordingly, an arrangement with Austria was essential and unavoidable, as was a return to something like the old German Confederation; but the restored Confederation should take greater account of Prussia's interest, strength, and influence. The main task that faced all German governments, however, was the 'restoration of authority from above and the elimination of authority from below'.[75]

After returning from a diplomatic mission to Munich in the late spring of 1849, Leopold von Gerlach was in the King's company almost daily. Adjutant-General Rauch had become seriously ill in 1849, and later that year returned to St Petersburg; his illness took a turn for the worse, however, and he died in June 1850. Thus Gerlach began to assume Rauch's daily duty of reading reports to the King, which he liked to do while the royal couple were drinking their morning coffee. He was keenly aware that the so-called 'coffee ministry' represented an excellent opportunity to present his views to the impressionable monarch at the very beginning of the day; and, of course, the Queen could invariably be counted on to back him up. In April 1850,

[72] Leopold von Gerlach, 'Promemoria', in diary (21 Oct. 1849), GA, 'Abschriften', vi. 489–94; Kondylis, *Konservativismus*, 295.

[73] Leopold von Gerlach, diary (23 Aug. 1849), GA, 'Abschriften', vi. 442; also his 'politisches Glaubensbekenntnis', 29 Jan. 1849, in Ernst Ludwig von Gerlach, *Von der Revolution zum Norddeutschen Bund: Politik und Ideengut der preußischen Hochkonservativen 1848–1866. Aus dem Nachlaß von Ernst Ludwig von Gerlach*, ed. Hellmut Diwald (2 vols.; Göttingen, 1970), ii. 622–3.

[74] Leopold von Gerlach to Radowitz, 24 May 1849, in Petersdorff, 'Radowitz', 56–7; Leopold von Gerlach, diary (20 May–3 June 1849), GA, 'Abschriften', vi. 366–79; his letters to FW IV of 21 and 24 May 1849, GStA Merseburg, HA Rep. 50 J Nr. 455, Bl. 37–40^v; and the documents in GStA Berlin, III. Hauptabteilung, Nr. 55.

[75] Leopold von Gerlach, 'Entwurf zu einem Promemoria', n.d. (Mar. 1850), GA, 'Abschriften', xx. 24–7; id., 'Promemoria', 1 July 1850, ibid. xx. 91–4; id., 'Promemoria . . . in bezug auf Radowitz' Einwendungen', early July 1850, ibid. xx. 95; Ludwig von Gerlach, 'Promemoria', 4 Aug. 1850, ibid. xx. 116–18; Leopold von Gerlach to Ludwig von Gerlach, 7 Apr. 1850, in E. L. von Gerlach, *Von der Revolution*, ii. 670–1.

shortly before Rauch's death, Gerlach was finally appointed Adjutant-General. His role in the royal entourage, which had always been very significant, now became official and even more powerful than before; and Radowitz and his allies, including Brandenburg and the Prince of Prussia, soon began to complain that Gerlach was abusing his position by speaking to the King about political as well as military matters.[76]

Leopold von Gerlach never overestimated his capacity to influence the King's policies, especially in 1849–50. With Rauch ill and then dead, Gerlach often felt isolated and depressed, and was convinced that he could not 'hold out' much longer.[77] Occasionally he thought of stepping down, especially when it became evident that he could not shake the King's devotion to Radowitz. Indeed, Frederick William often scolded Gerlach for doubting the wisdom of Radowitz's policies, 'for it proves to me that partisanship can even make such a gifted man as you blind and deaf and insignificant'.[78] Although Gerlach did not resign his post, he came close in the autumn of 1850, when his own influence reached its nadir and it appeared that Radowitz might in fact emerge triumphant.[79] Indeed, his own contribution—and that of the *Kreuzzeitung* party in general—to the events that led up to Radowitz's fall in November 1850 and the important Olmütz agreement later that month was rather limited. More important were external pressures, and, within Prussia itself, growing opposition from members of the Brandenburg cabinet.

The Russian court was, of course, mightily unhappy with Frederick William's entire Union project, and immensely distrustful of Radowitz himself. Though the Tsar almost certainly needed no prompting on this score, Prussia's representatives in Russia—Theodor Rochus von Rochow (brother of the late Interior Minister), Rauch, and, after Rauch's death, Count Hugo zu Münster-Meinhövel—were all close allies and confidants of the Gerlachs, and their contacts with Nicholas I only reinforced their antipathy to Radowitz's 'unhappy German business', which was leading Prussia down the road to catastrophe.[80] Despite his own deep-seated pessimism, Nicholas constantly hoped that the two German powers could reconcile their differences and return to the true path of Holy Alliance legitimism.[81] By the middle of May 1850, therefore, the Russians were playing a much more active role in

[76] See the exchange of letters between Brandenburg and Gerlach, 3–9 Feb. 1850, GA, 'Abschriften', xx. 5–8; Leopold von Gerlach, diary (28 May 1850), ibid. vii. 110; Leopold von Gerlach to Prince of Prussia, n.d. (May 1850), ibid. xx. 60–1; Radowitz to Leopold von Gerlach and Leopold von Gerlach to Radowitz, 22 Oct. 1850, ibid. xx. 204–5.

[77] e.g. see Leopold von Gerlach to Ludwig von Gerlach, 2 Apr., 5 Apr., 7 Apr., 17 May, and 13 June 1850, in E. L. von Gerlach, *Von der Revolution*, ii. 667, 669, 671, 676, 680.

[78] FW IV to Leopold von Gerlach, 18 Aug. 1850, GA, 'Abschriften', xxx. 6.

[79] Orr, 'Foundation', 484, 487; Kraus, 'Gerlach', i. 342–3, ii. 257–9.

[80] Rauch to Queen Elisabeth, 10 Nov. 1849, GStA Merseburg, HA Rep. 50 T Nr. 66, Bl. 1–2; cf. Rochow to Leopold von Gerlach, 23 Sept. 1849, BA Potsdam, 90 Ge 6 Nachlaß Leopold von Gerlach Nr. 42, Bl. 47–50. See also the voluminous correspondence between Gerlach, Münster, and Rochow in ibid., Nr. 42, and in GStA Merseburg, Rep. 92 Leopold von Gerlach, Nr. 4 and 10.

[81] Meinecke, *Radowitz*, 431; Theodor Schiemann, *Geschichte Rußlands unter Kaiser Nikolaus I.*, iv: *Kaiser Nikolaus vom Höhepunkt seiner Macht zum Zusammenbruch im Krimkriege 1840–1855* (Berlin, 1919), 220–1, 230–1; J. Hoffmann, 'Prokesch', 47.

trying to mediate the squabbles of their German neighbours by hosting a conference in Warsaw attended by the Tsar, Schwarzenberg, the Prince of Prussia, and Prince Carl; but the conversations ended inconclusively.[82]

The Warsaw talks, with their unsatisfactory outcome, were but one symptom of the growing hostility between Austria and Prussia, an estrangement that in the course of the year threatened to escalate into armed confrontation. Since agreeing to the 'Interim' in September 1849, the Austrians had incessantly expressed their dissatisfaction with the Prussian Union plan and had urged a return to the old Confederation of 1815. In late February 1850 Schwarzenberg presented a direct challenge to the Union by encouraging an Alliance of the Four Kings (*Vierkönigsbündnis*) of Saxony, Hanover, Bavaria, and Württemberg which called for the inclusion of the entire Habsburg Monarchy in a reconstituted Germany.[83] Finally, Schwarzenberg refused to renew the Interim after its expiration on 1 May 1850, calling instead for a conference in Frankfurt to re-establish the old Confederation. Representatives of ten German states showed up at that meeting on 10 May.[84] Although the Prussians did not participate, many prominent Prussian leaders, including Brandenburg himself, were not averse to the idea. The winds were clearly not blowing in Radowitz's favour. What he described as the 'moment of decision' was rapidly approaching, and a break with Austria seemed imminent, especially when, in early July, the Austrians proceeded with concrete plans to reconstitute the political structures of the pre-1848 German Confederation.[85] Within the Brandenburg cabinet itself, the deterioration of Austro-Prussian relations was causing some rapid rethinking; and Leopold von Gerlach was now joined in his furious opposition to Radowitz by War Minister August von Stockhausen and, most notably, by Interior Minister Otto von Manteuffel.

Neither man was a 'natural' ally of the Gerlachs or the *Kreuzzeitung* party. Though staunchly conservative, Stockhausen, who had become War Minister at the end of February 1850, was a rather blunt and even brutish man who had little sympathy for the 'pietists' around the King.[86] Manteuffel had pursued an administrative career before 1848 and seemed to be the very incarnation of a boring Prussian bureaucrat; he had absolutely none of the panache of his cousin Edwin. Until the spring of 1850 he had focused on domestic affairs and had followed Brandenburg's lead in matters of foreign policy. His experience at the Erfurt parliament, however, had made him increasingly sceptical of Radowitz's project: 'the house which they propose to build' would not result in real German unity, he feared, but was being designed according to the specifications of revolutionaries: 'All the same, Herr von

---

[82] Schiemann, *Kaiser Nikolaus*, iv. 222–5; Meinecke, *Radowitz*, 428–34; and esp. the daily dispatches of Edwin von Manteuffel to Leopold von Gerlach from Warsaw, 23 May to 1 June 1850, GStA Merseburg, Rep. 92 Leopold von Gerlach Nr. 10, Bl. 361–392ᵛ.

[83] Lutz, *Zwischen Habsburg und Preußen*, 315–17.

[84] Meinecke, *Radowitz*, 413–14; E. R. Huber, *Verfassungsgeschichte*, ii. 900–1; Orr, 'Foundation', 457.

[85] GStA Merseburg, Rep. 90a B III 2c Nr. 3 Bd. 1, Bl. 84–92; J. Hoffmann, 'Prokesch', 49–50.

[86] Ludwig Dehio, 'Zur November-Krise des Jahres 1850: Aus den Papieren des Kriegsministers von Stockhausen', *FBPG* 35 (1923), 134–6; Orr, 'Foundation', 463–4.

Radowitz seems determined to proceed with it. How he intends to do it exceeds my limited understanding.'[87] By June Manteuffel was beginning to articulate his concerns more forcefully, asserting on one occasion that he could not remain in the government if Radowitz persisted with his policies.[88]

In calling for a re-establishment of the German Confederation, Schwarzenberg had seemed to hold out a carrot to the Prussians by apparently hinting that he would not look askance at an expansion of Prussian power in northern Germany. That supposed concession finally convinced Stockhausen and Otto von Manteuffel that the time had come openly to repudiate Radowitz's Union project and dump the constitution of May 1849. To do otherwise, they contended, would constitute treason based on wilfulness and self-righteousness.[89] Even Brandenburg and the Foreign Minister, Baron Alexander von Schleinitz, whom Leopold von Gerlach had branded as the 'most servile' supporters of Radowitz's ideas, were now beginning to have doubts.[90] Finally, a Crown Council session on 19 August erupted into a full-scale confrontation between Radowitz and Manteuffel. The Interior Minister insisted that Prussia should publicly proclaim once and for all that the Union was being abandoned, and with it the 'supposedly revolutionary' constitution of May 1849. Prussia might legitimately seek to establish some sort of north German federal entity, but nothing more. Radowitz responded by asserting that the only alternatives to a German federal state were 'the revolutionary *unitary state* or the old form of a *confederation of states*', which during its thirty-three-year lifetime had been a showcase only for weakness and shame.[91] After this furious debate the differences between Radowitz and the ministers were again papered over, mainly because Frederick William could not bear the thought of breaking with his dear friend. But the Union itself had sputtered out, as Radowitz himself realized.[92]

The Autumn Crisis of 1850

In early September yet another crisis in Austro-Prussian relations emerged, as a result of which Radowitz briefly found himself elevated to Foreign Minister. For some months a dangerous situation had been brewing in Hesse-Kassel, a small state which

[87] Otto von Manteuffel to Leopold von Gerlach, 16 Apr. 1850, GA, 'Abschriften', xx. 48–9; cf. Manteuffel's vigorous defence of his activities at Erfurt at a Crown Council meeting on 14 Apr. 1850, GStA Merseburg, Rep. 90a B III 2c Nr. 3 Bd. 1, Bl. 67–72.

[88] Edwin von Manteuffel to Leopold von Gerlach, 5 June and 1 July 1850, GA, 'Abschriften', xx. 65, 96; Leopold von Gerlach to Ludwig von Gerlach, 29 June 1850, in E. L. von Gerlach, *Von der Revolution*, ii. 690.

[89] Edwin von Manteuffel to Leopold von Gerlach, 15 and 23 July 1850, GA, 'Abschriften', 20: 99–102.

[90] Leopold von Gerlach to Ludwig von Gerlach, 20 Apr. 1850, in E. L. von Gerlach, *Von der Revolution*, ii. 672; Edwin von Manteuffel to Leopold von Gerlach, 25 July 1850, GA, 'Abschriften', xx. 103; cf. Orr, 'Foundation', 460.

[91] GStA Merseburg, Rep. 90a B III 2c Nr. 3 Bd. 1, Bl. 175–176^v. See also Radowitz to Gräfin Louise Voß, 8 Aug. 1850, in id., *Briefe und Aufzeichnungen*, 280; Leopold von Gerlach, diary (16 and 19 Aug. 1850), GA, 'Abschriften', vii. 161–2, 163–4; and Otto von Manteuffel, 'Promemoria' (18 Aug. 1850), ibid. xx. 143–7.

[92] Meinecke, *Radowitz*, 445–52.

lay directly astride a strategically vital network of military roads connecting the Rhineland and Westphalia to the main bulk of Prussian territory in the east. For generations Hesse-Kassel had been a watchword for spectacular misrule and rather brutish authoritarianism. Finally, in 1850 the degenerate Elector of Hesse and his chief minister, the ultra-reactionary Camarilla-friend Daniel Hassenpflug, faced what amounted to an insurrection of their own civilian and military officials. On 17 September the Elector asked the German Confederation to intervene with force to quash the revolt and restore his authority. The Federal Diet had been restored, though without the participation of the Union states, on 2 September; and now Schwarzenberg saw an excellent opportunity to force Prussia to accept the Confederation's continued existence or face serious embarrassment, especially if non-Prussian troops were sent into Hesse-Kassel. Accordingly, on 21 September the Diet agreed to help the Elector.[93] This heavy-handed Austrian challenge in such a strategically sensitive area, with its Prussian-controlled military roads, temporarily united a divided Prussian cabinet; and in that moment Radowitz, who had stood firm in his resistance to Austrian pressures and to the old Confederation, was named Foreign Minister to replace Schleinitz. The Prince of Prussia, one of Radowitz's few remaining allies at court, had been urging this step for some weeks, and finally the King himself agreed. Although Radowitz was not optimistic about his prospects, with his appointment the Prussian government was serving notice that it would resist what Frederick William described as Schwarzenberg's '*jeu infame*' in Frankfurt and Hesse.[94]

Greatly vexed by Radowitz's appointment, Nicholas I was now inclined to lean toward Austria; after all, was not Schwarzenberg calling for concrete measures against the 'revolution' and on behalf of monarchical legitimacy? Meanwhile, Schwarzenberg himself increased the pressure on the Prussians, who, with the exception of Radowitz and the Prince of Prussia, were now desperately searching for a peaceful way to resolve the Hessian dilemma. On 26 October 1850 the Diet in Frankfurt ordered Bavarian and Hanoverian forces to carry out a 'federal execution' in Hesse-Kassel. Prussian troops, commanded by the King's friend Groeben, were poised on the Hessian frontier to resist such an incursion. Radowitz continued to urge a policy of firmness, based on his apparent belief that Prussia's adversaries were not serious about going to war. In the event of a federal execution, he hinted to Prokesch, the whole Prussian army might be mobilized.[95] Count Brandenburg himself, who had gone to Warsaw on Frederick William's behalf to negotiate some sort of peaceful settlement with Nicholas and Schwarzenberg, was dismayed when word of Radowitz's threatening language reached him. He was eager for accommodation; and at Warsaw Schwarzenberg in fact seemed to be willing to work out some sort of

[93] J. Hoffmann, 'Prokesch', 53.

[94] Rhyno Quehl to Otto von Manteuffel, 7 Aug. 1850, GStA Merseburg, Rep. 92 Otto von Manteuffel Tit. II Nr. 92, Bl. 3ᵛ; Leopold von Gerlach, diary (4 Sept. 1850), GA, 'Abschriften', vii. 170; Radowitz, *Briefe und Aufzeichnungen*, 296–302, 303–5, 310, 318–19; Meinecke, *Radowitz*, 449–51; Orr, 'Foundation', 477.

[95] Fritz Heinemann, *Die Politik des Grafen Brandenburg* (Berlin, 1909), 58, 60–1; Schiemann, *Kaiser Nikolaus*, iv. 225; J. Hoffmann, 'Prokesch', 54, 58–9.

arrangement that would be compatible with Prussia's honour. Radowitz's behaviour had embarrassed him, the angry Brandenburg believed, and had threatened Prussia's security as well. After his return from Warsaw on 31 October it thus seemed that Radowitz's resignation, after only a few weeks in office, was now a certainty.[96]

That same day Radowitz prepared his final report, in which he stated that the Warsaw discussions were bound to fail because of the Tsar's partisanship for Austria. At a cabinet meeting on 1 November Brandenburg, Manteuffel, and Stockhausen voted against Radowitz's arguments. Two more ministers, who were at first undecided, switched to the anti-Radowitz side at a Crown Council meeting later in the day. Only *Kultusminister* Ladenberg and Trade Minister von der Heydt continued to support him. That same evening word reached Berlin that the federal execution had begun; Bavarian troops had entered Hesse-Kassel.[97] The following morning, at a critical Crown Council session in Bellevue Palace, the majority of the ministers, led by Brandenburg and Manteuffel, announced their opposition to a full-scale Prussian mobilization in response to the Bavarian intervention. They also supported accepting the conditions for discussions which Schwarzenberg had laid down in Warsaw. Radowitz, the King, and the Prince of Prussia opposed the majority's view. Now, however, Frederick William turned Radowitz's strategy of self-effacement against its author. Though he disagreed with the cabinet's decision, he said, he would accept it, but the ministers would have to take full responsibility. He was himself shattered, he said, by the situation. Weeping bitterly, he complained to Leopold von Gerlach about the 'un-Prussian, craven attitude of his ministers. Under no circumstances did they want to mobilize the army; they wanted to deliver us without defences to the Austrians. Manteuffel was especially cowardly.' The 'weeping and scornful' Prince of Prussia 'cursed the ministers and their cowardice', but without effect. In anticipation of the outcome, Radowitz had already prepared his formal resignation. Shortly thereafter, he was sent on a 'special mission' to London to get him out of the country.[98]

But Schwarzenberg did not relent. He now demanded that Prussian troops evacuate the military roads on Hessian territory, and four days later the Prussian government reversed itself and reluctantly agreed to mobilize its whole army after all.[99]

---

[96] Radowitz, 'Die Katastrophe', n. d. (early Nov. 1850), in id., *Briefe und Aufzeichnungen*, 344. On the Warsaw conference, see Heinrich von Sybel, 'Graf Brandenburg in Warschau (1850)', *HZ* 58, NS 22 (1887), 245–78; Hans Julius Schoeps, *Von Olmütz nach Dresden 1850/51: Ein Beitrag zur Geschichte der Reformen am Deutschen Bund. Darstellung und Dokumente* (Cologne, 1970), 23–30; and Brandenburg's correspondence with the King and Radowitz in GStA Berlin, III. Hauptabteilung Nr. 74.

[97] Radowitz, *Briefe und Aufzeichnungen*, 339–42, 344; GStA Merseburg, Rep. 90a B III 2c Nr. 3 Bd. 1, Bl. 209–214^v (Crown Council session of 1 Nov. 1850); FW IV to Emperor Francis Joseph I, 1 Nov. 1850, GStA Merseburg, HA Rep. 50 J Nr. 939, Bl. 28–29^v.

[98] GStA Merseburg, Rep. 90a B III 2c Nr. 3 Bd. 1, Bl. 219–24 (Crown Council meeting of 2 Nov. 1850); Leopold von Gerlach, diary (2 Nov. 1850), GA, 'Abschriften', vii. 209, 210; Edwin von Manteuffel to Leopold von Gerlach, 3 Nov. 1850, ibid., xx. 217–18; Prince of Prussia to Radowitz, 4 Nov. 1850, in Wilhelm I., *Kaiser Wilhelms I. Briefe an Politiker und Staatsmänner*, ed. Johannes Schulze (2 vols.; 1930–1), i. 126–7; Radowitz to FW IV, 2 Nov. 1850, in Radowitz, *Briefe und Aufzeichnungen*, 345.

[99] J. Hoffmann, 'Prokesch', 59–61.

Count Brandenburg had become dangerously ill since his return from Warsaw, and, on the same day that Frederick William signed the mobilization orders, the Minister President suddenly died. 'Our brave and noble Brandenburg died this morning,' Frederick William wrote to Nicholas that evening. 'The blow is terrible, irreparable! And the cause of his death! I know positively that Schwarzenberg's treachery killed him.' An embittered Nicholas thought otherwise, exclaiming grimly to the Prussian Military Plenipotentiary that 'in Berlin they have done Rauch to his death, they've driven Brandenburg to his death, they really won't rest until every imaginable person has been driven to his death! How many people has the King used up already!'[100]

Otto von Manteuffel assumed control of the premiership and of the Foreign Ministry on a temporary and, after December, permanent basis. The situation remained critically dangerous, with Schwarzenberg refusing to back down and many prominent Prussians, foremost among them the Prince of Prussia, convinced that the time for action had come. On 8 November, shots were exchanged at Bronzell, on Hessian territory, between Austrian and Prussian forces.[101] On 21 November Frederick William opened the new session of parliament in Berlin with a bellicose speech denouncing the invasion of Hesse-Kassel and justifying the mobilization of the army.[102] Three days later Schwarzenberg issued an ultimatum calling for complete Prussian withdrawal from Hessian territory in forty-eight hours. War now seemed unavoidable.

But in fact it did not come. A detailed account of the events that led to the well-known Olmütz conference between Otto von Manteuffel and Schwarzenberg on 28–9 November 1850 lies outside the scope of this study. It is quite clear, however, that both Manteuffel and the Austrian emissary to Berlin, Count Prokesch, were desperate for a settlement. Manteuffel believed that a face-to-face meeting with Schwarzenberg was essential. Frederick William agreed, helped to arrange it diplomatically, and sent Manteuffel off to meet his Austrian counterpart in the Bohemian city of Olmütz. Though Schwarzenberg at first continued to pursue a harsh and uncompromising line, he had softened by the second day.[103] The result was the Punctation of Olmütz, in which Prussia proclaimed its willingness to participate in the federal execution against Hesse-Kassel, without, however, formally recognizing the resurrected German Confederation. Manteuffel agreed in effect to demobilize the Prussian army, and both sides also agreed to participate as equals in conferences to be held in Dresden on the reform and restructuring of the Confederation. Those conferences took place in the spring of 1851, and led to the formal restoration (with some modifications) of the old structures of 1815.[104]

---

[100] FW IV to Nicholas I, 6 Nov. 1850, in Willy Andreas, 'Der Briefwechsel zwischen König Friedrich Wilhelm IV. von Preußen und des Zaren Nikolaus I. von Rußland in den Jahren 1848 bis 1850: Ein Beitrag zur Geschichte der russisch-preußischen Beziehungen', *FBPG* 43 (1930), 163; Graf Münster to Leopold von Gerlach, 13 Nov. 1850, GStA Merseburg, Rep. 92 Leopold von Gerlach Nr. 10, Bl. 308.

[101] FW IV to Nicholas I, 10 Nov. 1850, GStA Merseburg, HA Rep. 50 J Nr. 1205, Bl. 134–5.

[102] Orr, 'Foundation', 518–19.

[103] J. Hoffmann, 'Prokesch', 64–7, 120–2; FW IV to Otto von Manteuffel, 25 Nov. 1850 (telegram), GStA Berlin, III. Hauptabteilung Nr. 75; Austensen, 'Policy', 872–3.

[104] Text of the Punctation in E. R. Huber (ed.), *Dokumente*, i. 449–50. See also FW IV to *Staatsministerium*, 30 Nov. 1850, GA, 'Abschriften', xx. 245–6; Francis Joseph to FW IV, 1 Dec. 1850,

[cont. on p. 210]

One historian has described the Olmütz Punctation as 'one of those events of such great symbolism for German history that it has been over-interpreted since the day after its conclusion'.[105] *Kleindeutsch* and national-liberal historians, like their earlier counterparts in the Prussian chambers, condemned it as a disgrace and a shame, while conservatives were divided on the issue. But the question of Olmütz's significance for German politics after the 1850s need not concern us here. More important is the question of immediate winners and losers. Otto von Manteuffel and the Austrian diplomat Prokesch were undoubtedly big winners; the latter had taken considerable political risks to urge a settlement with Prussia, while Manteuffel had come close to resignation on several occasions in November.[106] But he emerged victorious, and, although Frederick William IV never liked him very much, he officially became Minister President and Foreign Minister on 4 December 1850—posts which he kept for almost eight years, until the autumn of 1858. Despite being pilloried by *kleindeutsch* nationalists as the author of Prussia's worst disgrace since 1806, Manteuffel never doubted that he had made the right choice, that in the autumn of 1850 'we had no option but to choose between an alliance with the great powers of Europe or with the revolution; in that situation the choice was not in doubt'.[107]

Schwarzenberg was also a winner. He had never really intended utterly to humiliate Prussia. Rather, his principal aim had always been 'to get rid of the radical leadership in Prussia and to strike an agreement with conservatives with whom one could safely share power in Germany'.[108] Those conservatives, most notably Leopold von Gerlach and his friends, were, of course, also big winners. They were at last free of their nemesis Radowitz, though they themselves had contributed almost nothing to that outcome. Indeed, their influence during the autumn crisis of 1850 had been negligible. In contrast to November 1848, one could hardly speak of a court Camarilla at all, but rather of Gerlach as Adjutant-General assisted by his younger protégés Marcus Niebuhr and Edwin von Manteuffel. In September and October, when it appeared that Radowitz might triumph after all, Gerlach withdrew to his estate at Rohrbeck and, weary of the King's distrust and bad temper, attempted to resign.[109] But in the end, he and his friends in the *Kreuzzeitung* party had emerged victorious. His brother Ludwig took a grim satisfaction from this 'brilliant victory', and believed that it should be followed up quickly and ruthlessly: 'Radowitz's departure must be made great, important, and decisive.' Perhaps the time had come to get rid of Bunsen as well.[110] Leopold, always more world-weary and phlegmatic than his zealous

GStA Merseburg, HA Rep. 50 J Nr. 939, Bl. 36–39ᵛ. On the Dresden conferences, see Hans Julius Schoeps, *Von Olmütz nach Dresden*.

[105] Austensen, 'Policy', 872.   [106] J. Hoffmann, 'Prokesch', 66.

[107] Leopold von Gerlach, diary (7 Jan. 1851), GA, 'Abschriften', viii. 6; O. von Manteuffel, *Unter Friedrich Wilhelm IV.*, i. 383–5.

[108] Austensen, 'Policy', 872.

[109] See Leopold's correspondence with Ludwig from 25 Sept. to 16 Oct. in E. L. von Gerlach, *Von der Revolution*, ii. 708–13; Leopold von Gerlach to FW IV, 3 Nov. 1850, GA, 'Abschriften', xxx. 7–8; Orr, 'Foundation', 485–6.

[110] Ludwig von Gerlach to Leopold von Gerlach, 5 and 6 Nov., 11 Dec. 1850, GA, 'Abschriften', xx. 218, 220, 260; Leopold von Gerlach, diary (13 Dec. 1850), ibid. vii. 245.

younger brother, deplored Ludwig's 'shouts of victory'. A victory had indeed been achieved, but at what a price! In contrast to October 1848, when the King had been on their side, this time they had embarked on political combat without him, and the 'heroes of this battle' had all come away with serious wounds.[111] Moreover, the party of the victors had been remarkably small and weak, and its triumph had by no means been inevitable. People like the Prince of Prussia had been driven by 'intellectual poverty and fear' to be 'full of heroic determination against Austria and full of cowardice towards the revolution', while others, like Stahl, Bismarck, and even Marcus Niebuhr, had been waverers.[112]

'The future belongs to us', Radowitz supposedly remarked to Otto von Manteuffel upon his departure from office.[113] But in truth he and his erstwhile allies, the Gotha liberals and the Prince of Prussia, had suffered a major defeat—and in Radowitz's case it was irremediable. In January 1851, shortly before his return from England, he wrote to Frederick William that he could no longer be of use to him, and he yearned for nothing more 'than to withdraw into deep obscurity'.[114] His wish was fulfilled, at least to an extent. He never again occupied an important position in Prussian service; even his appointment as director of military education in 1852 aroused the ire of his enemies. He devoted part of his time to writing, with some success.[115] But the great efforts of his adult life—to build a 'social kingdom' and to forge an alliance between the monarchical principle and the 'cause of the nation'—had, to all appearances, been dismal failures. Spurned by his erstwhile friends at court, rejected by his one-time liberal allies, and only occasionally in contact with his royal mentor, he lived a secluded and quiet life. His health had never been robust, and on Christmas Day 1853 he died at the age of 56. Leopold von Gerlach noted in his diary that the death of his old friend and rival had filled him with sadness. Before Radowitz's body was removed to Erfurt for final burial, Frederick William IV broke with protocol by attending a memorial service for his friend at a church in Berlin, where, one observer remarked, he was 'moved in the deepest way, as everyone could see'.[116]

But how had Frederick William responded to his friend's earlier political demise? And what were the consequences of Radowitz's Union proposals, and their ultimate defeat, for the King's own monarchical project? Radowitz's departure, Brandenburg's sudden death, and the ups and downs of the autumn crisis with Austria had all shaken the monarch's never very steady nerves; but the loss of Radowitz was clearly the hardest blow for him. His mood was as bleak as in the

---

[111] Leopold von Gerlach to Ludwig von Gerlach, 7 Nov. 1850, in E. L. von Gerlach, *Von der Revolution*, ii. 718.

[112] Leopold von Gerlach, diary (7 Jan. 1851), GA, 'Abschriften', viii. 7.

[113] Leopold von Gerlach to Ludwig von Gerlach, 7 Nov. 1850, in E. L. von Gerlach, *Von der Revolution*, ii. 718.

[114] Radowitz to FW IV, 16 Jan. 1851, in Radowitz, *Briefe und Aufzeichnungen*, 380–1.

[115] Meinecke, *Radowitz*, 524–6.

[116] Leopold von Gerlach, diary (3 Jan. 1854), GA, 'Abschriften', xi. 1; Malsen to King Max II, 7 Jan. 1854, BayHStA, MA III 2634.

summer of 1848, and his behaviour very similar. Almost immediately after his friend's resignation he had spoken of effacing himself again, and even of abdication.[117] He was 'overcome and crushed' by grief, he wrote to Radowitz; and he compared his feelings at Radowitz's loss to his emotions at the time of his father's death a decade earlier.[118] During the next few weeks he was by turns depressed, apathetic, full of self-pity, and overwhelmed by utter despair. It was so bad in November 1850, in fact, that the 'constantly weeping' Queen asserted that she could not hold out much longer; only Olmütz had seemed to revitalize her.[119]

There can be no doubt that the autumn crisis of 1850 had left deep psychic wounds. 'Let God in His mercy prove that William, Radowitz, and I are wrong!', he had cried out on 4 November. 'I believe that we are not.' And when he was forced to admit defeat, it was almost unbearable. Count Prokesch, who saw him on the tenth, wrote that he was 'in a fearful condition, broken to the depths of his being'.[120] Thus he often seemed distracted, unable to concentrate on the job at hand. At Count Brandenburg's funeral on 9 November, for example, Frederick William picked up a small pillow that was intended to display the dead man's military decorations; using his index finger, the King then inscribed 'imaginary letters' on the pillow and raised it to heaven 'with loud sighs of devotion'. Why had he done this?, asked Varnhagen. 'A note to the dear Lord? A report? A recommendation? Pangs of conscience, or just for show? All of these things together.' Then the King suddenly wanted to leave, and the Queen had to remind him that he had forgotten to console the widow. Even or especially at the times when he was most depressed, Frederick William IV remained both theatrical and self-absorbed.[121] Above all, though, he was angry, and for several weeks after the events of early November he lashed out furiously at his ministers. They were a '*Hundepack*', he said, and War Minister Stockhausen in particular deserved to go before a court martial for his behaviour during the Hessian crisis; but it was Otto von Manteuffel who bore the brunt of the royal scorn.[122] This hostility was, Gerlach implied, one consequence of the King's continued feelings of affection and guilt towards Radowitz: 'And so the ruins and wreckage of Radowitz are still in our way, and especially in the heart of the King . . . '.[123]

Leopold von Gerlach once noted that Radowitz had brought the King 'into contradiction with himself'.[124] There is a lot of truth to this remark, as Radowitz himself seemed to recognize. More accurately, perhaps, Radowitz had forced the King, wit-

---

[117] Leopold von Gerlach to Edwin von Manteuffel, 4 Nov. 1850, GStA Merseburg, Rep. 92 Edwin von Manteuffel B II 19, Bl. 13; Leopold von Gerlach, diary (3 Nov. 1850), GA, 'Abschriften', vii. 212.

[118] FW IV to Radowitz, 2 Nov. 1850, in Radowitz, *Briefe und Aufzeichnungen*, 346; cf. FW IV to Radowitz, 5 Nov. 1850, GStA Berlin, BPH Rep. 50 Nr. 91.

[119] Leopold von Gerlach, diary (4 and 25 Nov. 1850), GA, 'Abschriften', vii. 213, 228.

[120] FW IV to Nicholas I, 4 Nov. 1850, in Andreas, 'Briefwechsel', 163; Prokesch to Schwarzenberg, 10 Nov. 1850, in Prokesch (ed.), *Aus den Briefen*, 180.

[121] K. A. Varnhagen, *Tagebücher*, ed. Ludmilla Assing, 2nd edn., vii. 404 (addendum to entry for 9 Nov. 1850).

[122] Leopold von Gerlach, diary (15 and 28 Nov., and 12 and 15 Dec. 1850), GA, 'Abschriften', vii. 219, 233, 246, 247.

[123] Leopold von Gerlach, diary (15 Dec. 1850), ibid. vii. 247.   [124] Meinecke, *Radowitz*, 495.

tingly or unwittingly, to face the consequences of those contradictions. We have argued repeatedly in this study that, in his innermost being, Frederick William IV remained consistently loyal to a complex and multifaceted vision or project of monarchy that we have likened to a *Gesamtkunstwerk*. Although his feelings about his project remained consistent, the project itself was not free of contradictions. He wanted a *ständisch* monarchy, and he wanted to be a popular, modern monarch; and at the same time that he wanted to embrace the national cause *and* expand Prussian power in Germany, he dreamed of a restored empire with a Habsburg emperor. Radowitz had become keenly aware of all these contradictions, and somehow hoped that, through his own advice and counsel, the King would too, and that he would resolve them.

Radowitz was one of the few members of Frederick William's entourage who was capable of sustained political growth and continuous intellectual development. By 1850 he had come a long way from the *ständisch*, Christian-German notions of his young adulthood. Leopold von Gerlach had not been far wrong when he argued in 1851 that Radowitz had really become a Gotha liberal.[125] In fact, had Radowitz lived longer, and had his political instincts been stronger and his opportunities more numerous, he might have become a kind of Tory democrat with strong constitutional-monarchical and Christian-social tendencies. But that is, of course, sheer speculation.[126] Frederick William IV could never follow such a path, as Radowitz himself acknowledged. Thus he had always been pessimistic about his own chances for success. Given the circumstances of the times, his own nature, and the personality of the King, Radowitz could never have become a Richelieu, a Kaunitz, a Metternich, and especially not a Bismarck. To his enemies Radowitz may have been a 'Cagliostro', 'the great wizard';[127] but Radowitz himself knew that Frederick William IV would never let himself be dominated or directed by any one individual, no matter how strong his personal attachment might be. In a real sense, then, Heinrich von Sybel's argument—that Frederick William was responsible, in a direct and personal way, for the actions and decisions taken in his reign—was largely correct.[128] A number of factors constrained and directed royal power in Prussia, which had never been absolute and which had been severely shaken by the upheavals of 1848–50. But it remained formidable, even in November 1850. How, though, would the structures of monarchy respond to the new institutions that had emerged as a result of those upheavals? How would those responses affect the structure and distribution of power within the Prussian state? In short, how would the changed economic and social circumstances of the post-1848 era affect the place of the monarchy in Prussian society? These were the critical questions that were to shape the last eight years of Frederick William's active reign.

---

[125] Leopold von Gerlach to Ludwig von Gerlach, 1 July 1851, in E. L. von Gerlach, *Von der Revolution*, ii. 749.

[126] See Meinecke's own reflections in his *Radowitz*, 525–36.

[127] Stockhausen to Leopold von Gerlach, 26 Oct. 1850, GA, 'Abschriften', xx. 206.

[128] Heinrich von Sybel, *Die Begründung des Deutschen Reiches durch Wilhelm I. Vornehmlich nach den preußischen Staatsakten*, i, 4th edn. (Munich, 1892), 104.

9
Becoming 'Constitutional': Reshaping Monarchy in a Post-Revolutionary Age, 1849–1854

An Oath and a Bullet, 1850

After 1848 Frederick William IV always felt that his native city, the home of his erst-while 'dear Berliners', had betrayed him in the March revolution, and he tried to keep his visits to that 'disloyal' place to a minimum. Certain royal activities in the city were, however, unavoidable. One of those occasions took place on 6 February 1850. After spending the previous night in Potsdam, the King travelled to the capital early on the morning of the sixth, and then appeared in the Knights' Hall of the royal palace in all the finery of his office: a uniform of Prussian blue, with sash and sabre, and wearing the splendid helmet of the Garde du Corps. But his majestic attire could not disguise the fact that he was about to do something which he found almost inde-scribably demeaning: take an oath to a written constitution, in the presence of his ministers, the royal princes, and the members of the country's two parliamentary chambers. How far he had come since that day, three years earlier, when he had opened the first United Diet in the same palace and had pledged that he would never permit a scrap of paper to come between himself and his people!

The King's oath-taking ceremony had been preceded by two months of bitter political wrangling over the constitution's final form and the nature of Frederick William's oath to it. Faced with the prospect of a constitutional oath that might for-ever dash his dream of a *ständisch* revival, Frederick William had embarked on a com-plex series of delaying manœuvres in late 1849 and early 1850. After several weeks of confused, exhausting, and bitter governmental crisis, an acceptable compromise was finally worked out.[1] The architect of that compromise was Joseph Maria von Radowitz. The major bone of contention concerned the composition of the First Chamber, the upper house of the parliament. Now, at Radowitz's urging, the actual reorganization of the First Chamber would be delayed until 1852. The King assent-

---

[1] On the constitutional crisis of Dec. 1849–Jan. 1850, see Erich Jordan, *Friedrich Wilhelm IV. und der preußische Adel bei Umwandlung der ersten Kammer in das Herrenhaus: 1850 bis 1854* (Berlin, 1909), 69–149; Anna Clausen, *Die Stellung Leopold von Gerlachs zum Abschluß des preußischen Verfassungswerkes unter Friedrich Wilhelm IV.* (Weida, 1914), 13–51; William J. Orr, jun., 'The Foundation of the *Kreuzzeitung* Party in Prussia, 1848–1850' (Ph.D. thesis; Wisconsin-Madison, 1971), 374–426; Günther Grünthal, *Parlamentarismus in Preußen 1848/49–1857/58: Preußischer Konstitutionalismus—Parlament und Regierung in der Reaktionsära* (Düsseldorf, 1982), 159–74; Wilhelm Füßl, *Professor in der Politik: Friedrich Julius Stahl (1802–1861). Das monarchische Prinzip und seine Umsetzung in die parlamentarische Praxis* (Götting, 1988), 275–84; Hans-Christof Kraus, 'Ernst Ludwig von Gerlach: Politisches Denken und Handeln eines preußischen Altkonservativen' (Diss.; 2 vols.; Göttingen, 1991), i. 324–34, ii. 245–52.

ed to the fundamentals of this arrangement; and so, despite the frantic opposition of Camarilla and *Kreuzzeitung*, Radowitz's timely intervention had saved the day.[2] The King publicly proclaimed the new constitution on 31 January, and a week later he showed up to take his oath.[3]

The ceremony began at 11 a.m. After all the deputies and ministers had assembled in the Knights' Hall, the King entered the room and proceeded directly to the throne, in front of which stood a table with a copy of the constitution. The speech that preceded the oath was, to put it mildly, ambivalent. Frederick William began by reminding the assembled deputies that the constitution had emerged in a year which future generations would wish to expunge from Prussian history 'in tears, but in vain'. Nevertheless, he continued, it represented the work of men who had rescued the throne and had earned his undying gratitude. He called upon the members of the chambers to help him resist those who would misuse their new freedom. The constitution, he affirmed, would make it possible for him to govern effectively, 'for in Prussia the King must govern, and I do not govern because I enjoy it, God knows!, but because it is part of the divine order of things . . .' Then he finally took the long-awaited oath. The whole thing was over in two hours. To Ludwig von Gerlach's great disgust, Frederick William made a point of chatting afterwards with a number of prominent liberal deputies.[4]

Three months later, on 22 May 1850, Frederick William IV was in his unloved capital city again. At noon, preparing to leave for Potsdam, he arrived with the Queen at the railway station when a man in an army uniform rushed up to him and fired a pistol at close range. The bullet penetrated the King's right forearm. Although no serious nerve-damage resulted, the wound bled profusely. Amid scenes of great confusion, the would-be assassin was viciously beaten and then arrested. He gave his name as Maximilian Joseph Sefeloge, a twenty-nine-year-old ex-artilleryman who had been discharged from the army for mental problems. The King was rushed to Charlottenburg, where he spent three weeks recuperating. This time, in contrast to Tschech's earlier assassination-attempt, there was comparatively little public outcry. Varnhagen asserted that many embittered Prussians, from aristocrats to peasants, were sorry that Sefeloge's bullet had missed its mark.[5] Indeed, some observers hinted that Sefeloge's action had been the work of disaffected ultra-rightists who

[2] Count Brandenburg to Radowitz, 29 Jan. 1850, GStA Merseburg, Rep. 92 Joseph Maria von Radowitz d. Ä. 1. Reihe Nr. 66, Bl. 35; Orr, 'Foundation', 412.

[3] Grünthal, *Parlamentarismus*, 167–74. Text of the constitution of 1850 in Ernst Rudolf Huber (ed.), *Dokumente zur deutschen Verfassungsgeschichte*, i: *Deutsche Verfassungsdokumente 1803–1850* (Stuttgart, 1961), 401–14.

[4] Friedrich Wilhelm IV., *Reden und Trinksprüche Sr. Majestät Friedrich Wilhelm des Vierten, Königes von Preußen* (Leipzig, 1855), 116–19; Herman von Petersdorff, *König Friedrich Wilhelm der Vierte* (Stuttgart, 1900), 168–70; Ludwig von Gerlach to Leopold von Gerlach, 9 Feb. 1850, GA, 'Abschriften', xx. 13.

[5] Leopold von Gerlach, diary (22 May 1850), GA, 'Abschriften', vii. 108–9; Adolf Streckfuß, *500 Jahre Berliner Geschichte: Vom Fischerdorf zur Weltstadt. Geschichte und Sage*, ii, 4th edn. (Berlin, 1886), 1291–4; Günter Richter, 'Zwischen Revolution und Reichsgründung (1848–1870)', in Wolfgang Ribbe (ed.), *Geschichte Berlins* (Munich, 1987), ii: *Von der Märzrevolution bis zur Gegenwart*, 643–4. K. A. Varnhagen von Ense, *Tagebücher*, ed. Ludmilla Assing, 2nd edn., vii. 197, 205 (25 and 30 May 1850).

wanted to make way for the Prince of Prussia. Both Varnhagen and Karl Marx believed that Sefeloge had belonged to a government-sponsored royalist organization, the Loyalty League with God for King and Fatherland, and speculated that leading members of the aristocracy and military had used the wretched ex-soldier as an instrument in a plot to kill the King. Even Leopold von Gerlach came around to the idea that it was possible that Sefeloge had been part of a conspiracy which 'is not located in Berlin's democratic movement but somewhere else, such as the reactionary party'.[6] Either out of bureaucratic negligence or through a cover-up, Sefeloge was declared incompetent to stand trial and was sent to a lunatic asylum near Halle, where he remained under close observation until his death in 1859.[7] Whatever the source of Sefeloge's crime, it heightened an obsession with security issues which had been growing in Frederick William IV since the spring of 1848. His old faith in the loyalty of his simple *Preußenvolk* was gone, while he also acknowledged the possibility that the assassination attempt may have been arranged by members of the very 'party' to which Leopold von Gerlach himself adhered.[8] Such suspiciousness, Gerlach feared, could lead to a 'tyrannical regime' in Prussia; and, indeed, Frederick William's government and police responded to Sefeloge's deed by raiding the houses of suspected radicals and issuing a restrictive press-law.[9]

The two incidents that we have just described—the King's oath to the constitution on 6 February 1850 and Sefeloge's assassination attempt in May—illustrate two different sides of the decade of reaction, the last decade of Frederick William IV's active reign. On the one hand, Prussia had emerged from the revolution of 1848 as a constitutional state with an elected parliament, a reality to which the King of Prussia had to accommodate himself, however unwillingly. On the other hand, the decade also witnessed a significant expansion of the state's repressive apparatus, with restrictions on freedom of assembly and association, a tightening of press censorship, intensified police-surveillance of alleged radicals, and the regular use of spies, agents, and press manipulation.

Frederick William's own position, as the two incidents that we have described suggest, was ambivalent. His power remained immense, but he had to accept real constitutional limits on that power. He still wanted to reorganize religious life along 'apostolic' lines, but his efforts along those lines were constantly frustrated, as we saw at the end of Chapter 4. He still yearned to be popular, but he had become deeply suspicious of his subjects and wary even of his closest associates. After 1850 he was no longer very effective in his occasional attempts to influence and shape public opin-

---

[6] Hubertus Fischer, 'Der "Treubund mit Gott für König und Vaterland": Ein Beitrag zur Reaktion in Preußen', *JGMOD* 24 (1975), 80–4; Leopold von Gerlach, diary (5 Feb. 1851), GA, 'Abschriften', viii. 37, 38.

[7] FW IV to Carl Wilhelm Saegert, 14 Feb. 1851, GStA Berlin, BPH Rep. 192 Carl Wilhelm Saegert Nr. 37; Carl Ludwig von Hinckeldey to Direktion der Prov.-Irren-Anstalt zu Halle, 25 Feb. 1851, GStA Berlin, BPH Rep. 50 Nr. 235, Bl. 1; FW IV to Saegert, 7 Feb. 1851, ibid., BPH Rep. 192 Carl Wilhelm Saegert Nr. 37.

[8] Leopold von Gerlach, diary (5 Feb. 1851), GA, 'Abschriften', viii. 36.

[9] A. Streckfuß, *500 Jahre*, ii. 1294–5.

ion. It was mainly in his annual Speech from the Throne at the opening of parliamentary sessions that he managed to show occasional flashes of his former rhetorical gifts.[10] On the surface, at least, he continued to adhere to his old views, and his ruling style seemed little changed. But in fact, Frederick William *did* change during those years. Although he held fast to his vision of a *ständisch* monarchy, he was far more adept at adjusting himself to new political and social realities than has usually been suggested. During the 1850s both court and parliament were the scenes of endless political conflicts which Frederick William was not always able to control, but which he often exploited for his own ends. His task was not easy: 'It's quite a job trying to rule in Prussia these days,' he sighed, with considerable justification, in 1852.[11] Certainly he made many mistakes, and there seems little doubt that the popularity of monarchical institutions declined during the 1850s. Nevertheless, during the 'decade of reaction' Frederick William IV helped to ensure that the sovereign and his court remained at the centre of the entire Prussian system. This chapter will first evaluate the new, post-revolutionary shape of Prussian society and Prussian politics during the reaction decade. Then it will consider how Frederick William IV tried to adapt the monarchy and monarchical institutions to the new conditions that he confronted, focusing first on his links to the country's security apparatus and then on his attempts to revise the constitution in his favour.

After the Revolution: Society and Politics during the Reaction Decade

During the decade of reaction Prussia's traditional rulers had to adjust themselves to far-reaching processes of demographic, economic, and social change. Those changes formed part of a longer evolutionary process which had begun before 1848; the revolutions of that year did not, for example, have a significant effect upon such things as population trends, rates of urbanization, or shifts in occupational structures.[12] In the early 1850s there also persisted what might be described as a 'continuity of misery'; until 1854 much of Germany was afflicted by poor harvests and rising prices, which were especially hard on some kinds of artisans and agricultural workers, and contributed to the massive emigration of those years.[13] These conditions could not obscure the fact, however, that the general economic situation, especially for business enterprise, did improve significantly in the 1850s.[14] The decade of reaction

[10] Grünthal, *Parlamentarismus*, 415.

[11] FW IV to Saegert, 18 May 1852, GStA Berlin, BPH Rep. 192 Carl Wilhelm Saegert Nr. 42.

[12] Jürgen Kocka, 'Zur Schichtung der preußischen Bevölkerung während der industriellen Revolution', in Wilhelm Treue (ed.), *Geschichte als Aufgabe: Festschrift für Otto Büsch zu seinem 60. Geburtstag* (Berlin, 1988), 390.

[13] Reinhard Rürup, *Deutschland im 19. Jahrhundert 1815–1871* (Göttingen, 1984), 208; Günther Grünthal, 'Crown and Parliament in Prussia 1848–1866', *Parliaments, Estates and Representation*, 5 (1985), 169–70.

[14] Among many descriptions, see esp. James J. Sheehan, *German History 1770–1866* (Oxford, 1989), ch. 12; Wolfram Siemann, *Gesellschaft im Aufbruch: Deutschland 1849–1871* (Frankfurt am Main, 1990), 89–121; and Wilhelm Treue, 'Preußens Wirtschaft vom Dreißigjährigen Krieg bis zum Nationalsozialismus', in Otto Büsch (ed.), *Handbuch der preußischen Geschichte*, ii: *Das 19. Jahrhundert und große Themen der Geschichte Preußens* (Berlin, 1992), 526–44.

coincided with a phase of economic expansion that continued, despite interruptions like the international financial crisis of 1857–8, until the crash of 1873. Examples of that expansion are legion. They include the rapid development of joint-stock companies and the establishment of new kinds of financial institutions—e.g., joint-stock and commandite banks—specializing in industrial investment. Most spectacular, perhaps, was the development of railways after mid-century. In 1849, for instance, 107 million Taler were invested in nineteen private railway companies in Prussia, but by 1856 that amount had increased to more than 273 million. And of course other industries could point to similarly impressive patterns of growth. Between 1850 and 1860 coal production in Prussia grew by 183 per cent; and in the Ruhr valley alone the number of individuals employed in coal-mines more than doubled during the same period.[15] The 1850s thus witnessed the beginning of Germany's 'take-off' into sustained industrial growth. These processes obviously worked to Prussia's long-term economic and financial advantage, especially *vis-à-vis* Austria.

Virtually all of Prussia's élites—old and new, political and economic, from the landed aristocracy, the military, and the bureaucracy to the *Wirtschaftsbürger* and local notables of various kinds—experienced a series of what German scholars like to call *Lernprozesse* during the reaction decade. The effects of those 'learning processes' are still ambiguous and a bit obscure. The landed aristocracy, for example, had been stripped of a number of privileges during the revolution; like the monarchy, to which they had been bound for generations, aristocrats had to adjust themselves to a changed constellation of social, political, and economic forces after 1849. To be sure, the reaction did make possible the recovery of some important aristocratic privileges which had been lost in the maelstrom of 1848. For example, the relatively liberal local and regional government laws of March 1850, which would have reduced Junker political influence in the countryside, were repealed in June 1852, and thereafter the Junkers were able to regain manorial police-powers and the right to designate village officials (*Schulzen* and *Schöffen*). The renewed police-powers of estate owners were confirmed in 1855 and largely remained in place until the First World War.[16] All the same, the aristocracy had to accept the permanence of many revolutionary innovations, such as the Commutation Law of 1850, which essentially completed the agrarian reforms of the early nineteenth century, and the elimination of patrimonial courts on the countryside.[17] Above all, perhaps, the aristocracy had to accept the permanence of parliamentary and constitutional arrangements; indeed, many aristocrats were quick to respond to the challenge of 1848 by creating quite

---

[15] James M. Brophy, 'Capitulation or Negotiated Settlement? Entrepreneurs and the Prussian State, 1848–1866' (Ph.D. thesis; Bloomington, Ind., 1991), 134; Sheehan, *German History*, 740.

[16] Albrecht Funk, *Polizei und Rechtsstaat: Die Entwicklung des staatlichen Gewaltmonopols in Preußen 1848–1918* (Frankfurt am Main, 1986), 58–9.

[17] Heinrich Heffter, 'Der nachmärzliche Liberalismus: Die Reaktion der fünfziger Jahre', in Hans-Ulrich Wehler (ed.), *Moderne deutsche Sozialgeschichte*, 4th edn. (Cologne, 1973), 181–3; William J. Orr, jun., 'The Prussian Ultra Right and the Advent of Constitutionalism in Prussia', *Canadian Journal of History/Annales canadiennes d'histoire*, 11 (1976), 307; Hans-Ulrich Wehler, *Deutsche Gesellschaftsgeschichte* (Munich, 1987–), ii: *Von der Reformära bis zur industriellen und politischen 'Deutschen Doppel-*
[cont. on p. 219]

modern forms of interest representation and articulation. These ranged from the *Kreuzzeitung* and its 'party' to pressure groups designed to defend the economic interests of East Elbian agrarians.[18] Even before 1848, as we have seen, many aristocrats had begun to adapt themselves to the exigencies of capitalist agriculture, while at the same time large numbers of landed estates were falling into the hands of non-aristocratic purchasers, a process which accelerated after 1848. By 1856 more than 5,000 of Prussia's 12,399 estates (*Rittergüter*) had been taken over by bourgeois owners.[19] These processes of change in the countryside do not mean, however, that Prussia's 'traditional' landed élite had changed its political orientation by the middle of the century, or that, despite the partial *embourgeoisement* of rural society and of aristocratic cultural values, it was yet merging with the country's *Bürgertum*.[20] For all their adaptability, throughout the 1850s Prussia's agrarian élites were characterized by an exclusive caste spirit and had become at best 'pseudodemocratized' (to use Hans Rosenberg's expression). The officer corps, the upper reaches of the bureaucracy, and the court all remained bastions of aristocratic privilege throughout the decade of the 1850s.

Nor is there much evidence to support the notion of a 'feudalization' of the Prussian bourgeoisie during the 1850s. This is not the place to recapitulate the extremely complex discussion concerning the relationship between aristocracy and bourgeoisie in nineteenth-century Germany, or the debate on whether or not that country experienced a 'bourgeois revolution'. Neither *Wirtschaftsbürger*, who were busily making money, nor practitioners of the free professions seemed inclined to imitate aristocratic values, outlooks, or conduct during that decade. Indeed, it has been suggested that in nineteenth-century Germany the bourgeoisie maintained its distance from other social formations and was much less integrated with traditional ruling groups than in other European countries.[21] Certainly that was the case in Prussia during the 1850s. Of course, many wealthy bourgeois did have the means to

revolution' 1815–1845/49, 776; Theodore S. Hamerow, *Restoration, Revolution, Reaction: Economics and Politics in Germany 1815–1871* (Princeton, NJ, 1958), 219–25. Some 640,000 peasants took advantage of the Commutation Law to end their remaining 'feudal' obligations. Francis L. Carsten, *Geschichte der preußischen Junker* (Frankfurt am Main, 1988), 114–15.

[18] Wolfgang Schwentker, *Konservative Vereine und Revolution in Preußen 1848/49: Die Konstituierung des Konservativismus als Partei* (Düsseldorf, 1988), 100–10; Hans Rosenberg, 'Die Pseudodemokratisierung der Rittergutsbesitzerklasse', in id., *Machteliten und Wirtschaftskonjunkturen: Studien zur neueren deutschen Sozial- und Wirtschaftsgeschichte* (Göttingen, 1978), 94 (art. orig. pub. 1958). On the celebrated *Junkerparlament* of Aug. 1848, see Schwentker, *Vereine*, 106–10; Klaus Klatte, 'Die Anfänge des Agrarkapitalismus und der preußische Konservativismus' (Diss.; Hamburg, 1974), 247–72; Gerhard Becker, 'Die Beschlüsse des preußischen Junkerparlaments von 1848', *ZfG* 24 (1976), 889–918.

[19] Rosenberg, 'Pseudodemokratisierung', 88. See also Carsten, *Junker*, 97; David Blackbourn and Geoff Eley, *The Peculiarities of German History: Bourgeois Society and Politics in Nineteenth-Century Germany* (Oxford, 1984), 182.

[20] Rosenberg, 'Pseudodemokratisierung', 91–2; cf. the qualifications of Jürgen Kocka, 'Bürgertum und bürgerliche Gesellschaft im 19. Jahrhundert: Europäische Entwicklungen und deutsche Eigenarten', in id. (with Ute Frevert) (ed.), *Bürgertum im 19. Jahrhundert: Deutschland im europäischen Vergleich* (3 vols.; Munich, 1988), i. 66; and David Blackbourn, 'The Discreet Charm of the German Bourgeoisie', in id., *Populists and Patricians: Essays in Modern German History* (London, 1987), 67–83, esp. 74–6.

[21] Kocka, 'Bürgertum', i, 68.

pursue a lavish and showy life-style after the revolutions of 1848, but such opulence was really 'more plutocratic than aristocratic'.[22] Despite the set-backs of 1848–50 and the political frustrations of the period from 1849 to 1858, the Prussian middle classes remained diverse, distinctive, and, for the most part, resiliently self-confident. For the middle classes during the 1850s, a conviction of unity, of belonging to an 'integrated bourgeois society', transcended differences of education, income, or occupation. One expression of that bourgeois unity was a continued feeling of both superiority and hostility towards the 'traditional' aristocracy and its pretensions.[23] Thus there were comparatively few signs during the reaction decade of an 'alliance', 'fusion', or 'class symbiosis' of bourgeois and aristocratic élites.[24]

It cannot be denied, of course, that many members of the middle classes and the aristocracy in Prussia shared a number of common fears and some common interests. For example, their mutual fear of radicalism and revolutionary republicanism persisted even after the removal, through repression, exile, or inner emigration, of radical democrats and republicans from the political stage. To many middle-class observers as well as to virtually all aristocrats, the continued existence of the monarchy was inextricably bound up with the maintenance of order, stability, the protection of property, and lawful government. Before and after 1848, anti-monarchical voices were relatively rare in Prussia; and, as we have seen, moderate liberals were willing to concede a great deal of decision-making power and authority to the Prussian crown, as long as the crown, for its part, was willing to abide by the principles of a constitutional order. Conditions in the 1850s were especially propitious for a renewal and strengthening of monarchical values; despite differences among Prussia's political and economic élites about the limits of royal authority, there was a general consensus that the country needed a strong and effective monarchy. But what kind of monarchy? Monarchical loyalty did not necessarily mean attachment to the person of the monarch, or acceptance of his particular vision of kingship. It is thus not surprising that the Prussia of the 1850s, far from being politically quiescent, witnessed the emergence of new kinds of political organization and the development of new forms of interest-group representation. In a time of dynamic social and economic change, the whole country was operating under a new set of political and institutional rules. The political setting was thus exceptionally fluid and dynamic, with political factions and alliances shifting in highly complex ways that are sometimes difficult to understand. Those shifts in turn reflect the various 'learning processes' that were going on during the reaction decade.

An inescapable reality for all political actors in Prussia—parliamentary or extra-parliamentary alike—was the permanence of the country's constitutional order. For all its limitations, and despite the desire of many conservatives to eliminate it or crip-

---

[22] Werner Mosse, 'Adel und Bürgertum im Europa des 19. Jahrhunderts: Eine vergleichende Betrachtung', in Kocka (ed.), *Bürgertum im 19. Jahrhundert*, ii. 278.

[23] Thomas Nipperdey, *Deutsche Geschichte 1800–1866: Bürgerwelt und Starker Staat* (Munich, 1983), 728–9.

[24] Brophy, 'Capitulation', chs. 1 and 7; but see also Mosse, 'Adel', esp. 276–8, 300–3, 311–14.

ple it, the constitution was there to stay. It had become a part of Prussia's public life because it offered something to just about everyone, except for adherents of old-fashioned bureaucratic absolutism. Even to ultra-conservatives it provided institutional safeguards against a return to that 'absolutism', which they had abhorred for so long. To a career bureaucrat like Minister President Otto von Manteuffel it offered guarantees against royal caprice and the machinations of the King's informal advisers. To moderate conservatives and moderate liberals it held out the promise of an institutionally secure state based on guaranteed principles of legality (*Rechtsstaat*) within which property rights and good order could be maintained; after all, moderate liberals were certainly not twentieth-century democrats, and the amended constitution's three-class suffrage-system could certainly be turned to their own political advantage.

Accordingly, the years from 1849 to 1858 witnessed the emergence of a new alignment of forces at the summit of the Prussian state: a new kind of relationship between monarchical structures, on the one hand, and cabinet, parliament, bureaucracy, and newly emergent forms of political organization and interest articulation on the other.[25] Although Prussia remained a monarchical state of soldiers and officials, the older 'monarchic-bureaucratic-aristocratic condominium' of the *Vormärz* years was being changed in fundamental and important ways. The historian James M. Brophy has argued that during the 1850s liberal entrepreneurs were engaged in elaborate processes of negotiation with the existing Prussian state and its traditional underpinning of monarchy, army, bureaucracy, and landed property. The result, he contends, was a 'negotiated settlement' from which both sides emerged with real gains. The process of negotiation between business interests and the state had been going on since the 1830s; but by the 1850s and early 1860s it had resulted in an 'amalgamation' of old and new élites. This amalgamation was not the result either of an alliance or a symbiosis of the two groups, but of conflict, political negotiation, and ultimate compromise. It was a process that took place both within and outside the parliamentary arena in a political setting characterized by 'fluid, ill-defined spheres of power'. As a result, Brophy asserts, political power in Prussia was transformed 'from bureaucratic control to a broad consensus between government and society'.[26] There were, of course, limits to that consensus. Many individuals and groups—including radicals, republicans, factory workers, and women—were excluded from it. Prussia remained an authoritarian *Überwachungsstaat* during the reaction decade; bureaucratic chicanery, police surveillance, and censorship, though mild by twentieth-century standards, were nevertheless very real and were significantly extended after 1848. Indeed, no organized group in Prussia—ultra-conservative and radical alike—could escape the embrace of the 'politics of bureaucratic reaction' after 1848–9.[27] Still, Brophy forcefully reminds us of one of the central realities of Prussian

---

[25] Dieter Langewiesche, *Liberalismus in Deutschland* (Frankfurt am Main, 1988), 65; see also John R. Gillis, *The Prussian Bureaucracy in Crisis 1840–1860: Origins of an Administrative Ethos* (Stanford, Calif., 1971), 146. On the concept of 'reaction', see Kraus, 'Gerlach', i. 355–6.

[26] Brophy, 'Capitulation', 272, 389, 399, 401.   [27] Funk, *Polizei*, 59.

history. Prussia always remained an artificial entity; and, just as its borders frequently shifted, so too was the Prussian state constantly being refashioned and re-created. Brophy's concept of a 'negotiated settlement' between bureaucratic and business élites can thus serve more generally as a metaphor to describe the processes by which the Prussian state was remade during the decade of reaction and the New Era that followed it.

His analysis also reminds us that there were limits to the coercive power of the state and its police, even in the early to mid-1850s. Business élites, for example, were constantly and vocally dissatisfied with the policies of August von der Heydt, Minister of Trade and Industry throughout the entire decade. They were frequently able to demonstrate considerable political influence, as in 1856, when the government's unconstitutional attempt to outlaw 'commandite' banks in Prussia was successfully thwarted. Those banks had been introduced as a response to the government's continued reluctance to charter joint-stock banks, which elsewhere on the Continent were demonstrating their extraordinary capacity to mobilize capital for large-scale investment. Frederick William IV and many of his advisers, however, regarded joint-stock financial institutions as dangerous 'French' innovations. Accordingly, by 1856 Prussian entrepreneurs were turning to large-scale commandite organizations, which could elude government regulation more easily than joint-stock institutions. The cabinet in turn responded by drawing up a decree which would have banned large-scale commandite banks. Minister President Otto von Manteuffel, however, believed that the decree was politically dangerous, and after much effort he was able to convince the King not to promulgate it.[28] As a result, the Prussian government had to abandon 'its authority to channel and restrict the availability of credit for financial institutions', just as it was also obliged during those same years to loosen its control over coal and iron production.[29] In short, even during the decade of reaction Prussian officials had to bow to the growing power of industrial capital, which for its part was increasingly able to evade older forms of state tutelage.

Prussia's Catholics were another group that remained politically active in important ways during the reaction years. Although Catholics shared many of the government's conservative sentiments, Catholic leaders were quite successful in their attempts to mobilize opposition to government policies which they viewed as hostile to the church. In 1852, for example, the pro-*Kreuzzeitung* Minister of Religious and Educational Affairs (*Kultusminister*), Karl Otto von Raumer, introduced a series of decrees which were intended to restrict the activities of the Jesuits, who had long been banned from Prussian territory but had been permitted to return after 1848. The 'Raumer Decrees' would have limited Catholic missionary activities in areas with large Protestant populations, and they would have required government permission for Prussians who wanted to study at the Collegium Germanicum in Rome.[30]

[28] Brophy, 'Capitulation', ch. 5; id., 'The Political Calculus of Capital: Banking and the Business Class in Prussia, 1848–1856', *CEH* 25 (1992), 149–76.
[29] Brophy, 'Political Calculus', 172.
[30] Ernst Rudolf Huber and Wolfgang Huber, *Staat und Kirche im 19. und 20. Jahrhundert: Dokumente*
[cont. on p. 223]

Although Frederick William IV seems to have been indifferent to his *Kultusminister*'s proposals, they did reflect a powerful spirit of Evangelical orthodoxy within the *Kreuzzeitung* party itself. The result was a political uproar which in turn influenced parliamentary elections later that year. In some cases, liberals even supported Catholic candidates on the grounds that they were defending constitutional propriety against unwarranted state intrusion into religious affairs. After the election sixty-two lower-house deputies established a *katholische Fraktion*, which in later years often opposed government policies. Ludwig von Gerlach, Raumer's cousin and political ally, believed that the *Kultusminister*'s decrees had gone too far, and he was able to work out a compromise by which the decrees remained on the books but were not enforced.[31]

While liberals and Catholics were not politically impotent during the reaction decade, another characteristic feature of the politically fluid 1850s was a conspicuous lack of political unity on the part of conservative élites; their various disagreements resulted in the emergence of competing conservative factions within and outside the parliament. These factions jockeyed endlessly with each other, with the King, and with Otto von Manteuffel for political advantage and influence. Although everyone seemed to dislike the Minister President, as we shall see in greater detail in the next chapter, he was himself a brilliantly successful political tactician, and he managed to make himself indispensable to his royal master.

Foremost among the various conservative factions was, of course, the circle of the Camarilla and the *Kreuzzeitung*, the celebrated 'small but powerful party' of the far right.[32] It is, in fact, difficult to speak of a functioning Camarilla at all after Rauch's death in 1850. Thereafter, its only real members included Leopold von Gerlach and Marcus Niebuhr, a Gerlach protégé and Privy Councillor. Both men, of course, openly avowed their allegiance to the *Kreuzzeitung* party. The Gerlach-Stahl factions in the chambers, headed by Ludwig von Gerlach and Friedrich Julius Stahl, represented its parliamentary wing, while Hermann Wagener edited the newspaper until 1853. In the aftermath of Olmütz the party was able to secure key positions for a number of its adherents. Thus two committed conservatives, Ferdinand von Westphalen (1799–1876) and Karl Otto von Raumer (1805–59), received the crucial portfolios of Interior Minister and *Kultusminister* respectively. Westphalen, the former district governor of Liegnitz in Silesia, was a solid supporter of the King's *ständisch* ideas, and became notorious for his attempts to increase political control over civil servants, his

zur Geschichte des deutschen Staatskirchenrechts, ii: *Staat und Kirche im Zeitalter des Hochkonstitutionalismus und des Kulturkumpfs 1848–1890* (Berlin, 1976), 69–72.

[31] Ludwig von Gerlach, diary (13 Sept. 1852), in Ernst Ludwig Von Gerlach, *Von der Revolution zum Norddeutschen Bund: Politik und Ideengut der preußischen Hochkonservativen 1848–1866. Aus dem Nachlaß von Ernst Ludwig von Gerlach*, ed. Hellmut Diwald (2 vols.; Göttingen, 1970), i. 313; Leopold von Gerlach, diary (14 Sept. 1852), GA, 'Abschriften', ix. 168–9; Jonathan Sperber, *Popular Catholicism in Nineteenth-Century Germany* (Princeton, NJ, 1984), 61, 105–6; Simon Hyde, 'Roman Catholicism and the Prussian State in the Early 1850s', *CEH* 24 (1991), 111–19; Grünthal, *Parlamentarismus*, 400–3; Kraus, 'Gerlach', i. 369–70, ii. 278.

[32] Kurt Borries, *Preußen im Krimkrieg (1853–1856)* (Stuttgart, 1930), ch. 2.

repressive press-policies, and his manipulation of elections. Raumer, a former district governor of Frankfurt an der Oder, was a cousin of the Gerlachs and a man whose theological and ecclesiastical notions were in such perfect accord with their own that Ludwig once called him the '*only* really reliable minister' in the cabinet. Nevertheless, he was tactically rather clumsy and even inept, and some of his initiatives backfired, as in the case of the 'Raumer Decrees' of 1852.[33] In 1851 another supporter of the *Kreuzzeitung*, Otto von Bismarck, became Prussia's representative to the Diet of the resuscitated German Confederation in Frankfurt am Main, and in the same year one of Stolberg's sons-in-law, the ultra-reactionary Hans Hugo von Kleist-Retzow (1814–92), replaced the moderately liberal former Minister President Rudolf von Auerswald as governor of the Rhine province. An ideological bull in a political china-shop, Kleist managed to antagonize Rhenish liberals and Catholics alike; and, like Karl von Raumer, his clumsy activities tended to encourage, rather than discourage, pro-constitutional political activity in the Rhineland. Then, in early 1852, Ludwig von Gerlach's brother-in-law, Baron Senfft von Pilsach, became governor of Pomerania. He turned out to be a vastly more effective administrator than Kleist, and during his long tenure he put a permanent stamp on his province. Although Leopold von Gerlach had at first been sceptical about this appointment, he quickly realized that Senfft's considerable persuasive powers with the King could often be extremely helpful to the so-called 'court party'.[34] Finally, the *Kreuzzeitung* party could also count on two strategically placed allies in St Petersburg: Theodor Rochus von Rochow, Prussian Minister to Russia and brother of the former Interior Minister; and Count Hugo zu Münster, Rauch's successor as Military Plenipotentiary to the Tsar's court. Their voluminous, and often brutally frank, correspondence with Leopold von Gerlach provided the Adjutant-General with detailed information to which not even the Minister President had access. Münster was also a close friend of Edwin von Manteuffel, who remained one of the King's aides-de-camp; even when Manteuffel received a regimental command in Düsseldorf, Frederick William continued to use him for delicate diplomatic missions.[35]

[33] Ludwig von Gerlach to Leopold von Gerlach, 27 Oct. 1851, GA, 'Abschriften', xxi. 170. On Westphalen, see, *inter alia*, *ADB*, xlii. 221–6 (Friedrich Thimme); and, on his political mobilization of civil servants, Gillis, *Bureaucracy*, 164–6, as well as the older analysis by Fritz Hartung, 'Studien zur Geschichte der preußischen Verwaltung', in id., *Staatsbildende Kräfte der Neuzeit: Gesammelte Aufsätze* (Berlin, 1961), 255–60. Westphalen's sister Jenny was married to Karl Marx. On Raumer, see *ADB*, xxvii. 418–20.

[34] On Bismarck's appointment, see, most recently, Lothar Gall, *Bismarck: The White Revolutionary*, trans. J. A. Underwood (2 vols.; London, 1986), i, ch. 3; Ernst Engelberg, *Bismarck: Urpreuße und Reichsgründer* (Berlin, 1985), 363–99; Otto Pflanze, *Bismarck and the Development of Germany*, i: *The Period of Unification, 1815–1871*, 2nd edn. (Princeton, NJ, 1990), 74–6. On Kleist-Retzow, see, above all, Herman von Petersdorff, *Kleist-Retzow: Ein Lebensbild* (Stuttgart, 1907), esp. 194–302. On Senfft's appointment, see Paul Haake, 'Ernst Freiherr Senfft von Pilsach als Politiker', *FBPG* 53 (1941), 90, and Herman von Petersdorff, 'Oberpräsident v. Senfft-Pilsach', in Petersdorff, *Deutsche Männer und Francn: Biographische Skizzen vornehmlich zur Geschichte Preußens im 18. und 19. Jahrhundert* (Berlin, 1913), 157–9; Leopold von Gerlach to Senfft, 24 Jan. 1853 and 16 Dec. 1854, GStA Merseburg, Rep. 92 Ernst Freiherr Senfft von Pilsach B 3, Bl. 44–44a, 49.

[35] See Münster's reports to Edwin von Manteuffel from 1850 to 1856, in *Deutsche Revue*, 38/1 (1913), 9–25, 172–93, 297–309; ibid. 38/2 (1913), 60–70, 183–97, 326–37. Cf. Orr, 'Foundation', 549–51.

Stahl and Ludwig von Gerlach, the parliamentary leaders of the *Kreuzzeitung* party, were also its leading intellectuals and political theorists. Despite some important differences between them, both men sought to learn from the mistakes of the *Vormärz* era and lay the foundations of a modern conservative movement which combined tactical flexibility with a fixed commitment to conservative, and especially monarchical, values. Although, as we have seen, neither Stahl nor Gerlach was ever personally close to the King, both continued to avow their loyalty to him, and especially to his office. In an essay of 1849 which has rightly been described as the first 'party programme' in the history of Prussian conservatism, Stahl affirmed the constitution as 'the legally guaranteed unitary order of the entire public realm'. At the same time, he insisted

We shall hold firmly, even in a constitutional state, to real, true monarchy. We do not want the king simply because he is regarded as a necessary or useful cog in the mechanism of the state, as academic theory would have it; rather, we want the king because of his holy right to the throne and because of our loyalty to him and because of the duty imposed by our oath to him. And we regard him as the highest authority, as the sovereign of our land, which he still remains even under the most extreme constitutional limitations . . . [36]

In short, both Stahl and Ludwig von Gerlach were convinced that a conservative politics of reaction had to be based both on a politics of principle and on a politics of 'conservative reform', a politics which was adapted to the realities and requirements of the present.[37] Despite the real contributions of Stahl and Gerlach to the development of a modern, monarchical-constitutional conservatism in Prussia, however, the *Kreuzzeitung* factions in the two houses of the Prussian parliament never managed to become a fully modern political party in the 1850s. Although the party's rise during that decade was meteoric, so too was its eclipse after 1858. Part of the problem was the difficulty its leaders encountered in trying to develop a working consensus among its component groups: 'Junkers, officers, pietists, and ultramontanes'.[38] Increasingly, to the disappointment of Stahl and the Gerlachs, the *Kreuzzeitung* party became less interested in the modernization of conservative principles and more interested in the defence of narrow, particularistic interests, especially the interests of what Ludwig called 'crude, absolutist Junkers and bureaucratic *Landräte*'.[39] According to the Gerlachs, their party's egotistical and short-sighted pursuit of narrow material interests undermined its ability to contribute positively to political reform, especially after 1854, and paved the way for its rapid decline in 1858. In any case, conservatives had long disagreed with each other over a variety of issues; and one of those disagreements had led to the first serious breach in their ranks and to the emergence of a second conservative 'party' after the early 1850s.

One piece of legislation favoured by the *Kreuzzeitung* party and by Frederick William himself was the reactivation, on a *ständisch* basis, of regional and provincial

[36] Füßl, *Professor*, 183–5; cf. Kraus, 'Gerlach', i. 450.   [37] Kraus, 'Gerlach', i. 356.

[38] Ibid. i. 444.

[39] Ibid. ii. 338. See also Kraus's summary history of the 'conservative party', ibid., i. 443–53, ii. 330–8.

diets. That proposal was not, however, congenial to all conservatives, and helped to precipitate a split in conservative ranks in 1851—a schism which had been latent since at least the time of the Union project and which had been exacerbated by Olmütz.[40] There were in fact many reform conservatives who believed, as Radowitz had once observed, that it was necessary to emerge from the revolution at the front and not in the rear. One of those was Moritz August von Bethmann-Hollweg (1795–1877). The scion of a family of Frankfurt bankers and grandfather of the controversial *Reich* Chancellor during the First World War, Bethmann-Hollweg was exactly the same age as Frederick William IV and Ludwig von Gerlach, with whom he had been on intimate terms for many years. A professor of law in Berlin and then in Bonn, and an advocate of Savigny's historical school of law, Bethmann-Hollweg had been profoundly shaped by the Awakening after 1815. He had been closely involved for many years with ecclesiastical and public affairs, serving in the Council of State, in the General Synod of 1846, and as founding president, along with Friedrich Julius Stahl, of the Evangelical Assembly (*Evangelischer Kirchentag*) after 1848. In 1848 he was associated with the League for King and Fatherland, but he was no political mossback. During the *Vormärz* years he had become sharply critical of Ludwig von Gerlach's rigid neo-orthodoxy, and in 1847 he had supported the United Diet as a move in the right constitutional direction. In the spring of 1849 he had urged the King not to respond too negatively to the deputation from the Frankfurt National Assembly, even though he understood that Frederick William could not accept the imperial crown under the conditions on which it had been proffered.[41] Finally, as a supporter of the constitution of 1850 he was convinced that the reintroduction of the old provincial diets was a step in the wrong direction, and he announced that he would never serve in such a diet.[42]

By late 1851 Bethmann-Hollweg's opposition to the ultra-conservatives had spawned both a newspaper, the *Preußisches Wochenblatt*, and a reformist-conservative parliamentary faction. Like the original *Kreuzzeitung* party, the *Wochenblatt* party was also a fluid and informal group, some of whose most important members drifted away after a couple of years.[43] Bethmann-Hollweg's efforts at first attracted considerable sympathy in high bureaucratic and diplomatic circles, especially among individuals like Bunsen who were closely involved with the shaping of Prussian foreign policy and who regarded the diplomacy of the Manteuffel government as a blot on Prussia's honour.

Outraged over the split in conservative ranks, Frederick William at first refused to receive Bethmann-Hollweg, whom he criticized for promoting a 'French constitutional regime'. And for their part, the leaders of the *Wochenblatt* party, though all

---

[40] Ernst Rudolf Huber, *Deutsche Verfassungsgeschichte seit 1789*, 3rd edn. (Stuttgart, 1988), iii: *Bismarck und das Reich*, 166–7.

[41] Bethmann-Hollweg to FW IV, 1 Apr. 1849, GStA Merseburg, HA Rep. 50 J Nr. 147, Bl. 15–16ᵛ.

[42] *NDB*, ii. 187–8 (Fritz Fischer); Fritz Fischer, *Moritz August von Bethmann-Hollweg und der Protestantismus (Religion-, Rechts- und Staatsgedanke)* (Berlin, 1937), esp. ch. 8.

[43] Michael Behnen, *Das Preußische Wochenblatt (1851–1861): National-konservative Publizistik gegen Ständestaat und Polizeistaat* (Göttingen, 1971), 60–79.

loyal monarchists, rejected both Frederick William's *ständisch* projects and his inter-pretation of the divine source of his office.[44] Nevertheless, the King sought to avoid an open break, tried in vain to induce Bethmann-Hollweg to return to the fold, and ultimately managed at least partially to reconcile himself with the party's leaders, whom he once described as 'loyal friends'.[45]

Although it never attracted much electoral support, the *Wochenblatt* party could count on the sympathy of one exceedingly important segment of Prussian society: the Prince and Princess of Prussia and their friends. Indeed, the court of William and Augusta can be regarded as a third conservative group or faction jockeying for power and influence throughout the 1850s. During the reaction decade that court was usu-ally situated in Koblenz, where William was serving as military governor of the Rhineland and Westphalia. Augusta herself was an unabashed Anglophile—her hus-band's siblings snidely called her 'Lady William'—who appreciated the *Wochenblatt* party's relative cosmopolitanism, which stood in such sharp contrast to the *Kreuzzeitung*'s Junker provincialism. For his part, William had undergone a remark-able political transformation since his London exile in 1848, and, arguing that 'you can't swim against the stream', now believed that it was necessary to adjust to consti-tutional realities. This was something which the *Kreuzzeitung* party, with its 'out-moded legalistic fancies', was unwilling to concede.[46] He had also sympathized with Radowitz and had become a stern critic of the Olmütz policy. Thereafter he became increasingly hostile to his brother's advisers and policies, which he was afraid would compromise Prussia's credibility as a great power, especially *vis-à-vis* Austria.[47]

The Koblenz court of William and Augusta thus became a centre of constant opposition to the policies both of Otto von Manteuffel and of the *Kreuzzeitung*; it can even be described as a 'counter-court', many of the members of which had personal connections or sympathies with the *Wochenblatt* group. Here the intellectually gift-ed Augusta, with her penchant for interesting conversation, was able to develop a court society which was vastly more glittering and stimulating than its counterpart in Berlin and Potsdam.[48] William and Augusta preferred to stay in Koblenz even during the winter season and arrange their own court spectacles; they regarded their obliga-tory sojourns in Berlin as 'a real torture' and tried to reduce them to a minimum. Augusta and Elisabeth had never liked each other, while William was on a bad polit-ical footing not only with Frederick William but also with Prince Carl, who since 1848 had dabbled with the idea of replacing William as the King's heir. The King and

[44] FW IV to Bethmann-Hollweg, 17 Oct. 1851 and 2 Apr. 1852, GStA Merseburg, HA Rep. 50 J Nr. 147, Bl. 28, 48–50ᵛ; Behnen, *Wochenblatt*, 61–2, 67–70, 75, 84–8, 136–48; E. R. Huber, *Verfassungs-geschichte*, iii. 178–9; Borries, *Krimkrieg*, 24–35.

[45] Marginal comment on report from Saegert, 28 Nov. 1851, GStA Berlin, BPH Rep. 192 Carl Wilhelm Saegert Nr. 37.

[46] Prince of Prussia to Leopold von Gerlach, 11 Feb. 1850 and 11 Feb. 1853, BA Potsdam, 90 Ge 6 Nachlaß Leopold von Gerlach Nr. 40, Bl. 11, 23.

[47] Elisabeth Richert, 'Die Stellung Wilhelms, des Prinzen von Preußen, zur preußischen Außen- und Innenpolitik der Zeit von 1848 bis 1857', (Diss.; Berlin, 1948), 47–79; Karl Heinz Börner, *Kaiser Wilhelm I. 1797 bis 1888: Deutscher Kaiser und König von Preußen. Eine Biographie* (Cologne, 1984), 104–9, 115–17.

[48] Börner, *Wilhelm I.*, 107, 109.

his advisers were constantly unhappy with William's court, which they regarded as a nest of subversion and 'democratic' infection. Frederick William harangued his brother endlessly on this subject, demanding that he purge his entourage and threatening to do so himself.[49] From time to time members of the King's own entourage schemed to get the Prince and Princess to return to Berlin, where they could be more readily observed and controlled; and there can be little doubt that the civil governor of the Rhineland, Hans Hugo von Kleist-Retzow, organized regular surveillance of the princely couple's activities.[50] Nevertheless, the counter-court remained in Koblenz, and until 1857 continued to serve as the focus of opposition to Manteuffel and to the *Kreuzzeitung*; it also assured the *Wochenblatt* party of more success than it might otherwise have been able to enjoy.

No Return to 'Normalcy': King and Court in the Reaction Decade

After 1849–50 Frederick William IV tried desperately to 'return to normalcy'; and, superficially at least, his behaviour, his style of governance, and his relationships with his friends and his subjects seemed little altered by the events of 1848. But, in his case at least, the more things stayed the same, the more they changed. Though he often showed flashes of his former wit, he was no longer the amusing, amiable raconteur of his younger days. Scorned by his enemies, chastised by his friends, he found it hard to accept responsibility for his own actions and for what had happened to Prussia since the beginning of his reign. The Gerlachs continued to complain constantly about the King's 'weakness' and 'unreliability', about his capacity for self-deception, and about his tendency to regard his associates and subordinates as 'cattle'. In Leopold's words, 'He takes the credit for everything that turns out all right; things which go bad he blames on his servants.'[51]

Many observers noted that after 1848 the King was never quite his old self again. Virtually everyone agreed that he was more nervous, forgetful, and irritable, often lashing out at his advisers over trifling matters. Self-control had, of course, always been one of his main problems, especially at times when he had to make critical decisions. As Ernest II, Duke of Saxe-Coburg-Gotha and brother of Britain's Prince Albert, once noted, before 1848 Frederick William had always been able to use his sardonic wit to 'joke away' the difficulties that his temper sometimes created. After 1848, though, things were different. Following every difficult decision, Ernest reported, the King succumbed to 'weakness and apathy. Then he fell apart physically, dragging his hand over his sweat-drenched brow, while his countenance assumed an expression of utter ruin.'[52] After his outbursts, which sometimes precipitated

---

[49] Prince of Prussia to Leopold von Gerlach, 14 and 20 Apr. 1851, BA Potsdam, 90 Ge 6 Nachlaß Leopold von Gerlach Nr. 40, Bl. 14–15.

[50] Börner, *Wilhelm I.*, 113; Georg Graf Esterházy von Galántha to Graf Buol, 18 Jan. 1856, HHStA, P. A. III Karton 56, Preußen. Berichte 1856 I–VI, fol. 39ʳ–39ᵛ.

[51] Leopold von Gerlach, diary (11 June 1851), GA, 'Abschriften', viii. 180.

[52] Ernst II., Herzog von Sachsen-Coburg-Gotha, *Aus meinem Leben und aus meiner Zeit* (3 vols.; Berlin, 1887–9), i. 614.

reproachful letters and offers of resignation from their victims, Frederick William was invariably conciliatory and full of self-recrimination. On one typical occasion in 1853, for example, Edwin von Manteuffel tried to resign after the King had 'blown up' at him. Frederick William rejected Manteuffel's resignation in revealing fashion: 'I am really a harmless creature, but a very harassed one, and I've got nerves.' When 'pricked with needles for an entire morning', he said, it was easy to become agitated.[53]

Frederick William's apologies were almost certainly sincere, for he had no desire to alienate his old friends and advisers. Prematurely ageing, nervous, frequently depressed, and increasingly suspicious, he was keenly aware that many of his subjects—especially high-ranking ones—held him in scorn and contempt. A voracious reader of newspapers, after 1848 he became hypersensitive to what he regarded as personal affronts from journalists and other mediators of public opinion. He also knew that it would take a heroic effort of will to salvage something of his *ständisch* project: and, as he was constantly reminded during those years, he was anything but a heroic character. As the burdens of his office and his feelings of guilt weighed more heavily upon him, he craved more than ever the intimate company of old friends and a regular daily routine.

His daily schedule had, of course, changed in certain respects by the 1850s. With his fear and hatred of the '*misérable public*' of post-1848 Berlin, the three palaces of Potsdam, Sanssouci, and Charlottenburg now became his principal residences.[54] At all of these places, he and the Queen favoured an extremely structured life-style. Almost every day, between 7.30 and 8.00 a.m., the royal couple took their breakfast with Leopold von Gerlach; as we noted in the last chapter, this was called the 'coffee ministry' or 'coffee report'. The Marshal of the Court, Count Keller, also usually appeared at breakfast to discuss the day's activities at court—who was going to be invited to table, who was going to be presented at court, plans for forthcoming royal visits or inspection tours, visits to the theatre, and matters of a similar nature. Frederick William and Elisabeth withdrew in mid-morning for short religious devotions, and then the stream of reports continued. Civil matters were usually presented by cabinet secretaries such as Emil Ernst Illaire, Marcus Niebuhr, or August Costenoble (1803–81), while military affairs were the domain of the adjutants or other officers with ready access to the King's presence.

The old Civil Cabinet, which before 1848 had functioned under the aegis of Thile's cabinet ministry, was transformed after the revolution. The former first section of the cabinet ministry was now responsible to the Minister President, and the veteran official who headed that section, August Costenoble, received the title of State Ministerial Councillor (*Staatsministerialrat*); with the right to report directly to the King, he served as the liaison between the ministers and the King. After 1850, in fact, Otto von Manteuffel increasingly allowed Costenoble to handle routine ministerial reports on his own, so that in effect he had assumed many of Thile's old

---

[53] Edwin von Manteuffel to FW IV, 11 Sept. 1853, GStA Merseburg, HA Rep. 50 J Nr. 795, Bl. 30–31; FW IV to Manteuffel, 13 Sept. 1853, GStA Merseburg, Rep. 92 Edwin von Manteuffel B II Nr. 44, Bl. 3.
[54] FW IV to Nicholas I, 3 June 1851, GStA Merseburg, HA Rep. 50 J Nr. 1205, Bl. 138.

activities. The second department of the old cabinet ministry or civil cabinet, headed by Emil Ernst Illaire, now more or less officially received the designation of 'Civil Cabinet', serving as the King's private secretarial bureau. Frederick William thus had several secretaries available to him, including Costenoble, Illaire, and his veteran Privy Chamberlain, Eduard Schöning.[55] His most influential secretary, though, was surely Marcus Niebuhr, son of the historian-diplomat Barthold Georg Niebuhr and protégé of the Gerlachs. Although Leopold often described Niebuhr as his 'best ally', other conservatives distrusted him as a self-righteous, vain religious zealot. For his part, the King admired the younger man's powerful intellect; Frederick William found Niebuhr's advice '*very valuable*', he said, 'for we both occupy the same ground (the historical)'.[56] In 1851 Niebuhr became a Privy Councillor and in 1853 a Cabinet Councillor. His position at court was both important and ill defined. He once described himself as the near-sighted monarch's 'physical eyes'; and as the confidant of Leopold von Gerlach and the *Kreuzzeitung* his daily proximity to Frederick William was very useful. Gerlach himself knew, however, that Niebuhr's influence over the King was limited; as Frederick William once remarked to his Adjutant-General, 'I need Niebuhr to write letters to the ministers, which he does superbly.'[57]

After a light lunch the King followed his doctors' orders and took a fairly long walk until 3 or 4 p.m., at which time the day's main meal took place. This was a rather informal and spontaneous occasion, in which anywhere from seven to fifty persons took part. The guest list was virtually unchanged since *Vormärz*: Keller, Leopold von Gerlach, Alexander von Humboldt, the architect August Stüler, Carl von Voß-Buch (who was now a Consistory Council president), the pious ladies-in-waiting Countess Münster, Countess Voß, and Countess Pauline Neale, and, during winter sojourns in Charlottenburg, the historian Leopold von Ranke. Of course, things did not always run as smoothly as this schedule suggests. After 1848 Frederick William was just as inefficient with his time, and just as likely to preoccupy himself with trivialities, as during the *Vormärz* years, and often the press of daily reports caused him to cut short his afternoon walk. Around 5 p.m. he frequently conferred with Otto von Manteuffel, and from time to time the War Minister as well; he rarely spoke individually with the other ministers. Finally, as in previous years a 'tea evening' usually followed at about 8 p.m.[58] The only important new face at these affairs belonged to Louis Schneider, a well-known Berlin actor, playwright, author of popular historical

[55] Heinrich Otto Meisner, 'Zur neueren Geschichte des preußischen Kabinetts', *FBPG* 36 (1924), 58–63; E. R. Huber, *Verfassungsgeschichte*, iii. 68–9; GStA Merseburg, Geheimes Zivilkabinett, 2.2.1., *Findbuch*, 3–4.

[56] Leopold von Gerlach to Ludwig von Gerlach, 26 Oct. 1851, 10 Aug. 1852, 7 Oct. 1857, in E. L. von Gerlach, *Von der Revolution*, ii. 766–7, 807, 930; FW IV to Saegert, 19 Dec. 1848, GStA Berlin, BPH Rep. 192 Carl Wilhelm Saegert Nr. 10; Eichhorn to FW IV, 6 Jan. 1849, GStA Merseburg, HA Rep. 50 J Nr. 350, Bl. 20–21ᵛ.

[57] Meisner, 'Geschichte', 60–1; Ludwig von Gerlach, diary (8–25 June 1849), in E. L. von Gerlach, *Von der Revolution*, i. 183; Leopold von Gerlach, diary (29 May 1851), GA, 'Abschriften', viii. 163.

[58] Bismarck-Bohlen, 'Aufzeichnungen', GStA Merseburg, HA Rep. 50 F 1 Nr. 6, Bl. 8ᵛ–11ᵛ; Prinz Kraft zu Hohenlohe-Ingelfingen, *Aus meinem Leben: Aufzeichnungen*, ii: *Flügeladjutant unter Friedrich Wilhelm IV. und König Wilhelm I. 1856–1863*, 8th edn. (Berlin, 1909), 25–6.

narratives, and conservative publicist. After 1849 he became a fixture as official reader (*Vorleser*) at the royal tea-evenings, especially on Saturdays. A man of second-rate
abilities and conventional monarchical sentiments, his presence was interpreted by
jealous critics like Humboldt as a sign of the court's intellectual decline after 1848.[59]

Between 1848 and 1850 the King had rarely left the Berlin-Potsdam region; after
the revolutionary years, however, he resumed his customary wanderings. As in previous years, he visited Rügen every August, followed by Erdmannsdorf in late
August or early September; he participated in army manœuvres and the various royal
hunts every autumn; and in the mid-1850s he added an annual trip to Marienbad to
take the waters. He frequently toured the western parts of the kingdom, and also met
other sovereigns on a fairly regular basis. For example, in 1851 he spent some time in
Warsaw with his Russian brother-in-law, Nicholas I, and at Hohenschwangau with
his Bavarian nephew, King Max II; in 1853 he visited another nephew, the young
Emperor Francis Joseph, in Vienna; and several months later he again journeyed to
Warsaw for meetings with Nicholas I. These kinds of activities continued until the
very end of his active reign. In 1857, for example, shortly before the onset of his illness, he visited Francis Joseph at Schönbrunn.[60]

Frederick William's frequent travels offered him an opportunity for psychological refreshment; they permitted him to escape the tedium of daily governance, see
new and interesting things, and bolster his self-esteem. As we know, however, art
and architecture were even more important sources of personal and ideological
renewal. Indeed, by the early 1850s Leopold von Gerlach was worrying that
Frederick William's 'constant though actually thoughtless preoccupation with art'
had become a form of escapism.[61] But Gerlach, who was largely indifferent to aesthetic pursuits, failed to understand that the King's artistic and architectural passions, especially in the Potsdam area that he loved more than any other, constituted
both an escape *and* an essential ingredient of his monarchical project—the most vivid
and concrete expression of his vision of monarchical authority and kingly tradition.
Throughout the 1850s Frederick William suffered from the belief that his authority
had been illegally circumscribed, that he was constrained by a 'miserable' constitution to which he felt bound by his oath of February 1850. There was thus a significant gap between his own perception of the real limits of his power, on the one hand,
and, on the other, the grandiose monumentality of his architectural projects during
those same years.

With one or two important exceptions, those projects were never completed.
They included plans for a monumental avenue, a *via triumphalis*, along the heights
just to the east, north, and north-west of Sanssouci. A network of bridges and

[59] Louis Schneider, *Aus meinem Leben* (3 vols.; Berlin, 1879), ii. 224–7, 244–53, 255–366; Lore
Schatten, 'Louis Schneider: Porträt eines Berliners', *Der Bär von Berlin: Jahrbuch des Vereins für die
Geschichte Berlins*, 8 (1959), 116–44.
[60] Leopold von Gerlach, diary (11 Sept. 1851), GA, 'Abschriften', viii. 252–3; GStA Merseburg, HA
Rep. 50 C 2 Nr. 58, Bl. 2–2ᵛ; FW IV to Elisabeth, 20–1 May and 3 Oct. 1853, ibid., HA Rep. 50 J Nr. 995
Fasz. 24, Bl. 25–25ᵛ, 24–24ᵛ, 8–11ᵛ; FW IV to Elisabeth, 9–10 July 1857, ibid., Fasz. 25, Bl. 162–4.
[61] Leopold von Gerlach, diary (22 June 1851), GA, 'Abschriften', viii. 196.

viaducts would connect a series of representative buildings, including an orangerie, a hippodrome, an antique theatre, a casino, and a *nymphaeum*. The King seems to have been especially fascinated by the idea of creating a kind of architectural and representational framework to surround the palace of Sanssouci, which had previously stood more or less by itself on its hill overlooking Potsdam.[62] The result would certainly have been a tasteful architectural ensemble that would also have emphasized the power, glory, and prestige of the dynasty. Although the King had begun to develop plans and sketches for his triumphal avenue during the 1840s, the revolution had slowed everything down, and the project was never finished. All that was completed was the Arch of Triumph (1851) at its proposed eastern outlet and, to the west of Sanssouci, the great Orangerie which was erected between 1851 and 1860. One of the most significant examples of Berlin-Potsdam architectural historicism, the Orangerie reflected the King's decades-long interest in High Renaissance Italian palace and villa architecture.[63] For all its magnificent qualities, however, it remained a torso, a constant reminder that it was the centrepiece of a much larger and unfinished architectural exercise in monarchical self-representation. Neither the Orangerie nor Frederick William's other unfinished projects from the 1850s—especially his plans for a palace complex on the Pfingstberg and for a 'retirement' villa at Lindstedt, both near Potsdam—ever fulfilled their original purpose.[64] These projects were the results of Frederick William's own fertile imagination, projections of his own will and of his desire publicly to assert his notions of monarchical splendour. Their very incompleteness can thus be regarded as a kind of metaphor for the monarchy in the 1850s: imposing but fragmentary. Above all, Frederick William's architectural projects after 1848 underscore his determination to maintain an image of stability, majesty, and historical continuity. That same craving for continuity was reflected in the personnel and structure of his court during the reaction era.

Throughout the last decade of his reign Frederick William IV continued to turn to old cronies from his days as Crown Prince to fill prominent positions at court or in the *maison militaire*. They included such long-time confidants as Leopold von Gerlach, Carl von der Groeben, and Anton Stolberg. We have already seen how Gerlach became a General *à la suite* in 1849 and Rauch's successor as Reporting Adjutant-General the following year. Groeben had held important field commands in 1849–50; and though he had not exactly distinguished himself on those occasions, he enjoyed the fierce loyalty of his royal master. Accordingly, in 1853 Groeben succeeded General von Prittwitz—whom the King detested—as Commanding General

---

[62] Friedrich Mielke, *Potsdamer Baukunst: Das klassische Potsdam*, 2nd edn. (Frankfurt am Main, 1991), 173–4.

[63] Ludwig Dehio, *Friedrich Wilhelm IV. von Preußen: Ein Baukünstler der Romantik* (Munich, 1961), 78; Götz Eckardt, *Die Orangerie im Park von Sanssouci*, 12th edn. (Potsdam-Sanssouci, 1984).

[64] L. Dehio, *Friedrich Wilhelm IV.*, 70–8, 90–6; Volker Duvigneau, 'Die Potsdam-Berliner Architektur zwischen 1840 und 1875. An ausgewählten Beispielen' (Diss.; Munich, 1987), 27–38; Mielke, *Baukunst*, 174–7; Marcus Kiefer, 'Schloß Lindstedt bei Potsdam-Sanssouci: Zur Baukunst und Gartengestaltung des nachschinkelschen "Klassizismus"' (*Magisterarbeit*; Bonn, 1993); Frederick William's Pfingstberg drawings and sketches in Plankammer Potsdam-Sanssouci, Sammlung Friedrich Wilhelm IV., Mappe III, Heft 2, Umschlag C.

of the Guard Corps, one of the most prestigious posts in the Prussian army and one which ensured that Groeben would frequently be in the King's company.[65]

Stolberg himself was named to the two highest court offices—Lord Chamberlain (*Oberkammerherr*) and Minister of the Royal House—after Wittgenstein's death in April 1851. Camarilla veteran Ludwig von Massow was undoubtedly better qualified to occupy those posts, but Frederick William had never been fond of Massow's boring personality, while in the 1850s he seemed to crave Stolberg's calm, reassuring physical presence even more than in the 1840s.[66] Although he was exceedingly conscientious, Stolberg—whom Leopold von Gerlach dismissed as little more than an old-fashioned 'court cavalier'—had never been a particularly effective administrator, and he left many details of the court's operation to Massow and to his son-in-law, Marshal of the Court Count Keller.[67] Stolberg was keenly aware of his own limitations, and only reluctantly accepted his new positions at court. But his selflessness, courtliness, and ultra-aristocratic demeanour made him perfect for the largely ceremonial job of Lord Chamberlain. He was also very helpful at moderating and controlling the King's increasingly frequent outbursts of rage; and he was able to induce Frederick William to back off from some of his wilder schemes, such as his plan to borrow 500,000 Taler from the state bank (*Seehandlung*) to finance his building projects.[68]

After Stolberg died in early 1854, Frederick William decided to separate more clearly the offices of Supreme Chamberlain and House Minister, which since 1819 had been held jointly. One of Prussia's most exalted grandees, Field Marshal Count Friedrich zu Dohna-Schlobitten (1784–1859), assumed the first office, while the long-serving Massow finally was named House Minister.[69] Thereafter the Supreme Chamberlain was responsible for all the King's personal affairs and for the ceremonial life of the court, including questions of etiquette and precedence, presentations at court, and the supervision of all the official royal retinues. These were tasks that were eminently suited for Dohna, an immensely dignified, handsome, and worthy old soldier who had never been much interested in politics or court intrigues. The real management of the court resided, as before, with Massow and Keller, the Camarilla veterans. The House Ministry remained responsible for the finances of the entire court; moreover, Massow and Eduard Schöning, Frederick William's private secretary, continued to administer the King's private funds and estates.[70]

[65] Leopold von Gerlach, diary (4 June 1853), GA, 'Abschriften', x. 78; Thun to Buol, 13 June 1853, HHStA, P. A. III Karton 48, VIII. Interna Preußens, fol. 27ʳ–32ʳ.

[66] AKO, FW IV to Stolberg, 14 May 1851, GStA Merseburg, Geheimes Zivilkabinett 2.2.1. Nr. 3150, Bl. 177–177ᵛ; Malsen to Max II, 25 Apr. 1851, BayHStA, MA III 2631.

[67] Leopold von Gerlach, diary (23 Aug. 1851), GA, 'Abschriften', viii. 243; Stolberg to FW IV, 30 May 1851, GStA Merseburg, Geheimes Zivilkabinett 2.2.1. Nr. 3150, Bl. 184–9.

[68] Leopold von Gerlach, diary (10 Feb. 1854), GA, 'Abschriften', xi. 16; Otto Graf zu Stolberg, *Anton Graf zu Stolberg-Wernigerode: Ein Freund und Ratgeber König Friedrich Wilhelms IV.* (Munich, 1926), 96–106.

[69] FW IV to Staatsministerium, 20 Mar. 1854, GStA Merseburg, Geheimes Zivilkabinett 2.2.1. Nr. 1683, Bl. 17.

[70] *Reglements* of FW IV, 'Ressort des Oberst-Kämmerers' and 'Ressort des Ministers des Königlichen Hauses', Apr. 1854, GStA Merseburg, Rep. 92 Leopold von Gerlach Nr. 27, Bl. 38–9; AKO, FW IV to Dohna and Massow, 15 May 1854, ibid., Bl. 40.

After a hiatus during the revolutionary years, court activities resumed their customary pattern in the 1850s. The atmosphere of these events could, however, be quite stifling. Before 1848 the court had never exactly been a scene of libertine spectacle, and during the 1850s it became steadily more boring and introverted. It was an ageing court led by an ageing monarch with an ageing retinue, and during the last decade of Frederick William's reign there were no great court galas comparable to the dazzling festivals of 1843 or 1846. Moreover, the Berlin of the 1850s was full of religious and moral zealots who maintained a watchful eye for what they regarded as sybaritic excess. In February 1852, for example, the ever-vigilant *Kreuzzeitung* criticized leading members of court society for holding Saturday-night balls that lasted into Sunday morning; it also complained that the Russian emissary, Baron Budberg, had organized a *déjeuner dansant* on a Sunday afternoon. As a result of the ensuing uproar, members of Berlin high society eliminated all organized social activities on Saturdays and Sundays. Most observers agreed, however, that ordinary Berliners were quite unaffected by these things and were not at all sympathetic to the 'Sabbath enthusiasts'.[71] Thus the court and court society inhabited an ever more narrow and circumscribed world, and one which exerted only limited influence on the development of popular tastes and fashions during the decade of reaction. In magnificence, glamour, and social impact it could not remotely compare with the sumptuous court of Second Empire France.

The Prussian court was, however, getting both larger and more expensive. Despite the stodginess of court life in the 1850s, that decade witnessed the beginnings of a steady 'inflation' of court structures and institutions which continued throughout the latter half of the nineteenth century.[72] During Stolberg's tenure Frederick William decided once again to reorganize the court. He had done so once before, in 1843. Now, ten years later, he decided to be both more thoroughgoing and more 'historic' by resuscitating old and largely forgotten court offices such as 'Royal Cup Bearer' or 'Supreme High Steward'. Existing positions were given grandiose new titles; so, for example, the Lord Chamberlain now became 'Supreme Chamberlain' (*Oberstkämmerer*). This reorganized court also required new arrangements for precedence and court rank. Previously all *Hofchargen* had been ranked behind infantry and cavalry generals, but now the Supreme Officials of the Court were given the same rank as such officers.[73] Frederick William also introduced a new court-uniform, 'a blue coat with black velvet collar which is the same for all ranks down to the buttons, which serve to distinguish the most important categories'.[74]

[71] *NPZ*, 47 (25 Feb. 1852); Varnhagen von Ense, *Tagebücher*, ix. 85–6, 94–5 (24–5 Feb., 1 Mar. 1852); Meysenbug to Rüdt, 28 Feb. 1852, GLA, Abt. 48/2649; Malsen to Max II, 10 Feb. 1853, BayHStA, MA III 2633.

[72] John C. G. Röhl, 'Hof und Hofgesellschaft unter Kaiser Wilhelm II.', in id., *Kaiser, Hof und Staat: Wilhelm II. und die deutsche Politik* (Munich, 1987), 78.

[73] AKO, FW IV to Stolberg, 13 Apr. 1853, GStA Merseburg, Geheimes Zivilkabinett 2.2.1. Nr. 1683, Bl. 12–12ᵛ; *Königlich-Preußischer Staats-Kalender für das Jahr 1853*, 16–17.

[74] Malsen to Max II, 10 Feb. 1853, BayHStA, MA III 2633; Massow to FW IV, 25 Feb. 1854, GStA Merseburg, Geheimes Zivilkabinett 2.2.1. Nr. 3279, Bl. 30–1.

The initiative for this project had come entirely from the King. Serving clear ideo-logical and political ends, it was consistent with his continued determination, even after 1848, 'to sustain historic, medieval reminiscences'. The new court-structure, though, did not make a very favourable impression. As the Austrian emissary, Count Thun, sarcastically commented, 'People regard the reintroduction of such useless medieval titles as inappropriate to the times, especially since the newly appointed supreme offices at court have been awarded to persons who do not enjoy a very high reputation.'[75]

Royal representation was also becoming increasingly costly. In 1848 the House Ministry ceased to be an official ministry or agency of the state. In effect, it was 'pri-vatized', and its expenses had to be borne by the monarch himself.[76] These changes added significant new expenses to the King's official budget, most of which was still derived from the 2.5 million Taler provided annually since 1820 by the *Kronfideikommißkasse*. Massow and Keller had always managed the budget very carefully, but after the early 1850s things got increasingly difficult.[77] In 1851 Keller was able to report that he had managed to make some savings thanks to the infre-quency with which the royal couple had travelled between 1848 and 1850, but by the mid-1850s 'the steady increase in the costs of all basic necessities' required extreme financial stringency.[78] Deficits had thus become unavoidable, while Massow vocifer-ously complained that an annual subsidy of 2.5 million Taler had been insufficient even during the last years of Frederick William III's reign. Moreover, after 1848 the King was no longer entitled freely to dispose of certain special funds, including reserves in the state bank, which in the past had sometimes been used to pay unex-pected bills. What should the King do about these problems? To go every year to the parliament for extra money would be most ill-advised, Massow believed, because it would undermine the independence of the crown. Extra funds granted by the parlia-ment would be analogous to the parliamentary 'civil lists' provided to royal houses in constitutional states and which, of course, were anathema to monarchical conserva-tives. Massow finally proposed that the Debt Law of 1820, which provided for the annual court-subsidy, and Article 59 of the constitution of 1850, which affirmed the independence of the crown, both be amended to make it possible to extract more than 2.5 million Taler a year from the nationalized crown demesnes. In the mean-time, the parliament should agree to supplement the King's budget with 500,000 Taler from state funds. The cabinet and parliament did not accede to Massow's orig-inal proposal, but after a series of delays they finally agreed in 1859 to provide the annual supplement of 500,000 Taler, which, the cabinet argued, should help cover all

---

[75] Thun to Buol, 23 Apr. 1853, HHStA, P. A. III Karton 48, VIII. Interna Preußens, fol. 1ᵛ–3ʳ.

[76] David E. Barclay, 'Hof und Hofgesellschaft in Preußen in der Zeit Friedrich Wilhelms IV. (1840 bis 1857): Überlegungen und Fragen', in Karl Möckl (ed.), *Hof und Hofgesellschaft in den deutschen Staaten im 19. und beginnenden 20. Jahrhundert* (Boppard am Rhein, 1990), 340–1.

[77] GStA Merseburg, Geheimes Zivilkabinett 2.2.1. Nr. 3368, Bl. 43–44ᵛ; Stolberg to FW IV, 13 Jan. 1853, ibid., Bl. 93–4; Massow to FW IV, 26 Jan. 1856, ibid., Bl. 98–99ᵛ.

[78] Keller to FW IV, 4 Feb. 1851, 11 Feb. 1856, and 5 Feb. 1857, GStA Merseburg, Geheimes Zivilkabinett 2.2.1. Nr. 3190, Bl. 85–6, 102–102ᵛ, 105–105ᵛ.

the court's expenses for many years to come.[79] After 1859, however, both the income and the expenses of the court increased dramatically. The subvention of 1859 was doubled in 1868 and increased again in 1889 and 1910; nevertheless, those growing state subsidies never served as a lever for increased parliamentary control over crown and court.[80]

Although Frederick William managed to avoid parliamentary control of his own purse and his own House Ministry, he was still obliged to work with constitutional ministers, which was never easy for him. He did manage to develop a fairly stable work-routine with Otto von Manteuffel, and he also met regularly in Crown Council sessions with the entire cabinet. Those meetings usually took place about once a month at Bellevue Palace, and, not surprisingly, they tended to be dominated by long-winded royal monologues.[81] But such routinized practices did not deter Frederick William from corresponding directly with his ministers, correcting them, scolding them, and repudiating them. For the rest of his life he continued to regard them as his own 'servants' and agents, and not as the representatives of a constitutional order; and his outrage knew no bounds when they persisted in 'disobeying' him. A minister's lot remained a hard and thankless one in Prussia, even though the rate of ministerial turnover was much lower after 1850 than during the King's first decade.

Not untypical was the experience of August von Stockhausen, War Minister between February 1850 and December 1851, whom we met in the last chapter. By June 1851, after the conclusion of the Dresden conferences, Stockhausen complained that the strain had become unbearable, that he was 'used up, fully and forever'. Part of the problem lay in his own quarrelsome personality and in disputes with the Finance Minister over military budgets. But the real difficulty, he suggested, lay in the King's tendency to go behind his ministers' backs, to let 'me go about my business peacefully, to let me go to the chambers and make statements about every possible sort of thing. Then he steps in and screams that the latter had directly violated his commands and was outrageously disobedient, that he retracts what I said as untrue, etc.'[82] Stockhausen finally resigned at the end of 1851 when Frederick William bypassed him and dealt directly with Colonel Friedrich von Schöler, head of the Personnel Division in the War Ministry, in a delicate matter concerning military justice.[83]

Stockhausen was by no means the only victim of royal wrath. Not only was Frederick William not a creature of the *Kreuzzeitung* party, whose policies Stockhausen had supported in 1850, he was often bitterly hostile to it and its

---

[79] Massow to FW IV, 24 June 1856, GStA Merseburg, Geheimes Zivilkabinett 2.2.1. Nr. 3395, Bl. 90–6; FW IV to Staatsministerium, 21 July 1856, ibid., Bl. 75–75ᵛ; *Staatsministerium* to FW IV, 31 Jan. 1858, ibid., Bl. 81–9; *Staatsministerium* to Prince of Prussia, 28 Apr. 1859, ibid., Bl. 101.

[80] Röhl, 'Hof', 80–7.

[81] See the minutes of those meetings in GStA Merseburg, Rep. 90a B III 2c Nr. 3 Vol. II; cf. Hintze, 'Staatsministerium', 594.

[82] Stockhausen to Leopold von Gerlach, 11 June and 14 Dec. 1851, GA, 'Abschriften', xxi. 89, 206.

[83] Leopold von Gerlach, diary (2 Jan. 1852), GA, 'Abschriften', ix. 1–2; Stolberg-Wernigerode, *Stolberg-Wernigerode*, 96–9.

members, especially Ludwig von Gerlach. Indeed, the King was subordinate to no group or faction at court or in the parliament, but continued to manœuvre among them. Thus the Prussian court during the reaction decade remained the site of ferocious, perpetual, and usually inconclusive personal rivalries and factional conflicts. Non-Prussian observers could hardly believe their eyes. As the British diplomat Lord Bloomfield caustically observed in 1854, 'There is perhaps no Court in Europe at the present moment where such a maze of intrigue is being carried out as at Berlin. . . . the King thinks that by not avowing his partiality for any particular Party, by playing fast and loose with all, that he maintains his own independence and freedom of action, and though he pleases none he also quarrels with none.'[84] A more seasoned observer like Ludwig von Gerlach had become resigned to the idea that disorder would always characterize the ruling style of Frederick William IV. In 1852 he wrote to Leopold, 'All we can do is accept this anarchy, as the French say; we must accommodate ourselves to the fact that it exists and that we can't get rid of it. Anarchy isn't totally intolerable for us. We've more or less got used to it.'[85] Leopold himself expressed similar sentiments two years later when he noted that 'anarchy moderated by good will has been a characteristic condition' in Prussia since the time of Frederick William II.[86] Frederick William himself explained his ruling style and his relationship to his advisers in early 1852: 'I am not like so many rulers . . . who act as though no one can influence them. I choose my ministers and my entourage so that they can exercise influence over me, but that has its definite limits; and on this point there is nothing more to be said.'[87]

As if to leave no doubt about his own independence from control by anyone, Frederick William did turn to two new advisers after 1848, neither of whom was in any way beholden to, or even associated with, his older friends and cronies from his days as Crown Prince: Carl Wilhelm Saegert and Carl Ludwig Hinckeldey. His relationship with these two individuals, especially Hinckeldey, says a great deal about the evolution of monarchical structures and the relationship of the monarchy to the repressive and coercive apparatus of the state during the reaction decade. Above all, it says a lot about the relationship between monarchy and the re-creation of what might be called an 'authoritarian *Rechtsstaat*' during the reaction decade.

Monarchy and State Security: Carl Wilhelm Saegert and Carl Ludwig von Hinckeldey

We have noted on several occasions that after 1848 Frederick William had become increasingly concerned, even obsessed, with security issues. Convinced that exiled

---

[84] Lord Bloomfield to Earl of Clarendon, 10 Feb. 1854, PRO, FO 64/368.

[85] Ludwig von Gerlach to Leopold von Gerlach, 16 July 1852, GA, 'Abschriften', xxii. 210.

[86] Leopold von Gerlach to Otto von Bismarck, early Feb. 1854, in Horst Kohl (ed.), *Briefe des Generals Leopold von Gerlach an Otto von Bismarck* (Stuttgart, 1912), 82; cf. Borries, *Krimkrieg*, 40–1; and Winfried Baumgart, 'Zur Außenpolitik Friedrich Wilhelms IV. 1840–1858', in Otto Büsch (ed.), *Friedrich Wilhelm in seiner Zeit: Beiträge eines Colloquiums* (Berlin, 1987), 146.

[87] Leopold von Gerlach, diary (5 Jan. 1852), GA, 'Abschriften', ix. 4–5.

revolutionaries were constantly hatching new plots, and worried about the danger of assassination, the King now turned to confidants like Saegert and Hinckeldey who could satisfy his thirst for intrigue and provide him with the information that he wanted. These individuals can only be described as social outsiders, people who enjoyed few of the connections to aristocracy and upper bureaucracy that character-ized the King's other advisers. They both made themselves indispensable to the King by deluging the monarch with confidential reports on the political and secur-ity situations; those reports served both to heighten Frederick William's suspicions and increase his personal reliance on his new friends. Although Leopold von Gerlach regretted his master's use of 'bureaucratic', police-state measures, he also under-stood their psychological source. He once described Hinckeldey's police reports to Frederick William as 'mostly quite unimportant. They contain a lot of absurd, con-tradictory stuff. But the King likes them, because he believes that they give him a chance to hear a point of view different from that of his entourage.'[88]

Carl Wilhelm Saegert (1809–79) could under no circumstances be regarded as part of the regular royal entourage; indeed, Frederick William's relationship to Saegert has to be regarded as one of the oddest in the entire annals of the Hohenzollern monarchy. The King came to trust him implicitly, and used him as a sounding-board, a source of information, and a partner in intrigue. Although Frederick William was frantically, almost pathetically devoted to him, Saegert never really turned into a Rasputin figure; the King was far too independent, and far too determined to take his advice from several quarters, to succumb utterly to Saegert's influence.[89] Still, that influence was formidable indeed, and after the spring of 1848 Saegert succeeded in becoming the leading figure in what Leopold von Gerlach him-self called a 'second Camarilla', which also included the King's secretary, Eduard Schöning, as well as the Queen's secretary, a man named Harder.[90]

The product of a family of non-commissioned officers, Saegert himself had become a teacher and eventually was named director of the Berlin Institute for the Deaf and Mute. In the early 1840s he had briefly tutored the Prince of Prussia's son, Prince Frederick William, in history. One day during the revolutionary upheavals of March 1848, Harder, impressed with Saegert's political views and supposed grass-roots contacts in the capital, introduced the school director to Schöning, who in turn began passing along Saegert's political observations to the King. Equally impressed by the apparent quality of Saegert's information, Frederick William secretly met Saegert in April 1848 and was immediately won over. Soon Saegert was writing mas-sive reports to the King, full of observations on every conceivable subject, which Frederick William returned to him with extensive marginal comments. Shortly

[88] Leopold von Gerlach to Edwin von Manteuffel, 18 July 1856, GStA Merseburg, Rep. 92 Edwin von Manteuffel B III 19, Bl. 79.

[89] Hans-Joachim Schoeps, 'Das preußische Krisenjahr 1854 im Spiegel des Briefwechsels Friedrich Wilhelm IV. mit Carl Wilhelm Saegert', in id., *Der Weg ins deutsche Kaiserreich* (Berlin, 1970), 13. For bio-graphical details, see Gerhard Kutzsch, 'Friedrich Wilhelm IV. und Carl Wilhelm Saegert', *JGMOD* 6 (1957), 133–72.

[90] Leopold von Gerlach, diary (29 Jan. 1852 and 18 Apr. 1856), GA, 'Abschriften', ix. 25 and xiii. 77.

thereafter the two men began meeting regularly on Sunday afternoons, and occasionally during the week as well. Finally, in the spring of 1849 the King arranged for Saegert's election to the First Chamber, where he served until 1852. His conversations and correspondence with Frederick William continued during that entire period.[91] Frederick William himself admitted that his relationship to Saegert was an unusual one, justified only by the extraordinary circumstances in which it had developed.[92] Almost immediately he became fervently devoted to the man he called '*Freund Saegert*' or '*Amice Saegertius*', and the fulsome quality of his adulation was matched or exceeded only by his effusions about Radowitz. According to Frederick William, Saegert was a '*rare man*' whose '*savoir-faire*', 'burning, true Prussian patriotism', and 'incomparable skill at observation' had secured him a place among the 'most clever individuals, sharpest thinkers, and most well-disposed Berliners'.[93] Indeed, Frederick William came to value Saegert's opinions so much that on one occasion he confessed to Schöning, 'I no longer make any decision, especially in important affairs, without Saegert's counsel.'[94]

The King was less than successful, however, in his efforts to convince his other advisers and confidants of the brilliance of Saegert's insights. Their reluctance to have anything to do with Saegert was well-founded. He was a self-important, quarrelsome, and arrogant opportunist who wildly exaggerated his political influence in Berlin and adapted his political views to the exigencies of his own career. Obsessed with his own professional and personal advancement, he exploited his relationship with the King in a relentless hunt for titles and honours. As a bourgeois social climber, he bitterly and perhaps understandably resented the caste exclusiveness of the court aristocracy and his own treatment at the hands of the King's other advisers. Not having attained the rank of a Privy Councillor, he could not hope to be presented at court. When it became evident to him in the spring of 1852 that his royal patron could not freely dispose of offices and promotions, he temporarily broke off his relationship with the King. That estrangement turned out to be short-lived, and Saegert's influence with Frederick William continued to grow, reaching its zenith during the Crimean War. His loyalty to the King was, however, always conditional; and there is something really pitiable about the passion with which the King of Prussia, desperate for friendship, affirmed his affection and his '*unexampled* loyal

[91] On the origins of the relationship between Frederick William and Saegert, see Eduard Schöning, 'Auszüge aus Aufzeichnungen des Geheimen Kämmeriers Schöning aus "Amtlich Erlebtem" (de 1840–1861) geschrieben im April 1872 und später', GStA Merseburg, HA Rep. 50 G 3 Nr. 5, Bl. 10–15; Carl Wilhelm Saegert, diary, Fassung C (21, 26 Mar. 1848; 13 and 16–20 Apr. 1848; 23 May 1848), GStA Berlin, BPH Rep. 192 Carl Wilhelm Saegert Nr. 6; Saegert to FW IV, 9 Mar. 1849, GStA Merseburg, HA Rep. 50 J Nr. 1244, Bl. 24–24ᵛ; FW IV to Adalbert von Ladenberg, 5 Aug. 1850, GStA Berlin, BPH Rep. 192 Carl Wilhelm Saegert Nr. 24; and a revealing court judgement from 18 Apr. 1856 in which one of Saegert's enemies was found guilty of slander: GStA Merseburg, Rep. 92 Graf Guido von Usedom B IV 27, Bl. 7–9.

[92] FW IV to Karl von Raumer, 13 June 1852, GStA Merseburg, HA Rep. 50 J Nr. 1109, Bl. 1–1ᵛ.

[93] FW IV to Wrangel, 4 Mar. 1849, GStA Berlin, BPH Rep. 192 Carl Wilhelm Saegert Nr. 16; FW IV to Prince of Prussia, 17 Nov. 1853, GStA Merseburg, HA Rep. 50 J Nr. 977, Bl. 35; Kutzsch, 'Saegert', 169.

[94] Schöning, 'Auszüge', GStA Merseburg, HA Rep. 50 G 3 Nr. 5, Bl. 15.

friendship' for the school director. Saegert was, he insisted, one of the only people who understood him; and when they spoke to each other, the King once wrote to him, it was always clear 'that in the conversation I was number two and you were number one'.[95]

Although Saegert's influence with the King was important and even remarkable, there can be little doubt that Carl Ludwig von Hinckeldey (1805–56) was a vastly more formidable and historically significant figure. That redoubtable policeman was one of the most remarkable and creative conservative officials in nineteenth-century Prussia, and in many ways he invites comparison with his better-known Parisian contemporary, Baron Haussmann. Despite belonging to a well-established family of officials which, like the Gerlachs, had been ennobled in the previous century, Hinckeldey was nevertheless shunned as a boorish outsider by most members of Berlin-Potsdam court society, and his most determined enemies could be found in the ranks of the *Kreuzzeitung* party and its allies. He spent his entire career in the Prussian bureaucracy, but was often quite indifferent to bureaucratic norms and procedures, especially that painstaking sense of order and 'legality' (*Rechtsstaatlichkeit*) which was so characteristic of the civil service. He was more than willing to bend the law in his zeal to crush 'subversion' and harass opponents of the government. At the same time, he envisaged a vastly expanded role for positive state action as part of a conservative strategy to mobilize popular support for the monarchical cause. With his mixture of rough authoritarianism and welfare paternalism, with his emphasis on the extension of state power and his simultaneous support for modern forms of economic activity, Hinckeldey represented an early form of Prussian crypto-Bonapartism, a variant of conservatism to which the King himself was strongly attracted and which he did not believe contradicted his own patrimonial-*ständisch* views. Frederick William himself eagerly embraced Hinckeldey's carrot-and-stick policies of political repression and socio-economic activism, meanwhile heaping lavish praise on the man he described as one of his 'most clever and efficient servants'. Indeed, Varnhagen was not exaggerating very much when he described the Berlin police chief as Prussia's 'second king' in the first part of the 1850s.[96] At the same time, however, there were real limits to Hinckeldey's influence. Although his contribution to the development of a modern form of bureaucratically regulated, legalistic, statist authoritarianism in Prussia was critically important, his own power ultimately hinged on his personal relationship to the monarch.[97]

Until 1848 Hinckeldey had pursued a successful if unexceptionable bureaucratic career. After studying law in Berlin and Göttingen, he had entered the Prussian civil service in 1826. His work as a district councillor (*Regierungsrat*) in the Liegnitz region of Silesia was so outstanding that in 1842 he was promoted to *Oberre-*

---

[95] FW IV to Saegert, 23 Jan. 1856, GStA Merseburg, HA Rep. 50 J Nr. 1244, Bl. 34; Kutzsch, 'Saegert', 169–70.

[96] FW IV to Leopold von Gerlach, 21 Feb. 1854, GA, 'Abschriften', xxx. 19; Berthold Schulze, 'Polizeipräsident Carl von Hinckeldey', *JGMOD* 4 (1955), 98; Frank J. Thomason, 'The Prussian Police State in Berlin 1848–1871' (Ph.D. thesis; Johns Hopkins, 1978), 142, 153–4.

[97] Funk, *Polizei*, 91–3.

gierungsrat, responsible for supervising the internal affairs of the Merseburg district in the province of Saxony. There he made such a name for himself as a pillar of conservative order that in November 1848 the Brandenburg-Manteuffel government summoned him to Berlin as Police President. He inherited a police force which, in the course of the revolution, had already been significantly reorganized; Hinckeldey continued the process, placing policemen in military-style uniforms and imposing a similarly martial discipline upon them.[98] Within weeks of his appointment he began systematically to observe the activities of reputed democrats, and shortly thereafter he gained the right to report in person to the King. Before long, he had become the monarch's chief adviser on security matters.[99] Taking advantage first of Berlin's official state of siege and later of the repressive legislation of the reaction period (including restrictions on the right of association as well as tightened provisions on censorship), Hinckeldey became notorious for the fervour with which he and his officers went about their work. Their regular methods included systematic surveillance of suspected 'subversives', house searches, strictly enforced identity-controls at Berlin's city gates and railway stations, deportations from the capital city, and the prohibition and seizure of newspapers and other published materials.[100]

Although he was formally subordinate to the Interior Ministry, Hinckeldey usually did what he pleased. His rather cavalier attitude towards the law and regular police-procedure occasionally got him into hot water, but such set-backs in no way dampened the King's confidence in his ruthless and ambitious servant. Hinckeldey personally provided the King with a steady stream of information on all manner of police topics, from the breakup of alleged revolutionary conspiracies to ordinary murder cases or problems in the regulation of Berlin's brothels; and, typically, Frederick William circumvented normal bureaucratic channels by issuing orders directly to the Police President.[101]

As a man who was extraordinarily sensitive to public opinion and the modern requirements of 'image-making', Frederick William was well aware of the importance of the press, and he consistently supported Hinckeldey's efforts to control and shape it. The most frequent victims of confiscation were, of course, newspapers of the 'left', including the well-known *National-Zeitung* and the more openly democratic *Urwähler-* (later *Volks-*) *Zeitung*; but even respectable and cautious newspapers like the venerable *Vossische Zeitung* could become the targets of royal tantrums and were treated by Hinckeldey accordingly.[102] But by far the most spectacular seizures

---

[98] Cf. *ADB*, xii. 437–8; B. Schulze, 'Hinckeldey', 81–108; Heinrich von Sybel's posthumous 'Carl Ludwig von Hinckeldey 1852 bis 1856', *HZ* 189 (1959), 108–23; Thomason, 'Police State', 142–207; Wolfram Siemann, *Deutschlands Ruhe, Sicherheit und Ordnung: Die Anfänge der politischen Polizei 1806–1866* (Tübingen, 1985), 342–55; Funk, *Polizei*, 63–7; Günter Richter, 'Friedrich Wilhelm IV. und die Revolution von 1848', in Büsch (ed.), *Friedrich Wilhelm IV. in seiner zeit*, 647–50.

[99] Friedrich Wilhelm von Rauch to Hinckeldey, 12 and 18 Dec. 1848, GStA Merseburg, HA Rep. 50 J Nr. 512, Bl. 4–7.

[100] E. R. Huber, *Verfassungsgeschichte*, iii. 169–70.

[101] FW IV to Hinckeldey, 1 Dec. 1849, GStA Merseburg, HA Rep. 50 J Nr. 512, Bl. 28; Hinckeldey to FW IV, 24 Mar. 1853, ibid., Bl. 78.

[102] Funk, *Polizei*, 77–9.

involved none other than the *Kreuzzeitung*, which was confiscated by Hinckeldey's police on seven occasions between 1850 and 1852 alone. Hinckeldey himself always insisted that he was simply performing his duty, that he appreciated the paper's services to the 'good cause' in 1848–9, but that its excessively violent prose was embarrassing to the government and subversive of good order.[103] As we already know, Frederick William was often incensed by the *Kreuzzeitung*'s articles, and he frequently warned its supporters at court that the paper and its editor, the brash and aggressive Hermann Wagener, were overstepping their bounds. The alacrity with which Hinckeldey responded to the King's concerns earned him the undying hatred not only of the leading members of the *Kreuzzeitung* party at court but also of their sympathizers within the Junker squirearchy and the officer corps.[104] The quarrel reached a high point in 1854, when issues of the paper containing Ludwig von Gerlach's well-known monthly review of the news were suppressed, eliciting a threat from him to resign from his judicial post in Magdeburg.[105]

Hinckeldey's actions against the representatives of agrarian, aristocratic, and military interests represented an enormous risk, for his only real protector was the King himself. Those measures did, however, gain him the support of many influential Berlin *Bürger* who were tired of revolution and desirous of effective government, yet full of resentment against the arrogant social pretensions of the aristocracy and the officer corps. Hinckeldey's boundless administrative energies also contrasted sharply with the sloth of Berlin's regular municipal authorities. Between 1848 and 1856 Hinckeldey thus managed to become a kind of urban boss, using the powers of his office to modernize Prussia's rapidly growing capital; among other things, he established a regular fire-brigade, opened public baths for the poor, updated the municipal street-cleaning system, and encouraged the construction of a new waterworks. He supported measures to guarantee a steady supply of cheap but healthy food to the city, and under his aegis the police were even used to plant trees on public thoroughfares. He was also responsible for introducing the familiar public-notice columns (*Litfaßsäulen*) that can still be seen in Berlin today. (Those columns were also effective instruments of bureaucratic social control, for they helped to assure that public authorities could regulate what could or could not be legally posted in public.)[106] All these examples of an effective public administration, which responded

---

[103] Hinckeldey to Ferdinand von Westphalen, 8 July 1852, GA, 'Abschriften', xxii. 200–4.

[104] Hinckeldey to Leopold von Gerlach, 12 May 1852, GA, 'Abschriften', xxii. 128–9; Hinckeldey to FW IV, 4 Jan. 1854 and 26 May 1855, GStA Merseburg, HA Rep. 50 J Nr. 512, Bl. 134–5, 472–3; unsigned police report, 21 Feb. 1854, ibid., Bl. 174–6; Lord Augustus Loftus to Earl of Clarendon, 8 Jan. 1854, PRO, FO 64/367.

[105] Ernst Ludwig von Gerlach, *Aufzeichnungen aus seinem Leben und Wirken 1795–1877*, ed. Jakob von Gerlach (2 vols.; Schwerin, 1903), ii. 182–8; Leopold von Gerlach to FW IV, 22 Feb. 1854, GA, 'Abschriften', xxiv. 41–2; Leopold von Gerlach to Ludwig von Gerlach, 9 Mar. 1854, in E. L. von Gerlach, *Von der Revolution*, ii. 858–9; Westphalen to Leopold von Gerlach, 11 July 1854 and n.d. (July 1854), GA, 'Abschriften', xxiv. 199–200; Hermann Wagener to Leopold von Gerlach, 13 July 1854, ibid. xxiv. 201; Hinckeldey to FW IV, 12 and 16 July 1854, GStA Merseburg, HA Rep. 50 J Nr. 512, Bl. 231–232ᵛ, 234–235ᵛ.

[106] Funk, *Polizei*, 71.

quickly and energetically to real public needs, dramatically enhanced Hinckeldey's popularity in the city, especially in middle-class circles. When the cornerstone of the new waterworks was laid in 1853, a group of prominent citizens sponsored a ball in Hinckeldey's honour; some 1,100 guests, including an admiring Prince of Prussia, attended. Hinckeldey's exemplary personal life—he never used his office to enrich himself, and he was happily married with seven children—was a model of bourgeois rectitude and almost certainly contributed to his growing popularity among the capital's *Bürgertum*.[107]

Above all, of course, Hinckeldey devoted himself to the reorganization of the police force, including the criminal police and regular street-patrols; but the expansion and modernization of the political police assumed especially impressive dimensions under his aegis. Hinckeldey helped to set up a police network that extended beyond Prussia to the territory of the larger German Confederation. Although one should not judge the ruthlessness or effectiveness of Hinckeldey's police state by twentieth-century standards, it was nevertheless a remarkable achievement, and one which enjoyed the King's unqualified support.[108] Indeed, Frederick William himself was directly responsible for many of Hinckeldey's more dubious activities, a fact of which his confidants were keenly and bitterly aware. How sad it was, sighed Leopold von Gerlach, that the man who as Crown Prince had deplored Interior Minister Rochow's excessive use of police power should now be responsible for a much more formidable apparatus of repression! Gerlach's concerns were well-founded; in the 1850s Frederick William turned out to be quite adept at using both constitutional forms and police-state techniques to advance his own ends.[109]

Hinckeldey was also a vain and ambitious man, constantly complaining that he was overworked, unappreciated, and underpaid. He asserted too that it had been far easier to work with Otto von Manteuffel as Interior Minister than with his successor, the *Kreuzzeitung* ally Ferdinand von Westphalen. Accordingly, in 1851 and again in the following year Hinckeldey asked to be reassigned to Liegnitz, his former home in Silesia, as district governor.[110] Alarmed that he might lose a man upon whom he had become so dependent, Frederick William responded with a two-year campaign to get Hinckeldey promoted, an affair which turned out to be an interesting example both of his own stubbornness and of the limits to royal authority in the face of concerted bureaucratic opposition.

First the King proclaimed his intention to offer Hinckeldey control of all police affairs in Prussia, as a separate department in the Interior Ministry, while at the same time allowing him to continue as Police President of Berlin. Since the Berlin police had essentially become the command centre for the political police in the entire

---

[107] G. Richter, 'Revolution', 650–4; Heinrich Lutz, *Zwischen Habsburg und Preußen: Deutschland 1815–1866* (Berlin, 1985), 344–5; B. Schulze, 'Hinckeldey', 92–5.

[108] Siemann, *Anfänge*, 355–99; Sheehan, *German History*, 722.

[109] Leopold von Gerlach, diary (15 July 1852), GA, 'Abschriften', ix. 124–5; Siemann, *Anfänge*, 346.

[110] Hinckeldey to Westphalen, 14 Mar. 1852, GStA Merseburg, Rep. 92 Marcus von Niebuhr IV 6, Bl. 3–4; Hinckeldey to FW IV, 30 May 1852, ibid., Bl. 16–16ᵛ; Hinckeldey to FW IV, 6 Nov. 1853, GStA Merseburg, HA Rep. 50 J Nr. 512, Bl. 113–114ᵛ.

country, Frederick William argued, Hinckeldey should have the right to participate and vote in meetings of the highest Interior Ministry officials. Both Manteuffel and Westphalen objected to this idea and managed to 'stonewall' the matter for a number of months. In 1853, however, frightened by an assassination attempt against his nephew Francis Joseph, the King tried again, announcing his decision to name Hinckeldey as 'General Director of Police' (*Generalpolizeidirektor*) for the whole monarchy. Hinckeldey would have special responsibility for political and security matters, and all Prussian police officials would be required to follow his orders. This time the entire cabinet as well as leading provincial authorities resisted the King's demand; and, in fact, the extent of the police chief's proposed powers would have been quite unprecedented in the history of the Prussian bureaucracy. Hinckeldey's formal promotion to that new position was delayed until 1854. By that time the police chief's foes in the Interior Ministry were legion, and when Frederick William tried to arrange once more for his protégé to get a high official position directly in the ministry itself, Westphalen offered to step down. Although Frederick William refused to accept Westphalen's resignation, he still insisted on Hinckeldey's appointment, which after further delays finally took place in 1855.[111] Hinckeldey had thus, in effect, become Prussia's Minister of State Security.

By encouraging these developments, Frederick William IV had also encouraged Hinckeldey in his efforts to create what has been described as a legitimation, based on codified procedure, for 'executive action' in the struggle against revolution: that is, to establish an expanded bureaucratic basis for legitimate state activity.[112] Whether he knew it or not, Frederick William's security obsessions after 1848 were helping to move him far beyond his original monarchical project—and, for that matter, beyond the real, existing structures of the *Vormärz* monarchy. His other great obsession after 1848 was the constitution, which he always insisted had been foisted upon him against his will; accordingly, one of his major goals during the reaction decade was radically to amend the constitution on terms favourable to himself. In the course of doing so, however, he ended up by accommodating himself, in an odd sort of way, to the very constitutional order which he so detested. His relentless struggle to reorganize the upper house of parliament is the best example of how the King himself became at least partially 'constitutional' after 1848.

From the 'First Chamber' to the 'House of Lords': The Struggle to Revise the Constitution, 1850–1854

Although, as Radowitz once sagely observed, Frederick William IV was the very antithesis of a constitutional monarch, he was also personally and ideologically incapable of being an absolutist, at least in any sustained way. Nor was it possible, under post-1848 conditions, to return to the older system of cabinet government and per-

---

[111] See the documents in GStA Merseburg, Rep. 92 Marcus von Niebuhr IV 6; Sybel, 'Hinckeldey', 111–18; Siemann, *Anfänge*, 347–55.
[112] Funk, *Polizei*, 91.

sonal rule. Thus Frederick William constantly had to manœuvre among the various factions and groups that surrounded him: cabinet, Camarilla and *Kreuzzeitung* party, the *Wochenblatt* party and the Koblenz court, Hinckeldey and the police, the 'second Camarilla', and, of course, the army, the bureaucracy, and the parliament. To achieve his aims, therefore, he had to develop skills as a political manager for which he had never been trained and to which he was temperamentally disinclined. He never became really adept at this game; and until his final illness in 1857–8 he often oscillated between surly self-effacement and querulous assertions of the prerogatives of his office. Nevertheless, he turned out to be a rather more effective player than has sometimes been realized. Despite his deep personal yearnings he was, of course, unable to revive his *ständisch* projects; nevertheless, he and his allies (whether permanent or temporary) were able, through a mixture of stubbornness, compromise, and political sagacity, effectively to sustain the 'monarchical principle' in the new constitutional state. In the summer of 1849, for example, Frederick William had been able to count on the support of the Camarilla and the *Kreuzzeitung* party in his efforts to maintain the royal right of exclusive command (*Kommandogewalt*) over the army, a principle embraced by all his successors down to 1918. In an extremely important advisory note (*Handbillett*) of 1 July 1849, Frederick William described to his ministers his notion—central to subsequent political and military developments in Prussia-Germany—of virtually unlimited royal authority over the military.[113] These views were, of course, in perfect accord with those of Rauch and Leopold von Gerlach, and in June 1849 they played a crucial role in helping to stiffen the King's resolve on this question.[114] The King and his vestigial Camarilla often disagreed, however, on other constitutional issues, the most notable example—and the one which sheds the most light on Frederick William's skills as a political manager—being the struggle between 1850 and 1854 over the reorganization of the First Chamber.

Before taking his constitutional oath in February 1850, Frederick William had toyed with the idea of simply suspending the constitution; but once he had given his royal word, to which he felt himself bound, the option of an anti-constitutional coup was no longer open to him.[115] He had to pay a high psychological price for this concession; he always complained that his oath had been extracted by his ministers in a

---

[113] Text of the *Handbillett* in 'Unveröffentlichte Handbillette des Königs Friedrich Wilhelm IV.', *Deutsche Revue*, 32/4 (Oct.–Dec. 1907), 155–6. See also Rudolf Schmidt-Bückeburg, *Das Militärkabinett der preußischen Könige und deutschen Kaiser: Seine geschichtliche Entwicklung und staatsrechtliche Stellung 1787–1918* (Berlin, 1933), 39–42; Manfred Messerschmidt, 'Die politische Geschichte der preußisch-deutschen Armee', in Militärgeschichtliches Forschungsamt (ed.), *Handbuch zur deutschen Militärgeschichte 1648–1939*, ii, sect. IV: *Militärgeschichte im 19. Jahrhundert 1814–1890*, pt. 1 (Munich, 1979), 166–8; E. R. Huber, *Verfassungsgeschichte*, iii. 76–7; Füßl, *Professor*, 284–6.

[114] See Leopold von Gerlach's diary for 18–27 June 1849, GA, 'Abschriften', vi. 387–92, and the documents in ibid. xix. 65–77, as well as the 'Promemoria des Prinzen von Preußen über die Stellung des preußischen Kriegsministers', 11 Dec. 1849, ibid. xix. 126–8.

[115] Grünthal, *Parlamentarismus*, 203–8. On the King's notion of suspending the constitution in 1849, see the notes of Prince Frederick William (Frederick III), n.d., GStA Merseburg, HA Rep. 50 F 1 Nr. 7, Bl. 1ᵛ–2.

'pact with the rebellious people'. Thus he was contantly on the look-out for some legal way to revise the constitution and reissue it as a 'royal patent' (*Königlicher Freibrief*) or 'sovereign investiture' (*souveraine Verleihung*) from himself, which would have been consistent with his own interpretation of the monarchical principle.[116] Unless the constitution were changed, his hands would be tied and his executive powers illegitimately shackled. Constitutional revision was thus, Frederick William declared to the Crown Council in 1853, an essential aspect of the process by which Prussia could work its way out of the 'muck of 1848'; after all, Frederick William insisted, 'a King of Prussia had to have his hands free to fulfil the calling given to him by God'.[117] The transformation of the elected upper house into a British-style 'House of Lords' occupied by hereditary and designated peers would be a step in the right direction.

The question of the First Chamber's final structure had cropped up repeatedly during the complicated debates leading up to the passage of the constitution of 31 January 1850 and the King's oath a week later. Article 65 of the constitution envisaged an upper house of 240 members, of which half were to be elected and no more than twelve named by the King. Article 66, however, had provided that Article 65 would only go into effect in August 1852, and until that time the electoral provisions of December 1848—according to which the First Chamber represented an élite of property rather than noble privilege—remained in force.[118] As August 1852 loomed closer, Frederick William increasingly focused his attention on the question of how to revise Article 65 and reorganize the upper house in accordance with his own peerage notions. By the end of 1851 it had become a question of consuming, almost obsessive importance to him, the touchstone by which the restoration of monarchical power in Prussia could be assessed. How ironic, then, that this issue should temporarily estrange him from his most conservative allies and lead to the further fragmentation of the conservative camp![119]

Frederick William insisted from the very outset that he was only demanding for himself the same rights that any self-respecting monarch enjoyed. The King of Prussia, he insisted in a Crown Council session in November 1851, should possess no less power than the sovereigns of Britain, Spain, Portugal, or Greece, all of whom had the right to name the members of their upper chambers. Thus Article 65 should be changed. The upper house should consist of mediatized nobles, other members of the high nobility, life peers named by himself, and elected representatives of Prussia's universities and a few cities.[120] It was crucial, he argued at another session on 30 December, to take account of the swing of public opinion in favour of 'old

[116] FW IV in Crown Council, 1 Apr. 1852, GStA Merseburg, Rep. 90a B III 2c Nr. 3 Vol. II, Bl. 63.

[117] FW IV in Crown Council, 7 July 1853, ibid., Bl. 102–102^v; cf. notes of Prince Frederick William (Frederick III), n.d., GStA Merseburg, HA Rep. 50 F 1 Nr. 7, Bl. 2; cf. Jordan, *Friedrich Wilhelm IV.*, 150–4.

[118] E. R. Huber, *Verfassungsgeschichte*, iii. 81–2.

[119] Grünthal, *Parlamentarismus*, 210–11; Füßl, *Professor*, 298–9.

[120] FW IV in Crown Council, 24 Nov. 1851, GStA Merseburg, Rep. 90a B III 2c Nr. 3 Vol. II, Bl. 31–31^v.

Prussian' values and those historically sanctioned rights and privileges which the constitutions of December 1848 and January 1850 had so grossly violated. Moreover, Frederick William seems to have decided, the time was propitious for an alteration of the constitution; after all, full-scale anti-constitutional *coups* had just taken place in Austria and France.[121] He himself did not have such a *coup* in mind. In fact, he argued, the initiative for a reorganization of the upper chamber should ideally come from the chambers themselves.[122]

After some initial hesitation by the cabinet and most parliamentary conservatives, a proposal to restructure the First Chamber was introduced in that body on 18 January 1852. That proposal, the Heffter Proposition, was supported by the Bethmann-Hollweg faction in the parliament. Frederick William himself knew well in advance about plans to introduce the proposition, and, although it did not exactly coincide with the King's ideas, it came close enough. Indeed, it would have given him 'virtually limitless influence over the composition of the chamber of peers'.[123] As we have seen, that was just what Frederick William wanted: in a widely circulated memorandum of 19 January 1852, the monarch declared, '*I demand to be the one and only organizer of the First Chamber*', an arrangement which he described as essential for the '*honour, prestige, and future of the Prussian crown*'.[124] These ideas were also related to his larger plan to get the chambers themselves to revise the constitution so that it could then be reissued as a royal patent.[125]

Convinced that Frederick William's notions about restructuring the upper house were foolish, Leopold von Gerlach was also appalled by the King's dream of a royal patent. The best thing to do, he believed, was simply to leave the constitution alone, for ultimately it would founder on its own contradictions.[126] Gerlach vigorously attempted to induce the King to abandon his schemes; but despite a series of what Frederick William himself called 'desperate' scenes between the two men, the monarch was not to be dissuaded.[127] Gerlach's allies in the *Kreuzzeitung* party were similarly disturbed, for what the King clearly had in mind was a grand House of Lords to which mainly titled aristocrats would have access and from which the gentry (*Ritterschaft*)—the Junker bedrock of the Prussian system, 'the heart of the country', as Gerlach called it—would be excluded. Gerlach and his friends feared that such an arrangement would lead to an open conflict and would further alienate the

[121] Jordan, *Friedrich Wilhelm IV.*, 156–7.

[122] FW IV in Crown Council, 30 Dec. 1851, GStA Merseburg, Rep. 90a B III 2c Nr. 3 Vol. II, Bl. 37–38ᵛ.

[123] Grünthal, *Parlamentarismus*, 240. See also Jordan, *Friedrich Wilhelm IV.*, 175–7; Füßl, *Professor*, 321–2.

[124] FW IV, 'Mein Verhältniß zur Frage über die Zusammensetzung der Ersten Kammer', 19 Jan. 1852, GStA Merseburg, HA Rep. 50 E 2 Nr. 9, Bl. 31–31ᵛ.

[125] Leopold von Gerlach, diary (11 Feb. 1852), GA, 'Abschriften', ix. 34. As Gerlach noted in this passage, and as Grünthal has further demonstrated, Frederick William's ideas on constitutional revision were strongly influenced by Ferdinand Walter, a professor of Catholic theology in Bonn. Grünthal, *Parlamentarismus*, 211–14.

[126] Leopold von Gerlach, diary (11, 15, and 23 Feb. 1852), GA, 'Abschriften', ix. 34, 37, 40.

[127] FW IV to Saegert, 16 Jan. 1852, GStA Berlin, BPH Rep. 192 Carl Wilhelm Saegert Nr. 42.

monarch from his conservative allies. Friedrich Julius Stahl pointed out that an appointed House of Lords would not be based on *ständisch* principles but would instead resemble the French peerage created by the despised usurper Louis-Philippe. Above all, however, Stahl agreed with Gerlach that the King's ideas represented a slap in the face of the Junkers, 'for power and prestige here are not based on the *grands seigneurs* but on the gentry'.[128]

The debate over the reorganization of the First Chamber thus turned out to be lengthy, bitter, and almost indescribably confused. The King could count, for a change, on his brother William's support as well as on a rather opportunistic alliance with Bethmann-Hollweg's faction.[129] Frederick William fruitlessly attempted to use these debates to heal the rift between *Kreuzzeitung* and *Wochenblatt*; the former castigated the latter as 'dynastic' leftists, while Stahl himself was full of disdain for what Ludwig von Gerlach called 'the King's confusion and arrogance' at a late January royal audience with Stahl, Kleist-Retzow, and Bethmann-Hollweg. For his part, Ludwig von Gerlach was fiercely determined to push for a retention of Article 65, despite Leopold's warning that it really wasn't worth all the trouble it was causing.[130] Within the cabinet, Otto von Manteuffel provided only lukewarm support for the King's efforts, while Interior Minister von Westphalen tried without much success to mediate among the King, cabinet, and the factions in the chamber. The result was that he tied himself into convoluted political knots; and where in 1851 he had been one of Frederick William's darlings, he now found himself the target of royal wrath and at one point threatened to resign.[131]

In February 1852 a group of conservative parliamentarians, including the Gerlach-Stahl faction, tried to revise the Heffter Proposition, which itself was defeated in committee. Negotiations immediately began with the King to work out a new compromise, the so-called 'Koppe Proposition'. During the course of deliberations in the First Chamber, that proposition was altered to accommodate the King's wishes almost entirely. When the revised Koppe Proposition was put to a vote in the First Chamber on 5 March, most of the right, including Stahl's supporters, voted against it; it passed all the same, by a vote of 82 to 56.[132] The King was, of course, incensed at this '*outrageous display of mistrust*' on the part of his so-called friends on the right; but his angry outbursts had no effect on the final outcome of the Koppe Proposition, which was killed in the lower house by a 142–125 margin.[133]

[128] Stahl to Leopold von Gerlach, 9 Jan. 1852, GA, 'Abschriften', xxii. 8. For Stahl's celebrated speech in the First Chamber on 5 Mar. 1852, see Füßl, *Professor*, 319–20, 332–6.

[129] Prince of Prussia in Crown Council, 22 Jan. 1852, GStA Merseburg, Rep. 90a B III 2c Nr. 3 Vol. II, Bl. 43–43ᵛ; cf. Jordan, *Friedrich Wilhelm IV.*, 166–7, 175–7.

[130] Ludwig von Gerlach, diary (30 Jan. 1852) in E. L. von Gerlach, *Von der Revolution*, i. 301; id., *Aufzeichnungen*, ii. 137–9. Cf. Grünthal, *Parlamentarismus*, 241; Füßl, *Professor*, 323–4.

[131] Bloomfield to Earl of Malmesbury, 6 and 18 May 1852, PRO, FO 64/342. On the quarrel between King and *Kreuzzeitung* party, see Meysenbug to Rüdt, 16 Mar. 1852, GLA, Abt. 48/2649.

[132] Jordan, *Friedrich Wilhelm IV.*, 175–218; Grünthal, *Parlamentarismus*, 242–52; Füßl, *Professor*, 322–31.

[133] FW IV, marginal comment on report from Saegert, 8 Mar. 1852, GStA Berlin, BPH Rep. 192 Carl Wilhelm Saegert Nr. 42.

Accordingly, in early August, just before the official deadline and after the adjournment of the two houses, the government issued a decree which essentially provided that the First Chamber would be selected on the basis of Article 65: that is, a proportion of its members would still be elected by a small number of wealthy notables.[134]

But the King was able to pluck victory from the jaws of humiliating defeat. His own stubbornness, plus disarray and exhaustion within the government and the conservative camps, encouraged a compromise which ultimately gave him just about everything he wished. In the autumn of 1852 a special committee began to consider Westphalen's ideas for a drastic constitutional revision, and the result of these deliberations was yet another proposal for the restructuring of the upper house. Essentially Stahl's work, it immediately garnered the King's praise; thus the parliamentary way had been paved for a formal constitutional revision on 7 May 1853, which led in turn to a decree in late 1854 altering the composition of the First Chamber. The upper house—which after 1855 was called the House of Lords (*Herrenhaus*)—no longer included any elected members. The King had the right to name members to that house, but he was obliged to select them from certain categories, including, as a concession to the Junkers, representatives of 'old and established landed property'. Thus the House of Lords would not be limited to titled aristocrats of the highest rank. Finally, of course, it also included hereditary members, among them royal princes, mediatized nobles, and members of the high aristocracy whose families had belonged to the Curia of Lords (*Herrenkurie*) at the 1847 United Diet.[135]

Friedrich Julius Stahl was no doubt right to believe that this arrangement represented a victory for the political interests that he represented. Nevertheless, the House of Lords was less the creation of the *Kreuzzeitung* party than of Frederick William IV himself;[136] and as an élite bastion of aristocratic privilege and monarchical sentiment, it was to play a crucial role in the history of the Prussian-German state until the monarchy itself collapsed in 1918. Few other institutions attested more clearly to the persistence of monarchical authority and the 'monarchical principle' in Prussia. As the complex struggle over the First Chamber indicated, the powers of the monarchy remained formidable; and the form that those powers assumed had largely been shaped by Frederick William's own behaviour, infuriating and mercurial though it appeared even to those who were closest to him.

On 4 March 1852, the day before the vote on the Koppe Proposition in the First Chamber, Frederick William IV proclaimed in a letter to the Prince of Prussia, 'I will not give up, and I will come back again and again until I have won. And my victory is

---

[134] Jordan, *Friedrich Wilhelm IV.*, 219–65; Grünthal, *Parlamentarismus*, 254–5, 295–9; Füßl, *Professor*, 331–2.

[135] E. R. Huber, *Verfassungsgeschichte*, iii. 83–5; Grünthal, *Parlamentarismus*, 312–13; Kraus, 'Gerlach', i. 374–9, ii. 281–5.

[136] FW IV to Senfft von Pilsach, 9 July 1854, GStA Merseburg, Rep. 92 Ernst Freiherr Senfft von Pilsach B Nr. 8, Bl. 12–14; Füßl, *Stahl*, 353–5; Jordan, *Friedrich Wilhelm IV.*, 301.

much less for me than for you and your son.'[137] As we have seen throughout this study, Frederick William was often given to bombastic declarations of intent that he then backed away from; but in this case he meant everything he said. Although he never made his peace with that constitution which so radically contradicted all his notions regarding the purpose and function of monarchy, he nevertheless succeeded in transforming the constitution without violating his oath to it. To achieve his ends he had been aggressive, theatrical, self-effacing, dilatory, lachrymose, vague, and conspiratorial by turns. In the end, through his 'anarchy moderated by good will', he got much of what he wanted for himself and his successors; but to do that he was also forced, however reluctantly, to adjust himself to constitutional norms. Especially revealing of the process by which he adapted himself psychologically and politically to the realities of post-1848 Prussia are his remarks in a letter of September 1853 to his nephew, the Austrian Emperor Francis Joseph. The King regretted that in 1850 he had been forced 'to take an oath to a miserable, French-modern constitution!!!!' But, he continued, 'it happened, and my word is sacred, and I will not break it. But with the help of the very laws to which I swore . . . I will *replace* and kill the "French ideologies" with real German, *ständisch* institutions. . . . However, as long as we are afflicted by the French constitution, and especially as we free ourselves from it, we still need majorities!!'[138]

As these comments reveal, Frederick William had no alternative but to rule through majorities, while his most important allies—and occasional rivals—in the *Kreuzzeitung* party had discovered that the constitution was a useful device which could help sustain conservative values. The 'high conservatives' around the Gerlachs, Stahl, and their friends had always regarded 'revolution' and 'absolutism' with equal distaste. As one scholar puts it, 'Trapped between the Scylla of revolution and the Charybdis of (Bonapartist) absolutism, the right chose . . . to cover their nakedness with the "rag" of the constitution'.[139] Thus there developed in the 1850s what has been trenchantly described as a 'pseudo-constitutionalization' of the Prussian right, the 'use of new forms to rescue old contents'.[140] And though Friedrich Julius Stahl's monarchical constitutionalism is the best-known and most important example of conservative adaptability to new circumstances after 1848, it was by no means the only one; the much more dogmatic and unbending Ludwig von Gerlach also became aware of the political utility of the new constitutional order. The constitution itself, Gerlach believed, could become an instrument in the struggle against the ideas of popular sovereignty.[141] The King himself was aware of what was going on. Thus he complained on various occasions after 1852 that people like Stahl and

---

[137] FW IV to Prince of Prussia, 4 Mar. 1852, GStA Merseburg, HA Rep. 50 J Nr. 976, Bl. 4ᵛ; cf. Petersdorff, *Friedrich Wilhelm der Vierte*, 177.

[138] FW IV to Francis Joseph, 28–9 Sept. 1853, GStA Merseburg, HA Rep. 50 J Nr. 939, Bl. 59ᵛ–60.

[139] Grünthal, *Parlamentarismus*, 315.

[140] Günther Grünthal, 'Bemerkungen zur Kamarilla Friedrich Wilhelms IV. im nachmärzlichen preußen', in Büsch (ed.), *Friedrich Wilhelm IV. in seiner Zeit*, 46; id., *Parlamentarismus*, 315.

[141] Id., 'Bemerkungen', 46.

the Gerlachs, indeed the entire *Kreuzzeitung* party had, 'may God have mercy!, suddenly become constitutional!!!'[142] Of course, the 'constitutionalism' of the *Kreuzzeitung* party, the government, the Prince of Prussia, and even, in an odd sort of way, the King himself was a constitutionalism of convenience. Above all, it created the institutional context within which the 'anarchy' of the Prussian court and state could be moderated, directed, and controlled, as we shall see in the next chapter.

[142] FW IV to Senfft von Pilsach, 9 July 1854, GStA Merseburg, Rep. 92 Ernst Freiherr Senfft von Pilsach B Nr. 8 Bl. 12ᵛ.

'Anarchy' and Monarchy, 1850–1861

A Prussian Watergate

For years Wilhelm Stieber had been one of Prussia's most ruthless and successful policemen. The son of a petty official from Merseburg, he had studied law and thereafter had risen fast in the Berlin police. Thoroughly familiar with the seamier sides of the city's underworld, after 1848 he had become attached to the Criminal Police, a branch of Hinckeldey's Police Presidium responsible for particularly sensitive investigations throughout the entire realm and even beyond its borders. Although the distinctions between criminal and political investigations were still quite blurred in those days, Stieber became an early prototype of the modern counter-intelligence agent. A man who did not hesitate to resort to physical intimidation, bribery, and perjury to achieve his object, Stieber was moving on a fast career-track during the security-obsessed decade of reaction, and in 1854 he became Director of the newly created Seventh Department for Criminal Police Affairs in the Berlin Police Presidium.[1]

Now, on 30 January 1856, Stieber had got his man again. He and his colleague, the veteran police inspector Friedrich Goldheim, had extracted a signed confession from Carl Techen, a former army lieutenant with an exceedingly shady reputation. In the past, the fiercely ambitious Stieber had often been able to attract his superiors' attention to his spectacular successes. This time, however, he would have to be very careful indeed, for the Techen case turned out to be exceptionally sensitive.

In October 1855 the police had revealed that certain private papers belonging to Leopold von Gerlach and Marcus Niebuhr had been secretly transcribed and their contents transmitted to third parties.[2] Suspicion immediately began to focus on Techen, who had previously been involved in espionage activities at the residence of the French minister in Berlin, and a man named Ferdinand Seiffart, Vice-President of the Fiscal Bureau in Potsdam. At the beginning of November two servants of Gerlach and Niebuhr were arrested and charged with making and selling copies of their masters' correspondence and diaries. Techen was temporarily arrested in late October, but was quickly released. It was soon discovered that Gerlach's servant had received about 10 Taler a month for his services, which dated back to mid-July 1853.[3] More importantly, many of the Gerlach–Niebuhr papers had landed in the French

---

[1] On Stieber, see Wilhelm J. C. E. Stieber, *Denkwürdigkeiten des Geheimen Regierungsrathes Dr. Stieber*, ed. Leopold Auerbach (Berlin, 1884); and esp. Wolfram Siemann, '*Deutschlands Ruhe, Sicherheit und Ordnung': Die Anfänge der Politischen Polizei 1806–1866* (Tübingen, 1985), 371–85.

[2] Leopold von Gerlach, diary (19 Oct. 1855), GA, 'Abschriften', xii. 129.

[3] Leopold von Gerlach, diary (7 Nov. 1855), ibid. xii. 134; Lord Augustus Loftus to Earl of Clarendon, 24 Nov. 1855, PRO, FO 64/399.

diplomatic mission in Berlin. They included highly sensitive reports from Gerlach's confidant Count Münster, Prussian Military Plenipotentiary in St Petersburg, a man intimately familiar with the details of Russian military planning. And, of course, all of these things were taking place in the midst of the Crimean War, a conflict in which Frederick William IV was desperately trying to stay neutral. The information that the French gleaned from Münster's dispatches was thus exceedingly helpful to them and to their British allies. Among other things, the Western powers were able to learn about the extent of Russian naval forces in the Baltic and about the low morale of Russian troops at Sebastopol.[4]

After several months of investigations, Techen was again arrested on 29 January 1856, and the following day he signed his confession in the presence of Stieber and Goldheim. Who had put him up to his crimes? That was the question that had been circulating for some months, and finally Techen provided an interesting if somewhat unsurprising answer: 'For a long time I have been employed as a secret agent of the Minister President, Baron von Manteuffel. I had to deliver reports to him on the situation in Potsdam, and for that I received indefinite payment.' Manteuffel had asked him to keep an eye on the activities of the *Kreuzzeitung* party, and especially on Marcus Niebuhr and the Gerlach brothers, 'since the Minister President believed that these persons were constantly intriguing against him'. As a result, Techen bribed two servants to steal their masters' correspondence so that they could then be copied. The copies, and in some cases original documents, were then passed on to Manteuffel. Unfortunately for Techen, however, Manteuffel's interest in the whole matter had begun to cool by early July 1855; besides, Manteuffel—'with Prussian frugality', as Bismarck sardonically put it in his memoirs—had never paid Techen very much.[5] He thus decided to go free-lance and take his information to the French mission in Berlin, a relationship which lasted until his arrest in the autumn.[6]

Although Manteuffel had given his 'word of honour' that he had not been involved with Techen or Seiffart in this sordid business, this assurance did not count for very much. Diplomats at the Prussian court had long observed, in the words of one of their number, that Manteuffel 'is not fundamentally a dissimulator, neither is he fundamentally believable, but likes to flirt with lies'. Leopold von Gerlach thus had good reason to be sceptical of Manteuffel's denials, and for a long time he remained suspicious that the Minister President was deeply involved in the whole affair—as, of course, he was. By December 1855, however, Gerlach claimed to have cast aside all his doubts and proclaimed that Manteuffel was not guilty. Why he did so is not clear. Certainly he wanted this whole embarrassing and potentially nasty matter to be covered up; after all, the disclosure of Manteuffel's involvement would

[4] Kurt Borries, *Preußen im Krimkrieg 1853–1856* (Stuttgart, 1930), 39–40; Meysenbug to Rüdt, 17 Mar. 1856, GLA, Abt. 48/2653.

[5] Otto von Bismarck, *Die gesammelten Werke*, xv: *Erinnerung und Gedanke: Kritische Neuausgabe auf Grund des gesamten schriftlichen Nachlasses*, ed. Gerhard Ritter and Rudolf Stadelmann (Berlin, 1932), 83.

[6] 'Protokoll der Vernehmung Techens', 30 Jan. 1856, in Winfried Baumgart (ed.), *Akten zur Geschichte des Krimkriegs*, Ser. II, *Preußische Akten zur Geschichte des Krimkriegs* (2 vols.; Munich, 1990–1), ii. 805–8; id., 'Einleitung', ibid. 40–1; and Stieber, *Denkwürdigkeiten*, 61–6.

inevitably have led to his resignation, which Gerlach thought was inopportune at that particular moment.[7] Unfortunately for both Gerlach and Manteuffel, however, the matter could not be resolved behind the scenes, but persisted in the open throughout much of the following year. Seiffart, of the Fiscal Bureau, attempted to defend himself by openly implicating the Minister President. In March 1856 a democratic parliamentarian from Breslau named Theodor Molinari distributed an anonymous pamphlet which, among other things, contained an official judicial statement by Seiffart exculpating himself and implicating Manteuffel. Molinari's pamphlet was sent to all the major newspapers and diplomatic missions in Berlin.

To make things worse, one of the Gerlach letters which had been stolen and transcribed was a report to him from a shady journalist in Minden, a certain Emil Lindenberg, who had spied on the Prince of Prussia while the latter was touring Westphalia. He concluded that the Prince was himself involved in a plot to discredit the King's conservative friends. When this report was disclosed, William instituted libel proceedings against Lindenberg, which dragged on for most of 1856. And as if all of these things were not bad enough, Police President Hinckeldey was shot and killed in a duel in mid-March. Although Hinckeldey's death was not linked to the Techen or Lindenberg cases, it was simply one more piece of evidence that all was not well in Prussia eight years after the revolution.[8]

These uproars represented far more than simply titillating and sordid *chroniques scandaleuses*. Many contemporary observers believed that they were symptomatic of the sorry condition of the Prussian state as a whole in the 1850s, despite the fact that the Prussian economy was healthy and the country had managed to stay out of the Crimean War. In the words of Lord Bloomfield, the British minister to Prussia, all these scandals and their aftermaths had lain 'bare the disgraceful system of intrigue and corruption which is carried on both in the avenues of the King's Palace, and also in the official regions'.[9]

Bloomfield was undoubtedly correct in suggesting that the scandals reflected some critical problems of governance in post-1848 Prussia. Especially complex were the difficulties that arose from the diffusion of power and authority in an early constitutional setting in which the rules of the political game were being recast and in

[7] Thun to Buol, 5 July 1853, HHStA, P. A. III Preußen Karton 48, I. Bundes-Angelegenheiten, fol. 47eᵛ; Leopold von Gerlach, diary (16 Oct., 3 Nov., 12 Nov., 29 Nov., 7 and 12 Dec. 1855), GA, 'Abschriften', xii. 128, 133, 136, 151, 152, 157, 158, and diary (18 June 1856), ibid. xiii. 115; Leopold von Gerlach to Otto von Manteuffel, 28 Nov. 1855, in Otto von Manteuffel, *Unter Friedrich Wilhelm IV.: Denkwürdigkeiten des Ministers Otto Freiherrn von Manteuffel*, ed. Heinrich von Poschinger (3 vols.; Berlin, 1901), iii. 84. Cf. Walter Bußmann, *Zwischen Preußen und Deutschland: Friedrich Wilhelm IV. Eine Biographie* (Berlin, 1990), 392; Winfried Baumgart, 'Zur Außenpolitik Friedrich Wilhelms IV. 1840–1858', in Otto Büsch (ed.), *Friedrich Wilhelm in seiner Zeit: Beiträge eines Colloquiums* (Berlin, 1987), 153; and Hans-Christof Kraus, 'Ernst Ludwig von Gerlach: Politisches Denken und Handeln eines preußischen Altkonservativen' (Diss.; 2 vols.; Göttingen, 1991), i. 431–5, ii. 323–5.

[8] Anon., *Der Potsdamer Depeschen-Diebstahl*, copies in several archives, e.g., BayHStA, MA III 2636; GLA, Abt. 48/2653; PRO, FO 64/413. See also Stieber's report of his investigation, 23 Mar. 1856, GStA Merseburg, Rep. 92 Leopold von Gerlach Nr. 31 Bd. III, Bl. 326–332ᵛ.

[9] Bloomfield to Clarendon, 28 Oct. 1856, PRO, FO 64/418; cf. Meysenbug to Rüdt, 14 Dec. 1855, GLA, Abt. 48/2652.

which the monarchy still occupied a central, though not always easily definable, position. As we saw in the last chapter, Prussia was groping towards a new model of political order in the 1850s. Thus that decade witnessed the emergence of a new kind of political culture and the formation of a new kind of state in Prussia. These structures of power and authority turned out to be remarkably persistent, and helped to shape the character of the Prussian-German state until its collapse in 1918. To help us understand these developments in greater detail, we shall first focus in this chapter on two individuals close to the King who, along with the monarch himself, helped to define the post-revolutionary monarchical order in Prussia: Leopold von Gerlach and Otto von Manteuffel. Their ideas about the nature of the modern monarchical state differed in significant ways; indeed, the two men anticipated many of the divisions and dilemmas within German conservatism down to the time of the First World War. As we know, Gerlach was the man of principle, the 'high conservative', the pietist, the defender of the *ständisch*, Christian-German state. Manteuffel was a product of the traditional bureaucracy and uninterested in the kinds of ideological and ecclesiastical issues that moved the King and the Gerlachs. Because of his efforts to adapt bureaucratic and executive practices to post-revolutionary realities, he has to be regarded as among the most important builders of the new Prussian state in the decade after 1848. In understanding the interactions of these two men and their relationship to the crown, we can learn much about the redefinition of the Prussian state and the place of monarchy in that state. To consider the contributions of Gerlach, Manteuffel, and the King himself to the emerging monarchical system of the 1850s, we shall focus on several key problems of that decade: (1) the new domestic order, especially the relationship between new kinds of formal and informal political structures (for example, parliament and press) on the one hand, and crown and court on the other; (2) the responses of Prussia's élites to the oriental crisis and the Crimean War; (3) related to that conflict, the 'state crisis' that emerged out of the quarrels between the King and his heir in 1854; (4) the scandals of 1855–6, which we have already briefly described; (5) the position of the King himself, especially in the context of his declining years, his disabling final illness, the establishment of the regency, and the launching of a so-called 'New Era' in 1858.

Two Visions of Monarchy and State Interest: Leopold von Gerlach and Otto von Manteuffel

Although the careers of Leopold von Gerlach and Otto von Manteuffel intersected in various ways throughout the 1850s, they otherwise had little in common, and were often temperamentally and ideologically opposed to each other. Gerlach was, of course, personally much closer to the King. Where his brother Ludwig was notable for his fiercely concentrated energy and wilful determination, Leopold had always been endowed with a phlegmatic disposition as well as a substantial dose of fatalism and even pessimism. Those tendencies became more pronounced during the 1850s. Five years older than the monarch, and in military service since 1806, Gerlach was already 60 when he became Adjutant-General in 1850; and, as he constantly stressed in his diary and correspondence, he was feeling his age. Short and immensely fat, after 1848 he also had increasingly severe problems with gout. More importantly, though, he frequently insisted that he had become too old to change his opinions, which had already been fixed for decades and which he did not believe in adapting to changed circumstances. He frequently proclaimed that he had grown weary of politics and that he yearned to return to the bucolic isolation of the family estate at Rohrbeck in the Neumark. From time to time he offered to resign, but Frederick William invariably turned down his requests; and, in any case, there was always something disingenuous about those offers. Gerlach was too attached to the King, too committed to an ideal of personal service to his monarch, and too much the political animal to consider seriously the life of a Junker squire.[10]

Gerlach's resignation attempts usually took place after one of his numerous spats with the King. Neither Leopold nor Ludwig believed in flattery or discretion in their dealings with Frederick William; the brothers were men of principle who made no attempt to alter their views according to the King's shifting moods. Thus Leopold was frequently the butt of royal displeasure, which in turn usually elicited harsh criticism from the Adjutant-General. Nevertheless, in contrast to the astringent Ludwig, who until the end of his life remained sharply critical of Frederick William and his behaviour, Leopold always professed his 'great love for the gentleman, who for all his weaknesses and mistakes has such a noble nature'. Part of the problem in their relationship, Leopold believed, was that the King so often deviated from his own principles, and thus the ever-consistent Gerlachs frequently provoked feelings of guilt and inadequacy in him.[11] Despite all his limitations, however, Frederick William was still vastly preferable to his younger brothers. The Prince of Prussia, Gerlach asserted, was characterized 'by complete mindlessness, Prince Carl by perversity, and both by the absolute absence of any concept of honour'.[12]

Gerlach recognized that it was, above all, shared political views which had bound him to Frederick William for so many years. In 1855 he wrote, 'I do not believe that there is anyone among the King's servants who so completely agrees with him politically, which His Majesty himself knows very well. From 1827 until 1840, indeed until 1848, I regarded him—precisely him—as the head of my party.'[13] For Leopold, as indeed for Frederick William IV, the primacy of religion, a devotion to 'historic' law, unremitting hostility to 'revolution' and 'absolutism', support for the Christian universalism embodied in the Holy Alliance, and an attachment to patrimonial notions of monarchical governance constituted the irreducible bases of political

[10] Leopold von Gerlach to FW IV, 27 Nov. 1851, 20 Mar. 1852, 9 May 1852, 28 June 1855, GStA Merseburg, HA Rep. 50 J Nr. 455, Bl. 62, 65–6, 70–70ᵛ, 107; FW IV to Leopold von Gerlach, 14 Mar. 1852, GA, 'Abschriften', xxx. 151; Nobbe, 'Einfluß', 47–8.

[11] Leopold von Gerlach, diary (13 Oct. and 6 Dec. 1855), GA, 'Abschriften', xii. 127, 157; Hans-Christof Kraus, 'Das preußische Königtum und Friedrich Wilhelm IV. aus der Sicht Ernst Ludwig von Gerlachs', in Büsch (ed.), *Friedrich Wilhelm IV. in Seiner Zeit*, 90.

[12] Leopold von Gerlach, diary (5 Dec. 1855), GA, 'Abschriften', xii. 155.

[13] Leopold von Gerlach, diary (13 Oct. 1855), ibid. xii. 127.

action.[14] Principle and morality should inform that action, not abstract or amoral calculations of state interest.

Thus it was with some distress that Gerlach contemplated the direction in which Otto von Bismarck was moving during his tenure as Prussia's representative to the Diet of the restored German Confederation. Bismarck had been closely associated with the *Kreuzzeitung* party since 1848 and had become one of Leopold's protégés. Their correspondence throughout the 1850s constituted a remarkable exchange of ideas and viewpoints, which reached a climax in 1857. The issues that year focused on Napoleon III, Bonapartism, and Prussia's policies toward the Second Empire in France. Bismarck had met the French Emperor in 1855, and believed that it was in the best interest of the Prussian crown and state to remain on a friendly footing with France, especially in view of Prussia's continuing disagreements with Austria. The legitimacy or illegitimacy of Napoleon III's dynastic pedigree was not an issue, Bismarck insisted; and anyway, it was wishful thinking to suppose that the 'legitimate' Bourbon pretender, 'Henry V', would ever mount the throne of France. Rather, he asserted, it was necessary to deal with France 'without regard to its current ruler, purely as a piece, an unavoidable piece in the chess game of politics, a game in which it is my duty to serve only *my* king and *my* country'.[15]

To Gerlach, of course, any accommodation with a Bonaparte was anathema. Like his royal master, Gerlach had been indelibly stamped by his experiences between 1806 and 1815, and half a century later he still regarded any Bonaparte, whether uncle or nephew, as 'the revolution incarnate' and thus 'our natural enemy'.[16] The two Napoleons were bound to the revolution, and as Gerlach expressed it to Bismarck in May 1857, 'My political principle is and remains the struggle against revolution. You will not persuade Bonaparte that he is not on the side of revolution.' And by 'revolution', of course, Gerlach understood popular sovereignty, the elimination of historic rights and liberties, levelling democracy, the denial of religion and divine authority, and aggressive wars of conquest. For all the quarrels and disagreements between King and Adjutant-General, these were views to which both men adhered and which had linked them inextricably for virtually their entire adult lives.[17]

[14] Stefan Nobbe, 'Der Einfluß religiöser Überzeugung auf die politische Ideenwelt Leopold von Gerlachs' (Diss.; Erlangen, 1970), 81, 84, 93–5, 142–5.

[15] Otto von Bismarck to Leopold von Gerlach, 2 May 1857, quoted in Lothar Gall, *Bismarck: The White Revolutionary*, trans. J. A. Underwood (2 vols.; London, 1986), i. 133.

[16] Leopold von Gerlach to Bismarck, 5 June 1857, in Horst Kohl (ed.), *Briefe des Generals Leopold von Gerlach an Otto von Bismarck* (Stuttgart, 1912), 218, 219; cf. Leopold von Gerlach to Edwin von Manteuffel, 2 Sept. 1856, GStA Merseburg, Rep. 92 Edwin von Manteuffel B II 19, Bl. 91–2.

[17] Leopold von Gerlach to Bismarck, 6 May 1857, in Kohl (ed.), *Briefe des Generals Leopold von Gerlach*, 211–12, and quoted in Gall, *Bismarck*, i. 130. On the Gerlach–Bismarck exchange and the evolution of the latter's ideas, see ibid. i. 131–40; Ernst Engelberg, *Bismarck: Urpreuße und Reichsgründer* (Berlin, 1985), 409–50; Otto Pflanze, *Bismarck and the Development of Germany*, i. *The Period of Unification 1815–1871*, 2nd edn. (Princeton, NJ, 1990), ch. 4, esp. 92–7; Frank-Lothar Kroll, 'Bismarck und Friedrich Wilhelm IV.', in Jost Dülffer, Bernd Martin, and Günter Wollstein (eds.), *Deutschland in Europa: Gedenkschrift für Andreas Hillgruber* (Frankfurt am Main, 1990), 205–28, esp. 221–2; Henry Kissinger, *Diplomacy* (New York, 1994), 124–30.

The struggle against 'Bonapartism' was, for Gerlach, only one aspect of a broader struggle against the 'revolution' in the 1850s. 'Absolutism' had long been yet another pernicious expression of the revolutionary spirit of the modern age. By no means identical with Bonapartism, it antedated the French Revolution and continued, according to both the Gerlachs, to pose a real danger to historic rights and freedoms. Absolutism in all its guises, whether bureaucratic or royal, had to be repudiated; and for that reason Gerlach and his fellow 'high conservatives' had never been uncritical Russophiles, for the empire of the tsars was the very embodiment of autocracy and 'military despotism'.[18] Similarly, the reader will recall that Gerlach and his friends had long criticized the 'arbitrary', bureaucratic despotism of Frederick William III's last years; and now, in the 1850s, Leopold was often concerned that absolutism was again rearing its head, and that its destructive potential was even greater than in the years before 1840. Like his brother and Friedrich Julius Stahl, by 1853 Leopold had reached the reluctant conclusion that the existing constitution, although only a feeble surrogate for a *ständisch* system, nevertheless offered the best institutional protection against both Bonapartism and the pretensions of irresponsible bureaucrats.[19]

The Minister President also discovered the utility of a constitution during those years. Like Gerlach, and in contrast to so many other royal officials during those years, Otto von Manteuffel enjoyed considerable longevity in office: he served as Interior Minister for two years and thereafter for eight more as Minister President and Foreign Minister—an astonishing feat indeed, especially considering that Frederick William never liked him very much. Adaptable, malleable, conciliatory, and discreet, he always appeared to his contemporaries and to subsequent generations as the very personification of the Prussian tradition of neo-absolutist, statist, bureaucratic conservatism. This judgement is no doubt true, as far as it goes, but it is also much too simplistic. Manteuffel was a complex, little-understood man, and he has long suffered from an unfavourable historical press that has failed to understand his real contributions to the negotiated re-creation of the Prussian state during the reaction decade.

Born in Lower Lusatia in 1805, Manteuffel was the son of a high-ranking Saxon official.[20] Orphaned at an early age, he and his younger brother Karl were brought up in the household of his uncle Hans, father of his cousin Edwin. After attending the renowned school at Schulpforta—which also produced, among many others, Leopold von Ranke and Friedrich Nietzsche—and university at Halle, Manteuffel entered the Prussian judicial service before transferring to the administrative branch. In 1833 he became *Landrat* of Luckau in his native Lower Lusatia as well as a gentry (*ritterschaftlich*) delegate to the provincial diet of the Mark Brandenburg and

[18] Leopold von Gerlach to Otto von Manteuffel, 20 July 1852 (draft), GA, 'Abschriften', xxii. 223–4.
[19] Leopold von Gerlach to FW IV, 20 Feb. 1853, GStA Merseburg, HA Rep. 50 J Nr. 455, Bl. 84–5; Leopold von Gerlach to Graf Münster, 27–30 May 1853, and to Edwin von Manteuffel, 29 Oct. 1858, in Nobbe, 'Einfluß', 109–14 and app. of sources 162–3, 180–2; Anna Clausen, *Die Stellung Leopold von Gerlachs zum Abschluß des preußischen Verfassungswerkes unter Friedrich Wilhelm IV.* (Weida, 1914), 76–8.
[20] For biographical details, see *ADB*, xx. 260–72; and esp. Günther Grünthal, 'Otto Freiherr von Manteuffel', unpub. ms. (1989). My thanks to Professor Grünthal for making this study available to me.

the Margravate of Lusatia. He was thereby able to gain direct experience of those *ständisch* institutions that were so admired in the Crown Prince's entourage.

Thereafter Manteuffel's rise up the bureaucratic ladder was sure and swift, with stops in Königsberg and Stettin until, in 1844, he became a councillor to the Prince of Prussia. Two years later he became a Director in the Interior Ministry, and in 1847 a delegate to the United Diet. His formidable administrative competence, combined with unbending loyalty to the crown, recommended him to the Camarilla and Count Brandenburg in the autumn of 1848, and in the next two years, as we have already seen, he was critically involved with all the major issues of the day, including the December 1848 constitution, the introduction of the three-class suffrage in 1849, the more or less final revision of the constitution in 1849–50, and, of course, the crises of 1850. Like Brandenburg himself, Manteuffel was never a creature of the Camarilla, the Gerlachs, or the *Kreuzzeitung*. Quite the contrary: agrarian and aristocratic interests, and with them the Camarilla and the *Kreuzzeitung*, were appalled by the communal and agricultural laws of 1850, which he had played a major role in drafting.[21] Indeed, conflicts between the Minister President and the 'high conservatives' persisted intermittently for years, and contributed significantly to that atmosphere of 'moderated anarchy' so characteristic of the Prussian state in the 1850s.

At first glance, Manteuffel hardly seemed to be made for intrigue. Short, bespectacled, fat, and otherwise completely undistinguished in appearance, he looked more like a petty office-clerk than the chief minister of one of Europe's great powers.[22] His personality was almost the exact opposite of his royal master's; where Frederick William could be almost uncontrollably garrulous, Manteuffel became notorious for his secretiveness and his brusque conversational style. As a result, he was especially unpopular within the diplomatic corps in Berlin. One irritated envoy spoke for most of his colleagues when he reported that Manteuffel 'has essentially no knowledge of the usual forms of courtesy, and in personal dealings he daily manages to give offence because of his inattention to customary considerations of politeness', while Queen Elisabeth herself remarked that the Minister President 'has something primitive about him'. Members of Berlin high society also poked fun at Manteuffel's wife for her poor breeding and her inability to speak French.[23] In fact, Manteuffel had few friends or confidants, and he was never associated with any particular faction or group at court; nor, in contrast to people like Leopold von Gerlach or Hinckeldey, was he ever really taken into the King's confidence. How, then, did he manage to stay in office so long?

Throughout the 1850s rumours constantly swirled through court and capital that Manteuffel was out of favour, that his political position was hopelessly weak, and that Frederick William intended to replace him. Yet he always survived. Many

[21] Hans Walter, *Die innere Politik des Ministers von Manteuffel und der Ursprung der Reaktion in Preußen* (Berlin, 1910), ch. 3 and pp. 140–7.

[22] Borries, *Krimkrieg*, 41.

[23] Leopold von Gerlach, diary (30 July 1853), GA, 'Abschriften', x. 114; Meysenbug to Rüdt, 21 June 1852, GLA, Abt. 48/2649; Malsen to Max II, 10 Oct. 1853, BayHStA, MA III 2633.

observers attributed his durability to adaptability and opportunism, suggesting that he never regarded anything as a matter of principle, that he was always willing to bend to the political winds, and that he consistently accommodated himself to the King's vagaries. Leopold von Gerlach believed that the problem with Manteuffel—whom he usually described, in puns on his surname, as 'Oberteufel' or 'Fra Diavolo'—was an unwillingness to ground his politics in Christian belief and moral-ity. Like Pontius Pilate, the Adjutant-General liked to say, Manteuffel washed his hands and asked, 'What is truth?' Other observers were even less charitable, con-tending that Manteuffel, who was not well-to-do, wanted to stay in office as long as possible in order to salt away substantial sums of money for future use.[24]

In the eyes of many potential or actual adversaries, Manteuffel often appeared to represent something of a lesser evil. In the regions of the court and the parliamentary chambers everyone realized that serving as Frederick William's chief minister was an exasperating and thankless job, and not many were eager to have it. Very few people possessed Manteuffel's thick skin, or could put up with the abusive treatment that Frederick William regularly meted out to him. Moreover, people like Leopold von Gerlach usually thought that the alternatives to Manteuffel—for example, someone like Bethmann-Hollweg—would be far worse, and so, despite their frequent dis-putes with the Minister President, they usually preferred to see him stay in office. In fact, Gerlach often insisted that Manteuffel was indispensable. Manteuffel himself skilfully exploited that indispensability to strengthen his own position at court and in the cabinet. In the late summer of 1852, for example, Frederick William decided to appoint Radowitz as head of the Prussian military education system. Typically, he had not bothered to inform his chief minister about his plans, even though he should have realized that rehabilitating Radowitz would be a red flag to the Russians and Austrians, and a political slap to Manteuffel himself. Thus the King issued the order directly to War Minister Eduard von Bonin, and simply ignored the Minister President. Again typically, Frederick William insisted that as supreme commander of the Prussian army he was not obliged to inform anyone, especially civilians, about his military decisions. To make things even worse, the King's decision became known while he was taking his annual holiday on the Baltic island of Rügen. It was all too much for Manteuffel, who journeyed to Rügen and threatened to resign. Frederick William immediately realized that he had committed a gaffe, effusively begged Manteuffel to stay, and on 8 September 1852 agreed to a cabinet order that systematized and dramatically increased the powers of the Minister President. That official now gained the right to proclaim the affairs of a single ministry to be a matter for general cabinet discussion. The order further stipulated that any minister who wished to report to the King should inform the Minister President first, so that the latter could, if he wished, attend the meeting. Finally, in most cases the Minister

[24] Leopold von Gerlach, diary (5 Oct. 1853), GA, 'Abschriften', x. 134; Leopold von Gerlach to Otto von Manteuffel, 20 July 1852 (draft), ibid. xxii. 224; Thun to Buol, 23 Apr. 1853, HHStA, P. A. III Preußen Karton 48, VIII. Interna Preußens, fol. 4aʳ–4eᵛ; Karl Enax, *Otto von Manteuffel und die Reaktion in Preußen* (Dresden, 1907), 45–6.

President would be the official who would pass cabinet reports on to the King. It had thus become much more difficult for the monarch to circumvent his chief minister. Manteuffel had turned a serious personal and political embarrassment into a major political victory, though he never managed to gain that complete control over the cabinet which he so desired. He would never become a Hardenberg, much less a Bismarck.[25]

As the Radowitz affair illustrates, one secret of Manteuffel's success was his skill as a resourceful and even ruthless political tactician. Like his sometime adversaries Friedrich Julius Stahl, Ludwig von Gerlach, and Hermann Wagener, he appreciated the ways in which public opinion could be manipulated and even won over for the monarchical-conservative cause. In Berlin, for example, he became famous for his unannounced visits to public houses, where he tossed back a few *Weißbiere* and talked politics with *Stammtisch* guests. On the first of these occasions, in October 1849, he appeared as 'Herr Müller'; but thereafter he made no attempt to disguise his identity, even when he showed up in a tavern frequented by politically radical machinists.[26]

Much more serious, and just as spectacular, were his attempts to manipulate the press, which, despite intensified censorship after 1851, managed to remain more vigorous, politically varied, and influential than in the *Vormärz* years. Almost immediately after assuming power in 1850 Manteuffel created a Central Office for Press Affairs (*Zentralstelle für Preßangelegenheiten (sic)*) which was supposed to monitor newspaper activities throughout the entire kingdom, plant 'inspired' articles in friendly publications, and supply money to accommodating editors. By January 1851 the Central Office was supporting sixty-four periodicals either through direct subventions or through specially lithographed Saturday supplements.[27] The office's director, Dr Rhyno Quehl (1821–64), quickly became one of the Minister President's most controversial acolytes.

A pastor's son from Erfurt, Quehl had worked as a journalist in Danzig until his support for the 'November ministry' in 1848 got him in hot water with the moderately liberal mercantile élite of that city. He then went to work in Berlin for the *Deutsche Reform*, a paper that sympathized with Manteuffel; thereafter he rose very rapidly indeed, directing not only the Central Office but also a new pro-Manteuffel newspaper called *Die Zeit*. Fiercely loyal to the Minister President, he fired editorial salvos with equal effect at liberals, democrats, Interior Minister Westphalen, and

[25] The cabinet order of 1852 played an important role in the events leading up to Bismarck's resignation in 1890. Leopold von Gerlach, diary (20 Aug. 1852), GA, 'Abschriften', ix. 152, 153–4; Prokesch to Buol, 26 and 28 Aug. 1852, HHStA, P. A. III Preußen Karton 46, VIII. Innere Angelegenheiten Preußens, fol. 69ʳ–69ᵛ, 71ʳ–71ᵛ; Gerlach's correspondence in August 1852 in GA, 'Abschriften', xxii. 246–60; FW IV to Elisabeth, 2 and 10 Sept. 1852, GStA Merseburg, HA Rep. 50 J Nr. 995 Fasz. 23, Bl. 9–11ᵛ, 20–22ᵛ; Manteuffel, *Unter Friedrich Wilhelm IV.*, ii. 242–51; Ernst Rudolf Huber, *Deutsche Verfassungsgeschichte seit 1789*, 3rd edn. (Stuttgart, 1988), iii: *Bismarck und das Reich*, 65; John R. Gillis, *The Prussian Bureaucracy in Crisis 1840–1860: Origins of an Administrative Ethos* (Stanford, Calif., 1971), 147.

[26] Manteuffel, *Unter Friedrich Wilhelm IV.*, i. 184–7, ii. 82.

[27] E. R. Huber, *Verfassungsgeschichte*, iii. 171; Manteuffel, *Unter Friedrich Wilhelm IV.*, i. 416.

Wagener's *Kreuzzeitung*. The result was a vituperative press-war which became even nastier as a result of Hinckeldey's various seizures of the *Kreuzzeitung*. The conflict reached a climax in 1852, when Quehl's papers lashed out at a series of prominent *Kreuzzeitung* supporters, including Bismarck, Kleist-Retzow, and Westphalen. Many of those supporters were, for their part, almost hysterical in their loathing of Quehl. The *Kreuzzeitung* thundered incessantly against what it called 'the Manteuffel-Quehl system'; and even Frederick William, whose spats with the *Kreuzzeitung* were common knowledge, characterized Quehl simply as a *'Scheißkerl'*.[28]

The Minister President responded to these attacks by placing himself firmly on the side of his press tsar and by announcing that he would himself step down rather than dismiss Quehl. Manteuffel seems to have thought that Quehl's activities could help him maintain his distance from the *Kreuzzeitung* party while making overtures to the *Wochenblatt* group and the Prince of Prussia. The Minister President also correctly suspected Leopold von Gerlach of intriguing to get copies of Quehl's correspondence, while at the same time he had become increasingly alienated from those cabinet colleagues—*Kultusminister* Raumer, Interior Minister Westphalen, and Finance Minister Karl von Bodelschwingh, brother of the *Vormärz* minister—who were associated with the *Kreuzzeitung* party. Indeed, personal relations within the cabinet had become so bad by the summer of 1853 that Manteuffel again tried to resign, while the King himself had to intervene in the Crown Council and urge his ministers 'to maintain unity among themselves'.[29]

An armistice was finally achieved in 1853 after Wagener left the *Kreuzzeitung* and Quehl was packed off to Copenhagen as Prussian consul.[30] Quehl's departure did not mean, however, that Manteuffel had abjured the use of agents and spies. Quehl was the least clandestine of the Minister President's various informants. At the very height of the Quehl–*Kreuzzeitung* conflict, in fact, Manteuffel had been in close contact with Georg Klindworth, one of the most notorious secret agents in nineteenth-century Europe and, at the time, an employee of the King of Württemberg.

[28] For Quehl's biography, see von Schaetzell to Leopold von Gerlach, 27 Nov. 1852, GA, 'Abschriften', xxii. 362–6. On the press wars of 1851–3, see *inter alia* Otto von Manteuffel to Leopold von Gerlach, 5 July 1851, and Hermann Wagener to Leopold von Gerlach, 6 July 1851, ibid., xxi. 107–8; Ludwig von Gerlach to Leopold von Gerlach, 21 July 1852, ibid., xxii. 228–30; Otto von Manteuffel to Leopold von Gerlach, 20 Nov. 1852, ibid., xxii. 345–6; Ludwig von Gerlach, diary (22 May 1852), in Ernst Ludwig von Gerlach, *Von der Revolution zum Norddeutschen Bund: Politik und Ideengut der preußischen Hochkonservativen 1848–1866. Aus dem Nachlaß von Ernst Ludwig von Gerlach*, ed. Hellmut Diwald (2 vols.; Göttingen, 1970), i. 309; Leopold von Gerlach, diary (17 May, 24 May, and 18 July 1852), GA, 'Abschriften', ix. 90, 96, 129–30; Manteuffel, *Unter Friedrich Wilhelm IV.*, ii. 217–19, 223–30, 367–8, 376–8; Quehl to Manteuffel, 18 Nov. 1852, GStA Merseburg, Rep. 92 Otto von Manteuffel Tit. II Nr. 92, Bl. 29–43ᵛ.

[29] Otto von Manteuffel to Leopold von Gerlach, 2 July 1853, GA, 'Abschriften', xxiii. 60–1; Manteuffel, *Unter Friedrich Wilhelm IV.*, ii. 371–6; Bloomfield to Earl of Clarendon, 15 July 1853, PRO, FO 64/356; FW IV in Crown Council, 7 July 1853, GStA Merseburg, Rep. 90a B III 2c Nr. 3 Vol. II, Bl. 102; Leopold von Gerlach, diary (3, 6, and 7 July 1853), GA, 'Abschriften', x. 95–8; Gerlach to Bismarck, 19 Feb. 1853, in Kohl (ed.), *Briefe des Generals Leopold von Gerlach*, 37.

[30] Malsen to Max II, 3 Sept. 1853, BayHStA, MA III 2633; Manteuffel, *Unter Friedrich Wilhelm IV.*, ii. 377–8; Kraus, 'Gerlach', i. 380–6, 393–9, ii. 286–91, 297–301.

Manteuffel clearly hoped that Klindworth could serve as a useful intermediary in sensitive negotiations concerning the renewal of the Prussian-dominated German Customs Union (*Zollverein*). And of course, as we already know, by 1853 Manteuffel had hired Techen to spy on Leopold von Gerlach and Marcus Niebuhr.[31]

Manteuffel was thus a rather gifted and often unscrupulous player of the political game. But he was not just a ruthless tactician or a smooth 'operator'. Nor is it sufficient to describe him as a man who, in the words of his ultra-conservative rivals, had 'grown great as a bureaucrat'.[32] And, despite the dark suspicions and accusations of the Gerlachs and their friends, he was not a 'Bonapartist'. Though his reflections about the nature and place of monarchy in post-1848 Prussia were never very original, he thought clearly and consistently about these matters; and the conclusions he reached represented an important, if not altogether happy or successful, attempt to adjust monarchical conservatism to mid-century conditions.

Manteuffel always remained a child of the Prussian bureaucracy. Prussia was, he insisted, a state dominated by soldiers and officials. That reality had made Prussia great; and if there was any ideal form of government to which he looked, it was the enlightened absolutism of Frederick II, which, he hoped, could be rejuvenated and adapted to the needs of the present. For Manteuffel was no Romantic reactionary. Though he was a conservative who wanted to preserve historically legitimate institutions, he was also a realist who had little patience with quixotic battles against the trends of the times. The real task of the conservative statesman, he believed, should be to preserve as much as possible of the effective authority of the crown and of an efficient civil service. Without them, Prussia would cease to be a great power. Thus the maintenance of state power was the highest obligation of all Prussians, and took priority over everything else.[33]

The interests of the state did not require a reversion to *ständisch* institutions. Indeed, Manteuffel argued in 1852, those institutions reflected the warlike values of the feudal age, and so were not really appropriate to the peaceable needs of modern commerce, agriculture, and industry. He did not discount his own experience with the *Stände* of Lower Lusatia, and in fact thought that corporative institutions at the communal level were rather a good thing. But it was illusory to assume that such institutions could play a useful role at higher levels of state life, for 'the *Prussian* state, the great power *Prussia*, has never been based on them, and never will be'. Thus Manteuffel had never been enamoured of the provincial diets, especially as they had developed between 1823 and 1840, nor did he wish to revert to the United Diet of 1847. It was necessary to come up with modern responses to recent economic and social changes. The Minister President was not being disingenuous when he

---

[31] Correspondence between Manteuffel and Klindworth in GStA Merseburg, Rep. 92 Otto von Manteuffel Tit. II Bd. 58 Vol. I and II; cf. Alfred Stern, 'Georg Klindworth: Ein politischer Geheimagent des neunzehnten Jahrhunderts', *Historische Vierteljahrschrift*, 25 (1929–30), 430–58, esp. 441–2; Loftus to Clarendon, 3 Jan. 1854, PRO, FO 64/367.

[32] Enax, *Manteuffel*, 43; Grünthal, 'Manteuffel' (ms.), 2.

[33] Manteuffel, *Unter Friedrich Wilhelm IV.*, iii. 99.

insisted that Prussia should 'hang on to the past but look to the present and thereby repudiate reaction as such'.[34]

Manteuffel also believed that it would be possible to govern with the existing constitution, but like most conservatives of the 1850s he was fearful that the emergent parliamentary system would seriously, perhaps fatally, undermine the monarchy and with it the bases of Prussian state power. In the early 1850s, accordingly, he was determined to resuscitate the old Council of State (*Staatsrat*) of 1817 as a politically neutral, informed body of expert decision-makers standing above the rest of society. Such a council could control and divert, and even 'absorb', constitutional tendencies in Prussian society.[35] The *Kreuzzeitung* conservatives strongly opposed the Minister President's plan, contending that the Council of State would only amount to an 'Olympus of bureaucrats', a refuge for mediocrities.[36] In early 1852 Frederick William named Manteuffel to head the Council of State, which had never been dissolved in 1848 and so had never legally ceased to exist; but the body was only formally reconstituted two years later, and it never regained the importance it had enjoyed under Frederick William III.[37]

In developing his views of monarchical government, Manteuffel was attracted to some of the ideas of the well-known publicist Constantin Frantz, who in the early 1850s advocated patently Bonapartist solutions to modern problems. At the same time, however, the Minister President shied away from Frantz's more radical ideas, especially his support for a Caesarist, plebiscitary state. Manteuffel's own view of Germany's social condition was more strongly influenced by the conservative writer Wilhelm Heinrich Riehl, whose analysis of civil society, *Die bürgerliche Gesellschaft*, appeared in 1851. Riehl contended that German society was now essentially composed of four groups: the peasantry and the aristocracy, or the 'powers of conservation', and the *Bürgertum* and the 'fourth estate', or the 'powers of movement'. The art of government, Manteuffel believed, lay in recognizing those fundamental divisions; pretending that they could not or should not exist, or organizing government to the exclusive advantage of one group, would be wrong-headed and potentially disastrous. A stable monarchy could be built upon the co-operative efforts of peasantry, aristocracy, *and* an autonomous *Bürgertum*, thereby isolating a potentially revolutionary underclass. Government itself should stand above and mediate conflicts among the various 'bodies' (*Körperschaften*) of society. Such a political system, he believed, would represent a *via media* between *ständisch* and constitutional structures, and thus the best guarantor of a stable monarchical order.[38]

---

[34] Manteuffel to Leopold von Gerlach, 18 July 1852, GA, 'Abschriften', xxii. 220; Manteuffel to Gerlach, 4 Sept. 1852, in Manteuffel, *Unter Friedrich Wilhelm IV.*, ii. 240–1.

[35] Leopold von Gerlach, 'Auszug aus dem mir am 16. Juli 1852 mitgeteilten Promemoria des Ministers Manteuffel über den Staatsrat', GA, 'Abschriften', xxii. 215–18.

[36] Leopold von Gerlach to Ludwig von Gerlach, n.d. (mid-July 1852), in E. L. von Gerlach, *Von der Revolution*, ii. 798; Ludwig von Gerlach to Leopold von Gerlach, 14 June 1852, GA, 'Abschriften', xxii. 170.

[37] Enax, *Manteuffel*, 36–7; E. R. Huber, *Verfassungsgeschichte*, iii. 167–9.

[38] This discussion largely follows the excellent analysis in Günther Grünthal, *Parlamentarismus in*
[*cont. on p. 265*]

Manteuffel's vision of a neutral bureaucratic state never quite came to fruition in the 1850s. Bismarck pointed out in his memoirs that Manteuffel always found himself on the defensive, and he could never count on the wholehearted support of his royal master. Like all the other 'cattle' who had to work with that monarch, Manteuffel complained about the absence of 'a clear and plain course in which one can take confidence'. The King's lack of trust in his advisers had undermined their capacity to rise above the petty divisions of the day and give him the impartial advice that he so badly needed. Thus his government was divided and demoralized, while Prussia's credibility as a great power was sorely threatened. Even worse, Manteuffel thundered in his 'Testament' of 1856, was the King's persistent tendency to maintain an alternative cabinet next to his official one, composed of cabinet councillors, adjutants, and secretaries. As a result the King's government had become a plaything of the *Kreuzzeitung*, 'whose open policy—to replace the kingdom by the Grace of God with a regime of Junkers and pietists—has earned it the hatred and scorn of the nation'. Though Manteuffel often felt overwhelmed, he said, by the perpetual intrigues and backbiting of the royal court, he also believed strongly that he was obliged, as the King's servant, to accommodate himself as much as possible to his master's wishes. Like Leopold von Gerlach, Manteuffel was deeply fatalistic. It was his destiny, he sighed in August 1852, to be 'used up' by his sovereign; and so, despite endless problems and innumerable setbacks, he hung on stubbornly to his thankless job.[39]

The Oriental Crisis and the Domestic Crisis of Monarchical Authority, 1853–1856

If Manteuffel failed to emerge victorious from the intrigues and conflicts of the reaction decade, the same is true of his rivals. As we have just seen, Leopold von Gerlach and Otto von Manteuffel advocated alternative conservative responses to post-1848 conditions; Hinckeldey's crypto-Bonapartism, Friedrich Julius Stahl's constitutional monarchism, and the 'liberal' conservatism of the *Wochenblatt* party represented three more. The first three—Gerlach's *ständisch* patrimonialism, Manteuffel's statist neo-absolutism, and Hinckeldey's authoritarianism—were constantly competing for the King's favour, but none ever really managed to achieve it. Frederick William himself did not like to make a choice among the varieties of conservatism that his advisers proposed to him. The *ständisch* conservatism of the Gerlachs and the *Kreuzzeitung* party was undoubtedly closest to his heart; but as we have repeatedly seen, the King was never able to resolve a persistent tension between his own affirmation of '*ständisch* freedom', on the one hand, and his elevated notions of his own authority on the other. Those notions invariably clashed with the

Preußen 1848/49–1857/58: Preußischer Konstitutionalismus—Parlament und Regierung in der Reaktionsära (Düsseldorf, 1982), 281–6, and id., 'Manteuffel' (ms.), 10–11.

[39] Otto von Manteuffel to Leopold von Gerlach, 16 June 1852, GA, 'Abschriften', xxii. 175–6; Manteuffel, *Unter Friedrich Wilhelm IV.*, iii. 103–4, 105; Leopold von Gerlach, diary (4 Sept. 1852), GA, 'Abschriften', ix. 162; Enax, *Manteuffel*, 13–17, 48–9.

Hallerian views of the high conservatives, for whom, as Ludwig von Gerlach loved to repeat, every man (or at least every *paterfamilias*) was a king. Frederick William, in contrast, expected 'obedience' from his subjects, and, when he failed to get it, railed against their 'disloyalty'. In many ways he felt more comfortable with the police-state conservatism of a Hinckeldey, which managed to combine social control and administrative efficiency with a modicum of popularity. The statist or bureaucratic conservatism of a Manteuffel, however, was always far less appealing to him, though it was in some ways the most imaginative conservative alternative offered in the 1850s, and the one most in accord with Prussia's genuine traditions.

During the reaction decade Frederick William was never able to reconstruct that 'personal rule' which he had established during the last *Vormärz* years. After 1848 there were real limits to his power, manifested most obviously in his oath to the constitution but also in the capacity of other groups to thwart or forestall his wishes. Nevertheless, he remained the focal point of the Prussian state, and his non-committal tactics helped to sustain, rather than diminish, the power of his office. That authority was nowhere better illustrated than in the conflicts over Prussia's foreign policy at the time of the oriental crisis and the Crimean War from 1853 to 1856. During that crisis Prussia literally found itself caught in the middle, with powerful internal and external pressures to opt either for the Western powers or for the Russians. But Prussia stayed neutral throughout, a policy which was Frederick William's own, sustained by him and imposed by him upon his officials and advisers, virtually all of whom had their own particular foreign-policy agendas.[40]

Frederick William's behaviour throughout the oriental crisis reflected both considerations of ideology and calculations of interest.[41] Thus he could not excuse Russia's invasion of the Danubian principalities in 1853, nor, for obvious reasons, could he condone the 'folly' of supporting the Ottoman Empire and thereby '*Islam against Christians!*'[42] He also was genuinely fearful of the incalculable consequences of a general European war, and concluded that such a conflict could not possibly be to Prussia's benefit. In early 1854 he proclaimed, 'The war that is breaking out is an *unjust* one on both sides. And *I will not let Prussia be forced into an unjust war.*' Therefore, 'Prussia should remain firmly neutral.'[43] In that policy Frederick William generally enjoyed the support of the vestigial Camarilla—that is, Leopold von Gerlach and Niebuhr—and its allies. A man like Gerlach could, of course, never tolerate the idea of co-operation with a Bonaparte, and he would have preferred to support the Russians openly. Since that would not be politically feasible, he opted for Frederick William's neutrality policy as a lesser evil; after all, a neutral Prussia, with its long common border with Russia, would work more to the Tsar's advantage than

[40] Baumgart, 'Außenpolitik', 139; Bußmann, *Friedrich Wilhelm IV.*, 353.

[41] Baumgart, 'Einleitung', in id. (ed.), *Preußische Akten*, i. 31–42.

[42] FW IV to Bunsen, 20 Nov. 1853, GStA Merseburg, HA Rep. 50 J Nr. 244a, Bl. 183–185ᵛ; FW IV to Bunsen, 25 Feb. 1854, in Borries, *Krimkrieg*, 351.

[43] Documents in Borries, *Krimkrieg*, 352, 353–4, 361–2; FW IV to Victoria, 7 Mar. 1854, GStA Merseburg, HA Rep. 50 J Nr. 359, Bl. 3–4ᵛ.

to his adversaries'.[44] Throughout the conflict, however, Gerlach also liked to emphasize that it was wrong to regard him and his friends as unconditional Russophiles. In July 1855 he wrote, 'Our goal is and always was the struggle against a Bonapartism and an absolutism based on the revolution and revolutionary ideas. There is no such thing as a *parti moscovite*. The King, Ludwig, Stahl, and I do not have the remotest Russian sympathies. In Russia we see only the opposition to Bonaparte as well as our proven ally in the coming struggle.'[45]

In contrast to the Gerlachs, Otto von Manteuffel had no particular ideological axes to grind, and was prepared to deal with Napoleon III as an emperor '*comme tous les autres*'. In early 1854 he leaned toward the Western powers, but that flirtation was short-lived. On the whole, the Minister President followed the King's lead and supported the policy of neutrality, from which Prussia might be able to derive some political advantages.[46] Although that placed him more or less on the side of the Camarilla and the *Kreuzzeitung*, he was more suspicious of Russia and also much more inclined to base his views on considerations of state interest than on ideology. He was also keenly aware that the King frequently circumvented him and that his rivals Gerlach and Niebuhr had regular access to information that was not available to him.

It was, in fact, the *Wochenblatt* party which raised the first serious internal challenge to Prussia's policy of neutrality. Bethmann-Hollweg and his supporters were ideologically inclined to the West rather than to the East. In addition, they were convinced that it was essential for Prussia to cast off its dependence on Austria and develop a more assertive foreign policy that would allow Prussia to regain the initiative in German affairs. With its emphasis on moderate reformism and Prussian patriotism, the *Wochenblatt* party could rely on important sympathizers in powerful places, including veteran diplomats like Count Albert von Pourtalès, Robert von der Goltz, or Count Guido von Usedom. As the oriental crisis deepened in 1853 and early 1854, the *Wochenblatt* could also count among its sympathizers the Prince of Prussia, War Minister Eduard von Bonin, and our old acquaintance Bunsen, still Prussia's envoy in London. As a result of his long years in England, Frederick William commented, Bunsen had become 'more Whiggish than the Whigs'.[47] Now Bunsen was determined to take concrete action to ensure closer ties between his own country and Britain, and thus to place Prussia squarely on the side of the Western powers. At the end of 1853 it seemed that such an arrangement might well be possible. In December Prussia joined with Austria, France, and Britain in a note to Russia calling for the maintenance of the Ottoman Empire's territorial integrity. Bunsen believed that this note could pave the way for a military convention among the four powers.[48]

[44] Borries, *Krimkrieg*, 22.

[45] Leopold von Gerlach, diary (11 July 1855), GA, 'Abschriften', xii. 105; cf. Kraus, 'Gerlach', i. 406–15, ii. 305–10.

[46] Borries, *Krimkrieg*, 36–43; Baumgart, 'Außenpolitik', 149–50; id., 'Einleitung', in id. (ed.), *Preußische Akten*, i. 44–8.

[47] FW IV to Victoria, 24 May 1854, in Borries, *Krimkrieg*, 355.   [48] Ibid. 76–85.

On 1 March 1854 Bunsen presented an elaborate memorandum which he hoped could serve as a basis for negotiations with the British Foreign Secretary, Lord Clarendon. Among other things, it called for a concerted attempt to halt Russian expansion, to restrict that country to its 'natural borders in Europe', and radically to redraw the map of the Continent. If Prussia did not act soon to join this cause, it would once again lose the diplomatic initiative to Austria.[49] Unfortunately for Bunsen, he had no authorization to proceed with negotiations of this sort, and a storm of indignation erupted when word of his activities reached Berlin. By early March Frederick William, who had been distressed by the entrance of British and French vessels into the Black Sea, had abandoned the idea of a military convention with the Western powers and had become determined to preserve Prussia's strict neutrality. At the same time, the Gerlachs and their friends demanded Bunsen's head.

Frederick William decided to respond to these developments by sending his old confidant Carl von der Groeben on a special mission to London to investigate the charges against Bunsen and reaffirm Prussia's neutral position. But Groeben's mission only delayed the inevitable. Bunsen had always had powerful enemies back home, and now, through his active support for the Western powers, he had fatally exposed himself. On 19 April 1854, aware that the tide had turned against him in Berlin and Potsdam, he asked the King to relieve him of his post. The reluctant monarch was finally pressured by his advisers at home, especially the pro-*Kreuzzeitung* Supreme Chamberlain Count Dohna, to dismiss Bunsen and name Count Bernstorff, one of Manteuffel's associates, to replace him. Shortly thereafter, the highly regarded, pro-*Wochenblatt* War Minister Bonin was also dismissed for making an ill-advised statement about the impossibility of a Prussian arrangement with Russia. Within the course of a few weeks, then, the most articulate supporters of a pro-Western foreign policy had been purged from office, while Manteuffel, who had been playing with similar ideas, beat a hasty retreat. Ludwig von Gerlach was speaking for all his friends when he gleefully described Bunsen's fall as a 'great victory' which had 'amortized' the King's favourite once and for all. Unbeknownst to most contemporary observers, the rout of the *Wochenblatt* party was also a victory for Carl Wilhelm Saegert. The ambitious school director's influence now reached its zenith. Saegert consistently urged the King to pursue an uncompromising policy of neutrality, even if it meant breaking with the leaders of both the *Wochenblatt* and the *Kreuzzeitung* parties. The Prince of Prussia, fearful that a second Olmütz was in the offing, now erupted with almost hysterical anger at his allies' dismissal. The result was a temporary breach with his older brother which brought Prussia to the brink of a serious internal crisis.[50]

---

[49] Text of *Denkschrift* in Frances Baroness Bunsen, *Christian Carl Josias Freiherr von Bunsen: Aus seinen Briefen und nach eigener Erinnerung geschildert von seiner Witwe*, ed. Friedrich Nippold (3 vols.; Leipzig, 1868, 1869, 1871), iii. 337–43.

[50] Ibid. iii. 352–63; Borries, *Krimkrieg*, 46–9, 108–34; Klaus Groß, 'Die deutsch-englischen Beziehungen im Wirken Christian Carl Josias von Bunsens (1791–1860)' (Diss.; Würzburg, 1965), 246–76, 290–312; Peter Rassow, *Der Konflikt König Friedrich Wilhelms IV. mit dem Prinzen von Preußen*
[cont. on p. 269]

Although William had been on exceptionally friendly terms with Bunsen since the time of his London exile in 1848, he did not unconditionally support the Prussian diplomat's rash and ill-conceived diplomatic initiatives in early 1854; nor did he endorse the *Wochenblatt* party's aversion to co-operation with Austria. Still, he felt that Bunsen's gaffe did not warrant his resignation. Bonin's dismissal in early May was, however, the last straw for the man who had long regarded himself as the embodiment and guardian of the Prussian army. The King's Russophile advisers, he believed, were trying to neutralize him politically and at the same time undermine Prussia's political and military autonomy. In a violent letter to 'Fritz' on 5 May, William asserted that this was all part of a plan to move Prussia 'into the Russian camp'. He also noted that in the past he had always been consulted whenever Frederick William was about to appoint a new War Minister. This time, however, he had been kept in the dark. 'I must regard Bonin's fall as directed against myself', he asserted, 'and thus, as the first officer of the army, I herewith submit a most firm protest against his release, and beseech you at this important moment to retract Bonin's dismissal immediately, for *your* own good, that of the *army*, and for *your own political position.*' If not, William continued, he would immediately leave Prussia and go to Baden in order to regain his nerves and dissociate himself from the King's policies.[51]

William was quite clearly guilty of a grave act of military disobedience, as Frederick William himself pointed out by noting that his younger brother had no right to protest in the name of the army against a decision taken by the commander-in-chief; and, indeed, the heir to the Prussian throne could well have been liable for a court martial and perhaps even the death penalty, so grievous was his insubordination. In this entire affair, however, the supposedly 'unstable' and 'emotional' Frederick William showed himself to be far more statesmanlike and conciliatory than his 'calm' and 'steady' brother. Although reprimanding him for his behaviour, Frederick William decided otherwise to 'ignore' the Prince's act of defiance, temporarily relieve him of his army command, and grant him leave to go to Baden. Though William denied that he was guilty of insubordination, he at first continued to protest against the King's policies and to insist that the Gerlachs and their friends were intent on forging a dangerous alliance with Russia. The King still hoped that a reconciliation could be achieved, if only to preserve the line of succession and block the ambitions of the unsavoury (and fiercely pro-Russian) Prince Carl, who again, as in 1848, sensed succession possibilities for himself and his son.[52] Some expression of regret from William would be necessary, however, for 'you have set a very wicked example for my army and my subjects'. Although he continued to believe that his

im Jahre 1854: Eine preußische Staatskrise (Wiesbaden, 1961), 24–5, 39–40; Ludwig von Gerlach to Leopold von Gerlach, 27 Apr. 1854, GA, 'Abschriften', xxiv. 152; Elisabeth Richert, 'Die Stellung Wilhelms, des Prinzen von Preußen, zur preußischen Außen- und Innenpolitik der Zeit von 1848 bis 1857' (Diss.; Berlin, 1948), 95–104; Baumgart, 'Außenpolitik', 151–2; id., 'Einleitung', in id. (ed.), *Preußische Akten*, i. 52–3.

[51] Prince of Prussia to FW IV, 5 May 1854, in Rassow, *Konflikt*, 41–2.

[52] Ibid. 56–60; Carl to FW IV, 8 May 1854, GStA Merseburg, HA Rep. 59 I J Nr. 3 1854–9, Bl. 2.

own views were correct, the Prince of Prussia finally conceded that he was indeed the King's subject and so apologized for his actions. William returned to Berlin to be reconciled with the King on 7 June, the anniversary of their father's death.[53]

Although the affair ended peacefully, it had been far more than a storm in a teacup. In his determination not to deviate from his policy of neutrality, Frederick William had accepted the political disgrace of one of his closest friends and had come close to an irreparable breach with the heir to the throne, which, coming in the midst of a European conflict, might well have precipitated internal upheavals of incalculable proportions.[54] Despite their public reconciliation, relations between the royal brothers remained strained, with Frederick William frequently scolding William for his dyspeptic hostility to '*my* politics and *my* rule'.[55] The crisis of 1854 also contributed to the rapid decline of the *Wochenblatt* party, a process which was sealed the following year by its disastrous defeat in elections to the lower house of the reorganized Prussian Diet. Those elections were carefully managed by government officials, especially Interior Minister von Westphalen, to ensure a politically 'favourable' outcome. Only 16 per cent of the qualified electorate actually voted; and the result was a lower house in which 205 of 352 deputies were reckoned to be 'vigorously pro-government'. Seventy-two members of the new parliament were politically reliable *Landräte*, so that the new parliament—or *Landtag*, as it was now called—has gone into history books as the '*Landrat* chamber'. In the midst of the Crimean War crisis, the reaction in Prussia had gained its most notable victory since the autumn of 1848. The constitution, it seemed, had become a pliable instrument in the hands of monarchical conservatives; while such bold conservative strategists as Friedrich Julius Stahl and Ludwig von Gerlach had apparently proved correct in their assumption that the constitution could be appropriated on behalf of 'the good cause'.[56]

The King himself seems to have found relatively little consolation in these results. Rather, as the Crimean conflict got bogged down, he remained determined to maintain his foreign-policy course—a policy which, he argued, had been '*one and the same* since the beginning of this unholy conflict'.[57] Unfortunately, his policy was not nearly as clear as he insisted, mainly because of his persistent and confusing tendency to conduct a highly personalized diplomacy. So, for example, he had a penchant for sending emissaries on special missions to other capitals, often without the prior knowledge or approval of Manteuffel or other officials. The Groeben mission to London was an example; so too were several delicate missions to Vienna by Edwin von Manteuffel. The most spectacular and silly of these missions, however, was the

---

[53] Documents in Rassow, *Konflikt*, 64–5, 71; Prince of Prussia to Grand Duke Carl Alexander of Saxe-Weimar, 11 and 25 May 1854, in Wilhelm I., *Kaiser Wilhelms I. Weimarer Briefe*, ed. Johannes Schultze (2 vols.; Berlin, 1924), i. 263–4, 265–6; FW IV to Victoria, June 1854, GStA Merseburg, HA Rep. 50 J Nr. 359, Bl. 18–18ᵛ; Richert, 'Stellung', 115–19.

[54] Rassow, *Konflikt*, 79–84.

[55] FW IV to Prince of Prussia, 16 Dec. 1856, GStA Merseburg, HA Rep. 50 J Nr. 980, Bl. 37–37ᵛ.

[56] Grünthal, *Parlamentarismus*, 415–49; Thomas Nipperdey, *Deutsche Geschichte 1800–1866: Bürgerwelt und starker Staat* (Munich, 1983), 681–2.

[57] FW IV to Victoria, 24 May 1854, in Borries, *Krimkrieg*, 361.

ill-fated Usedom-Wedell mission to London and Paris in late 1854 and early 1855. The background to that mission was the unilateral Austrian decision in December 1854 to sign an alliance agreement with the Western powers. Although it did not oblige Austria to commence hostilities against Russia, it was a complete surprise to the Prussians and seemed contrary to the spirit of the protective alliance (*Schutz- und Trutzbündnis*) of 1854, which had committed the two German powers to the maintenance of their boundaries and the preservation of peace in Central Europe. Frederick William complained that Austria had committed an 'infamous betrayal', an act of 'high treason', while Prussia itself was now threatened with diplomatic isolation. That isolation became painfully obvious when Prussia was excluded from an abortive peace-conference in Vienna in the spring of 1855.[58]

At that point none other than Carl Wilhelm Saegert proposed to Frederick William that Count Guido von Usedom be sent to London to explore the possibility and the conditions of a Prussian arrangement with the Western powers.[59] The King followed his 'friend's' advice; indeed, during those months Saegert's influence on the shaping of Prussian foreign policy reached its zenith.[60] The mission turned out to be a complete fiasco. Usedom himself was a veteran diplomat, a schoolfriend of Otto von Manteuffel, and one of the few Prussian bluebloods who was friendly with Saegert. Leopold Heinrich von Wedell was commander of the fortress at Luxembourg and a man with virtually no experience of diplomacy. Usedom was sent to London, then to Paris to join Wedell. His aims, according to Frederick William, were to press for Prussian participation in the forthcoming Vienna peace-discussions, to 'offer a hand to England, but *solely* in Prussia's capacity *as a European power*', and to demonstrate that without Prussian backing Austria would be unable significantly to help the Western powers.[61] Usedom himself had long supported the *Wochenblatt* party and was especially hostile to Austria. Accordingly, he viewed his and Wedell's mission as an opportunity to demonstrate that Frederick William was not a Russophile marionette of the *Kreuzzeitung* party. Indeed, the King himself assured Usedom, 'Let Lord Clarendon, let the Queen with all her ministers know that *I am not inclined towards Russia*; I am *not* flirting with Russia. The Russian character is not to my taste.'[62]

Usedom and Wedell encountered difficulties with their mission at every turn. Frederick William had not been terribly enthusiastic about Saegert's idea in the first place. Then he proceeded to carry it out behind Manteuffel's back; and, in any case, he regarded it largely as a device to confuse the Western powers without in reality

[58] Kroll, *Friedrich Wilhelm IV.*, 172–4; Hans-Joachim Schoeps, 'Das preußische Krisenjahr 1854 im Spiegel des Briefwechsels Friedrich Wilhelm IV. mit Carl Wilhelm Saegert', in id., *Der Weg ins deutsche Kaiserreich* (Berlin, 1970), 36–7; Borries, *Krimkrieg*, 250–3.

[59] Hans-Joachim Schoeps, 'Saegert', 40–6.

[60] Walter Bußmann, 'Friedrich Wilhelm IV. und Carl Wilhelm Saegert in der Krisis des Krimkrieges', *Forschungen zur brandenburgischen und preußischen Geschichte*, NS 1 (1991), 101–10; Baumgart, 'Einleitung', in id. (ed.), *Preußische Akten*, ii. 29–39.

[61] FW IV to Usedom, 9 Jan. 1855, GStA Merseburg, Rep. 92 Graf Guido von Usedom B IV 1, Bl. 88–89^v, 91–91^v.

[62] FW IV to Usedom, 5 July 1855, ibid., Bl. 110.

making serious overtures to them, hoping in the meantime that the mission would ensure Prussia a continuing diplomatic role commensurate with its great-power status.[63] Napoleon III and his government regarded the mission as a bit of a joke, while Usedom sighed that in London he had found 'nothing but the most boundless mistrust towards the King and his government'.[64] And in fact the mission suggested to the Western leaders that Frederick William was unreliable and talking out of both sides of his mouth. Virtually none of the major players in Berlin and Potsdam placed any faith in the mission, while Usedom and Wedell complained that the regular Prussian envoys to London and Paris were conspiring to sabotage their efforts. Finally, after many months of pointless discussions, Usedom and Wedell were summoned home. By now they had become convinced that Manteuffel had torpedoed the mission, and an especially nasty vendetta, which dragged on for almost two years, ensued. Before the King himself managed to settle the conflict, Usedom even threatened his old schoolfriend with a duel. Saegert, for his part, huffily informed the King that he would no longer supply him with political advice but would instead devote the rest of his career to the service of humanity.[65]

Despite such embarrassments, Frederick William persisted with his policy of neutrality until the end, sustained in his determination both by Leopold von Gerlach and Otto von Manteuffel. He also turned out to be the lucky beneficiary of events over which he had no control. The Vienna peace-discussions ended without result, but the fall of Sebastopol in the autumn of 1855, a forthright ultimatum by Austria to Russia in December 1855, and the decision of the young Tsar Alexander II to cut his losses all created new possibilities for talks, which culminated in the Peace of Paris in 1856.[66] This time Prussia was invited to participate, albeit late and with some reluctance on the part of the other powers; and in March 1856 a grateful Frederick William awarded the Order of the Black Eagle to his Minister President, whose position at court and in the government had become unassailable.[67] Prussia had stayed out of war, and above all had managed to remain on a friendly footing with Russia— which in turn would pay political dividends for Prussia in the 1860s. Still, it had been a close-run thing, and Prussia emerged from the peace conference without glory or prestige. Moreover, recent studies have shown that Frederick William was very lucky that the war ended when it did. Had the conflict persisted, the policy of neutrality could not have been sustained, and a weakened Prussia might have found itself

   [63] Baumgart, 'Einleitung', in id. (ed.), Preußische Akten, ii. 37.
   [64] Quoted in Hans-Joachim Schoeps, 'Saegert', 45.
   [65] Ibid. 48–53; FW IV to Usedom, 9 Sept. 1855, 15 May 1857, and 7 June 1857, GStA Merseburg, Rep. 92 Graf Guido von Usedom B IV 1, Bl. 116–19, 125–125ᵛ, 126–7; Borries, Krimkrieg, 262–75, 279–83; Otto von Manteuffel, Preußens auswärtige Politik 1850 bis 1858: Unveröffentlichte Dokumente aus dem Nachlasse des Ministerpräsidenten Otto Frhrn. v. Manteuffel, ed. Heinrich von Poschinger (3 vols.; Berlin, 1902), iii. 132–6, 148–52, 156–60, 303–4, 337–40; Otto von Manteuffel to Leopold von Gerlach, 22 July 1855, GA, 'Abschriften', xxv. 175–176a; Leopold von Gerlach, diary (6 Apr. 1857), BA Potsdam, 90 Ge 6 Nachlaß Leopold von Gerlach, Bd. 32, Bl. 55.
   [66] Baumgart, 'Einleitung', in id. (ed.), Preußische Akten, ii. 42–5.
   [67] Bloomfield to Clarendon, 1 and 26 Apr. 1856, PRO, FO 64/413.

dangerously isolated, as in 1806. The conflict did not end disastrously for Prussia, but that was more the result of good fortune than of good statesmanship.[68]

The Inglorious End of a Monarchical Project? The Last Years of Frederick William IV, 1856–1861

What should have been a moment of sweet triumph for Manteuffel was soured by the persistence of scandal and intrigue at home. The Potsdam dispatch affair dragged on throughout the year 1856, culminating in a trial and an eight-year sentence for the agent Techen. The Minden editor Lindenberg also had to go to trial in connection with the libel suit filed against him by the Prince of Prussia. Leopold von Gerlach was required to testify for the prosecution, and on the basis of that evidence Lindenberg was found guilty and sentenced to nine months in prison plus court costs. He received a royal pardon shortly thereafter. Struggles for advantage and sordid intrigues had apparently become a normal and unavoidable feature of life at the top during the last years of Frederick William IV's reign; and in the case of Carl Ludwig von Hinckeldey, those struggles had a lethal outcome.[69]

The Berlin police chief's rough-and-ready style had gained him a galaxy of prominent enemies, especially among Prussia's aristocratic and military élites. Their conflict boiled over in 1855, when the police moved to suppress the gambling activities of aristocratic Guard officers in the capital city. The focus of those activities was the Jockey Club, an exclusive establishment located in the private rooms of Hans von Rochow-Plessow, a young member of the House of Lords. Frederick William had long been dismayed by the 'immoral' gambling habits of Prussian bluebloods, and when he heard that certain discharged officers were frequenting the Jockey Club, he ordered Hinckeldey to remove them from Berlin. On the night of 22–3 June 1855 the police raided Rochow's suite at the posh Hôtel du Nord. The presiding officer, a Lieutenant Damm, treated the gambling officers brusquely, and then proceeded to arrest them. Although they were quickly released, Damm's action provoked a storm of criticism from the officer corps, which, caste-conscious as always, argued that it was both illegal and inappropriate for a non-military official to behave in such a way towards gentlemen of high birth and good breeding. Two days later, Rochow and one of his friends visited Hinckeldey to demand an explanation. He insisted, correctly, that he had been following the King's orders. He also realized that his aristocratic enemies would try to use this *contretemps* to unseat him, and he begged Frederick William—in vain, as it turned out—to stand behind him. Although he and his family had now become outcasts in Berlin court society, the police chief was determined to carry out his duties as before; so that in the summer and autumn of 1855 Berliners were frequently exposed to the odd sight of public disputes and altercations between the police and the army.[70]

---

[68] Baumgart, 'Außenpolitik', 144–5; id., 'Einleitung', in id. (ed.), *Preußische Akten*, i. 30–1.

[69] Richert, 'Stellung', 127; Stieber, *Denkwürdigkeiten*, 71; Prince of Prussia to FW IV, 9 Feb. 1857, GA, 'Abschriften', xxvii. 18; Ludwig von Gerlach to Leopold von Gerlach, n.d. (3 Feb. 1857), ibid. xxvii. 36.

[70] Hinckeldey to FW IV, 8 July 1855, GStA Merseburg, HA Rep. 50 E 3 Nr. 56, Bl. 36–36^v, 65–65^v;

[*cont. on p. 274*]

'I have known for a year', Frederick William wrote to Groeben at the beginning of March 1856, 'that Hinckeldey's fall was solemnly sworn to after the accursed Jockey Club story broke loose.' And to Hinckeldey himself he insisted, '*I will sustain you in this struggle.*'[71] In fact, however, the King of Prussia left his Police Director in the lurch. He denied that he had issued an order to move against the Jockey Club, so that Hinckeldey now found himself in an untenable position. After all, he had assured Rochow that the King had issued such an order; and now, to 'cover' for his sovereign, the police chief had to retract his earlier statement and assert that no direct order had been given. This was the opening that Rochow and his friends needed. Rochow asserted that the whole incident proved that Hinckeldey was a liar, which in turn left the Police Director with no honourable recourse but to challenge his tormentor to a duel.[72] In early March 1856 the King and his advisers were informed that the duel would take place soon, but they did nothing to stop it. A direct order from Frederick William would have sufficed, but for reasons that remain unclear, he dithered until it was too late. The outcome was almost inevitable, for the near-sighted Hinckeldey barely knew how to fire a pistol. When the confrontation finally occurred in the early morning of 10 March 1856 at the Jungfernheide near Berlin, Rochow killed the police chief with a direct shot to the chest.[73]

An enormous wave of popular revulsion greeted the news of Hinckeldey's death. Rochow was arrested but was released, pending trial, to his family estate near Potsdam. The man who in life had embodied police-state authoritarianism was transformed in death into a bourgeois hero, a blameless family man who had been murdered by a degenerate aristocratic clique and betrayed by the fickle monarch whom he had served so faithfully. A popular subscription was quickly launched to raise money for his financially strapped widow and her seven children, while tens of thousands attended Hinckeldey's funeral in a massive demonstration of the Berlin bourgeoisie 'against the Junkers and the *Kreuzzeitung*'—and, it seemed, against the disloyal monarch himself.[74] In fact, some members of the circles close to the *Kreuzzeitung* immediately realized that the Hinckeldey affair had demonstrated a dangerous gap between monarchy, aristocracy, and officer corps on the one hand, and an increasingly disaffected bourgeoisie and bureaucracy on the other. The latter two groups, it was suggested, regarded themselves as victims of the reaction era; accordingly, Edwin von Manteuffel argued, something needed to be done to allevi-

'Referat in den Beschwerden des Yokey-Clubs wider den Polizei-Leutnant Dam', 2 July 1855, ibid., Bl. 47–62ᵛ; Berthold Schulze, 'Polizeipräsident Carl von Hinckeldey', *JGMOD* 4 (1955), 103.

⁷¹ FW IV to Groeben, 3 Mar. 1856, GStA Merseburg, Rep. 92 Graf Carl von der Groeben B Nr. 4ᵍ 1855–1857, Bl. 30; FW IV to Hinckeldey, 19 Nov. 1855, ibid., HA Rep. 50 J Nr. 514, Bl. 53.

⁷² B. Schulze, 'Hinckeldey', 103–5; Heinrich von Sybel, 'Carl Ludwig von Hinckeldey 1852 bis 1856', *HZ* 189 (1959), 120–2; FW IV to Groeben, 11 July 1855, GStA Merseburg, Rep. 92 Graf Carl von der Groeben B Nr. 4ᵍ 1855–7, Bl. 5–6.

⁷³ Leopold von Gerlach, diary (7 and 8 Mar. 1856), GA, 'Abschriften', xiii. 48–9; Hinckeldey to FW IV, 3, 4, 8, and 9 Mar. 1856, GStA Merseburg, HA Rep. 50 J Nr. 514, Bl. 14–15, 17–18, 20–21ᵛ, 73–82, 85–85ᵛ, 89–89ᵛ; FW IV to Groeben, 9 Mar. 1856, GStA Merseburg, Rep. 92 Graf Carl von der Groeben B Nr. 4ᵍ 1855–7, Bl. 35; Sybel, 'Hinckeldey', 123.

⁷⁴ B. Schulze, 'Hinckeldey', 105.

ate their grievances. Hinckeldey had been acting in his capacity as a royal official, Manteuffel said, and should not have been allowed to go ahead with the duel. Therefore, everyone who was associated with it should be prosecuted to the fullest extent. The aristocracy itself, he observed insightfully, had become too isolated from the rest of society during the years of reaction, and the King had favoured them too much. He could begin to remedy the situation by ennobling a large number of deserving bourgeois subjects.[75]

Frederick William, of course, did no such thing. His own response to Hinckeldey's death, like his behaviour just before the duel, was contradictory. Leopold von Gerlach reported that the King had been 'very distressed but calm' when he heard of Hinckeldey's death; Varnhagen tells us, however, that upon viewing the body he burst into 'frightful weeping and wailing'. He was especially appalled to learn that the Berlin public was blaming him for the tragedy: 'The public regards me as *the one* who sacrificed my beloved Hinckeldey to myself, as though I were a Moloch!!!' At the same time he asserted that Hinckeldey was 'too plebeian for me' and hoped that his successor would demonstrate 'a more refined character'.[76] The King's contradictory reactions in March 1856 have been interpreted by one historian as a foretaste of the illness that ended his active reign a year and a half later.[77] Frederick William was indeed a sick and prematurely ageing man in 1856; but Leopold von Gerlach probably identified the problem more correctly when he pointed out that Hinckeldey had been a victim of his own misplaced confidence in the King and of Frederick William's well-known indifference to the 'instruments' who were supposed to execute his will. Moreover, Gerlach pointedly observed, there were real similarities between Hinckeldey's fate and that of Radowitz: both men had succumbed, despite the King, to the 'small but powerful party'.[78]

In contrast to Hinckeldey, both Leopold von Gerlach and Otto von Manteuffel had shown themselves to be political as well as literal survivors, despite years of having to bear the burden of Frederick William's 'self-deception and contempt for others'.[79] They had outlasted people like Thile, Bodelschwingh, Radowitz, Bunsen, and Hinckeldey. They had learned to adapt themselves to the King's passions and *idées fixes*, and had made themselves indispensable in the process. Their relationship to each other had always been an odd one. After the dispatch-theft affair they had become temporarily reconciled—Gerlach spoke often of his 'old love' for the Minister President—but in 1857 major differences again flared up between the two men, this time as a result of the last political crisis of Frederick William IV's active reign, the Neuchâtel affair of 1856-7.

[75] Edwin von Manteuffel to Leopold von Gerlach, 19 Mar. 1856, GA, 'Abschriften', xxii. 66-7. Ironically, Manteuffel was himself involved in a controversial duel several years later.

[76] Leopold von Gerlach, diary (11 Mar. 1856), GA, 'Abschriften', xiii. 49; K. A. Varnhagen von Ense, *Tagebücher*, ed. Ludmilla Assing, 2nd edn., xii. 399 (10 Mar. 1856); FW IV to Groeben, 25 Mar. 1856, GStA Merseburg, Rep. 92 Graf Carl von der Groeben B Nr. 4^g 1855-1857, Bl. 38-38^v.

[77] B. Schulze, 'Hinckeldey', 107.

[78] Leopold von Gerlach, diary (23 and 25 June 1856), GA, 'Abschriften', xiii. 120, 121; diary (27 Feb. 1857), BA Potsdam, 90 Ge 6 Nachlaß Leopold von Gerlach Nr. 32, Bl. 40.

[79] Meysenbug to Rüdt, 14 Dec. 1855, GLA, Abt. 48/2652.

The reader will recall that the King had been personally shattered by the republican insurrection in early 1848 which had brought an end to Hohenzollern authority in Neuchâtel and had paved the way for that canton's integration into the Swiss Confederation. With characteristic stubbornness, Frederick William had refused to accept the loss of Neuchâtel and for years had barraged his fellow rulers with missives calling attention to his claims to the canton. Their support had never been forthcoming, and Britain had more or less actively sided with the Neuchâtel republicans and the Swiss Confederation. In September 1856 a group of Neuchâtel royalists tried to stage a coup in the canton, but their efforts fizzled out immediately, and their leaders were arrested. Full of 'grief for my beloved Neuchâtel', Frederick William announced that he would support the royalists to the hilt.[80] A diplomatic row quickly emerged which involved not only Prussia and Switzerland but also France, Austria, Britain, and the medium-sized states of southern Germany.

Otto von Manteuffel and most other Prussian diplomats were not eager for their country to be involved in an international dispute as a result of Frederick William's personal attachment to Neuchâtel. By the end of 1856 it appeared that a mutually acceptable solution to the crisis could be arranged with the assistance of Napoleon III. The royalist prisoners would be released and Neuchâtel's membership in the Swiss Confederation would be guaranteed. Unfortunately, the Swiss authorities rejected certain Prussian preconditions for negotiation, and at the end of 1856 Frederick William considered sending a force of 130,000 men to attack the Confederation. Faced with tremendous pressure from the great powers to relent, yet assured of British support for its independence and neutrality, Switzerland agreed to release the prisoners. It appeared that war had been averted and that the outstanding issues between Prussia and Switzerland could be peacefully resolved.

In late January 1857, however, Leopold von Gerlach threatened to undo the whole thing. Indeed, his behaviour during the Neuchâtel crisis is an excellent example both of the ideological character of his politics and of his capacity to swing Frederick William around to his own views. Gerlach had spent most of the previous autumn at the family estate in Rohrbeck, where, preoccupied with his daughter's lingering illness and his wife's poor health he had hardly concerned himself with politics at all. The dispatch-theft and Lindenberg cases had left him deeply depressed, and once again he seriously considered resignation. After his daughter's death, however, he returned to the capital and insisted to the impressionable monarch that, in exchange for giving up Neuchâtel, Frederick William should demand that the political system of the entire Swiss Confederation be restored to its *Vormärz*, 'Christian-German' condition. Otherwise Switzerland would continue to be a dangerous bastion of subversive and democratic values. Moreover, Gerlach was deeply annoyed by Manteuffel's willingness to co-operate with Napoleon III—further evidence, he believed, of the Minister President's 'unreliability', lack of principle, and willingness to flirt with

---

[80] FW IV to Elisabeth, 7 Sept. 1856, GStA Merseburg, HA Rep. 50 J Nr. 995 Fasz. 25, Bl. 42. On the origins of the 1856 crisis, see the documents in ibid., Rep. 92 Marcus von Niebuhr I Nr. 9, and Edgar Bonjour, *Vorgeschichte des Neuenburger Konflikts 1848–1856* (Berne, 1932).

'Bonapartism'. The King immediately responded positively to Gerlach's proposals, and by late January was insisting that 'he will never, ever give up Neuchâtel. He would rather die.' Manteuffel had in effect been shunted aside in what can only be described as an effective display of the Adjutant-General's continuing influence. But Gerlach was not willing to push his advantage too far. The British energetically resisted his notions, and indicated that they would not participate in any international conference that interfered in the internal affairs of Switzerland as a whole. No one in Prussia seriously wanted a confrontation with Britain over this issue. Accordingly, a conference to mediate the crisis finally opened in Paris in March 1857. After much resistance Frederick William gave in to the united opposition of the European powers, which regarded his obsession with Neuchâtel as quixotic. He renounced his rights to the canton, while the Swiss proclaimed an amnesty for the rebels and agreed to pay all the costs associated with the royalist uprising.[81]

The loss of Neuchâtel was almost as painful to Frederick William as his humiliation in March 1848, for it was one more piece of evidence that time had passed him by, that his vision of a *ständisch* monarchy in an anti-revolutionary, monarchist Europe was *passé*, and that, indeed, the entire structure of his monarchical project lay in ruins. He had become an old man, increasingly unresponsive to the currents of his time. The monarch who before 1848 had appreciated the importance of railways, had understood Radowitz's warnings about the 'social question', had supported the Industrial Exposition of 1844, and had used modern techniques of mobilizing opinion to sway the public had no comprehension whatsoever of the financial and economic changes of the late 1850s. Neither in Frederick William's own writings nor in those of Leopold von Gerlach is there any reference at all to an event of far greater magnitude and historical significance than the Neuchâtel affair—the great international financial crash of 1857. And to many members of the *Wirtschafisbürgertum* directly affected by the crash, the King, and his various ideas and concerns, must surely have seemed irrelevant at best. Cut off from the world of the present, the unhappy monarch looked glumly into the future, burdened with a keen sense of his own failure and his many shortcomings. He had never overcome the shock of 1848, despite his grim and consistent efforts throughout the 1850s to restore the bases of his monarchical authority.[82] In the end he was convinced that he had lost. 'The revolution is stalking the world once more', he wrote to his friend Groeben in the summer of 1857. 'May God have mercy!'[83]

The King wrote to Groeben from Marienbad, where his doctors had sent him to take the waters. His health had been declining noticeably for several years. He was

[81] Erwin von Blume, *Die preußische Politik in der Neuenburger Frage (1856–1857): Ein Beitrag zur Geschichte Friedrich Wilhelms IV.* (Hamburg, 1930), 89–94; Edgar Bonjour, *Der Neuenburger Konflikt 1856/57: Untersuchungen und Dokumente* (Basle, 1957).

[82] See esp. Dirk Blasius, *Friedrich Wilhelm IV. 1795–1861: Psychopathologie und Geschichte* (Göttingen, 1992), 236, 243–5.

[83] FW IV to Groeben, 29 June 1857, GStA Merseburg, Rep. 92 Graf Carl von der Groeben B Nr. 4ᵍ 1855–7, Bl. 45–6.

greatly overweight and, as we have seen, had rightly been suspected of overindulging with snuff and champagne. For many years he had suffered—like many of his contemporaries—from a variety of ailments, including a persistent and virtually incurable case of the sniffles. After 1853 more serious problems developed. He began to have problems with his once formidable memory, often forgetting the names of familiar people and places. On some occasions he appeared exhausted and passive, while on others he suffered from extreme nervous agitation and irritability, often culminating in unpredictable outbursts of rage.[84] Symptomatic was an incident in early October 1855, when the King and Queen were returning to Berlin by train after a visit to the Rhineland. When passing through the Westphalian city of Hamm, the royal couple were greeted at the station by a delegation of local notables. When one of them mentioned the name 'Vincke' (presumably the well-known Westphalian politician Georg von Vincke), Frederick William turned 'deep red' and began screaming uncontrollably that Vincke was his enemy and the enemy of Prussia. After several minutes Elisabeth managed to calm him down, and in an atmosphere of almost unbearable embarrassment the train pulled out of the station.[85] A month later Frederick William heatedly dismissed as 'perfidy' various rumours that he had suffered a slight stroke.[86]

In the summer of 1856 his doctors sent him to Marienbad for the first time, and, relieved of the stress of daily work, his condition improved markedly. After early 1857, however, his nervous agitation and forgetfulness increased. In May, on the occasion of a visit from Prince Napoleon, cousin of Napoleon III, he was unable to recall the name of the veteran Adjutant-General Neumann. He himself was aware of his problem. He felt 'weak and without energy', he admitted to Elisabeth in mid-May. 'I am quite melancholy!! and in a nervous bad mood!'[87] The King's second stay in Marienbad, in June 1857, did not provide much relief, and in July he made the mistake of undertaking a strenuous official visit to Vienna. While staying with his Saxon in-laws at Pillnitz on the way back to Berlin, he suffered what was described as a 'light stroke'. Although he seemed, superficially at least, to recover fairly quickly, at the end of July he complained to Leopold von Gerlach about the 'decline of his energies, inability to work, and loss of memory, especially the impossibility of remembering names'.[88] The early autumn of 1857 was especially busy, with annual army manœuvres and a state visit by the King's Russian nephew, the young Alexander II, on the programme. On 6 October he was about to set off on a trip to Silesia and Saxony with the Tsar and King John of Saxony when, while still in Berlin, he felt so ill that he returned immediately to Potsdam. Two days later, suffering from fever and what was

---

[84] Bismarck-Bohlen, 'Aufzeichnungen', GStA Merseburg, HA Rep. 50 F 1 Nr. 6, Bl. 12.

[85] My thanks to Professor Günther Grünthal for describing this incident to me, which is detailed in Staatsarchiv Osnabrück, Dep. 45^b, v. Vincke-Ostenwalde, Nr. 676.

[86] FW IV to Hinckeldey, 5 Nov. 1855, GStA Merseburg, HA Rep. 50 J Nr. 512, Bl. 544.

[87] FW IV to Elisabeth, 15 May 1857, GStA Merseburg, HA Rep. 50 J Nr. 995 Fasz. 25, Bl. 120. See also Friedrich Vogel, 'Die Krankheit Friedrich Wilhelms IV. nach dem Bericht seines Flügeladjutanten', in Büsch (ed.), *Friedrich Wilhelm IV. in seiner Zeit*, 260.

[88] Leopold von Gerlach, diary (30 July 1857), BA Potsdam, 90 Ge 6 Nachlaß Leopold von Gerlach Nr. 32, Bl. 110. See also Manteuffel, *Unter Friedrich Wilhelm IV.*, iii. 199–201; and Alfred von Reumont, *Aus König Friedrich Wilhelms IV. gesunden und kranken Tagen*, 2nd edn. (Leipzig, 1885), 453–84.

described as 'congestion', he temporarily lost consciousness and appeared to be near death. After regaining his consciousness he remained unable to attach proper words to people or objects. Although his condition began to stabilize, everyone realized that, at the very least, it would be a long time before he could resume the activities of his office. The question of a regency—that is, the assumption of the King's powers by the sixty-year-old Prince of Prussia—could not be long avoided.[89]

Leopold von Gerlach was acutely aware that his position depended entirely on his relationship to the King, and that a regency would mean the end of his career. When the King became ill Gerlach was in mourning for his wife, who had died the previous month; while Marcus Niebuhr, whom he had often described as his closest ally, had become the victim of what were called 'epileptic chest-seizures' and apparent mental collapse.[90] Although Leopold admitted to Ludwig that he could still count on important supporters, such as Edwin von Manteuffel, Ludwig von Massow, and Supreme Chamberlain Count Dohna, he was certain that he had become politically isolated and that his public life was almost over. On 7 October he confided to his diary just how much he would miss Frederick William, despite all the irritations over so many years: 'It seems that this year is predestined to put paid to all the recollections of my youth. If this immensely gifted man dies or deteriorates, how much will end with him? *Stände*, the United Diet, the House of Lords, the Supreme Church Council, Sanssouci and its buildings, artists, friendships, humour, and above all that truly Christian feeling of one's own sinful nature.'[91]

Gerlach would not give up without a fight. Determined to remain in power as long as possible, he played with the idea of arranging for a regency to be declared as soon as possible; a surprised Prince of Prussia would have no alternative but to keep him in office, while at the same time he could count on the support of the huge conservative majority in the Prussian parliament. The Queen quickly made it clear, however, that she believed that her husband would regain his health and that a quick regency was out of the question; so Gerlach shifted course and thereafter tried to delay the introduction of an official regency as long as possible.[92] But it could not be put off indefinitely. After all, as he put it later in the autumn, the major themes of his career as Adjutant-General since 1849–50 had been the struggle against the revolution, against Radowitz, against an alliance with the Western powers, and, in the end, the assurance of a smooth transfer of power to the King's successor.[93] Now the time had come to arrange for the latter. On 23 October 1857 Frederick William IV signed a document giving his younger brother authority to govern (*Vollmacht*) for a

---

[89] Manteuffel, *Unter Friedrich Wilhelm IV.*, iii. 201; reports on the King's health from Oct. to Dec. 1857, GStA Merseburg, HA Rep. 50 K 1 Nr. 1.

[90] Anna Niebuhr to Leopold von Gerlach, 20 Oct. 1857, GA, 'Abschriften', xxvii. 205–6.

[91] Leopold von Gerlach to Ludwig von Gerlach, 20 Oct. 1857, in E. L. von Gerlach, *Von der Revolution*, ii. 930–2; Leopold von Gerlach, diary (7 Oct. 1857), BA Potsdam, 90 Ge 6 Nachlaß Leopold von Gerlach Nr. 32, Bl. 134.

[92] Günther Grünthal, 'Das Ende der Ära Manteuffel', *JGMOD* 39 (1990), 183–5.

[93] Leopold von Gerlach, diary (18 Nov. 1857), BA Potsdam, 90 Ge 6 Nachlaß Leopold von Gerlach Nr. 32, Bl. 166. His brother Ludwig believed that the regency should be established quickly, and that

[cont. on p. 280]

three-month period. This was not a full-scale regency as described in Article 56 of the constitution; the Prince had no control over the affairs of the royal household, nor could he really alter the composition of his brother's cabinet. It was, in effect, a private agreement between the King and the Prince, not a matter of public law.[94]

The three-month *Vollmacht* was renewed on several occasions, but by the autumn of 1858 it had become obvious that Frederick William's condition would never significantly improve. The parliament, which had theretofore been excluded from the private arrangements within the royal house, now demanded that William's position be regularized and legitimized. Finally, on 7 October 1858 the enfeebled monarch signed the cabinet order that brought an official end to his active reign. The Prince of Prussia became Regent, with the full power of the crown and the authority to make policy within the limits defined by the constitution. Interior Minister von Westphalen, the unpopular symbol of police-state despotism, was dismissed the next day. Within weeks the Regent had also dismissed Otto von Manteuffel and replaced him with a government headed by the mildly liberal Prince Karl von Hohenzollern-Sigmaringen.[95] Most of Manteuffel's ministers, especially those who were closely associated with the reactionary policies of the previous decade, were gone; the most significant hold-over was Trade Minister August von der Heydt. The real leader of the new cabinet was Rudolf von Auerswald, the old Minister President of 1848, and among its other members were *Wochenblatt* stalwarts and members of the Prince's Koblenz circle. Bethmann-Hollweg replaced Karl von Raumer, the Gerlachs' trusted cousin, as *Kultusminister*. Ignoring his older brother's advice and the wishes of conservative hardliners like Edwin von Manteuffel, the Regent took his oath to the constitution before the assembled houses of parliament on 26 October 1858. Liberal public opinion took heart from these developments, and soon it was being said that Prussia was embarking on a 'New Era' of moderate, constitutional-monarchical government.[96] That assumption seemed to be vindicated by parliamentary elections in November, in which the conservative factions suffered massive losses; the *Kreuzzeitung* faction, excluded from the cabinet and deprived of its access to the institutions of monarchy, was facing a crisis of survival. Ludwig von Gerlach and Hermann Wagener both lost their parliamentary seats. The reaction seemed to have been swept away overnight, and with it the conservative forces that had dominated the post-revolutionary decade. As one historian recently observed, 'Seldom in German political history has a party which had risen so rapidly to influence and

William should take his oath to the constitution forthwith so as to avoid the danger of 'liberal' absolutism. Ludwig von Gerlach to Leopold von Gerlach, 17 Oct. 1857, GA, 'Abschriften', xxvii. 201–2; Grünthal, 'Ende', 189–90; Kraus, 'Gerlach', i. 440–1, ii. 328–9.

[94] Manteuffel, *Unter Friedrich Wilhelm IV.*, iii. 302–8; copy of *Vollmacht* in GStA Merseburg, HA Rep. 50 J Nr. 981, Bl. 24; Leopold von Gerlach to Ludwig von Gerlach, 24 Oct. 1857, in E. L. von Gerlach, *Von der Revolution*, ii. 933–5.

[95] Grünthal, 'Ende', 204–7, 210–17.

[96] Ibid. 206–7; Wolfram Siemann, *Gesellschaft im Aufbruch: Deutschland 1849–1871* (Frankfurt am Main, 1990), 190–4; Karl Heinz Börner, *Kaiser Wilhelm I. 1797 bis 1888: Deutscher Kaiser und König von Preußen. Eine Biographie* (Cologne, 1984), 126–34.

importance experienced a more precipitous decline' than the conservative party after 1858.[97] The New Era government responded to these developments with a series of measures designed to appeal to moderately liberal business-interests. They included a sharp reduction in state influence over railways and coal-mining, a new Commercial Code, a free-trade agreement with France, and the elimination of property-tax exemptions in the eastern parts of the kingdom. As a result of the latter, eastern landowners were 'further brought under the jurisdiction of a centralized, bureaucratic modern state'. In short, the policies of the New Era, while breaking with some of the more extreme actions of the Manteuffel era, represented the continuation— and to a certain extent the liberal culmination—of that continuing process of 'negotiation' which, as James Brophy reminds us, had been going on since at least the 1830s. The end of Frederick William IV's reign thus witnessed the emergence of what Brophy has suggestively called a Prussian *juste milieu*. Even before the dramatic constitutional conflict which ended the New Era and launched the age of Germany's first unification, the Prussian state had reached an accommodation with the new élites of capital and industry.[98]

Otto von Manteuffel's policies had, to all appearances, been utterly repudiated; his political career over, he lived in relative obscurity until his death in 1882. Leopold von Gerlach remained in service as the stricken monarch's chief adjutant. His political influence, however, had disappeared completely. Frederick William himself continued to decline, despite occasional if short-lived improvements. In the first part of 1858 he was still able to write, though in a shaky, almost child-like hand.[99] He spent much of the summer of 1858 at the Tegernsee in Bavaria and the following winter in Italy, where, accompanied by his old friend Alfred von Reumont, a distinguished Prussian diplomat and art historian, he was able to revisit many of his favourite sites. After returning to Germany he suffered two strokes in the second half of 1859. Thereafter he was confined to a wheelchair at Sanssouci, and by late 1860 he was unable to speak. Sometimes in a semi-comatose condition, he had also become incontinent.[100]

The real nature of Frederick William's lingering illness will probably never be known. However, the textbook accounts which describe it as 'madness' or 'insanity' are certainly inaccurate. One recent study suggests that Frederick William suffered from a cerebral condition, probably advanced arteriosclerosis in the brain, which manifested itself in speech difficulties, loss of memory, and embolism-induced losses of consciousness; the situation was further exacerbated by the two strokes in 1859. There is also a possibility that the King may have suffered from Alzheimer's disease. Whatever the case may be, his condition deteriorated rapidly in December 1860.[101]

[97] Kraus, 'Gerlach', i. 443.

[98] James M. Brophy, 'Politics of the *Juste Milieu*: Entrepreneurs in the New Era', unpub. paper presented at German Studies Association, 17th annual meeting, 7–10 Oct. 1993 (Washington, DC). My thanks to Professor Brophy for his permission to cite this important paper.

[99] See his diary from 1858 in GStA Merseburg, HA Rep. 50 K 1 Nr. 1a.

[100] See the detailed account of his travels in Reumont, *Aus gesunden und kranken Tagen*, 486–509, 520–74; and the descriptions of his condition in Leopold von Gerlach's diary, GA, 'Abschriften', xiv–xvi, *passim*.

[101] F. Vogel, 'Krankheit', 262–5, 266–70; Bußmann, *Friedrich Wilhelm IV.*, 412–30, esp. 418. See the

[cont. on p. 282]

On 1 January 1861 the serving *Flügeladjutant*, Prince Kraft zu Hohenlohe-Ingelfingen, reported to William that the King's death 'is possible at any moment'.[102] Frederick William's top advisers and the entire royal family gathered in Sanssouci around the unconscious monarch, who died quietly in the early hours of 2 January 1861. The new King wept. The dowager Queen announced that she had lived only for the King, and that her work was over; and she asked Frederick William's relatives and friends to take their leave of him while his body was still warm. Despite his own grief, the ever-political Leopold von Gerlach noted that same day that 'King William is still entirely the old Prince William', and that he would undoubtedly be dominated by the new Queen Augusta, 'which is extremely dangerous in view of her strange, agitated, passionate, and insincere character'.[103]

Always a punctilious observer of ceremony, Frederick William IV had carefully prepared the details of his funeral and burial. They would be held at the two places he had loved most: Sanssouci and the Friedenskirche, where he was to be interred. The final ceremonies took place on a wintry seventh of January with a procession from Sanssouci to the church. Field Marshal Count Wrangel, carrying the '*Reich* Banner' (*Reichspanier*), preceded the new King and Queen; he was accompanied by the dead King's senior adjutants, Lindheim and Leopold von Gerlach.[104]

Before the funeral Gerlach had stood guard over the King's body, and the strain had been almost too much for the seventy-year-old man. For hours he had worn a heavy helmet, which had slightly injured his forehead. The doctor thereupon ordered him not to attend the funeral, but of course he would hear none of that. The ceremony was long, and the temperature was well below freezing. Gerlach came down with a cold, and when he took a fever he had to be confined to his rooms near Sanssouci. He became delirious and lost consciousness, and on 10 January 1861 he died, eight days after the King. His own funeral took place in the Friedenskirche, and on 17 January he was laid to rest at Rohrbeck 'in a light snowfall'. Many years later, in a frequently quoted passage of his memoirs, Otto von Bismarck recalled the circumstances of Gerlach's death: 'His end is reminiscent of the followers of an old Germanic chief, whose followers chose to die with him.' Leopold von Gerlach had been the King's man to the end.[105]

doctors' bulletins to the Prince of Prussia in GStA Merseburg, HA Rep. 50 K 1 Nr. 3, esp. Bl. 550, 554, and 559.

[102] Ibid., Bl. 562.

[103] See the descriptions of the deathbed scene by Leopold von Gerlach, with additions by Edwin von Manteuffel from 1876, in 'Der zweite Januar 1861 zu Sanssouci', BA Potsdam, 90 Ge 6 Nachlaß Leopold von Gerlach Nr. 39, Bl. 92–101; also Crown Princess Victoria to Queen Victoria and Prince Albert, 2 Jan. 1861, *The Letters of Queen Victoria: A Selection from Her Majesty's Correspondence between the Years 1837 and 1861*, ed. Arthur Christopher Benson and Viscount Esher (3 vols.; London, 1907), iii. 540–4.

[104] *Reglement zu dem feierlichen Leichenbegängnisse Seiner Hochseeligen Majestät Friedrich Wilhelms IV., König von Preußen uc. in der Friedenskirche bei Sanssouci am 7. Januar 1861*, printed version in BLHA, Pr. Br. Rep. 37 Herrschaft Boitzenburg, Nachlaß Adolf Heinrich von Arnim-Boitzenburg Nr. 4141.

[105] Bismarck, *Erinnerung und Gedanke*, 37; see also E. L. von Gerlach, *Aufzeichnungen aus seinem Leben und Wirken 1795–1877*, ed. Jakob von Gerlach (2 vols.; Schwerin, 1903), ii. 237–9.

Conclusion:
Frederick William IV and Monarchical
Institutions in Prussia

At the time of his death in January 1861, Frederick William IV had disappeared from public view and from public consciousness. More than two years had elapsed since William had permanently assumed the regency, and much had changed. The New Era of 1858 had given way to new tensions and problems, as William's determination to reform the Prussian army had brought on a major confrontation with the resurgent forces of parliamentary liberalism. In the context of that developing constitutional crisis, the dead monarch already seemed like a figure from a relatively remote past. Few of his subjects paid much attention to his death. According to one newspaper obituary, he had been an anachronism since 1848, condemned after the revolution 'to survive only as the wreckage of his former self'.[1]

But not everyone was ready to consign Frederick William to historical forgetfulness. What lessons might be learned from his reign? And, above all, how had he shaped the monarchy in Prussia? What sort of monarchical system had he left to his successors? How successful or unsuccessful was he in his efforts to put the monarchical system on a new footing? These were questions of particular interest to Frederick William's favourite nephew, Maximilian II, King of Bavaria since the abdication of his father, Ludwig I, in 1848. Like his father and his uncle, King Max was keenly interested in history. As a young prince he had lived in Berlin, where he had studied with Leopold von Ranke. The circumstances of his succession to the Bavarian throne in the midst of the revolutionary upheavals in 1848 convinced him and his advisers that far too many of his subjects had been lured to the cause of national-liberal German patriotism; too many, he believed, had been indifferent to the Wittelsbach dynasty and to the continued existence of Bavaria as a separate and distinct monarchy. Therefore, between 1848 and 1864 Max and his advisers embarked on a systematic programme to capture the loyalty of ordinary men and women and turn them into committed, conservative, assertively *Bavarian* monarchists and patriots. Indeed, few better examples can be found in nineteenth-century Europe of a king so devoted to the 'invention' of a monarchical tradition.[2]

As part of his effort to understand the negative 'forces of the age' and counter them more effectively, Max consulted regularly with academics and intellectuals, among them a highly successful writer of popular histories named Franz Löher.[3] In

---

[1] *Volks-Zeitung* (Berlin), 3 Jan. 1861.

[2] See the excellent analysis of Maximilian II's programme to 'raise Bavarian national feeling' in Manfred Hanisch, *Für Fürst und Vaterland: Legitimitätsstiftung in Bayern zwischen Revolution 1848 und deutscher Einheit* (Munich, 1991).

[3] Ibid. 65–6, 99–100.

the summer of 1861 the King asked Löher to prepare a 'résumé' for him on the career of his uncle, Frederick William IV, who before and after 1848 had also confronted the 'forces of the age'. Having assessed Frederick William's goals and achievements in the areas of domestic policy, German policy, foreign policy, religion, and intellectual life, Löher reached two conclusions: '1. Frederick William IV fought against the revolutionary spirit of the century in church and state. In the area of politics he had to submit to that spirit; but he also contributed significantly to the emergence of resolutely conservative religious and political views among a portion of the people. 2. This King did not at all increase the glory and power of Prussia and Germany, but he kept Germany out of civil wars and from involvement in European wars.'[4]

Löher's assessment of Frederick William IV, though critical of his handling of particular issues, was sympathetic to his larger goals. Similarly friendly in their judgements, though by no means entirely uncritical, were some of the old monarch's academic acquaintances, especially Friedrich Julius Stahl and Leopold von Ranke. In March 1861 Stahl assessed Frederick William's career in a memorial lecture. The late King's reign, he admitted, had not been blessed by fortune. 'His lot was hostility, misunderstanding, defamation, and ingratitude from all sides.' He died unhappy, Stahl said, but convinced that he had tried to carry out his mission as a Christian king to struggle against his age's spirit of negation, 'call it what you will: revolution, technical civilization, rationalism, "liberalism", or the ideas of 1789'. It would nevertheless be false, Stahl continued, to describe Frederick William simply as 'a counter-revolutionary, a conservative, a restorationist'. He was not a partisan politician who followed party programmes; indeed, he was not doctrinaire at all: 'He did not utterly reject the movements of our time, he did not fail to appreciate the great truths which lie hidden within them and which constitute the real aims and commandments of our age.' He was a creative statesman driven not by the passion for power but by a commitment to divinely revealed truth. And that commitment sustained the King, Stahl believed, in the most difficult years of his life, the decade of reaction. During those years Frederick William pursued a grim struggle against the revolution: 'The government no longer displayed its devotion to the popular will, to the press, or to progress . . .' In the end, Stahl concluded, the King had really succeeded. He had defeated the revolution and had been Prussia's moral example, its 'standard-bearer' in the struggle against the 'apostasy of the age'.[5]

Despite Stahl's attempts to evaluate Frederick William positively, his speech in fact betrayed a tone of real melancholy, a sense that the monarch had indeed failed to live up to his own expectations, that he had ended his reign embittered, unloved, isolated, and overtaken by events. Writing more than a decade later, Leopold von Ranke reached similarly ambivalent conclusions. It was the King's 'curious fate',

---

[4] Franz Löher, 'Friedrich Wilhelm IV.', July 1861, GHA, Nachlaß König Max II., 74/6/17.

[5] Friedrich Julius Stahl, *Zum Gedächtniß Seiner Majestät des hochseligen Königs Friedrich Wilhelm IV. und seiner Regierung: Vortrag gehalten im evangelischen Verein zu Berlin am 18. März 1861* (Berlin, 1861), 5–6, 16, 21.

Ranke noted, 'that his actions had long-term effects but failed to provide him with any satisfaction'. Frederick William 'combined remarkable flexibility in handling individual issues with unflinching firmness in regard to the main issue. Perhaps these qualities permitted him to withstand the revolutionary storms of his age without surrendering the monarchy.' In the end, though, the King was out of touch with the times. 'His idealized view of the world frequently clashed with the realities of things. And in his personal disposition lay something that aroused opposition to him. He was far from feeling happy; most of his pronouncements from his later years have a painful quality to them.'[6]

Younger commentators took a more distanced and less sympathetic view. As we noted at the outset of this study, after the 1880s most writers tended to assess Frederick William IV's reign in the context of the *Reichsgründung* of 1871; because, as Löher had put it, the King had apparently contributed little to his country's 'glory and power', his legacy was found wanting. Faced with the demands and needs of a rapidly changing society, Heinrich von Sybel wrote, Frederick William had seemed like 'the son of a past age, the citizen of another world, the speaker of a foreign tongue', doomed to fail and to disappoint.[7] Even harsher—but perhaps more typical—was the judgement of the Bonn historian Wilhelm Maurenbrecher, who in the late 1870s taught the young Prince William (later William II) that Frederick William IV had been thoroughly 'un-Prussian', that it was a 'misfortune for Prussia and for Germany that he occupied Prussia's throne in such a critical time'.[8] And down to the present, historical opinion has continued to be unkind to that unhappy monarch, regarding him as inconstant, erratic, unsteady, impractical, effete, and even 'psychopathic'.[9]

This study has reached somewhat different conclusions about Frederick William IV and the nature of the monarchical system over which he presided. Instead of regarding his reign mainly as a prelude to the events of the 1860s and 1870s, it has attempted to locate Frederick William within the specific context of his own times—and, in particular, within the context of what we described as the persistence and even revival of monarchical authority in many parts of nineteenth-century Europe. Frederick William's own culture and society remained profoundly affected by monarchical institutions and by the political, ideological, and symbolic expressions of royal power. Accordingly, without understanding the extent to which nineteenth-century Europe remained a continent of monarchs, it is impossible to understand the nature and character of Prussia's particular monarchical system.

The monarchical revival in nineteenth-century Europe must also be understood

---

[6] Leopold von Ranke, 'Friedrich Wilhelm IV., König von Preußen', in *ADB*, vii. 774, 776.

[7] Heinrich von Sybel, *Die Begründung des Deutschen Reiches durch Wilhelm I. Vornehmlich nach preußischen Staatsakten*, i, 4th edn. (Munich, 1892), 103.

[8] Quoted in John C. G. Röhl, *Wilhelm II.: Die Jugend des Kaisers 1859–1888* (Munich, 1993), 314.

[9] e.g. see the finely drawn characterization in Jerome Blum, *In the Beginning: The Advent of the Modern Age—Europe in the 1840s* (New York, 1994), 283–4. Cf. Dirk Blasius, *Friedrich Wilhelm IV. 1795–1861: Psychopathologie und Geschichte*, (Göttingen, 1992), for a somewhat different view of Frederick William as a 'psychopath'.

within the broader context of the struggle by many of the Continent's 'traditional' élites against what Wilhelm Heinrich Riehl called 'the forces of movement'. The renewal and revitalization of royal authority in many parts of Europe thus constituted an integral part of a process of conservative élite mobilization. The struggle against the 'revolution' required that conservatives make use both of traditional techniques of dominance and more modern forms of cultural representation, political mobilization, and interest articulation. One of the most important and modern among the latter was the weapon of ideology.

Frederick William IV and many of his closest advisers were, of course, ideologues *par excellence*. Throughout this book we have seen how Frederick William viewed the world almost exclusively through ideological and aesthetic lenses. Still, it is not easy—and is probably misleading—to categorize him according to particular forms or typologies of conservative thought, or to point too insistently to the obvious inconsistencies in his views and behaviour. It is more useful to consider his ideas *and* his feelings about the world in terms of *generalized* strategies of conservative defence and mobilization. As one historian has recently noted, nineteenth-century conservatism was not so much about a coherent set of 'principles' and 'ideas' as it was about the defence of 'a way of life, a view of the world, a system of relationships, and a complex interplay of tradition and innovation'.[10] And to defend that way of life Frederick William devised an elaborate vision of the world which we have likened to a *Gesamtkunstwerk* and which, as he himself once admitted, had come 'together like a stream from many sources'.[11]

Frederick William's *Gesamtkunstwerk*—his monarchical project—was thus more than simply the emanation of an eccentric and overheated Romantic imagination. Rather, it was the outgrowth of an all-embracing vision of ideological, cultural, political, moral, and religious regeneration in Germany, and of the King's determination to modernize monarchy while creating a total and positive alternative to 'the revolution'. That determination helps to explain his quest for popularity, his embrace of the 'national' cause, and, above all, his tendency to draw upon the ideas of such diverse individuals as Radowitz, Bunsen, the Gerlachs, Hinckeldey, Otto von Manteuffel, or even Carl Wilhelm Saegert. The result was a vision which, though often contradictory in its particulars, was consistent in its aspirations and its aims.

This study has also shown that, during the *Vormärz* years, there was in fact an undeniable and significant discrepancy between Frederick William's relative success at publicly representing his grandiose vision, on the one hand, and the often rather aimless quality of government policy on the other. The modernization of monarchical ritual, ceremonial, and representation was effective, within limits; but it could not offset the consequences of governmental disorganization. The gap between image

---

[10] James Retallack, '"Ideology without Vision"? Recent Literature on Nineteenth-Century German Conservatism', *German Historical Institute London, Bulletin*, 13/2 (1991), 6.
[11] FW (IV) to Bunsen, 24 Mar. 1840, in Leopold von Ranke, *Aus dem Briefwechsel Friedrich Wilhelms IV. mit Bunsen* (Leipzig, 1873), 47, 49.

and reality was substantial, especially during the period of Frederick William's personal rule after 1842; and it contributed in important ways to the crisis of the monarchical system between 1847 and 1850. As a result of that crisis, Frederick William's monarchical project seemed to be in ruins, just as his architectural projects for Potsdam were to remain unfinished torsos. Indeed, many members of Prussia's traditional ruling élite had always doubted that the King could ever be successful. In the autumn of 1850, for example, Count Brandenburg argued that the King's *ständisch* vision had been quixotic and had never corresponded to Prussia's genuine, bureaucratic and centralizing political traditions. For that reason, he hinted, it was probably doomed to failure.[12] Subsequent events seemed to justify that prognostication; for nothing could possibly be more alien to Frederick William's vision of a Christian monarchy than the secular, constitutional, parliamentary order to which he had to swear allegiance in February 1850.

Despite the obvious shortcomings, contradictions, and failures of his monarchical project, Frederick William IV was, nevertheless, more successful *in his own terms and in the context of his own ideas* than has often been realized. In contrast to so many of his fellow monarchs, he did not fall from his throne in 1848; and thereafter the basic structures of monarchical power remained intact, even as Frederick William was reluctantly presiding over his country's transition to a form of constitutionalism. In the complex struggles of the reaction decade, when it seemed to many observers that the King's vision had lost its relevance, his fiercely stubborn adherence to it helped to keep him going, and helped above all to assure the ultimate success of the monarchical cause in a way that would not have been possible without his ideological doggedness. The Prussia over which Frederick William presided during the decade of reaction witnessed the successful adaptation of traditional court and service élites to changed social, economic, and political circumstances.[13] His own intense ideological commitment was an essential ingredient of that larger process; and his role in it—with all its consequences for the future of the Prussian-German state—should not be overlooked.

In what condition had he left the monarchy? In subsequent decades Prussia remained what it had become in the 1850s: 'half autocratic monarchy, half constitutional state'.[14] The complexities of that ultimately unstable condition were symbolized during the first great ceremonial occasion of William I's reign, his coronation in Königsberg in October 1861. To the scorn and dismay of many conservatives, the new King agreed to dispense with the traditional ceremonies of homage and replace them with an outright coronation. This decision clearly reflected the wishes of many liberals, who argued that the homage ceremonies, with their evocations of a *ständisch* past, were anachronistic in the new constitutional and parliamentary age. At the same time, William was just as convinced as his late brother that the throne should

[12] Brandenburg to FW IV, 4 Sept. 1850, GStA Merseburg, HA Rep. 50 J Nr. 212, Bl. 74.
[13] Wolfram Siemann, *Gesellschaft im Aufbruch: Deutschland 1849–1871* (Frankfurt am Main, 1990), 142–3.
[14] Ibid. 309.

continue to occupy the strategic centre of the Prussian state. Although he had accommodated himself to the new constitutional realities, he wanted publicly to affirm the authority and dignity of his position, and above all to emphasize the intimate relationship between crown and army in Prussia. Many liberals praised the ceremony, especially its more 'popular' features, but it nevertheless was suffused with a 'mixture of courtly and military splendour', culminating with the act of coronation itself, in which William placed the crown on his own head. A ceremony which was supposed to assuage liberal feelings had instead witnessed an affirmation of kingship 'by the Grace of God'.[15]

That same monarchical self-consciousness manifested itself in the constitutional conflict of those years, which culminated in Bismarck's compromise of 1866–7 that in turn helped to assure the future of the monarchical principle and of effective crown authority in Prussia-Germany. The fundamental sources of that authority remained where they had been since the 1850s: in the court, the army, and the higher civil service; in the monarch's control of foreign policy and the structures of the military; and in the persistence of popular support for the monarchy, which William I's own modesty, simplicity, and dignity, so reminiscent of Frederick William III, did much to encourage.[16]

That popularity endured and even grew despite the fact that William found it difficult to come to terms with the imperial title that he obtained in January 1871, and always regarded himself first and foremost as King of *Prussia*. His court thus remained a Prussian court, with Prussian rituals and ceremonial; and, despite its continued growth and expense, it remained notable mostly for its lack of ostentation and even for its gracelessness.[17] Still, there can be little doubt that when William died in 1888 the prestige of the monarchy had reached new heights, or that attachment to crown and dynasty was widespread in many circles far beyond the traditional élites represented in the high society of the court.[18] Even in Baden, where the 'Grapeshot Prince' had drowned the revolution in blood in 1849, he had become a respected, patriarchal figure. Indeed, Carl Schurz, the old Forty-Eighter who had emigrated to the United States, admitted that William was the most popular monarch that the nineteenth century had produced. He had come a long way indeed from 1848, when

[15] Walter Bußmann, 'Die Krönung Wilhelms I. am 18. Oktober 1861: Eine Demonstration des Gottesgnadentums im preußischen Verfassungsstaat', in Dieter Albrecht, Hans Günter Hockerts, Paul Mikat, and Rudolf Morsey (eds.), *Politik und Konfession: Festschrift für Konrad Repgen zum 60. Geburtstag* (Berlin, 1983), 189–212; Karl Heinz Börner, *Kaiser Wilhelm I. 1797 bis 1888: Deutscher Kaiser und König von Preußen. Eine Biographie* (Cologne, 1984), 149–51; David E. Barclay, 'Ritual, Ceremonial, and the "Invention" of a Monarchical Tradition in Nineteenth-Century Prussia', in Heinz Duchhardt, Richard A. Jackson, and David Sturdy (eds.), *European Monarchy: Its Evolution and Practice from Roman Antiquity to Modern Times* (Stuttgart, 1992), 217–19.

[16] Siemann, *Gesellschaft*, 80.

[17] Isabel V. Hull, 'Prussian Dynastic Ritual and the End of Monarchy', in Carole Fink, Isabel V. Hull, and MacGregor Knox (eds.), *German Nationalism and the European Response, 1890–1945* (Norman, Okla., 1985), 18–19; Börner, *Wilhelm I.*, 264–70.

[18] Karl-Ferdinand Werner, 'Fürst und Hof im 19. Jahrhundert: Abgesang oder Spätblüte?', in id. (ed.), *Hof, Kultur und Politik im 19. Jahrhundert: Akten des 18. Deutsch-französischen Historikerkolloquiums Darmstadt vom 27.–30. September 1982* (Bonn, 1985), 48.

he had fled to London and his house had been proclaimed 'property of the nation' by angry Berliners; and after his death, more than 200,000 of his subjects filed past his coffin.[19] The power and authority of the Hohenzollern monarchy thus seemed assured.

That turned out, of course, to be an illusion. The old Emperor's grandson, William II, represented a new kind of national-imperial monarchy, and he tried to invest the Prussian-German crown with new forms of symbolic and political meaning, many of which revolved around his own person.[20] But his efforts to merge Prussian tradition with contemporary German modernity fell short, despite the gargantuan expansion of the court and the unparalleled splendour, even gaudiness, of Wilhelmine court society. The court itself remained at the heart of the Wilhelmine political system, in which 'the central structures of the Reich, the Foreign Office, and the army' continued to be intertwined.[21] It was in no position, however, seriously to address or resolve the innumerable contradictions of the Wilhelmine state. Moreover, as one recent historian has trenchantly observed, through its inability to create a truly national ritual in place of older, Prussian-dynastic ones, the Wilhelmine court ultimately failed either to capture the nationalism of the German bourgeoisie or to ease the growing anxieties of the country's traditional élites.[22] In short, William II was unable successfully to adapt the monarchy to changing circumstances, despite the enormous power that continued to reside in his office and in the court that surrounded him; and at the same time he managed to use up what Friedrich von Holstein called the 'royalist capital' that his forebears, especially his grandfather, had accumulated for many years.[23] Finally, of course, he was swept away by a catastrophe far greater than that which his great-uncle had confronted seventy years earlier. His entourage, his court, his officials, and his army could not save him or his fellow rulers.[24] Seven decades after 1848, and only a few years after the monarchical revival of the nineteenth century had reached its zenith, monarchy was dead in Germany.

That outcome had not been entirely unforeseen by some perspicacious conservatives. In fact, many nineteenth-century conservatives—Stahl, the Gerlachs, and others—had long sensed that they were swimming against the currents of history. Even the modernization of conservatism, and its political victories during the second

[19] Günter Richter, 'Kaiser Wilhelm I.', in Wilhelm Treue (ed.), *Drei deutsche Kaiser: Wilhelm I.—Friedrich III.—Wilhelm II. Ihr Leben und ihre Zeit 1858–1918* (Freiburg, 1987), 74–5.

[20] Elisabeth Fehrenbach, 'Images of Kaiserdom: German Attitudes to Kaiser Wilhelm II', in John C. G. Röhl and Nicolaus Sombart (eds.), *Kaiser Wilhelm II: New Interpretations: The Corfu Papers* (Cambridge, 1982), 269–85.

[21] Werner, 'Fürst und Hof', 47; John C. G. Röhl, 'Hof und Hofgesellschaft unter Kaiser Wilhelm II.', in id., *Kaiser, Hof und Staat: Wilhelm II. und die deutsche Politik* (Munich, 1987).

[22] Hull, 'Ritual', 36–41.

[23] Quoted in Bernd Sösemann, 'Der Verfall des Kaisergedankens im Ersten Weltkrieg', in John C. G. Röhl (with Elisabeth Müller-Luckner) (ed.), *Der Ort Kaiser Wilhelms II. in der deutschen Geschichte* (Munich, 1991), 148.

[24] See the thoughtful remarks in Isabel V. Hull, *The Entourage of Kaiser Wilhelm II. 1888–1918* (Cambridge, 1982), 293–306.

half of the reign of Frederick William IV, did little to overcome conservative pessimism and a growing feeling among them of inevitable social and political marginal-
ization.[25] Bismarck himself succumbed to those moods from time to time. Writing in
1893, during the bitter years after his resignation, he observed, 'It could be that God
has planned yet another time of decay for Germany, and thereafter a new age of glory
on a new basis, the republic. But that won't affect me anymore.'[26]

---

[25] Retallack, 'Conservatism', 14.
[26] Bismarck to Baroness Spitzemberg, March 1893, quoted in Lothar Gall, 'Bismarck: Preußen,
Deutschland und Europa', in Deutsches Historisches Museum (ed.), *Bismarck: Preußen, Deutschland und
Europa*, 2nd edn. (Berlin, 1990), 34.

BIBLIOGRAPHY

ARCHIVAL SOURCES

1. *Bayerisches Hauptstaatsarchiv, Munich (BayHStA)*

Abteilung II: Neuere Bestände (19./20. Jahrhundert):
    MA III 2618–37. Preußen. Politische Berichte der K. Bayer. Gesandtschaft 1840–1857
    Gesandtschaft Berlin 505, 522, 630, 641. Berichte
Abteilung III: Geheimes Hausarchiv (GHA):
    Nachlaß König Ludwig I
    Nachlaß König Max II

2. *Brandenburgisches Landeshauptarchiv Potsdam (BLHA; formerly Staatsarchiv Potsdam)*

Pr. Br. Rep. 37: Herrschaft Boitzenburg, Teil II: Familienarchiv:
    Nachlaß Adolf Heinrich von Arnim auf Boitzenburg

3. *Bundesarchiv, Außenstelle Frankfurt am Main (BA Frankfurt/M.)*

FSg. 1: Biographische Sammlung zur deutschen Einheits- und Freiheitsbewegung im 19. Jahrhundert
    FSg. 1/112: Wilhelm Freiherr Hiller von Gärtringen
    FSg. 1/144: Bürgermeister Naunyn von Berlin
    FSg. 1/154: Joseph Maria von Radowitz
    FSg. 1/210: Erzherzog Johann von Österreich
ZSg. 6: Karikaturen

4. *Bundesarchiv, Abteilungen Potsdam (BA Potsdam; formerly Zentrales Staatsarchiv Potsdam)*

90 Ge 6 Nachlaß Leopold von Gerlach
90 Wa 3 Nachlaß Hermann Wagener

5. *Geheimes Staatsarchiv Preußischer Kulturbesitz Berlin (GStA Berlin)*

Brandenburg-Preußisches Hausarchiv (BPH)
    BPH Rep. 50: König Friedrich Wilhelm IV. (1840–1861) und Gemahlin
    BPH Rep. 59 I: Prinz Carl und Familie
    BPH Rep. 192: Nachlässe: Carl Wilhelm Saegert; Wilhelm Fürst zu Sayn-Wittgenstein-Hohenstein
I. Hauptabteilung: Preußische und neue Reposituren:
    I. Hauptabteilung Rep. 90: Staatsministerium
    I. Hauptabteilung Rep. 92: Nachlässe: von Auerswald II. Papiere Rudolfs von Auerswald; Carl Ernst Wilhelm Freiherr von Canitz und Dallwitz; Gustav von Rochow; Constantin Freiherr von Zedlitz-Neukirch; Theodor von Schön; Rudolf Vaupel

I. Hauptabteilung Rep. 109: Seehandlung
III. Hauptabteilung: Auswärtiges Amt
XX. Hauptabteilung: Staatsarchiv Königsberg
    Rep. 300 v. Brünneck I. Nachlaß Theodor von Schön.

6. *Geheimes Staatsarchiv Preußischer Kulturbesitz, Abteilung Merseburg (GStA Merseburg;*
formerly Zentrales Staatsarchiv, Dienststelle Merseburg)

Hausarchiv (HA):
    HA Rep. 49: König Friedrich Wilhelm III. und Familie
    HA Rep. 50: König Friedrich Wilhelm IV. und Gemahlin
    HA Rep. 51: Kaiser Wilhelm I. und Familie
    HA Rep. 59 I: Prinz Karl von Preußen
    HA Rep. 192: Nachlässe: M Edwin von Manteuffel; R Georg Wilhelm von Raumer
2.2.1. Geheimes Zivilkabinett
2.2.10. Ministerium des Königlichen Hauses
Rep. 77: Ministerium des Innern
    Tit. 95: Hof- und Hofstaatssachen, I. Reihe
    Tit. 96: Hof- und Hofstaatssachen, II. Reihe
    Tit. 327: Majestätsverbrechen
    Tit. 499: Volksfeste und Feierlichkeiten
Rep. 90a: Staatsministerium
    B III 2c Nr. 3: Protokolle der Kronratssitzungen
Rep. 92: Nachlässe: Alexander Heinrich von Arnim (-Suckow); Christian Carl Josias Freiherr
von Bunsen; Leopold von Gerlach; Graf Carl von der Groeben; Edwin von Manteuffel; Otto
von Manteuffel; Familienarchiv von Massow; Marcus von Niebuhr; Joseph Maria von
Radowitz d. Ä.; Gustav von Rochow; Ernst Freiherr Senfft von Pilsach; Ludwig Gustav
von Thile; Graf Guido von Usedom; Graf Karl von Voss-Buch
Rep. 94: Kleine Erwerbungen:
    IV.O.a. Friedrich Wilhelm IV. 1840–1847
    IV.O.c. Friedrich Wilhelm IV. 1850–1861

7. *Generallandesarchiv Karlsruhe (GLA)*

Abt. 48: Großherzogliches Haus- und Staatsarchiv III. Staatssachen. Diplomatische
Korrespondenz. Preußen, 2594–2600, 2640–2655 (1840–1857)
Abt. 49: Großherzogliches Haus- und Staatsarchiv IV. Gesandtschaften, Nr. 2162 (1850)

8. *Gerlach-Archiv am Institut für politische Wissenschaft der Friedrich-Alexander-Universität*
Erlangen-Nürnberg (GA)

Fasz. I–XIX: Korrespondenz Ernst Ludwig von Gerlachs
Fasz. 2/a: Ernst Freiherr Senfft von Pilsach an Ernst Ludwig von Gerlach
Fasz. BF: Tagebuch Leopold von Gerlachs 1.3.1848–23.12.1848—Abschrift des Landrats
von Oschersleben
Fasz. CK/a: Hans von Kleist-Retzow an Ernst Ludwig von Gerlach
Fasz. CS: Leopold von Gerlach an Ernst Ludwig von Gerlach 1822–1844
Fasz. CT: Leopold von Gerlach an Ernst Ludwig von Gerlach 1845–1851

Casz. CU: Leopold von Gerlach an Ernst Ludwig von Gerlach 1852–1861
Neg J/I/e: Kopien aus dem Bodelschwingh'schen Hauptarchiv Bethel.
Beilagen zur Familiengeschichte, Mappe i–iii
Tagebücher Ernst Ludwig von Gerlachs, Bd. i–ix
Abschriften aus dem Nachlaß Leopold von Gerlachs, vols. i–xxxv

9. *Österreichisches Staatsarchiv, Vienna: Haus-, Hof- und Staatsarchiv (HHStA)*

Staatskanzlei. Preußen (St. K. Preußen): Karton 177, 180, 183, 186, 190, 192, 196
Politisches Archiv III Preußen (P.A. III): Karton 41, 42, 46, 48, 50, 54, 56, 59

10. *Public Record Office, Kew (PRO)*

FO 64. Foreign Office. General Correspondence before 1906. Prussia and Germany 1781 to 1905:
    Nrs. 229, 231, 233, 234, 235, 238, 239, 243, 249, 256, 263, 273, 285, 286, 290, 292, 307, 314, 321, 322, 340, 341, 342, 343, 344, 345, 353, 354, 355, 356, 257, 367, 368, 371, 381, 389, 399, 400, 412, 413, 414, 417, 418, 440, 441, 460.

11. *Staatsbibliothek Preußischer Kulturbesitz Berlin, Handschriftenabteilung (StaBi Berlin)*

Nachlaß Ernst Wilhelm Hengstenberg

12. *Stiftung Schlösser und Gärten Potsdam-Sanssouci, Plankammer*

Sammlung Friedrich Wilhelm IV. (Slg. FW IV.): Mappe I, Mappe II, Mappe III, Mappe IV, Mappe VI, Mappe X

PRINTED SOURCES

1. *Published Speeches and Correspondence of Frederick William IV*

Andreas, Willy, 'Der Briefwechsel König Friedrich Wilhelms IV. von Preußen und des Zaren Nikolaus I. von Rußland in den Jahren 1848 bis 1850: Ein Beitrag zur Geschichte der russisch-preußischen Beziehungen', *FBPG* 43 (1930), 129–66.
Bailleu, Paul, 'Kronprinz Friedrich Wilhelm im Ständekampf 1820', *HZ* 87, NS 51 (1901), 67–73.
Brandenburg, Erich (ed.), *König Friedrich Wilhelms IV. Briefwechsel mit Ludolf Camphausen* (Berlin, 1906).
Breitenborn, Konrad, 'Aus dem Briefwechsel zwischen Friedrich Wilhelm IV. von Preußen und Graf Anton zu Stolberg-Wernigerode im Jahre 1848', *ZfG* 30 (1982), 224–44.
Friedrich Wilhelm IV., König von Preußen, *Reden, Proklamationen, Botschaften, Erlasse und Ordres Sr. Majestät des Königs Friedrich Wilhelm IV: Vom Schlusse des Vereinigten ständischen Ausschusses, am 6. März 1848, bis zur Enthüllungs-Feier des Denkmals Friedrichs des Großen, am 31. Mai 1851* (Berlin, 1851).
—— *Reden und Trinksprüche Sr. Majestät Friedrich Wilhelm des Vierten, Königes von Preußen* (Leipzig, 1855).

Friedrich Wilhelm IV., *Reden Seiner Majestät des Königs Friedrich Wilhelm des Vierten seit seiner Thronbesteigung: Zusammengestellt und zum Besten des Nationaldanks herausgegeben von Dr. J. Killisch, Dirigent einer concessionirten Militär-Vorbereitungs-Anstalt*, 5th edn. (Berlin, 1861).

Geiger, Ludwig (ed.), *Bettine von Arnim und Friedrich Wilhelm IV: Ungedruckte Briefe und Aktenstücke* (Frankfurt am Main, 1902).

Granier, Herman (ed.), *Hohenzollernbriefe aus den Freiheitskriegen 1813–1815* (Leipzig, 1913).

—— (ed.) *Prinzenbriefe aus den Freiheitskriegen 1813–1815: Briefwechsel des Kronprinzen Friedrich Wilhelm (IV.) und des Prinzen Wilhelm (I.) von Preußen mit dem Prinzen Friedrich von Oranien* (Stuttgart, 1922).

Haenchen, Karl (ed.), *Revolutionsbriefe 1848: Ungedrucktes aus dem Nachlaß König Friedrich Wilhelms IV. von Preußen* (Leipzig, 1930).

Heckel, Johannes, 'Ein Kirchenverfassungsentwurf Friedrich Wilhelms IV. von 1847', in id., *Das blinde, undeutliche Wort 'Kirche': Gesammelte Aufsätze*, ed. Siegfried Grundmann (Cologne, 1964), 434–53.

Johann Georg, Herzog zu Sachsen, and Ermisch, Hubert (eds.), *Briefwechsel zwischen König Johann von Sachsen und den Königen Friedrich Wilhelm IV. und Wilhelm I. von Preußen* (Leipzig, 1911).

Knesebeck, Ludwig Gottschalk von dem, 'Unveröffentlichte Briefe Friedrich Wilhelm IV. und Wilhelm I. an Landrat Fritz von Berg', *FBPG* 42 (1929), 300–15.

Kretzschmar, Hellmut, 'König Friedrich Wilhelms IV. Briefe an König Friedrich August II. von Sachsen', *Preußische Jahrbücher*, 227 (1932), 28–50, 142–53, 245–63.

Krusch, Bruno, 'Letters of Queen Victoria to Frederick William IV, 1848–49', *English Historical Review*, 40 (1925), 106–10.

Küntzel, Georg (ed.), *Briefwechsel zwischen König Friedrich Wilhelm IV. und dem Reichsverweser Erzherzog Johann von Österreich (1848–1850)* (Frankfurt am Main, 1924).

Linz, Bernhard, 'Mörike und Friedrich Wilhelm IV.: Mit ungedruckten Briefen des Dichters an den König und dessen Antworten', *Deutsche Rundschau*, 220 (1929), 232–7.

Meusel, Friedrich, 'Ernst Moritz Arndt und Friedrich Wilhelm IV. über die Kaiserfrage', *Hohenzollern-Jahrbuch*, 12 (1908), 231–9.

Ow-Piesing, A. Freiherr von, 'Ein unbekannter Brief König Friedrich Wilhelms IV. von Preußen', *Gelbe Hefte*, 17 (Dec. 1940), 87–8.

Poschinger, Heinrich von, 'Aus der unveröffentlichten Korrespondenz des Königs von Preußen Friedrich Wilhelm IV.', *Deutsche Revue*, 31/4 (1906), 1–7.

—— 'Friedrich Wilhelm IV. und Wilhelm I.: Charakterzüge aus unveröffentlichten Briefen beider Könige', *Konservative Monatsschrift für Politik, Literatur und Kunst*, 64 (June 1907), 820–32.

—— 'Ein Brief des Kaisers Nikolaus I. an den König Friedrich Wilhelm IV.', *Konservative Monatsschrift für Politik, Literatur und Kunst*, 64 (Sept. 1907), 1114–17.

—— 'Aus der unveröffentlichten Korrespondenz des Königs Friedrich Wilhelm IV.', *Konservative Monatsschrift für Politik, Literatur und Kunst*, 67 (Nov. 1909), 117–20.

Ranke, Leopold von, *Aus dem Briefwechsel Friedrich Wilhelms IV. mit Bunsen* (Leipzig, 1873).

Rellstab, L[udwig], *Zwei Gespräche mit Seiner Majestät Friedrich Wilhelm dem Vierten (am 23sten November 1847, und am 19ten März 1848) in geschichtlichen Rahmen gefaßt* (Berlin, 1849).

Schiemann, Theodor, 'Kaiser Nikolaus I. und Friedrich Wilhelm IV. über den Plan, einen vereinigten Landtag zu berufen', in Verein für Geschichte der Mark Brandenburg (ed.), *Festschrift zu Gustav Schmollers 70. Geburtstag* (q. v.), 275–85.

Stock, Friedrich, 'Aus dem Briefwechsel Friedrich Wilhelms IV. mit Carl Friedrich von Rumohr', *Jahrbuch der Königlich Preußischen Kunstsammlungen*, 35, suppl. (1914), 1–84.

'Unveröffentlichte Handbillette des Königs Friedrich Wilhelm IV.', *Deutsche Revue*, 32/4 (Oct.–Dec. 1907), 154–8.

2. *Reference Works, Handbooks, Parliamentary Minutes, and Government Documents*

Allgemeine Deutsche Biographie (56 vols.; Berlin, 1967–71 [repr. of orig. edn., 1875–1912]).

Anschütz, Gerhard, *Die Verfassungsurkunde für den preußischen Staat vom 31. Januar 1850: Ein Kommentar für Wissenschaft und Praxis* (Aalen, 1974; repr. of 1912 edn.).

Arnim, Hans von, and Below, Georg von (eds.), *Deutscher Aufstieg: Bilder aus der Vergangenheit und Gegenwart der rechtsstehenden Parteien* (Berlin, 1925).

Baumgart, Winfried (ed.), *Akten zur Geschichte des Krimkriegs*, ser. I: *Österreichische Akten zur Geschichte des Krimkriegs* (3 vols.; Munich, 1979–80).

—— (ed.), *Akten zur Geschichte des Krimkriegs*, ser. III: *Englische Akten zur Geschichte des Krimkriegs*, iv: *10. September 1855 bis 23. Juli 1856* (Munich, 1988).

—— (ed.), *Akten zur Geschichte des Krimkriegs*, ser. II: *Preußische Akten zur Geschichte des Krimkriegs* (2 vols.; Munich, 1990–1).

Bleich, Eduard (ed.), *Der Erste Vereinigte Landtag in Berlin 1847* (4 vols.; Berlin, 1847; repr. Vaduz, 1977).

Ceremonial-Buch für den Königlich Preußischen Hof [Rudolf Graf von Stillfried-Alcantara] (12 vols.; Berlin, 1877–85).

Dehio, Georg, and Gall, Ernst (eds.), *Handbuch der deutschen Kunstdenkmäler: Bezirke Berlin/DDR und Potsdam*, new edn. by Abteilung Forschung des Instituts für Denkmalpflege (Munich, 1983).

Dehio, L., Hölk, E., and Jagow K. (eds.), *Übersicht über die Bestände des Brandenburg-Preußischen Hausarchivs zu Berlin-Charlottenburg* (Leipzig, 1936).

Gesetz-Sammlung für die Königlich Preußischen Staaten (Berlin, 1840–57).

Handbuch über den Königlich Preußischen Hof und Staat (7 vols.; Berlin, 1841–8).

Hubatsch, Walther (ed.), *Grundriß zur deutschen Verwaltungsgeschichte 1815–1945*, ser. A: *Preußen*, xii, pt. a: *Preußische Zentralbehörden*, ed. Friedrich Wilhelm Wehrstedt (Marburg, 1978).

Huber, Ernst Rudolf (ed.), *Dokumente zur deutschen Verfassungsgeschichte*, i: *Deutsche Verfassungsdokumente 1803–1850* (Stuttgart, 1961); ii: *Deutsche Verfassungsdokumente 1851–1918* (Stuttgart, 1964).

—— and Huber, Wolfgang, *Staat und Kirche im 19. und 20. Jahrhundert: Dokumente zur Geschichte des deutschen Staatskirchenrechts*, i: *Staat und Kirche vom Ausgang des alten Reiches bis zum Vorabend der bürgerlichen Revolution* (Berlin, 1973); ii: *Staat und Kirche im Zeitalter des Hochkonstitutionalismus und des Kulturkampfs 1848–1890* (Berlin, 1976).

Institut für Denkmalpflege der DDR (ed.), *Die Bau- und Kunstdenkmale in der DDR: Bezirk Potsdam* (Munich, 1979).

Köllmann, Wolfgang (ed.), *Quellen zur Bevölkerungs-, Sozial- und Wirtschaftsstatistik Deutschlands 1815–1875*, i: *Quellen zur Bevölkerungsstatistik Deutschlands 1815–1875*, ed. Antje Kraus (Boppard am Rhein, 1980).

Königlich Preußischer Staats-Kalender (Berlin, 1850–5).

Malortie, C. E. von, *Der Hof-Marschall: Handbuch für Einrichtung und Führung eines Hofhalts*, 2nd edn. (Hanover, 1846).

Meisner, Heinrich Otto, *Archivalienkunde vom 16. Jahrhundert bis 1918* (Göttingen, 1969).

Neue Deutsche Biographie (17 vols. to date; Berlin, 1953–).

Petersdorff, Herman von, *Deutsche Männer und Frauen: Biographische Skizzen vornehmlich zur Geschichte Preußens im 18. und 19. Jahrhundert* (Berlin, 1913).

Priesdorff, Kurt von (ed.), *Soldatisches Führertum* (10 vols.; Hamburg, 1937–42).

Stenographische Berichte über die Verhandlungen der . . . Kammern: Erste Kammer (15 vols.; Berlin, 1849–54).

Stenographische Berichte über die Verhandlungen der . . . Zweiten Kammer (21 vols.; Berlin, 1849–55).

Stenographische Berichte über die Verhandlungen der . . . beiden Häuser des Landtages: Herrenhaus (2 vols.; Berlin, 1856–7).

Stenographische Berichte über die Verhandlungen der . . . beiden Häuser des Landtages: Haus der Abgeordneten (6 vols.; Berlin, 1856–7).

Verhandlungen der Preußischen National-Versammlung zu Berlin: Stenographische Berichte (4 vols.; Berlin, 1848).

Wigard, Franz (ed.), *Stenographischer Bericht über die Verhandlungen der deutschen constituirenden Nationalversammlung zu Frankfurt am Main* (9 vols.; Frankfurt am Main, 1848–9).

3. *Diaries, Memoirs, Published Documents and Correspondence*

'Aktenstücke zur preußischen Regentschaftsfrage vom Jahre 1858', *Konservative Monatsschrift für Politik, Literatur und Kunst*, 65 (Apr. 1908), 689–92.

Albert, *Letters of the Prince Consort 1831–1861*, ed. Kurt Jagow and trans. E. T. S. Dugdale (New York, 1938).

Augusta, Deutsche Kaiserin, *Aus dem literarischen Nachlaß der Kaiserin Augusta*, ed. Paul Bailleu and Georg Schuster, 2nd edn. (Berlin, 1912).

Below, Georg von, 'Aus der Zeit Friedrich Wilhelms IV.: Briefwechsel des Generals Gustav von Below', *Halbmonatshefte der Deutschen Rundschau*, 109 (1901), 114–46, 302–16, 340–57.

Bernstorff, Gräfin Elise von, geborene Gräfin von Dernath, *Ein Bild aus der Zeit von 1789 bis 1835: Aus ihren Aufzeichnungen*, 2nd edn. (2 vols.; Berlin, 1896).

Bismarck, Otto von, *Die gesammelten Werke*, xiv: *Briefe*, 1: *1822–1861*, ed. Wolfgang Windelband and Werner Frauendienst (Berlin, 1933); xv: *Erinnerung und Gedanke: Kritische Neuausgabe auf Grund des gesamten schriftlichen Nachlasses*, ed. Gerhard Ritter and Rudolf Stadelmann (Berlin, 1932).

Börner, Karl-Heinz, 'Prinz Wilhelm von Preußen über die Berliner Märzrevolution 1848', *ZfG* 41 (1993), 425–36.

Bunsen, Frances Baroness, *Christian Carl Josias Freiherr von Bunsen: Aus seinen Briefen und nach eigener Erinnerung geschildert von seiner Witwe*, ed. Friedrich Nippold (3 vols.; Leipzig, 1868, 1869, 1871).

—— *Memoirs of Baron Bunsen, Late Minister Plenipotentiary and Envoy Extraordinary of His Majesty Frederic William IV at the Court of St. James. Drawn Chiefly from Family Papers by his Widow*, 2nd edn. (2 vols.; London, 1869).

Canitz und Dallwitz, Carl Ernst Wilhelm Freiherr von, *Denkschriften* (2 vols.; Berlin, 1888).

Central-Comité zur Errichtung der Königin-Elisabeth-Vereins-Stiftung, *Gedenkbuch an die silberne Jubel-Hochzeitsfeier Ihrer Königlichen Majestäten Friedrich Wilhelm IV. und Elisabeth Ludovika von Preußen zu Potsdam am 29. November 1848* (Berlin, 1849).

Dehio, Ludwig, 'Zur November-Krise des Jahres 1850: Aus den Papieren des Kriegsministers von Stockhausen', *FBPG* 35 (1923), 134–45.

Delbrück, Friedrich, *Die Jugend des Königs Friedrich Wilhelm IV. von Preußen und des Kaisers
und Königs Wilhelm I.: Tagebuchblätter ihres Erziehers Friedrich Delbrück (1800–1809)*, ed.
Georg Schuster (3 vols.; Berlin, 1907).

Diest, Gustav von, *Meine Erlebnisse im Jahre 1848 und die Stellung des Staatsministers von
Bodelschwingh vor und an dem 18. März 1848* (Berlin, 1898).

'Erinnerungen an den Kabinettsrat von Niebuhr', *Deutsche Revue*, 13/4 (1888), 166–72.

Ernst II., Herzog von Sachsen-Coburg-Gotha, *Aus meinem Leben und aus meiner Zeit* (3 vols.;
Berlin, 1887–9).

Fontane, Theodor, *Von Zwanzig bis Dreißig*, ed. Walter Keitel (Frankfurt am Main, 1980).

Friedrich III., Deutscher Kaiser, *Kaiser Friedrich III: Tagebücher von 1848–1866*, ed.
Heinrich Otto Meisner (Leipzig, 1929).

Gerlach, Ernst Ludwig von, *Aufzeichnungen aus seinem Leben und Wirken 1795–1877*, ed.
Jakob von Gerlach (2 vols.; Schwerin, 1903).

—— *Von der Revolution zum Norddeutschen Bund: Politik und Ideengut der preußischen
Hochkonservativen 1848–1866. Aus dem Nachlaß von Ernst Ludwig von Gerlach*, ed. Hellmut
Diwald (2 vols.; Göttingen, 1970).

Gerlach, Leopold von, *Denkwürdigkeiten aus dem Leben Leopold von Gerlachs, Generals der
Infanterie und General-Adjutanten König Friedrich Wilhelms IV.*, ed. Agnes von Gerlach (2
vols.; Berlin, 1891–2).

Hare, Augustus J. C., *The Life and Letters of Frances Baroness Bunsen* (2 vols.; New York, 1879).

Harnisch, Hartmut, 'Aus den Papieren des Grafen von Arnim-Boitzenburg: Zur
Widerspiegelung der Revolution von 1848/49 im Briefnachlaß eines Junkers', *ZfG* 22
(1974), 539–55.

Hohenlohe-Ingelfingen, Prinz Kraft zu, *Aus meinem Leben: Aufzeichnungen*, ii: *Flügeladjutant
unter Friedrich Wilhelm IV. und König Wilhelm I. 1856–1863*, 8th edn. (Berlin, 1909).

Humboldt, Alexander von, *Briefe Alexander von Humboldt's an Ignaz v. Olfers Generaldirektor
der Kgl. Museen in Berlin*, ed. E. W. M. von Olfers (Nuremberg, n. d.).

—— *Briefe von Alexander von Humboldt an Varnhagen von Ense aus den Jahren 1827 bis 1858.
Nebst Auszügen aus Varnhagen's Tagebüchern, und Briefen von Varnhagen und Andern an
Humboldt*, ed. Ludmilla Assing, 5th edn. (Leipzig, 1860).

—— *Briefe von Alexander von Humboldt an Christian Carl Josias Freiherr von Bunsen* (Leipzig,
1869).

—— *Alexander von Humboldt und das preußische Königshaus: Briefe aus den Jahren 1835–1857*,
ed. Conrad Müller (Leipzig, 1928).

—— *Gespräche Alexander von Humboldts*, ed. Hanno Beck (Berlin [East], 1959).

—— *Vier Jahrzehnte Wissenschaftsförderung: Briefe an das preußische Kultministerium
1818–1859*, ed. Kurt-R. Biermann (Berlin [East], 1985).

Keyserling, Leonie von, *Studien zu den Entwicklungsjahren der Brüder Gerlach. Mit Briefen
Leopolds von Gerlach und seiner Brüder an Karl Sieveking* (Heidelberg, 1913).

Koglin, Olaf Karl Friedrich, 'Die Briefe Friedrich Julius Stahls' (Diss.; Kiel, 1975).

Kohl, Horst (ed.), *Bismarcks Briefe an den General Leopold v. Gerlach* (Berlin, 1896).

—— (ed.) *Briefe des Generals Leopold von Gerlach an Otto von Bismarck* (Stuttgart, 1912).

Liermann, Hans, and Schoeps, Hans-Joachim, *Materialien zur preußischen Eherechtsreform im
Vormärz: Aus dem Briefwechsel Savigny, Puchta und Bethmann Hollweg mit Ludwig von
Gerlach* (Göttingen, 1961).

Luise, Königin von Preußen, *Königin Luise von Preußen: Briefe und Aufzeichnungen 1786–1810*, ed. Malve Gräfin Rothkirch (Munich, 1985).

Manteuffel, Edwin von, 'Briefe des Generalfeldmarschalls Edwin v. Manteuffel an seinen Sohn Hans Karl', *Deutsche Revue*, 38/3 (1913), 190–201, 314–25.

Manteuffel, Otto von, *Unter Friedrich Wilhelm IV.: Denkwürdigkeiten des Ministers Otto Freiherrn von Manteuffel*, ed. Heinrich von Poschinger (3 vols.; Berlin, 1901).

—— *Preußens auswärtige Politik 1850 bis 1858: Unveröffentlichte Dokumente aus dem Nachlasse des Ministerpräsidenten Otto Frhrn. v. Manteuffel*, ed. Heinrich von Poschinger (3 vols.; Berlin, 1902).

Meyendorff, Peter von, *Ein russischer Diplomat an den Höfen von Berlin und Wien: Politischer und privater Briefwechsel 1826–1863*, ed. Otto Hoetzsch (3 vols.; Berlin, 1923).

Münster, Graf Hugo zu, 'Politische Briefe des Grafen Hugo zu Münster an Edwin v. Manteuffel aus den Jahren 1850 und 1851', *Deutsche Revue*, 38/1 (1913), 9–25.

—— 'Politische Briefe des Grafen Hugo zu Münster an Edwin v. Manteuffel aus den Jahren 1850 bis 1852', *Deutsche Revue*, 38/1 (1913), 172–93.

—— 'Politische Briefe des Grafen Hugo zu Münster an Edwin v. Manteuffel aus den Jahren 1852 und 1853', *Deutsche Revue*, 38/1 (1913), 297–309; 38/2, (1913), 60–70.

—— 'Politische Briefe des Grafen Hugo zu Münster an Edwin v. Manteuffel aus der Zeit des Krimkrieges', *Deutsche Revue*, 38/2 (1913), 183–97, 326–37.

Natzmer, Gneomar Ernst von, *Unter den Hohenzollern: Denkwürdigkeiten aus dem Leben des Generals Oldwig v. Natzmer. Allen deutschen Patrioten gewidmet von Gneomar Ernst v. Natzmer*, iii: *Aus der Zeit Friedrich Wilhelms IV. 1840–1848* (Gotha, 1888) and iv: *Aus der Zeit Friedrich Wilhelms IV. 1848–1861* (Gotha, 1889).

Persius, Ludwig, *Das Tagebuch des Architekten Friedrich Wilhelms IV. 1840–1845*, ed. Eva Börsch-Supan (Munich, 1980).

Petersdorff, Herman von, 'Briefe Ludwigs von Gerlach an seinen Bruder Leopold', *Konservative Monatsschrift für Politik, Literatur und Kunst*, 63/1 (Oct. 1905), 68–80.

—— 'Zur Geschichte König Friedrich Wilhelms IV: Vierzehn Aktenstücke aus dem Nachlaß des Generals Leopold v. Gerlach', *Konservative Monatsschrift für Politik, Literatur und Kunst*, 65/1 (1907), 19–29; 65/2 (1907), 110–21.

Poschinger, Heinrich von, 'Verhandlungen zwischen Preußen und dem päpstlichen Stuhle unter Friedrich Wilhelm IV. und Pius IX.', *Deutsche Revue*, 31/2 (1906), 317–28.

—— 'Aus der Korrespondenz des russischen Reichskanzlers Graf Nesselrode 1852 bis 1853', *Deutsche Revue*, 32/4 (1907), 64–72.

—— 'Vor fünfzig Jahren: Diplomatisches aus allen Welten', *Konservative Monatsschrift für Politik, Literatur und Kunst*, 67/3 (1909), 227–34.

Prittwitz, Karl Ludwig von, *Berlin 1848: Das Erinnerungswerk des Generalleutnants Karl Ludwig von Prittwitz und andere Quellen zur Berliner Märzrevolution und zur Geschichte Preußens um die Mitte des 19. Jahrhunderts*, ed. Gerd Heinrich (Berlin, 1985).

Prokesch von Osten, Anton Graf, *Aus den Briefen des Grafen Prokesch von Osten, k. u. k. österr. Botschafters und Feldzeugmeisters (1849–1855)*, ed. Anton Graf Prokesch von Osten (not id.) (Vienna, 1896).

Radowitz, Joseph Maria von, *Gesammelte Schriften* (5 vols.; Berlin, 1853).

—— *Ausgewählte Schriften und Reden*, ed. Friedrich Meinecke (Munich, 1921).

—— *Nachgelassene Briefe und Aufzeichnungen zur Geschichte der Jahre 1848–1853*, ed. Walter Möring (Stuttgart, 1922).

Reumont, Alfred von, *Aus König Friedrich Wilhelms IV. gesunden und kranken Tagen*, 2nd edn. (Leipzig, 1885).

Rochow, Caroline von, and La Motte-Fouqué, Marie de, *Vom Leben am preußischen Hofe 1815–1852*, ed. Luise von der Marwitz (Berlin, 1908).

Rochow, Theodor Heinrich Rochus von, *Briefe des Königlich Preußischen Generals und Gesandten Theodor Heinrich Rochus von Rochow an einen Staatsbeamten*, ed. Ernst Kelchner and Karl Mendelssohn-Bartholdy (Frankfurt am Main, 1873).

Rothkirch, Gräfin Malve, *Prinz Carl von Preußen: Kenner und Beschützer des Schönen 1801–1883. Eine Chronik aus zeitgenössischen Dokumenten und Bildern* (Osnabrück, 1981).

Schiemann, Theodor, 'Vertrauliche Briefe des Freiherrn Peter v. Meyendorff an seine Brüder Georg und Alexander', *HZ* 86, NS 50 (1901), 445–63.

Schneider, Louis, *Aus meinem Leben* (3 vols.; Berlin, 1879–80).

Schoeps, Hans-Joachim, 'Aus dem Briefwechsel Leopold von Gerlachs mit Edwin von Manteuffel', in Ernst Heinen and Hans Julius Schoeps (eds.), *Geschichte in der Gegenwart: Festschrift für Kurt Kluxen* (Paderborn, 1972), 129–60.

—— 'Unbekanntes aus dem Gerlachschen Familienarchiv', in id., *Ein weites Feld: Gesammelte Aufsätze* (Berlin, 1980), 265–78.

—— (ed.) *Aus den Jahren preußischer Not und Erneuerung: Tagebücher und Briefe der Gebrüder Gerlach und ihres Kreises 1805–1820* (Berlin, 1963).

—— (ed.) *Neue Quellen zur Geschichte Preußens im 19. Jahrhundert* (Berlin, 1968).

Schultz, Hartwig (ed.), *Der Briefwechsel Bettine von Arnims mit den Brüdern Grimm 1838–1841* (Frankfurt am Main, 1985).

Schultze, Johannes, 'Prinz Wilhelm im Sommer 1848: Briefe an den Ministerpräsidenten Rudolf von Auerswald', *FBPG* 39 (1927), 123–33.

Stern, Alfred, 'Ein apokrypher Brief des Prinzen von Preußen', *HZ* 87, NS 51 (1901), 73–5.

—— 'König Friedrich Wilhelm IV. von Preußen und Fürst Metternich im Jahre 1842', *Mitteilungen des Instituts für österreichische Geschichtsforschung*, 30 (1909), 120–35.

Stieber, Wilhelm J. C. E., *Denkwürdigkeiten des Geheimen Regierungsrathes Dr. Stieber*, ed. Leopold Auerbach (Berlin, 1884).

—— *Spion des Kanzlers: Die Enthüllungen von Bismarcks Geheimdienstchef* (Munich, 1981).

Stoll, Adolf, *Friedrich Karl v. Savigny: Ein Bild seines Lebens mit einer Sammlung seiner Briefe*, i: *Der junge Savigny: Kinderjahre, Marburger und Landshuter Zeit Friedrich Karl von Savignys. Zugleich ein Beitrag zur Geschichte der Romantik* (Berlin, 1927); ii: *Friedrich Karl v. Savigny: Professorenjahre in Berlin 1820–1842* (Berlin, 1929); iii: *Friedrich Karl v. Savigny: Ministerzeit und letzte Lebensjahre 1842–1861* (Berlin, 1939).

Streckfuß, Karl, *Der Preußen Huldigungsfest, nach amtlichen und andern sichern Nachrichten und eigener Anschauung zusammengestellt* (Berlin, 1840).

Varnhagen von Ense, K. A., *Tagebücher*, ed. Ludmilla Assing, 2nd edn.: i–vi (Leipzig, 1862); vii–viii (Zurich, 1865); ix–xiv (Hamburg, 1868–70); xv (Berlin, 1905).

Victoria, *The Letters of Queen Victoria: A Selection from Her Majesty's Correspondence between the Years 1837 and 1861*, ed. Arthur Christopher Benson and Viscount Esher (3 vols.; London, 1907).

Wagener, Hermann, *Die Politik Friedrich Wilhelm IV.* (Berlin, 1883).

—— *Erlebtes: Meine Memoiren aus der Zeit von 1848 bis 1866 und von 1873 bis jetzt* (2 vols.; Berlin, 1884).

[——] 'Aus den Aufzeichnungen eines alten preußischen Staatsmannes', *Deutsche Revue*, 13/2 (1888), 318–28; 13/3 (1888), 92–103.

Wilhelm I., Deutscher Kaiser, *Kaiser Wilhelms des Großen Briefe, Reden und Schriften*, ed. Ernst Berner (2 vols.; Berlin, 1906).

—— 'Aus der unveröffentlichten Korrespondenz Kaiser Wilhelms I.', *Deutsche Revue*, 33/3 (1908), 129–32.

—— *Briefe Kaiser Wilhelms des Ersten. Nebst Denkschriften und anderen Aufzeichnungen in Auswahl*, ed. Erich Brandenburg (Leipzig, 1911).

—— *Kaiser Wilhelms I. Weimarer Briefe*, ed. Johannes Schultze (2 vols.; Berlin, 1924).

—— *Kaiser Wilhelms I. Briefe an Politiker und Staatsmänner*, ed. Johannes Schultze (2 vols.; Berlin, 1930–1).

Wolff, Adolf, *Berliner Revolutions-Chronik: Darstellung der Berliner Bewegungen im Jahre 1848 nach politischen, socialen und literarischen Beziehungen* (3 vols.; Berlin, 1851, 1852, 1854; repr. Vaduz, 1979).

4. Newspapers

Allgemeine Preußische Zeitung; after 1 May 1848 *Preußischer Staatsanzeiger* (Berlin, 7 Jan. 1848–31 Dec. 1848).

Allgemeine Zeitung (Augsburg, 7 Nov. 1846–Apr. 1849).

Berlinische Nachrichten von Staats- und gelehrten Sachen (*Spenersche Zeitung*) (Berlin, 3 Jan. 1848–9 Mar. 1849).

Constitutionelle Zeitung (Berlin, 1 Jan. 1851–30 June 1852).

Deutsche Reform (Berlin, 1 Jan. 1849–10 Mar. 1851).

Königlich privilegirte Berlinische Zeitung von Staats- und gelehrten Sachen (*Vossische Zeitung*) (Berlin, 1847–61).

National-Zeitung (Berlin, 1848–61).

Neue Preußische [Kreuz-] Zeitung (Berlin, 1848–61).

Urwähler-Zeitung; after 9 Apr. 1853 *Volks-Zeitung* (Berlin, 1849–61).

5. Secondary Literature

ANDREAS, WILLY, *Die russische Diplomatie und die Politik Friedrich Wilhelms IV. von Preußen* (Berlin, 1927).

ARCH, NIGEL, and MARSCHNER, JOANNA, *Splendour at Court: Dressing for Royal Occasions since 1700* (London, 1987).

ARNIM, BETTINE VON, *Bettina von Arnims Armenbuch*, ed. Werner Vordtriede (Frankfurt am Main, 1981).

—— *Dies Buch gehört dem König*, ed. Ilse Staff (Frankfurt am Main, 1982).

AUSTENSEN, ROY A., 'Einheit oder Einigkeit? Another Look at Metternich's View of the German Dilemma', *German Studies Review*, 6 (1983), 41–57.

—— 'The Making of Austria's Prussian Policy, 1848–1852', *Historical Journal*, 27 (1984), 861–76.

—— 'Metternich, Austria, and the German Question, 1848–1851', *International History Review*, 13 (1991), 21–37.

BADSTÜBNER-GRÖGER, Sibylle, *Die Friedenskirche zu Potsdam*, 4th edn. (Berlin [East], 1986).

BAHNE, SIEGFRIED, 'Die Verfassungspläne König Friedrich Wilhelms IV. von Preußen und die Prinzenopposition im Vormärz' (*Habilitationsschrift*; Bochum, 1971).

BAK, JÁNOS M. (ed.), *Coronations: Medieval and Early Modern Monarchic Ritual* (Berkeley, Calif., 1990).

BARCLAY, DAVID E., 'König, Königtum, Hof und preußische Gesellschaft in der Zeit Friedrich Wilhelms IV. (1840–1861)', in Büsch (ed.), *Friedrich Wilhelm IV. in seiner Zeit* (q. v.), 1–21.

—— 'The Soldiers of an Unsoldierly King: The Military Advisers of Frederick William IV, 1840–1858', in Treue (ed.), *Geschichte als Aufgabe* (q. v.), 247–66.

—— 'Hof und Hofgesellschaft in Preußen in der Zeit Friedrich Wilhelms IV. (1840 bis 1857): Überlegungen und Fragen', in Möckl (ed.), *Hof und Hofgesellschaft* (q.v.), 321–60.

—— 'Ritual, Ceremonial, and the "Invention" of a Monarchical Tradition in Nineteenth-Century Prussia', in Heinz Duchhardt, Richard A. Jackson, and David Sturdy (eds.), *European Monarchy: Its Evolution and Practice from Roman Antiquity to Modern Times* (Stuttgart, 1992), 207–20.

—— 'The Court Camarilla and the Politics of Monarchical Restoration in Prussia, 1848–58', in Jones and Retallack (eds.), *Between Reform, Reaction, and Resistance* (q. v.), 123–56.

—— 'Denkmal und Revolutionsfurcht: Friedrich Wilhelm IV. und die Verherrlichung des preußischen Feldzugs in Südwestdeutschland 1849. Monumentale Beispiele im Potsdamer Raum', *Jahrbuch für brandenburgische Landesgeschichte*, 44 (1993), 130–60.

—— 'Gartenintendant und konservativer Hofpolitiker: Ludwig von Massow (1794–1859)', *Mitteilungen der Pückler Gesellschaft*, NS 9 (1993), 6–30.

BAUMGART, WINFRIED, 'Zur Außenpolitik Friedrich Wilhelms IV. 1840–1858', in Büsch (ed.), *Friedrich Wilhelm IV. in seiner Zeit* (q. v.), 132–56.

BECK, HANNO, *Alexander von Humboldt* (2 vols.; Wiesbaden, 1959, 1961).

BECK, HERMANN, 'Conservatives, Bureaucracy, and the Social Question in Prussia (1815–1848)' (Ph.D. thesis; Los Angeles, 1988).

—— 'The Social Policies of Prussian Officials: The Bureaucracy in a New Light', *Journal of Modern History*, 64 (1992), 263–98.

—— 'State and Society in Pre-March Prussia: The Weavers' Uprising, the Bureaucracy, and the Association for the Welfare of Workers', *CEH* 25 (1992), 303–31.

—— 'Conservatives and the Social Question in Nineteenth-Century Prussia', in Jones and Retallack (eds.), *Between Reform, Reaction, and Resistance* (q. v.), 61–94.

BECKER, GERHARD, 'Die Beschlüsse des preußischen Junkerparlaments von 1848', *ZfG* 24 (1976), 889–918.

BEHNEN, MICHAEL, *Das Preußische Wochenblatt (1851–1861): National-konservative Publizistik gegen Ständestaat und Polizeistaat* (Göttingen, 1971).

BENDIX, REINHARD, *Kings or People: Power and the Mandate to Rule* (Berkeley, Calif., 1978).

BENZ, ERNST, *Bischofsamt und apostolische Sukzession im deutschen Protestantismus* (Stuttgart, 1953).

BERCKENHAGEN, EKHART, and WAGNER, GRETEL (eds.), *Der bunte Rock in Preußen: Militär- und Ziviluniformen 17. bis 20. Jahrhundert in Zeichnungen, Stichen und Photographen aus dem Bestand der Kunstbibliothek Berlin* (Berlin, 1981).

BERDAHL, ROBERT M., *The Politics of the Prussian Nobility: The Development of a Conservative Ideology 1770–1848* (Princeton, NJ, 1988).

BERGMANN, JÜRGEN, *Das Berliner Handwerk in der Frühphase der Industrialisierung* (Berlin, 1973).

BIERMANN, KURT-R., *Alexander von Humboldt*, 3rd edn. (Leipzig, 1983).

BIGLER, ROBERT M., *The Politics of German Protestantism: The Rise of the Protestant Church Elite in Prussia, 1815–1848* (Berkeley, Calif., 1972).

BISSING, WILHELM MORITZ FREIHERR VON, *Königin Elisabeth von Preußen (1801–1874): Ein Lebensbild* (Berlin, 1974).

—— 'Sein Ideal war der absolut regierte Staat: Prinz Carl von Preußen und der Berliner Hof', *Der Bär von Berlin: Jahrbuch des Vereins für die Geschichte Berlins*, 25 (1976), 124–44.

BLACKBOURN, DAVID, *Populists and Patricians: Essays in Modern German History* (London, 1987).

—— and ELEY, GEOFF, *The Peculiarities of German History: Bourgeois Society and Politics in Nineteenth-Century Germany* (Oxford, 1984).

—— and EVANS, RICHARD J. (eds.), *The German Bourgeoisie: Essays on the Social History of the German Middle Class from the Late Eighteenth to the Early Twentieth Centuries* (London, 1991).

BLASIUS, DIRK, *Bürgerliche Gesellschaft und Kriminalität: Zur Sozialgeschichte Preußens im Vormärz* (Göttingen, 1976).

—— *Geschichte der politischen Kriminalität in Deutschland (1800–1980): Eine Studie zu Justiz und Staatsverbrechen* (Frankfurt am Main, 1983).

—— *Ehescheidung in Deutschland 1794–1945: Scheidung und Scheidungsrecht in historischer Perspektive* (Göttingen, 1987).

—— *Friedrich Wilhelm IV. 1795–1861: Psychopathologie und Geschichte* (Göttingen, 1992).

BLED, JEAN-PAUL, *Franz Joseph*, trans. Teresa Bridgeman (Oxford, 1992).

BLEIBER, HELMUT, *Zwischen Reform und Revolution: Lage und Kämpfe der schlesischen Bauern und Landarbeiter im Vormärz 1840–1847* (Berlin [East], 1966).

—— SCHMIDT, WALTER, and WEBER, ROLF (eds.), *Männer der Revolution von 1848*, ii (Berlin [East], 1987).

BLUM, JEROME, *In the Beginning: The Advent of the Modern Age. Europe in the 1840s* (New York, 1994).

BLUME, ERWIN VON, *Die preußische Politik in der Neuenburger Frage (1856–1857): Ein Beitrag zur Geschichte Friedrich Wilhelms IV.* (Hamburg, 1930).

BOCK, HELMUT, and HEISE, WOLFGANG (eds.), *Unzeit des Biedermeiers: Historische Miniaturen zum Deutschen Vormärz 1830 bis 1848* (Cologne, 1986).

BOHLE-HEINTZENBERG, SABINE, and HAMM, MANFRED, *Ludwig Persius: Architekt des Königs* (Berlin, 1993).

BOLDT, HANS, 'Zwischen Patrimonialismus und Parlamentarismus: Zur Entwicklung vorparlamentarischer Theorien in der deutschen Staatslehre des Vormärz', in Ritter (ed.), *Gesellschaft, Parlament und Regierung* (q. v.), 77–100.

—— *Deutsche Staatslehre im Vormärz* (Düsseldorf, 1975).

—— 'Die preußische Verfassung vom 31. Januar 1850. Probleme ihrer Interpretation', in Puhle and Wehler (eds.), *Preußen im Rückblick* (q. v.), 224–46.

BONJOUR, EDGAR, *Vorgeschichte des Neuenburger Konflikts 1848–56* (Berne, 1932).

—— *Der Neuenburger Konflikt 1856/57: Untersuchungen und Dokumente* (Basle, 1957).

BÖRNER, KARL HEINZ, *Die Krise der preußischen Monarchie von 1858 bis 1862* (Berlin [East], 1976).

—— 'Voraussetzungen, Inhalt und Ergebnis der Neuen Ära in Preußen', *Jahrbuch für Geschichte*, 14 (1976), 85–123.

—— *Kaiser Wilhelm I. 1797 bis 1888: Deutscher Kaiser und König von Preußen. Eine Biographie* (Cologne, 1984).

—— 'Prinz Wilhelm von Preußen: Kartätschenprinz und Exekutor der Konterrevolution', in Bleiber *et al.* (eds.), *Männer der Revolution von 1848*, ii (q. v.), 487–512.

BORNHEIM GEN. SCHILLING, WERNER, *Schloß Stolzenfels*, 3rd edn. (Mainz, 1980).

—— 'Stolzenfels als Gesamtkunstwerk', in Trier and Weyres (eds.), *Kunst des 19. Jahrhunderts im Rheinland* (q. v.), ii. 329–41.

BORRIES, KURT, *Die Romantik und die Geschichte: Studien zur romantischen Lebensform* (Berlin, 1925).

—— *Preußen im Krimkrieg (1853–1856)* (Stuttgart, 1930).

BÖRSCH-SUPAN, EVA, *Berliner Baukunst nach Schinkel 1840–1870* (Munich, 1977).

—— 'Wachstum und Schicksal der Berliner Museen', *Der Bär von Berlin: Jahrbuch des Vereins für die Geschichte Berlins*, 29 (1980), 7–42.

—— 'Friedrich August Stüler', in Wolfgang Ribbe and Wolfgang Schäche (eds.), *Baumeister—Architekten—Stadtplaner: Biographien zur baulichen Entwicklung Berlins* (Berlin, 1987), 195–218.

BÖRSCH-SUPAN, HELMUT, *Marmorsaal und blaues Zimmer: So wohnten Fürsten* (Berlin, 1976).

—— 'Wohnungen preußischer Könige im 19. Jahrhundert', in Werner (ed.), *Hof, Kultur und Politik im 19. Jahrhundert* (q. v.), 99–120.

BOTHE, ROLF, *Burg Hohenzollern: Von der mittelalterlichen Burg zum national-dynastischen Denkmal im 19. Jahrhundert* (Berlin, 1979).

BOTTING, DOUGLAS, *Humboldt and the Cosmos* (New York, 1973).

BOTZENHART, MANFRED, 'Die Parlamentarismusmodelle der deutschen Parteien 1848/49', in Ritter (ed.), *Gesellschaft, Parlament und Regierung* (q. v.), 121–43.

—— *Deutscher Parlamentarismus in der Revolutionszeit 1848–1850* (Düsseldorf, 1977).

—— 'Das preußische Parlament und die deutsche Nationalversammlung im Jahre 1848', in Ritter (ed.), *Regierung, Bürokratie und Parlament* (q. v.), 14–40.

—— *Reform, Restauration, Krise: Deutschland 1789–1847* (Frankfurt am Main, 1985).

BRAMSTED, ERNEST K., *Aristocracy and the Middle-Classes in Germany: Social Types in German Literature 1830–1900*, rev. edn. (Chicago, 1964).

BRANDENBURG, ERICH, *Untersuchungen und Aktenstücke zur Geschichte der Reichsgründung* (Leipzig, 1916).

BRANDT, HARTWIG, *Landständische Repräsentation im deutschen Vormärz: Politisches Denken im Einflußfeld des monarchischen Prinzips* (Neuwied, 1968).

BRANIG, HANS, 'Kronprinz Friedrich Wilhelm (IV.) und Rudolph von Stillfried in den Jahren von 1836–1838', in Gerd Heinrich and Werner Vogel (eds.), *Brandenburgische Jahrhunderte: Festgabe für Johannes Schultze zum 90. Geburtstag* (Berlin, 1971), 189–99.

—— *Fürst Wittgenstein: Ein preußischer Staatsmann der Restaurationszeit* (Cologne, 1981).

BRAUN, RUDOLF, 'Taxation, Sociopolitical Structure, and State-Building: Great Britain and Brandenburg-Prussia', in Charles Tilly (ed.), *The Formation of National States in Western Europe* (Princeton, NJ, 1975), 243–327.

—— and GUGERLI, DAVID, *Macht des Tanzes—Tanz der Mächtigen: Hoffeste und Herrschaftszeremoniell 1550–1914* (Munich, 1993).

BREDERLOW, JÖRN, *'Lichtfreunde' und 'Freie Gemeinden': Religiöser Protest und Freiheitsbewegung im Vormärz und in der Revolution von 1848/49* (Munich, 1976).

BRENNECKE, HANNS CHRISTOF, 'Eine heilige apostolische Kirche: Das Programm Friedrich Wilhelms IV. von Preußen zur Reform der Kirche', *Berliner Theologische Zeitschrift*, 4 (1987), 231–51.

BROPHY, JAMES M., 'Capitulation or Negotiated Settlement? Entrepreneurs and the Prussian State, 1848–1866' (Ph.D. thesis; Bloomington, Ind., 1991).

—— 'The Political Calculus of Capital: Banking and the Business Class in Prussia, 1848–1856', *CEH* 25 (1992), 149–76.

—— 'Politics of the *Juste Milieu*: Entrepreneurs in the New Era', unpub. paper, German Studies Association, 17th annual meeting, 7–10 Oct. 1993 (Washington, DC).

BROSE, ERIC DORN, *The Politics of Technological Change in Prussia: Out of the Shadow of Antiquity, 1809–1848* (Princeton, NJ, 1993).

BRÜCKMANN, REMIGIUS, ' "Es ginge wohl, aber es geht nicht": König Friedrich Wilhelm IV. von Preußen und die politische Karikatur der Jahre 1840–1849', in *Berlin zwischen 1789 und 1848: Facetten einer Epoche. Ausstellung der Akademie der Künste vom 30. August bis 1. November 1981* (Berlin, 1981) 147–61.

BRUNNER, MAX, *Die Hofgesellschaft: Die führende Gesellschaftsschicht Bayerns während der Regierungszeit König Maximilian II.* (Munich, 1987).

BRUNNER, OTTO, 'Vom Gottesgnadentum zum monarchischen Prinzip: Der Weg der europäischen Monarchie seit dem hohen Mittelalter', in id., *Neue Wege der Verfassungs- und Sozialgeschichte*, 2nd edn. (Göttingen, 1968), 160–86.

BUCHHEIM, KARL, 'Die Partei Gerlach-Stahl', in Alfred Herrmann (ed.), *Festschrift zum 70. Geburtstag von Ludwig Bergstraesser: Aus Geschichte und Politik* (Düsseldorf, 1954), 41–56.

BUNSEN, CHRISTIAN CARL JOSIAS, *Die Zeichen der Zeit: Briefe an Freunde über die Gewissensfreiheit und das Recht der christlichen Gemeinde* (2 vols., Leipzig, 1855–6).

BÜSCH, OTTO, *Industrialisierung und Gewerbe im Raum Berlin-Brandenburg 1800–1850: Eine empirische Untersuchung zur gewerblichen Wirtschaft einer hauptstadtgebundenen Wirtschaftsregion in frühindustrieller Zeit* (Berlin, 1971).

—— (ed.), *Untersuchungen zur Geschichte der frühen Industrialisierung vornehmlich im Wirtschaftsraum Berlin-Brandenburg* (Berlin, 1971).

—— (ed.,), *Friedrich Wilhelm IV. in seiner Zeit: Beiträge eines Colloquiums* (Berlin, 1987).

—— (ed.), *Handbuch der preußischen Geschichte*, ii: *Das 19. Jahrhundert und große Themen der Geschichte Preußens* (Berlin, 1992).

BUSSCHE, ALBRECHT VON DEM, *Heinrich Alexander von Arnim: Liberalismus, Polenfrage und deutsche Einheit. Das 19. Jahrhundert im Spiegel einer Biographie des preußischen Staatsmannes* (Osnabrück, 1986).

BUßMANN, WALTER, *Das Zeitalter Bismarcks*, 4th edn. (Frankfurt am Main, 1968).

—— 'Eine historische Würdigung Friedrich Wilhelms IV.', in id., *Wandel und Kontinuität in Politik und Geschichte: Ausgewählte Aufsätze zum 60. Geburtstag*, ed. Werner Pöls (Boppard am Rhein, 1973), 289–304.

—— 'Die Krönung Wilhelms I. am 18. Oktober 1861: Eine Demonstration des Gottesgnadentums im preußischen Verfassungsstaat', in Dieter Albrecht, Hans Günter Hockerts, Paul Mikat, and Rudolf Morsey, (eds.), *Politik und Konfession: Festschrift für Konrad Repgen zum 60. Geburtstag* (Berlin, 1983), 189–212.

—— 'Friedrich Julius Stahl', in Martin Greschat (ed.), *Gestalten der Kirchengeschichte*, ix: *Die neueste Zeit I* (Stuttgart, 1985), 325–43.

—— 'Das Scheitern der Revolution in Preußen 1848', in Karl Dietrich Erdmann *et al.*, *Preußen: Seine Wirkung auf die deutsche Geschichte* (Stuttgart, 1985), 153–77.

—— 'Probleme einer Biographie Friedrich Wilhelms IV.', in Büsch (ed.), *Friedrich Wilhelm IV. in seiner Zeit* (q. v.), 22–38.

—— *Zwischen Preußen und Deutschland: Friedrich Wilhelm IV. Eine Biographie* (Berlin, 1990).

—— 'Friedrich Wilhelm IV. und Carl Wilhelm Saegert in der Krisis des Krimkrieges', *Forschungen zur brandenburgischen und preußischen Geschichte*, NS 1 (1991), 101–10.

BÜTTNER, WOLFGANG, 'Der Weberaufstand in Schlesien 1844', in Helmut Reinalter (ed.), *Demokratische und soziale Protestbewegungen in Mitteleuropa 1815–1848/49* (Frankfurt am Main, 1986), 202–29.

CANIS, KONRAD, 'Der preußische Militarismus in der Revolution 1848' (Diss.; Rostock, 1965).

—— 'Ideologie und politische Taktik der junkerlich-militaristischen Reaktion bei der Vorbereitung und Durchführung des Staatsstreiches in Preußen im Herbst 1848', *Jahrbuch für Geschichte*, 7 (1972), 459–503.

—— 'Leopold von Gerlach', in Seeber and Noack (eds.), *Preußen in der deutschen Geschichte nach 1789* (q. v.), 153–72.

—— 'Joseph Maria von Radowitz: Konterrevolution und preußische Unionspolitik', in Bleiber *et al.* (eds.), *Männer der Revolution von 1848*, ii (q. v.), 449–86.

CANNADINE, DAVID, 'The Context, Performance and Meaning of Ritual: The British Monarchy and the "Invention of Tradition", *c.*1820–1977', in Hobsbawm and Ranger (eds.), *The Invention of Tradition* (q. v.), 101–64.

—— and PRICE, SIMON (eds.), *Rituals of Royalty: Power and Ceremonial in Traditional Societies* (Cambridge, 1987).

CANNON, JOHN, and GRIFFITHS, RALPH, *The Oxford Illustrated History of the British Monarchy* (Oxford, 1988).

CARSTEN, FRANCIS L., *Geschichte der preußischen Junker* (Frankfurt am Main, 1988).

CASPARY, ANNA, *Ludolf Camphausens Leben. Nach seinem schriftlichen Nachlaß* (Stuttgart, 1902).

CECIL, LAMAR, *Wilhelm II: Prince and Emperor, 1859–1900* (Chapel Hill, 1989).

CERVELLI, INNOCENZO, *Liberalismo e conservatorismo in Prussia 1850–1858* (Bologna, 1983).

CLARK, CHRISTOPHER M., 'The Politics of Revival: Pietists, Aristocrats, and the State Church in Early Nineteenth-Century Prussia', in Jones and Retallack (eds.), *Between Reform, Reaction, and Resistance* (q. v.), 31–60.

CLAUSEN, ANNA, *Die Stellung Leopold von Gerlachs zum Abschluß des preußischen Verfassungswerkes unter Friedrich Wilhelm IV.* (Weida, 1914).

COLLEY, LINDA, 'The Apotheosis of George III: Loyalty, Royalty and the British Nation 1760–1820', *Past and Present*, 102 (Feb. 1984), 94–129.

CRAIG, GORDON A., 'Military Diplomats in the Prussian and German Service: The Attachés, 1816–1914', *Political Science Quarterly*, 64 (1949), 65–94.

—— 'Portrait of a Political General: Edwin von Manteuffel and the Constitutional Conflict in Prussia', *Political Science Quarterly*, 66 (1951), 1–36.

—— *The Politics of the Prussian Army 1640–1945* (New York, 1964; orig. 1955).

DALLINGER, GERNOT, *Karl von Canitz und Dallwitz: Ein preußischer Minister des Vormärz. Darstellung und Quellen* (Cologne, 1969).

DE BRUYN, GÜNTER, 'Ein märkischer Don Quijote,' in Friedrich de la Motte Fouqué, *Ritter und Geister: Romantische Erzählungen*, ed. Günter de Bruyn (Frankfurt am Main, 1981), 267–303.

DEHIO, LUDWIG, 'Edwin von Manteuffels politische Ideen', *HZ* 131 (1925), 41–71.

—— 'Benedict Waldeck', *HZ* 136 (1927), 25–57.

—— *Friedrich Wilhelm IV. von Preußen: Ein Baukünstler der Romantik* (Munich, 1961).

DEMETER, KARL, *The German Officer-Corps in Society and State, 1650–1945*, trans. Angus Malcolm (New York, 1965).

DIBELIUS, OTTO, 'Friedrich Wilhelm IV. und die Idee des christlichen Staates', *Die Furche*, 22 (1936), 40–8.

DICKENS, A. G. (ed.), *The Courts of Europe: Politics, Patronage and Royalty 1400–1800* (London, 1977).

DITTMER, LOTHAR, *Beamtenkonservativismus und Modernisierung: Untersuchungen zur Vorgeschichte der Konservativen Partei in Preußen 1810–1848/49* (Stuttgart, 1992).

DOEBERL, M., *Bayern und das preußische Unionsprojekt* (Munich, 1926).

DOLLINGER, HEINZ, 'Das Leitbild des Bürgerkönigtums in der europäischen Monarchie des 19. Jahrhunderts', in Werner (ed.), *Hof, Kultur und Politik im 19. Jahrhundert* (q. v.), 325–64.

—— *Friedrich II. von Preußen: Sein Bild im Wandel von zwei Jahrhunderten* (Munich, 1986).

DREWITZ, INGEBORG, *Bettine von Arnim: Romantik—Revolution—Utopie*, 4th edn. (Munich, 1982; orig. 1969).

DRONKE, ERNST, *Berlin*, ed. Rainer Nitsche (Darmstadt, 1974; orig. 1846).

DUMONT, GEORGES-HENRI, *Léopold II* (Paris, 1990).

DUVIGNEAU, VOLKER, 'Die Potsdam-Berliner Architektur zwischen 1840 und 1875. An ausgewählten Beispielen' (Diss.; Munich, 1966).

ECKARDT, GÖTZ, *Die Orangerie im Park von Sanssouci*, 12th edn. (Potsdam-Sanssouci, 1984).

ECKERMANN, JOHANN PETER, *Gespräche mit Goethe in den letzten Jahren seines Lebens*, 3rd edn. (Berlin [East], 1987).

EICKENBOOM, PETER, 'Der preußische Erste Vereinigte Landtag von 1847' (Diss.; Bonn, 1976).

ELIAS, NORBERT, *The Court Society*, trans. Edmund Jephcott (New York, 1983).

ENAX, KARL, *Otto von Manteuffel und die Reaktion in Preußen* (Dresden, 1907).

ENGEL, HELMUT, 'Friedrich Wilhelm IV. und die Baukunst', in Büsch (ed.), *Friedrich Wilhelm IV. in seiner Zeit* (q. v.), 157–203.

ENGELBERG, ERNST, *Bismarck: Urpreuße und Reichsgründer* (Berlin, 1985).

ENGLER, F., *Revolution und Reaktion in Anhalt-Dessau-Cöthen: Ein Beitrag zur Geschichte Anhalts in den Jahren 1848–61* (Dessau, 1929).

ERICHSEN, JOHANNES and PUSCHNER, UWE, (ed.), *'Vorwärts, vorwärts sollst du schauen . . .': Geschichte, Politik und Kunst unter Ludwig I.* (Munich, 1986), i (with Michael Henker): *Katalog zur Ausstellung*; ii (with Uwe Puschner): *Aufsätze*; iii (with Ursula Huber): *Schauspiele von König Ludwig I.*

FEHRENBACH, ELISABETH, 'Images of Kaiserdom: German Attitudes to Kaiser Wilhelm II', in John C. G. Röhl and Nicolaus Sombart (eds.), *Kaiser Wilhelm II: New Interpretations: The Corfu Papers* (Cambridge, 1982), 269–85.

FISCHER, FERDINAND, *Preußen am Abschlusse der ersten Hälfte des neunzehnten Jahrhunderts: Geschichtliche, culturhistorische, politische und statistische Rückblicke auf das Jahr 1849* (Berlin, 1876).

FISCHER, FRITZ, *Moritz August von Bethmann-Hollweg und der Protestantismus (Religion, Rechts- und Staatsgedanke)* (Berlin, 1937).

FISCHER, HUBERTUS, 'Der "Treubund mit Gott für König und Vaterland": Ein Beitrag zur Reaktion in Preußen', *JGMOD* 24 (1975), 60–127.

—— 'Konservatismus von unten: Wahlen im ländlichen Preußen 1849/52—Organisation, Agitation, Manipulation', in Stegmann *et al.* (eds.), *Deutscher Konservatismus im 19. und 20. Jahrhundert* (q. v.), 69–127.

FISCHER, L[EOPOLD] H[ERMANN], 'Ludwig Tieck am Hofe Friedrich Wilhelms IV.', in id., *Aus*

Berlins Vergangenheit: Gesammelte Aufsätze zur Kultur- und Litteraturgeschichte Berlins (Berlin, 1891), 107–41.

FISCHER, WOLFRAM, KRENGEL, JOCHEN, and WIETOG, JUTTA, *Sozialgeschichtliches Arbeitsbuch*, i: *Materialien zur Statistik des Deutschen Bundes 1815–1870* (Munich, 1982).

FLASHAR, HELLMUT, 'F. Mendelssohn-Bartholdys Vertonung antiker Dramen', in Willmuth Arenhövel and Christa Schreiber (eds.), *Berlin und die Antike. Aufsätze: Architektur— Kunstgewerbe—Malerei—Skulptur—Theater und Wissenschaft vom 16. Jahrhundert bis heute* (Berlin, 1979), 353–6.

FLEISCHER, MANFRED P., 'Deus Praesens in Jure: The Politics of Ludwig von Gerlach', *Zeitschrift für Religions- und Geistesgeschichte*, 39 (1987), 1–23.

FLOCKEN, JAN VON, *Luise: Eine Königin in Preußen. Biographie* (Berlin [East], 1989).

FRAHM, FRIEDRICH, 'Entstehungs- und Entwicklungsgeschichte der preußischen Verfassung (vom März 1848 bis zum Januar 1850)', *FBPG* 41 (1928), 248–301.

FREY, LINDA, and FREY, MARSHA, *Frederick I: The Man and his Times* (Boulder, Col., 1984).

FRIEDJUNG, HEINRICH, *Österreich von 1848 bis 1860*, 3rd edn. (2 vols.; Stuttgart, 1908).

FRÜH, WALTER, *Radowitz als Sozialpolitiker: Seine Gesellschafts- und Wirtschaftsauffassung unter besonderer Berücksichtigung der sozialen Frage* (Berlin, 1937).

FUNK, ALBRECHT, *Polizei und Rechtsstaat: Die Entwicklung des staatlichen Gewaltmonopols in Preußen 1848–1918* (Frankfurt am Main, 1986).

FÜBL, WILHELM, *Professor in der Politik: Friedrich Julius Stahl (1802–1861). Das monarchische Prinzip und seine Umsetzung in die parlamentarische Praxis* (Göttingen, 1988).

GAILUS, MANFRED, 'Zur Politisierung der Landbevölkerung in der Märzbewegung von 1848', in Peter Steinbach (ed.), *Probleme politischer Partizipation im Modernisierungsprozeß* (Stuttgart, 1982), 88–113.

—— 'Soziale Protestbewegungen in Deutschland 1847–1849', in Heinrich Volkmann and Jürgen Bergmann (eds.), *Sozialer Protest: Studien zu traditioneller Resistenz und kollektiver Gewalt in Deutschland vom Vormärz bis zur Reichsgründung* (Opladen, 1984), 76–106.

—— *Straße und Brot: Sozialer Protest in den deutschen Staaten unter besonderer Berücksichtigung Preußens, 1847–1849* (Göttingen, 1990).

GALL, LOTHAR, *Bismarck: The White Revolutionary*, trans. J. A. Underwood (2 vols.; London, 1986).

—— ' " . . . ich wünschte ein Bürger zu sein": Zum Selbstverständnis des deutschen Bürgertums im 19. Jahrhundert', *HZ* 245 (1987), 601–23.

—— *Bürgertum in Deutschland* (Berlin, 1989).

—— 'Bismarck: Preußen, Deutschland und Europa', in Deutsches Historisches Museum (ed.), *Bismarck: Preußen, Deutschland und Europa*, 2nd edn. (Berlin, 1990), 25–34.

GARTON ASH, TIMOTHY, 'Eastern Europe: The Year of Truth,' *New York Review of Books*, 37/2 (15 Feb. 1990), 17–22.

GEERTZ, CLIFFORD, 'Centers, Kings, and Charisma: Reflections on the Symbolics of Power', in Wilentz (ed.), *Rites of Power* (q. v.), 13–38.

GEIST, JOHANN FRIEDRICH, and KÜRVERS, KLAUS, *Das Berliner Mietshaus 1740–1862: Eine dokumentarische Geschichte der 'von Wülcknitzschen Familienhäuser' vor dem Hamburger Tor, der Proletarisierung des Berliner Nordens und der Stadt im Übergang von der Residenz zur Metropole* (Munich, 1980).

GELDBACH, ERICH (ed.), *Der gelehrte Diplomat: Zum Wirken Christian Carl Josias Bunsens* (Leiden, 1980).

[GERLACH, ERNST LUDWIG VON,] *Zwölf politische Monats-Rundschauen vom Juli 1848 bis dahin 1849* (Berlin, 1849).

[GERLACH, ERNST LUDWIG VON,] *Zwölf politische Monats-Rundschauen vom Juli 1849 bis dahin 1850* (Berlin, 1850).

—— *Zwölf politische Monats-Rundschauen vom Juli 1850 bis dahin 1851* (Berlin, 1851).

GERSDORFF, BERNHARD VON, *Ernst von Pfuel: Freund Heinrich von Kleists, General, Preußischer Ministerpräsident 1848* (Berlin, 1981).

GEYER, ALBERT, 'König Friedrich Wilhelm IV. und seine Bauten', *Mitteilungen des Vereins für die Geschichte Berlins*, 42/7–9 (1925), 81–8.

GILLIS, JOHN R., *The Prussian Bureaucracy in Crisis 1840–1860: Origins of an Administrative Ethos* (Stanford, Calif., 1971).

GIRARD, LOUIS, *Napoléon III* (Paris, 1986).

GOLLWITZER, HEINZ, *Die Standesherren: Die politische und gesellschaftliche Stellung der Mediatisierten 1815–1918. Ein Beitrag zur deutschen Sozialgeschichte*, 2nd edn. (Göttingen, 1964).

—— 'Zum Fragenkreis Architekturhistorismus und politische Ideologie', *Zeitschrift für Kunstgeschichte*, 42 (1979), 1–14.

—— *Ludwig I. von Bayern: Königtum im Vormärz. Eine politische Biographie* (Munich, 1986).

GREW, RAYMOND, 'The Nineteenth-Century European State', in Charles Bright and Susan Harding (eds.), *Statemaking and Social Movements: Essays in History and Theory* (Ann Arbor, Mich., 1984), 83–120.

GRIEWANK, KARL, 'Vulgärer Radikalismus und demokratische Bewegung in Berlin 1842–1848', *FBPG* 36 (1924), 14–37.

—— 'Ursachen und Folgen des Scheiterns der deutschen Revolution von 1848', *HZ* 170 (1950), 495–523.

GRIMM, DIETER, *Deutsche Verfassungsgeschichte 1776–1866: Vom Beginn des modernen Verfassungsstaats bis zur Auflösung des Deutschen Bundes* (Frankfurt am Main, 1988).

GROH, JOHN E., *Nineteenth Century German Protestantism: The Church as Social Model* (Washington, DC, 1982).

GROß, KLAUS, 'Die deutsch-englischen Beziehungen im Wirken Christian Carl Josias von Bunsens (1791–1860)' (Diss.; Würzburg, 1965).

GRÜNTHAL, GÜNTHER, 'Konstitutionalismus und konservative Politik: Ein verfassungspolitischer Beitrag zur Ära Manteuffel', in Ritter (ed.), *Gesellschaft, Parlament und Regierung* (q. v.), 145–64.

—— 'Das preußische Dreiklassenwahlrecht: Ein Beitrag zur Genesis und Funktion des Wahlrechtsoktrois vom Mai 1849', *HZ* 226 (1978), 17–66.

—— *Parlamentarismus in Preußen 1848/49–1857/58: Preußischer Konstitutionalismus—Parlament und Regierung in der Reaktionsära* (Düsseldorf, 1982).

—— 'Grundlagen konstitutionellen Regiments in Preußen 1848–1867: Zum Verhältnis von Regierung, Bürokratie und Parlament zwischen Revolution und Reichsgründung', in Ritter (ed.), *Regierung, Bürokratie und Parlament* (q. v.), 41–55.

—— 'Crown and Parliament in Prussia 1848–1866', *Parliaments, Estates and Representation*, 5 (1985), 165–74.

—— 'Zwischen König, Kabinett und Kamarilla: Der Verfassungsoktroi in Preußen vom 5.12.1848', *JGMOD* 32 (1983), 119–74.

—— 'Bemerkungen zur Kamarilla Friedrich Wilhelms IV. im nachmärzlichen Preußen', in Büsch (ed.), *Friedrich Wilhelm IV. in seiner Zeit* (q. v.), 39–47.

—— 'Otto Freiherr von Manteuffel', ms. of lecture at Universität Karlsruhe, 14 Jan. 1989.

—— 'Das Ende der Ära Manteuffel', *JGMOD* 39 (1990), 179–219.

GÜNTHER, HARRI, *Peter Joseph Lenné: Gärten—Parke—Landschaften* (Berlin [East], 1985).

HAAKE, PAUL, *Johann Peter Friedrich Ancillon und Kronprinz Friedrich Wilhelm IV. von Preußen* (Munich, 1920).

—— 'Ernst Freiherr Senfft von Pilsach als Politiker', *FBPG* 53 (1941), 43–90, 296–323.

HAAS, EVE, and HENNING, HERZELEIDE, *Prinz August von Preußen* (Berlin, 1988).

HAENCHEN, KARL, 'Die Berufung der Brüder Grimm nach Berlin', *FBPG* 54 (1943), 11–42.

HAESLER, MAURICE, *De la situation de Neuchâtel vis-à-vis de la Prusse et de la Confédération suisse (1848–1857)* (Saint-Aubin [Neuchâtel], 1958).

HAHN, ADALBERT, *Die Berliner Revue: Ein Beitrag zur Geschichte der konservativen Partei zwischen 1855 und 1875* (Berlin, 1934).

HAMANN, BRIGITTE, 'Der Wiener Hof und die Hofgesellschaft in der zweiten Hälfte des 19. Jahrhunderts', in Möckl (ed.), *Hof und Hofgesellschaft* (q. v.), 61–78.

HAMEROW, THEODORE S., *Restoration, Revolution, Reaction: Economics and Politics in Germany, 1815–1871* (Princeton, NJ, 1958).

HAMMER, KARL, 'Die preußischen Könige und Königinnen im 19. Jahrhundert und ihr Hof', in Werner (ed.), *Hof, Kultur und Politik im 19. Jahrhundert* (q. v.), 87–98.

HANISCH, MANFRED, *Für Fürst und Vaterland: Legitimitätsstiftung in Bayern zwischen Revolution 1848 und deutscher Einheit* (Munich, 1991).

HANSEN, JOSEPH, *König Friedrich Wilhelm IV. und das liberale Märzministerium Camphausen-Hansemann i.J. 1848* (Trier, 1913).

HARDTWIG, WOLFGANG, *Vormärz: Der monarchische Staat und das Bürgertum* (Munich, 1985).

HARNISCH, HARTMUT, *Kapitalistische Agrarreform und industrielle Revolution: Agrarhistorische Untersuchungen über das ostelbische Preußen zwischen Spätfeudalismus und bürgerlich-demokratischer Revolution von 1848/49 unter besonderer Berücksichtigung der Provinz Brandenburg* (Weimar, 1984).

—— 'Die Gutsherrschaft: Forschungsgeschichte, Entwicklungszusam-menhänge und Strukturelemente', *Jahrbuch für Geschichte des Feudalismus*, 9 (1985), 189–240.

HARTUNG, FRITZ, 'Verantwortliche Regierung, Kabinette und Nebenregierungen im konstitutionellen Preußen 1848–1918', *FBPG* 44 (1932), 1–45, 302–73.

—— 'Studien zur Geschichte der preußischen Verwaltung', in id., *Staatsbildende Kräfte der Neuzeit: Gesammelte Aufsätze* (Berlin, 1961), 178–344.

HASENCLEVER, ADOLF, 'König Friedrich Wilhelm IV. und die Londoner Konvention vom 15. Juli 1840', *FBPG* 25 (1912), 143–58.

—— 'Zur Geschichte der Neuenburger Frage in den Jahren 1856 und 1857', *FBPG* 27 (1914), 517–44.

HASSEL, PAUL, *Joseph Maria von Radowitz*, i: *1797–1848* (Berlin, 1905).

HEFFTER, HEINRICH, 'Der nachmärzliche Liberalismus: Die Reaktion der fünfziger Jahre', in Hans-Ulrich Wehler (ed.), *Moderne deutsche Sozialgeschichte*, 4th edn. (Cologne, 1973), 177–96.

HEINEMANN, FRITZ, *Die Politik des Grafen Brandenburg* (Berlin, 1909).

HEINIG, KURT, *Hohenzollern: Wilhelm II. und sein Haus. Der Kampf um den Kronbesitz* (Berlin, 1921).

HEINRICH, GERD, *Geschichte Preußens: Staat und Dynastie* (Frankfurt am Main, 1981).

HEINRICH-JOST, INGRID, 'Die politische Publizistik Adolf Glaßbrenners', *Jahrbuch des Instituts für Deutsche Geschichte*, 12 (1983), 203–27.

HEINTZE, JOHANNES, 'Die erste preußische Generalsynode', *Jahrbuch für Berlin-Brandenburgische Kirchengeschichte*, 41 (1966), 122–41.

HENDERSON, CAROLYN REBECCA, 'Heinrich Leo: A Study in German Conservatism' (Ph.D. thesis; Wisconsin-Madison, 1977).

HERDT, GISELA, 'Der württembergische Hof im 19. Jahrhundert: Studien über das Verhältnis zwischen Königtum und Adel in der absoluten und konstitutionellen Monarchie' (Diss.; Göttingen, 1970).

HERTZ, DEBORAH, *Jewish High Society in Old Regime Berlin* (New Haven, Conn., 1988).

HERZ, HANS, 'Kreuzzeitungspartei (Kzp) 1848–1867', in Dieter Fricke *et al.* (eds.), *Lexikon zur Parteiengeschichte: Die bürgerlichen und kleinbürgerlichen Parteien und Verbände in Deutschland (1789–1945)* (Leipzig, 1985), iii. 321–4.

HERZFELD, HANS, 'Ernst Ludwig von Gerlach', in Historische Kommission für die Provinz Sachsen und für Anhalt (eds.), *Mitteldeutsche Lebensbilder* (Magdeburg, 1930), v. 275–98.

HILSCHER, ELKE, *Die Bilderbogen im 19. Jahrhundert* (Munich, 1977).

HINSLEY, F. H., *Sovereignty*, 2nd edn. (Cambridge, 1986).

HINTZE, OTTO, *Die Hohenzollern und ihr Werk: Fünfhundert Jahre vaterländischer Geschichte* (Berlin, 1915).

—— 'Die Epochen des evangelischen Kirchenregiments in Preußen', in id., *Gesammelte Abhandlungen, iii: Regierung und Verwaltung: Gesammelte Abhandlungen zur Staats-, Rechts- und Sozialgeschichte Preußens*, ed. Gerhard Oestreich, 2nd edn. (Göttingen, 1967; art. orig. pub. 1906), pp. 56–96.

—— 'Das preußische Staatsministerium im 19. Jahrhundert', in id., *Gesammelte Abhandlungen, iii: Regierung und Verwaltung: Gesammelte Abhandlungen zur Staats-, Rechts- und Sozialgeschichte Preußens*, ed. Gerhard Oestreich, 2nd. edn. (Göttingen, 1967; art. orig. pub. 1908), 530–619.

—— 'Das monarchische Prinzip und die konstitutionelle Verfassung', in id., *Gesammelte Abhandlungen, i: Staat und Verfassung: Gesammelte Abhandlungen zur allgemeinen Verfassungs-geschichte*, ed. Gerhard Oestreich, 3rd edn. (Göttingen, 1970; art. orig. pub. 1911), 359–89.

HOBSBAWM, ERIC, and RANGER, TERENCE (eds.), *The Invention of Tradition* (Cambridge, 1981).

HÖCKER, WILMA, *Der Gesandte Bunsen als Vermittler zwischen Deutschland und England* (Göttingen, 1951).

HOFFMANN, HANS, and MÖLLER, RENATE, *Schloß Charlottenhof und die Römischen Bäder*, 2nd edn. (Potsdam-Sanssouci, 1985).

HOFFMANN, JOACHIM, 'Die Berliner Mission des Grafen Prokesch-Osten 1849–1852' (Diss.; Freie Universität Berlin, 1959).

HOFMANN, HANNS HUBERT, 'Eliten und Elitentransformation in Deutschland zwischen der französischen und der deutschen Revolution', *Zeitschrift für bayerische Landesgeschichte*, 41 (1978), 607–31.

HOFMANN, JÜRGEN, *Das Ministerium Camphausen-Hansemann: Zur Politik der preußischen Bourgeoisie in der Revolution 1848/49* (Berlin [East], 1981).

HUBATSCH, WALTHER, *Grundlinien preußischer Geschichte: Königtum und Staatsgestaltung 1701–1871*, 3rd edn. (Darmstadt, 1988).

HUBER, ERNST RUDOLF, *Deutsche Verfassungsgeschichte seit 1789*, 3rd edn. (Stuttgart, 1988), ii: *Der Kampf um Einheit und Freiheit 1830 bis 1850*; iii: *Bismarck und das Reich*.

HULL, ISABEL V., *The Entourage of Kaiser Wilhelm II 1888–1918* (Cambridge, 1982).

—— 'Prussian Dynastic Ritual and the End of Monarchy', in Carole Fink, Isabel V. Hull, and MacGregor Knox (eds.), *German Nationalism and the European Response, 1890–1945* (Norman, Okla., 1985), 13–41.

HYDE, SIMON, 'Roman Catholicism and the Prussian State in the Early 1850s', *CEH* 24 (1991), 95–121.

JANY, CURT, *Geschichte der preußischen Armee vom 15. Jahrhundert bis 1914*, iv: *Die Königlich Preußische Armee und das Deutsche Reichsheer 1807 bis 1914*, 2nd edn., ed. Eberhard Jany, Osnabrück, 1967; repr. of 1933 edn.).

JENSEN, GWENDOLYN EVANS, 'Official Reform in *Vormärz* Prussia: The Ecclesiastical Dimension', *CEH* 7 (1974), 137–58.

JOHNSON, HUBERT C., *Frederick the Great and his Officials* (New Haven, Conn., 1975).

JONES, LARRY EUGENE, and RETALLACK, JAMES (eds.), *Between Reform, Reaction, and Resistance: Studies in the History of German Conservatism from 1789 to 1945* (Providence, 1993).

JORDAN, ERICH, *Die Entstehung der konservativen Partei und die preußischen Agrarverhältnisse von 1848* (Munich, 1914).

—— *Friedrich Wilhelm IV. und der preußische Adel bei Umwandlung der ersten Kammer in das Herrenhaus: 1850 bis 1854* (Berlin, 1909).

KAEBER, ERNST, *Berlin 1848: Zur Hundertjahrfeier der Märzrevolution* (Berlin, 1948).

—— 'Henriette Paalzow, die Lieblingsschriftstellerin Friedrich Wilhelms IV.', *JGMOD* 5 (1956), 251–71.

—— 'Bodelschwingh und die Berliner Märzrevolution', in id., *Beiträge zur Berliner Geschichte: Ausgewählte Aufsätze*, ed. Werner Vogel (Berlin, 1964), 160–80.

KAELBLE, HARTMUT, *Berliner Unternehmer während der frühen Industrialisierung: Herkunft, sozialer Status und politischer Einfluß* (Berlin, 1972).

KAHAN, ALAN, 'Liberalism and *Realpolitik* in Prussia, 1830–52: The Case of David Hansemann', *German History*, 9 (1991), 280–307.

KANTZENBACH, FRIEDRICH WILHELM, *Die Erweckungsbewegung: Studien zur Geschichte ihrer Entstehung und ersten Ausbreitung in Deutschland* (Neuendettelsau, 1957).

—— 'Gerd Eilers und Kultusminister Eichhorn: Zur Beurteilung der Ära Friedrich Wilhelms IV. (1840–1848) und seines Ministeriums', in Oswald Hauser (ed.), *Zur Problematik 'Preußen und das Reich'* (Cologne, 1984), 247–97.

KAUFMANN, GEORG, 'Ranke und die Beurteilung Friedrich Wilhelms IV.', *HZ* 88 (1902), 436–73.

KECK, KARL HEINRICH, *Das Leben des General-Feldmarschalls Edwin von Manteuffel* (Bielefeld, 1890).

KEINEMANN, FRIEDRICH, *Das Kölner Ereignis: Sein Widerhall in der Rheinprovinz und in Westfalen* (2 vols.; Münster, 1974).

—— *Preußen auf dem Wege zur Revolution: Die Provinziallandtags- und Verfassungspolitik Friedrich Wilhelms IV. von der Thronbesteigung bis zum Erlaß des Patents vom 3. Februar 1847. Ein Beitrag zur Vorgeschichte der Revolution von 1848* (Hamm, 1975).

KEKULÉ VON STRADONITZ, STEPHAN, 'Gedanken über eine Um- und Ausgestaltung des Adelswesens in Deutschland', *Deutsche Revue*, 35/1 (Jan.–Mar. 1910), 295–305.

KETTIG, KONRAD, *Friedrich Wilhelm IV. Stellung zu Frankreich bis zur Errichtung des 2. französischen Kaiserreiches (2. Dezember 1852)* (Berlin, 1937).

KIEFER, MARCUS, 'Schloß Lindstedt bei Potsdam-Sanssouci: Zur Baukunst und Gartengestaltung des nachschinkelschen "Klassizismus" ' (*Magisterarbeit*; Bonn, 1993).

KISER, EDGAR, 'The Formation of State Policy in Western European Absolutisms: A Comparison of England and France', *Politics and Society*, 15 (1986–7), 259–96.

KISSINGER, HENRY, *Diplomacy* (New York, 1994).

KLATTE, KLAUS, 'Die Anfänge des Agrarkapitalismus und der preußische Konservativismus' (Diss.; Hamburg, 1974).

KLIEM, MANFRED, 'Genesis der Führungskräfte der feudal-militaristischen Konterrevolution 1848 in Preußen' (Diss.; Humboldt-Universität zu Berlin, 1966).

—— 'Die Rolle der feudaljunkerlichen Reaktion in der Revolution von 1848/49', *ZfG* 17 (1969), 310–30.

KLINGENBURG, KARL-HEINZ, *Der Berliner Dom: Bauten, Ideen und Projekte vom 15. Jahrhundert bis zur Gegenwart* (Berlin [East], 1987).

KOCH, RAINER, *Deutsche Geschichte 1815–1848: Restauration oder Vormärz?* (Stuttgart, 1985).

KOCH, URSULA E., 'Prolegomena zu einer Geschichte des Berliner politischen Witzblattes', in Treue (ed.), *Geschichte als Aufgabe* (q. v.), 519–66.

KOCKA, JÜRGEN, 'Zur Schichtung der preußischen Bevölkerung während der industriellen Revolution', in Treue (ed.), *Geschichte als Aufgabe* (q. v.), 357–90.

—— (with Ute Frevert) (ed.). *Bürgertum im 19. Jahrhundert: Deutschland im europäischen Vergleich* (3 vols.; Munich, 1988).

KOHLMANN, THEODOR, with KINDERMANN, PETER-LUTZ, *Neuruppiner Bilderbogen* (Berlin, 1981; exhib. cat.).

KONDYLIS, PANAJOTIS, *Konservativismus: Geschichtlicher Gehalt und Untergang* (Stuttgart, 1986).

KOPISCH, AUGUST, *Die königlichen Schlösser und Gärten zu Potsdam: Von der Zeit ihrer Gründung bis zum Jahre MDCCCLII* (Berlin, 1854).

KOSELLECK, REINHART, *Preußen zwischen Reform und Revolution: Allgemeines Landrecht, Verwaltung und soziale Bewegung von 1791 bis 1848*, 3rd edn. (Stuttgart, 1981).

KOSER, REINHOLD, 'Zur Geschichte der preußischen Politik während des Krimkrieges', *FBPG* 2 (1889), 233–43.

—— 'Zur Charakteristik des Vereinigten Landtags von 1847', in Verein für Geschichte der Mark Brandenburg (ed.), *Festschrift zu Gustav Schmollers 70. Geburtstag* (q. v.), 287–331.

—— *Zur preußischen und deutschen Geschichte: Aufsätze und Vorträge*, ed. Elisabeth Koser (Stuttgart, 1921; orig. 1899).

KRAUS, HANS-CHRISTOF, 'Das preußische Königtum und Friedrich Wilhelm IV. aus der Sicht Ernst Ludwig von Gerlachs', in Büsch (ed.), *Friedrich Wilhelm IV. in seiner Zeit* (q. v.), 48–93.

—— 'Ernst Ludwig von Gerlach: Politisches Denken und Handeln eines preußischen Altkonservativen' (Diss.; 2 vols.; Göttingen, 1991).

—— 'Leopold von Gerlach: Ein Rußlandanwalt', in Mechthild Keller (ed.), *West-Östliche Spiegelungen*, ser. A, iii: *Russen und Rußland aus deutscher Sicht. 19. Jahrhundert: Von der Jahrhundertwende bis zur Reichsgründung (1800–1871)* (Munich, 1991), 636–61.

KRETZSCHMAR, HELLMUT, 'Das sächsische Königtum im 19. Jahrhundert: Ein Beitrag zur Typologie der Monarchie in Deutschland', *HZ* 170 (1950), 457–93.

KRIEGE, ANNELIESE, 'Geschichte der Evangelischen Kirchen-Zeitung unter der Leitung Ernst-Wilhelm Hengstenbergs (vom 1. Juli 1827 bis zum 1. Juni 1869) (Ein Beitrag zur Kirchengeschichte des 19. Jahrhunderts)' (Diss.; Bonn, 1958).

KROLL, FRANK-LOTHAR, 'Politische Romantik und romantische Politik bei Friedrich Wilhelm IV.', in Büsch (ed.), *Friedrich Wilhelm IV. in seiner Zeit* (q. v.), 94–106.

—— 'Bismarck und Friedrich Wilhelm IV.', in Jost Dülffer, Bernd Martin, and Günter Wollstein (eds.), *Deutschland in Europa: Gedenkschrift für Andreas Hillgruber* (Frankfurt am Main, 1990), 205–28.

—— *Friedrich Wilhelm IV. und das Staatsdenken der deutschen Romantik* (Berlin, 1990).

KROSIGK, KLAUS VON, and WIEGAND, HEINZ, *Glienicke* (Berlin, 1984).

KRÜGER, HILDEGARD, *Preußens innenpolitische Zustände von 1840 bis 1846 im Urteil des österreichischen Botschafters in Berlin, Grafen Trauttmannsdorf* (Leipzig, 1936).

KUHLOW, KURT, *Das königliche Schloß Charlottenhof bei Potsdam baugeschichtlich und kunstgeschichtlich dargestellt unter besonderer Berücksichtigung der Handzeichnungen König Friedrich Wilhelms IV.* (Berlin, 1912).

KUNAU, HEINRICH, *Die Stellung der preußischen Konservativen zur äußeren Politik während des Krimkrieges (1853–1856)* (Halle, 1914).

KUTZSCH, GERHARD, 'Friedrich Wilhelm IV. und Carl Wilhelm Saegert', *JGMOD* 6 (1957), 133–72.

LANCIZOLLE, CARL WILHELM VON, *Ueber Königthum und Landstände in Preußen* (Berlin, 1846).

LANGER, WILLIAM L., *Political and Social Upheaval 1832–1852* (New York, 1969).

LANGEWIESCHE, DIETER, 'Republik, konstitutionelle Monarchie und "Soziale Frage": Grundprobleme der deutschen Revolution von 1848/49', *HZ* 230 (1980), 529–48.

—— 'Die deutsche Revolution von 1848/49 und die vorrevolutionäre Gesellschaft: Forschungsstand und Forschungsperspektiven', *Archiv für Sozialgeschichte*, 21 (1981), 458–98.

—— *Die deutsche Revolution von 1848/49* (Darmstadt, 1983).

—— *Europa zwischen Restauration und Revolution 1815–1849* (Munich, 1985).

—— *Liberalismus in Deutschland* (Frankfurt am Main, 1988).

—— ' "Staat" und "Kommune": Zum Wandel der Staatsaufgaben in Deutschland im 19. Jahrhundert', *HZ* 248 (1989), 621–35.

—— 'Die deutsche Revolution von 1848/49 und die vorrevolutionäre Gesellschaft: Forschungsstand und Forschungsperspektiven, Teil II', *Archiv für Sozialgeschichte',* 31 (1991), 331–443.

LEES, ANDREW, *Revolution and Reflection: Intellectual Change in Germany during the 1850's* (The Hague, 1974).

LEHMANN, JOACHIM, 'Die politischen Berichte der preußischen Gesandtschaft in Petersburg von 1815 bis 1867 und ihre Erschließung', *Archivmitteilungen*, 36 (1986), 18–26.

LENMAN, ROBIN, 'Painters, Patronage and the Art Market in Germany 1850–1914', *Past and Present*, 123 (May 1989), 109–40.

LEVINGER, MATTHEW, 'Hardenberg, Wittgenstein, and the Constitutional Question in Prussia 1815–22', *German History*, 8 (1990), 257–77.

—— 'Imagining a Nation: The Constitutional Question in Prussia, 1806–1825' (Ph.D. thesis; Chicago, 1992).

LEWALTER, ERNST, *Friedrich Wilhelm IV.: Das Schicksal eines Geistes* (Berlin, 1938).

LIEVEN, DOMINIC, *The Aristocracy in Europe, 1815–1914* (New York, 1992).

LILL, RUDOLF, *Die Beilegung der Kölner Wirren 1840–1842. Vorwiegend nach Akten des Vatikanischen Geheimarchivs* (Düsseldorf, 1962).

LOWENTHAL-HENSEL, CÉCILE, GRIESBACH, LUCIUS, and LUDWIG, HORST, *Preußische Bildnisse des 19. Jahrhunderts: Zeichnungen von Wilhelm Hensel* (Berlin, 1981; exhib. cat.).

LÜDTKE, ALF, *Police and State in Prussia, 1815–1850*, trans. Pete Burgess (Cambridge, 1989).

LUKES, STEVEN, 'Political Ritual and Social Integration', in id., *Essays in Social Theory* (New York, 1977), 52–73, 205–10.

LUTZ, HEINRICH, *Zwischen Habsburg und Preußen: Deutschland 1815–1866* (Berlin, 1985).

MACHTAN, LOTHAR, and MILLES, DIETRICH, *Die Klassensymbiose von Junkertum und Bourgeoisie: Zum Verhältnis von gesellschaftlicher und politischer Herrschaft in Preußen-Deutschland 1850–1878/79* (Frankfurt am Main, 1980).

MACK SMITH, DENIS, *Italy and its Monarchy* (New Haven, Conn., 1989).

Mähl, Hans, *Die Überleitung Preußens in das konstitutionelle System durch den zweiten Vereinigten Landtag* (Munich, 1909).

Maltzahn, Christoph Freiherr von, *Heinrich Leo (1799–1878): Ein politisches Gelehrtenleben zwischen romantischem Konservatismus und Realpolitik* (Göttingen, 1979).

Mann, Bernhard, 'Das Ende der deutschen Nationalversammlung im Jahre 1849', *HZ* 214 (1972), 265–309.

Mansel, Philip, *Louis XVIII* (London, 1981).

—— 'Monarchy, Uniform and the Rise of the *Frac* 1760–1830', *Past and Present*, 96 (Aug. 1982), 103–32.

—— *The Eagle in Splendour: Napoleon I and his Court* (London, 1987).

—— *The Court of France 1789–1830* (Cambridge, 1988).

Marcks, Erich, *Der Aufstieg des Reiches: Deutsche Geschichte von 1807–1871/78* (2 vols.; Stuttgart, 1936).

—— '1848', in id., *Männer und Zeiten: Aufsätze und Reden zur neueren Geschichte*, ed. Gerta Andreas, 7th edn. (2 vols.; Stuttgart, 1942), i. 251–94.

—— *Kaiser Wilhelm I.*, 9th edn. (Leipzig, 1943).

Marrinan, Michael, *Painting Politics for Louis-Philippe: Art and Ideology in Orléanist France, 1830–1848* (New Haven, Conn., 1988).

Martin-Fugier, Anne, *La Vie élégante ou la formation du Tout-Paris 1815–1848* (Paris, 1990).

Matthew, H. C. G., *Gladstone 1809–1874* (Oxford, 1986).

Mayer, Arno J., *The Persistence of the Old Regime: Europe to the Great War* (New York, 1981).

Mehlhausen, Joachim, 'Friedrich Wilhelm IV.: Ein Laientheologe auf dem preußischen Königsthron', in Henning Schröer and Gerhard Müller (eds.), *Vom Amt des Laien in Kirche und Theologie: Festschrift für Gerhard Krause zum 70. Geburtstag* (Berlin, 1982), 185–214.

Meinecke, Friedrich, *Das Leben des Generalfeldmarschalls Hermann von Boyen* (2 vols.; Stuttgart, 1896, 1899).

—— *Radowitz und die deutsche Revolution* (Berlin, 1913).

—— *Preußen und Deutschland im 19. und 20. Jahrhundert: Historische und politische Aufsätze* (Munich, 1918; orig. 1902).

—— *Cosmopolitanism and the National State*, trans. Robert B. Kimber (Princeton, NJ, 1970).

—— *Brandenburg—Preußen—Deutschland: Kleine Schriften zur Geschichte und Politik*, ed. Eberhard Kessel (Stuttgart, 1979).

Meisner, Heinrich Otto, 'Zur neueren Geschichte des preußischen Kabinetts', *FBPG* 36 (1924), 39–66, 180–209.

—— *Der Kriegsminister 1814–1914: Ein Beitrag zur militärischen Verfassungsgeschichte* (Berlin, 1940).

—— *Militärattachés und Militärbevollmächtigte in Preußen und im Deutschen Reich: Ein Beitrag zur Geschichte der Militärdiplomatie* (Berlin [East], 1957).

—— 'Die monarchische Regierungsform in Brandenburg-Preußen', in Richard Dietrich and Gerhard Oestreich (eds.), *Forschungen zu Staat und Verfassung: Festgabe für Fritz Hartung* (Berlin, 1958), 219–45.

—— *Die Lehre vom monarchischen Prinzip im Zeitalter der Restauration und des Deutschen Bundes* (Aalen, 1969; orig. Breslau, 1913).

Messerschmidt, Manfred, 'Die politische Geschichte der preußisch-deutschen Armee', in Militärgeschichtliches Forschungsamt (ed.), *Handbuch zur deutschen Militärgeschichte 1648–1939*, ii, sect. IV: *Militärgeschichte im 19. Jahrhundert 1814–1890*, pt. 1 (Munich, 1979), 9–380.

Meyer, Dora, *Das öffentliche Leben in Berlin im Jahr vor der Märzrevolution* (Berlin, 1912).

MIECK, ILJA, 'Von der Reformzeit zur Revolution (1806–1847)', in Wolfgang Ribbe (ed.), *Geschichte Berlins* (Munich, 1987), i: *Von der Frühgeschichte bis zur Industrialisierung*, 405–602.

—— 'Preußen von 1807 bis 1850: Reformen, Restauration und Revolution', in Büsch (ed.), *Handbuch der preußischen Geschichte* (q. v.), ii. 3–292.

MIELKE, FRIEDRICH, *Potsdamer Baukunst: Das klassische Potsdam*, 2nd edn. (Frankfurt am Main, 1991).

MITTENZWEI, INGRID, *Friedrich II. von Preußen: Eine Biographie* (Cologne, 1980).

—— and HERZFELD, ERIKA, *Brandenburg-Preußen 1648–1789: Das Zeitalter des Absolutismus in Text und Bild*, 3rd edn. (Berlin, 1990).

MÖCKL, KARL, 'Der deutsche Adel und die fürstlich-monarchischen Höfe 1750–1918', in Hans-Ulrich Wehler (ed.), *Europäischer Adel 1750–1950* (Göttingen, 1990), 96–111.

—— (ed.), *Hof und Hofgesellschaft in den deutschen Staaten im 19. und beginnenden 20. Jahrhundert* (Boppard am Rhein, 1990).

MORRIS, WARREN B., jun., 'The Prussian Plan of Union: Traditional Policy by "Revolutionary" Means', *The Historian*, 39 (1977), 515–30.

—— *The Road to Olmütz: The Career of Joseph Maria von Radowitz* (New York, 1976).

MOSSE, WERNER, 'Adel und Bürgertum im Europa des 19. Jahrhunderts: Eine vergleichende Betrachtung', in Kocka (ed.), *Bürgertum im 19. Jahrhundert* (q. v.), ii. 276–314.

MULLEN, RICHARD, and MUNSON, JAMES, *Victoria: Portrait of a Queen* (London, 1987).

MÜLLER, F. MAX, *Chips from a German Workshop* (London, 1870).

MÜLLER, HANS, *Die militärische Wirksamkeit des Prinzen Wilhelm von Preußen* (Hamburg, 1937).

MÜLLER, HARALD, 'Der Blick über die deutschen Grenzen: Zu den Forderungen der bürgerlichen Opposition in Preußen nach außenpolitischer Einflußnahme am Vorabend und während des ersten Preußischen Vereinigten Landtags von 1847', *Jahrbuch für Geschichte*, 32 (1985), 203–38.

MÜNCHOW-POHL, BERND VON, *Zwischen Reform und Krieg: Untersuchungen zur Bewußtseinslage in Preußen 1809–1812* (Göttingen, 1987).

NÄF, WERNER, 'Die Idee der Heiligen Allianz bei Leopold von Gerlach', *Zeitschrift für schweizerische Geschichte / Revue d'histoire suisse / Rivista storica svizzera*, 11 (1931), 459–72.

NETZER, HANS-JOACHIM, *Albert von Sachsen-Coburg und Gotha: Ein deutscher Prinz in England* (Munich, 1988).

NEUGEBAUER, WOLFGANG, 'Die Protokolle des ost- und westpreußischen Huldigungslandtages von 1840', *JGMOD* 41 (1993), 235–62.

NEUMANN, SIGMUND, *Die Stufen des preußischen Konservatismus: Ein Beitrag zum Staats- und Gesellschaftsbild Deutschlands im 19. Jahrhundert* (Berlin, 1930).

NIPPERDEY, THOMAS, 'Nationalidee und Nationaldenkmal in Deutschland im 19. Jahrhundert', *HZ* 206 (1968), 529–85.

—— 'Der Kölner Dom als Nationaldenkmal', *HZ* 233 (1981), 595–613.

—— *Deutsche Geschichte 1800–1866: Bürgerwelt und starker Staat* (Munich, 1983).

NITHACK-STAHN, WALTHER, 'Die preußische Landeskirche unter Friedrich Wilhelm IV.', *Preußische Jahrbücher*, 128 (Apr.–June 1907), 191–208.

NOBBE, STEPHAN, 'Der Einfluß religiöser Überzeugung auf die politische Ideenwelt Leopold von Gerlachs' (Diss.; Erlangen, 1970).

'NOVALIS' [FRIEDRICH VON HARDENBERG], 'Glauben und Liebe oder Der König und die

Königin', in id., *Fragmente und Studien: Die Christenheit oder Europa*, ed. Carl Paschek (Stuttgart, 1984), 42–58.

OBENAUS, HERBERT, 'Die Immediatkommission für die ständischen Angelegenheiten als Instrument der preußischen Reaktion im Vormärz', in Mitarbeiter des Max-Planck-Instituts für Geschichte (eds.), *Festschrift für Hermann Heimpel zum 70. Geburtstag am 19. September 1971* (3 vols.; Göttingen, 1971–2), i. 410–46.

—— *Anfänge des Parlamentarismus in Preußen bis 1848* (Düsseldorf, 1984).

OBERMANN, KARL, BECKER, GERHARD, SCHMIDT, SIEGFRIED, SCHUPPEN, PETER, and WEBER, ROLF, (eds.), *Männer der Revolution von 1848*, i (Berlin [East], 1970).

—— *Die Wahlen zur Frankfurter Nationalversammlung im Frühjahr 1848: Die Wahlvorgänge in den Staaten des Deutschen Bundes im Spiegel zeitgenössischer Quellen* (Berlin [East], 1987).

O'BOYLE, LENORE, 'Some Recent Studies of Nineteenth-Century European Bureaucracy: Problems of Analysis', *CEH* 19 (1986), 386–408.

ONCKEN, HERMANN, 'Zur Genesis der preußischen Revolution von 1848', *FBPG* 13 (1900), 123–52.

ORR, WILLIAM J., JUN., 'The Foundation of the *Kreuzzeitung* Party in Prussia, 1848–1850' (Ph.D. thesis; Wisconsin-Madison, 1971).

—— 'König Friedrich Wilhelm IV. und der Sturz des Ministeriums Auerswald-Hansemann', *JGMOD* 25 (1976), 124–44.

—— 'The Prussian Ultra Right and the Advent of Constitutionalism in Prussia', *Canadian Journal of History/Annales canadiennes d'histoire*, 11 (1976), 295–310.

—— 'Königsberg und die Revolution von 1848', *Zeitschrift für Ostforschung*, 26 (1977), 271–306.

—— 'East Prussia and the Revolution of 1848', *CEH* 13 (1980), 303–31.

PARENT, THOMAS, *Die Hohenzollern in Köln* (Cologne, 1981).

PARET, PETER, *Clausewitz and the State* (New York, 1976).

—— *Art as History: Episodes in the Culture and Politics of Nineteenth-Century Germany* (Princeton, NJ, 1988).

PERROT, MICHELLE (ed.), *A History of Private Life*, iv: *From the Fires of Revolution to the Great War*, trans. Arthur Goldhammer (Cambridge, Mass., 1990).

PERTHES, OTTO, 'Beiträge zur Geschichte der Märztage 1848', *Preußische Jahrbücher*, 63 (Jan.–June 1889), 527–43.

PETERSDORFF, HERMAN VON, *König Friedrich Wilhelm der Vierte* (Stuttgart, 1900).

—— 'Joseph v. Radowitz und Leopold v. Gerlach', *Deutsche Rundschau*, 130 (1907), 43–61.

—— *Kleist-Retzow: Ein Lebensbild* (Stuttgart, 1907).

—— 'Graf Albrecht von Alvensleben-Erxleben', *HZ* 100 (1908), 263–316.

—— 'Der älteste Sohn der Königin Luise und sein erster Erzieher', *Hohenzollern-Jahrbuch*, 14 (1910), 192–223.

PETITPIERRE, JACQUES, *Neuchâtel et la Confédération suisse devant l'Europe: L'Insurrection royaliste et le Traité de Paris. A propos du centenaire d'une capitulation royale 1856–1857* (Neuchâtel, 1958).

PFLANZE, OTTO, *Bismarck and the Development of Germany*, i: *The Period of Unification, 1815–1871*, 2nd edn. (Princeton, NJ, 1990).

POENSGEN, GEORG, *Die Bauten Friedrich Wilhelms IV. in Potsdam* (Berlin, 1930).

POGGI, GIANFRANCO, *The Development of the Modern State: A Sociological Introduction* (Stanford, Calif., 1978).

PRERADOVICH, NIKOLAUS VON, *Die Führungsschichten in Österreich und Preußen (1804–1918)*.

Mit einem Ausblick bis zum Jahre 1945 (Wiesbaden, 1955).

PRESS, VOLKER, 'Adel im 19. Jahrhundert: Die Führungsschichten Alteuropas im bürgerlich-bürokratischen Zeitalter', in Reden-Dohna and Melville (eds.), *Der Adel* (q. v.), 1–19.

PRUTZ, ROBERT, *Zehn Jahre: Geschichte der neuesten Zeit. 1840–1850* (2 vols.; Leipzig, 1850, 1856).

PUHLE, HANS-JÜRGEN, 'Conservatism in Modern German History', *Journal of Contemporary History*, 13 (1978), 689–720.

—— and WEHLER, HANS-ULRICH (eds.), *Preußen im Rückblick* (Göttingen, 1980).

RACHFAHL, FELIX, *Deutschland, König Friedrich Wilhelm IV. und die Berliner Märzrevolution* (Halle, 1901).

—— 'König Friedrich Wilhelm IV. und die Berliner Märzrevolution im Lichte neuer Quellen', *Preußische Jahrbücher*, 110 (Oct.–Dec. 1902), 264–309, 413–62.

—— 'Zur Beurteilung König Friedrich Wilhelms IV. und der Berliner Märzrevolution', *Historische Vierteljahrschrift*, 5 (1902), 196–229.

—— 'Österreich und Preußen im März 1848: Aktenmäßige Darstellung des Dresden-Potsdamer Kongreßprojektes', *Historische Vierteljahrschrift*, 6 (1903), 357–86, 503–30; 7 (1904), 192–240.

—— 'Zur Berliner Märzrevolution', *FBPG* 17 (1904), 193–236.

—— 'Die Opposition des Generals von Prittwitz', *FBPG* 18 (1905), 252–7.

—— *Die deutsche Politik König Friedrich Wilhelms IV. im Winter 1848/49* (Munich, 1919).

RAILLAT, LANDRIC, *Charles X: Le Sacre de la dernière chance* (Paris, 1991).

RAKOW, PETER-JOACHIM, 'Staat, Verfassung und Regierung von Mecklenburg-Schwerin im Spannungsfeld von Revolution und Konterrevolution 1848–1850: Ein Beitrag zur Problematik der Machtfrage in der bürgerlichen Umwälzung in Deutschland' (Diss.; Rostock, 1981).

RARISCH, ILSEDORE, *Das Unternehmerbild in der deutschen Erzählliteratur der ersten Hälfte des 19. Jahrhunderts: Ein Beitrag zur Rezeption der frühen Industrialisierung in der belletristischen Literatur* (Berlin, 1977).

RASSOW, PETER, *Der Konflikt König Friedrich Wilhelms IV. mit dem Prinzen von Preußen im Jahre 1854: Eine preußische Staatskrise* (Wiesbaden, 1961).

RATHKE, URSULA, 'Ein Sanssouci am Rhein: Bemerkungen zur Entwicklung der preußischen Burgenromantik am Rhein', in Renate Wagner-Rieger and Walter Krause (eds.), *Historismus und Schloßbau* (Munich, 1975), 87–102.

—— *Preußische Burgenromantik am Rhein: Studien zum Wiederaufbau von Rheinstein, Stolzenfels und Sooneck (1823–1860)* (Munich, 1979).

—— 'Schloß- und Burgenbauten', in Trier and Weyres (eds.), *Kunst des 19. Jahrhunderts im Rheinland* (q. v.), ii. 343–62.

—— 'Die Rolle Friedrich Wilhelms IV. von Preußen bei der Vollendung des Kölner Doms', *Kölner Domblatt*, 47 (1982), 127–60; 48 (1983), 27–68; 49 (1984), 169–73.

REDEN-DOHNA, ARMGARD VON, and MELVILLE, RALPH (eds.), *Der Adel an der Schwelle des bürgerlichen Zeitalters 1780–1860* (Stuttgart, 1988).

REHM, HERMANN, *Modernes Fürstenrecht* (Munich, 1904).

REIF, HEINZ, 'Der Adel in der modernen Sozialgeschichte', in Wolfgang Schieder and Volker Sellin (eds.), *Sozialgeschichte in Deutschland: Entwicklungen und Perspektiven im internationalen Zusammenhang*, iv: *Soziale Gruppen in der Geschichte* (Göttingen, 1987), 34–60.

RETALLACK, JAMES N., ' "Ideology without Vision"? Recent Literature on Nineteenth-Century German Conservatism', *German Historical Institute London, Bulletin*, 13/2 (May 1991), 3–22.

REULECKE, JÜRGEN, *Sozialer Frieden durch soziale Reform: Der Centralverein für das Wohl der arbeitenden Klassen in der Frühindustrialisierung* (Wuppertal, 1983).

RICHARDS, THOMAS, 'The Image of Victoria in the Year of Jubilee', *Victorian Studies*, 31 (1987), 7–32.

RICHERT, ELISABETH, 'Die Stellung Wilhelms, des Prinzen von Preußen, zur preußischen Außen- und Innenpolitik der Zeit von 1848 bis 1857' (Diss.; Berlin, 1948).

RICHTER, GÜNTER, 'Friedrich Wilhelm IV. und die Revolution von 1848', in Büsch (ed.), *Friedrich Wilhelm IV. in seiner Zeit* (q. v.), 107–31.

—— 'Kaiser Wilhelm I.', in Wilhelm Treue (ed.), *Drei deutsche Kaiser: Wilhelm I.—Friedrich III.—Wilhelm II. Ihr Leben und ihre Zeit 1858–1918* (Freiburg, 1987), 14–75.

—— 'Zwischen Revolution und Reichsgründung (1848–1870)', in Wolfgang Ribbe (ed.), *Geschichte Berlins* (Munich, 1987), ii: *Von der Märzrevolution bis zur Gegenwart*, 603–87.

RICHTER, LUDWIG, *König Friedrich Wilhelm IV. und die Verfassung der evangelischen Kirche* (Berlin, 1861).

RIEHL, W., 'Die Friedenskirche bei Sanssouci', *Mittheilungen des Vereins für die Geschichte Potsdams*, 2 (1866), 53–74.

RIEHL, WILHELM HEINRICH, *Die bürgerliche Gesellschaft*, ed. Peter Steinbach (Frankfurt am Main, 1976).

RITTER, EMIL, *Radowitz: Ein katholischer Staatsmann in Preußen. Verfassungs- und konfessionsgeschichtliche Studie* (Cologne, 1948).

RITTER, GERHARD, *Staatskunst und Kriegshandwerk: Das Problem des 'Militarismus' in Deutschland*, i: *Die altpreußische Tradition (1740–1890)*, 3rd edn. (Munich, 1965).

RITTER, GERHARD A. (ed.), *Gesellschaft, Parlament und Regierung: Zur Geschichte des Parlamentarismus in Deutschland* (Düsseldorf, 1974).

—— (ed.), *Regierung, Bürokratie und Parlament in Preußen und Deutschland von 1848 bis zur Gegenwart* (Düsseldorf, 1983).

[ROBOLSKY, HERMANN,] *Die Damenpolitik am Berliner Hof 1850–90: Ein Beitrag zur Geschichte des Deutschen Reiches* (Berlin, 1897).

—— *Politische Generale am preußischen Hofe seit 1848* (Berlin, 1897).

ROBSON-SCOTT, W. D., *The Literary Background of the Gothic Revival in Germany: A Chapter in the History of Taste* (Oxford, 1965).

RÖHL, JOHN C. G., 'Hof und Hofgesellschaft unter Kaiser Wilhelm II.', in id., *Kaiser, Hof und Staat: Wilhelm II. und die deutsche Politik* (Munich, 1987), 78–115.

—— *Wilhelm II.: Die Jugend des Kaisers 1859–1888* (Munich, 1993).

ROSENBERG, HANS, *Bureaucracy, Aristocracy, and Autocracy: The Prussian Experience 1660–1815* (Cambridge, Mass., 1966).

—— 'Theologischer Rationalismus und vormärzlicher Vulgärliberalismus', in id., *Politische Denkströmungen im deutschen Vormärz* (Göttingen, 1972), 18–50.

—— 'Die Pseudodemokratisierung der Rittergutsbesitzerklasse', in id., *Machteliten und Wirtschaftskonjunkturen: Studien zur neueren deutschen Sozial- und Wirtschaftsgeschichte* (Göttingen, 1978), 83–101.

ROTHFELS, HANS, *Theodor v. Schön, Friedrich Wilhelm IV. und die Revolution von 1848* (Halle, 1937).

ROTHKIRCH, MALVE GRÄFIN, *Der 'Romantiker' auf dem Preußenthron: Porträt König Friedrich Wilhelms IV.* (Düsseldorf, 1990).

RUPPEL, HANS-RUDOLF, FOERSTER, FRANK, and BECKER, HANS (eds.), *Universeller Geist und guter Europäer: Christian Carl Josias von Bunsen 1791–1860. Beiträge zu Leben und Werk des 'gelehrten Diplomaten'* (Korbach, 1991).

RÜRUP, REINHARD, *Emanzipation und Antisemitismus: Studien zur 'Judenfrage' der bürgerlichen Gesellschaft* (Göttingen, 1975).

—— *Deutschland im 19. Jahrhundert 1815–1871* (Göttingen, 1984).

RUVILLE, ALBERT VON, 'Die Lösung der Neuenburger Frage im Winter 1856/57', in Verein für Geschichte der Mark Brandenburg (ed.), *Festschrift zu Gustav Schmollers 70. Geburtstag* (q. v.), 333–61.

SAß, FRIEDRICH, *Berlin in seiner neuesten Zeit und Entwicklung 1846*, ed. Detlef Heikamp (Berlin, 1983; orig. 1846).

SAUER, PAUL, *Der schwäbische Zar: Friedrich, Württembergs erster König* (Stuttgart, 1984).

SCHAMA, SIMON, 'The Domestication of Majesty: Royal Family Portraiture, 1500–1850', *Journal of Interdisciplinary History*, 17 (1986), 155–83.

SCHAPER, EWALD, *Die geistespolitischen Voraussetzungen der Kirchenpolitik Friedrich Wilhelms IV. von Preußen* (Stuttgart, 1938).

SCHÄRF, HARTMANN MANFRED, *Die klassizistischen Landschloßumbauten Karl Friedrich Schinkels* (Berlin, 1986).

SCHARFF, ALEXANDER, 'General Carl Graf von der Groeben und die deutsche Politik König Friedrich Wilhelms IV.', *FBPG* 48 (1936), 1–47.

—— 'König Friedrich Wilhelm IV., Deutschland und Europa im Frühjahr 1849', in Martin Göhring and Alexander Scharff (eds.), *Geschichtliche Kräfte und Entscheidungen: Festschrift zum fünfundsechzigsten Geburtstage von Otto Becker* (Wiesbaden, 1954), 138–75.

SCHATTEN, LORE, 'Louis Schneider: Porträt eines Berliners', *Der Bär von Berlin: Jahrbuch des Vereins für die Geschichte Berlins*, 8 (1959), 116–41.

SCHIEDER, THEODOR, *Friedrich der Große: Ein Königtum der Widersprüche* (Frankfurt am Main, 1983).

SCHIEMANN, THEODOR, *Geschichte Rußlands unter Kaiser Nikolaus I.*, iv: *Kaiser Nikolaus vom Höhepunkt seiner Macht zum Zusammenbruch im Krimkriege 1840–1855* (Berlin, 1919).

SCHISSLER, HANNA, *Preußische Agrargesellschaft im Wandel: Wirtschaftliche, gesellschaftliche und politische Transformationsprozesse von 1763 bis 1847* (Göttingen, 1978).

SCHMIDT, ARNO, *Fouqué und einige seiner Zeitgenossen: Biographischer Versuch* (Zurich, 1987; orig. 1958).

SCHMIDT, SIEGFRIED, 'Junkertum und Genesis des deutschen Konservativismus im 19. Jahrhundert', *ZfG* 27 (1979), 1058–72.

SCHMIDT-BÜCKEBURG, RUDOLF, *Das Militärkabinett der preußischen Könige und deutschen Kaiser: Seine geschichtliche Entwicklung und staatsrechtliche Stellung 1787–1918* (Berlin, 1933).

SCHMIDT-CLAUSEN, KURT, *Vorweggenommene Einheit: Die Gründung des Bistums Jerusalem im Jahre 1841* (Berlin, 1965).

SCHMITZ, ELISABETH, *Edwin von Manteuffel als Quelle zur Geschichte Friedrich Wilhelms IV.* (Munich, 1921).

SCHNABEL, FRANZ, *Deutsche Geschichte im neunzehnten Jahrhundert*, iv: *Die religiösen Kräfte*, 3rd edn. (Freiburg, 1955).

SCHNEIDER, REINHOLD, 'Das Schicksal Friedrich Wilhelms IV.', in id., *Macht und Gnade: Gestalten, Bilder und Werte in der Geschichte* (Munich, 1964), 16–21.

SCHOEPS, HANS-JOACHIM, *Der Weg ins Deutsche Kaiserreich* (Berlin, 1970).

—— 'Der Erweckungschrist auf dem Thron: Friedrich Wilhelm IV.', in Friedrich Wilhelm Prinz von Preußen (ed.), *Preußens Könige* (Munich, 1971), 159–72.

SCHOEPS, HANS-JOACHIM, *Ein weites Feld: Gesammelte Aufsätze* (Berlin, 1980).

—— *Das andere Preußen: Konservative Gestalten und Probleme im Zeitalter Friedrich Wilhelms IV.*, 5th edn. (Berlin, 1981).

—— *Preußen: Geschichte eines Staates. Bilder und Zeugnisse* (Frankfurt am Main, 1981).

SCHOEPS, HANS JULIUS, *Von Olmütz nach Dresden 1850/51: Ein Beitrag zur Geschichte der Reformen am Deutschen Bund. Darstellung und Dokumente* (Cologne, 1972).

SCHOEPS, JULIUS H., 'Agenten, Spitzel, Flüchtlinge: Wilhelm Stieber und die demokratische Emigration in London', in Horst Schallenberger and Helmut Schrey (eds.), *Im Gegenstrom. Für Helmut Hirsch zum Siebzigsten* (Wuppertal, 1977), 71–104.

SCHROEDER, JOHANN KARL VON, 'Standeserhöhungen in Brandenburg-Preußen 1663–1918', *Der Herold: Vierteljahrsschrift für Heraldik, Genealogie und verwandte Wissenschaften*, 9 (1978), 1–18.

SCHULT, RICHARD, 'Partei wider Willen: Kalküle und Potentiale konservativer Parteigründer in Preußen zwischen Erstem Vereinigten Landtag und Nationalversammlung (1847/48)', in Stegmann *et al.*, (eds.), *Deutscher Konservatismus im 19. und 20. Jahrhundert* (q. v.), 33–68.

SCHULZE, BERTHOLD, 'Polizeipräsident Carl von Hinckeldey', *JGMOD* 4 (1955), 81–108.

SCHULZE, HAGEN, 'Preußen von 1850 bis 1871: Verfassungsstaat und Reichsgründung', in Büsch (ed.), *Handbuch der preußischen Geschichte* (q. v.), ii. 293–372.

—— *Der Weg zum Nationalstaat: Die deutsche Nationalbewegung vom 18. Jahrhundert bis zur Reichsgründung* (Munich, 1985).

SCHULZE, HERMANN, *Die Hausgesetze der regierenden deutschen Fürstenhäuser* (Jena, 1883), iii, pt. 2.

SCHÜMANN, CARL-WOLFGANG, *Der Berliner Dom im 19. Jahrhundert* (Berlin, 1980).

SCHÜTZ, CHRISTIANE, *Preußen in Jerusalem (1800–1861): Karl Friedrich Schinkels Entwurf der Grabeskirche und die Jerusalempläne Friedrich Wilhelms IV.* (Berlin, 1988).

SCHÜTZ, RÜDIGER, *Preußen und die Rheinlande: Studien zur preußischen Integrationspolitik im Vormärz* (Wiesbaden, 1979).

SCHWENTKER, WOLFGANG, *Konservative Vereine und Revolution in Preußen 1848/49: Die Konstituierung des Konservativismus als Partei* (Düsseldorf, 1988).

SCURLA, HERBERT, *Alexander von Humboldt: Eine Biographie* (Frankfurt am Main, 1984).

SEEBER, GUSTAV, and NOACK, KARL-HEINZ (eds.), *Preußen in der deutschen Geschichte nach 1789* (Berlin [East], 1983).

SEILER, MICHAEL, 'Die Entwicklungsgeschichte des Landschaftsgartens Klein-Glienicke 1796–1883' (Diss.; Hamburg, 1986).

SHEEHAN, JAMES J., *German Liberalism in the Nineteenth Century* (Chicago, 1978).

—— *German History 1770–1866* (Oxford, 1989).

SHILS, EDWARD, *Center and Periphery: Essays in Macrosociology* (Chicago, 1975).

SIEMANN, WOLFRAM, *Die deutsche Revolution von 1848/49* (Frankfurt am Main, 1985).

—— *'Deutschlands Ruhe, Sicherheit und Ordnung': Die Anfänge der politischen Polizei 1806–1866* (Tübingen, 1985).

—— *Gesellschaft im Aufbruch: Deutschland 1849–1871* (Frankfurt am Main, 1990).

SKED, ALAN, *The Decline and Fall of the Habsburg Empire 1815–1918* (London, 1989).

SONDHAUS, LAWRENCE, 'Schwarzenberg, Austria, and the German Question, 1848–1851', *International History Review*, 13 (1991), 1–20.

SORKIN, DAVID, *The Transformation of German Jewry, 1780–1840* (Oxford, 1987).

SÖSEMANN, BERND, 'Der Verfall des Kaisergedankens im Ersten Weltkrieg', in John C. G. Röhl (with Elisabeth Müller-Luckner) (ed.), *Der Ort Kaiser Wilhelms II. in der deutschen Geschichte* (Munich, 1991), 145–70.

—— (ed.), *Gemeingeist und Bürgersinn: Die preußischen Reformen* (Berlin, 1993).

SPERBER, JONATHAN, *Popular Catholicism in Nineteenth-Century Germany* (Princeton, NJ, 1984).

—— 'State and Civil Society in Prussia: Thoughts on a New Edition of Reinhart Koselleck's *Preußen zwischen Reform und Revolution*', *Journal of Modern History*, 57 (1985), 278–96.

—— *Rhineland Radicals: The Democratic Movement and the Revolution of 1848–1849* (Princeton, NJ, 1991).

SPREE, REINHARD, and BERGMANN, JÜRGEN, 'Die konjunkturelle Entwicklung der deutschen Wirtschaft 1840–1864', in Hans-Ulrich Wehler (ed.), *Sozialgeschichte Heute: Festschrift für Hans Rosenberg zum 70. Geburtstag* (Göttingen, 1974), 289–325.

SPRINGER, ANTON, *Friedrich Christoph Dahlmann* (2 vols.; Leipzig, 1870, 1872).

SRBIK, HEINRICH RITTER VON, *Deutsche Einheit: Idee und Wirklichkeit vom Heiligen Reich bis Königgrätz*, 3rd edn. (4 vols.; Munich, 1940, 1942).

STAATLICHE ARCHIVVERWALTUNG DER DDR and STAATLICHE SCHLÖSSER UND GÄRTEN POTSDAM-SANSSOUCI (eds.), *Potsdamer Schlösser in Geschichte und Kunst*, 2nd edn. (Leipzig, 1984).

STAHL, FRIEDRICH JULIUS, *Das monarchische Princip: Eine staatsrechtlich-politische Abhandlung* (Heidelberg, 1845).

—— *Zum Gedächtniß Seiner Majestät des hochseligen Königs Friedrich Wilhelm IV. und seiner Regierung: Vortrag gehalten im evangelischen Verein zu Berlin am 18. März 1861* (Berlin, 1861).

STAMM-KUHLMANN, THOMAS, 'War Friedrich Wilhelm III. von Preußen ein Bürgerkönig?', *Zeitschrift für historische Forschung*, 16 (1989), 441–60.

—— 'Der Hof Friedrich Wilhelms III. con Preußen 1797 bis 1840', in Möckl (ed.), *Hof und Hofgesellschaft* (q. v.), 275–319.

—— *König in Preußens großer Zeit: Friedrich Wilhelm III. Der Melancholiker auf dem Thron* (Berlin, 1992).

—— 'Die Rolle von Staat und Monarchie bei der Modernisierung von oben: Ein Literaturbericht mit ergänzenden Betrachtungen zur Person König Friedrich Wilhelms III.', in Bernd Sösemann (ed.), *Gemeingeist* (q. v.), 261–78.

STEGMANN, DIRK, WENDT, BERND-JÜRGEN, and WITT, PETER-CHRISTIAN, (eds.), *Deutscher Konservatismus im 19. und 20. Jahrhundert. Festschrift für Fritz Fischer zum 75. Geburtstag und zum 50. Doktorjubiläum* (Bonn, 1983).

STEKL, HANNES, 'Der Wiener Hof in der ersten Hälfte des 19. Jahrhunderts', in Möckl (ed.), *Hof und Hofgesellschaft* (q. v.), 17–60.

STERN, ALFRED, 'Georg Klindworth: Ein politischer Geheimagent des neunzehnten Jahrhunderts', *Historische Vierteljahrschrift*, 25 (1929–30), 430–58.

STOLBERG-WERNIGERODE, OTTO GRAF ZU, *Anton Graf zu Stolberg-Wernigerode: Ein Freund und Ratgeber König Friedrich Wilhelms IV.* (Munich, 1926).

—— 'Der monarchische Gedanke in Deutschland', *Politische Studien*, 9 (1958), 833–41.

STRAUß, DAVID FRIEDRICH, *Der Romantiker auf dem Throne der Cäsaren, oder Julian der Abtrünnige: Ein Vortrag* (Mannheim, 1847).

STRECKFUß, ADOLF [ADOLPH CARL, pseud.] *Das freie Preußen! Geschichte des Berliner Freiheits-Kampfes vom 18. März 1848 und seiner Folgen*, i: *Geschichte Berlins vom 18. März bis 22. Mai* (Berlin, 1848); ii: *Geschichte Berlins vom 22. Mai bis 5. Dezember* (Berlin, 1849).

—— [ADOLPH CARL, pseud.] *Die Staats-Umwälzungen der Jahre 1847 und 1848* (3 vols.; Berlin, 1848, 1849).

STRECKFUß, ADOLF, *500 Jahre Berliner Geschichte: Vom Fischerdorf zur Weltstadt. Geschichte und Sage*, ii, 4th edn. (Berlin, 1886).

—— *1848. Die März-Revolution in Berlin: Ein Augenzeuge erzählt*, ed. Horst Denkler with Irmgard Denkler (Cologne, 1983).

STREITER, KARL HEINK, *Die nationalen Beziehungen im Grossherzogtum Posen (1815–1848)* (Berne, 1986).

SYBEL, HEINRICH VON, 'Graf Brandenburg in Warschau (1850)', *HZ* 58, NS 22 (1887), 245–78.

—— 'Aus den Berliner Märztagen 1848', *HZ* 63, NS 27 (1889), 428–53.

—— *Die Begründung des Deutschen Reiches durch Wilhelm I. Vornehmlich nach preußischen Staatsakten*, iii–iv, 4th edn. (Munich, 1892).

—— 'Carl Ludwig von Hinckeldey 1852 bis 1856', *HZ* 189 (1959), 108–23.

THIMME, FRIEDRICH, 'General von Prittwitz und der 18./19. März 1848', *FBPG* 17 (1904), 588–601.

TOCQUEVILLE, ALEXIS DE, *Recollections*, trans. George Lawrence, ed. J. P. Mayer and A. P. Kerr (Garden City, NY, 1970).

TOWNSEND, MARY LEE, 'The Politics of Humor: Adolph Glassbrenner and the Rediscovery of the Prussian *Vormärz* (1815–48)', *CEH* 20 (1987), 29–57.

—— *Forbidden Laughter: Popular Humor and the Limits of Repression in Nineteenth-Century Prussia* (Ann Arbor, Mich., 1992).

TREITSCHKE, HEINRICH VON, *Deutsche Geschichte im neunzehnten Jahrhundert*, 2nd edn., v: *Bis zur März-Revolution* (Leipzig, 1894).

TREUE, WILHELM (ed.), *Geschichte als Aufgabe. Festschrift für Otto Büsch zu seinem 60. Geburtstag* (Berlin, 1988).

TRIER, EDUARD, and WEYRES, WILLY (eds.), *Kunst des 19. Jahrhunderts* (Düsseldorf, 1980), i: *Architektur I: Kultusbauten*; ii: *Architektur II: Profane Bauten und Städtebau*.

TRIPPEN, NORBERT, 'Das Kölner Dombaufest 1842 und die Absichten Friedrich Wilhelms IV. von Preußen bei der Wiederaufnahme der Arbeiten am Kölner Dom: Eine historische Reflexion zum Domfest 1980', *Annalen des Historischen Vereins für den Niederrhein insbesondere das alte Erzbistum Köln*, 182 (1979), 99–115.

TROX, ECKHARD, *Militärischer Konservativismus: Kriegervereine und 'Militärpartei' in Preußen zwischen 1815 und 1848/49* (Stuttgart, 1990).

VALENTIN, VEIT, *Geschichte der deutschen Revolution von 1848–1849* (2 vols.; Cologne, 1977; orig. 1931–2).

VEHSE, EDUARD, *Preußische Hofgeschichten*, ed. Heinrich Conrad (4 vols.; Munich, 1913).

—— and 'Vehse redivivus', *Illustrierte Geschichte des preußischen Hofes, des Adels und der Diplomatie vom Großen Kurfürsten bis zum Tode des Kaisers Wilhelm I.* (2 vols.; Stuttgart, n. d. [1901]).

VEREIN FÜR GESCHICHTE DER MARK BRANDENBURG (ed.), *Festschrift zu Gustav Schmollers 70. Geburtstag. Beiträge zur brandenburgischen und preußischen Geschichte* (Leipzig, 1908).

VERWALTUNG DER STAATLICHEN SCHLÖSSER UND GÄRTEN BERLIN (ed.), *Schloß Glienicke: Bewohner, Künstler, Parklandschaft. Schloß Glienicke 1. August bis 1. November 1987* (Berlin, 1987; exhib. cat.).

VIERHAUS, RUDOLF, ' "Vormärz": Ökonomische und soziale Krisen, ideologische und politische Gegensätze', *Francia*, 13 (1985), 355–68.

VOGEL, BARBARA, *Allgemeine Gewerbefreiheit: Die Reformpolitik des preußischen Staatskanzlers Hardenberg (1810–1820)* (Göttingen, 1983).

—— 'Beamtenkonservatismus: Sozial- und verfassungsgeschichtliche Voraussetzungen der

Parteien in Preußen im frühen 19. Jahrhundert', in Stegmann *et al.*, (eds.), *Deutscher Konservatismus im 19. und 20. Jahrhundert* (q. v.), 1–31.

VOGEL, FRIEDRICH, 'Die Krankheit Friedrich Wilhelms IV. nach dem Bericht seines Flügeladjutanten', in Büsch (ed.), *Friedrich Wilhelm IV. in seiner Zeit* (q. v.), 256–71.

VOLKMANN, HEINRICH, and BERGMANN, JÜRGEN (eds.), *Sozialer Protest: Studien zu traditioneller Resistenz und kollektiver Gewalt in Deutschland vom Vormärz bis zur Reichsgründung* (Opladen, 1984).

WALTER, HANS, *Die innere Politik des Ministers von Manteuffel und der Ursprung der Reaktion in Preußen* (Berlin, 1910).

WARRACK, JOHN, 'Gesamtkunstwerk', in Denis Arnold (ed.), *The New Oxford Companion to Music* (2 vols.; Oxford, 1983), i. 759.

WEGGE, HANS, *Die Stellung der Öffentlichkeit zur oktroyierten Verfassung und die preußische Parteibildung 1848/49* (Berlin, 1932).

WEHLER, HANS-ULRICH, *Deutsche Gesellschaftsgeschichte* (Munich, 1987–), i: *Vom Feudalismus des Alten Reiches bis zur defensiven Modernisierung der Reformära*; ii: *Von der Reformära bis zur industriellen und politischen 'Deutschen Doppelrevolution' 1815–1845/49*.

WENDLAND, WALTER, 'Studien zur Erweckungsbewegung in Berlin (1810–1830)', *Jahrbuch für brandenburgische Kirchengeschichte*, 19 (1924), 5–77.

—— 'Die Entstehung des Evangelischen Ober-Kirchenrates', *Jahrbuch für brandenburgische Kirchengeschichte*, 28 (1933), 3–30.

WERNER, KARL FERDINAND, 'Fürst und Hof im 19. Jahrhundert: Abgesang oder Spätblüte?', in id. (ed.), *Hof, Kultur und Politik im 19. Jahrhundert* (q. v.), 1–53.

—— (ed.), *Hof, Kultur und Politik im 19. Jahrhundert: Akten des 18. Deutsch-französischen Historikerkolloquiums Darmstadt vom 27.–30. September 1982* (Bonn, 1985).

WIEGAND, HANNS-JÜRGEN, *Das Vermächtnis Friedrich Julius Stahls: Ein Beitrag zur Geschichte konservativen Rechts- und Ordnungsdenkens* (Königstein, 1980).

WIENFORT, MONIKA, *Monarchie in der bürgerlichen Gesellschaft: Deutschland und England von 1640 bis 1848* (Göttingen, 1993).

WILENTZ, SEAN (ed.), *Rites of Power: Symbolism, Ritual, and Politics since the Middle Ages* (Philadelphia, 1985).

WITTE, HERMANN, *Die pommerschen Konservativen: Männer und Ideen 1810–1860* (Berlin, 1936).

WITZMANN, GEORG, *Die Gothaer Nachversammlung zum Frankfurter Parlament im Jahre 1849 (Das 'Gothaer Parlament'): Eine Studie aus der Vorgeschichte der Reichsgründung und der Jugendzeit des deutschen Parlamentarismus* (Gotha, 1917).

WOLF, CHRISTA, 'Nun ja! Das nächste Leben geht aber heute an: Ein Brief über die Bettine', in Bettina von Arnim, *Die Günderode* (Frankfurt am Main, 1983), 545–84.

WOLFF, ARNOLD, 'Der Kölner Dom', in Trier and Weyres (eds.), *Kunst des 19. Jahrhunderts im Rheinland* (q. v.), i. 55–73.

WORTMAN, RICHARD, 'Rule by Sentiment: Alexander II's Journeys through the Russian Empire', *American Historical Review*, 95 (1990), 745–71.

ZORN, WOLFGANG, 'Wirtschafts- und sozialgeschichtliche Zusammenhänge der deutschen Reichsgründungszeit (1850–1870)', in Hans-Ulrich Wehler (ed.), *Moderne deutsche Sozialgeschichte*, 4th edn. (Cologne, 1973), 254–70.

ZUCHOLD, GERD-H., 'Friedrich Wilhelm IV. und die Byzanzrezeption in der preußischen Baukunst', in Büsch (ed.), *Friedrich Wilhelm IV. in seiner Zeit* (q. v.), 205–31.

ZUCHOLD, GERD-H., ' "Und ein talentvoller König wird vergebens deklamieren!" Friedrich Wilhelm IV. in der Sicht Heinrich Heines', *Jahrbuch preußischer Kulturbesitz*, 24 (1987), 403–16.

—— Der 'Klosterhof' des Prinzen Karl von Preußen im Park von Schloß Glienicke in Berlin (2 vols.; Berlin, 1993).

—— *Die Triumphstraße König Friedrich Wilhelms IV. von Preußen in Potsdam: Das Triumphtor* (Berlin, 1994).

ZUNKEL, FRIEDRICH, *Der Rheinisch-Westfälische Unternehmer 1834–1879: Ein Beitraag zur Geschichte des deutschen Bürgertums im 19. Jahrhundert* (Cologne, 1962).

INDEX